Understanding the Law

Understanding the Law

Donald L. Carper, J.D.
Professor of Legal Environment

Norbert J. Mietus, J.D.
Professor of Law, Emeritus

T. E. Shoemaker, Ph.D.
Professor of Government

Bill W. West, J.D.
Professor of Law and Real Estate

all of California State University, Sacramento

West Publishing Company
St. Paul   New York   Los Angeles   San Francisco

COPYEDITING: Gail Miller, Lorretta Palagi

COMPOSITION: Parkwood Composition

COVER ART: *Jury Duty* by Muriel Doggett

Library of Congress Cataloging-in-Publication Data

Understanding the law / Donald L. Carper ... (et al.).
        p.   cm.
     Includes bibliographical references and index.
     ISBN 0-314-80723-3 (hard)
        1. Law—United States.   I. Carper, Donald L.
KF386.U53   1991
349.73—dc20
(347.3)   90-23355
                                                             CIP

Table of Contents

Preface

In today's society law affects most human activities. Consequently its influence increases as the population expands and concentrates in and around cities, where people engage in more complex activites, often involving governmental regulation. Moreover, a growing awareness of real and imagined rights has generated an unprecedented volume of litigation in most metropolitan areas. In this environment, a person needs a basic knowledge of legal fundamentals to be properly informed of his or her rights and duties for practical application in social and business life.

This pervasiveness of law in American society demands that an educated person understand the basic structure of our legal system, its processes and the fundamental rules of law which govern our nation. It is our opinion that the general education of every university student would be enriched and strengthened with the inclusion of a minimum of one course containing significant and generalized content in law.

This textbook provides an appropriate lower division introduction to law. It presents fundamental principles, introduces legal reasoning, and applies selected legal rules in problem areas of concern to all students. Many can and will go on to further studies in the law, but upon completion of a course using *Understanding the Law* all will be much better prepared for successful life in our legally influenced and complex society.

In the text, we utilize a transactional approach consistent with a course of study so broadly focused. Judicial reasoning is exemplified with numerous actual and hypothetical legal controversies and situations, and with a representative conventional case at the end of each chapter. This approach permits a fast-paced course that maintains student interest through coverage of a variety of important and obviously relevant legal issues.

Understanding the Law is a response to the need of all students to understand the law that will govern their social, economic and political relations with others throughout life and serves the multifaceted needs of the educated citizen. In a modified Socratic fashion, every chapter is organized and presented with a series of provocative key questions which raise recurrent legal problems. The text which follows explains the answers in a friendly, non-legalistic, non-pretentious, readable style. However, accuracy has not been sacrificed for simplicity; the text is college level. Some topics covered are controversial; some are challenging.

In orderly sequence, the seven chapters of Part I describe our legal system, its constitutional foundation, and basic principles of the triumvirate of common law:

crimes, torts and contracts. A chapter on administrative law reflects the phenomenal growth of government agencies which now regulate much of our economic, social, and political life. The eight chapters of Part II apply the described principles to areas of daily life which directly or indirectly concern all members of our society in their customary roles as family members, as employees and as employers, as owners and operators of small businesses, as owners and operators of motor vehicles, as renters and landlords, as homeowners and estate planners. Most of us at some time may require specific legal advice, or become the plaintiffs, or defendants, or jurors in trials, and so the final chapter discusses the attorney-client relationship. Everyone should be able to recognize when professional legal counsel is needed.

The legal principles and rules cited usually express the generally accepted positions unless otherwise noted. We have drawn on the law of many individual states, as well as on the United States Supreme Court and lower federal courts, which have national and regional applicability. Of course, important differences exist in identified rules among the 50 states and at the federal level. All reflect life and law in action in courts and legislative halls.

Supplements

Instructor's Manual with Test Bank

The *Instructor's Manual* was written by the authors. Each chapter of the manual provides a chapter overview and teaching suggestions. The *Test Bank* has 15 multiple-choice questions, a minimum of 10 true and false questions, and 3 to 5 essay questions per chapter.

Educational Legal Software

 West Publishing Company's educational software LEGAL CLERK is available for student research and learning. Several cases discussed in the text, identified by the special computer logo shown here, can be researched further using the LEGAL CLERK software. LEGAL CLERK is a user-friendly, interactive software package that simultaneously introduces students to the rudiments of computer-aided legal research and reinforces many of the underlying concepts presented in *Understanding the Law*. LEGAL CLERK is available for IBM-PC and compatible personal computers. Ask your West sales representative for details.

Acknowledgements

We are indebted to many persons who have assisted the authors with this textbook. Don Carper would like to acknowledge the valuable research assistance of former students Huong Tran and Debra Mack. All authors appreciate the vision of Clyde Perlee Jr., Editor-in-Chief who has supported this progressive approach to undergraduate legal education. We recall his reflective yet immediate response: "This book should be published, and West should publish it." Jan Lamar gave us early help. Stephen Schonebaum made many gentle suggestions and diplomatically transmitted all reviewers comments without shattering the feelings of the authors. LeeAnne Storey supervised the very helpful editing and production process.

Several reviewers provided helpful suggestions to drafts of this edition. We were assisted by all, and are most grateful. They are: Thomas M. Apke, California State University, Fullerton; Jane Bennett, Orange Coast College; Joyce Birdoff, Nassau Community College; Thomas Brucker, University of Washington; James Ford, California State Polytechnic University, Pomona; John Guarino, North Essex Community College; Susan Helf, Seattle Central Community College; Deborah Howard, University of Evansville; Mike LaFrance, Kirkwood Community College; Donald Mayer, Oakland University; Richard Mills, Cypress College; H. Randall Rubin, California State Polytechnic University, Pomona; R. Bankole Thompson, Kent State University; Thomas Van Devort, Middle Tennessee State University; and Don Wirries, Moorhead State University.

UNIT
1

The Legal System
and Basic
Principles of Law

1

Introduction to Law

Welcome to the study of law for your general education. In this text, we focus your attention on selected topics of the law commensurate with their relevance, value, and interest to you. Do not feel short-changed that *all* topics of law are not included in this text or in the law course you are taking. As you soon will learn, the world of the law is far too vast to permit a thorough and in-depth presentation of all its aspects. Students seeking careers as lawyers usually spend three years in law school, following college, in preparation for the professional practice of law—and even they do not study every branch of the law! Selection of the topics presented in this text has been responsive to the many expressions of interest made by students in our introductory law classes.

We do not assume you are interested in becoming attorneys in the future, although that is a noble calling and many of you might surprise yourselves by eventually opting for law school and becoming members of the bar (lawyers). We know you are interested in becoming better-informed persons with an understanding of the rationale of the laws that will be affecting you on a day-to-day basis during the rest of your lives. *Understanding the Law* is designed to assist you in attaining that goal.

Already you have learned something about the law, simply by experiencing life. You know that intentionally injuring another person, stealing, or damaging someone else's property is unlawful. You know that in an automobile collision, the careless driver is held responsible (sometimes both drivers may have been careless, and therefore share the blame). You know that divorce creates issues of alimony, property division, and sometimes child support and custody. You know you must conform to rules while casting your vote or registering in college, speeding is illegal, and using certain drugs is criminal.

You probably could write a reasonable definition of law. Perhaps you would correctly conclude that laws are rules that must be obeyed to avoid the imposition of sanctions (legal penalties). More precisely, law is a body of rules of conduct prescribed by controlling authority, and having binding legal force.[1]

As you leave college and begin your careers, possibly marry and start families, the laws of our society will play an ever-increasing role in your lives. In Unit 1 you will learn about our legal system and basic legal principles. You should be familiar with these institutions, processes, and concepts, if only to better express your views with well-informed votes. Our legal system, applying established principles of law, is charged with the ultimate responsibility of deciding the most controversial issues of the day, whether they are abortion rights, flag-burning limitations, society's legal obligation to the homeless, rights to invade (or rescue) countries (such as the Republic of Panama or Kuwait), the right to die, or criminal's and victim's rights, to name but a few.

In Unit II we have anticipated which areas of the law will most likely affect you directly. These topics include the legal problems that confront members of our society on a daily basis.

Preview to Unit I: The Legal System and Basic Principles of Law

The U.S. Constitution

Ours is a constitutional form of government; a society governed by laws rather than the preferences of some supreme ruler or oligarchy. College graduates especially should be familiar with our Constitution and the protection it provides us from possible abuse by those who govern, while defining the structure and legitimate powers of the federal government. Why college graduates? Because it is you who will be primarily responsible for maintaining and managing our democracy in the years to come.

Can the police routinely enter your home to search for drugs? Can your state enforce a law prohibiting you from owning a handgun? Can government regulate or prohibit abortion? What if your land is zoned by your local government prohibiting the house you want to build? Can your university deprive you of a right to appeal an arbitrary grade received in a class? Can you be deprived of the effectiveness of your vote through gerrymandering?* We examine our Constitution in Chapter 2.

Courts

Most of you will be required to go to court sooner or later. Courts exist to resolve disputes. Innumerable disputes (called *cases,* once in court) are handled by courts every business day. Disputes vary in content from simple traffic tickets to bitter

---

* *Gerrymandering* is the intentional drawing of political districts by a party that is in power so as to give itself a majority of voters in as many districts as possible while concentrating the voting strength of the other party into as few districts as possible. With this technique an incumbent party may control a legislature, although it generates only the same number of (or even fewer) votes as the other party in each election.

divorce proceedings. They range from arguments over price fixing between national corporations involving tens of millions of dollars to accusations of murder and violent crime. Your appreciation of the breadth of court decisions will be greatly enhanced by this course.

Your personal involvement in court will probably be as a juror or witness. Hopefully none of you will appear in criminal court as a defendant or victim, but this too could happen. You may have civil disputes with business associates, strangers, or even with friends or relatives who you believe have violated your rights, or you may end up in court to resolve family issues.

From time to time proposals to change our courts will appear on election ballots. For example, delays in court proceedings are becoming legendary. The longest criminal trial in history took place in California where two defendants were accused of molesting dozens of children at their family-run preschool. The trial began in April 1987 and resulted in final verdicts in 1990, costing taxpayers more than $12 million.[2] Generally criminal trials take precedence over civil trials, which therefore may be delayed for years (especially in large metropolitan areas) waiting for an available courtroom and judge. For example, litigants can expect to wait for five years to have a civil case heard in Los Angeles. Unfortunately, drug-related cases are overloading many of our metropolitan courts as we enter the 1990s. We can expect proposals to achieve economies in time and money by reduction in the size of juries, and even by their elimination from certain types of cases. Basic changes in court procedures should be carefully and thoughtfully made.

Clearly it is important and useful to know where your courts are located, how they function, and the important role they play in our society. You should consider visiting a court in your community while a trial is in session; almost always they are open to the public. We examine courts in Chapter 3.

Criminal Law

Some conduct is so offensive it is deemed threatening to society in general, even though there may be but a single victim injured by the perpetrator. Congress, and state legislatures, have codified (prohibited by statute) such conduct and have set forth penalties applicable to those guilty of its commission. Enforcement of the criminal law is almost exclusively the responsibility of various law enforcement bodies (e.g., the Federal Bureau of Investigation and state and local police departments). Private citizens normally do not enforce the criminal law, although there are laws authorizing citizen's arrest under specified circumstances. Members of the public sit on juries that determine the guilt or innocence of persons accused of crimes, and in that manner participate in the enforcement of the criminal law. Those convicted of crime may be punished in a wide variety of ways, including the ultimate penalty of death. We consider the laws governing crimes in Chapter 4.

Civil Tort Law

Some conduct may cause injury to another person although no crime is involved. For example, negligent (careless) operation of an automobile often is the cause of serious injury. But such negligent conduct is not considered to threaten society in general, and therefore is not treated as criminal conduct.* Nonetheless, the injured person may be entitled to take legal action seeking monetary compensation. It is a basic principle of law that there is some remedy for every wrong. Private wrongs, called *torts,* are explored in Chapter 5.

Contracts

Contracts are essential in getting the world's work done. Businesses and consumers alike need to rely on promises concerning the manufacture, distribution, and sale of goods and services. Contract law governs promises made for commercial purposes, including complex remedies designed to keep the nation's businesses operating. Contracts are the backbone of business as well as consumer purchasing. You will examine the laws of contracts in Chapter 6.

Administrative Law

You cannot qualify as a well-informed college graduate unless you are familiar with our form of government and its legal structure. Of course you're familiar with the three basic branches of government: legislative, executive, and judicial. But how the functions of these branches interact in implementing and enforcing our statutory laws in the governance of our country is both complex and significant. In addition to state and federal lawmakers, hundreds of federal and state administrative agencies share responsibility to regulate the day-to-day business of our society. It is an established principle that lawmakers can delegate lawmaking functions to these specialized agencies, which are assigned specific areas to govern. These agencies form a major part of our legal system.

Sometimes the perceived local interests of particular jurisdictions (scope of power to govern) clash. For example, Staten Island, a borough of New York, is home of the world's largest dump, accepting the trash of 7 million New Yorkers. Citizens there complain also of poor roads, poor public transportation, and an inadequate sewer system. Staten Island is under the jurisdiction (power to govern) of New York, but Congress has authorized Staten Island voters to decide in a *referendum vote* whether they want autonomy.[3] (A ballot measure initiated by a legislative body is a referendum vote.) In Chapter 7 we will explore how our federal, state, and local governments and administrative agencies function and often cooperate in the complex task of running the public business of the country.

How the fundamental institutions and the principles of laws they administer apply directly to the individual comprises the second half of the text.

---

* Some careless conduct is so reckless as to constitute a willful disregard for the safety of the public. Such gross negligence will be treated as a crime. Causing a vehicular accident while under the influence of alcohol or drugs is an example of such conduct.

Preview to Unit II: Applications of the Law to the Individual

Family Law

What is required for a person to be legally married? If you get divorced someday, what are your rights and obligations concerning family property, alimony, child support, and custody? Must you hire an attorney to get a divorce? What is a common-law marriage and is it valid and binding on parties in all states? Can members of the same sex legally marry? Should you have a premarital agreement? Should it be in writing? Family law is examined in Chapter 8.

Employee Law

Suppose you leave your job without notice, breaking your employment contract. Are you in serious trouble? Can your employer fire you without good cause? Can you sue if you are injured on the job? What are your remedies if you are sexually harassed at work? Must you comply with orders that go beyond the scope of your job classification? Must you join a union? The law of employee rights and duties is explained in Chapter 9.

Small Business Law

Suppose you want to own your own small business, such as a boutique. What must you do to open shop? Must you hire union members? What licenses and permits do you need? Should you select a corporate form of doing business? What taxes do small businesses have to pay? What is the Small Business Administration? The laws governing the small entrepreneur are explained in Chapter 10.

Automobile Law

Virtually every adult and many minors drive automobiles. Who is responsible when accidents occur? What insurance must you have? What happens if you do not have insurance? What should you do if involved in an accident? If your passenger is injured, will your insurance company pay his or her medical expenses? Is no-fault insurance an appropriate idea? Laws pertaining to automobiles are presented in Chapter 11.

Renter and Landlord Law

Many of you are renting an apartment or sharing a rented home during college. Most of you probably will be renting housing accommodations for some years after college while saving for a down payment to buy a home. What are your rights as a tenant, and what duties do you owe your landlord? Can the landlord raise the rent? What if your landlord doesn't fix a leaking roof? If your belongings are stolen from your apartment, are you legally entitled to receive compensation from the landlord? Can your landlord secretly enter your apartment? What happens if you break your lease? The laws pertaining to renters and landlords are described in Chapter 12.

Home Ownership

A few years after college, almost all of you will be pursuing the "American dream" of owning your own home. How do you locate, finance, and purchase a home? Can two unrelated persons qualify for home financing? How large will your monthly payments be? Can your monthly payments increase? What happens if you miss a payment? Do you need the services of a real estate broker or sales agent when buying? When selling? What is a homestead and how do you obtain one? We consider the practices and laws affecting the "American dream" in Chapter 13.

Wills, Trusts, and Probate Laws

Unfortunately, not all of the significant events in our lives are happy ones. Death must someday come to family members and others that we love. But life goes on and the law provides means of ensuring survivors that important financial matters of the deceased are properly handled. Are you prepared to share in these responsibilities? Who should have a will? Should property be left equally, share and share alike, to heirs? When is a trust helpful in preparing for the financial aftermath of death? Is an attorney needed when a family member dies? Under what circumstances can a will be contested? How are family assets taxed when death occurs? We present the law of probate matters in Chapter 14.

Laws Concerning Your Attorney

Because of the complexities of modern life it is very likely that you will, from time to time, require the services of an attorney. How will you locate and hire an attorney? What are customary attorney's fees for typical types of services? Can you contest the payment of fees if the service you receive is unsatisfactory? What if you are unhappy with the legal services you are receiving—can you fire your attorney? What if your attorney fails to keep you informed on the progress of your case? What is legal malpractice? Our study of the law ends in the arena of lawyers in the final chapter, Chapter 15.

Before proceeding to the specific legal topics found in Unit I and Unit II, some familiarity with the ancestry of our laws and our legal system will help you better grasp their significance.

The English Source of Our Law

Before the eleventh century, England was an Anglo-Saxon society, a unified and relatively prosperous nation living mostly in villages. The economy was agricultural and the people were self-sufficient, growing grain, spinning wool, and even brewing beer for home consumption. Their kings headed powerful and wealthy aristocracies. Wealth was primarily tied to their landholding feudal system. Serfdom was common—the serfs were bound to the aristocratic lords and required to work the lords' hereditary land. Throughout the Saxon period, law essentially was a matter of local custom changing very slowly. Their laws mostly were unwritten, but reflected long-established customs and shared values; kings rarely issued nationwide laws. Established legal systems provided monetary compensation for private wrongs and criminal prosecution for public wrongs. Generally, a person accused of a crime had either been caught in the act or found guilty in a strange proceeding during which witnesses and the accused engaged in "oath-swearing." This was a complicated procedure not related to evidence so much as to the character of the accused. There were no lawyers, no legal profession, and no jury trial. Needless to say, this was not a sophisticated system.

The Normans (Vikings who originally came from Scandinavia and then Northern France) were French in language,* viewpoint, and culture, including their system of law, which was based on the ancient **Roman civil law,** expressed mostly in detailed codes (systematic collections of rules). These were imposed by the ruler from above, in contrast to the Saxon practice of developing rules from below, based on customs of the people.

In 1066 William, Duke of Normandy, led 5,000 men and 2,500 cavalry across the English Channel to defeat the Saxons in the Battle of Hastings. The Duke became William the Conqueror. Although there followed decades of regional uprisings and resistance characterized by uncontrolled murder, oppression, famine, and fear, William was known generally for his zeal for law, order, and justice. The Normans retained the English common law of unwritten customs, except that Church Courts were introduced with authority limited mainly to spiritual matters and domestic (family) relations. England gradually underwent positive changes. A sense of national instead of local unity ensued, which led to a national system of law derived from both Anglo-Saxon and Norman influences. The Normans already had been influenced by the French, and the linking of England with the European continent, brought about by the conquest, led to the introduction of elements of Roman civil law. Ultimately, following numerous regional battles, William accepted the crown, becoming King of England, and obtained the allegiance of the people. Gradually, intermarriage became frequent. As before, local justice continued to be the concern of local sheriffs, and the common law (law universal throughout the country) was characterized even then by equality before the law (the law applied the same to every person), respect for established rights, and impartial justice.

The King's Courts dealt with the common law (civil and criminal matters); the new Church Courts dealt with the canon law and all aspects of marriage and succession. Disputes existed in some areas, such as legitimization of illegitimate children, which was not possible under canon law. Under common law, legitimization was accomplished by subsequent marriage of the parents. This was an important matter because it affected rights of succession to land.

By the twelfth century, sheriffs were being displaced by judges who periodically visited places in the country to dispense justice. These circuits were precursors to U.S. circuit and district courts. The itinerant judges dealt with crimes such as murder, robbery, forgery, and arson. One judge, Glanvil, is credited with writing the *Treatise on the Laws and Customs of the Kingdom of England,* the first

---

* Norman French is very different from the French language of today.

serious book on the evolving **common law.** In 1215, King John was forced to accept the *Magna Charta* (Latin: Great Charter), the basis of modern English constitutional liberty, commanding reform of the courts and free elections, and barring imprisonment without a trial by peers. Trial by jury had evolved into permanency in the Magna Charta, and ultimately was incorporated into the U.S. Constitution. The Magna Charta essentially decreed supremacy of law over personal authority of the king and his aides. It was a precursor of our constitutional democracy.

For several hundred years the English system of courts and jurisdictions evolved, influenced by conflicts and political interventions. High-ranking clergymen served as chancellors to the king; when the King's Courts, sitting with a jury, were unable to provide a just solution to a legal problem, and the wronged citizen appealed to the king, he would be referred to the chancellor. As a man committed to justice and equity, the chancellor was authorized to decide the case without assistance of a jury. An example would be a dispute over the sale of a parcel of land in which the seller refused to transfer the title. The King's Courts could do no more than award monetary damages. The chancellor could, and would order the seller to relinquish possession. Such decree of specific performance, to this day, remains an equitable remedy and is available in regular courts sitting without juries. Ultimately jurisdictional conflicts refined the fundamental distinction between courts at law and courts in equity. This distinction endures today and determines important questions. However, unlike England, where courts in law and in equity were physically separated, each court today is empowered to render either equitable or legal relief. Equity is explained further in Chapter 3.

The eighteenth century brought England from medieval to modern times. The Industrial Revolution greatly affected the law as England changed from an agricultural society where land was the principal form of wealth to a society more based on industry. Machinery produced more goods at less cost with less labor; prices dropped, resulting in greater demand for goods. England prospered as trade expanded, and the law rapidly evolved responding with the many new principles of business law. But the transition was marred by many difficulties and abuses. By the end of the eighteenth century the state of the law was described by an eminent historian, Sir Thomas Erskine May, in these probably pessimistic words:

> Heart-breaking delays and ruinous costs were the lot of suitors. Justice was dilatory, expensive, uncertain and remote. To the rich it was a costly lottery: to the poor a denial of right, or certain ruin. The class who profited most by its dark mysteries were the lawyers themselves. A suitor might be reduced to beggary or madness, but his advisers revelled in the chicane and artifice of a lifelong suit and grew rich.[4]

Over hundreds of years the common law of England had evolved into a framework of principles, found in both customs and statutes that were brought to the New World by the early colonial settlers. When the United States broke away from England after the Revolutionary War, we adopted the entire body of English common law as it existed in the eighteenth century, to the extent it did not conflict with laws of the United States or laws that were from time to time created by each state. And that is the situation today; principles of the English common law are in effect throughout the country. Only Louisiana, purchased in 1803 from Napoleon, retained a variation of the Roman civil law that had been used in France.

In Chapters 2 and 3 you will review how our form of government is a federalism, or union of states under a federal government, that includes both federal and state courts. Both federal and state courts apply principles of the common law.

Federal courts either apply the common law of the state in which they sit, or apply federal law to constitutional questions and congressional acts. Most often federal courts resolve disputes through the application of state common law. Federal common law is limited to disputes involving obligations of the United States, interstate and international disputes, and admiralty cases. Most common law is state law, which varies from state to state.

Some principles of law derived through the common law do apply to both state and federal court systems. For example, the doctrine of *stare decisis* (Latin: to stand by things settled) commands that once a principle of law is determined to be applicable to a particular set of facts involved in a case, it will be applied to all future cases that have similar facts. This doctrine binds courts of equal or junior rank to the senior court that first applies the principle. Essentially, lower state courts are bound to the principles established by higher appellate courts within the same state; lower federal courts are bound to the principles established by higher appellate courts within their respective jurisdictions. (We will consider courts and their hierarchy in Chapter 3.)

This important doctrine leads to stability and predictability in the law. For example, if a high court establishes the principle that a promise to marry is not enforceable or compensable in court, then routine legal research will alert all attorneys to the existence of the rule. If a similar case arises, they will not waste time and money litigating the question—they know their court will be bound by the same earlier outcome under the doctrine of stare decisis.* The appellate court's decision thus has become a part of the common law of that particular state.

Stare decisis is not a straitjacket, however. Once a principle has outlived its usefulness, or has grown inapplicable because of changing social standards and circumstances, it may be overruled. Often a modern case is not controlled by a principle previously applied in an earlier case simply because the two cases are distinguishable on their facts. The unenforceable marriage-vow example above would be distinguishable from a case where one of the prospective spouses had incurred considerable related expenses before the promise of marriage was broken. The earlier principle, therefore, may not apply to or bind the court's decision, which may establish a new principle and authorize compensation (an award of damages) in this later situation.

The common law of today is the body of rules derived from usages and customs of antiquity, particularly as they appeared in medieval England, and from modern judgments of appellate courts recognizing and applying those customs in specific cases. Since thousands of appellate cases are decided each year the body of common law is enormous, even though most of these cases define no new principles. In preparing their cases, lawyers spend much time and effort searching the common law for principles that might be applicable. Thanks to computer

---

* The doctrine of stare decisis also is commonly called the *doctrine of precedents*. Once a common law principle is applied in a case it becomes a "precedent" to and binding on future courts.

technology the task is less laborious today, but the information at the attorney's fingertips is nonetheless overwhelming in volume, let alone complexity.

Originally the common law of England was called *unwritten law,* because it evolved from the decisions of judges based on unwritten customs. It also was not recorded or printed in books; often judges exchanged their rulings verbally. In contrast, codes and statutes (enacted by the king or a legislative body) were usually written (printed). Today, of course, most additions to the common law, made in appellate court decisions, are published in books, called *reporters,* and are referred to as *case law.* If case law was unwritten, attorneys, and the public as well, would be ignorant of what decisions were made and what the appellate court's rationale was for those decisions.

Modern Sources of Our Law

Ours is a constitutional form of government, as will be explained fully in Chapter 2. In one sense, our Constitution is the ultimate source of our laws because it contains those principles according to which our nation is governed, and limits the power of government in making and applying laws. Here we are concerned with those institutions of government that create the laws of our land.

Most educated adults are familiar with the basic structure of our federal government, which our Constitution divides into three branches: the legislative, the executive, and the judicial. Knowledge of this structure facilitates understanding of how and where our laws are made, and how they are classified for clarity and comprehension. State and local governments also are structured into these three branches and they operate in a manner similar to that of the federal system. We will explore government and these branches in greater detail in Chapter 7. Here we briefly consider the sources of our laws.

Lawmaking by Legislators

Legislators, both state and federal, enact laws called **statutes.** * Local legislative bodies enact laws called **ordinances.** Collectively these statutes and ordinances are called the *written law,* as contrasted to case law (judicial decisions). The written law covers a staggering number of subjects, such as crimes, civil rights, housing, health, and indeed all matters that the legislative branch has the constitutional power to govern. But it is important to understand that federal statutory law is limited to matters of federal **jurisdiction,**† state statutory law is limited to matters of statewide jurisdiction, and a similar limitation is true for local ordinances.

---

* Often statutes are assigned titles, such as the Federal Racketeer Influence and Corrupt Organizations Act, called RICO.
† Jurisdiction of the Congress or a state legislature refers to the subject matter over which the Congress or legislature is empowered to enact laws. For example, Congress has jurisdiction to regulate the transportation of goods in interstate commerce; state legislatures do not. Court jurisdiction is explained fully in Chapter 3.

The preceding jurisdictional rules may sound straightforward, but extremely difficult conflicts of jurisdiction have occurred. Article I, Section 8 of the U.S. Constitution enumerates everything over which the federal government has jurisdiction. Its language has been interpreted by federal courts in an expansive way. Some argue that the federal government intrudes on state's rights; others argue that the federal reach should be extended even further, perhaps into such matters as shelter for the homeless. (We consider the mysteries of constitutional law in detail in Chapter 2.) When conflicts arise between federal and state jurisdictions, the federal Supreme Court makes the ultimate judicial decision through its interpretation of the U. S. Constitution.

Even when jurisdictions overlap, that is, both a state and the federal government have jurisdiction, conflicts arise. The two may pass contradictory statutes. When that happens, the **Doctrine of Supremacy** applies, and the federal law prevails to the extent that the state law conflicts with federal law. For example, Amtrak routinely dumps its sewage on top of its tracks and roadbed as trains roll across the country. Permission for this dates back to early federal laws designed to encourage railroad construction. Florida initiated a criminal nuisance charge against Amtrak contending it dumped sewage on fishermen in a boat under a railroad trestle. In retaliation for the suit, Amtrak has threatened to discontinue rail service to Florida. Amtrak does not want to set a precedent by bowing to state law. Supported by the Doctrine of Supremacy, as of this writing, Amtrak continues dumping sewage along all its tracks. We predict that Amtrak will prevail until a *federal* lawmaking body determines to overrule Amtrak's policy.

Similar jurisdictional conflicts may exist between state and local governments. For example, local governments usually exercise exclusive jurisdiction over the zoning of real estate. Zoning laws restrict how land may be used. What if a state enacted a statute that authorized *state* officials to re-zone real estate, regardless of local government rules? Does that differ from the common practice whereby state laws require suburban communities to accept construction of treatment centers for drug addicts? Just as state law bows to federal law, local ordinances bow to state statutes.

Although proposed statutes are studied before their enactment, and although the end sought to be achieved is usually desirable and even necessary in the minds of proponents, the validity of a statute or ordinance still remains in doubt until determined by an appropriate court. There is a presumption that a newly enacted statute or ordinance is constitutional, and few are held invalid by courts. Nonetheless, it is possible to be sentenced to jail for violation of a statute that later is determined to be unconstitutional and therefore void.

The question of the validity of a statute can be very complex. Is a statute or ordinance that prohibits sleeping overnight in a public place constitutional? What if its stated purpose is to maintain sanitary and safe public sidewalks and parks? But what if its true purpose is to drive homeless people out of the inner cities? Is the legal effect of the statute more or less important than its stated purpose? As you can readily see, the wise enactment of proper statutes by our legislators is no easy task.

Once the legislative branch enacts a law, uncertainty technically remains until the law is applied and judicially approved as constitutional. A statute or ordinance will not be ruled on by a court unless it is challenged by someone affected by its application, because courts do not render decisions based on hypothetical conflicts. There must be a case or controversy properly presented to a court before judicial action will be taken.

Lawmaking by the Executive Branch

The executive branch of government, at the federal, state, and local levels, joins with the legislative branch in the adoption of statutes. However, even if the President (or a governor), as head of the executive branch, vetoes a proposed statute, the legislators have the power to override such action, usually with a two-thirds vote. This partnership in lawmaking is part of our system of checks and balances that encourages negotiation and compromise. The executive branch also makes certain laws by itself. The President, state governors, and heads of local governments all have authority to issue certain directives that have the force and effect of law.*

Of much wider applicability and impact is the lawmaking power of thousands of federal and state administrative agencies, which are specialized bodies created by Congress or state legislatures and empowered to regulate specific activities. Administrative agencies investigate problems within their respective jurisdictions (an executive function); make laws called *rules* and **regulations** (a legislative function); and conduct hearings (similar to trials) to determine if their rules have been violated, and, if so, what penalties should be imposed (a judicial function). There are hundreds of important federal administrative agencies, hundreds of state agencies in each state, and a lesser number of agencies within each local government. These agencies comprise much of what is referred to as "the ruling bureaucracy." They all make rules that have the force and effect of law.

You are probably already somewhat familiar with such federal administrative agencies as the Central Intelligence Agency (CIA), Drug Enforcement Administration (DEA), Environmental Protection Agency (EPA), Farm Credit Administration (FCA), Food and Drug Administration (FDA), and the National Bureau of Standards (NBS) [which has recently changed its name to the National Institute of Standards and Technology (NIST)]. Thousands of federal, state, and local administrative agencies continue to make and enforce innumerable laws each year on myriad subjects. We present the law of administrative agencies in Chapter 7.

Lawmaking by Courts

Federal and state judges conduct trials to settle legal controversies that are brought before them by the parties in litigation. At the conclusion of each trial, the judge renders judgment in favor of one or the other of the litigants. Sometimes these judgments are based on a jury verdict. When there is no jury, the judgment is

---

* For example, in 1986 then-President Ronald Reagan ordered the random drug testing of certain employees working in interstate transportation. In 1990 President George Bush ordered the activation of certain military reserve units for duty in the Middle East.

based on the trial court judge's evaluation of the evidence and his or her application of the law to the facts as found. The vast majority of these judgments are
never appealed. They resolve specific controversies and, to that extent, usually
apply existing law. Occasionally, however, if the case is unique and the first of its
kind in that jurisdiction, the trial judge may formulate and apply a new rule of
common law. Such a rule may then be reviewed by an appellate court, and
accepted or rejected for all courts in that jurisdiction.

Usually when judgments are appealed to appellate courts, the essential
question on appeal is whether or not the trial court judge made a *prejudicial
error*. Error exists when a trial court judge misapplies the law in the conduct of
the trial. For example, a trial judge may have erred by permitting the jury to consider irrelevant evidence. Not all errors of trial courts taint the outcome of the trial;
only those that reasonably could have affected the outcome of the trial are prejudicial. Much irrelevant testimony can be taken that is not prejudicial because it
could not reasonably have affected the jury verdict.

When error is claimed and an appeal is taken, the appellate court may affirm
the lower court's decision, reverse it, send it back for a new trial, or simply modify
the trial court judgment in some manner. Whichever result is appropriate, the
appellate court usually writes and publishes a written opinion which typically (1)
describes the nature of the controversy, (2) states what result was reached in the
lower court, (3) reveals the basis upon which the appellant is appealing, and (4)
declares and elaborates on its own decision, or "holding." In its decision the court
states the applicable "rules of law" as well as the rationale underlying its decision.

In making rulings, appellate courts interpret and apply relevant statutory law
together with appropriate rules of common law derived from prior cases under the
doctrine of stare decisis. If there is no controlling statute or principle of common
law, which occasionally happens, the appellate court will create or extend an
existing principle and apply it to the case. That new principle becomes a part of
the continually evolving common law to be followed by other courts in future
cases. New law is thereby created. For example, if the United States Supreme
Court declared that states could constitutionally prohibit the possession of
handguns by all citizens, is there any doubt that it would be new law?

Judges who purposefully expand on the law in their decisions are often
referred to as *judicial activists*. Judges who narrowly interpret the law by relying
heavily on the doctrine of stare decisis are often referred to as *strict construc-
tionists*. Either way, the interpretations of law set forth by judges constitute "judge-
made" law, or common law. Sometimes court-made law is called *decisional law* or
case law, since it is found in decisions of courts. Courts are reactive institutions;
judges must wait for litigation to reach them so they can render a decision.
Legislative bodies, on the other hand, can initiate new laws on any subject at any
time they choose. Nonetheless, the judicial system has been responsible for many
of the great social changes that have occurred in the United States.

Not all the language used by appellate courts in their written opinions becomes
part of the common law. Much of it is explanatory, analyzing the facts of the case
and elaborating on various legal principles that may or may not directly apply.
Legal issues addressed in the opinion that are not logically necessary to support
the ruling in the case are called *dicta*. Being unnecessary language, dicta does not

become part of the common law, although it may reveal a clue about how that judge's philosophy might be applied in future cases.

Sometimes it is quite clear which statutory language or principle of common law is applicable to a case. But how it should be applied may be quite complex. For example, in a murder trial there may be no disagreement about the applicability of a statute declaring that an unlawful killing with malice is murder. But the question of whether or not the particular defendant, who was severely impaired with drugs at the time of the crime, can be legally capable of harboring malice, may be an extremely complex legal question. Following the trial (in which the trial court judge will have ruled one way or the other on the issue), opposing appellate attorneys persuasively argue in favor of their contradictory positions when presenting their appeals to the appellate court in written briefs and during oral arguments. Ultimately the legal controversy will be decided by an appellate court and a precedent will be set.

Through this decisional process, both federal and state appellate judges are making new law on a daily basis. With judges throughout the country "making law," can we expect decisions to be consistent?

> . . . critical legal scholars—or simply 'crits'—. . . contend that decisions conflict with one another because they are based on different, and controversial, moral and political ideals. Lawyers cannot give a simple answer to a question, the crits say, because the legal system, like our society at large, cannot reconcile the contradictory instincts people feel when they confront social problems.[5]

Does this mean the rule of law is flexible, depending on who is declaring it? If so, does that give added significance to the political appointment process underlying the selection of judges?

To assist you in understanding the way our appellate courts make and apply the law, excerpts from various important appellate cases are presented at the end of every chapter.

Types and Classifications of Law

Already you have considered the medieval sources of our contemporary law. You also have identified people and institutions that continually make and update our laws to help manage our highly complex modern society. Now you are ready to consider some definitions and classifications of our law, broadening your perspectives and enhancing your appreciation of its pervasiveness.

We have distinguished between common law and statutory law. **Federal law** consists of the U.S. Constitution, statutes enacted by Congress, treaties and Presidential orders, rules promulgated by federal agencies, and decisions of federal courts. **State law** consists of state constitutions, statutes enacted by state legislatures, rules promulgated by state agencies, and the decisions of state courts. **Civil law** is the body of law, both federal and state, that pertains to civil or private rights enforced by civil actions. For example, the laws governing contracts are civil laws. Breach of a contract may result in a civil action for money damages to reimburse the person wronged for any financial loss suffered. **Criminal law**, as contrasted to civil law, is the body of statutory law, both federal and state, that declares what conduct is criminal and prescribes penalties for its commission. For example, a statute may define murder as an unlawful killing "with malice afore-thought." The precise definition of malice aforethought may change through inter-pretation by courts over a period of years, and thus courts may be said to define conduct that is criminal in nature.

The statutory law of individual states concerning crimes is collected in books called *Penal Codes*. Civil laws, in general, are collected in books called *Civil Codes*. In addition, there are numerous specialized codes in the states that group together statutes pertaining to particular subjects, such as a Vehicle Code, a Health and Welfare Code, a Corporations Code, and a Business and Professions Code. These codes (often with slightly different titles) are generally available in the public law library usually located in county courthouses. **Private law** is the body of law regulating the rights and duties that exist between private persons (a term that includes corporations). Contract law is an example of private law. **Public law** on the other hand, includes constitutional, administrative, criminal, and interna-tional law, all more directly concerned with public rights and obligations. **International law** is the law governing relations among sovereign nations.

Procedural law consists of all the rules, or mechanisms, for processing civil and criminal cases through the judicial system. Some call it "lawyer's law," since its complexities arguably are designed to provide full employment for attorneys. Different procedural laws govern each court system, both state and federal.

Procedural law, in its pre-trial aspects, may dictate the dates and time limits within which papers must be filed, the size of paper to be used by attorneys, the size of print to be used on the specified paper, the fees that must be paid for the various documents upon filing, what information must be contained in legal papers, how witnesses and parties can be orally examined before trial, when and where the trial shall be, what witnesses may be called, what issues may be pre-sented to the trial court, and so on.

In its trial aspects, procedural law dictates what evidence may be offered to the jury, how the jury may be selected, where the parties may sit in the courtroom and even if they may stand, what questions may be asked of witnesses, and so on.

Finally, there is a separate body of procedural law governing the mechanics of processing appeals.

Procedural law for civil cases differs from that for criminal cases. In short, the procedural law is as complex as it is vast, and cases that might have been won on their merits have been lost because of faulty lawyering with the applicable proce-dural law. A frequent type of attorney malpractice involves procedural law mis-takes, such as missing a critical deadline. If an attorney fails to comply with the civil procedural law, the court may, as a penalty, dismiss the case, with the result that the attorney's client loses. If a prosecutor fails to comply with the criminal procedural law, the court may dismiss the case and set the defendant free. Some of you may already have experienced this happy event when you went to court to challenge a citation for a traffic infraction, the citing officer was too busy with other duties, did not appear to testify, and your case was dismissed.

Procedural law is so important that it receives basic constitutional protection in the Sixth Amendment to the U.S. Constitution (made applicable to the states by the Fourteenth Amendment, as explained in Chapter 2). The Sixth Amendment as interpreted by the U.S. Supreme Court requires that the government provide each citizen with procedural due process in criminal proceedings, including the right to have the advice of an attorney even if you are indigent, the right to confront your accusers in a speedy and public trial by an impartial jury, and the right to be heard and present a defense.

Clearly the challenge of providing the mechanics for the processing of myriad cases of widely different nature has resulted in a complex body of procedural law. State and federal procedural laws are created by statute and by the courts themselves in publications called *rules of court.*

The **substantive law,** as contrasted to the procedural law, defines duties, establishes rights, and prohibits wrongs. Murder is prohibited by the substantive law; a license is required before entering the real estate sales business; there are speed limits and registration requirements for automobiles—all are duties imposed by the substantive law.

Law also is often classified on the basis of subject matter. Consider these distinct types of law: *corporation, admiralty, business, real estate, family, environmental, constitutional, labor, probate, corporate securities,* and *immigration.* There are dozens of other specialties and the list keeps growing. For example, a recent addition is *elder law,* pertaining to unique rights and duties of senior citizens. Lawyers often refer to themselves in terms like: "trial lawyer," "corporate lawyer," "labor lawyer," or "lobbyist."* As noted in Chapter 15, when you need an attorney, you may need a specialist. Most specialists in the law have their own professional organizations, such as Trial Lawyers Associations, and the National Academy of Elder Law Attorneys. A licensed attorney may practice in any field of law, but in California, for example, the official State Bar permits only those lawyers who have met certain standards of education and experience to become certified and to advertise themselves as certified specialists in the following fields: criminal law; family law; immigration and nationality law; taxation law; workers' compensation law; and probate, estate planning, and trust law. Other attorneys may practice law in those areas, but they cannot hold themselves out as certified specialists.

Examples of Legal Issues in the 1990s

Law is dynamic, always changing and evolving, always meeting new issues. Our legal system is charged with making the "hard" decisions. This conclusion seems especially relevant when issues on the cutting edge of modern life become politically too hot to handle. Perhaps the best current example is the issue of abortion; elected officials at all levels of government increasingly are faced with the

---

* Not all lobbyists are lawyers, but since legislators are constantly concerned with passage of new laws, and the amendment or repeal of old laws, lawyers are especially qualified for this endeavor. Oddly enough, if they are hired and paid as legal counsel, they generally need not register as professional lobbyists, and are not subject to the rules that require lobbyists to disclose sources and amounts of income received.

dilemma of stating their personal positions on the question, either pro or con. Whatever their choice, politicians fear the loss of many votes by constituents who disagree. The number could be decisive. Understandably most politicians would be happy to see the issue resolved by the U.S. Supreme Court, removing it as a factor in future elections. This sort of political bombshell is one reason why Supreme Court Justices are appointed for life. They are accustomed to both praise and criticism, but never have to yield to public pressure or special interest groups. As of this writing, many court observers predict that the Supreme Court will return the abortion issue to the states for closer study and varied legislative and judicial treatment. Abortion is only one extraordinarily difficult issue facing our society in the 1990s. Many important future legislative actions and judicial decisions will profoundly affect different segments of our society. Many critics argue that some of the issues are relatively unimportant (e.g., flag-burning, and prayers in schools); but to sincere partisans, the same issues involve fundamental tenets in our constitutional democracy.

Most people become aware of new issues when reading newspapers or news magazines, or while watching television reports of current events. One of the benefits you will gain from your study of the law will be an improved ability to formulate and defend reasoned opinions about new and controversial issues of the day. Perhaps you already have strong convictions about some of these issues, or are directly affected by them. We present a short selection of these issues of the 1990s, both as examples and for your reflection.

● *Should a city's homeless people be jailed or cited for sleeping in public places?* Homelessness has reached shocking levels in major cities in the United States. One reason for this tragic development has been the deinstitutionalization of the mentally ill who, if properly treated with medications, pose little danger to themselves or society. Unfortunately, without close supervision, many fail to take the prescribed drugs. Other persons live on the streets because of chronic unemployment and a lack of affordable, decent housing. Drug and alcohol addiction also contributes to the problem. Should cities be permitted to disperse and drive away their homeless residents by passing ordinances prohibiting sleeping in public places? At least one court has upheld such ordinances.[6]

● *Should herbicides be sprayed on marijuana plants in foreign countries when their residue causes incurable lung damage to users in the United States?* Herbicides, especially the potent paraquat (forbidden for use in the United States) is sprayed on marijuana plants in foreign countries, especially Mexico, for eradication purposes. But a significant percentage of the marijuana used in New York, Atlanta, Chicago, Dallas, and Los Angeles is contaminated with residue in amounts capable of causing irreversible lung damage. Is paraquat simply a normal risk of using illegal drugs? Would your answer be affected if the government admitted that one purpose of paraquat spraying was to punish users by damaging their health? Would such a response violate the principle that all accused are presumed innocent until proven guilty in a court of law?

● *Should a university prohibit on-campus verbal speech that belittles students because of their race, religion, or sexual orientation?* Almost no one approves of or condones seriously offensive speech. But what is seriously offensive speech? And is the proper antidote for such speech a prohibitory law—or simply "good" counter-speech? In a more sophisticated sense, does the First Amendment to the U.S. Constitution protect all speech, or only "good" speech? The University of Michigan tried to create a harassment-free environment by prohibiting racially offensive speech. It was struck down by a federal court as violating the First Amendment to the Constitution. Stanford has adopted a more restrictive ban, prohibiting only "fighting words," which are epithets likely to evoke a violent response. Even those words are forbidden only if they are understood to convey hatred or contempt for humans of the sex, race, or sexual orientation in question. Will courts uphold the ban? Is there a clear-cut rule of law to apply?

Nina Wu, while residing as a student in a University of Connecticut dormitory, placed a sign on her door that described four categories of people, one of which included those who would be "shot on sight." That group included "homos," "bimbos," "preppies," "men without chest hair," and "drunk skunks." Her fellow students complained and Wu was evicted. She also was denied cafeteria privileges. Has her right to free speech been violated? Wu thinks so, and has filed suit in federal court.[7]

● *Should there be a "Right to Die?"* Nancy Cruzan, now in her 30s, is unconscious in a persistent vegetative state—"awake but unaware"—as a result of devastating brain injuries suffered in an automobile accident when she was only 25. Her eyes open sometimes and she breathes without aid. She receives nourishment through a surgically inserted feeding tube. Nancy is permanently disabled. All four of her limbs are severely contracted; her fingernails cut into her wrists. Nancy is incontinent. The most intimate aspects of her existence are exposed to and controlled by strangers. She has no chance for recovery but could be maintained for another 30 years. Since Nancy is not a minor, Missouri taxpayers bear the $130,000 annual cost of keeping her alive. Her parents testified that Nancy would prefer death to technological life.

The Missouri Supreme Court held that under state law there was no clear and convincing evidence that Nancy would prefer to die.* The U.S. Supreme Court held there is no constitutional "right to die" and that state law, not federal law, controls the circumstances under which medical treatment can be discontinued.[8] An estimated 10,000 people linger in a persistent vegetative state within the United States, and are being keep alive in a manner similar to Nancy Cruzan.[9]

Unlike Nancy Cruzan, Larry McAfee is awake and a rational adult, although he is paralyzed from the neck down by a motorcycle accident. A Georgia Superior Court has responded to McAfee's request by ruling he has a right to shut off the ventilator that is sustaining his life. The local judge ruled that McAfee's right to refuse life-sustaining treatment outweighs the state's interest in preserving life.[10]

This literally vital issue is discussed in Chapter 14 in connection with living wills. Do such rulings encourage ending a life rather than striving for a meaningful existence? The right to die from discontinuance of treatment is quite different from the direct taking of a life for merciful reasons. Euthanasia, so-called "mercy

---

* Thirteen states have durable power of attorney statutes that authorize a person to appoint a surrogate to make medical treatment decisions. A *durable power of attorney* is a written form of authorization that survives any mental disability of the person who otherwise would elect to discontinue or decline treatment.

killing," has not been sanctioned by courts, although many courts award minimum or reduced sentences to persons convicted of such crimes.

Assisting a person in a merciful suicide is a crime in some states; in other states it is not. The U.S. Supreme Court has not been presented with such a case as of this writing.

● *Should lawyers be required to reveal the identities of their clients who pay large fees in cash?* As you will learn in Chapter 15, there is an attorney-client privilege that prohibits attorneys from revealing communications received from their clients. This is an ancient rule of law designed to promote full and honest disclosure from client to attorney, without the risk of self-incrimination or other disadvantage. The Internal Revenue Service is not concerned with communications from clients, only with tracing profits from illicit sources, often drug-related. Enforcement of this law would, no doubt, reveal much "laundered drug money"* as well as the identity of some tax evaders. Is revealing the nature of payment received different than revealing information about some event? Does such information seem to violate the privilege against self-incrimination? Couldn't clients pay with checks or money orders? Or is cash preferred because negotiable paper is easily traceable by investigative authorities? Do cash payments encourage attorneys to commit tax evasion? Congress enacted a statute requiring the disclosure of large cash fees, but the IRS has attempted to enforce it only once, in Detroit. Some lawyers complied, others did not. The law remains on uncertain ground and litigation is pending.[11]

● *Who should be granted ownership of frozen embryos?* Some otherwise fertile women need to have some of their ova (eggs) surgically removed for in vitro (Latin: in glass, i.e., in a laboratory vessel) fertilization. Rather than endure surgery more than once, it is common to remove and fertilize many eggs for future use, keeping them frozen in a procedure called *cryopreservation.* The world's first test-tube "orphans" lost their mother and father in a plane crash in South America. If successfully implanted and born, they would inherit a multi-million dollar estate. What disposition should be made of these fertilized eggs? There are thousands of fertilized eggs in America which could survive for 100 years or more. Unfortunately, some have been abandoned by mothers who do not want additional children, some have been abandoned for unknown reasons, and some parents have simply failed to pay storage bills that average about $200 per year. Should fertilized embryos be sold? Given to women who need them to have children? Who should get the embryos upon divorce? Some fertility laboratories destroy unwanted embryos by rapid thawing or simply flushing them down the sink. Should we have a national and comprehensive statutory scheme dealing with frozen embryos? Or should court-made law resolve the problem? How does this problem affect the larger issue of abortion? What should the law require?

● *Should author-prisoners have the right to sell articles about prison life to newspapers?* Federal prison rules (made by the U.S. Bureau of Prisons, an administrative agency) prohibit prisoners from selling by-lined articles (i.e., with the author identified in print) about prison conditions to newspapers. Dannie Martin,

---

* Laundered money is cash that has had its illegal source "washed away" by infusing it into some legitimate business enterprise.

serving time at the Lompoc federal facility on a conviction for attempted bank robbery, wrote a number of such articles, which were purchased by and published in the *San Francisco Chronicle*. One, titled the "Gulag Mentality," reported rising tensions in the prison and criticized the warden. Martin was summarily placed in solitary confinement for a week, and then transferred to another facility outside California. Martin joined with the newspaper in suing in U.S. District Court, contending the prison rule infringed on his freedom of speech as protected by the First Amendment. Prison officials contend that continued publication would create an intolerable situation in managing the prison. Is Martin being additionally punished for "committing journalism" or for violating reasonable prison rules, or both? Should the public have a right to know—by learning the facts from prisoners, prison personnel, unannounced visitors, or grand juries, if need be—what is happening inside prison walls? Should newspapers be joining, and possibly financing, litigation brought against prison officials by disgruntled prisoners? At the time of this writing, a U.S. District Judge has ruled that the prison rules are rationally related to the legitimate penological objective of prison security, and therefore are constitutional. An appeal to a higher court is pending.

● *Should a "resident child molester" law be enacted permitting conviction of defendants when young victimized children cannot testify as to when or where each alleged act occurred?* A young child who has been molested repeatedly by someone living in the house might not be able to distinguish the time and place of one act from another. On the other hand, such a failure to pinpoint the alleged acts may deny the defendant any reasonable chance to contest the charges, which may violate due process of law. Proposed "resident child molester" laws would make conviction possible without proof as to specific time, place, or other particulars. Testimony about three abusive sexual acts with a child under 14 by a resident of the house within any three-month period would constitute the crime.[12] Would this rule of evidence be an improper "bending" of the law, which could lead to conviction of innocent persons, to achieve the socially desirable goal of protecting defenseless children? Would such a rule render an alibi defense impossible? Would it allow a conviction without requiring jurors to agree on what the defendant had done, violating the right to a unanimous verdict? What if you were the innocent defendant?

● *Should standardized psychological tests be used in criminal cases as evidence that the accused does not have a personality type likely to have committed the charged crime?* Suppose a defendant's personality profile does not conform to the profile displayed by the average child molester, robber, rapist, etc. Should personality test results be accepted as evidence of a defendant's innocence? In other words, should personality profile test results be used the same as blood tests and voice prints? What if personality tests are accurate 70 percent of the time? Or 50 percent of the time? Should the prosecution be entitled to call its own witnesses about the defendant's profile? Would the emphasis of the trial shift to experts testifying about test results? Is it relevant to this problem that visual profiles of persons entering the U.S. from foreign countries have been used successfully by customs officers in identifying drug smugglers? Of course, many who fit such profiles are not "druggies." One high court has permitted the introduction of personality test results in the defense of a husband and wife accused of committing lewd acts with minors.[13] All states, except New Mexico, ban lie detector test results from use as evidence in criminal trials. One visiting professor at Brandeis University, Leonard Saxe, a leading opponent of polygraph testing, publicly declared "You might as well flip a coin."[14] His opinion regarding psychological profile test results is unknown.

Public Perceptions of Our Legal System

Our legal system may be defined in a broad sense, encompassing all institutions and people involved in making, applying, and enforcing law. Members of the legislative branches of federal, state, and local governments; judges; lawyers; law enforcement officials; penologists (prison management officials); most governmental bureaucracies; and even our law schools all form parts of our legal system. This legal system is the backbone of our constitutional democracy and guarantees traditional notions of fair play and justice to the society it serves. Or does it? How does our society perceive and measure our legal system?

Most people become personally aware of our legal system when it directly enters their lives. An audit notice is received from the Internal Revenue Service. A parking ticket is found on the windshield of one's car. A car is burglarized. An important issue, such as abortion, is presented in a case before the Supreme Court and is given extensive coverage by the media. Often such personal experiences produce disturbingly unpleasant reactions in our minds. To sue or be sued is always a traumatic experience. But our perceptions of the legal system are derived largely from the news media: television, newspapers, or news magazines. News, by its very nature, focuses on current events of the day—often catastrophes, tragedies, and political issues—not on processes routinely accomplished by millions of people doing their daily work within the legal system. Society's perceptions clearly focus on what the electronic and print media deliver (i.e., the topics presented) and how they deliver it (i.e., the focused viewpoint).

The public may be expected to measure our legal system by generally accepted ethical principles: *honesty, integrity, fidelity, fairness, respect for others, accountability, promise-keeping, responsible citizenship, the appearances of propriety, and courage to do what is right rather than what is expedient.*

Following are widely publicized events dealing with our legal system as we have defined it above. Are these events evidence of general ethical malaise within our legal system? Or do they distort reality by focusing on the one rotten apple in the barrel? Whichever you agree with, both views feed public suspicions about how many "guilty" public officials and private attorneys aren't being exposed.

Lawmakers

Following years of unprecedented and highly publicized examples of unethical and criminal behavior in Washington, D.C. (from Watergate to the Savings and Loan industry debacle), it would not be surprising if the public gave most politicians low grades in fulfilling their responsibilities within the legal system. Dave Barry, Pulitzer-winning syndicated humor columnist, visited Congress to look into what he calls "this ethics thing." He observed: "Ten lawmakers got more than

$200,000 each from special interests last year, even though nobody was running against them . . . ." Continuing: "People tend to view members of Congress pretty much the way they view body odors. They can tolerate their own, but they can't stand anybody else's."[15] Why would a congressional representative need campaign funds if there is no campaign? Perhaps because campaign funds can be transferred to personal funds when the lawmaker retires, often amounting to hundreds of thousands of dollars.*

One businessman, blank checks in hand, appeared on the floor of the Texas state senate while legislation in which he was interested was pending. He handed out nine personal checks for $10,000 each, with the payee's name left blank. He said they were "political contributions" and not "bribes." Eight senators later returned their checks; one who didn't said "I've received campaign contributions that size before. If the principle's wrong, it don't matter if it's a dollar or a million, right?"[16] Do you think it was significant that the checks were made out blank, with no named payee? Assuming the blank check event was a legal political contribution, what are the *appearances of propriety* of contributions made in such manner?

Annually, Public Citizen, a consumer advocacy group founded by Ralph Nader, reports publicly on foreign travel by U.S. lawmakers as a part of their congressional business. However, Congress requires little *accountability:* its members report only the dates, destinations, and certain expenses of their public-financed trips; neither justification for nor accomplishments of foreign travel is required. One representative visited 39 countries on 14 different trips in one year. Total cost to taxpayers of foreign travel by members of Congress in a recent year: $13 million.[17] Are ethical constraints likely to be as effective as laws in restricting the improper use of public funds for personal travel?

Congress historically has exempted itself from federal employment and anti-discrimination laws, including the Civil Rights Act, the Equal Opportunity Act, the Equal Pay Act, the Occupational Safety and Health Act, and the Fair Labor Standards Act. One result is that clerical and blue-collar workers are denied overtime pay that federal law enacted by Congress requires other employers to provide. Is it reasonable to see in this a lack of *fairness?* What about hypocritical lawmaking?

At least partly in response to growing public distrust, and even hostility toward Congress because of disclosures of questionable conduct by some of its members, the senators and representatives passed the Ethics Reform Act of 1989, which ". . . contains important reforms that strengthen federal ethical standards," according to President George Bush. It also raised House members' salaries from $89,500 to $125,000 (with restrictions on honoraria); senators' salaries increased from $89,500 to $98,400 (with right to receive honoraria up to $38,800). All federal judges and top executive branch officials also received major increases.[18] Is it basic *honesty* to disguise legislation, titling it an "Ethics Reform Act," when its dominant impact is a general salary increase? What difference, if any, does such mislabeling make?

---

* The practice of transferring unused campaign funds into personal accounts upon retirement will end in 1993, pursuant to the Ethics Reform Act of 1989.

No issue involving the ethics of lawmakers has received more public attention than the multi-billion dollar fiasco of Lincoln Savings & Loan, also called the "Keating Five" case.* American Continental Corp. owned many corporations, including Lincoln Savings & Loan and its 29 branch offices. In 1987, federal regulators in San Francisco were pressing an investigation into the alleged reckless lending practices of Lincoln preliminary to a U.S. seizure to prevent further losses of federally insured funds. The chairman of the Federal Home Loan Bank Board (FHLB), which was in charge of investigations of member savings and loans, was summoned at that time to a now-infamous meeting with five U.S. senators who had received a combined total of $1.4 million in campaign contributions from Keating. There is dispute about what was said at the meeting, but there is no dispute as to the questionable *propriety* of a meeting between five U.S. senators and one bureaucrat concerning an ongoing investigation. Soon after, a new chairman of the FHLB ordered the investigation transferred to Washington, D.C. The transfer somehow delayed the closing of Lincoln for two years while its losses continued to grow. Moreover, during this two-year period Lincoln, through its branch offices, encouraged investors to buy "junk bonds."†

In 1989, one day after American Continental Corp. filed for bankruptcy, and two years after the noted meeting of senators, the FHLB ordered the seizure of Lincoln to protect it from further federally insured losses. The FHLB chairman who ordered the investigation transfer has since resigned. Continental's junk bonds are worthless, Lincoln's losses of insured funds exceed $2 billion. Investors accuse the five senators of derailing the California investigation into Lincoln that might have resulted in government intervention before they lost their money. Others contend the delay in the investigation and closure caused Lincoln's insured losses to escalate by more than $1.3 billion.[19] At the time of this writing, a U.S. Senate ethics committee is investigating and a maze of litigation is underway. Regardless of the outcomes, the image of five U.S. senators meeting with a key administrator about a pending investigation into fraudulent practices involving hundreds of millions of

---

* Charles Keating controlled Lincoln Savings and Loan; the ethical standards of five U.S. senators are involved: Cranston (California), DeConcini (Arizona), Glenn (Ohio), McCain (Arizona), and Riegle (Michigan). Among other acts, Keating is accused of defrauding some 23,000 small investors, mostly older people, of some $250 million. Many lost their life's savings. Furthermore, Lincoln's losses, which must be paid by taxpayers' money because Lincoln was insured by the Federal Savings and Loan Insurance Corporation (FSLIC), total $2.5 billion dollars or more, equal to $10 for each man, woman, and child in the U.S. At this writing Charles Keating is in jail with bail set at $5 million pending trial on various criminal charges.

† A junk bond is the slang term for a corporate debenture bond, which is a security given to a creditor (small investor, in this case) who is lending money to a borrower (American Continental Corp., in this case). Debentures are analogous to promissory notes. Repayment of the borrowed money is guaranteed only by the credit worthiness of the borrower; the debt is not secured with collateral. Only risky debentures that carry extraordinarily high interest rates, such as 15 or more percent, are commonly referred to as "junk bonds." Holders of risky junk bonds are usually the last creditors entitled to be paid when and if all other creditors of the borrowing corporation are paid. In a nutshell, junk bonds are riskier than other forms of debt securities, and are especially unsuitable as investments for older and retired persons. Most of the elderly investors in Continental's now-worthless junk bonds were led to believe their investments were insured by the government's FSLIC, just like deposits of savers. That belief turned out to be unfounded.

dollars can only lower the public's perception of our lawmakers' prudence, if not their *integrity,* while participating in our legal system. Is this an example of media distortion of five U.S. senators, or is the focus of public attention especially warranted because the appearances of *impropriety* of five senators involves 5 percent of the entire 100-member U.S. Senate? What would be reasonable *accountability* for the involvement of five U.S. senators in the scandal?

The Executive Branch

The world-famous scandals known as Watergate and Iran-Contra involved unethical and even criminal behavior primarily by members of the executive branch. Iran-Contra continues into the 1990s with the appeal of John Poindexter, former National Security Adviser to President Ronald Reagan, of his conviction for lying to Congress. Poindexter was the only Iran-Contra defendant to receive a jail sentence (six months)* As of this writing, one of North's convictions has been reversed. North's and Poindexter's remaining appeals are still pending, as are the public's perceptions of unethical conduct in the executive branch.

Perhaps the most expensive example of executive misconduct concerns the mishandling of the funds of the Department of Housing and Urban Development (HUD). A panel of congressional representatives is investigating charges of fraud, mismanagement, and influence peddling, prompted by anticipated losses in the hundreds of millions of dollars. Samuel Pierce, as Secretary of HUD (a cabinet-level position), has refused to testify before Congress concerning the disposition of millions earmarked for shelter for low-income citizens. The Fifth Amendment to our Constitution protects everyone in our society from self-incrimination, even cabinet-level officers. Nevertheless, much has already surfaced. For example, former Interior Secretary James Watt placed eight telephone calls and attended one 30-minute meeting and received $300,000 in lobbying fees for obtaining a HUD contract for a Maryland housing project.[20] Does the public's perception that in politics what counts is who you know, not what you know, appear to be correct? As much as $100 million in taxpayers' money was stolen from foreclosure proceeds by escrow agents. One agent alone admitted stealing $5.6 million.[21] The Department of Justice continues its nationwide investigation of HUD as the decade of the 1990s begins. What impact does unethical conduct by the highest officials in the executive branch have on the public's perception of the behavior of all members in government and in the bureaucracy? Because unethical behavior of a few tarnishes the reputation of thousands who perform their tasks in proper manner, should this multiplier effect be a factor in determining just punishment of the few who are exposed and convicted of criminal conduct? What is a reasonable *accountability* for senior management officials who oversee the wholesale theft of millions of dollars of public money?

---

* Other executive branch defendants include Oliver North (former National Security Council aide), who was found guilty by jury trial of three felonies; Robert McFarlane (former National Security Adviser), who pleaded guilty to four misdemeanors; and Richard Secord (retired Air Force general), who pleaded guilty to lying to Congress. McFarlane and Secord each were sentenced to two years' probation. North was fined $150,000 and ordered to perform community service. North is appealing his conviction contending that the prosecution improperly used information obtained from his previous testimony to Congress, which was given under a grant of immunity. Testimony given under a grant of immunity cannot be used against the witness.

In California it is illegal to provide clean needles to drug addicts to help slow the spread of AIDS. In San Francisco, volunteers exchange about 2,500 needles per week with the tacit approval of local enforcement officials, making it a larger program than the legal one in New York City. Regardless of the merit or lack of merit of the program, what becomes of the ethical principle of *fidelity* when officials who are sworn to uphold the law look the other way.[22] Who gets to decide on which occasions officials need not enforce the law?

Judges

Most judges accept appointments to the bench out of a sincere commitment to public service, not to get rich. But judges everywhere publicly contend they are underpaid, and some are threatening to leave the bench for more profitable jobs. Justices of the highest state court in New York receive $115,000; their Michigan counterparts receive $100,000. The national average is $77,231. Judges of the general trial courts in New York receive $95,000; their Michigan counterparts get $84,600. The national average for these lower court judges is $69,439.[23] Similar to state court systems, there are also three basic levels of courts in the federal system. Federal court judges received a raise from Congress in 1989 to $96,570 for District Court judges, $102,505 for justices of Courts of Appeal, and $118,690 for U.S. Supreme Court justices. An important factor in supporting the pay raises for federal judges was a supposed migration from the bench, threatening to result in the appointment of less qualified judges. This migration would thus, so the argument goes, threaten the quality of justice delivered by our legal system. Where would these migrating judges go? Would private law firms absorb them all? Would there be no adequate replacements for such a migration? Is it reasonable to draw such a dramatic conclusion without a scientifically accurate study concluding that there are not enough qualified attorneys who are willing to accept federal judgeships for salaries at even the former level of $89,500? *Honesty* is a basic precept of ethical conduct, as is *courage* to do what is right and not necessarily expedient.

In 1989 the U.S. Congress impeached a U.S. District Court judge, Alcee Hastings, for conspiring to accept a $150,000 bribe from two criminal defendants in exchange for lenient sentences. Following his impeachment, Hastings announced his candidacy for governor of Florida: "Negative celebrity brings one into the fray the same as positive celebrity does," he said. "I'm at least well known."[24] Conviction for flagrant unethical conduct does not appear to be a factor in Hastings' decision to campaign for his state's highest office. Is ethical conduct of public officials as unimportant to the voters as this candidate assumes? *Integrity* is a basic precept of ethical conduct.

U.S. District Court judge Robert Aguilar, who sits in San Jose, California, has been indicted on charges that he attempted to influence other judges in two criminal cases, leaked government surveillance information to felons, and lied to federal agents. His first trial occurred in 1990, and Aguilar was acquitted on one count. The jury was "hung," that is, deadlocked on seven other counts, of which two were dropped by the U.S. Attorney. On retrial, later in 1990, a jury convicted Judge Aguilar of leaking wire tap information to a former mobster and of lying to FBI agents to derail a federal grand jury investigation into his conduct. He may receive up to ten years in prison and up to a $500,000 fine for the felony convictions, nonetheless he will receive his full salary of $96,523 per year pending the

Is character a criterion for judges?

outcome of his appeal. Judge Aguilar has continued sitting as an active judge through much of the pre-trial and post-trial periods. If Judge Aguilar's convictions are upheld on appeal, we predict he will resign his lifetime appointment or face impeachment by the United States Congress.[25] U.S. judges are among the most powerful, well-paid, and respected public officials, with lifetime appointments subject to removal only through impeachment and conviction by Congress. Would you object to submitting your case, civil or criminal, to a judge who was awaiting his own felony criminal trial? _Respect for others_ is another precept for ethical conduct. Would you favor a law requiring temporary suspension of official duties for judges awaiting their own criminal trials, instead of relying on the ethical behavior of indicted judges? Should it be necessary to enforce all basic ethical precepts with laws?

The perception of the public, as measured by a 1989 Gallup poll, is that criminals are being treated too leniently (83 percent) and that courts are unable to properly convict and sentence criminals (73 percent).[26] Whether the public is displeased with the court system, judges, or both, the result of the poll reflects a poor public perception of the judicial branch.

Lawyers

Lawyers are the touchstone between society and its legal system. They give advice attempting to guide clients around controversy. They perform negotiating services to resolve problems; they steer disputes through settlement processes, and through litigation if necessary. They work long hours and bear overwhelming responsibilities while serving their clients. Many still find time for **pro bono** (Latin: for the public good) contributions of time to indigent persons. Most lawyers seldom see the inside of a courtroom; instead they are researching, advising, negotiating, and ministering to the demands of clients. Some people blame the legal profession for the proliferation of law, lawyers, and lawsuits; others blame a litigious, mean-spirited, and greedy society. In a sense, attorneys are simply the tools of society, reflecting its demands for victory. They are the so-called "hired guns."

Attorneys know well that criticism is inevitable, since in every case one side loses: the attorney, the client, and possibly others who are allied with them. When one doctor loses a medical malpractice case, other doctors reading of the outcome or hearing of it from colleagues may take umbrage at the actual or supposed aggressive tactics of the winning lawyer and the size of the verdict. Certainly the public's perception of the ethical conduct of attorneys is poor, as reflected by the increasing popularity of hostile "lawyer jokes."

In a sense, the adversary system of justice (See Chapter 15 for further explanation) compels public perceptions of skepticism toward the legal profession. The underlying assumption of the adversary system is that truth is most likely to be ascertained if advocates aggressively present evidence in support of all conceivable opposing theories to a neutral judge or jury.

In criminal cases, critics of the adversary system point to the differences between resources and legal talent available to the poor or even the middle class, and the wealthy. Doesn't the defendant in a criminal trial want to hide the truth if he or she is guilty? Isn't it the defense attorney's job, according to the adversary system, to help conceal that truth? And isn't the prosecutor tempted to hide the truth about any illegal means through which evidence used in the case was obtained? In civil cases, do attorneys on contingent fee contracts, who may win a "piece of the pie," have vested interests in truth or in generous verdicts? These examples of negative perceptions and suspicions flowing from court cases are difficult for the legal profession to overcome. Supposed easy answers to these questions are likely to ignore the reality that all attorneys are officers of the court in which they practice, and are ethically bound to numerous written rules of conduct.

The public is aware that, through objections by attorneys, even the jury is not trusted with all the truth in either civil or criminal cases. Why is much evidence withheld from the jury (such as the existence of insurance covering the liability of the civil defendant or existence of a criminal record or an improperly obtained confession of the criminal defendant)? Lawyers know that any value in revealing such matters to juries would be more than offset by the prejudices that would likely impact the juries' verdicts. But members of the public are likely to focus on the fact that somehow lawyers make sure that juries do not hear all the truth.

Long before a trial begins, lawyers compete for clients, just as other profit-motivated persons do. Advertising by attorneys has become commonplace. On a national basis, millions of dollars are spent by lawyers on TV advertisements alone.[27] "Ambulance chasing" is the unethical practice of soliciting legal business at the scene of some tragedy. Following the crash of a Delta L-1011 airplane at the Dallas-Fort Worth airport in 1985, lawyers descended on the scene seeking clients amid the chaos, meandering among emergency-relief workers and hospital aides. They entered Parkland Memorial Hospital handing out name cards to families of the survivors. Is this ethical, proper, or necessary? Is at-the-scene solicitation *respectful* of the sensitivities of others?

By 1989, state bar officials were ready when a United DC-10 airplane crashed in Sioux City, Iowa (dubbed "Sue City" by the media). They set up an office at the nearby health center and ran newspaper ads asking people to call if they knew of any unethical contacts. Self-policing resulted in no visible ambulance chasing.

Why might an attorney solicit business at the scene of a recent tragedy? The average jury verdict for loss of life from an air crash is nearly $600,000, usually resulting in an attorney's fee of $200,000 or more. One lawyer in the Delta crash won a $7.9 million judgment, far in excess of the average. Payoff in such case is assured; the real issue on trial is "how much?"[28]

> . . . lawyers have no regard for the truth or fairness; in the pursuit of winning they will manipulate, distort, mischaracterize, or conceal facts to gain an advantage. You can't really trust a lawyer, they are too clever. They are tricky and sneaky and they can make black look white. They have an arsenal of procedural technicalities to stymie the truth at every turn.[29]

Unfortunately, the preceding quotation may well reflect the public's perception of the legal profession.

In Houston, Texas, officials tallied the top 100 traffic ticket offenders and discovered that 41 of them were lawyers, responsible for at least 3,000 citations issued but unpaid during the preceding four years. Lawyers averaged 88 unpaid tickets; one lawyer owed $30,000 for parking violations.[30] Is this *responsible citizenship?* Are the offenders scofflaws or professional persons dedicated to upholding "equal justice under law" (the words inscribed in marble above the entrance to the U.S. Supreme Court building in our nation's capital)? Or are parking fines an improper basis for the public's perception of attorneys? Certainly attorneys are not the only category of persons dodging the payment of parking tickets. Consider these parking tickets unpaid as of this writing: Los Angeles, $249 million; San Francisco, $39 million; and New York, $1.9 billion.[31] Lawyers aren't accountable for *all* of them!

Can the public be wrong in its perceptions of ethics within the legal system? And if so, do our universities and colleges, as well as the media, have any ethical obligation to enlighten the public about the law and rights and duties under it? Already the legal profession has more extensive written codes of ethics than any other profession, together with enforcement and disciplining agencies (see Chapter 15). Furthermore, disciplined attorneys often are required to pursue continuing education, including subjects involving ethics. Other professions completely ignore the issue of ethics or continuing education. There is no code of ethics and no continuing education requirement for university professors, for example. Nor is there any for politicians.

Conclusion

At the beginning of this chapter we welcomed you to the study of law for your general education. Already you have been presented with an overview of the law; an historical perspective of our common law; how modern laws are made, classified, and defined; what wide variety of legal issues face us in the decade of the 1990s; and how our society perceives the various segments of our legal system. Next it is appropriate for a more detailed examination of the foundations of our legal system, which will be dealt with in the next several chapters.

Case 1

TEXAS v. JOHNSON
U.S. Supreme Court, 491 U.S._____, 109 S.Ct. 2533 (1989)

During a political demonstration at the 1984 Republican National Convention in Dallas, Texas, defendant Johnson doused a U.S. flag with kerosene and set it on fire. While the flag burned, protesters chanted "America, the red, white, and blue, we spit on you." Johnson was convicted of desecration of a venerated object in violation of a Texas penal code section. After *a trial Johnson was convicted, sentenced to one year in prison, and fined $2,000. On appeal, his conviction was held unconstitutional.*

Justice Brennan (for the majority). . . conduct may be sufficiently imbued with elements of communication to fall within the scope of the First and Fourteenth Amendments.

Hence we have recognized the expressive nature of students' wearing of black armbands to protest American involvement in Vietnam; of a sit-in by blacks in a "whites only" area to protest segregation, . . . and of picketing about a wide variety of causes. . . . Pregnant with expressive content, the flag . . . signifies this Nation as does the combination of letters found in "America. . . ." The expressive, overtly political nature of [the flag burning] was both intentional and overwhelmingly apparent. Texas claims that its interest in preventing breaches of the peace justifies Johnson's conviction. . . . [But] a principal function of free speech . . . is to invite dispute. It may indeed best serve its high purpose when it induces a condition of unrest, creates dissatisfaction with conditions as they are, or even stirs people to anger. . . . Nor does Johnson's expressive conduct fall within that small class of "fighting words" that are likely to provoke the average person to retaliation, and thereby cause a breach of the peace. *Chaplinsky v. New Hampshire,* 315 U.S. 568 (1942).

We are tempted to say, in fact, that the flag's deservedly cherished place in our community will be strengthened, not weakened, by our holding today. Our decision is a reaffirmation of the principles of freedom and inclusiveness that the flag best reflects, and of the conviction that our toleration of criticism such as Johnson's is a sign and source of our strength. Indeed, one of the proudest images of our flag, the one immortalized in our own national anthem, is of the bombardment it survived at Fort McHenry. . . . The way to preserve the flag's special role is not to punish those who feel differently. . . . It is to persuade them that they are wrong.

Chief Justice Rehnquist (with whom Justice White and Justice O'Connor join, dissenting)

(Following a stirring account of the historical role of the U.S. flag in our society, the dissent continued): The Court upheld *Chaplinsky's* [referring to the precedent cited in the majority opinion] conviction under a state statute that made it unlawful to "address any offensive, derisive or annoying word to any person who is lawfully in any street or other public place." *Chaplinsky* had told a local marshal, "You are a God damned racketeer" and a "damned Fascist and the whole government of Rochester are Fascists or agents of Fascists." Here it may equally well be said that the public burning of the American flag by Johnson was no essential part of any exposition of ideas, and at the same time it had a tendency to incite a breach of the peace.

Justice Stevens dissented separately.

Note that the Johnson *case was a 5 vote to 4 vote divided court decision. Dissenting justices often, as here, write separate opinions explaining why they cannot vote with the majority. Also note the use of the* Chaplinsky *case as a precedent. In that case the U.S. Supreme Court held that "fighting words" are not protected by the First Amendment. In the* Johnson *case the majority opinion distinguished it as not applicable, while the minority justices contended it was a binding precedent under the doctrine of* stare *decisis.*

QUESTIONS AND PROBLEMS

1. Florida recently has adopted a statute pursuant to which parents can be fined and/or jailed if their child obtains a loaded household gun and injures or kills someone with it. What pros and cons to this law come to your mind?

2. Many persons are intensely interested in the public proceedings (oral arguments) of the U.S. Supreme Court. People often line up for hours after traveling to Washington, D.C., hoping to gain entrance to the proceedings that offer only limited seating for the public. Should especially news-worthy case proceedings be televised? What pros and cons can you think of?

3. Should non-lawyer "legal technicians" be authorized to provide simple legal services to the public? Paralegals are employees of attorneys. Legal technicians would be authorized to deal directly with the public. What are some of the pros and cons concerning this proposal?

4. Under West Virginia law, the driver's license of a high school dropout can be suspended. In California, the driver's license of any person under 21 who is convicted of a drug- or alcohol-related offense can be suspended for one year. What are the pros and cons of suspension of a driver's license in these situations?

5. Cheap wine, fortified with alcohol up to 21 percent, sells for about $1 a bottle. Buyers are street people, often alcoholics, who sometimes beg passersby for money and who may engage in unsanitary practices in public places. What are the pros and cons of a law banning the sale of such cheap, fortified wine in stores located in areas where street-alcoholics congregate?

6. Persons who are injured by the negligence of another may sue for various kinds of damages. We will explore such damages in detail in Chapter 5, where you will learn that in most states juries can award money to injured victims for "pain and suf-fering" in addition to out-of-pocket expenses, such as lost wages. Now there is a proposal to permit the award of money damages to victims for any fun they won't be able to have because of their injury or death. What pros and cons come to your mind concerning this proposal?

7. New York provides clean needles to drug addicts in an exchange program to help stop the spread of AIDS. What might some of the pros and cons be concerning this law?

8. Do you believe there is a different standard of justice for the rich and the poor in criminal cases? What factors do you believe contribute to your con-clusion? Is your conclusion the same with respect to civil cases?

9. Suppose that over a 10-year period the deci-sions of the U.S. Supreme Court reflected the fact that the majority of five justices were conservatives and the minority of four justices were liberal. If a conservative justice retired and a new liberal justice was appointed by the President and confirmed by the Senate, what do you believe should be the binding status of the 5–4 decisions rendered by the so-called "conservative" court? Should lower court judges, when considering the doctrine of stare decisis, dilute the thrust of the conservative court decisions because they probably will be reversed or modified in the coming years by the new, so-called "liberal" court? Why or why not? If a lower court judge did ignore the command of stare decisis for the stated reason, would that be an example of judicial activism or strict construction?

10. Identify two most significant *legal* issues that you believe will be of major significance to society during the next few years. Can you identify how they are significant, such as direct impact on many individuals or indirect impact through taxation or psychological factors?

FURTHER READING

1. Craft, C., *Too Old, Too Ugly, and Not Deferential to Men*. Rocklin: Prima Publishing, 1988. A trou-bling description of discrimination in employment based on appearances.

2. Forer, L., *Money and Justice*. New York: Norton, 1984.

3. Hall, Kermit. *The Magic Mirror: Law in American History*. Oxford University Press, 1989.

4. Moore, K., *Pardons, Justice, Mercy and the Public Interest*. Oxford University Press, 1989.

5. Rembar, C., *The Law of the Land*. New York: Simon & Schuster, 1980. An interesting account of the evolution of common law.

6. Spence, G., *With Justice for None*. New York: Times Books, 1989. An interesting criticism of how our system of justice functions.

7. Traver, R., *Anatomy of a Murder*. New York: St. Martin's Press, 1958.

8. Turow, S., *Presumed Innocent*. New York: Farrar, Straus, Giroux, 1987.

9. Woodward, B. and C. Bernstein, *All the President's Men*. New York: Simon & Schuster, 1974.

NOTES

1. *Black's Law Dictionary,* 5th ed. (St. Paul, MN: West, 1979).

2. Thomson, M., "Waiting for Judgment Day," *California Lawyer,* August, 1989.

3. *San Francisco Examiner,* September 24, 1989.

4. Plucknett, T. *A Concise History of the Common Law,* 5th ed. (Boston: Little, Brown, 1956), quoting Sir Thomas Erskine May, *Constitutional History.*

5. Frug, "Why Courts Are Always Making Law," *Fortune Magazine,* September 1989, p. 245.

6. *People* v. *Davenport,* 222 Cal.Rptr. 736 (1985), cert. den. 475 U.S. 1141 (1986). See also *Portland* v. *Johnson,* 651 P.2d 1384 (Oregon 1983), pet. den. 660 P.2d 681 (1983). For a possible solution, see Lawrence and Kass, "Homelessness in America: Looking for the Right to Shelter," 19 *Columbia Journal of Law & Social Problems* (1985), p. 305.

7. *San Francisco Chronicle,* October 12, 1989.

8. *Cruzan* v. *Director, Missouri Dept. of Health,* 110 S.Ct. 2841 (1990).

9. *Time,* December 11, 1989, p. 80.

10. *Time,* September 18, 1989, p. 67.

11. *San Francisco Chronicle,* March 10, 1990.

12. Egelko, R., "Society's Child," *California Lawyer,* October, 1989, p. 22.

13. *San Francisco Chronicle,* December 19, 1989.

14. *San Francisco Chronicle,* December 25, 1989.

15. *USA Today,* June 26, 1989.

16. *San Francisco Chronicle,* June 28, 1989.

17. *San Francisco Chronicle,* July 13, 1989.

18. *Time,* November 27, 1989, p. 24.

19. *Time,* November 27, 1989, p. 29.

20. *Time,* June 26, 1989, p. 18.

21. *Time,* September 18, 1989, p. 20 and *San Francisco Examiner,* January 28, 1990.

22. *San Francisco Examiner,* January 7, 1990.

23. *San Francisco Chronicle,* June 22, 1989.

24. *San Francisco Chronicle,* October 24, 1989.

25. *San Francisco Chronicle,* December 14, 1989.

26. *San Francisco Chronicle,* June 21, 1989. The poll, conducted on June 8–11, 1989, was based on telephone interviews with 1,235 adults. Its publicized margin of error was plus or minus 4 percentage points.

27. Attorneys across the nation spent $39.8 million on local TV ads in the first six months of 1989. *California Lawyer,* December, 1989.

28. *Time,* August 7, 1989, p. 42.

29. "Unloved Lawyers," *Ethics, Easier Said Than Done,* vol. 1, no. 4, 1989.

30. "Familiarity Breeds Contempt," *California Lawyer,* November, 1989.

31. *San Francisco Chronicle,* April 16, 1990.

2

Our Constitution

A constitution is a system of fundamental principles by which a nation is governed.[1] The Constitution of the United States is a good example. Written in the spring and summer of 1787, it is the world's oldest written Constitution that is still functioning.* But it is distinctive for many reasons far more important than age.

What Is a Written Constitution?

A written **constitution,** sometimes referred to as a *social contract,* sets forth fundamental principles of governance to which the citizens have voluntarily consented. Our Constitution derives its power, authority, and legitimacy—its right to govern—from the people it governs. However, nations are governed by people, whether one, few, or many. A "pure" democracy in which all or most of the people govern all the time is possible only in small political entities such as New England towns or small republics. Accordingly, a large republic such as ours requires a representative form of governance.[2] We, the people, elect congressional representatives and the President and Vice President who rule us at the national level. We have similar ruling structures at the state and local levels.

---

* For over two millennia, constitutions have existed in unwritten form. The Magna Carta, A.D. 1215, was rudimentary and incomplete. However, it laid the foundation for the "social contract" definition of the relationship between rulers and the ruled, and the precedent that such relationships should be in writing. State constitutions are written, and some preceded the U.S. Constitution. After the ratification of the U.S. Constitution, those states rewrote their constitutions.

What Is Constitutionalism?

Constitutionalism means limits on the exercise of governmental power. Many nations have constitutions, but that does not mean their citizens enjoy the fruits of *constitutionalism*. Constitutionalism means ". . . a fundamental law, or a fundamental set of principles, and . . . [an] institutional arrangement, which would [actually] restrict arbitrary power and ensure a 'limited government.' "[3]

For example, a constitution that permits unlimited political power whether in the hands of one, few, or many does not produce constitutionalism. The Fascists' constitutions of Italy and Germany in the 1930s contain no expressions of limited governmental power. Their constitutions were meaningless with regards to limitations on arbitrary and capricious uses of political power by the rulers. Even a constitution that stipulates limited political power, but in reality establishes no mechanism to restrain the ruler's exercise of that power, fails to provide constitutionalism. For instance, a "freedom of the press" Article in the Argentinian Constitution failed to prevent Juan Peron (1945–1955) from destroying the world's largest Spanish-language newspaper, *La Prensa*, located in Buenos Aires.

The people enjoy constitutionalism only to the degree that their constitution limits power by specific provisions that effectively control the behavior of the ruling governors. One such control is having the judiciary serve as a watchdog on the exercise of governmental powers and enforcing limitations on such powers. For example, in 1952 President Harry Truman ordered the Secretary of Commerce to seize and operate our country's steel mills when the United Steel Workers Union threatened to strike and stop production. The President believed the strike would impair his ability to conduct the Korean War. Was the seizure order within the President's power? No. The Supreme Court held "that this seizure order cannot stand" for the following reasons:

1. The President's power, if any, to issue the order must stem either from an act of Congress or from the Constitution itself. The Supreme Court of the United States could find no statute nor Constitutional provision that expressly authorizes the President to take possession of property as he did in this case.
2. Moreover, prior to this controversy, when the Taft-Hartley Act was under consideration in 1947, Congress had refused to adopt the seizure method of settling labor disputes that Truman used.
3. The order cannot be sustained as an exercise of the President's military power as Commander in Chief of the armed forces. He does not have the power as Commander in Chief to take possession of private property in order to keep labor disputes from stopping production. The nation's lawmakers, not military authorities, should regulate labor disputes declared the Court.[4]

The power of the national Supreme Court to dictate to President Truman and have him obey provides one of the ways the people of the United States live under a meaningful constitutionalism.

What Is Constitutional Law?

Constitutional law in the United States has a variety of meanings. The founders of our nation believed in what is known as *natural law*. From their view, natural law was the higher law "which is in accordance with nature, applies to all men, and is unchangeable and eternal."[5] The founders believed that they had incorporated natural law principles into the Constitution. The natural law doctrines found in the Constitution are reflected in the following fundamental beliefs, and they dictate the parameters within which legitimate governmental authority must be exercised.[6]

1. The rights of the people are inalienable and indestructible.

2. Of paramount importance is the natural law doctrine, which stipulates that the most fundamental rights of all human beings are life, liberty, and property.[7]

3. Legitimate governments are obligated (by natural law) under their contracts (constitutions) to protect and guarantee these rights to each person in their respective jurisdictions.

4. The higher law acknowledges and promotes the principle of private domain into which governments should not intrude. Under this doctrine the individual is free to do anything he or she chooses, unless specifically prohibited or circumscribed by law.* By contrast, most countries in the turbulent world of today allow their citizens to do only that which is permitted by their government-declared rules and decrees. All else is deemed prohibited.

5. No person is allowed to be a judge in his or her own cause.[8] Thus a justice of the United States Supreme Court who has a personal interest in a controversy under appeal will refuse to participate in the case.

6. No person is above the law—not legislators, not presidents, not judges.

Important elements of the natural law were included in the Declaration of Independence and later incorporated into the United States Constitution.† In January of 1776, George Washington had written of ". . . the propriety of separation [from England on the basis of] . . . the sound doctrine and unanswerable reasonable reasoning contained in the pamphlet *Common Sense*."‡ The author of *Common Sense,* Thomas Paine, summed up the spirit of the time in these lofty words:

> But where, say some, is the King of America? Yet that we may not appear to be defective even in earthly honors, let a day be solemnly set apart for proclaiming the charter; let it be brought forth placed in the divine law, the word of God; let a crown be placed thereon, by which the world may know, that so far as we approve of monarchy, that in America *the law is king*.[9] [Emphasis added]

The quest for freedom, and a recognition of human rights and individual dignity under law, is neverending. The evidence is great that oppressed peoples

---

* This means that one may violate ethical standards, hallowed conventions, and holy writ, unless certain behavior involved has been prohibited or circumscribed by law. Legality v. morality is a continuing debate in our society. For example, the Robert Mapplethorpe photographic exhibit and the music albums of Madonna and 2 Live Crew. (These cases were widely publicized in 1989 and 1990. See, for example, *Los Angeles Times,* June 14, 1990, and June 18, 1990, Section F.)

† "We hold these truths to be self-evident, that all men are created equal, that they are endowed by their Creator with certain unalienable Rights, that among these are Life, Liberty and the pursuit of Happiness. That to secure these rights, Governments are instituted among Men, deriving their just powers from the consent of the governed. That whenever any Form of Government becomes destructive of these ends, it is the Right of the people to alter or to abolish it, and to institute new Government, laying its foundation on such principles and organizing its powers in such form, as to them shall seem most likely to effect their Safety and Happiness."

‡ Letter from George Washington to Joseph Reed of Pennsylvania, dated January 31, 1776.

around the world—from South Africa to Tiananmen Square to Eastern Europe—are trying to enthrone liberty under the law as king.

When we speak of constitutional law today we mean the fundamental law or the supreme law of the land, the highest "earthly" law. Constitutional principles accorded special designation as Constitutional law are: (1) judicial review, (2) separation of powers, (3) federalism, and (4) civil rights and liberties.

What Is Judicial Review?

Judicial review is the power invested in the Supreme Court to declare acts of the federal government (also state laws) that violate constitutional law null and void, meaning unconstitutional. Despite the absence of judicial review in Article III (the Judiciary Article of the Constitution), some form of judicial review was envisioned by the Framers (those who wrote the Constitution). According to Alexander Hamilton, the Court is the "least dangerous branch" because it controls neither sword nor purse.[10] Nevertheless, he did say the Supreme Court and not the Congress or the President should be the custodian of the Constitution. Further, he argued that the Court has the power to declare the acts of the legislature that are contrary to the Constitution null and void.[11] What *judicial review* meant, however, was not articulated until 1803, in the case of *Marbury* v. *Madison*.[12]

Marbury's suit was docketed in the Supreme Court under a provision of the Judiciary Act of 1789, which gave power to the Supreme Court to issue writs of mandamus (a legal writ issued by a court forcing a public official to act in some legal capacity). Marbury was suing because he did not get his appointment to a federal judgeship. He went to the Supreme Court asking that a writ of mandamus be issued on his behalf forcing James Madison (whose responsibility it was, as Secretary of State) to deliver the appointment. Madison refused to deliver it. What was the Court to do?

Marshall's decision was delayed for several years, letting passions subside. When it finally was delivered, Marshall avoided the showdown with Jefferson's Secretary of State, Madison, and established for the Supreme Court power equal to that of the other branches of the national government. Was Marbury duly appointed? Was Marbury entitled to his appointment? To these questions the Court answered yes. Was the Supreme Court empowered to force the Secretary of State to deliver the appointment? To this question the Court answered no, because Section 13 (issuance of writs of mandamus) of the Judiciary Act of 1789 was unconstitutional. The Supreme Court reasoned that its jurisdiction* was limited to only those cases and controversies outlined in Article III (the Judicial Article), Section 2 of the Constitution. Congress cannot add to the categories stated in the Judicial Article.† To permit Congress to do so is to grant Congress the power to amend the Constitution by mere legislative action.

---

* *Jurisdiction* is the right and authority given to a court to hear a case. In *Marbury* v. *Madison* the Supreme Court distinguished between *original jurisdiction*—the right to hear a case in first instance (for the first time)—and *appellate jurisdiction*—the right to hear a case on appeal from a lower court.
† For example, Marbury obviously did not fall within any of the categories mentioned in Article III, Section 2 of the Constitution (Ambassadors, ministers, consuls, etc.), for which the Supreme Court has original jurisdiction.

Marbury v. *Madison* did more than establish a judicial review of legislative enactments. Marshall enunciated a sweeping power for the Court: (1) the Supreme Court is the sole interpreter and custodian of the Constitution, to the exclusion of the President and Congress; and (2) it is the duty of the Court to say what the Constitution means and what it does not mean. The Court's power through judicial review has not ceased to govern us and, from the beginning, judicial review has not ceased to be controversial.[13]

What Is Separation of Powers?

Separation of powers is an indispensable part of the checks and balance system built into our charter of government. The Constitution demands that the powers of government be divided according to function. The functional divisions are: legislative (law making), executive (law enforcing), and judicial (law judging).[14]

The Constitution delegates power to the national government in portions according to function. This mechanism guarantees that different persons are given unique and specific power. Thus powerful, ambitious persons inhabit and function in the major national branches of government. The ingenious feature is that each branch will function under the direction of different persons. They check and balance each other if attempts are made to consolidate an inordinate amount of power in any one division.[15] This institutional structure, while restraining governors' natural tendency toward tyranny, permits them to retain sufficient power to execute faithfully their constitutionally delegated functions.

The Constitutional doctrine of separation of powers speaks of the relationships between and among the national divisions of government: the relationships of the legislative, the executive, and the judicial branches of government with each other. While there are indeed exclusive functions assigned to each (e.g., tax bills must begin in the House of Representatives), much of the work engaged in by the three branches of government is shared (see Figure 2–1), or decisions of one are subject to scrutiny, review, and approval of the other two branches.

FIGURE 2–1   Separation of Powers

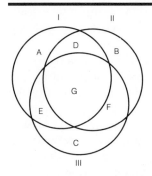

A. Exclusive legislative function
B. Exclusive executive function
C. Exclusive judicial function
D. Functions shared by legislature and executive
E. Functions shared by legislature and judiciary
F. Functions shared by executive and judiciary
G. All functions performed exclusively by all three branches of the national government

Circle I alone represents all power to legislate that rests with Congress
Circle II alone represents all power to execute law that rests with the President
Circle III alone represents all power to judge that rests with the Judiciary.

The purpose of Figure 2–1 is to show that the Framers intended only to separate power and distribute distinct grants of power to different officials in order that "[a]mbition . . . be made to counteract ambition."[16] As Figure 2–1 shows, most of the functions of government are shared. And they are shared in a variety of ways. For example, the legislature executes laws as well as makes them, and the executive makes laws as well as executes them (as depicted by the letter D in the figure). Notice, for example, that the letter G shows that all three branches of government perform all three functions independently. However, the sharing of functions has caused as much conflict as it has provided harmony in government operations.

Congress may pass a law; the President may sign or veto the law. Congress may override the veto and enact the law. The Supreme Court may strike down the statute as unconstitutional. If necessary, Congress may initiate a campaign to have the Constitution amended to accomplish the purpose of the statute, or more likely it may attempt to pass a new statute that is in conformity with the Constitution[17] Note too that the President may be able to appoint new members to the Supreme Court (with the advice and consent of the Senate) who are sympathetic to his or her views. It is reassuring to note that in the final analysis the power to decide an issue rests with the people, who may use their votes—"the power of the ballot box"—to elect representatives who will do the expressed will of the people.

How Is the National Government Organized?

Legislative Branch

Article I of the Constitution delineates the organization and functions of the legislature. The legislative branch is bicameral, having two parts: an upper house (the Senate) and a lower house (the House of Representatives). Members of the Senate originally were appointed by state legislatures, but in 1913 the Seventeenth Amendment changed the system to popular vote. The Senate has 100 members, two from each state.

Members of the House of Representatives are elected to 435 seats that are allocated to the states on the basis of population, as determined in the decennial national census. California is the most populous state as of this writing, and therefore has the largest number of members in the House. After the 1990 census, California, because of its continued growth in population, is expected to gain up to five new members, bringing its total up to 50.[18]

The function of the legislative branch is to enact laws. This is usually accomplished by majority vote, for or against enactment, amendment, or repeal of specific laws. Powers of the legislature are spelled out in Article I, Section 8 of the Constitution. They include the power to tax and borrow money, to regulate interstate commerce, to make laws regulating bankruptcies, to coin money, to establish post offices, to establish courts inferior to the Supreme Court, to declare war, and to govern the District of Columbia (the nation's capital). However, great latitude is given to Congress in its detailed application of these enumerated powers by its constitutional authority: "to make all laws which shall be necessary and proper for carrying into execution the foregoing powers."[19]

Once the legislature enacts a law, its job is usually done. Someone else must apply the law and, if necessary, determine whether it is compatible with the national Constitution. The determination of constitutionality is not as simple as it may sound. For example, Congress passed a law releasing alien Chinese students studying in the United States from the requirement of returning to China upon the expiration of their visas (a visa is a document that grants a person of a foreign country legal permission to live, work, or study in the host country.) This was done because Congress believed that the Chinese government would punish most of these students for supporting the 1989 student uprising in Tiananmen Square and elsewhere in China. However, President George Bush vetoed the legislation on the grounds that Congress was meddling in foreign policy matters (his province). Moreover, the students were protected against forced repatriation by his executive order. The President claimed he ordered the Immigration and Naturalization Service to extend the Chinese student visas indefinitely. When the bill was returned to the Congress the House voted to override, but the Senate upheld the President's veto.

The Executive Branch (The Presidency)

The President and Vice President are each elected to a term of four years, with a limit of two consecutive full terms.* The Constitutional process for choosing the Chief Executive and his or her running mate is cumbersome because the method is indirect, with state electors actually electing the President by casting electoral votes. The number of electors in each state is determined by the number of representatives the state has in Congress plus its two senators. For example, Alaska has 3 electors; New York, 36; and California, 47. To become president, the candidate must attract a combination of states with sufficient electoral votes to make a majority in the electoral college: 270 electors. The states with the greatest populations command the most attention from the candidates. This makes good political sense since each state gives all electoral votes to the candidate receiving the majority of the popular vote.

Thus the campaign is really for all of the electoral votes: 435 from Congress, 100 from the Senate, and 3 from the District of Columbia (totalling 538). The winner needs a majority, at least 270 of those electoral votes. (Note that presidential elections and vacancies are also regulated by amendments to the Constitution).[20]

Constitutionally Defined Powers

Section 2 of Article II of the Constitution specifies the following as presidential powers. First and foremost of the President's power, and of great importance during most of the twentieth century, is the power of the President as

---

* No person shall be elected to the office of the president more than twice, and no person who has held the office of president, or acted as president for more than two years of a term to which some other person was elected president, shall be elected to the office of the president more than once. (U.S. Constitution, Twenty-second Amendment)

"Commander in Chief of the Armed Forces of the United States and of the militia of the several states, when called into actual service of the United States. . . ."[21] As some state governors were opposed to the national government's foreign policy in Central America, they tried to block President Ronald Reagan's deployment of a number of National Guard units to Honduras for training exercises in the mid 1980s. In response, Congress passed a law prohibiting governors of the respective states from blocking a call-up of national guard troops (militia) because they didn't like guard units training on foreign soil. The Supreme Court sustained Congress' power to grant the President complete control over national guard units.[22] While Congress retains to itself the power to declare war, the power "to make war" is granted solely to the President. It was during the Civil War that the Commander in Chief was declared to be the sole determiner of whether the hostilities are of ". . . such alarming proportions as will compel him to accord to them the character of belligerent . . ."[23] and whether he shall engage the armed forces of the United States in such hostilities. Modern technology has changed the character of war and has increased greatly the power of the President to make war.

Presidential powers dealing with the faithful execution of the law have led to many conflicts with Congress. President Richard Nixon refused to spend monies appropriated by Congress. Since he did not have the power of a *line item veto* (the power to remove selected items from a bill without vetoing the whole bill) he accomplished the same effect by impounding funds that Congress had appropriated for other projects that the President felt were unnecessary or that contributed to deficits.

Early in President George Bush's administration, the President showed great skill using his veto power over legislation he didn't like. Congress did not manage to override a single veto in 13 attempts.* (This was remarkable, since Bush's party, the Republicans, was not the majority party in the Senate or the House of Representatives.)

The Constitution grants to the President the power to make treaties, but all must be approved by a two-thirds vote of the Senate. With the advice and consent of the Senate,[24] the President may also appoint ambassadors, public ministers and consuls, Supreme Court justices, and presidential advisors. Congress can grant additional appointment power to the President, by which he or she may choose other federal officers and commission heads. In the Judiciary Act of 1789, Congress gave presidents power to nominate appellate and district court judges in the federal court system. In 1876, Congress established four-year terms for postmasters and gave the President power to appoint and remove them from office with the advice and consent of the Senate.

The President has the power to appoint, and this power is enhanced or weakened by the kinds of people he or she appoints as advisers. This also applies to the choice of a running mate. The President is the leader of his or her party. Ronald Reagan was the most formidable of party leaders because of his ability to raise money for the party coffers. His presence alone guaranteed that any fundraising event would be a success.

---

* January 1989 to June 30 1990.

The Supreme Court

At the center of the doctrine of separation of powers is the Supreme Court of the United States. At the time the Constitution was ratified, the role of the Court was not clearly defined. It remained for the justices to create and refine the "proper" place of the Court within the federal government.

Article III, the Judicial Article, declares: "The Judicial power of the United States shall be vested in one Supreme Court, and in such inferior courts as the Congress may from time to time ordain and establish."[25] All federal judges hold office for life and good behavior. The present average age of the justices on the Supreme Court is over 67 years, making it the oldest Court in its history.

Federal judges can be removed from their courts only by death, voluntary retirement, or impeachment by the Congress of the United States.

The Honorable I. M. Deceptione, a Federal district judge in Des Moines, Iowa, was tried and convicted of cheating on his income tax by filing a false return. He was sentenced to federal prison, where he served eighteen months. He promptly paid all fines, penalties, and underpayment of taxes, amounting to $52,000. Then he immediately asked to be restored to his former position. Was he given his job back?

Yes. But he was finally removed from the court by impeachment eight months after returning to his job. Nevertheless, he received his federal salary for the 26 months following his conviction.[26]

Congress is reluctant to use the impeachment procedure to remove public officials from office because it is cumbersome, time-consuming, and often more political than legal in nature. Nevertheless, impeachment is the only way to remove from the payroll federal judges who are guilty of criminal conduct. Fortunately, criminal acts that call for impeachment of federal judges are rare.[27]

Congress sets the salaries for all federal employees, including judges. However, once the salaries for federal judges are set by Congress they can never be reduced for any reason during the judges' tenure on the court.[28]

The Honorable Seymore Merit, federal district judge in Salt Lake City, Utah, sued in federal district court for a pay raise that he thought he was entitled to because Congress had not raised the salaries of federal judges for several years. Did Judge Merit get his raise?

Yes. The court said that failure to raise the judge's salary equal to the annual rate of inflation was unconstitutional, because the Constitution prohibits the reduction of the salary of federal judges.[29] Loss of purchasing power is the equivalent of a salary reduction. As a result all federal judges had their salaries raised.

The Supreme Court has far-reaching powers, not only over the conduct of affairs between the Presidency and Congress, but over the states as well. Since the tenure of Chief Justice John Marshall (1801–1835), the Supreme Court has been extremely active in regulating the relationship between state governments and the national government.

What Is Federalism?

Federalism is defined as a political arrangement in which two or more levels of government direct the affairs of the same people in the same location. For example, Iowans are governed by their state governments as well as by the national government.

Scholars estimate that there are more than 80,000 state and local* governments, all of which exist to meet the needs and wants of an extremely complex technologically driven society. This profusion of governments meets human needs and resolves human conflicts in a climate of political pressures, not the least of which involves competition and cooperation among the various governors in their hierarchical positions. The United States Constitution demanded this complexity from its beginning, when it retained limited sovereignty for the original 13 states of the union. The relationship of the national government to state and local governments is called *federalism*.

In any event, as a practical matter we are a people subject to governments' rule, from the sweeping mandates of our national Congress to the narrowly defined rules of our local school board and mosquito abatement district.

The Constitution dictates the division of powers between the national government and the state governments. The national government has only those powers delegated to it, and such other powers that naturally flow from these. Congress shall have the power "to make all laws which shall be necessary and proper for carrying into Execution the foregoing powers."[30] Some of these powers are exclusive as to the national government, such as "to coin Money" and "to make Treaties."[31] But other powers are shared such as taxing and spending. As noted, all other powers "are reserved to the States respectively, or to the people."[32]

Our Constitution also limits the power of the national government; for example, it is prohibited from denying a writ of Habeas Corpus (a formal written order that a person be brought before a court, usually to protect against incarceration).[33] Powers are also denied to the state, such as the power to make a treaty. Finally, there are powers denied to both, such as the passage of *bills of attainder* (an act of the legislature punishing a named individual(s) or a member of a specific group) and *ex post facto law* (a retroactive law designed to punish a particular individual or group of individuals. For example, an ex post facto law makes a particular behavior a crime that was not a crime when the act was committed).

---

* All governments within states were (are) created by the state legislatures under provisions in their respective state constitutions. The governments of cities, boroughs, and counties are most commonly recognized by citizens. Other varieties of local governments are school districts, flood control districts, mosquito abatement districts, and park districts. Under their charters of government (granted by state legislatures) they have budgets, collect taxes, and govern themselves.

FIGURE 2–2 Federalism

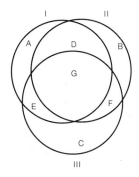

I. Powers of the national government
II. Powers of state governments
III. Powers of the people

A. Powers *delegated* to national government
B. Powers *reserved* to the states
C. Powers *reserved* to people
D. Concurrent powers shared by both national and state governments
E. Powers *denied* to the *national* government
F. Powers denied to *state* government
G. Powers denied to both national and state governments
(Also power denied to the people)

What Constitutional Powers Belong to the Citizens?

Although much power is delegated to the national government and great power is reserved to states, it is the people that possess the ultimate power in our Constitution system (see Figure 2–2). One of the great powers of the people is their power to vote.[34]

Every politician wishing to govern must engage in a competitive struggle against political opponents and win his or her privilege of governing by receiving a majority of the people's vote. ". . . [T]hose who make public policy [laws] in this society are privileged to do so because they have won the struggle against others who seek the privilege of making policy."[35] By popular vote lawmakers and governors are chosen.

not in RI

Some state constitutions give the people the right (power) to bypass the usual lawmaking process of state and local governments to make laws directly. This legislative process is called the *initiative process*. The initiative process, the referendum petition, and the recall petition* are devices of direct democracy, and for the better part of the twentieth century these practices have given the people power to collectively control some aspects of their lives.

However, these practices (especially the initiative process), once reserved to the people, are presently being used with great success by powerful lobbyists, special interest groups, businesses, and professions to pass laws that favor their narrow interests. This unforeseen use of the initiative process has become a growth

---

* (a) The *direct initiative* empowers the people themselves to originate and pass laws, ordinances, and amendments to their respective constitutions without recourse to the legislature.
(b) The *referendum petition* is used by the people to "veto" laws already passed by the legislature and signed by the governor (or a veto overridden by the legislature).
(c) The *recall petition* is a political device by which the people may remove from office any elected state or local official before the expiration of his or her term.

industry in California since the passage of the property tax limitation initiative (Proposition 13) in the latter part of the 1970s.

Public relations firms (PRFs) are hired to conduct the initiative process and run the campaign for the passage of the desired legislation. With the use of direct-mail fundraising and signature gathering, the PR firms easily qualify their initiatives for the ballot. All persons who have signed petitions then are sent absentee ballots to make it easy for the same people to vote on a particular proposal. Despite this apparent abuse, the people are busy using the initiative process.

> Citizens in the 1980s have turned to the initiative process to [establish a state-wide lottery in California], to protect the moose in Maine, to encourage the death penalty in Massachusetts, to approve the sale of wine in local grocery stores in Colorado, to abolish daylight savings time in North Dakota, and to pressure the national government for some type of nuclear freeze.[36]

Critics have condemned the initiative process as presently used. Controversial issues make their way onto the ballot and are often written in a manner so confusing that the people cannot possibly understand how they are to vote. The confusion frequently is increased by slick media advertising. Nevertheless, the democratic devices of the initiative, the referendum, and the recall will remain important processes for the people throughout the 1990s.

Those who wrote the Constitution, along with the states that ratified it, did not intend that the national government have power over the everyday lives of the people. James Madison believed that this limitation on the power of the national government was one of the virtues of federalism, meaning that the states' great reservoir of police power* was reserved to them and the states had no need to fear any intrusions by the national government into their affairs. Under the Constitution, the national government's power to regulate, control, and circumscribe human conduct is specifically tied to one or more of its delegated powers.[37] For example, the Federal Aviation Administration was established to provide for safety regulation in the manufacture of aircraft as a "necessary and proper" extension of Congress' power to regulate interstate commerce. The interstate commerce clause is one of the most important sources of the national government's police power.†

What Is the Supremacy Clause?

The United States Constitution declares:

> This Constitution and the laws of the United States which shall be made in pursuance thereof; and all treaties made, or which shall be made, under the authority of the United

---

* The police power of a government is to promote order, safety, health, morals, and general welfare within its constitutional limits, and, as such, it is an essential attribute of government.
† The importance of the commerce clause came early in our history. See the case of *Gibbons v. Ogden* 22 Wheaton 1 (1823).

States, shall be the *Supreme Law of the Land;* and the judges in every state shall be bound thereby, *anything in the Constitution or laws of any state to the contrary not withstanding.*[38] [Emphasis added]

The Supreme Court of the United States has added U.S. Supreme Court decisions to the categories of supreme law. No state law can stand contrary to Supreme Court decisions. The significance of the supremacy doctrine is that it invalidates any conflicting state law by virtue of preemption, meaning that the federal law takes precedence over state law.[39]

The Supreme Court of the United States was confronted with the issue of national power over state power early in our history. In two cases—*Martin* v. *Hunter's Lessee* (1816) and *Cohens* v. *Virginia* (1821)—the Supreme Court, relying on the supremacy clause, declared forcefully that national law is superior to state law and federal tribunals have the authority to review the judgment of state courts.

In this regard, Justice Oliver Wendell Holmes wrote: "I do not think the United States would come to an end if we lost our power to declare an act of Congress void. I do think the Union would be imperiled if we could not make that declaration as to the laws of the states."[40]

Other "supreme powers" accrue to the national government as extensions of Congress' power to regulate commerce and Congress' power to tax.

In 1912, the state of Arizona passed a law making it unlawful to operate a train of more than 14 passenger cars or 70 freight cars. The law was a safety measure passed under the state's police power. Was state regulation of train lengths lawful?

No. The state of Arizona cannot place an undue burden on interstate commerce adverse to the national interest. However, if state regulation affects interstate commerce only slightly, or if the national interests are best served, then states are permitted to regulate interstate commerce.[41]

In the famous case *McCulloch* v. *Maryland,* Chief Justice John Marshall observed that "The power to tax involves the power to destroy."[42] But it is more. Taxes are primarily revenue-raising measures, but taxes are also used to control and regulate the movement of people and the production and distribution of products and services. Is the power to tax equally shared by both federal and state governments? Not quite. It depends on what the states want to tax.

Maryland's legislature attempted to tax banks and bank branches not chartered by the state legislature. The Bank of the United States operated a branch in Baltimore. McCullock, the bank's cashier, refused to pay the tax assessed against the bank. Must McCullock comply with Maryland state law?

No. The Supreme Court said: "The government of the United States . . . though limited in its powers, is supreme . . . "[43] over the states, and the power of

Congress to charter a bank implies the power to operate the bank successfully and without interferences from the states.

Today there is no argument about the supremacy of the national government. Most debate about proper state and federal roles has to do with "effectiveness": Should it be done nationally, or can it be done better locally? The availability of necessary funds and adequate resources are also important factors. States, counties, and cities that are "strapped for cash" eagerly seek federal funding for local projects such as public housing, mass transit construction, education, care for the aged, and health care. The fight for a cure for AIDS is a good example that in real crises we look to Washington, D.C., not to state capitals.

Finally, constitutional law covers the United States Supreme Court's decisions defining the scope and meaning of the Bill of Rights.

What Is the Bill of Rights?

The Bill of Rights mandates specific and general restraints on the national government to protect all persons from arbitrary and capricious acts by federal authority. Originally the Bill of Rights applied only as a restraint on the national government; states were not bound by any of the provisions found therein, except insofar as specified in their state constitutions.[44]

Following the Civil War several amendments were added to the Constitution to protect and assist the newly freed slaves. The most powerful of these was the Fourteenth Amendment, which has been instrumental in the nationalization of the Bill of Rights:

> No state shall make or enforce any law which shall abridge the privileges or immunities of citizens of the United States; nor shall any state deprive any person of life, liberty, or property, without *due process* of law, nor deny to any person within its jurisdiction the *equal protection* of the laws.[45] [Emphasis added]

The due process of law and equal protection of the law clauses of the Fourteenth Amendment have been used to restrict the reserved powers of the states; police powers and education are most notable. To oversimplify, the court defines due process as the equivalent of "fundamental fairness" and equal protection as the prevention of "invidious discrimination."

The Nationalization of the Bill of Rights

Most of the first ten amendments of the U.S. Constitution—called the Bill of Rights—have been incorporated into the Fourteenth Amendment (through its *due process of laws* and *equal protection of law* clauses) by the Supreme Court. This has encouraged Congress to pass whatever laws are necessary and proper to implement the Bill of Rights not only at the national level of government, but also at the state and local levels.[46]

The Incorporation Doctrine

In its momentous decision in *Gitlow* v. *New York* in 1925, the U.S. Supreme Court announced: ". . . we may and do assume that freedom of speech and of press— First Amendment protections—are among the fundamental personal rights and 'liberties' protected by the due process clause of the Fourteenth Amendment from impairment by the States."[47]

With the *Gitlow* decision, the Supreme Court began systematically imposing on the states the guarantees found in the Bill of Rights. The purpose was to bind both national and state governments to the same standard of compliance regarding these guarantees.

The First Amendment

The First Amendment contains what is known historically as *primary rights*. It is no accident that this Amendment begins with the phrase: "Congress shall make no law . . . ." Nor is it accidental that first among our primary rights is freedom of speech and press. They are "the matrix, the indispensable condition, of nearly every other form of freedom."[48] As Justice Hugo Black remarked: "Freedom to speak and write about public questions is as important to the life of our government as is the heart to the human body. . . . If that heart be weakened, the result is debilitation; if it be stilled, the result is death."[49]

Freedom of Speech and Press

The Supreme Court has decided incrementally that the states must also guarantee to their citizens First Amendment rights of freedom of speech and press.[50] Nevertheless, even our most basic rights are not absolute. For "compelling" reasons governments may constitutionally restrict certain forms of speech.

John Deviling became bored with the movie he was watching at the Grand Palace Theater. Although very crowded, Deviling felt that most of the patrons were as bored as he. As he was about to exit the theater, he decided to "shake up the audience a bit."

Instead of exiting, he returned and ran partway down the aisle shouting: "Fire! Fire! Fire!" He turned and ran from the theater.

Was Deviling's speech and behavior protected by the First Amendment? No. Justice Oliver Wendell Holmes, speaking for the Court, said:

> The character of every act depends upon the circumstances in which it is done. The most stringent protection of free speech would not protect a man in *falsely shouting* fire in a theater and causing panic . . . . The question in every case is whether the words used are used in such circumstances and are of such a nature as to create a *clear and present danger* that they will bring about the substantive evils that Congress [and every state] has a right to prevent.[51] [Emphasis added]

In attempting to balance the need for preserving the social interests of peace, order, and morality against the most liberal interpretations of free speech and press, the Court has been unable to define free speech with anything close to precision.

The Court has moved successively through a number of legal expedients called "tests", as follows:

1. The "clear and present danger" test was explained in *Schenck*.[52]

2. The "bad tendency" test was exemplified in *Abrams*. Here the Court accorded little importance to the guarantee of free speech, focusing almost solely on the effect the challenged speech had on the war (WWI) effort.[53]

3. The "preferred position" test was articulated in Justice Harlan Stone's famous footnote in the *Carolene Products* case. Stone articulated the view that free speech enjoyed a preferred position in relation to other constitutional guarantees, calling for a more precise and searching scrutiny of legislation that might curtail "political processes."[54]

4. During the "Cold War" of the late 1940s and 1950s, the Court adopted the "clear and probable danger" test. This was done to curtail the speech and activities of American Communists, and the Court was willing to uphold such legislation.[55]

5. Political dissent during the late 1960s and early 1970s found the Court using the "ad hoc balancing'" test. Using the clear and present danger test, the Court weighed the competing interests of free speech and law and order. Every ordinance attempting to serve the interests of the state must be drawn with "reasonable specificity toward the [speech] and conduct prohibited. . . ."[56]

In spite of the Reagan-era Court's conservative drift, free speech continues to receive high and substantial protection. Even the Rehnquist Court is careful to protect expressive activity and symbolic speech, which the Courts have traditionally held to be Constitutional.[57] Flag burning as political speech cannot be restricted by the states, nor by the Congress of the United States.[58]

Freedom of Religion

Religious pluralism is a hallmark of American life, together with our commitment to religious freedom. In many parts of the world, governments maintain "official" religions and official religions maintain governments. In the United States we erected a wall between church and state; any significant breach of that wall by either government or church, no matter how compelling, is generally suspect. Yet attempts are made from time to time in spite of the Constitution's declaration that "Congress shall make no law respecting an establishment of religion, or pro-hibiting the free exercise thereof." What should be the government's position respecting religion? The Supreme Court has answered. The First Amendment (on religion) means this:

> Neither a state nor the federal government can set up a church. Neither can pass laws which aid one religion, aid all religions, or prefer one religion over another. Neither can force nor influence a person to go to or to remain away from church against his will or force him to profess a belief or disbelief in any religion. No person can be punished for entertaining or professing religious beliefs or disbeliefs, for church attendance or nonat-tendance. No tax in any amount, large or small, can be levied to support any religious activities or institutions, whatever they may be called, or whatever form they may adopt to teach or practice religion. Neither a state or the federal government can, openly or secretly, participate in the affairs of any religious organizations or groups and vice versa . . . the [religious] clause was intended to erect "a wall of separation between church and state."[59] *1947 Everson vs Bd. of Education*

Recently our government has been charged with being anti-religious.[60] The anti-religious sentiment arose because of a series of decisions made by the Supreme Court. For example, in a number of decisions[61] the Supreme Court declared unconstitutional state attempts to promote "religious values" in public schools. The Court said that even a one-minute period of silence for "meditation or voluntary prayer" is constitutionally impermissible.[62]

In 1984 Congress passed the Equal Access Act, making it unlawful for any public high school receiving federal assistance (funds) to keep student groups from using school facilities for religious activities. If other student-initiated gath-erings were permitted to meet at a high school, then there could be no denial of on-campus meetings for student-initiated religious activities. The Supreme Court had already declared constitutional student-initiated religious worship at state uni-versities and colleges.[63]

Could Guns Be Banned?

The Second Amendment states:

> A well regulated militia, being necessary to the security of a free state, the right of the people to keep and bear arms, shall not be infringed.[64]

It should be noted that the word "state" in the Second Amendment is a generic term and does not refer to a state of the union, as it is frequently interpreted. When this amendment was penned, the common practice of national states was to have large standing armies. In America, there was a strong sentiment that a large permanent army should not be part of the national government. Also, the amendment was designed to prevent Congress from disarming and abolishing state militias.

The Supreme Court has sustained this sentiment. "The Second Amendment guarantees *no right* to keep and bear a firearm that does not have some reasonable relationship to the preservation or efficiency of a well-regulated militia.[65]

States as well as the federal government may regulate some or all firearms if they so choose. The Court has declared:

> There is under our decisions no reason why stiff laws governing the purchase and possession of pistols may not be enacted. There is no reason why pistols may not be barred from anyone with a police record. There is no reason why a state may not require a purchaser of a pistol to pass a psychiatric test. There is no reason why all pistols should not be barred to everyone except the police.[66] 1972

The Courts have held that the states, as well as the federal government, may regulate any and all firearms as they deem necessary for a well-ordered society. There is no constitutional bar to such practice.

Freedom From Unreasonable Searches

Other Bill of Rights guarantees were imposed on the states during the "judicial revolution" of the 1960s. As Justice John Marshall wanted to establish national supremacy in commerce and banking, so it was that Justice Earl Warren wanted to create national supremacy in the exercise of police power—the inherent right to regulate in the interests of public health, safety, and morals.

The Fourth Amendment rights to be free from unreasonable searches and seizures and to have excluded from criminal trials any evidence illegally seized are guaranteed by the states as well as the federal government. As a result, most searches must be conducted as prescribed by a prior, judicially issued warrant.[67] However, there are a number of exceptions incident to a lawful arrest. For example, there are exigent circumstances and plain view doctrines exempting the warrant requirement.

In two cases, *Wolf* v. *Colorado*[68] (1949) and *Mapp* v. *Ohio*[69] (1961), the Supreme Court imposed on the states the same standards of care in search and seizure procedures and the exclusion of evidence illegally obtained as that imposed by the Constitution on the national government. The Court said that we have a "right to privacy" and to be "free from unreasonable state intrusions. . . . We hold that all evidence obtained by search and seizures in violation of the Constitution is, by the same authority, inadmissable in a state Court."[70] This is known as the **exclusionary rule.** Warrantless searches and seizures are generally viewed as unconstitutional. Any arrests and evidence seized without warrants are usually declared by the trial judge as behavior violative of the Constitution.

No rule exists that requires the use of a warrant to make a valid arrest. Necessarily, judicial decisions have focused "almost exclusively on search warrants."[71] Warrants are issued by judicial authority and conform to the following requirements: (1) specify place to be searched, (2) specify the items to be seized, (3) specify the time the warrant is to be executed (generally prescribed by law),

(4) specify person(s) to be searched and/or arrested, and (5) execute the warrant (forced entry limited, except in searches for narcotics).[72]

Rights of the Accused to Due Process of Law

Rights guaranteed under the Constitution to be free of compelled testimony and self-incrimination have been mandated to the states since 1964.[73]

A police undercover agent was placed in a cellblock with a Mr. Perkins who was in jail for aggravated assault. However, Perkins was under investigation for murder. When asked by the undercover agent if he (Perkins) had ever killed anybody, Perkins made statements implicating himself in the murder. Is this testimony voluntarily given by Mr. Perkins unknowingly to a police officer inadmissable as evidence because of the way it was obtained?

No. The U.S. Supreme Court held that an undercover police officer posing as an inmate has no obligation to warn an incarcerated suspect of any of his rights before asking questions whose response could be legally incriminating.[74] *1990*

The United States Supreme Court has, through a series of decisions, imposed on the states most of the guarantees found in the Fifth and Sixth Amendments. The Fourteenth Amendment now requires the states to guarantee the right to a speedy[75] and public[76] trial by an unbiased jury.[77] A speedy, public trial conducted before an unbiased jury are among our most fundamental rights. However, the Court, in order to make a fair trial possible, also incorporated the right to have compulsory process for obtaining witnesses for the accused's defense,[78] and have the assistance of counsel in all cases[79] and at all stages[80] of criminal procedures to which the defendant is subjected, except in appellate procedures, where the prisoner is on his or her own (although, in fact, appellants are generally assisted by counsel).[81]

Equal Protection and Education

The nationalization of equality, especially equality of opportunity, continues to be a major priority. Nowhere is the federal government more committed to equality of opportunity than in the field of education at all levels. Social custom, economic conditions, and housing patterns as developed during the nineteenth century created segregated educational programs and facilities. "Separate but equal" was the standard claimed by local educators, and the Supreme Court affirmed the segregated system not only in education, but in many other aspects of life.[82] "Jim Crow" laws, as they were called, forced blacks to live separately from whites throughout most of the southern United States.

Using the Fourteenth Amendment's Equal Protection of the Law clause, blacks filed suits challenging segregation as unconstitutional. In 1954 the Supreme Court declared segregated education "inherently unequal,"[83] and a year later ordered school districts to desegregate with "all deliberate speed."[84]

Congress passed the Civil Rights Act of 1964 in which Title VI requires that all federal funds must be withdrawn from any school, college, or university that is guilty of discrimination on the "grounds of race, color, or national origin in any program or activity receiving federal financial assistance." (Gender, the disabled and handicapped, age, Vietnam veterans, and disabled veterans were later added to the list).

Christian National College, a private, coeducational liberal arts institution, refused to accept any state or federal financial assistance in order to preserve its autonomy. However, many of its students received Basic Educational Opportunity Grants (BEOG) from the U.S. Department of Education. The Department required every institution participating in financial assistance programs to file a report certifying that no sex discrimination existed on its campus.

Christian National refused to file the certification. The Department of Education sought to cancel the students' BEOGs. Christian National brought suit. Must Christian National file the required certification or lose its BEOG funds?

Yes. Failure to file a statement assuring compliance with the requirements of nondiscrimination on the basis of gender is evidence of an intent to discriminate in violation of the law.[85] In similar cases involving tax-exempt organizations, such as religious schools, a failure to comply with legal orders to eliminate discrimination has resulted in action by the Internal Revenue Service threatening to remove the tax-exempt status.[86] Loss of tax-exempt status could cause the closure of many worthwhile organizations.

May a state take unilateral action to eliminate sex-discrimination, the Supremacy Clause notwithstanding? Yes. In Minnesota, the legislature established a civil rights commission (an administrative agency) to deal with questions of discrimination. The state chapter of the United States Jaycees, a male-only organization of businessmen, disobeyed an order from Minnesota's civil rights commission to admit women. As this was a violation of the national Jaycees rules, litigation followed.

The U.S. Supreme Court agreed with the state of Minnesota, holding that the state interest in eradicating sex discrimination was sufficiently compelling to override the organization's freedom of political association.[87] In 1987, the Court extended its decision in *Jaycees* to include the Rotary Club as well.[88] 1987

Leroy Irvis, an invited guest and African American, was refused service because of his race at the Harrisburg, Pennsylvania, chapter of the Moose Lodge. Irvis sued in federal court for injunctive relief (a writ issued by a court prohibiting an action deemed illegal by the person requesting the writ) alleging state involvement, because the Lodge possessed a liquor license issued by the Pennsylvania Liquor Board. Can the Lodge's liquor license be revoked until its discriminatory practices cease?

No. The Supreme Court dismissed challenges to its exclusive membership requirement on the grounds "that where the impetus for discrimination is private, the State must have 'significantly involved itself' . . . in order for the discriminatory action to fall within the gambit of the constitutional prohibition."[89] 1972

Equal Protection and Affirmative Action

Minorities have sought special consideration in access to educational institutions and employment opportunities since Justice Harlan Stone enunciated his position on affirmative action in a now-famous footnote in the *Carolene Products* case:

> Principles outlawing the irrelevant or pernicious use of race [are] inappropriate to racial classifications that provide benefits to minorities for the purpose of remedying the present effects of past racial discrimination. Such classifications may disadvantage some whites, but whites as a class lack the "traditional indicia of suspectness": the class is not *saddled with such disabilities* or subjected to such a history of *purposeful unequal treatment,* or relegated to such a *position of political powerlessness* as to command extraordinary protection from the majoritarian political process.[90] [Emphasis added]
>
> 1938

So controversial is affirmative action policy that it has displaced busing as a national political issue in the fight for integration in education.* Three main areas have been selected for *affirmative action:* employment, government contracts, and higher education. We deal here only with higher education.

To achieve affirmative action goals, federal and state courts have adopted race-conscious remedies.[91] Critics of the courts' decisions claim that what began as reasoned argument to overcome past discriminatory practices soon emerged as a series of numerical goals, quotas, and timetables, created to bring blacks, Asians, Hispanics, Orientals, and Native Americans into the colleges and universities of the country. While there is much opposition to the way it is being done, there is no question that affirmative action is the law of the land (as of this writing).[92] But is it constitutional? No policy issue is more hotly debated. The Supreme Court is as divided as the nation.

The *Bakke* case is the major source of law in affirmative action relative to the Court. In this 1978 case, the legality of a University of California–Davis (UCD) Medical School affirmative action program was tested. The program had set aside 16 positions for minority applicants. Bakke, a white male and a top student at the University of Minnesota and at Stanford, applied for admission to UCD Medical School and was rejected twice; both times students with lower test scores, lower grade point averages, and inferior interviews were admitted over him, under the

---

* Busing is an anti-segregation procedure requiring that schoolchildren be transported by school bus from school districts in which they reside to other school districts, to achieve court-mandated racial balances in all schools.

university's special admittance program. After his rejection in 1974, he brought suit, claiming he was excluded because of race, contrary to the Constitution's equal protection requirements and the Civil Rights Act of 1964, Title VI.

The Supreme Court found for Bakke and declared the admissions scheme of UCD unconstitutional. The Court was divided as to the reasons for its finding for Bakke. The constitutional problem with the UCD plan was that it excluded whites solely on the basis of race. While declaring this scheme unconstitutional, the Court allowed that diversity among the medical students was an appropriate goal and that race could be one of the factors taken into consideration when applicants were considered for admission.[93]

There have been no decisions by the Court to clarify this language. In fact, United States Supreme Court Justice Byron White said recently: "Agreement upon a means for applying the Equal Protection Clause to an affirmative action program has eluded this Court every time the issue has come before us."[94]

The Right to Privacy

The right to privacy is the right to be left alone by other persons and by government. It is generally recognized as an essential component of personal dignity, peace of mind, and independence. Nevertheless, a right to privacy has not always been implicitly recognized and respected as a constitutionally protected right. There is no reference to privacy, as such, in the Constitution or the Bill of Rights. Indeed, it was not until 1965 that the U.S. Supreme Court recognized "the new constitutional right of privacy," in the words of Justice William O. Douglas. In the case of *Griswold* v. *Connecticut,* the Court held invalid a Connecticut statute that made it a criminal offense for married persons to use any drug or instrument to prevent conception. The Court held that the statute violated the First, Third, Fourth, Fifth, and the Ninth Amendments, plus the Equal Protection clause of the Fourteenth.[95]

The nation's highest court subsequently has used the declared and implicit right of privacy to affirm (1) the right of unmarried persons to have access to contraceptives, (2) the rights of black persons to marry white persons as a vital right (also protected by the Due Process and Equal Protection clauses of the Fourteenth Amendment), (3) the right of a woman to have an abortion under certain conditions, an (4) the right to possess obscene materials in one's home.[96]

Ohio passed a law making it a crime to possess obscene materials that depict children having sex in any form or manner. Osborne was arrested for having such outlawed materials in his home. Should Osborne be punished for his crime?

Yes. The U.S. Supreme Court upheld the accused's conviction. The Court said that the possession of photographs showing children engaging in sex acts is not protected under the Constitution even if you keep them in your residence.[97]

The Court has held that the right of privacy does not extend to ". . . places of public accommodation" and therefore adults do not have a constitutional right to acquire pornographic materials in bookstores or theaters.[98]

In *Eisenstadt* v. *Baird,* the Supreme Court tacitly recognized the right of heterosexual activity between consenting adults.* Does this apply to homosexual adult males? No. Georgia's statute prohibiting homosexual acts between adult males was found to be constitutional, on the grounds that the Constitution does not contain "a fundamental right to engage in homosexual sodomy,"[99] 1986 even in one's own home. Left undecided was whether sodomy between heterosexuals—husband and wife—is also unconstitutional.

Do "coerced" polygraph tests administered by the private sector violate the right to privacy? Yes, at least in California. In the largest settlement of its kind (an out-of-court settlement), the Federated Groups agreed to pay $12.1 million to job applicants forced to take polygraph ("lie detector") tests as a condition of employment. The right to privacy is guaranteed by California's Constitution.[100]

New Exercises of State Police Power

The decade of the 1980s saw the emergence of a number of hotly contested issues pitting individual rights against the police power of the state to protect the public. State constitutions can require more stringent protective laws than are required by the U.S. Constitution. However, no state constitution or law can relax standards established by federal law, because of the doctrine of supremacy.

Among these problems none is more difficult to resolve than the disease of AIDS—Acquired Immune Deficiency Syndrome. Should there be a mandatory AIDS testing program, especially for persons who work in certain high-risk areas, or with high-risk persons? The general answer is no.†

The Supreme Court confronted the issue for the first time in a case where a statute required AIDS tests for state employees who care for the mentally retarded in the state of Nebraska. The Supreme Court without comment upheld a federal appeals court decision that mandatory blood tests required by the statute were a violation of the Fourth Amendment's protection against unreasonable search and seizures.[101]

For now, the Supreme Court seems content to accept the doctrine that AIDS testing must meet the same constitutional requirements of reasonableness as other warrantless search and seizure practices.

---

* The state could not prevent the distribution of contraceptives to college students, many of them unmarried. Sexual acts between consenting unmarried adults is still illegal in some states.
† Mandatory AIDS testing, like mandatory drug testing, involves an invasion of one's privacy that the Fourth Amendment seeks to protect.

Critics of universal blood testing charge that the Fourth Amendment "right of the people to be secure in their persons, houses, papers and effects, against unreasonable searches and seizure . . ." is violated by indiscriminate blood testing (i.e., taking blood from one's body is a search). However, the Supreme Court said it was not unconstitutional to take blood from a person without his or her permission if that person is believed to be driving under the influence. (In this case, the person in question was convicted of drunken driving on the basis of the amount of alcohol in his blood.)[102]

Another area of constitutional conflict is mandatory drug testing. The legal status of drug testing in the private sector varies from state to state. While the Supreme Court has ruled that certain governmental drug testing plans are constitutional, some authorities believe that the states will have to make their own decisions about drug testing. As long as drug testing meets a reasonableness test as to safeguards, such as providing sufficient notice and keeping the test results secret, the business community apparently will be permitted to continue testing employees and job applicants.[103]

The Constitution is a truly dynamic instrument, a bulwark of our freedom and independence. But it will always need to be reconsidered in light of technological change and social evolution.

Our Constitution embodies the fundamental principles that govern our society. The world never has seen a more perfect example of constitutionalism than is found in the United States of America. It endures because it embodies long-established customs, beliefs, political doctrines, and shared values of our society. It is a stabilizing force, yet it is dynamic, continually being interpreted by our legal system, always changing, and managing important questions that face us from day to day. Understandably, the U.S. Supreme Court does not react immediately to public concerns; it takes the time necessary to be reflective and cautious in interpreting the supreme law of the nation.

Case 2

ALLEGHENY COUNTY v. AMERICAN CIVIL LIBERTIES UNION
U.S. Supreme Court, 492 U.S. ___, 109 S.CT. 3086 (1989)

This case concerns the constitutionality of the annual holiday display placed on government property by Allegheny County of Pennsylvania. The display was composed of a creche depicting the Christian nativity scene and a sign proclaiming "Gloria in Excelsis Deo," placed in the "Grand Staircase" of the County Courthouse. Also an 18-foot Chanukah menorah or candelabrum was placed outside of the Courthouse beside a 45-foot decorated Christmas tree. The creche is owned by the Holy Name Society, a *Roman Catholic group. The menorah is owned by Chabad, a Jewish group. The American Civil Liberties Union brought suit, charging Allegheny County with violating the establishment of religion clause of the First Amendment of the U.S. Constitution.*

Justice Harry Blackman delivered the opinion of the Court. [A] "practice which touches upon religion, if it is to be permissible under the Establishment Clause," must not, *inter alia,* "advance [or] inhibit religion in its principal or primary effect." Although, in refining the definition of governmental action that unconstitutionally "advances" religion, the Court's subsequent decisions have variously spoken in terms of "endorsement," "favoritism," "preference," or "promotion," the essential principle remains the same: The Clause, at the very least, prohibits government from appearing to take a position on questions of religious belief or from "making adherence to a religion relevant in any way to a person's standing in the political community. . . .

When viewed in its overall context, the creche display violates the Establishment Clause. The creche angel's words endorse a patently Christian message: Glory to God for the birth of Jesus Christ. [N]othing in the crech's setting detracts from that message. Although the government may acknowledge Christmas as a cultural phenomenon, it may not observe it as a Christian holy day by suggesting that people praise God for the birth of Jesus. . . .

[We hold] that the menorah display does not have the prohibited effect of endorsing religion, given its "particular physical setting." Its combined display with a Christmas tree and a sign saluting liberty does not impermissibly endorse both the Christian and Jewish faiths, but simply recognizes that both Christmas and Chanukah are part of the same winter-holiday season, which has attained a secular status in our society. The widely accepted view of the Christmas tree as the preeminent secular symbol of the Christmas season emphasizes this point. The tree, moreover, by virtue of its size and central position in the display, it clearly the predominant element, and the placement of the menorah beside it is readily understood as simply a recognition that Christmas is not the only traditional way of celebrating the season.

The absence of a more secular alternative to the menorah negates the inference of endorsement. Similarly, the presence of the Mayor's sign confirms that in the particular context the government's association with a religious symbol does not represent sponsorship of religious beliefs but simply a recognition of cultural diversity. Given all these considerations, it is not sufficiently likely that a reasonable observer would view the combined display as an endorsement or disapproval of his individual religious choices.

The Court held in a 5 to 4 decision that the religion clause in the First Amendment was violated by the display of a creche inside the county courthouse, but not by the display of a menorah, a Christmas tree and a sign saluting liberty in front of the city–county office building.

QUESTIONS AND PROBLEMS

1. Is the Constitution a blueprint for government or a rule book for citizens?

2. From what you have read on the Constitution, which branch of the national government is presently most powerful? Why?

3. It has been recommended that the electoral college be eliminated. Are you in favor or against such suggestion? Why?

4. High school student Joe I. Needmore, upon receiving his final in calculus, cried "Oh God! Oh God!" He then bowed his head in silence in what the teacher thought was an attitude of prayer. What should the teacher do? Should the student be punished? Why?

5. You have been asked to prepare an amendment to the Constitution. Write out your amendment, and then write an essay discussing the problem to be rectified and how your proposal will solve the problem.

6. The State of Delaware authorized its Highway Patrol officers to make random stops of automobiles for the sole purpose of apprehending unlicensed drivers and unsafe vehicles. Mr. Prouse was stopped and produced a valid driver's license and was found driving a safe vehicle. He claimed that his rights under the Fourth Amendment were violated. Is Prouse correct in his claim? [*Delaware* v. *Prouse,* 440. U.S. 648 (1979)]

7. What is the meaning of *liberty* according to the United States Constitution? Citizen George Nastee put up a sign on one of the columns of the Supreme Court building in Washington, D.C., calling for the impeachment of every member of the Supreme Court. He stationed himself in front of the visitor's entrance in order to pass out his hate literature to those who attempted to enter. He was arrested by the security police. What possible defense under the First Amendment could he raise?

8. At a demonstration protesting the U.S. government's involvement in the Vietnam War, O'Brien made a speech denouncing the United States as "Fascist" and our soldiers as "murderers." At the conclusion of his speech, he burned his draft registration card, all the time shouting repeatedly: "Hell no, we won't go!" Was O'Brien's verbal and symbolic speech protected by the First Amendment? [*U.S.* v. *O'Brien,* 391 U.S. 367 (1968)]

9. Police received an anonymous tip by telephone indicating that Vanessa White was leaving a specified apartment at a particular time in a particular vehicle and would be carrying cocaine with her to a specified motel. Police placed the apartment under surveillance and saw a woman enter and drive off in an automobile like the one described by the informant. Just short of the motel the police stopped her vehicle. A consent search of the vehicle revealed marijuana. White was arrested and cocaine found in her purse. Is this a lawful search without a warrant for both the marijuana and the cocaine? [*Alabama* v. *White,* 110 S.Ct. 2412 (1990)]

10. The city of San Diego passed a city ordinance confining all outdoor display and sign advertising to the premises of the business advertised. An outdoor advertising firm sued, claiming a denial of First Amendment rights to freedom of expression. The city's claim is that beautification and public safety take precedence over and against the business of outdoor advertising. Discuss. *Metro Media* v. *San Diego,* 453 U.S. 490 (1980).

FURTHER READING

1. Bork, R. *The Tempting of America.* New York: The Free Press, 1990. One of America's erudite and prominent scholars, Bork recounts and defends his conception and interpretation of the Constitution.

2. Ducat, C. R. & H. W. Chase, *Constitutional Interpretation.* St. Paul, MN: West Publishing Co., 1988.

3. *The Federalist Papers.* Modern Library Edition. Next to the Constitution itself, the *Federalist Papers* is our most important source showing what the founders intend for our Constitution to mean.

4. Keenan, Joseph T. *The Constitution of the United States.* Chicago: The Dorsey Press, 1988. This book

is an indispensable study aid, containing basic facts and essential concepts about the Constitution.

5. Peltason, Jack. *Understanding the Constitution.* New York: Holt, Rinehart and Winston, 1988. One of the finest explanations of Constitutional power. Always current because of periodic updates. One of the nation's foremost Constitutional scholars, Peltason discusses our "national charter of government" not only as "symbol and instrument," but also as "the cement of the union."

6. Peters, William. *A More Perfect Union.* New York: Crown Publishers, 1987. A contemporary historian's "story" of the Constitution. This text is inspiring and elevating.

NOTES

1. *Webster's New Twentieth Century Dictionary,* 1983 ed.

2. *The Federalist,* No. 51, Modern Library Edition.

3. Sartori, "Constitutionalism: A Preliminary Discussion," *The American Political Science Review,* December 1962.

4. *Youngstown Sheet and Tube Co.* v. *Sawyer,* 343 U.S. 579, 72 S.Ct. 863 (1952).

5. See Marcus Tullius Cicero, *The Republic,* III 22, translated by George Sabine and Stanley Smith (Columbus, 1929).

6. Corwin, Edward, *The "Higher Law" Background of American Constitutional Law* (Ithaca, NY: Cornell University Press, 1967).

7. Locke, John, *Two Treatises on Civil Government,* (New York: Classic Club edition, 1947). All references to Locke are from this edition. See also Shoemaker, T. E., *Readings in Ideology, the Judiciary and Law* (Boston: Ginn & Co., 1985), pp. 12–14.

8. *The Federalist,* op. cit. No. 51.

9. Paine, Thomas, *Political Writings* (1837), pp. 45–46.

10. *The Federalist,* op. cit. No. 78.

11. Ibid.

12. I CRANCH 137 (1803).

13. *Eakin* v. *Raub,* 12 Sergeant and Rawle (Pennsylvania Supreme Court) 330 (1825). Judicial review continues to be controversial, see Robert Bork, *The Tempting of America* (New York: The Free Press, 1990).

14. See U.S. Constitution: Art. I, Art. II, Art. III.

15. *The Federalist,* op. cit. No. 51.

16. Ibid.

17. See *U.S.* v. *Eichman* and *U.S.* v. *Haggerty,* 110 S.Ct. 2404 (1990). See also *The New York Times,* pp. A1, 13 (June 12, 1990).

18. Walters, Dan, *The New California* (California Journal, 1986).

19. U.S. Constitution, Art. I, Sec. 8.

20. U.S. Constitution, Twentieth Amendment, 1933; Twenty-second° Amendment, 1951; Twenty-fifth Amendment, 1967.

21. U.S. Constitution, Art. II, Sec. 2.

22. *Perpich* v. *Department of Defense,* 110 S.Ct. 2418 (1990).

23. *Prize Cases,* 67 U.S. 635 (1863).

24. U.S. Constitution, Art. II, Sec. 2.

25. U.S. Constitution, Art. III, Sec. 1.

26. Impeachment of U.S. District Judge, *Facts on File* (Yearbook Publication, 1986).

27. Specter, "Impeachment: Another Look," *National Law Journal* 12 (1989), p. 1.

28. U.S. Constitution, Art. III, Sec. 1.

29. *U.S.* v. *Will,* 449 U.S. 200, 101 S.Ct. 471 (1979).

30. U.S. Constitution, Art. I, Sec. 8.

31. Ibid., Art. II, Sec. 2.

32. Tenth Amendment.

33. U.S. Constitution, Art. I, Sec. 9.

34. U.S. Constitution, Twenty-fifth Amendment, Nineteenth Amendment, Twenty-third Amendment, Twenty-fourth Amendment, and Twenty-sixth Amendment.

35. Krinsky, Fred and Gerald Rigby, *Theory and Practice of American Democracy* (Belmont, Ca: Dickenson Publishing Co., 1967), p. 105.

36. Burns, James, Jack Peltason, and Tom Cronin, *Government by the People* (Englewood Cliffs, NJ: Prentice-Hall, 1989), p. 606.

37. *The Federalist,* op. cit. No. 51.

38. U.S. Constitution, Art. VI.

39. *Martin* v. *Hunters Lessee,* 1 Wheaton 304 (1816) and *Cohens* v. *Virginia,* 6 Wheaton 264 (1821).

40. Quoted in Ducat, C. R. & H. W. Chase, *Constitutional Interpretation* (St. Paul, MN: West Publishing Co., 1988), p. 7.

41. *Southern Pacific* v. *Arizona,* 325 U.S. 761, 65 S.Ct. 1515 (1945), and *Edwards* v. *California,* 314 U.S. 160, 62 S.Ct. 164 (1941).

42. *McCulloch* v. *Maryland,* 4 Wheaton 316 (1819).

43. Ibid.

44. *Barron* v. *Baltimore,* 7 Peters 243 (1833).

45. The Fourteenth Amendment, 1868.

46. Examples are Civil Rights Act, 1964 and the Voting Rights Act, 1965.

47. *Gitlow* v. *New York,* 268 U.S. 652, 45 S.Ct. 625 (1925).

48. *Palko* v. *Conn.,* 302 U.S. 319, 58 S.Ct. 149 (1937)

49. *Milk Wagon Drivers Union* v. *Meadowmoor Dairies,* 312 U.S. 287, 60 S.Ct. 259 (1941).

50. *Near* v. *Minnesota,* 283 U.S. 697, 51 S.Ct. 625 (1931), and *Bridges* v. *California,* 314 U.S. 252, 62 S.Ct. 190 (1941). Frequently tied to free speech. See also *De Jonge* v. *Oregon,* 299 U.S. 353, 57 S.Ct. 255 (1937), and *Cox* v. *Louisiana,* 379 U.S. 536, 85 S.Ct. 466 (1965).

51. *Shenck* v. *United States,* 249 U.S. 47, 39 S.Ct. 247 (1919).

52. Ibid.

53. *Abrams* v. *United States,* 250 U.S. 616, 40 S.Ct. 17 (1919).

54. *United States* v. *Carolene Products,* 304 U.S. 144, 58 S.Ct. 778 (1938).

55. *Dennis* v. *United States,* 341 U.S. 494, 71 S.Ct. 857 (1951).

56. *Coates* v. *Cincinnati,* 402 U.S. 611, 91 S.Ct. 1686 (1971).

57. *Hazelwood School District* v. *Kuhlmeir,* 108 S.Ct. 562 (1988) and *Frisby* v. *Shultz,* 108 S.Ct. 2495 (1988).

58. *United States* v. *Haggerty* and *United States* v. *Eichman,* 110 S.Ct. 2404 (1990).

59. *Everson* v. *Board of Education,* 330 U.S. 1, 67 S.Ct. 504 (1947).

60. Francis Canavan, "The Pluralist Game," *Law and Contemporary Problems,* Vol. 44, No. 2 (Spring 1981), pp. 23–38. See also Dallin H. Oaks, "Religion in Public Life," *Ensign* (July 1990), pp. 6–13.

61. *Engel* v. *Vitale,* 370 U.S. 421, 82 S.Ct. 1261 (1962), *Abington School District* v. *Schemp,* and *Murray* v. *Curlett,* 374 U.S. 203, 83 S.Ct. 1560 (1963).

62. *Wallace* v. *Jaffree,* 472 U.S. 38, 105 S.Ct. 2479 (1985).

63. *Board of Education of the Westside Community Schools* v. *Mergens,* 110 S.Ct. 2356 (1990).

64. U.S. Constitution, Second Amendment.

65. *Lewis* v. *United States,* 445 U.S. 55, 100 S.Ct. 915 (1980).

66. *Adams* v. *Williams,* 407 U.S. 143, 92 S.Ct.1921 (1972).

67. *Mapp* v. *Ohio,* 367 U.S. 643, 81 S.Ct. 1684 (1961).

68. *Wolf* v. *Colorado,* 338 U.S. 25, 69 S.Ct. 1359 (1949).

69. *Mapp* v. *Ohio,* 367 U.S. 643, 81 S.Ct. 1684 (1961).

70. Ibid.

71. Inbou, Fred E., et al., *Criminal Procedure* (New York: The Foundation Press, 1974), p. 59.

72. Ibid., 59–64.

73. *Malloy* v. *Hogan,* 378 U.S. 1, 84 S.Ct. 1489 (1964) and *Miranda* v. *Arizona,* 384 U.S. 436, 86 S.Ct. 1602 (1966), Miranda will be discussed in Chapter 4 on criminal law.

74. *Illinois* v. *Perkins,* 110 S.Ct. 2394 (1990).

75. *Klopher* v. *North Carolina,* 386 U.S. 213, 87 S.Ct. 988 (1967).

76. In re *Oliver,* 333 U.S. 257, 68 S.Ct. 499 (1948).

77. *Parker* v. *Gladden,* 385 U.S. 363, 87 S.Ct. 468 (1966) and *Duncan* v. *Louisiana,* 391 U.S. 145, 88 S.Ct. 1444 (1968).

78. *Washington* v. *Texas,* 388 U.S. 14, 87 S.Ct. 1920 (1967).

79. *Argersinger* v. *Hamblin,* 407 U.S. 25, 92 S.Ct. 2006 (1972), and *Gideon* v. *Wainwright,* 372 U.S. 335, 83 S.Ct. 792 (1963).

80. Ibid.

81. Chapter 4 on criminal law will speak to these issues more thoroughly. We mention them here to show the process of how these guarantees were forced on the states by the Supreme Court.

82. *Plessy* v. *Ferguson,* 163 U.S. 537, 16 S.Ct. 1138 (1896).

83. *Brown* v. *The Board of Education,* 347 U.S. 483, 74 S.Ct. 686 (1954).

84. *Brown* v. *The Board of Education,* 349 U.S. 294, 75 S.Ct. 753 (1955).

85. *Grove City College* v. *Bell,* 555 U.S. 535, 104 S.Ct. 1211 (1984).

86. Ibid.

87. *Roberts* v. *United States Jaycees,* 468 U.S. 609, 104 S.Ct. 3244 (1984).

88. *Rotary International* v. *Rotary Club of Duarte,* 481 U.S. 537, 107 S.Ct. 1940 (1987).

89. *Moose Lodge No. 107* v. *Irvis,* 407 U.S. 163, 92 S.Ct. 1965 (1972).

90. *U.S.* v. *Carolene Products,* 304 U.S. 144, 58 S.Ct. 778 (1938).

91. *Swann* v. *Charlotte Necklenburg,* 402 U.S. 1, 91 S.Ct. 1267 (1971).

92. *Steelworkers* v. *Weber,* 443 U.S. 193, 99 S.Ct. 2721 (1979), *Sheet Metal Workers* v. *Equal Employment Opportunity Commission,* 478 U.S. 421, 106 S.Ct. 3019 (1986), and *Firefighters* v. *Cleveland,* 478 U.S. 501, 106 S.Ct. 3063 (1986).

93. *University of California Regents* v. *Bakke,* 438 U.S. 265, 95 S.Ct. 2733 (1978).

94. *Wygant* v. *Jackson Board of Education,* 476 U.S. 267, 106 S.Ct. 1842 (1986).

95. *Griswold* v. *Connecticut,* 381 U.S. 479, 85 S.Ct. 1678 (1965).

96. *Eisenstadt* v. *Baird,* 405 U.S. 438, 92 S.Ct. 1029 (1972), *Loving* v. *Virginia,* 388 U.S. 1, 388 U.S. 1, 87 S.Ct. 1817 (1967), *Roe* v. *Wade,* 410 U.S. 113, 93 S.Ct. 705 (1973), *Doe* v. *Bolton,* 410 U.S. 179, 93 S.Ct. 739 (1973), and *Stanley* v. *Georgia,* 394 U.S. 557, 87 S.Ct. 1243 (1969).

97. *Osborne* v. *Ohio,* 110 S.Ct. 1691 (1990).

98. *Paris Adult Theater I* v. *Slayton,* 413 U.S. 49, 93 S.Ct. 2628 (1973).

99. *Bowers* v. *Hardwick,* 478 U.S. 186, 106 S.Ct. 284 (1986).

100. *The Wall Street Journal,* June 23, 1989.

101. *Washington Post,* October 31, 1989. Also see Lifson, "History of HIV Infection," *San Francisco Chronicle,* December 27, 1989.

102. *Schmerber* v. *California,* 384 U.S. 757, 86 S.Ct. 1826 (1966).

103. "Drug Testing Becomes a Corporate Mine Field," *The Wall Street Journal,* December 21, 1989.

3

The Court System

A government of laws, and not of men

—Words written in 1774 by John Adams, first Vice President and second President of the United States.[1]

Introduction

It is often stated and generally believed that people in the United States of America are governed by law, not people. What does this mean? It means that decisions establishing and affecting rights and duties are not made arbitrarily by individuals; rather, such decisions are made according to existing rules, using fair and impartial processes. Like all generalizations, there are exceptions and short-comings to this fundamental idea. The frequently heard lament about "red tape" is a veiled criticism of the rule of law.

To provide for the application of the rule of law in a fair, impartial, and con-sistent manner, while remaining efficient, is a difficult task. The diversity of ethnic origins and cultural backgrounds of the United States compounds the problem of achieving consensus on fair solutions to many complex issues subject to law.

The recognition and creation of human rights and duties is a responsibility shared by the legislative, executive, and judicial branches of government. However, the nature and manner in which law is created and shaped differs dra-matically depending on the source of its creation. Probably no other country relies more on its judiciary and courts. One hundred and fifty years ago, French political scientist Alexis de Tocqueville noted the special importance of courts in the American political system. His observations, containing a mixture of praise and reproval, still ring true today. "Restricted within its limits, the power granted to American courts to pronounce on the constitutionality of laws is yet one of the most powerful barriers ever erected against the tyranny of political assemblies."[2]

Application of the rule of law requires an independent neutral forum, where facts are determined and rules applied, to resolve legal disputes. In the United States this function is accomplished through the *court system. Courts* are governmental facilities open to both private persons and government agencies. The courts offer their tax-supported services practically free to users, as they are subsidized by the government. Under the U.S. Constitution the courts are for the most part independent of any other branch of government. This independence provides an important restraint on governmental interference with individual liberties by the executive or legislative branches.

What Is a Court?

A **court** is both a place and a system. It is a place where you may go to peacefully resolve your disputes with other persons. The word *court* is commonly used to describe a place ("I'll see you in court!"); all participants, including judge, attorneys, clerks, witnesses, parties, and the public ("Court is in session"); and sometimes the judge or justice ("If the court please, may I be heard at this time?").

Courts are also part of a system, as there are different courts for different legal disputes with different specified procedures. Some courts determine the facts of individual disputes; other courts review decisions of lower courts for correctness, consistency, and fairness. To understand the courts, it is useful to recognize some of their different functions.

Trial and Appellate Courts

What are the differences between trial and appellate courts? **Trial courts** conduct the initial proceedings. The trial court proceeding has three distinct purposes: (1) to determine the facts of the dispute ("What happened between the competing parties?") (2) to determine what rules of law should be applied to the facts, and (3) to apply those rules to the facts.

After a trial court's decision, some cases are appealed to an **appellate court** for review and either approval or an order for corrective action. There may be more than one level of appellate courts. Thus a case may be further appealed from an intermediate appellate court. Appellate courts do not hear new **evidence*** or make new determinations of facts. Instead, they focus on whether the law was correctly stated or applied to the facts as found by the trial court. Most cases are

---

*Examples of evidence are testimony of witnesses, photographs, documents, handwriting samples, dented fenders, etc.

not appealed. The cost of an appeal can be prohibitive in time, money, and peace of mind. Although not always pleased with the outcome, the parties have had their "day in court" in the original trial. Also, even when an error of law is made in the trial, it may be insufficient to appeal the case. Clearly the trial is crucial. It is the powerful and final dispenser of justice for most persons involved in litigation.

Marguerite Martinez signed up for ski instruction at Heavenly Mountain in Idaho. Gary Graf, a certified ski instructor, fitted Marguerite with rental skis. He then taught her how to snowplow. During the afternoon after her lesson, Marguerite decided to show her new skills to Luther Thomas, whom she had met during lunch. Her show was short. Marguerite fell and suffered a spiral fracture of her right leg, just above the ankle. Her bindings had failed to release her boot from the skis when she fell. She decided to sue Graf in a civil action for damages, alleging that he had carelessly adjusted the bindings too tightly. Who will win?

No one knows who will win because the facts have not yet been judicially determined. Did Gary secure the bindings too tightly? Did Marguerite, or anyone else, tamper with the bindings after they were set by Gary? Did the bindings fail because they were too tight, or because Marguerite had allowed ice to accumulate beneath her boot? Were the bindings defective? Was there a contract where liability was properly disclaimed or limited? A civil trial will determine the answers to these and all other relevant factual and legal contentions. In the trial Marguerite is the **plaintiff,** since she is seeking to recover **damages** (money) from Gary, the **defendant.** The entire proceeding, ultimately resulting in a resolution of the controversy, is called a *lawsuit* or **litigation.**

The example of Marguerite's misfortune and her attempt to collect damages from Gary is one example of a **civil dispute** or *case*. Civil disputes involve private disputes between persons. A civil dispute is sometimes defined broadly by stating what it is not. It is not a matter involving criminal law. A *criminal dispute* or *case* is a determination of whether a defendant is guilty of an act committed or omitted in violation of a penal statute.

Civil and criminal matters are usually considered separate systems; in large cities, attorneys and judges often specialize in one or the other. There are similarities and differences in civil and criminal matters. Both criminal and civil trials are formal proceedings before a court. Both are conducted to resolve disputed questions of fact and law that will, in turn, define applicable rights and duties. Different terms are, however, often used; a defendant found to be responsible in a civil trial is said to be *liable*, and in a criminal trial such person is said to be *guilty*.

In a criminal trial, the public is usually represented by an attorney from the local governing unit (county) on behalf of the state (e.g., a public prosecutor or district attorney). If a federal crime is involved, the Department of Justice represents the public. While government can be a party in either a civil or criminal matter, only the government can be the plaintiff (prosecutor) in a criminal action, because crimes are public offenses against all society. The accused is the defendant. Criminal actions have substantially different rules and procedures. The focus of this chapter is on the civil court system with only an occasional reference to the criminal system. (See Chapter 4 for a discussion of criminal procedure.)

With very few exceptions, civil trials are open to the public and the press. Public attendance can be restricted for security reasons, when one or both parties request privacy, and when there is no overriding reason why the public should be informed of the details of the dispute. Cases involving children, who might be affected unfavorably by a public hearing, may be held in private. If the trial is closed to the public, the press is excluded. Much of what you read in the press regarding the legal problems of public figures is based on reporters' access to public trials and legal documents.

Criminal trials may be conducted in private only in extraordinary situations. However, juvenile court proceedings, which are considered matters in equity (to be discussed later in this chapter), have long been conducted in private.

The Attorney General of the State of Maryland filed suit against Cottman Transmission Systems, Inc., relating to allegations of fraudulent activities. (Allegedly Cottman had removed automobile transmissions for inspection and maintenance when the costly action was unnecessary.) The Attorney General distributed news releases listing the charges against Cottman. When the Attorney General instituted further charges, Cottman asked the court to close the courtroom except for parties directly involved in the proceeding. Was Cottman successful?

Yes and no. Cottman's counsel convinced the trial court judge that the releases to the press were harmful to their ability to get a fair trial, and so the public was barred. On appeal, the trial court judge's decision was reversed. The Maryland appeals court stated:

> To close a court to public scrutiny of the proceedings is to shut off the light of the law. How else will the citizenry learn of the happenings in the courts—their government's third branch—except through access to the courts by the people themselves or through reports supplied by the media? A . . . corporate entity involved as a party to a civil case is entitled to a fair trial, not a private one.[3]

As previously stated, an appellate court reviews the decisions and proceedings of lower courts. The appellate court works from a verbatim record (court transcript) of what was said in the lower court. The appellate court does not listen to witnesses, accept evidence, or have a jury. It accepts as true the facts found in the trial court, which had considered all the testimony of all witnesses along with all other evidence. The appellate court decides whether rules of substantive and procedural law were properly applied by the trial judge. Appellate judges may also "weigh," or evaluate, the factual evidence as presented in the trial court and then decide whether, as a matter of law, the facts are sufficient to justify the verdict.

If the appellate court concludes that the trial court erroneously applied or interpreted the law, it may modify or reverse the judgment, and either enter a new judgment or remand (send) the case back to the trial court for a new trial or other proceedings in compliance with the appellate court's instructions. Merely finding an error made at the trial court level is not considered sufficient to overturn the trial court's verdict. The error found must be a serious one, requiring correction by the appellate court in order to avoid a miscarriage of justice. In the *Cottman* case, the appellate court vacated an order of the trial court, doing so even before the trial had taken place, because of the importance of the trial judge's order closing the trial to the public.

What Is the Adversary System?

In the **adversary system,** parties to legal actions (usually acting through legal counsel) are opponents. The judge is a neutral and usually passive participant. This is a fairly simple concept, but it has enormous ramifications. Courts make decisions based on facts brought to their attention by the parties. A contrasting system, sometimes called the *inquisitorial system,* exists in many other countries as diverse as the Soviet Union and France. Under that system, judges need not be dependent on the testimony of the parties once the matter is before the court. The judge can investigate the matter, question witnesses, and independently seek out evidence.

In the *adversary system,* opponents are responsible for producing evidence supporting their view of the dispute. Each party is openly partial for its own side, and against the opponent. Each party earnestly asserts every available supporting reason to merit victory. Every theory revealed and asserted is a theory considered and subject to attack by the opponent. Truth depends on openness in the public forum. Deceit depends on concealment. A deliberate lie by a witness who is under oath to tell the truth is called **perjury,** and is punishable as a crime. The adversary system makes deceit in the courtroom extremely difficult. In effect, the judge acts much as a referee in a sporting contest, to ensure that the procedural rules are properly followed.

Another major feature of the adversary system is the requirement of a **moving party.** In civil matters, legal questions are not considered by a court unless a private party brings the problem to the attention of the courts by filing a lawsuit. Each party is then independently responsible for presenting its case. In general, staff of the court (clerks, etc.) will not assist a litigant (person involved in a lawsuit) in any stage of the proceeding, except to provide the place and the process for the dispute to be resolved.

The adversary system is the backbone of what may be the most just legal system the world has ever known. It also has its shortcomings and critics. The adversary system places a premium on advocacy skills and thus encourages the use of lawyers in the resolution of legal disputes. Access to the system is critically important—redress is not possible if access is denied.

State and Federal Courts

Federalism exists in the United States court system as well as in the executive and legislative branches of government. Simply put, we have both federal and state court systems. Although there is much in common in the two systems, each is an independent, although interrelated, system.

How Are State Court Systems Organized?

Every state has a system of trial courts and one or more appellate courts. Unfortunately, titles of courts are not uniform; names of courts in one state frequently apply to quite different courts in another state. Confusion can be avoided by focusing on the function a court performs: appellate or trial? Table 3–1 shows the most common titles of courts and their respective functions.

Which court has *jurisdiction* (power or authority) over a given matter is a question of procedural law, as defined in the constitution and/or statutes of the respective states. Among the common distinctions used to determine which court has jurisdiction is the nature of the dispute and the type of relief or amount of remuneration sought. The location of the appropriate court within the state to hear the case is also determined by procedural law. This location is determined by the residence of the defendant, the location of real property involved, or the place of an accident.

Most states provide two levels of appeal. Because of the complexity of legal issues and of court procedures, people generally need the services of a lawyer to represent them in court.

TABLE 3–1   State Court System

Type of Court	Function	Representative Titles[1]
Appellate court	To review results reached in trial	
Highest		Supreme Court, or Court of Appeals
Intermediate[2]		Court of Appeals, or Appellate Division
Trial court	To conduct trials	
General jurisdiction		Superior Court, Circuit Court, or District Court
Limited jurisdiction[3]		Municipal Court, Magistrate Court, District Court, or Small Claims Court

[1] In many instances the titles of courts in one state describe quite different courts in other states. For example, the court of appeals may be the title of either the highest appellate court or an intermediate appellate court.
[2] Nearly half of the states do not have an intermediate appellate court. In those states the trial court of general jurisdiction may perform the appellate function of reviewing certain types of trial court decisions.
[3] There are many courts with limited jurisdiction to perform special functions—for example, probate court, juvenile court, police court, and family court. Courts are sometimes specialized to promote efficiency in administering justice.

What Are Small Claims Courts?

Court procedures are devised to handle a great variety of legal problems ranging from the most complex to the most simple. Not surprisingly, the usual manner of handling legal matters is not efficient for small or simple cases. If you have a legal claim for $1,500 worth of minor damage to your automobile in an accident, the cost of hiring an attorney to help you recover that amount through court action would no doubt exceed your expected recovery.

To promote peaceful resolution of disputes where conventional litigation is prohibitively expensive, most states have created a special trial court, the **small claims court.** Small claims courts are designed to provide a speedy, inexpensive, and informal method of settling minor civil claims. They may be a separate court or a designated sub-division of another court. Because they are the creation of each state, particulars vary widely. The maximum amount of damages recoverable ranges from $250 to more than $5,000, depending on the state. The most common maximum range is $1,500–$2,500. Many state legislatures are currently increasing the dollar limits of these courts to keep pace with inflation.*

The purpose of the small claims court is the same as any other trial court, to determine facts and apply the law. But the dynamics of the court are very different. Most cases involve a dispute over money, although some are concerned with matters such as eviction. Divorce actions are not permitted in small claims court. The procedural rules differ from those of traditional trial courts. Legal documents are kept to a minimum; often the only formal document required of the plaintiff is a simple preprinted form with boxes to check. There are no formal rules of evidence and no juries. In the interests of economy and simplicity, most states do not permit attorneys to represent litigants in small claims court. Corporations are artificial, legal persons, and so when they use small claims courts to collect debts they must be represented by employees. Most states will not allow attorneys to appear for litigants even in such corporate situations, unless the attorney is the sole shareholder and/or an officeholder of the corporation.

Each party tells his or her version of the dispute, calling on witnesses for corroboration or for added facts, and presenting any supporting documents or other physical evidence. The judge may ask questions and then, without any elaborate argument or research, decides the case, sometimes immediately, usually later by mail.

The small claims courts are there to help "the little person" get his or her "day in court" without the delays and costs that accompany use of traditional courts. However, because businesses often have a substantial number of small claims, they are the most frequent plaintiffs in small claims court actions.† Small claims courts have been popularized in recent years by the television program *People's*

---

*For example, the current maximum recoveries are indicated in this sample of states: California is currently $2,000, rising to $2,500 in January, 1991; Texas, $1,000 in counties with populations below 400,000 and $2,500 above 400,000; Illinois, $2,500; Indiana, $3,000; Massachusetts and North Carolina, $1,500.

†Apparently about one-half of the plaintiffs are businesses. See "The Role of the Small-Claims Court," *Consumer Reports,* November 1979, p. 666.

Court, where Judge Wapner presides. Technically, that television proceeding is an *arbitration* (use of a third party selected by parties to a dispute to hear and resolve the dispute) rather than a trial, but it illustrates the types of disputes heard and resolved in small claims court.

What Is the Federal Court System?

Trial Courts

The federal government has one basic trial court called the *U.S. district court.* The country is divided into 93 districts, each with a court. In populous areas, the districts are geographically small; in rural areas, they are large. There is at least one district court in every state and territory in the United States, even though individual court boundaries may include more than one state. U.S. district courts conduct trials concerning federal matters, such as federal crimes, enforcement of federal statutes, and certain **diversity of citizenship** cases. Diversity of citizenship jurisdiction exists when a plaintiff is a citizen of one state and the defendant is a citizen of another state, or when one party is a foreign country or a citizen of a foreign country and the other is a citizen of a state. The amount of claimed damages in a diversity of citizenship case must be at least $50,000.[4] In settling such diversity of citizenship controversies, the particular U.S. district court involved applies federal **procedural law** and the **substantive law** of the appropriate state, usually the state where the court is located.   *Basic law of rights & duties as opposed to methods (procedures)*

Appellate Courts

The United States has two principal appellate courts, the *U.S. Courts of Appeal* and the *U.S. Supreme Court.* The country is divided into 11 circuits or areas, each with a Court of Appeals. The Courts of Appeal review the decisions of the U.S. district courts located within their respective circuits. Like state appellate courts, the U.S. Courts of Appeal consider cases brought to the court's attention by parties contending that an error of law was made by the federal trial judge.

In addition to appeals from the Courts of Appeal, the U.S. Supreme Court may review cases from the highest court of any state by a process called **certiorari** (Latin: to be informed) when a federal question is involved. The Supreme Court is not required to consider and decide cases submitted to it. The Court selects to hear and decide cases that involve interpretation of federal law (including the Constitution) arising in either the federal or state court systems. If the court agrees to hear the case it issues an order—a *writ of certiorari*—to the lower court, requiring the record of the case. When the Supreme Court refuses to review a case the practical effect is to affirm the lower court decision, which continues to be binding on the parties. The Court is able to hear only a small percentage of the cases filed.

Figure 3–1 depicts the federal court structure, which, in addition to the principal courts, includes the court of military appeals, court of claims, court of customs and patent appeals, customs court, tax court, and bankruptcy court. Each of these is a special court restricted to hearing particular types of cases.

FIGURE 3-1 U.S. Court System

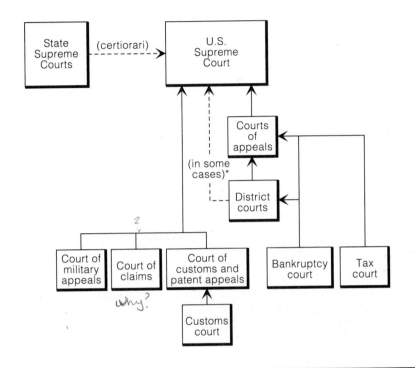

* For example, when a district court has held a federal law to be unconstitutional and an agency of the government is a party.

Trial Proceedings

How Is a Case Begun?

Civil If Marguerite Martinez decides to sue Gary Graf for the broken leg she suffered while skiing, her attorney will start the case by filing a document called a **complaint** with the county clerk. Martinez is the plaintiff, and the complaint is prepared by her attorney, who is satisfied that she has a **cause of action** (adequate basis for suing). The complaint will briefly state the facts she believes justify her claim and ask for damages or other relief. These are called **allegations of fact.**

County Clerks maintain files, in alphabetical order, of every case filed in their respective counties. These records are open to the public. A filing fee (from $15 to $100 or more) is charged at the time of filing. When the complaint is filed, the clerk issues a **summons** (prepared by the plaintiff's attorney) by endorsing it on behalf of the court. The summons states, in effect, that the defendant has a prescribed time (for example, 30 days) to respond to the complaint. If the defendant fails to respond, the plaintiff may win the case by **default,** and a **judgment,** the final decision of the court, may be awarded to the plaintiff.

Marguerite's attorney will arrange with a *process server* to have a copy of the summons and complaint personally served on the defendant, Gary Graf. A process server is in the business of serving legal documents on defendants or plaintiffs and witnesses. If Gary cannot be found, or if he evades service of the process, he may nonetheless be "constructively served" by a combination of notification by mail and publication of a summons in a local newspaper. Serving a copy of summons and complaint (or publication of summons) gives Gary notice that he has been sued and gives the proper court jurisdiction (or power) over his person to decide the controversy. The court must also be the appropriate forum (have jurisdiction) as to the subject matter and type of dispute involved.

Upon receipt of the summons and complaint, Graf would typically hire an attorney to represent his interests. Graf's attorney would file with the county clerk a document called an **answer,** and mail a copy to the plaintiff's attorney. In the answer, Graf may admit any allegations of the complaint that he believes are true, and deny the rest.

Instead of an answer, Graf's attorney could file another type of responsive pleading, asking for a dismissal of the complaint. This is called a **demurrer** or **motion to dismiss** and is used when the complaint, even if true, is legally insufficient to justify an answer. This is often called a "so what" motion, as its legal effect is to say that even if all of the plaintiff's allegations are true, no legal duty was breached by the defendant. A demurrer could also raise procedural defenses, such as that the action is barred by the **statute of limitations.** A statute of limitations provides that a particular legal action must be begun within a limited period of time.

In his complaint, plaintiff Archibald Cantwell alleged that defendant "wrongfully, viciously, and wantonly stuck out her tongue at the plaintiff, causing great and severe mental anguish." Has Archie stated a cause of action in his complaint?

No. Even if the plaintiff's allegations were admitted by the defendant, there would be no legal recovery (judgment) for the plaintiff because simply sticking out one's tongue is not against the law. Therefore, the defendant would be well advised to file a demurrer or motion to dismiss, which would be **sustained** (agreed to) by the court, and the complaint would be dismissed. A **motion** is a formal request to a court for some action. If Archibald filed an answer, the case would continue on to trial, wasting the time of both the defendant and the court.

Once both Marguerite's complaint and Graf's answer, called *pleadings,* are on file, the factual contentions of each party are stated. Typically, the parties will disagree in their versions and interpretations of the facts; it is these factual disputes that must be resolved at trial.

It is also possible that Graf could simply not respond to the complaint. He could ignore the complaint and see what happens. This non-action would pave the way for Marguerite to obtain an uncontested judgment, called a *default judgment.* As there is no opposition, Marguerite's attorney could obtain such a judgment after a minimal showing of supporting evidence. This is not a smart course of action for Graf, unless he agrees that he was at fault. Even then, he should answer the complaint and try to negotiate a compromise as to the damages rather than rely on the court to find and fix his liability.

Criminal   In contrast, a criminal case is formally commenced by the making of an *accusation*. An accusation can be made by the district attorney (usually called an *information*) or the grand jury (called an *indictment*). In misdemeanor cases, the accusation is usually called a *complaint*. A more complete explanation of criminal procedure appears in Chapter 4.

What Proceedings Take Place Before Trial?

Civil   Once a civil lawsuit begins, it may be a year or more until the date of the trial. In some jurisdictions, shortages of judges cause crowded court calendars, which in turn routinely cause delays as long as five years before the trial. In rural and less populous jurisdictions, the trial may occur as soon as the opposing attorneys are prepared. Courtroom delay has become one of the most serious problems facing this country's legal system. In recent years, many states have begun experimenting with new judicial methods to expedite the process. Many states actively encourage alternatives to litigation, such as arbitration. Many judges enjoy serving as arbitrators, for a fee, following their retirement. The legal system is flexible enough to allow for alternatives to the courts in many situations. These alternatives to litigation are called **alternative dispute resolution** (ADR) and are discussed later in this chapter.

Discovery   Although courtroom availability is the most common reason for delay, counsel for one or both the parties may seek to delay the trial. Particularly important is the need for time to take full advantage of discovery procedures. During the period before trial, both parties have the right to engage in **discovery** practices designed to (1) educate each party as to the facts surrounding the controversy, (2) promote voluntary settlement of the controversy by revealing strengths and weaknesses in the cases of each party, and (3) eliminate surprises that might otherwise arise at the trial and lead to a miscarriage of justice. **Depositions** and **interrogatories** are the most common types of discovery.

Marguerite Martinez hired Sally Sharpe as her attorney in the case against Gary Graf. Sally drafted a complaint and had the summons and complaint served on Graf. The defendant Graf hired Perry Darrow as his attorney, and Perry prepared and filed an answer. In his answer Graf admitted that he had adjusted Marguerite's bindings, but alleged that he was not negligent (careless) and had done it properly. The answer further alleged that Marguerite was also negligent as she was under the influence of alcohol at the time of her injury and had carelessly allowed ice to form beneath her boots. The pleadings were filed and the issues of fact joined. What is the status of the proceedings?

Sally is seeking a money judgment against Graf to compensate Marguerite for her injury on the theory that Graf was negligent. Perry, on behalf of Graf, is contending that Graf was not negligent and that even if he was, Marguerite was equally careless as to her own safety and, for both reasons, should be denied a money judgment. Both Sally and Perry will need more information in order to prepare their respective cases properly.

Depositions   Sally wants to know the exact setting Graf had used in adjusting Marguerite's bindings; then she can seek expert advice as to what should have been the proper setting. Sally could mail a *notice of taking deposition* to Graf's attorney, requesting that Graf appear in Sally's office at a stated time to be questioned under oath with a court reporter present. The court reporters will use mechanical shorthand to record all testimony. In many states electronic shorthand equipment and recording machines also are used. During this deposition, which Graf must attend, Sally could ask him what setting he had used. Of course, Graf's attorney will also probably take Marguerite's deposition.

At Marguerite's deposition, Perry asked the following question: "Miss Martinez, do you date frequently?" Sally immediately objected, shouting that she would not allow her client to be subjected to irrelevant questions by Perry. Must Marguerite answer the question?

At the deposition, Perry cannot force Marguerite to answer a question if she refuses. His remedy is to obtain a court order requiring her to answer the question if the question is deemed relevant by the judge. If she then refuses, her entire case may be dismissed or another sanction imposed. Perry will need to explain to a judge why the question is relevant, as relevance is not obvious.

After the deposition, the court reporter prepares a typewritten transcript of all questions and answers. This document is sent to the opposing counsel for review by the witness, who may make necessary corrections and sign and return it. If the witness is unavailable at the trial or is present but changes the version of the story given at the deposition, the transcript itself may be introduced as evidence and used to discredit (impeach) the witness. In complex cases, depositions may require several days of testimony under oath. The cost of taking depositions is a major expense of litigation and one significant reason why alternatives to litigation are often sought.

Written Interrogatories   After the deposition, Perry thought of some questions that he had failed to ask. He sent the following *written interrogatories* to Marguerite through her attorney:

1. Please state in writing the address of Luther Thomas.
2. Please state in writing each date you visited a doctor and your total medical bill expense.
3. Please state whether or not your medical bills are being paid by an insurance company. If so, please give the company's name and the applicable policy number.

What will happen if Marguerite fails to answer the written interrogatories? Graf's attorney may seek assistance from the court to compel answers or dismiss Marguerite's case. Courts have the power to compel the parties to comply with the discovery procedures. Attorneys may serve hundreds of written interrogatories in preparation of a complex case. They are less expensive than depositions, as no court reporter is needed, and since they are written, they tend to be far more succinct than the ramblings that frequently accompany oral interrogation. A disadvantage is that they allow a witness to consult with counsel and draft an answer that, although true, discloses little and seeks to answer questions as favorably as possible. The questioning attorney is not present to detect signs of uneasiness and possible evasion or concealment, nor is he or she able to immediately pursue promising leads.

Perry believed that Marguerite's diary would provide something of importance. He therefore filed a *motion to produce* with the court. It requested an order compelling Marguerite to deliver her diary to Perry for inspection. Will the motion be granted?

Motion to Produce   Not unless Perry can demonstrate to the court specifically what may be contained in the diary that would be relevant to the issues in the case. That appears doubtful unless, for example, Perry has proof of a deception by Marguerite that he has reason to believe would be confirmed by the diary. The purpose of such a motion is to compel production of evidence important to your case that is in someone else's possession.

At the time of trial, either attorney may ask the court for a **subpoena** (Latin: under penalty), a written order directing a person to appear in court and testify as a witness. If it is believed that the witness has books or documents needed for a full disclosure of the facts, the court may issue a **subpoena duces tecum** (Latin: under penalty bring with you), requiring that identified documents or physical evidence be brought to court.

Motion for Summary Judgment   If there are no factual contentions that need resolution, it is possible that the case can be decided without a trial. A *motion for summary judgment* argues that there are no significant questions of fact and that the applicable law requires the moving party to be awarded judgment. This motion might be made to the court after discovery, when a party believes discovery has shown there is no real dispute as to the facts. If the motion is granted no trial takes place.

Criminal Trials   It has been said that "justice delayed is justice denied." This is sometimes true, such as when a suspect is arrested and cannot post bail or obtain release on personal **recognizance** (i.e., agreement to appear for the trial without having to post a bond). The suspect must remain in jail awaiting a trial where he or she may be acquitted (declared not guilty). The U.S. Constitution requires a speedy trial for all criminal actions unless this right is waived by the defendant.

Usually, "speedy" is considered 60 days. One of the major reasons for delay in civil trials is that trial priority must be given to criminal matters in order to comply with this right to a speedy trial.

A defendant may waive the right to a speedy trial and ask for time for counsel to thoroughly investigate the case or deal with their own work schedule conflicts. (TV lawyers don't seem to have these conflicts even though they participate in major trials every week, but real lawyers do.) Sometimes delay is useful when a crime has aroused hostile public opinion and the defendant, although not convicted of the crime and therefore presumed to be innocent, is the object of the public's anger and hostility. After some delay, emotions usually cool, and the possibility of receiving a fair, dispassionate trial is improved.

In a criminal case, discovery is limited because of the defendant's **privilege against self-incrimination.** This constitutional privilege, in brief, means that a defendant cannot be compelled to testify against him/herself in a criminal case. The prosecutor does not have the same privilege. Therefore, the district attorney must allow examination of the state's evidence against the defendant, including names of witnesses against the defendant. The Sixth Amendment to the U.S. Constitution gives the accused the right "in all criminal prosecutions, to be confronted with the witnesses against him." Physical evidence (such as weapons, clothing, and stolen goods) may be impounded (seized and held) by the district attorney, pending trial. But the defendant has the right to inspect all such evidence before trial. This apparent advantage to the criminal defendant is more than counterbalanced by the state's extensive ability to independently investigate facts surrounding alleged criminal activity.

When Do Parties Have the Right to Trial by Jury?

Any party to a civil lawsuit in the federal court system has the constitutional right (by the Seventh Amendment) to trial by jury in cases at law, ". . . where the value in controversy shall exceed twenty dollars. . . ." A right to a jury trial in a civil case in state courts is not guaranteed by the federal Constitution,[5] although state constitutions usually provide this right. A jury is a constitutional right (by the Sixth Amendment) in any criminal matter, federal or state, where a serious penalty such as a jail sentence or imprisonment of more than six months may be the punishment.[6] Defendants often waive their right to a jury trial for various reasons, such as a plea bargain to admit guilt to a lesser offense. A judge will then make the necessary findings of fact and impose a sentence.

Juries

If there is no jury, the trial judge decides **questions of fact;** if there is a jury, the jury makes such evaluations and decisions. **Questions of law,** on the other hand, are raised in the trial court whenever the judge rules on objections made by attorneys. The judge is making a ruling of law when he or she permits or disallows certain evidence, rules on motions, or instructs the jury what legal principles should be applied to the facts during their deliberations. Of course, a question of law, not fact, arises whenever the constitutionality of a law is an issue. Thus, a jury does not decide whether a statute is constitutional.

The **jury** is a group of persons selected from a panel of randomly designated citizens of the local region assembled to decide a particular civil or criminal case. A jury is generally considered the most fair instrument of justice because no person—not even a highly educated, coldly analytical, scrupulously honest, professional scientist—is totally objective. The jury is thought to eliminate or neutralize individual bias from the courtroom by drawing together a number of persons of diverse interests and backgrounds. The combination of differing perspectives hopefully will provide the balance needed for just decisions. Judges, lawyers, witnesses, scholars—and most important, litigants themselves—generally agree that the jury system works well most of the time.

Certainly in emotionally charged cases, both civil and criminal, the consensus of a jury of one's peers (one's equals) is to be preferred to the decision of one judge. On the other hand, in complex business litigation, a jury can be overwhelmed and thoroughly confused by a flood of technical evidence, often presented in technical language. Often parties in such cases waive their right to a jury trial and rely on the expertise of the judge.

Prospective Jurors   It is important that the jury selection process be random. Otherwise, people will justifiably suspect the integrity of the jury. In criminal cases especially, the jury is sometimes the sole barrier between the individual and the awesome power of the prosecuting government. The selection begins with preparation of a list or panel of prospective jurors. Most states prepare such lists from voter registrations. Some states look to telephone directories, hunting and fishing license lists, utility lists, census rolls, and even volunteers. Because minorities, the poor, and the very young do not register to vote at the same rate as the rest of the population, there can be an undesirable distortion in the selection process when voter registration lists are used exclusively. Some states are experimenting with other sources of names for prospective jurors, such as driver registration records. The Jury Selection and Service Act regulates jury selection in federal cases. This act provides that names selected from voters' lists should be supplemented with names from additional lists to help ensure selection of juries that better represent a diverse community.

Exemptions   A few classes of people are automatically exempt, or disqualified, from jury duty in most states. In federal courts, disqualified groups include noncitizens; minors; residents of less than one year; persons unable to read, write, and understand English; persons with mental or physical infirmities that would impair their capability as jurors; and convicted felons. States have adopted similar exemptions. Persons may be temporarily excused or indefinitely exempted for good reason, as when absence from a job or family would cause an unreasonable hardship.

It is unconstitutional for an employer to penalize or discriminate against an employee for serving as a juror, such as docking vacation time. Some employers continue to pay the salary or wage of jurors, less the modest fees received from the court, but this is not compulsory. Jurors are presently paid $30 per day in the federal court system and usually less in state courts. Such small sums are inadequate pay for most jurors. Consequently, jury duty that may last for weeks or longer may mean a significant financial sacrifice for the juror. Jury service is a citizen's duty in a democracy. Refusal to serve without an acceptable excuse will be found to be contempt of court and may be punished with fines and/or imprisonment.

Voir Dire   *Voir dire* (to say the truth) is the process of questioning prospective jurors to expose possible bias. Understandably, each attorney tries to seat (select) jurors whom he or she believes to be sympathetic to his or her client's position as plaintiff or defendant. Thus an accountant accustomed to arithmetic precision may not be welcomed by a defendant relying on an unverified alibi in a criminal trial. A clerk who earns a low salary may be considered undesirable by the plaintiff in a civil action where damages sought for loss of future earning power exceed a million dollars.

In large cities, private companies are available to research potential juror lists. A research firm may provide past juror voting records to attorneys to assist them in identifying favorable prospective jurors. In major trials, where the stakes are high, sociologists and psychologists have been hired by lawyers to analyze the physical appearance, education, social status, economic condition, personality, and general cultural background of each prospective juror. The idea is to predict attitude and probable voting conduct in the forthcoming trial. Such assistance in jury selection raises many questions about the accuracy of character evaluation and the ethical propriety of this practice, especially if only one side has access to such information.*

On behalf of Marguerite, Sally demanded a jury trial. On the day set for trial, Sally and Perry met with Judge Miller in chambers. Sally requested permission to personally voir dire the prospective jurors. Perry did not object. Will Judge Miller grant this request?

Possibly. Historically, judges have had the power to either conduct voir dire themselves or allow the attorneys to do so. The trend in many states is to follow the lead of the federal court system. In federal jury selection, voir dire is conducted only by the judge, but after considering specific questions offered by the attorneys. This usually expedites questioning, and is more likely to avoid undesirable questions in selection.

Judge Miller granted Sally's request and ordered that the voir dire be conducted by the two attorneys. One of the questions Sally asked each prospective juror was whether he or she had ever been a ski instructor. One person answered "yes." Is this sufficient evidence of bias, and what recourse does Sally have?

---

* Litigation Science, Inc., the nation's largest legal consulting firm, provides "pre-trial opinion polls, creates profiles of 'ideal jurors,' sets up mock trials and shadow juries, coaches lawyers and witnesses, and designs courtroom graphics." Assuming such assistance is valuable, its availability creates serious questions about a jury of one's peers. *The Wall Street Journal,* October 24, 1989.

Prior experience or knowledge of a situation may or may not show a person is biased. Indeed, everyone possesses inclinations and opinions consistent with his or her culture, education, family background, experience, and so forth. What matters is whether this experience or inclination tends to make a person unable to fairly decide a particular case. If bias is evident, the judge may excuse the prospective juror for cause. In Marguerite's trial, a prospective juror who was once a ski instructor would probably not be as impartial as someone without this experience. The judge might properly excuse that prospective juror for cause.

There is no limit on the number of challenges for cause. In the jury selection for a trial concerning a highly publicized Brink's warehouse robbery in Boston, some one thousand prospective jurors were excused for cause. Because of newspaper accounts over the years before the first arrest in the case, most of those excused had definite opinions as to the guilt of the defendant.

Even if no bias is demonstrable, each attorney in either a civil or criminal action can challenge peremptorily (without cause) and thereby excuse from service a limited number of prospective jurors (six, for example, in civil actions, and generally more in criminal actions). The purpose of **peremptory challenges** is to permit parties to eliminate some prospective jurors for any reason or for no reason. Although no reason need be stated for a peremptory challenge, they cannot be used to accomplish a legally impermissible purpose such as the exclusion of persons on the basis of race; a well-known ditty goes:

"I do not like Dr. Fell;
the reason why I cannot tell.
But this I know and know full well,
I do not like Dr. Fell."

Once peremptory challenges are exhausted or waived (given up or unused), the 12 or fewer seated jurors are sworn to fulfill their duty faithfully, and the trial begins. If the trial is expected to last very long, one, two, or more extra jurors are selected and remain throughout the trial. They vote only if a regular juror dies or withdraws because of illness or family hardship. If by the end of a trial a sufficient number of jurors do not remain to render a verdict, a mistrial results unless the parties agree to accept the verdict of the smaller panel.

 The McMartin preschool molestation case in Los Angeles took over 2¹/₂ years before the jury adjourned to consider their verdicts. Although the jury started with six alternates, by the end of testimony there were no more alternates left. If the jury had lost another juror before the verdicts were rendered, a mistrial would have been likely in the trial that had cost over $15 million.[7] Was there a mistrial?

After three months of deliberations the jury reached verdicts on 65 counts (separate criminal charges) against two defendants. One defendant was found not guilty on all charged counts. The other defendant was found not guilty on all but 13 counts. As to these counts the jury was unable to reach a verdict. As the jury was able to finish its deliberations without losing another juror there was no mistrial.[8] After a second three-month trial, the second jury also dead-locked as to the guilt or innocence of Raymond Buckey. The L.A. County district attorney decided not to retry the case.

Jury Size and Vote   Since the middle of the fourteenth century, juries in England have been composed of 12 persons. The U.S. Constitution, in referring to juries in civil cases, commands that "the right of trial by jury shall be preserved" (Seventh Amendment). In criminal cases, it commands that ". . . the accused shall enjoy the right to . . . trial by an impartial jury" (Sixth Amendment).

Laypersons as well as scholars had long assumed the Constitution referred to a jury consisting of 12 persons. The U.S. Supreme Court has stated otherwise; juries in state courts need not be composed of 12 persons in either civil or criminal cases. As few as six may be allowed,[9] but a jury of five in a criminal case has been disallowed.[10] For reasons of efficiency and economy, about one-fourth of the states have reduced the size of juries to six or eight jurors in both civil and criminal matters. In addition, although the United States is indebted to the United Kingdom for its commitment to trial by jury, in 1933 the United Kingdom significantly curtailed the right to juries in civil cases. This action was a response to the growing complexity of civil law, and the time and expense consumed by the jury process. A civil jury is now the exception in the United Kingdom.[11]

Traditionally, to reach a verdict in criminal cases a jury vote must be unanimous. Thus, in criminal actions one person has been able to block the prosecutor's attempt to convict the accused. Such power is an affirmation of the importance of each juror. A few states allow for a guilty verdict in many criminal actions with less than a unanimous verdict (i.e., Oregon which allows for a conviction by ten out of twelve jurors). In most civil cases, a three-fourths majority (9 of 12 jurors) is sufficient.

The U.S. Supreme Court held that the Constitution also requires a unanimous vote for a verdict in a criminal case by a six-person jury.[12] Theoretically, it would seem logical that a vote by seven members of a 12-person jury should suffice to convict or acquit a defendant, but the prevailing practice calls for unanimity.[13] No state provides for fewer than 12 jurors in cases where the death penalty could be imposed, although that may be constitutionally permissible. Federal criminal courts continue to seat 12 jurors. However, many of the district courts have reduced the number of jurors in a civil case to six. According to the U.S. Supreme Court, this reduction to six jurors in a civil case satisfies the Seventh Amendment.[14]

Clearly, a reduction in jury size together with relaxed voting requirements for a verdict will do much to change the role of the jury in our society. In addition, some states are reducing the type of cases in which a jury is considered appropriate. For example, states with no-fault automobile insurance plans largely bypass the jury process in automobile-related personal injury cases.

Furthermore, the Constitution does not provide for jury trials in matters in equity. Most laypersons are not aware of what a matter in equity is.

What is a Matter in Equity?

The United States legal system, like that of the United Kingdom, distinguishes between disputes **at law** and **in equity.** The distinction between law and equity is not based on logic but on history. In English medieval history, certain types of cases were decided by chancellors rather than in the king's court. The chancellors were often clergyman aides to the king who were also trusted by the people. Chancellors decided these matters as a matter of good conscience and equity or fairness. A person who was unable to obtain relief from a regular court would appeal to the king, who would refer the citizen to the king's chancellor.

In most disputes, an aggrieved person could seek and obtain monetary relief from a regular king's court. In the king's court a judge would decide the case, sometimes with the assistance of a jury. Such were matters at common law and usually money damages were the only relief available from the king's courts. As a general proposition, chancellors only became involved when there was no adequate remedy at law, when monetary damages were not sought or did not satisfy the need of the party seeking relief. These actions became known as actions at equity.

Today, U.S. courts have combined powers of law and equity. Distinctions in the two methods of relief remain in the form of procedural rules, available remedies, and different methods of handling certain types of disputes. For instance, matters involving the family were and are matters in equity. Thus if a dispute involves a divorce or dissolution, adoption, name change, or juvenile problem, a court sits in equity without a jury and usually with different procedural rules.

Examples of civil cases at law include (1) an action to recover money for injury caused by negligence of the defendant, (2) an action for money for loss of earnings caused by defamation of character by the defendant, (3) an action to recover money lost as the result of the defendant's fraud and deceit, and (4) an action to recover money for profits lost due to breach of contract by the defendant.

Examples of civil cases in equity are (1) an action for dissolution of a marriage, (2) an action requesting the court to order the defendant to comply with his or her contract by performing as promised (e.g., when the subject of the sales contract is unique, such as an original painting by Renoir or a parcel of land, the buyer wants **specific performance,** not monetary damages), (3) an action requesting the court to rescind an agreement to sell one's home entered into through the undue influence of a relative **(rescission),** and (4) an action to bar a person from continuing to hunt unlawfully on someone else's property or to end an unlawful strike by a union **(injunction).** Note that in each example no money damages are sought. The remedy at law is inadequate or unavailable. However, if a court takes a case as an equity action, it will strive to give full relief requested, including monetary damages if appropriate. A court could grant an injunction barring an infringer from using someone else's copyrighted song and also order the wrongdoer to pay dollar damages for prior illegal use of the copyrighted song.

No criminal cases are heard as matters in equity.* There is no right to trial by jury in equity cases, because historically the chancellor relied on his own good conscience and sense of what was just and equitable. Historically juries were

---

* If a juvenile commits an act that would be criminal for an adult, the matter is considered a matter in equity. It is technically not considered a criminal matter, although a deprivation of liberty can and often does result. Because it is a matter in equity there is no right to a jury.

available at law, and if a person sought relief in equity he or she waived his or her right to the processes of law. In most states today, a judge in equity may use an advisory jury, without any obligation to take its advice. A judge sitting in a matter in equity has awesome power. The judge is both the finder of fact and law and controls the powerful remedies available only in equity. To defy the judge's order places that person in *contempt of court* and subject to summary arrest and imprisonment. Some of the most controversial cases in the history of law have involved the exercise of this power.

Dr. Elizabeth Morgan was a party to a legal action involving visitation rights concerning her minor female child. She maintained that her daughter had been sexually abused by the child's father. Although he strenuously denied this allegation, Morgan refused to obey a visitation order in favor of her husband, and placed the girl in hiding. Judge Herbert Dixon held Morgan in contempt of court. What happened to Dr. Morgan?

Dr. Morgan was taken to the District of Columbia jail, where she spent the next 759 days while continuing to refuse to disclose the whereabouts of her child. She was finally released after a special law was enacted by Congress and signed by President George Bush. As the court matter was in equity, no jury had been involved. Dr. Morgan had been legitimately jailed for her continuing refusal to follow the court's order, even though she had committed no crime.[15]

An even more dramatic case involved prison inmates in Texas. The United States district court for the southern district of Texas held that the conditions of confinement in the state violated the U.S. Constitution. To implement and ensure compliance with the court order, the entire prison system of Texas was put under the control of a Special Master of the court. At the time, Texas had the nation's largest prison system, confining more than 33,000 inmates.[16]

Since Marguerite's case against Graf is at law, either party may demand a jury trial. If neither party demands a jury, the right is waived and the trial proceeds with the judge alone determining the truth of all factual contentions.

How Is a Trial Conducted?

After the jury is selected in a civil case, the plaintiff's attorney proceeds first as the plaintiff has the **burden of proof.** The civil burden of proof is satisfied by presenting a *preponderance of evidence* in support of the party's position. If the jury feels that more likely than not the plaintiff is right, the burden is met and they must return a verdict for the plaintiff. In a criminal case, however, the burden of proof is much greater. The state, represented by a prosecutor, has the burden of proving the guilt of the defendant *beyond a reasonable doubt* and to a moral certainty.

While Marguerite Martinez was in the hospital, she told her father that Gary Graf took her wallet after she fell. This incensed Hernando Martinez, Marguerite's father, who demanded that Graf be prosecuted for theft. The criminal case came to trial months before the civil case and the jury found Graf not guilty. Does this mean that Marguerite will lose her civil case?

No. Marguerite's civil case concerns negligence in adjusting the ski bindings. The criminal case concerned later, unrelated acts. In some situations the identical act can result in civil liability and criminal penalty. For example, if Gary had deliberately struck Marguerite in the face, he would have been civilly liable for damages and criminally responsible for battery. Theoretically, he could win the criminal case and lose the civil case. Such a result could happen because of the different burdens of proof involved. Moreover, the trials take place at different times with different personnel and for different reasons. The law allows both victims their "day in court"; society (the state) is hurt by the alleged public crime, and Marguerite (a private party) is hurt civilly by the alleged private tort of negligence. There is no *double jeopardy* (being tried twice for the same offense), which would be unconstitutional as violative of the Fifth Amendment.

Criminal trial procedures are substantially the same as those for a civil case. However, a defendant in a criminal case cannot be compelled to testify under the U.S. Constitution (by the Fifth Amendment). This is not true in a civil case, unless the testimony would tend to incriminate and possibly subject the defendant to prosecution for some crime.

Opening Statements   The plaintiff's attorney begins the trial by making an *opening statement*—a summary of what the plaintiff expects to prove in the trial. Afterwards, the defendant's attorney may, but need not, make an opening statement describing what the defendant expects to prove. Such statements are often used to inform the jury, in broad outline, of what they can expect to hear in the trial.

Evidence   After the opening statements, the plaintiff's attorney presents the plaintiff's **case-in-chief.** This involves calling witnesses and introducing into evidence documents, photographs, or whatever bears on the issues. *Evidence* is everything that the *finder-of-fact* (the jury, or judge when there is no jury) is entitled to consider in arriving at a determination of the facts. For example, the oral testimony of witnesses presented under oath is evidence; remarks of the attorney are not. Attorneys are hired after the events in question have taken place and are thus not competent to testify as witnesses. Their role is to elicit evidence, comment on it, and argue about its significance. Of course, if the attorney's interpretation of the testimony of the witnesses is persuasive, the jury will be influenced by it.

The judge rules on all objections attorneys may make as to the admission of particular evidence, since these are questions of law. Evidence is admitted if it is of the kind that a jury is entitled to consider. There are many rules concerning what evidence is and is not admissible. For example, to be admitted, evidence must be **relevant** (related to the fact in dispute). **Irrelevant evidence** (evidence not related to the fact in dispute) is not admissible.

Sally called Marguerite as her first witness. Marguerite recited her story. Sally sat down and Perry began his cross-examination. "Isn't it a fact, Ms. Martinez, that immediately before you fractured your leg you got drunk on wine with a gentleman, Luther Thomas, whom you picked up in the bar?" Sally objected to the question. Will the objection be sustained or overruled?

The objection will be *sustained* (the judge will not allow the question to be answered). The question is compound; that is, it contains two questions, one concerning sobriety, the other concerning how she met Luther Thomas. It also contains a conclusion which is inflammatory: "drunk." Perry will probably be instructed to rephrase or drop the question. The question appears to be designed more to intimidate the witness than to elicit information. The ruling by the judge is a ruling on a question of law.

"Isn't it a fact, Ms. Martinez, that immediately before you fractured your leg you were drinking wine?"
"Yes, sir."
"With whom were you drinking wine?"
"Luther Thomas."
"And did you know him previously?"
"No."

After Sally has called all plaintiff's witnesses and introduced into evidence all relevant documents and other physical evidence (such as the ski boots), she *rests* (ends) the plaintiff's case. The defendant may *move to dismiss* the case, claiming that the plaintiff has failed to establish a **prima facie** (Latin: at first sight; on the fact of it) case. A plaintiff is required to introduce facts that prove a prima facie case before a defendant is required to put on a defense. The court will grant such a motion only if the plaintiff has failed to produce evidence about some significant aspect of the case. If this motion is denied by the judge, the defendant's attorney may make an opening statement (provided that it was not made at the beginning of the trial).

The defendant's case-in-chief begins by calling witnesses. Of course, the plaintiff's attorney has the right to cross-examine the defendant's witnesses immediately after their direct examination, as the defendant's attorney did when the plaintiff's case was presented. After the defense rests, the plaintiff may offer additional evidence limited to rebutting the defense, but not opening new issues. And, of course, the defense has one final opportunity to rebut, limited to whatever was presented in the plaintiff's rebuttal.

Motion for a Directed Verdict   After the parties have rested their respective cases-in-chief, either may ask the judge to decide the matter by making **a motion for a directed verdict.** The judge could, for example, properly direct a verdict in favor of the plaintiff if, despite the evidence presented by the defendant, no reasonable person could agree with the defendant. This situation is unusual. Even if the evidence appears to be legally conclusive for one party, the judge normally allows the jury to provide its independent opinion.

Summation   After all the evidence is in, each attorney *argues* the case before the jury. In other words, each attorney tells the jury what he or she believes was proved in the trial and tries to persuade the jury to agree. The summation is not evidence or even a discussion; rather, it is a speech made by the attorney designed to persuade the jury. The plaintiff's attorney begins, followed by the defendant's, and then the plaintiff's attorney concludes. Marguerite's attorney, Sally, might argue as follows:

"Ladies and gentlemen of the jury, you have heard all the evidence. It is now your duty to determine the facts. I believe we have shown by a preponderance of the evidence that the injury was caused by Mr. Graf. I remind you that Ms. Martinez's medical bills were $3,742.53. She missed one month of work, at her rate of pay of $3,195 a month. She had to wear a cast from her waist to her toes for six months. Why all this expense and all this pain and anguish? Why? Because the defendant, this careless ski instructor, Gary Graf, fastened the bindings down on Ms. Martinez's foot with unprofessional disregard for her safety and well being. The evidence is clear: Gary Graf was not thinking about bindings. Gary Graf did not pay attention to his serious duty. Gary Graf was clearly negligent. And so it is now your duty to reduce the harm he caused. Simple justice requires you to return a verdict in favor of Ms. Martinez."

Perry might argue to the jury:

"Ladies and gentlemen, it is our duty to pierce the veil of passion with which counsel is attempting to surround us. Let us look at the facts. Unfortunately, the plaintiff was injured. No one feels good about that. However, the fact she was injured is not enough to hold Gary Graf responsible. Skiing is a sport with risks. Marguerite cannot transfer responsibility for her own safety to another person if the risk materializes. She decided to ski. She failed to exercise the appropriate care that would have prevented her accident. Feeling sorry for her is natural. We all feel sorry for her. But this does not justify a verdict against Mr. Graf. The simple facts are that Ms. Martinez was not thinking about skiing; she was more interested in impressing her date after spending a good part of the day drinking wine. She was injured not because of any negligence of Gary Graf. Bindings don't work if they are icy, and had she been sober she would have seen the ice when she put her skis back on. She was negligent. Now she is trying to create responsibility at the expense of my client, a hard-working, sincere, very professional gentleman. Ladies and gentlemen of this jury, you know your duty: return a verdict for Gary Graf."

Instructions to the Jury   After the summation, Judge Miller will instruct the jury in the law that must be applied to the facts (*jury instructions*) that the jury accepts as true. Typically each attorney will submit proposed instructions to the judge. The judge decides the instructions to give to the jury. The instructions might include the following, but would be considerably more exhaustive:

"You are instructed that statements of witnesses, sworn to tell the truth, constitute evidence that you may consider. Comments of the attorneys are not evidence. You are instructed that if the defendant failed to use reasonable care and secured the bindings too tightly, he was negligent. You are further instructed that if the accident was caused by ice between the boot and ski, and not by the adjustment to the bindings, the defendant was not negligent."

Deliberation and Verdict   After the instructions, the jury will retire to a jury room to *deliberate,* and by vote (usually a three-fourths majority is decisive in a civil case) return a **verdict,** the jury's decision.

If the jury returns with a verdict deemed to be wrong as a matter of law, the judge may render a contrary judgment, sometimes called a **Judgment N.O.V.** or a **judgment non obstante veredicto** (Latin: notwithstanding the verdict). In effect, the judge is the 13th juror, with the power to veto the others' decision and to substitute a different one. (In a criminal case, the judge can never veto a verdict of "not guilty.")

After a verdict, the judge may grant a motion made by the losing party for a new trial. The judge will not grant a *motion for a new trial* unless some serious mistake of law (called *error*) has occurred. Sometimes the judge may think that the damages awarded by the jury are excessive or inadequate and may therefore grant a motion for a new trial unless the plaintiff or defendant, as the case may be, agrees to a modified award. To avoid the costs and uncertainties of another trial, the parties may compromise and agree to the modified award.

How Does an Appellate Court Differ from a Trial Court?

Procedures before a federal or state appellate court differ widely from trial court procedures. Appellate courts hear appeals from trial courts and do not conduct trials. The only question on appeal, as a general proposition, is whether or not the law was applied correctly by the judge during the trial proceedings. If so, the judgment of the trial court is *affirmed,* or upheld.

The jury found Jack Malum guilty of possession of cocaine. During the trial, the judge instructed the jury, in part, as follows: "I instruct you that a crime is committed when one attends a party at which cocaine is being used, regardless of whether or not the defendant did participate in such activity." Will an appeal by Mr. Malum succeed?

Yes. An appellate court would conclude that the court's instruction to the jury was an erroneous statement of the law. Mr. Malum did not receive a fair trial because mere attendance at a party is not in itself a crime, yet the jury was instructed to the contrary. On appeal, Malum would be called the **appellant** or petitioner, and the state would be the **appellee** or *respondent.*

Appellate courts consist of three or more judges, called **justices.** Most work of the justices is done in private and consists of reading *transcripts* (official copies of the proceedings in the trial court) of cases on appeal. The appellate court accepts all facts found by the trial court to be true. In order to make the court's decision, they will study the law and examine briefs filed by the attorneys for the appellant and the appellee. A **brief** is a written legal argument addressed to the appellate court discussing or arguing why the judgment from below should be affirmed or reversed, modified, or perhaps *remanded* (sent back) to the trial court for further specified action. Before the appellate court makes its decision, oral arguments are often made by the respective attorneys.

How Is a Case Ended?

The concluding pronouncement of a court is its *judgment*. A judgment may declare a status (e.g., divorced), order one to do or not do something (e.g., pay money damages or transfer a title to land), impose a sentence (e.g., go to jail), or otherwise resolve a controversy.

In an auto accident case, the jury became convinced that the plaintiff should be compensated for her left leg, which was crushed and had to be surgically removed. The accident was caused by the negligent operation of a truck by the defendant. The jury returned its verdict in the plaintiff's favor for $1,300,000. Is the verdict the voice of the court?

No. The verdict is the expressed opinion of the jury. Based on the verdict, the court will usually issue a judgment for damages. As noted earlier, if the court concludes that the jury verdict is unreasonable, it can prevent a miscarriage of justice by ordering a new trial or by rendering a judgment notwithstanding a verdict.

In divorce proceedings, the judgment of the court will be termination of the marriage. In a paternity case, the judgment of the court will be a declaration that the defendant is or is not the father. In a suit to end mass picketing and violence in a strike, the judgment of the court will be an injunction. In a suit to compel someone to do something that was promised by contract, the judgment of the court will be a decree of specific performance. In criminal cases, the verdict will be guilty or not guilty. The judgment of the court must correspond to a verdict of not guilty; however, to avoid a miscarriage of justice, the court may overrule a jury and acquit a person declared guilty, or may order a new trial. In most cases, the judge also could impose a sentence, then suspend it, and place the defendant on probation.

Once a party has received a judgment, the judicial branch of government has completed its work, unless the matter is appealed. Sometimes a party to the action may return to court if the order of the court is not obeyed. In divorce, for example, after support payments have been ordered, either party may return and request an increase or decrease in support payments because of changed circumstances, needs, or ability to pay.

Collecting a Judgment If the defendant does not appeal and the time for appeal passes, a losing defendant is considered a **judgment debtor** (one against whom a judgment has been entered but payment has not been made). The judgment debtor may voluntarily pay the judgment, or pay the judgment after the plaintiff demands payment. However, if the judgment debtor fails to pay, the legal system provides a method of satisfying the debt provided the defendant has assets that can be identified and seized. Statutory law generally provides for interest (usually between 6 percent and 10 percent) to accrue on the balance of any unpaid judgment until it is fully paid.

Assistance in satisfying the judgment is provided by the executive branch of government, usually the county sheriff or federal marshal. The nature of our adversary system of justice should again be noted. Officials will not do anything simply because you have won a lawsuit and have not been paid. A **judgment creditor** (one who has won a judgment but is as yet unpaid) will need to provide a copy of a final judgment, identify assets owned by the judgment debtor, and provide specific instructions to a sheriff or marshal before he or she will assist in collecting the judgment. A court order directing the sheriff to confiscate property of the defendant is called a **writ of execution.** Such a writ may be used to **garnish** (confiscate) part of the wages earned by the judgment debtor. After receiving payment in full, the judgment creditor must provide the judgment debtor with a signed **satisfaction of judgment** document as evidence that the debt has been paid.

Judicial means exist for requiring cooperation in identifying assets of the judgment debtor (e.g., **order of examination**). It is, however, a fact of legal life in this country that if a plaintiff wins a case but the defendant does not have sufficient assets or insurance to pay the judgment, the plaintiff will recover little or nothing. The U.S. Constitution (Article I, Section 8) gives Congress the exclusive right "To establish . . . uniform laws on the subject of Bankruptcies." Under federal statutes almost all debts, including most judgments, can be discharged by the bankruptcy of the defendant debtor. In addition, federal bankruptcy laws and state consumer statutes provide that certain property is exempt from debt collection by judicial or other means. Thus the bankrupt is not stripped of all possessions (see Chapter 6). The possibility or impossibility of collection, although the last step in an ordinary civil lawsuit, should be one of the first considerations before deciding to sue. The steps in a civil dispute resolved by court action are set forth in Figure 3–2 on pages 92 and 93.

A criminal trial is procedurally very similar to a civil trial and is explored in Chapter 4. Trial procedures in the U.S. district courts are governed by the Federal Rules of Civil and Criminal Procedure and closely resemble state procedures.

Alternative Dispute Resolution

As stated earlier, processes for judicial resolution of disputes are available for complicated cases as well as for simple ones. There are processes to protect fundamental liberties of free speech, press, assembly and religion, as well as to decide who gets to keep the "Blue Chip" stamp books in a dissolution of marriage.* Small claims courts provide relief from complicated and costly legal procedures for matters involving small amounts of money. Individuals and businesses may wish to avoid the complications and burdens of litigation in court for reasons other than the amount of money at stake, and they can do so through innovative alternate methods of dispute resolution.

---

* The issue of who got custody of Blue Chip stamp books (stamps collected with the purchase of goods, which could be exchanged for merchandise) was a matter of major contention and anger between two divorcing parties in the first case tried by the author of this chapter. I went to law school for that?

Alternative dispute resolution (ADR) is a broad term describing methods of resolving disputes through means other than traditional judicial process. In Anglo-American jurisprudence, the most significant developments in ADR have occurred in the past 15 years.

A recent book on dispute resolution suggested that the modern focus on alternatives to courtroom process emphasizes four goals:

1. to relieve court congestion as well as undue cost and delay;
2. to enhance community involvement in the dispute resolution process;
3. to facilitate access to justice; and
4. to provide more "effective" dispute resolution.[17]

The first of these reasons is probably the most important. Clearly the delay in receiving trial dates is more than an inconvenience for the parties. Between 1976 and 1986, state civil court filings increased 47 percent. In the state of Virginia alone, filings increased 104 percent.[18] Whether this increase was caused by population growth, too many persons wanting to sue, too many laws, or too many lawyers, the increased volume of filings has greatly extended the time necessary to resolve disputes. Delay is also caused by a shortage of judges and other court personnel, and especially by an even greater increase in criminal matters in the courts. Criminal matters take priority over civil matters and thus occupy the time of judges who otherwise would be available to hear civil cases. Delay imposes economic, social, and emotional costs.

Scott Donald not only liked rap music, he liked it loud and late. Occupying his first house, he really appreciated freedom from repeated parental insistence that he "turn the damn thing down." Evan and Nita Rufus lived next door in the house they had purchased 40 years before. After one week of 3 A.M. Fat Boys concerts, Evan was unable to hide his anger. Dressed in his robe, he stormed over to Scott's house and shouted "Turn the damn thing off!" Scott was annoyed and shouted back "I didn't move to get new parents. Anyway, it's a free country!" Then he turned the volume up. How do Evan and Nita get some sleep?

Evan and Nita have a number of legal options. They can phone the police, who will ask Scott to show more consideration for his neighbors. Scott probably is violating a public criminal statute against disturbing the peace, and the Rufuses could file a criminal complaint. They can seek civil redress by suing for damages for past harm and request an injunction (equitable relief) prohibiting the loud music as a continuing nuisance. The practical problem with all these remedies is that they are costly in time, money, and tranquility. Moreover, they ignore the fact that the parties will still live next door to each other after completion of the legal actions.

"Enhancing community involvement" and "providing more 'effective' dispute resolution" both suggest that problems such as the one above require a mutual understanding that is usually not achieved through either the criminal or civil court process. The root of many problems referred to the courts is a defective

FIGURE 3–2   Steps in a Civil Case

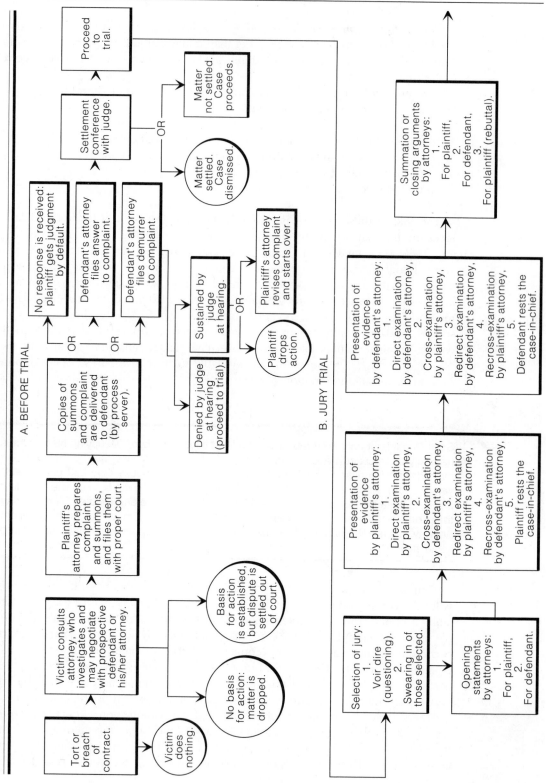

FIGURE 3–2 Steps in a Civil Case (continued)

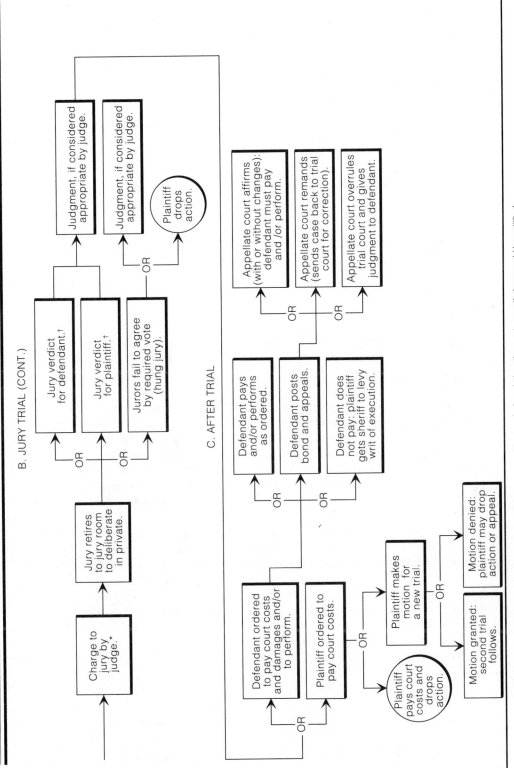

B. JURY TRIAL (CONT.)

Charge to jury by judge.* → Jury retires to jury room to deliberate in private. → OR

Jury verdict for defendant.† — Judgment, if considered appropriate by judge.

Jury verdict for plaintiff.† — Judgment, if considered appropriate by judge.

Jurors fail to agree by required vote (hung jury). — OR — Plaintiff drops action.

C. AFTER TRIAL

Defendant ordered to pay court costs and damages and/or to perform.

Plaintiff ordered to pay court costs.

Plaintiff pays court costs and drops action.

Plaintiff makes motion for a new trial.

Motion granted: second trial follows.

Motion denied: plaintiff may drop action or appeal.

Defendant pays and/or performs as ordered.

Defendant posts bond and appeals.

Defendant does not pay: plaintiff gets sheriff to levy writ of execution.

Appellate court affirms (with or without changes): defendant must pay and/or perform.

Appellate court remands (sends case back to trial court for correction).

Appellate court overrules trial court and gives judgment to defendant.

* A judge may direct a jury to return a certain verdict when, if all testimony on one side were believed, the other party nonetheless would be entitled to win.

† In rare cases, a judge may grant a judgment *non obstante veredicto* (Latin: notwithstanding the verdict), setting aside the jury's verdict because in the judge's opinion it is wrong as a matter of law.

human relationship. A poor relationship may continue and grow worse after judicial intervention. The adversarial proceeding of a trial usually aggravates and exaggerates existing hard feelings. Neighbors living close to one another often find new reasons to argue and find themselves in renewed conflict. Likewise, court resolution of business-related disputes may not be in the best interest of the parties. Examples include consumer product disputes that affect company public relations and product reception, and environmental disputes that will affect community and governmental relations for years. With increasing frequency, business and government agencies are using ADR techniques in such cases instead of and in addition to the courts.

"Facilitating access to justice" is achieved if methods other than the courts are available and either easier or cheaper to use. A problem such as the Rufuses' and Scotts' can often be solved without attorneys, courts, and complex procedures, at either no cost or at low cost. It may also be solved in a way that leads to improved long-term understandings and amity.

ADR can be classified in a variety of ways. The most common types of ADR are:

- Arbitration
- Mediation
- Private judging
- Ombudsman
- Negotiation

Arbitration

Arbitration is a formal process where the **disputants,** parties in conflict, select a neutral third party, the **arbitrator,** to hear and decide their dispute. Parties may agree to use an arbitrator as one part of an existing contract (e.g., in a lease agreement). In other words, the parties agree that if a dispute arises regarding their contractual relationship, they wish to substitute arbitration as the means of resolving the dispute rather than use the courts. Parties without such a prior contract (note: in most tort actions the parties do not have a prior contract relationship) might agree to arbitrate after the dispute arises.

An important difference between arbitration and court proceedings is that an arbitration is private, whereas the courts are public. An arbitrator also acts as finder of both law and fact, as judge, and as jury. The term **arbitration** usually means that a third party (or parties) will make a decision that is binding and final for the disputants, but variations of the process include *non-binding arbitration* (including *court-annexed arbitration*) and *issue arbitration.** In its purest form, however, arbitration provides a final resolution of the dispute, outside the public court system. It is often referred to as an informal process, because procedural rules before and during the hearing are more relaxed (e.g., rules of evidence and

---

* Non-binding arbitration means the arbitrator's finding is not binding on the parties. Court-annexed arbitration is the use of non-binding arbitration as a requirement before trial. The arbitration is often heard by an attorney. Although the finding is not binding, there may be some risks (responsibility for court costs if the award is not improved at trial) in not accepting the finding. Issue arbitration means the arbitration jurisdiction is limited to certain issues and not the entire dispute.

exclusion or limitation of discovery). Although an arbitration is often informal when compared to the judicial process, it is the most formal ADR process.

Parties may agree on any number of arbitrators, but it is most common to have one. The next likely number is three. Legal qualifications of arbitrators are limited to contractual capacity (See Chapter 6), impartiality, and voluntary selection by the parties. Typically arbitrators are chosen because of their known expertise in disputes of similar nature to the one being arbitrated. Every state and the federal government have statutes that allow for judicial enforcement of private arbitrator decisions if enforcement should prove to be necessary. Such statutes may also provide for the procedural processes to be used in arbitrations. Third-party associations such as the *American Arbitration Association* also provide procedural rules and administrative assistance for parties seeking arbitration. Standard procedural rules can be incorporated by reference in contracts by the parties.

Mediation

Mediation is the use of a neutral third party to assist parties in voluntarily resolving their dispute. A mediator facilitates communication between contending parties. The mediator has no power to impose a resolution to a dispute. One key to being a successful mediator is to not take a side in the dispute. Although mediation has been used in labor disputes for many years, its acceptance in commercial and other types of disputes is a recent development.

Because the process does not lead to any findings or conclusions by the mediator, its form can vary substantially. However, appropriate behavior and techniques have been identified by organizations that seek to expand acceptance of the process. For example, a mediator may meet with each party in separate caucuses to hear facts, opinions, and positions that someone might otherwise be reluctant to disclose with all parties present. The mediator may act, with the approval of both parties, as a messenger to carry possible positions and resolutions between the parties, so they can avoid face-to-face confrontation. To encourage its use, several states have provided that communications by the parties during mediation may not be used in later court proceedings.

The dispute between the Rufuses and Scott is one that may be best solved through mediation. *Neighborhood dispute centers,* common in major metropolitan areas, provide trained mediators to assist parties in resolving problems such as loud music at 3 A.M. Although any resolution assisted by a dispute center would be voluntary, the settlement success of neighborhood mediation has been remarkable and substantially more effective than court resolution.[19]

Private Judging

Private judging is a form of arbitration with a legally trained arbitrator. Formal judicial procedures are followed and the parties retain their conventional rights at law as to motions and appeals. Private judging is a significant variation of arbitration because in the usual arbitration the right to appeal an award is limited and restricted to issues of due process or procedure. The "private judge" is generally either a retired judge or, less frequently, a distinguished practicing attorney.

Private judging differs from a normal trial in that it provides more flexibility and privacy. This may be the most controversial ADR process, because it allows wealthy disputants to bypass the trial calendar. A wait for a trial date may mean a delay of three or more years. With private judging, the parties can immediately schedule the trial and still have access to usual trial procedures, and may appeal adverse rulings through the normal judicial process. Unlike other trials, the costs are not paid by the public; the responsibility for the costs of a private judging trial are borne solely by the disputants.

Ombudsman

An **ombudsman** differs from a mediator in that an ombudsman is proactive and involved in determining the facts and suggesting possible resolutions to the dispute. The ombudsman is a third party usually selected by *one* of the parties in an attempt to facilitate a resolution. An ombudsman will investigate, propose and advocate solutions, and often make public his or her independent findings and recommendations. In some organizations, the ombudsman is a permanent employee who processes and resolves disputes within the group on a regular basis. An ombudsman, like a mediator, has no authority to compel a solution. Both the mediator and the ombudsman start as neutrals, but ombudsmen, unlike mediators, are not expected to remain neutral.

Negotiation

Negotiation is a dispute resolution method used at some time by everybody, but with varied success. Negotiation has been defined as "communication for the purpose of persuasion." With the recent publication of several books (perhaps the most significant of which is Fisher and Ury's *Getting to Yes*),[20] the importance and art of negotiation seems to have been rediscovered. Perceiving negotiation as a form of ADR is useful because it legitimizes informal problem resolution by the client and even by the lawyer.

Typically, by the time a dispute is referred to a lawyer, negotiation is thought to have failed. Although negotiation may well continue after a lawsuit is filed, it is considered part of litigation strategy rather than negotiation. Identifying negotiation as an ADR technique suggests a serious professional, not casual, approach to dispute resolution, which may well enhance the possibilities of a successful negotiation. Also, it may encourage negotiation efforts by the lawyer earlier in the dispute, perhaps prior to filing the lawsuit.

In our hypothetical problem, Evan did not try to negotiate with Scott when he tried to get Scott to reduce the volume of his music; he issued an order. Negotiation may well have been more successful. If Evan tried negotiation and/or mediation and it did not work, he could still complain to the authorities (criminal action) and bring suit (civil action). Only if Evan arbitrated his claim (this would require Scott's agreeing to arbitrate as well) would he be substituting an ADR method for the traditional trial process.

ADR, as an approach to conflict resolution, capitalizes on the fact that litigation is risky (uncertain as to outcome), time-consuming for attorneys and clients, and costly. Emotional injury from litigation is a probable consequence. This does not suggest one should not litigate, but a decision to sue should be well considered because of the substantial direct and indirect costs involved.

A Sample Court Decision

The case below is a New Jersey state appellate case. Although we provide an edited case at the end of each chapter, this chapter presents a virtually complete appellate case in the words of the court. Space and time prevent inclusion of the full text of most cases. However, this is an interesting case decided on procedural grounds that will provide some exposure to a complete analysis.

Immediately below the case name, *Trustees of Columbia University* v. *Jacobsen,* is a **citation** to the case. A citation includes the symbols that describe to a reader where the full text of a case may be found. The first part of a citation refers to the volume, then the book, then the page, and last the date of decision. In this case the citation is 148 A. 2d 63 (1959). The case appears in volume 148 of the *Atlantic Reporter,* second edition (A.2d), on page 63. The case was decided in 1959.

The first part of the case identifies the pleadings made and the rulings of the trial court. The second part presents the underlying facts of the dispute. The third part presents the analysis and conclusion of the court.

Case 3

TRUSTEES OF COLUMBIA UNIVERSITY v. JACOBSEN

New Jersey Superior Court, Appellate Division, 148 A.2D 63 (1959)

This is an action by Columbia University against a student to recover on two notes given by the student representing the balance of his tuition owed by the student. The student filed a counterclaim for deceit based on alleged false representations by the university as to what it would teach.

Judge Goldmann, Superior Court of New Jersey Appellate Division, delivered the opinion of the court: Defendant appeals from a summary judgment of the Superior Court Law Division, dismissing his counterclaim with prejudice and denying his counter-motion for summary judgment . . .

I.

Columbia brought suit in the district court against defendant and his parents on two notes made by him and signed by them as co-makers, representing the balance of tuition he

owed the University. The principal due amounted to $1,049.50, but plaintiff sued for only $1,000, waiving any demand for judgment in excess of the jurisdictional limit of the court. Defendant then sought to file an answer and counterclaim demanding, among other things, money damages in the sum of $7,016. The counterclaim was in 50 counts which severally alleged that plaintiff had represented that it would teach defendant wisdom, truth, character, enlightenment, understanding, justice, liberty, honesty, courage, beauty and similar virtues and qualities; that it would develop the whole man, maturity, well-roundedness, objective thinking and the like; and that because it had failed to do so it was guilty of misrepresentation, to defendant's pecuniary damage.

The district court clerk having refused to accept the pleading because of the amount demanded, defendant moved to transfer the action to the Superior Court. Plaintiff consented, but before an order could be entered defendant's mother paid the amount due and plaintiff thereupon discontinued its action. After transfer to the Superior Court defendant filed a supplement to this answer and counterclaim in which he [further demanded] Columbia to return the sum paid by his mother.

Plaintiff then moved in the Superior Court for an order dismissing the counterclaim and for the entry of summary judgement . . . . (Defendant) appeared pro se throughout the entire proceedings below as he does here.

Following oral argument the Law Division judge . . . concluded that the statements attributed by defendant to plaintiff did not constitute a false representation. The judgment under appeal was then entered.

II.

Following a successful freshman year at Dartmouth defendant entered Columbia University in the fall of 1951. He continued there until the end of his senior year in the spring of 1954, but was not graduated because of poor scholastic standing. Plaintiff admits the many quotations from college catalogues and brochures, inscriptions over University buildings and addresses by University officers cited in the schedules annexed to the counterclaim. The sole question is whether these statements constitute actionable misrepresentation.

. . . Although the remedy of summary judgment is admittedly drastic and cautiously granted . . . the remedy should not be withheld where, as here, there is no genuine issue of material fact.

The attempt of the counterclaim, inartistically drawn as it is, was to state a cause of action in deceit. The necessary elements of the action are: a false representation, knowledge or belief on the part of the person making the representation that it is false, an intention that the other party act thereon, reasonable reliance by such party in so doing, and resultant damage to him.

We are in complete agreement with the trial court that the counterclaim fails to establish the very first element, false representation, basic to any action in deceit. Plaintiff stands by every quotation relied on by defendant. Only by reading into the imagined meanings he attributes to them can one conclude—and the conclusion would be a most tenuous insubstantial one—that Columbia University represented it could teach wisdom, truth, justice, beauty, spirituality and all the other qualities set out in the 50 counts of the counterclaim.

A sampling from the quotations cited by the defendant will suffice as illustration. Defendant quotes from a Columbia College brochure stating that

. . . Columbia College provides a liberal arts education . . . . A liberal arts course . . . has extremely positive values of its own. Chief among these, perhaps, is something which has been a principal aim of Columbia College from the beginning: It develops the whole man. . . . [Columbia's] aim remains constant: to foster in its students a desire to learn, a habit of critical judgment, and a deep-rooted sense of personal and social responsibility. . . . [I]ts liberal arts course pursues this aim in five ways. (1) It brings you into firsthand contact with the major intellectual ideas that have helped to shape human thinking and the course of human events. (2) It gives you a broader acquaintance with the rest of the world. (3) It guides you toward an understanding of people and their motivations. (3) It leads you to a comprehending knowledge of the scientific world. (5) It helps you acquire facility in the art of communication. . . .

He then cites the motto of Columbia College and Columbia University: "In lumine tuo videbimus lumen" ("In light we shall see light") and the inscription over the college chapel: "Wisdom dwelleth in the heart of him that hath understanding." He also refers to an address of the president of Columbia University at its bicentennial convocation:

There can never have been a time in the history of the world when men had greater need of wisdom * * * I mean an understanding of man's relationship to his fellow men and to the universe * * * To this task of educational leadership in a troubled time and in an uncertain world, Columbia, like other great centers of learning in free societies, unhesitating dedicates itself. * * *

We have thoroughly combined all the statements upon which defendant relies in his counterclaim, as well as the exhibits he handed up to the trial judge, including one of 59 pages setting out his account of the circumstances leading to the present action. They add up to nothing more than a fairly complete exposition of Columbia's objectives, desires and hopes, together with factual statements as to the nature of some of the courses included in its curricula. As plaintiff correctly observes, what defendant is seeking to do is to assign to the quoted excerpts a construction and interpretation peculiarly subjective to him and completely unwarranted by the plain sense and meaning of the language used . . . .

At the heart of defendant's counterclaim is a single complaint. He concedes that

> I have really only one charge against Columbia: that it does not teach Wisdom as it claims to do. From this charge ensues an endless number of charges, of which I have selected fifty at random. I am prepared to show that each of these fifty claims in turn is false, though the central issue is that of Columbia's pretense of teaching Wisdom.

We agree with the trial judge that wisdom is not a subject which can be taught and that no rational person would accept such a claim made by any man or institution. We find nothing in the record to establish that Columbia represented, expressly or even by way of impression, that it could or would teach wisdom or the several qualities which defendant insists are "synonyms for or aspects of the same Quality." The matter is perhaps best summed up in the supporting affidavit of the Dean of Columbia College, where he said that "All that any college can do through its teachers, libraries, laboratories and other facil-

ities is to endeavor to teach the student the known facts, acquaint him with the nature of those matters which are unknown, and thereby assist him in developing mentally, morally and physically. Wisdom is a hoped-for end product of education, experience and ability which many seek and many fail to attain."

Defendant's extended argument lacks the element of fraudulent representation indispensable to any action of deceit. We note, in passing, that he has cited no legal authority whatsoever for his position. Instead, he has submitted a dictionary definition of "wisdom" and quotations from such works as the Bhagavad-Gita, the Mundaka Upanishad, the Analects of Confucius and the Koran; excerpts from Euripides, Plato and Menander, and references to the Bible. Interesting though these may be, they do not support defendant's indictment. If his pleadings, affidavit and exhibits demonstrate anything, it is indeed the validity of what Pope said in his Moral Essays:

> A little learning is a dangerous thing;
> Drink deep, or taste not the Pierian spring . . . .

The papers make clear that through the years defendant's interest has shifted from civil engineering to social work, then to physics, and finally to English and creative writing. In college he became increasingly critical of his professors and his courses; in his last year he attended classes only when he chose and rejected the regimen of examinations and term papers. When his non-attendance at classes and his poor work in the senior year were called to his attention by the Columbia Dean of Students, he replied in a lengthy letter that "I want to learn, but I must do it my own way. I realize my behavior is non-conforming, but in these times when there are so many forces that demand conformity I hope I will find Columbia willing to grant some freedom to a student who wants to be a literary artist." In short, he chose to judge Columbia's educational system by the shifting standards of his own fancy, and now seeks to place his failure at Columbia's door on the theory that it had deliberately misrepresented that it taught wisdom.

III.

In light of our conclusion that defendant has failed to state a cause of action in deceit based on fraudulent representation, we need not deal with plaintiff's further contentions that (1) even assuming an unequivocal representation by Columbia that it would teach wisdom, this amounted to nothing more than a promise to do something in the future and therefore was not an actionable misrepresentation of fact; and (2) the counterclaim is defective for failure properly to plead the particulars of the alleged fraud.

The judgment is affirmed.

QUESTIONS AND PROBLEMS

1. Concerning the case of *Trustees of Columbia University* v. *Jacobsen*:
   a. Was there a trial in this case? Why or why not? *No - "Summary Judgment"*
   b. The court said the defendant appeared *pro se*. What does that mean, and what effect did it have on the case? *in person appeared for self*
   c. What legal result was the plaintiff trying to accomplish by this action? The defendant?
   d. Why did the plaintiff reduce its claim to $1,000? *Excess - outside jurisdiction*
   e. Did either the plaintiff or defendant present evidence in this proceeding?

2. Why do states usually not permit attorneys to represent litigants in small claims proceedings?

3. What are the differences between the television program *People's Court* and a real small claims proceeding? The success of popular television programs such as *People's Court* is not without controversy—what are the pros and cons of these types of programs?

4. An indigent defendant in a criminal case is entitled to free representation by an attorney. This fundamental right is derived from the U.S. Constitution.
   a. Does the Constitution treat defendants in civil cases differently?
   b. Do the rich always win because they can afford to hire very talented and expensive lawyers?
   c. Should poor defendants be assigned the most experienced and most effective attorneys, who usually command the highest fees?

5. Without provocation, Greg Buntz hit Tony Kulish in the mouth, knocking out his front teeth.
   a. What are the legal consequences, civil and criminal? *Civil - damages, criminal - assault*
   b. Are the remedies mutually exclusive? *battery*
   c. Could Greg be civilly liable to pay damages and yet not be criminally responsible? *yes*

6. Walter Martin brought an employment discrimination suit against the New York Department of Mental Hygiene and Dr. Stuart Keill, a regional director of the department. Although Dr. Keill knew of the lawsuit and the nature of the claim, he was not served with a copy of the complaint and a summons. A motion to dismiss the claim against Dr. Keill is made. Will it be granted? [*Martin* v. *N.Y. State Department of Mental Hygiene,* 588 F.2d 371 (1978)]

7. The typical arbitration is a binding proceeding. That means it cannot be appealed, except for very limited reasons. What are the negative aspects to arbitration because of this lack of appeal?

8. How is an ombudsman different from a mediator? Which role would be more difficult? Give your reasons.

9. The federal Constitution provides that any party to civil lawsuit has a right to a trial by jury in federal cases at law, "where the value in controversy shall exceed $20." The federal Constitution had its 200th anniversary in 1987. What was the reason for providing a minimum dollar limitation? Is that purpose still served? Discuss the implications of providing rights tied to dollar amounts specified in constitutions.

10. The Hembrees purchased a home. The purchase contract included the following clause, "Any controversy or claim arising out of or relating to this contract, or the breach thereof, shall be settled by arbitration in the city of contract origin, in accordance with the rules of the American Arbitration Association." The claim was arbitrated and the arbitrator found for the Hembrees on breach of implied warranty for a defective roof.

Such a warranty is a guarantee not expressly stated in the contract. The seller and seller's realtor challenged the arbitrator's award in court, claiming the arbitrator exceeded his authority because the theory of recovery was not part of the contract and they argued the arbitrator's finding was a clear error of law. Is the arbitrator's authority strictly limited to the terms of the contract? If the arbitrator is clearly wrong as to the application of law, will the award be overturned by the court? [*Hembree* v. *Broadway Realty Trust Company, Inc.,* 728 P.2d 288 (1986)]

FURTHER READING

1. Fisher, R., and W. Ury. *Getting to Yes: Negotiating Agreement Without Giving In.* New York: Penguin Books, 1983. A very popular and important book that promotes the idea of principled negotiation.

2. Goldberg, S., E. Green, and F. Sander. *Dispute Resolution.* Boston: Little Brown, 1985. "All you ever want to know and more" about alternative dispute resolution.

3. Hall, R., ed. *The Courts in American Life: Major Historical Interpretations.* New York: Garland Pub., 1987. Enlightening collection of essays about the United States court system.

4. Ulmer, S., ed. *Courts, Law and Judicial Processes.* New York: Free Press, 1981. Detailed discussion of topics presented in this chapter.

5. Warner, R. *Everybody's Guide to Small Claims Court.* Berkeley: Nolo Press, 1988. From an irreverent counterculture publisher, Nolo Press, an excellent self-help aid to small claims courts. Highly recommended.

6. Wishman, S. *Anatomy of a Jury.* New York: Penguin Books, 1986. Discussion of the jury system and more, with facts, figures, and analysis presented in relation to a murder trial.

NOTES

1. "Novanglus Papers," *Boston Gazette,* 1774, No. 7. "Novanglus" was a pseudonym used by John Adams.

2. Tocqueville, A., *Democracy in America,* J. Mayer and M. Lerner (editors) (New York: Harper and Row, 1966), p. 93.

3. *Maryland* v. *Cottman Transmission Systems Inc.,* 542 A.2d 859 (Maryland, 1988).

4. 28 U.S.C. §§ 1331 & 1332.

5. *Minneapolis and St. Louis R.R. Co.* v. *Bombolis,* 241 U.S. 211, 36 S.Ct. 595 (1916).

6. *Duncan* v. *Louisiana,* 391 U.S. 145, 88 S.Ct. 1444 (1968).

7. *Sacramento Bee,* August 14, 1989, Sect. II, p. 5 and *Los Angeles Times,* September 8, 1989, p. B4.

8. 76 *American Bar Association Journal* 28 (April 1990).

9. *Williams* v. *Florida,* 399 U.S. 78, 90 S.Ct. 1893 (1970), a non-capital criminal case, and *Cooley* v. *Strickland,* 459 F.2d 779 (1972), a civil case.

10. *Ballew* v. *Georgia,* 435 U.S. 223, 98 S.Ct. 1029 (1978).

11. Woolf and Williams, *Juries,* Justice for a Generation, Plenary Sessions American Bar Association, The Senate of the Inns of Court and the Bar, and The Law Society of England and Wales, American Bar Association Conference, London, England 1985, p. 9.

12. *Burch* v. *Louisiana,* 441 U.S. 130, 99 S.Ct. 1623 (1979).

13. *Apodaca* v. *Oregon,* 406 U.S. 404, 92 S.Ct. 1628 (1972).

14. *Colgrove* v. *Battin,* 413 U.S. 149, 93 S.Ct. 2448 (1973).

15. See *Washington Post,* September 26, 1989.

16. *Ruiz* v. *Estelle,* 679 F.2d 115 (1982).

17. Goldberg, S., E. Green, and F. Sander, *Dispute Resolution* (Boston: Little, Brown, 1985) p. 5.

18. Marvell, "Caseload Growth—Past and Future Trends," Vol. 71 *Judicature* p. 151 (1987).

19. See "Talk Don't Sue," *Changing Times,* August 1986, p. 49–52, which reports a settlement rate for mediation centers as high as 85 percent to 90 percent. Also see "Neighborhood Courts," *California Lawyer* (June 1982), p.

45, and "The Use of Mediation in the Resolution of Small Claims, *Landlord/Tenant and Neighborhood Disputes* (St. Louis Bar Journal Supplement, 1986) p. 34. But also see "Mediating Neighborhood Conflict: Conceptual and Strategic Considerations," 3 *Negotiation Journal* 397 (1987). The authors point out that such centers often hear cases referred by the police or the courts. These agencies impose pressure to resolve the matter. The authors further suggest that such centers have to monitor recurring problems to really achieve success.

20. Fisher, R. and W. Ury, *Getting to Yes: Negotiating Agreement Without Giving In* (New York: Penguin Books, 1983).

4

Crimes: Public Wrongs

No area of law provokes more intense public reaction than criminal law. Publicized cases frequently focus on issues that are controversial, perplexing, and provocative. Media capitalizes on the public's interest in crime, which borders on morbid fascination. Unfortunately, many controversial issues are frequently obscured by emotions. Is society morally responsible for criminal conduct, or is it victimized by repeat offenders who are punished too leniently, if at all? Is street crime condemned while white collar crime is condoned? Are there different standards of justice for the rich and the poor? Is capital punishment barbaric, justified, or both? Should so-called victimless crimes (e.g., prostitution and gambling) be prosecuted at all? Why does insanity, even temporary insanity, excuse even the most heinous criminal conduct?

The purpose of this chapter is to familiarize you with the pervasiveness and complexity of these dilemmas as we survey general concepts of criminal law. We cannot offer perfect solutions to anti-social behavior, but we can broaden your understanding and sharpen your thinking about crime and punishment.

What Is a Crime?

Most wrongful behavior, such as carelessly injuring another, is a private offense between the persons involved. Although the injured person may be seriously hurt, society itself is not threatened by the wrongdoer's conduct. It is called tortious conduct, or simply a **tort.** The victim may obtain compensation from the wrongdoer in the civil law. (Torts are covered in detail in Chapter 5.) Certain wrongful behavior, however, is deemed so offensive as to be threatening to society in general. Such conduct is therefore prohibited by statute. Violation of such a prohibitory statute is a **crime,** or public offense. Criminals, unlike persons who commit torts, face a wide range of possible penalties, including monetary fines and forfeitures, community service, incarceration, and even death.

Most crimes are also torts: A person who burglarizes a home, for example, not only has committed burglary, but also the tort of trespass, and probably the tort of conversion (theft) of another's property. In such a situation, the victim has the right to seek monetary compensation in the civil law even though society, through criminal law, punishes the wrongdoer. Under the U.S. Constitution, criminal statutes must describe the forbidden conduct clearly and precisely, so that all persons may know what is prohibited. For example, a law prohibiting "loitering" is unconstitutionally vague. The underlying principle is that no one shall be held criminally responsible for conduct that could not reasonably be recognized as forbidden.

With the exception of certain types of regulatory offenses (e.g., failing to keep a restaurant kitchen adequately clean) and criminally negligent conduct, an action requires **criminal intent** to be considered a crime. No one definition of criminal intent is universally accepted. However, generally the term means evil or wrongful purpose or design. Intent also may be specific, as the intent to commit robbery. Intent does not mean **motive,** which is a need, desire, or purpose that impels a person to act. A prosecutor need not prove the existence of an evil motive, and a good motive can never justify a criminal act.

Marilyn Harrell, a real estate broker in Maryland, publicly admitted unauthorized diversion of $5.7 million in proceeds from sales of federally insured properties that had been fore-closed. But she insisted that the bulk of the stolen money was used to provide housing for needy families as well as food for the poor. She had been entrusted with the money by the U.S. Department of Housing and Urban Development (HUD). Are her commendable purposes a legal defense to the crime of theft (also known as embezzlement)?

No. Robin Hood's classic motive to help the poor was no defense for Marilyn, who has been dubbed "Robin HUD." She has been convicted and sentenced to a prison term of 46 months.[1]

Criminal negligence is conduct that is without criminal intent and yet sufficiently careless or reckless to be punished as a crime. Causing injury when driving a vehicle while under the influence of drugs or alcohol is an example of criminal negligence.

Violation of food quality regulations is an example of a **regulatory offense,** in which criminal intent is irrelevant (i.e., not applicable) and therefore need not be proved.

Derick Dagger planned to murder his wife, Evelyn, so he could inherit her money. Over a period of time he developed and refined in his head an elaborate scheme to commit the murder. Is he guilty of any crime?

No. Criminal intent, in the absence of any supportive overt act, is not a crime. This is true even if one confesses to such an intent. The desire to inherit money is Derick's motive, not a crime.

In furthering his plan, Derick asked his lifelong friend, Patrick O'Leary, to assist him in murdering Evelyn. Has a crime occurred?

Yes. Regardless of Patrick's response, Derick is guilty of the crime of **solicitation.**

Suppose Patrick declined to assist, but loaned his revolver to Derick for use in accomplishing the murder. Has another crime occurred?

Yes. Patrick is guilty of **criminal facilitation,** because he knowingly and substantially increased the probability that the crime would be committed (i.e., he made it easier for Derick to realize his plan). Patrick, unlike a gun dealer in a normal retail sale, knew of Derick's intended crime and intended to assist in its commission.

Suppose Patrick O'Leary responded that he would be happy to assist in the murder. Has another crime occurred?

No. An agreement to commit a crime, standing alone, is not a crime in most jurisdictions. There is a constitutional difficulty in criminalizing mere thought when there is no conduct in furtherance of the conspiracy. There must be some manifestation of the conspiratorial intent by what is called an overt act.

Patrick then demonstrated how to load and fire his gun, and Derick agreed to divide the inheritance with him. Has another crime occurred?

Yes. Derick and Patrick are now guilty of the crime of **conspiracy.** An agreement to commit a crime becomes a criminal conspiracy once some act of preparation is performed by one or more of the conspirators in furtherance of their plan. Teaching how to load and use the gun is such an overt act.

Early that evening, while his wife was preparing supper, Derick aimed the loaded gun at her through the kitchen window, but she kept moving, providing a poor target. Derick did not fire. Have any more crimes occurred?

Yes. Derick committed the crime of **attempting to commit murder** because he committed an act of perpetration. Because conspirators share each other's guilt, Patrick is also guilty of that crime.

If Derick and Patrick actually did all of the assumed acts, they would not necessarily be chargeable with nor punishable for each separate act. Some crimes are said to be included within and merge into the ultimate crime. For example, the crime of solicitation would merge into and become a part of the ultimate crime of attempted murder, for which both Patrick an Derick would be punishable.

Duress may negate the intent necessary to find a crime has been committed. *Duress* is the forced participation in what otherwise would be a crime.

Russell Pena and his girlfriend Sara were asleep at 4 A.M. in a car parked on private property. They had been to a Halloween party. Patrolman Webb approached the car, smelled alcohol, and ordered Russell and Sara to get out. Sara was wearing only a fur coat over a sheer nightgown; Officer Webb, searching for weapons, closely examined Sara's body with his flashlight. Webb ordered Sara to enter his vehicle so he could take her home for protection, and departed leaving Russell alone in the parked car. Fearing for Sara's safety, Russell followed and was subsequently arrested by Webb for driving while under the influence. His blood alcohol turned out to be .15 percent. Russell contends he drove under duress, fearing for Sara's safety. Otherwise he would not have driven. Therefore, he argues, he did not voluntarily commit the offense. Is this a valid defense?

Yes. It is no crime to commit an act under duress arising from threats of harm to oneself or to another.[2] This case also magnifies the problem facing juries in ascertaining the truth when faced with bizarre circumstances (a problem constantly recurring in the criminal law). Note that killing another person cannot be justified even under duress.

Federal Crimes

As previously noted, a crime is conduct that is proscribed by a statute enacted by the legislative branch of government. If the conduct violates a state statute, it is a state crime punishable by the state. If, on the other hand, the conduct violates a federal statute, it is a federal crime punishable by the United States government. Examples of federal crimes are transportation of contraband (illegal property, such as drugs) across state lines, bank robbery, forgery of a federal check, failure to obey draft laws, violation of certain civil rights that are protected by federal laws, wrongful interference with or theft of mail, federal income tax evasion, theft of U.S. government property, violation of federal securities laws, and physical violence on government property.

Who Are Parties to a Crime?

In an attempt to identify the degree of culpability (blameworthiness) of a participant in a crime, criminals historically have been classified as either a *principal* or an *accessory*. Principals receive more severe sentences than accessories. Under such classifications, a person who actually commits the crime, such as robbing a liquor store, is a **principal in the first degree.** Another person not as directly involved (waiting in the getaway car, for example) is classified as a **principal of the second degree.** A person who participated in the planning but who was not personally present at the scene of the crime is an **accessory before the fact.** One who assists the principals in evading capture is called an **accessory after the fact.**

A recent trend in the federal system and in such states as California and Illinois, is to classify all participants in a crime, the planner, actual perpetrator, and the aider or abettor as principals. A "lookout" is **aiding and abetting** in a crime, and thus would be considered a principal.[3] Anyone who knowingly hides a fugitive, under this modern view, is called an accessory.

In a notorious case in California in 1971, Charles Manson was charged with the murder of the pregnant movie star Sharon Tate and others. Although not present at the scene of the crime, Manson, possessing hypnotic-like powers over members of his cult, commanded certain cult members to commit the atrocity. Is Manson a principal or an accessory?

Although Manson never appeared at the scene of the crime, he was convicted as a principal to the crime of murder and sentenced to death.*

The particular manner in which one's own state classifies criminal activity is not as important as an understanding that in all states even slight participation in the commission of crime may result in serious criminal penalty.

What Is the Corpus Delicti?

The **corpus delicti** (Latin: body of a crime) is not the body of the deceased. The term refers to both essential elements of every crime: (1) the material being or substance upon which a crime has been committed (e.g., in homicide, a dead person; in arson, a burned building), and (2) evidence of some person's criminal conduct (e.g., in homicide, a bullet hole in the corpse; in arson, glass fragments from a Molotov cocktail found at the scene).

A body washed up on a beach near Fort Lauderdale. An autopsy indicated that death had occurred by drowning. It was a widely known fact that the decedent was hated by Orval Swenson. Can Swenson be tried for murder?

---

* The death penalty of Charles Manson was reduced to life imprisonment following the abolition of the death penalty by the Supreme Court in *Furman* v. *Georgia,* 408 U.S. 238, 92 S.Ct. 2726 (1972). Although the death penalty was thereafter restored by statute, its effect was prospective and did not affect the life sentence of Manson, who remains in prison to the day of this writing.

No. The general law is that no person may be tried for any crime unless and until the prosecutor has established a corpus delicti. In the example above there is no clear evidence that a crime has occurred, and the corpus delicti cannot, therefore, be established. The drowning could have been accidental. However, if the corpse had a head injury apparently inflicted by a weapon, Swenson might be investigated and, if there were corroborating evidence, accused of and tried for **homicide** (an unlawful taking of a human life).

Goldie Millar's $340,000 ranch home was discovered burned to the ground. Her body was never found. Her grandson, Michael Pyle, lived in the vicinity and was known to believe he was the sole beneficiary of her will. The sole evidence of wrongdoing was a telephone call by Michael to his wife reporting the fire and death of his grandmother two hours before these events actually took place. Can Michael be convicted of homicide even though no trace of Goldie's body was ever found?

Yes, because neither production of the body of the missing person or evidence of the means used to produce death is essential to the establishment of the corpus delicti or to sustain a murder conviction. Michael's premature display of knowledge of the fire and his grandmother's death was a critical factor supporting the first degree murder conviction.[4] Whenever a victim's body is missing, the corpus delicti must be established by other evidence (for example, the testimony of an eyewitness). In any crime, the corpus delicti must be established before a criminal prosecution can take place against anyone.

What Is the Difference Between a Felony and a Misdemeanor? What Is an Infraction?

States generally classify crimes on the basis of blameworthiness as felonies or misdemeanors. The determinant is usually the severity of the criminal act, which in turn affects the penalty imposed. Generally, a **felony** is a crime that is punishable by death or by imprisonment in a state prison for a year or longer. In some instances, felonies are divided into capital crimes (punishable by death or imprisonment) and non-capital crimes (punishable by imprisonment only). Statutes may declare that a certain crime, such as robbery, is a felony. If the statute is silent, but incarceration in a state prison is the prescribed punishment, the crime is a felony. Some statutes prescribe punishment as imprisonment in either a state prison or a county jail. These "wobblers" are public offenses that may be either a felony or a misdemeanor depending on the actual punishment ordered by the judge.[5]

Some states have refined their system of classification of crimes. For example, in Illinois murder is one separate category of felony. The penalty can be death, or incarceration up to one's natural life. After this comes various classes of less culpable crimes:

- *Class X felonies:* Examples are solicitation of murder, aggravated sexual assault, and kidnapping for ransom. Minimum sentence 20 years—maximum 60 years.
- *Class 1 felonies:* Examples are non-aggravated sexual assault and second degree murder. Minimum sentence 4 years—maximum 15 years.
- *Class 2 felonies:* An example is armed escape from prison. Minimum sentence 3 years—maximum 7 years.
- *Class 3 felonies:* Examples are involuntary manslaughter, incest, and aggravated battery. Minimum sentence 3 years—maximum 5 years.
- *Class 4 felonies:* An example is bigamy. Minimum sentence 1 year—maximum 3 years.

Actual sentences imposed in Illinois are determined by the circumstances surrounding the crime, such as whether or not serious bodily injury or a prior conviction is involved.[6]

A **misdemeanor** typically is punishable either by fine, incarceration in a jail for less than a year, or both. Some states have an additional classification for petty offenses, called **infractions** or *violations*. An infraction carries no moral stigma and is punishable only by fine. Common infractions are illegal gaming, disturbing the peace, possession of alcohol by a minor, and presenting false evidence of age.[7] Illinois refines misdemeanors into three categories: Class A (e.g., prostitution, up to 1 year in jail); Class B (e.g., obstructing service of process, up to 6 months in jail); and Class C (e.g., inhaling glue, up to 30 days in jail).[8] These refinements in classification are examples of attempts to distinguish between criminal acts on the basis of culpability, leading to appropriate distinctions in penalties imposed.

Federal Law

The Sentencing Reform Act of 1984 abolished the system of **indeterminate sentencing** formerly applied in federal criminal cases. The indeterminate sentencing system had given federal judges broad discretion in setting the type and extent of punishment imposed on offenders. This resulted in great disparities in time actually served as well as sentences imposed, because parole officers made actual release decisions tailored to the supposed amenability of each prisoner to rehabilitation. The subjective quality of an indeterminate release date was resented by many prisoners.

Historically, rehabilitation had been a primary goal of indeterminate sentencing. The Sentencing Reform Act of 1984 rejects imprisonment as a means of rehabilitation. Rather, it states that punishment should serve retributive (to punish), educational (to help prepare for legitimate employment), deterrent (to discourage repetition through fear), and incapacitive (to prevent repetition through confinement) goals. The new law abolishes **parole** (suspension of part of a jail sentence) and makes all sentences determinate with reduction of sentence allowed only for credits earned by good behavior while in custody. Binding sentencing guidelines now are established by the new U.S. Sentencing Commission, an administrative agency placed within the judicial branch of government. Felony and misdemeanor distinctions are unimportant, as all criminal behavior is ranked in 43 different classes of severity that have corresponding sentences depending on the record of prior convictions of the defendant.

Minnesota, Washington, and Pennsylvania have also created sentencing commissions composed of experts who establish guidelines for their courts in rendering sentences. The other states vary widely in the severity of the punishment that a sentencing judge may impose for a particular crime. Some statutes prescribe determinate sentences, as in the Illinois example noted above with its range of minimums and maximums. In all jurisdictions, a felony is substantially more blameworthy and is more severely punished than a misdemeanor. More about sentencing for felonies and misdemeanors appears later in this chapter.

What Are Crimes Against the Person?

To be free of physical attack is of paramount value to all members of society. Perhaps the right to life and physical security is the matrix of all the other inalienable rights of a person. Often violence grows out of emotions that are difficult to control. As a result there are distinctions in moral culpability, and they are often subtle and difficult to apply. Nonetheless, general rules have evolved designed to measure culpability as an aid in fashioning appropriate penalties.

Murder

Murder is the unlawful killing of a human being with *malice*. Malice (sometimes called **malice aforethought**) is the highest degree of mental culpability or blameworthiness—an evil, cold-blooded state of mind. Both a killer for a fee and the person who did the hiring exemplify such state of mind.

For purposes of the Fourteenth Amendment to the U.S. Constitution, a fetus is not a person entitled to the full range of constitutional protections. For example, in a now outdated California case, a boyfriend stomped his pregnant girlfriend while accusing her of infidelity. The life of the fetus was terminated by the beating. The defendant was found not guilty of murder because, under the California statute existing at that time, murder was the unlawful killing of a human being with malice aforethought. Since the fetus was not yet a human being, the only crime committed was assault and battery to the girlfriend. California, and a minority of other states (e.g., Illinois) amended their murder statutes to include a fetus as a human being.[9] The U.S. Supreme Court has declared abortion legal throughout the country, but has also declared that the states can regulate abortions in the interest of protecting the "potentiality" of life.[10]

State laws classify murder into at least two categories, typically murder of the *first degree* (or capital murder) and murder of the *second degree* (noncapital murder). Murder in the first degree may be punishable by death, or imprisonment for life with or without possibility of **parole** (suspension of imprisonment for rehabilitation purposes). Murder in the second degree may be punishable by imprisonment for less than life.

Generally, any murder perpetrated by means of poison or torture; by ambush; during the commission of a dangerous felony; or by any other kind of wilful, deliberate, or premeditated killing is murder of the highest degree. All other kinds of murder, as when some provocation exists, are deemed murder of a lesser degree. Premeditation is an important factor in determining the highest degree of murder and does not necessarily require any certain period of time to occur. A cold, calculated decision to kill may be arrived at in a short period of time. On the other hand, a sudden rash impulse, even though it includes an intent to kill, is not such deliberation and premeditation as will fix an unlawful killing as "murder one." To constitute a deliberate and premeditated killing, with malice afore-thought, the slayer must weigh and consider the question of killing and the reasons for and against such a choice, and, having in mind the consequences, decide to and then actually commit the unlawful act, causing death. These rules are not always easy to apply, as demonstrated by the following case.

Ernest Martinez found his live-in girlfriend, Julie Ann, in his apartment in a compromising position with another man. Ernest climbed in the bathroom window and chased Julie Ann and her friend out the front door into the streets. Martinez managed to hit the man on the head several times with a shower curtain rod, and then cornered Julie Ann in the rear alley. He beat her savagely in the alley until a neighbor asked what was going on. Martinez replied that he had "caught her in the act." He then dragged her back into his apartment, turned up the stereo, and beat her to death. Martinez was very jealous and often had warned Julie Ann about infidelity. Martinez contends he is only guilty of voluntary manslaughter due to the passion and rage he felt under the circumstances. What should be the result?

Martinez was found guilty of murder in the first degree on two separate theories: (1) there was evidence of premeditation, and (2) this was murder by torture.[11] The intervention of the neighbor coupled with the act of turning up the stereo deprived the defendant of that intensity of passion that alone could have sufficed to reduce murder to voluntary manslaughter. There had been a "cooling-off period," supporting the finding of malice.

There are three general situations in which a defendant can be convicted of murder without personally killing anyone. The major drawback to these laws is that a relatively blameless defendant may receive the same severe punishment as a hardened killer.

Vicarious Murder Rule Assume that A, B, and C all have conspired to kill the victim, but only A pulls the trigger. B and C are vicariously guilty of murder in the first degree. They are aiders and abettors, and as such, are principals.

Felony-Murder Rule Assume that A, B, and C have conspired to commit some inherently dangerous felony (such as armed robbery) but do not intend to kill anyone. Nonetheless, A pulls the trigger of her gun and kills the salesperson. B and C are also guilty of murder in the first degree, even though they never intended that anyone be killed.* Even an aider and abettor (who, therefore, is also a principal) acting as "lookout" in the getaway car may be guilty of "murder one."[12]

---

* This rule is disfavored by courts, although most states have felony-murder statutes. Some states have reduced its classification to second degree (Louisiana, New Hampshire, New York, and Pennsylvania) or third degree (Maine and Wisconsin) murder. Hawaii, Kentucky, and Michigan have abolished it.

Provocative Act Rule   Assume that A, B, and C, although committing some dangerous crime, do not intend to kill anyone, and none of them pulls the trigger of their guns. Instead, A waves his gun and provokes some third party to fire the fatal bullet that kills C. A and B are guilty of murder in the first degree. This situation typically occurs with criminals fleeing the scene of their crime while being pursued by police. One defendant commits some act, such as firing a gun, that provokes the police to kill one of the criminals. The surviving perpetrators are guilty of murder.[13] The **Provocative Act Rule** has been rejected in many states.[14]

The preceding rules involving vicarious responsibility are intended to deter criminal activity in which there is a high likelihood of a death occurring, even if the killing is unintentional (negligent) or accidental.

Note that an aider and abettor to a felony that results in a homicide (such as a lookout or driver of a getaway car) who personally does not kill and who is not present at the killing, and who does not intend or anticipate the use of lethal force, may not be sentenced to death. Such punishment would violate the Eighth Amendment, which prohibits cruel and unusual punishment.[15] However, a "getaway" driver who has no intent to kill, and who does not personally commit a homicide, *but who has a reckless indifference to life* (such as evidenced by watching others perform a murder), can be sentenced to death.[16]

Juveniles Fernando and his two friends left their hideaway and drove into a rival gang's neighborhood intending to shoot "Cypress Park" members. On the first driveby, shots were exchanged among Fernando's car, a rival gang member's car, and shooters in a nearby house. On a second driveby, Caesar Sala, Fernando's shooter who was riding in the passenger seat, was fatally hit. Of what crime is Fernando guilty?

Fernando was found guilty of murder in the first degree under the Provocative Act Rule.[17] In many states Fernando would not be guilty of murder.

Lawrence Hernandez entered Mr. and Mrs. Wolfe's coin shop in the afternoon, brandished a gun, and robbed them of coins and currency. He did not touch them, but Mr. Wolfe died of a heart attack during the robbery. Of what crimes is Hernandez guilty?

Hernandez is, of course, guilty of armed robbery. In some states he is also guilty of murder in the first degree under the **felony-murder rule,** which, as noted, is designed to deter negligent or accidental deaths as well as intentional homicides.[18] If an accomplice had been waiting in the car, acting as a "lookout," he would be a principal and guilty with Hernandez.

Robert Rosenkrantz, 18, was a "closet" homosexual primarily because of fear of reprisal from his father and family. His brother, Joey, discovered the truth and, along with his friend Steven, substantiated and revealed the truth to the family. Robert, under great mental strain, purchased an Uzi semi-automatic carbine, tracked down Steven, and killed him with a fusillade of bullets. Psychiatrists agreed that Robert was suffering from acute emotional disturbance. Robert appealed a second degree murder conviction, arguing he was guilty only of voluntary manslaughter because there was no evidence of malice. What result?

The second degree murder conviction was affirmed on appeal.[19] Malice may be implied when, as here, the jury determines that no considerable provocation existed. Robert also unsuccessfully appealed that his sentence of 15 years to life plus 2 years for using a firearm was cruel and unusual punishment for an 18-year-old and in violation of the Eighth Amendment to the U.S. Constitution.

Manslaughter

There are two general categories of **manslaughter,** both involving the unlawful killing of a person under emotional circumstances. *Voluntary manslaughter* is the most blameworthy, because it is an intentional killing of a person. *Involuntary manslaughter* is an accidental killing. There is one further category in many states, *vehicular manslaughter,* specifically relating to deaths caused by the reckless driving of automobiles.

Voluntary manslaughter is an intentional killing in the heat of passion as a result of severe provocation. In the *Rosenkrantz* case above, it is clear that there must be a considerable heat of passion at the time of the killing as the result of some substantial provocation; otherwise the homicide is murder. Rosenkrantz was simply not in the heat of passion at the time of the killing. For example, he had purchased the Uzi many days before the killing, allowing plenty of time to "cool off."

Darwin Britcher agreed to drive Tony and Harry home from a teenage beer party. Darwin later testified that he had only nine beers and that it usually took eighteen beers to impair his driving. His blood alcohol later was determined to be .14 percent. Darwin was speeding when his car left the road, hitting an embankment, a tree, and finally a telephone pole. Darwin and Tony were seriously hurt; Harry died. Darwin was 19 years old. Can Darwin be found guilty of and sentenced for all three of the following crimes: (1) homicide by vehicle while driving under the influence of alcohol, (2) homicide by vehicle (for reckless driving), and (3) involuntary manslaughter?

Yes, even though our Constitution prohibits double jeopardy (twice being convicted for the same crime). There is no double jeopardy because the different crimes all contain different elements of proof, although only a single accident was involved. For example, Darwin was recklessly speeding and he also was driving while intoxicated.[20] However, in most states Darwin's sentences on the various crimes would run concurrently (each year served in prison would count as a year served on each sentence) rather than consecutively. In some states, Darwin could only be sentenced on one conviction because they're all transactionally related.

In addition to voluntary manslaughter (an intentional killing but without malice), there is involuntary manslaughter (an unintentional or accidental killing), as well as a special category of manslaughter involving automobiles. As the Darwin Britcher case indicates, one drunken driving exhibition can result in several felonies, because different crimes are involved. In some states, if the manner in which a vehicle is driven is grossly reckless and careless of human life, malice may be implied and the charge then becomes murder in the second degree.

Robert Watson, having been out drinking, ran a red light at high speed and narrowly missed another car by skidding to a stop. He took off, again at high speed, and collided with a Toyota at another intersection, skidding 292 feet before coming to a stop. The driver of the Toyota and his 6-year-old daughter were killed. Watson's blood alcohol was .23 percent. Watson was charged with murder, but contended he could be tried only for manslaughter because there is no showing of malice. Is Watson correct?

No. Malice may be implied when there is any act that involves a high probability that it will result in a death, and it is done in wanton disregard for human life. Watson was speeding through city streets while legally intoxicated, an act presenting a great risk of death. He narrowly avoided one accident only to cause another. These factors support a finding of implied malice. The jury verdict, guilty of murder in the second degree, was affirmed.[21]

Biance Green was born a "cocaine baby" and died two days later of oxygen deprivation. Cocaine was found in the baby's urine, as well as the bloodstream of her 24-year-old mother, and was believed to be the cause of her death. Her mother Melanie has been charged with involuntary manslaughter and supplying drugs to a minor. Should the law intervene in cases of prenatal cocaine use by the mother?

Prosecutors estimate there are 375,000 fetuses a year who have been exposed to illegal drugs; they are more likely than nonexposed fetuses to be born prematurely or to die before birth. They tend to be abnormally small and face increased risk of deformities and crib death. Should cocaine-using mothers be prosecuted for a crime upon the fetus? Opponents argue that a "prenatal police force" would have to decide whom to arrest for maternal misbehavior against the fetus. Only users of cocaine? But alcohol is also known to damage fetuses. Smokers, and perhaps women who must stand on their feet all day at their place of employment, may also cause damage to their fetuses. A related question is, if a woman who chooses to carry a fetus to term has legal obligations, how could she at the same time have the right to abort the fetus?[22] Or does this final question fail to acknowledge the distinction between a woman who chooses to carry her fetus to term and one who does not?

In Florida, where the law concludes that a fetus is not a person until birth, a judge found a mother guilty of supplying cocaine to her child after birth but before the umbilical cord was cut, a period of 60 to 90 seconds. The maximum penalty possible is 30 years in prison, but the final outcome is unknown at the time of this writing.[23] This case characterizes the many complexities that can occur when the criminal laws are used to achieve a socially desirable result, such as the birth of healthy babies.

Rape

Rape is sexual intercourse without the consent of the victim. If the victim is a consenting minor, the crime is often called **statutory rape.** The purpose of statutes prohibiting sexual intercourse between adults and minors is to protect children, who presumably cannot, because of their minority, make an informed decision.

The crime of rape has received much public attention in recent years. Generally, attention has focused on the involvement of the victim in the administration of justice; that is, how the victim is treated immediately after the crime and to what extent the victim must endure humiliating trial tactics, often dealing with her prior sexual experience(s). Additionally, penalties sometimes seem inadequate; many felons have repeated sex-related offenses; and juries seem skeptical unless the victim literally fights for her life, risking death or severe bodily injury. There has been much reform, and more is to be anticipated. For example, most states have enacted **rape shield statutes** protecting victims from courtroom questioning about prior sexual experience(s) with persons other than the defendant. For another example, consider these enhancements to rape sentences that are in effect in California at the time of this writing: (1) using a firearm during rape, 3 extra years, (2) inflicting great bodily harm, 5 extra years, (3) knowingly having AIDS, 3 extra years, (4) one prior conviction for rape, 5 extra years plus a $20,000 fine, (5) two or more prior convictions for rape, 10 extra years plus a $20,000 fine.[24] In Florida, forcible rape is a life felony, (maximum sentence, life imprisonment).[25] Imposition of a death penalty for the rape of an adult woman has been held as cruel and unusual punishment in violation of the Eighth Amendment. Regardless of the seriousness of the crime of rape, capital punishment is an unconstitutional penalty when no life has been taken.[26] But a sentence of up to 20 years for statutory rape has been held constitutional.[27] *1976*

This is an exclusion of evidence

 During a trial for forcible "date" rape, there was evidence that the victim, Ms. M, initially consented to sexual intercourse with defendant David Vela, but changed her mind during the act. She told him to "stop." D nonetheless forcibly continued against her will. Is David guilty of any crime?

David is not guilty of forcible rape, because Ms. M consented when penetration first occurred. The essence of the crime of rape is the outrage to the person and feelings of the female resulting from the nonconsensual violation of her womanhood. When a female consents, there can be no such outrage. If she retracts her consent during intercourse, but the male continues, the female may certainly feel outrage, but of less magnitude than from completely nonconsensual intercourse. However, the male who persists once consent is withdrawn may be guilty of another crime, such as assault or battery.[28]

As noted, statutory rape involves sexual intercourse between an older person and a consenting minor. For example, in New York, it is third degree rape, which is a *class E felony,* if a male or female over 21 years of age engages in sexual intercourse with a person to whom they are not married who is under 17 years of age. The respective ages are over 18 and under 14 for the more serious second degree rape, a *class D* felony. A reasonable but mistaken belief that the minor is of legal age is no defense.[29] In 1964, the first American court held that a reasonable but mistaken belief that a minor girl was 18 is a defense to statutory rape.[30] However, the defense is not available under federal rape statutes or under most state statutory rape laws.[31] In California, sexual intercourse between an adult male and a female under 18 years of age, not the wife of the perpetrator, is statutory rape. But a reasonable belief that the victim was at least 18 is a complete defense.[32] In Florida, it is a capital felony if a person 18 years or older commits sexual battery involving penetration on a person 11 years or younger. However, there is no death penalty for this "capital felony." The penalty is life imprisonment with a minimum of 25 years served. If the perpetrator is under 18 years, the crime is reduced to a life felony (without a minimum time-served requirement, so that earlier discharge is possible). Ignorance of the victim's age is no defense, even if the victim lied.[33]

Rape of a spouse is usually a "wobbler" crime (can be a misdemeanor or felony), punishable by either a maximum of 1 year in county jail or a term of years (8 years maximum, in California) in state prison, depending on the circumstances involved.

Extortion and Kidnapping

Richard Alday telephoned the father of a 7-year-old boy to say that he had kidnapped the child. Alday demanded $15,000, threatening that the child would be "hurt bad" unless the money was paid. Before the payment of any ransom, it was discovered that the boy had not been kidnapped but had become lost when he wandered away from the family summer cabin. Alday was arrested. During prosecution for extortion, his attorney argued that no crime had been committed because no kidnapping had occurred. Did a crime occur?

Yes. The **extortion** (obtaining money or property by threatening future injury to the victim or to his family) took place when the defendant posed as a kidnapper.[34] No actual kidnapping need occur, which would be a separate crime if it did. Extortion is the obtaining of money by the wrongful use of force or fear. It is recognized as an inherently vicious crime. Extortion is unlike **robbery,** which is the taking of property against the will of the victim. Some states confine extortion to the unlawful taking by an official under color of his or her office (e.g., "pay me or I'll cause you to be arrested"), while *blackmail* refers to an unlawful taking of money under threat by a private person.[35] The threat may be to accuse the victim of a crime, or to expose some deformity, previous crime, or important secret of the victim. And, of course, as in the *Alday* case above, any threat to injure the victim or related person is also extortion. It is no defense to extortion if the facts threatened to be revealed are true. It is the threat in exchange for money that is wrongful.

Simple **kidnapping** involves the use of force (or threat of force) in taking a person from one place to another against his or her will. Aggravated kidnapping occurs when an additional crime is involved, such as kidnapping to commit robbery, to collect a ransom or reward, or to commit extortion. A typical sentence for aggravated kidnapping without serious injury is life imprisonment with the possibility of parole. Any homicide occurring during a kidnapping will trigger the felony-murder rule, elevating it to murder of the first degree.

Robbery

Robbery is the taking of personal property from the person or presence of another by means of force or fear. A specific intent to steal is a necessary element of the crime. Robbery commands a greater penalty than **theft** (stealing without confrontation) because there is a greater possibility of violence when the victim and offender are face-to-face.

Mayhem

A person who wrongfully dismembers; disfigures; maims; cuts out the tongue; puts out an eye; or slits the nose, ear, or lips of another person is guilty of **mayhem.**

Bernie Lopez threw a beer bottle into a car, hitting Raul Morales and rendering him legally blind in the left eye. Bernie did not intend to damage Raul seriously, let alone render him partially blind. Is he guilty of battery or mayhem?

Bernie is guilty of mayhem. Specific intent to maim is not an element of the crime. All that is necessary is a general wrongful or criminal intent, such as existed when Bernie threw the beer bottle.[36]

Assault and Battery

Assault is an unlawful attempt, coupled with a present ability, to commit a violent injury upon the person of another. If the assault is successful and injury results, a **battery** has occurred. There can be no battery without an assault because battery is a completed assault. There must be a present ability to injure for there to be an assault. A menacing gesture with an unloaded gun is not an assault in criminal law, although the result is different in civil law. An unloaded gun simply cannot injure the victim; there is no present ability to cause physical injury. On the other hand, one who fires at a service station attendant who is protected by bullet-proof glass is guilty of assault. The shooter has the ability to strike out, and by shooting does in fact strike, even though the bullets cannot reach the intended victim.[37]

a purist definition [handwritten annotation]

→ may violate gun laws [handwritten annotation]

What Are Crimes Against Property?

Arson is the classic crime against property, the wrongful burning (either intentionally or recklessly) of real or personal property. Punishment for arson typically varies with the type of property burned. For example, arson of an inhabited structure is more serious than arson of a vacant storage building. It is not arson to burn one's own property unless there is some fraudulent purpose (e.g., obtaining casualty insurance proceeds) or damage to the property of others.

Burglary is the unlawful entry into premises, structures, and vehicles with intent to commit larceny (theft) or any other felony.

Theft is the modern catchall crime that embraces the unlawful taking of any personal property of another person. It includes the common law crime of **larceny;** the fraudulent taking of property lawfully entrusted to the criminal (historically called **embezzlement**), and the fraudulent acquisition of property through some scheme. **Grand theft** is a felony involving the taking of something of substantial value, as defined by statute (e.g., $400 or more), or the taking of a certain kind of property, such as vehicles, firearms, or farm animals. Theft of personal property worth less than the statutory definition of substantial value, such as $400, is a misdemeanor.

Receiving stolen property is a crime. To be complete, the accused must have known, or should have known, that the property was stolen. Proof of knowledge may be inferred from the circumstances, such as adequacy of the price paid, the character of the vendor, the time and place of delivery, and so on. Ownership of the stolen property does not change; an innocent purchaser of stolen property must return it to the real owner, and may seek reimbursement only from the thief from whom it was obtained.

Misuse of a credit card, issuing a check knowing there are insufficient funds at the bank, and malicious mischief (vandalism) are examples of other crimes against property. "Keying" a car (scratching its paint with a key) is an example of malicious mischief. If these examples of crimes involve small amounts of money or damage, they are misdemeanors. When victims suffer financial loss as a result of the crime, courts usually order the defendant to make full restitution of money in addition to fulfilling the criminal penalty imposed.

What Are Crimes Against Public Health, Safety, and Welfare?

All states have adopted either the *Uniform Controlled Substances Act* or the *Uniform Narcotic Drug Act.* These laws classify drugs in schedules depending on their harmfulness. For example, *Schedule I* drugs have a high potential for abuse and no accepted medical use; they include heroin, LSD, marijuana, mescaline, peyote, PCP, and cocaine base. *Schedule II* drugs have some accepted medical use, and include opium, codeine, morphine, and amphetamines. *Schedule V* drugs have a low potential for abuse, although they may lead to some psychological or physical dependence. Drugs containing low levels of codeine are included in this group.

Penalties are related to the activity (such as manufacturing or simply using) and the class of drug involved in the crime, and range from misdemeanors to felonies. For example, in California using or being under the influence of cocaine, heroin, or marijuana is a misdemeanor with a maximum sentence of one year in county jail plus five years probation. On the other hand, possession for sale of these drugs is a felony punishable by up to four years in state prison.[38] In Florida, it is no crime to be using or under the influence of a controlled substance. However, selling, buying, or manufacturing cocaine or heroin (*Schedule I* drugs) is a felony in the second degree with a penalty up to 15 years plus a $10,000 fine.[39]

Some conduct that endangers the public health or safety is a misdemeanor. Examples are (1) going to the scene of an emergency for viewing when it results in impeding official personnel, (2) discarding a refrigerator with its door intact, (3) exhibiting the deformities of another person in exchange for money, (4) killing a farm animal while hunting, (5) operating machinery too close to high-voltage wires, (6) attaching a burning candle to a balloon and releasing it, (7) donating blood or body organs while knowingly having AIDS, (8) violating laws regulating food, liquor, drugs, and cosmetics, (9) violating fish and game laws, (10) allowing animals with known vicious propensities to be loose, (11) adulterating candy with laxatives or other chemicals, (12) cutting public shrubs, and (13) selling alcoholic beverages after hours. In some states one or more of these crimes may be felonies, depending on all the circumstances involved.

What Are Crimes Against Public Decency and Morals?

This is one of the most controversial classifications of criminal behavior. Examples of crimes in this category are unlawful sexual intercourse, sodomy, and oral copulation. California does not restrict sexual activities between consenting adults in private places. Some other states prohibit all "unnatural and lascivious" acts.[40] In some states "sodomy" statutes proscribe both anal and oral intercourse. Other examples that are crimes in some or all states include **incest** (intercourse between specified classes of related persons), lewd conduct with children, **adultery** (intercourse between a married and unmarried person), **bigamy** (marriage to more than one person at the same time), obscenity and indecency, prostitution and pimping (arranging for the prostitution of another), seduction, abortion (except pursuant to each state's law), child stealing by a parent, child neglect, failure to support a dependent, and gambling (except as specifically authorized by statute). Sex perversion is a catch-all crime that includes sodomy as well as lewd or lascivious acts with a child. Conviction of sex perversion or any other crime involving lascivious activity (such as rape, pimping, or prostitution) results in some jurisdictions as a continuing duty to register with the local police as a sex offender, in addition to the applicable criminal penalty.

Some people contend that undue and unnecessary amounts of public law enforcement money and police attention are devoted to what they call "crimes without victims": deviant sexual behavior, fornication, homosexuality between consenting adults, cohabitation, prostitution, criminal abortion, illegal gambling, drunkenness in public, and drug abuse (especially when involving the use of marijuana); other people seek to justify the battle against each of these offenses. Deviant sexual behavior and homosexuality are said by some to be unnatural and unhealthful. Many people contend that prostitution debases women and contributes to widespread venereal disease and other crimes, such as drug abuse. Others contend that criminal abortion threatens maternal life as well as destroying fetal life. Many contend that both illegal and legal gambling not only divert funds from food and other necessities but commonly involve tax evasion. An alcoholic can be arrested (under certain circumstances) for his or her own protection and "drying out." Hard drugs are physically and mentally ruinous, although the full effects of marijuana remain to be determined. Moreover, when individuals fall by the wayside because of one or more of these abuses, society is forced to finance their care and rehabilitation.

John V., 16, screamed "f___ing bitch" at his neighbor, Nancy W., who was driving past his house. Complaint was made and John was charged with violating a statute that prohibits "offensive words in a public place which are inherently likely to provoke an immediate violent reaction." Nancy had become angry, and then furious. She became incoherent, enraged, and humiliated, although she had "flipped off" John on prior occasions. John was convicted and placed on probation. He contended the law is unconstitutionally overbroad and vague, and appealed. What should be the result?

John lost.[41] The right of free speech is not absolute. Not protected are the lewd and obscene, the profane, the libelous, and insulting or "fighting" words. For fighting words to be a crime, they must be uttered, as here, in a provocative manner, so there is a clear and present danger that an immediate breach of the peace will erupt. Such words are not protected because they are of such slight social value as a step to truth that any benefit is clearly outweighed by the social interest in order and morality.[42] Obviously these are distinctions that are difficult to make, especially on a consistent basis.

What Are Some Examples of Other Crimes?

White-Collar Crime

White-collar crime refers to criminal acts committed by persons while engaged in business or a professional occupation (e.g., an attorney or an engineer). There is a widespread perception that state and local prosecutors are swamped with traditional "street" crimes and show little interest in active pursuit of business crimes committed by white-collar professionals. Business crimes can be very complicated and difficult to prove beyond a reasonable doubt. Many believe that even those convicted of such crimes receive light sentences.*

---

* Defendants recently convicted of multi-million dollar white-collar crimes involving securities, and their respective sentences, are David Bloom (mail and securities fraud, 8 years); Paul Bilzerian (securities and tax fraud, 4 years plus $1.5 million fine); Stephen Wang, Jr. (insider trading, 3 years), and John Galanis (federal tax-shelter fraud, 27 years, and state securities fraud, 7 to 21 years, concurrently). (*San Francisco Chronicle,* December 10, 1988, and *The Wall Street Journal,* October 26, 1988, and September 28, 1989.)

In 1970, Congress passed the **Racketeer Influenced and Corrupt Organizations Act (RICO)** for use against organized crime and labor corruption. But federal prosecutors have begun to utilize the law on a widespread basis against white-collar criminals with astounding success. Anyone involved in an enterprise that engages at least twice in 10 years in any of numerous specified criminal acts is chargeable with "racketeering."* RICO penalties include heavy prison sentences (up to 20 years) and forfeiture of any ill-gotten monetary gains.

The RICO statute recently was used to convict a famous trial lawyer, E. Robert Wallach (former president of the San Francisco Bar Association), of accepting illegal payoffs to influence government officials. He was sentenced to six years in prison and fined $250,000. At this writing he remains free, pending the outcome of his appeal. Because the conviction involved crimes of moral turpitude (depravity), Wallach's license to practice law also is temporarily suspended, pending appeal.

Recently RICO has been used with success against violators of securities laws. For example, charges against junk-bond billionaire Michael Milken of scheming to manipulate stock prices, trading on inside information, and defrauding customers resulted in a guilty plea to six felony charges. As of this writing, Milken has not been sentenced—he faces up to 28 years in prison. Milken also agreed to pay $600 million to settle the government's civil fraud case. His investment banking firm, Drexel Burnam Lambert, facing a RICO indictment, pleaded guilty to lesser charges and was fined $650 million.

Under RICO, the assets of an accused can be temporarily seized before a trial begins, including funds otherwise available to pay defense attorneys. There has been much criticism about the expanding use of RICO into the areas of white-collar crime.[43]

Miscellaneous Crimes

There are a myriad of miscellaneous crimes (activities that legislatures have seen fit to proscribe by written laws). Some examples are (1) abusing animals; (2) conducting cockfights; (3) altering telegrams; (4) "beating" vending machines or pay telephones; (5) removing articles from a corpse; (6) loitering around public schools; (7) offering a "dead or alive" reward; (8) tatooing a minor under the age of 18; (9) harassing another person by telephone; (10) carrying a switchblade knife; (11) perjury (lying while sworn to tell the truth), and subornation of perjury (getting someone else to commit perjury); (12) killing protected species of birds; (13) bribing (paying money to a public official in return for some special consideration); and (14) defacing public property.

This list shows the diversity in criminal laws deemed necessary to maintain peace and order in a politically organized, civilized society. There are thousands of miscellaneous crimes "on the books," including many outdated ones that are never enforced; but ignorance of the law is not a defense. If it were, no doubt most persons accused of crime would plead such ignorance. Generally, the rules are reasonable and conform to standards of good conduct. The human conscience, or

---

* The list of 40 criminal acts that underlie RICO includes murder, robbery, securities fraud, and use of the mail or telephone for illegal purposes. Lying twice on the telephone concerning a business contract theoretically could trigger a RICO indictment or lawsuit.

one's innate knowledge of what is sometimes called "natural law," normally provides a workable guide to what is, in the eyes of society, right and lawful, and what is wrong and hence a crime.

Self-Defense *only get to respond in kind*

Violent conduct, which would otherwise be criminal behavior, is justified when used in defense of oneself or of certain other persons. All states recognize some form of the privilege of **self-defense.**

Harry Holland and his girlfriend, Shirley Snow, were listening to records in her apartment. A noisy party was underway next door. Suddenly there was a banging on Shirley's unlocked door and it was flung open. There stood Butch Meen, butcher knife in one hand and beer bottle in the other. Harry's first thought was to run out the back door, but Shirley grabbed her pistol from the table drawer, aimed it at Butch's heart, and stared him right in the eye. When Butch lunged toward her, Shirley, fearful of imminent and serious personal harm, killed him with a single, well-aimed shot. Was the killing unlawful?

No. When confronted with a genuine and reasonable fear of imminent danger of great bodily injury, the privilege of self-defense arises. Deadly resistance is justified when the imminent peril is great. Since Butch held a butcher knife and bottle, Shirley's fear of great and imminent harm, including possible death, was reasonable and her defense was reasonable. If Butch had retreated, stepping backward, the killing would not have been justified and Shirley would be guilty of manslaughter. If Butch had lunged toward Harry alone, the killing would still be justified because Shirley was entitled to defend Harry as well as herself.

Generally, the right to self-defense extends to members of one's immediate family or household and to others whom one is under a legal or socially recognized duty to protect. The fact that the acts occurred in Shirley's apartment increases the scope of the privilege of self-defense. Defense of habitation is rooted in the ancient principle that one's home is one's castle. It does not mean that a killing is justified merely because it takes place in the home of the accused. However, one is not obliged to retreat, whereas outside one's home (or apartment) one might be expected to do so, if possible without added risk of harm (i.e., there is a general duty to retreat rather than to kill in self-defense). Even in the home, the killing must be in defense of life or to prevent probable grievous bodily injury, such as rape.

Deadly force may not be used in defense against nondeadly force, such as slapping. Nor may it be used in defense of property when life is not threatened. Thus, one may not set a deadly spring gun to fire if a door or window is broken into when one is not at home. If an intruder is hurt or killed, the person who set the gun is guilty of either murder or manslaughter, and is also liable in a civil action for injury or wrongful death. Whether the crime was murder or manslaughter would be determined by the presence or absence of malice in the mind of the defendant who set the spring gun.

The privilege of self-defense is never a "license" to kill. If force less than a killing is all that is reasonably required, then a killing in defense becomes unlawful and punishable as a crime

Melody Downes lived with several roommates, including Kelsey Gleghorn. She also rented her garage to Michael Fairall for $150 per month plus use of a stereo. When Michael demanded return of his stereo, Melody said she had sold it. Michael became upset, smashed all the windows in Melody's car, and slashed its tires. Kelsey, upon learning of Michael's behavior, broke into Michael's room in the garage and set a small fire trying to burn Michael out of the rafters where he was hiding. Michael, happening to have a bow and quiver of arrows available in the rafters, shot an arrow into Kelsey's back, climbed down, and attempted to put out the fire by slapping it with his bare hands. Kelsey proceeded to beat up Michael, breaking his jaw, tearing his lips, knocking out ten teeth, and mangling two fingers, all the while with an arrow in his back. Is Kelsey innocent of crime by reason of self-defense?

Kelsey argued that since his acts prior to being shot by the arrow constituted only a simple assault, Michael, hiding in the rafters, could not legally defend himself using deadly force (the arrow). But since Michael did use deadly force, so the argument goes, Kelsey was entitled to defend himself by responding with deadly force. Kelsey lost his argument and stands convicted of both simple assault and battery with infliction of serious injury.[44] The right of self-defense is based on the appearance of imminent peril, such as experienced by Michael while in the rafters. While slapping the fire, Michael was not attacking Kelsey, hence Kelsey had no basis for self-defense, let alone the lengthy beating he administered. Once the danger is over, there is no justification for further retaliation.

Victims' Rights

For too long, the victims of crime have been the forgotten persons of our criminal justice system. Rarely do we give victims the help they need or the attention they deserve. Yet the protection of our citizens—to guard them from becoming victims—is the primary purpose of our penal laws. Thus each new victim personally represents an instance in which our system has failed to prevent crime. Lack of concern for victims compounds that failure. (Proclamation signed by President Ronald Reagan when declaring the first annual Crime Victims' Week, April 1981.)

In response to the growing concern for victims' rights, the United States Congress enacted the Omnibus Victim and Protection Act of 1982, providing (among other things) for victim impact statements at sentencing, protection from intimidation, restitution from offenders, and a general tightening of bail procedures.

The states have not stayed on the sidelines. Since 1985, there has been an explosion of new legislation supportive of victims' rights in the criminal system.

Most states have adopted a variety of statutes creating various victims' benefits. These victims' rights statutes typically require notice be provided to all victims, or members of deceased victims' families, prior to sentencing proceedings. During these proceedings they may express verbally (or in writing or by videotape, if they prefer) their views about the crime, the convicted felon, and the need for restitution. Victim impact statements are often required for the judge's use in sentencing. They typically contain information about the victim's economic loss, physical and psychological injuries, and how the crime caused changes in the victim's employment. Some statutes restrict plea bargaining in cases involving violence or serious felonies. Some statutes require the state to provide the victim with information about possible civil remedies against the defendant, as well as the procedures to recover compensation from the Innocent Victim Restitution Fund. So called "Son of Sam" laws impound the proceeds of sales by notorious criminals of their "story" to the media, such as movie and book rights.* Funds are escrowed until victims have ample opportunity to sue in civil proceedings and obtain a judgment, which then may be satisfied from the impounded funds. Any excess is returned to the felon. New York also created a Crime Victims' Board to administer all state programs dealing with crime victims. Some legislators express concern about legislation expanding victims' rights because of the increased costs of imposing a myriad of new procedural duties on the criminal justice system, which already handles the paperwork for thousands and thousands of cases.

When Are Police Permitted to Search?

The Fourth Amendment to the U.S. Constitution prohibits unreasonable **searches and seizures.** It is aimed at protecting the privacy of people from unreasonable intrusions by government, but it does not provide for any penalty against government officials when they violate its shield. However, decisions of the U.S. Supreme Court have established the so-called *"exclusionary rule,"* which acts as a deterrent to unreasonable searches by police. The **exclusionary rule** prohibits a prosecutor from using improperly obtained evidence against an accused during a trial.

Few rules have generated more public outcry than the exclusionary rule. Frequently the public hears or reads in the news that a clearly guilty person has been released simply because the incriminating evidence was produced through an illegal search.

To a very limited extent and subject to certain immunities, the victim of an unreasonable search, in addition to quashing (i.e., suppressing) use of the evidence discovered, may in a civil proceeding sue the officer involved. The purpose of the exclusionary rule that forbids the use of tainted evidence in trial is, as

---

* During 1977, New York was terrorized by multiple random shootings of young women and their companions, committed by a killer dubbed the "Son of Sam" by the press. The killer, David Berkowitz, sold book rights to his story. This prompted the state to enact the first "Son of Sam" escrow law. (*New York Times,* Aug. 11, 1977, and New York Exec. Law, § 632-a(1), McKinney 1982.)

noted, to deter the police from such activities.[45] At this writing there appears to be a trend in the U.S. Supreme Court toward relaxing the exclusionary rule, thereby creating a greater probability of evidence being deemed admissible. Significantly, such a rule is not found in England, where relevancy remains the essential test of admissibility.

A search for and seizure of evidence may be authorized in advance by issuance of a search warrant by a proper judge or magistrate based on probable cause that incriminating evidence will be found. A search warrant, or authorization to perform electronic or telephonic eavesdropping, is granted only upon preparation of an affidavit containing the basis on which the requesting law enforcement agency believes there is probable cause.

A search and seizure may also be justified and legal in the absence of a search warrant, when circumstances necessitate prompt, decisive action. The various states have developed many different rules with fine distinctions as to when a *warrantless search* is permitted. The states are free to adopt more stringent rules restricting searches than are required under federal law, but no state can permit searches that are prohibited by the Fourth Amendment. The following illustrative situations serve as a guide to when a search may be permitted, even though a search warrant has not been obtained.

● *Consent.* A person may freely consent to a search. Another occupant of one's apartment may also consent to a search of shared areas within the dwelling. In addition, police may search if they receive consent from someone who does not have the authority to give consent (such as a former roommate) if they reasonably believe the consent was legitimate.

● *Incident to a Lawful Arrest.* During a lawful arrest a defendant is taken into custody. The arresting officer then may make a search, generally limited to an "arm's length" area in which the defendant could reach for a weapon or destructible evidence. Once at the police station, during booking procedures, the warrantless search may take the form of a strip search for weapons or contraband.

● *Motor Vehicles.* A vehicle may be searched if there is probable cause to believe it contains contraband. The mobility of the vehicle underlies this exception to the rule requiring a search warrant in advance. Note that a traffic offense, such as speeding, may not be used as a pretext to justify a search for evidence of a different crime, but the observation of something "in plain view" is not an unreasonable search. Indeed, it is not considered a search at all and thus is not subject to the confines of the Fourth Amendment. For example, a handgun lying on the floor behind the front seat, if seen by the officer, would justify a search of a vehicle that had been stopped for a routine traffic offense. The only restriction on the "plain view" doctrine is that when the observation is made, the officer must have a right to be in that place.*

---

* Sobriety checkpoints set up by highway patrols to detect drunk drivers do not violate the Fourth Amendment, despite the absence of any individualized suspicion that a particular driver is under the influence. Neither the magnitude of the drunk driving problem nor the state's interest in eradicating it can be disputed. In contrast, the intrusion on motorists stopped briefly at sobriety checkpoints is slight [*Michigan Dept. of State Police* v. *Sitz,* ___U.S. ___, 110 S.Ct. 2481 (1990). Contraband in plain view during a sobriety checkpoint stop clearly will be admissible in evidence against the accused.

- *Stop and Frisk.* If an officer has a reasonable suspicion of criminal activity, a suspect of a felony or a dangerous misdemeanor may be detained, questioned, and "frisked" or "patted down" for a weapon.
- *Hot Pursuit.* A fleeing suspect may be pursued into a private building without a search (or arrest) warrant.
- *Emergency.* Under emergency situations it may not be possible to obtain a search warrant. An example would be a break-in to rescue the victim of a crime, seen through a window to be in need of assistance.
- *Open Field.* An officer may search an open field suspected to contain contraband so long as there is no reasonable expectation of privacy therein (as there would be in one's back and side yards). Observations from airplanes or helicopters (e.g., of fields suspected of being used to grow marijuana) generally do not require a search warrant.
- *Abandoned Property.* An officer may search an abandoned automobile or dwelling, or personal property discarded by a suspect.

[handwritten margin note: Time a factor when crime was committed.]

Jenny Stracner, a police investigator, examined the trash in a bag that Billy Greenwood and Dyanne Van Houten placed on the sidewalk near their home and discovered evidence of narcotics use. She used this evidence to obtain a search warrant of the house where quantities of narcotics were found. Was the warrantless search of the garbage constitutional?

Yes. There is no reasonable expectation of privacy of trash placed outside for collection. Therefore the search does not violate the Fourth Amendment.[46]

- *Customs and Immigration.* Customs and immigration officers do not need a search warrant in certain situations. For example, searches near the border of or places of entry to the United States are exempt from the general requirements of probable cause. That is, those officers can detain and search persons if they have a "mere suspicion." Body ("skin") searches must be based on "real, or reasonable suspicion," and even a body cavity search (i.e., an intrusion beyond the body's surface) requires only a "clear indication," which is much less than probable cause.[47] Conforming to a drug carrier's profile, behaving nervously, and wearing bulky clothing are typical bases for conducting a strip search.
- *Mail.* Although domestic first-class mail cannot be searched, there is an exception made for U.S. mail to and from prisons, which is subject to search.
- *Private Citizens.* The Fourth Amendment is a restraint on government, not on individuals. Accordingly, evidence obtained from a search by a private citizen is admissible.
- *Administrative Inspections.* Certain businesses (e.g., food establishments) are subject to various inspections by administrative personnel as part of licensing rules. No search warrant is necessary and evidence discovered during such a search is accordingly admissible, even if unrelated to the inspection.
- *Banks.* Banks and financial institutions supply information to government agencies pursuant to the Bank Secrecy Act without the necessity of a search warrant.

- *Probation and Parole*. As a condition to granting probation or parole, convicted felons waive their right to a search warrant, and searches can take place at any time and any place.

The states are free to establish more stringent restraints on the police than are required by the U.S. Constitution. Most have done so. Consequently, federal officers possess somewhat more latitude in performing warrantless searches than state officials. Determining the validity of a search is one of the most perplexing legal problems. It involves weighing the interests of the state in preventing crime against the interests of each person in maintaining privacy and freedom.

It is widely believed and probably true that some police officers, under the strain of daily action with dangerous and disagreeable suspects, are not always scrupulously considerate of the constitutional rights of the persons they search and arrest. Police can be and sometimes are sadistic bullies, guilty of brutal and illegal behavior, and courts are reluctant to believe the stories of arrested persons when flatly denied by officers. Comparatively few defendants have the means or the inclination to thoroughly challenge the propriety of police conduct.

On the other hand, law enforcement is improving, with rising salary scales attracting better-educated, higher-caliber personnel. Increased public respect for the men and women who engage in this necessary but difficult work will help even more.

What Procedures Lead to a Criminal Trial?

Criminal procedures can affect the quality of justice dispensed by our legal system. Procedural safeguards are important and also can be frightening and mysterious. The professional assistance of an attorney is necessary as early as possible in the criminal process. As soon as an investigation has included an individual, he or she should consult an attorney. The U.S. Supreme Court has declared a constitutional right in favor of indigent accused persons to an attorney, usually a public defender, at public expense.

All citizens should be generally familiar with the procedures facing every accused person, if for no other reason than to better understand these highly publicized and controversial areas of the criminal law.

Accusatory Pleading

Federal Crimes A **complaint** may be prepared by a federal official (such as a U.S. marshall or U.S. attorney) and submitted to a U.S. magistrate, charging there is probable cause to arrest a suspect. (A private person cannot file such a complaint but may enlist the assistance of a U.S. attorney in instigating criminal proceedings.) The magistrate then may issue a **warrant** for the arrest of the accused. Of course, law-enforcement persons can make an arrest for a crime committed in their presence without an arrest warrant.

After arrest, the accused must be formally charged by federal **information** or **indictment.** A federal information is prepared by the U.S. attorney to formally charge persons accused of crimes for which the penalty is one year or less in a penitentiary. More serious crimes are prosecuted by federal indictment, which is a formal charge made by a federal **grand jury** composed of between 16 and 23 citizens who decide whether a crime has been committed and whether to institute criminal proceedings against a specific person. The federal grand jury listens to testimony and considers evidence presented by the U.S. attorney before making its decision. Many defendants waive their right to an indictment and choose to proceed by information for reasons of expediency.

Defendants accused of federal crimes are tried in the U.S. district court before a federal judge (and jury, if a jury has been demanded). Incarceration for a federal offense is in a federal rather than a state penitentiary.

State Crimes   A person suspected of committing a state crime becomes an accused following the issuance of an **accusatory pleading.** There are various types of these documents: *information* (or affidavit), *indictment,* and *complaint.* Although the federal system uses documents with similar names, state criminal procedures are somewhat different.

In some felony cases, the district attorney will prepare a complaint and file it with a judicial officer (usually called a **magistrate,** who is an official with some but not all of the powers of a judge) authorized to issue arrest warrants. If there is probable cause for the charges made against the accused, an arrest warrant will be issued. Following the arrest, a **preliminary hearing** will be conducted by a judge or magistrate to determine if an *information* should be issued binding the defendant for subsequent trial in the superior (trial) court.

In other felony cases, the district attorney will request that the local grand jury (a group of selected citizens, not the type of jury sitting in jury trials) convene and, following a secret session, issue an *indictment* charging the suspect with commission of a crime. The indictment is issued only if the grand jury is persuaded that there is probable cause that a crime has been committed by the defendant. Although the grand jury will hear evidence before issuing an indictment, the process has been widely criticized as being a mere "rubber stamp" procedure because the evidence in defense, if any, may be withheld by the prosecutor. Indeed, the suspect usually is not even aware the proceeding is taking place. After an indictment is issued, a warrant for the arrest of the accused will follow. A trial will follow the defendant's apprehension.

The decision to proceed against a suspect by the process of *complaint–preliminary hearing–information–trial,* or more directly by the process of *indictment–trial* is left to the discretion of the prosecuting attorney. Frequently, if the suspect is a prominent person or political figure, the elected district attorney may prefer the indictment procedure, thereby delegating the decision to prosecute to a body of private citizens. In either case, it is important to recognize that there is some kind of a hearing to evaluate the prosecutor's case before the defendant is held for trial. This prevents an overzealous prosecutor from arbitrarily subjecting an accused to a criminal trial.

Regardless of the name of the accusatory documents utilized in your state, they all provide the defendant with a clear understanding of the offenses charged so he or she may prepare a defense.

There are no indictments by grand jury of persons suspected of committing misdemeanors. Rather, such suspects are accused by documents usually called *complaints*.

Arrest

After formal accusation by indictment or complaint, a warrant for the **arrest** of the accused will be issued and the arrest made. To arrest is to take into custody for the purpose of bringing the person before a court. It is made by physical restraint or by one's voluntary submission to custody.

Arrest may also occur in certain specified situations, before any accusatory pleading has been issued. This procedure differs slightly among the states. Generally, law officers may make a warrantless arrest (1) for a felony or a breach of the peace (perhaps a misdemeanor, such as simple assault) committed in their presence, (2) upon the accusation by a private person accusing another of a felony, or (3) upon probable cause or official information that the person arrested has committed a felony at some earlier time.

A private person can never obtain a warrant for the arrest of another. However, all states have either retained the common law rules, or some variation thereof, whereby a private citizen may make a warrantless arrest (known as a **citizen's arrest**). Generally, such an arrest may be made for a felony committed in the person's presence or for a misdemeanor currently in progress that constitutes a breach of the peace. Whenever possible, arrests should be left to trained law enforcement officers. A citizen attempting an arrest faces the problem of restraining the arrestee, the possibility of violence, and the hazard of mistake, which could lead to a civil suit and damages for the tort of false imprisonment (arrest).

An officer or citizen making an arrest may search the arrestee if reasonably necessary to prevent destruction of evidence or to detect and confiscate any weapon or article useful to the arrestee in making an escape. The search must be reasonable. Indeed, an officer is privileged to stop and frisk (by pat-down) any person being lawfully questioned as a criminal suspect. The pat-down is acceptable if it is reasonably necessary for the officer's own protection. Such a suspect, however, never can be locked in jail for questioning or investigation if there is inadequate basis to make a valid arrest. There is no adequate basis for an arrest for simple failure to identify oneself or to explain one's presence satisfactorily.

An officer making an arrest may use all force reasonably necessary to accomplish the restraint. The modern view is to discourage the use of deadly force in making an arrest. A private citizen may not use deadly force in making an arrest, except when the arrestee is guilty of a violent felony (e.g., murder, arson, rape, or robbery). On the other side of the coin, it is the legal duty of everyone, innocent or guilty, to submit to a lawful arrest; improper resistance is a separate crime.

Arrests are unnecessary in many situations involving illegal acts that occur in the presence of an officer, specifically misdemeanors, petty offenses, and infractions. The best example of an alternative to arrest is the ordinary traffic ticket, which is similar to the summons used in civil proceedings. The traffic violator is not a criminal and usually will abide by a written promise to respond to the citation. In a growing number of misdemeanors, including shoplifting and some narcotics violations, the summons is being used instead of arrest to facilitate and streamline the procedures for handling large numbers of cases.

Booking

After an arrest, the accused may be booked. **Booking** involves searching, finger-printing, photographing, testing for alcohol or drugs, and reasonable related activities. With respect to crimes involving the operation of motor vehicles while under the influence, states have statutes establishing prohibited levels of blood-alcohol content. State maximum levels range from a low of .08 percent to .10 percent.* Even lower levels, such as .04 percent, have been adopted for truck drivers and ship captains in some states. In Chapter 11 we have set out a guide to how many drinks result in various levels of blood-alcohol content.

Under increasing criticism is the practice of strip searching arrestees for the purpose of finding any concealed weapon, contraband, or evidence. This practice obviously is demeaning and humiliating. It also is of dubious value when the soon-to-be-released arrestee is charged with an offense not involving drugs, contraband, a weapon, violence, or any other factor that would indicate a strong possibility of the presence of a concealed object. At least partly due to public outcry, California has restricted the police in conducting strip searches as an incident to booking procedures.†

The accused has certain rights after arrest, including the right to be promptly taken before a judge or magistrate, the right to be allowed bail (except in certain cases), the right to remain silent, and, in serious criminal cases, the right to have an attorney present (a telephone call must be permitted for this purpose). The right of an accused to be promptly taken before a judge or magistrate limits the possibility of unreasonable police interrogation ("the third degree") and affords an opportunity for the accused to have bail set (if it has not been set and stated in the arrest warrant), to have constitutional rights explained, and to have an attorney appointed if he or she cannot afford private legal services.

Bail

An accused who is arrested is physically taken to jail. But the state has no right to punish the arrestee, because of the constitutional (Fifth Amendment) presumption of innocence. The purpose of **bail** is merely to guarantee the person's presence for trial and, if the person is found guilty, for punishment. Bail refers to the security given the court by the accused to ensure his or her later appearance for trial, in exchange for immediate release from custody. The amount of bail must be specified in the arrest warrant, or, if arrest is without warrant, the magistrate will set bail after the arrest and booking. All crimes are "bailable," but there are exceptions for certain situations. For example, the court may deny bail where there is a

---

* The trend is towards reduced permissible levels. California, Utah, Oregon, and Maine already use the lower .08 level.

† The restrictions apply only to pre-arraignment detainees arrested for infractions or misdemeanors. There can be no strip search or visual body search unless the misdemeanor involves weapons, controlled substances, or violence, or unless a peace officer has a "reasonable suspicion" it is necessary and obtains written authorization from some supervising officer on duty. There can be no touching of private body parts, and searches must be conducted in a private place by an appropriate person of the same sex as the accused. Those arrested for felonies still may be and are strip searched (Calif. Penal Code § 4030).

great likelihood the defendant will flee, as when it's a capital offense and the evidence of guilt is overwhelming.[48] Bail may be denied a person accused of a federal crime if the offense was committed while the accused (1) is on bail in a state or federal court, (2) is on parole or probation, (3) may flee, or (4) is a danger to the community.[49] In all cases the policy is to be liberal in setting bail before any conviction takes place. Freedom while appealing a conviction is easily distinguishable because there no longer is a presumption of innocence.

A **bail bond** is a document signed by both the accused and a bail bondsman binding them to pay to the state a specified sum if the accused fails to appear in court as directed. Bail bondsmen charge substantial fees in exchange for making such a promise (typically 10 percent of the sum specified as bail). They rarely lose money because they secure their risk with collateral (such as stocks, bonds, mortgages, jewelry, or other valuables) and later go to great lengths to recover from the clients who "jump bail" (i.e., fail to appear in court as promised).

Every accused person is presumed innocent until proven guilty beyond a reasonable doubt and to a moral certainty, and therefore is entitled to be released on bail with only limited exceptions, as noted above. Under the Eighth Amendment, a judge or magistrate may not demand "excessive" bail, but any amount may be too much for a poor person. Accordingly, at the federal level and in a number of progressive states, reforms have been enacted to permit release of the poor on their own *recognizance*, whereby the accused person simply promises in writing to appear for the trial.[50] The court can attach other conditions to the prisoner's release, such as a promise not to contact the victim of the crime. Failure to fulfill conditions of release may lead to rearrest and may involve an obligation to pay a specified sum of money to the court.

Arraignment

After being formally charged with a crime by the filing of an accusatory pleading (information, indictment or complaint), the accused must be **arraigned;** that is, called into court, informed of the charge, and given an opportunity to make a response or plea. Also, a public defender will be appointed to defend any accused who cannot afford private counsel. In general, the defendant's plea may be either guilty, not guilty, **nolo contendere** (Latin: I will not contest it), or not guilty by reason of insanity. A plea of nolo contendere in criminal law is comparable to a plea of guilty. The only real distinction justifying its use is that a guilty plea can be used against the defendant as an admission against interest in subsequent civil litigation, whereas a plea of nolo contendere generally cannot. A guilty plea standing alone presumes that the defendant was sane at the time the crime was committed. Hence, the question of insanity must be raised by special plea, namely "not guilty by reason of insanity." In felony cases, a preliminary hearing (unless waived by the defendant) and trial will follow the defendant's plea. There is no preliminary hearing in misdemeanor cases. If the plea is guilty in either a felony or misdemeanor case, sentencing will then follow.

Plea Bargain

Often, following arraignment, the district attorney or county prosecutor will decide that it is in the best interests of justice to offer a **plea bargain** to a defendant. The interests of justice are served when the time, expense, and uncertainty of a trial can be avoided. For example, it may be uncertain whether a conviction for murder in the second degree or voluntary manslaughter can be obtained. It may be preferable to accept a guilty plea to the lesser charge than to incur the expense and difficulty of trial. There is an unending stream of cases to be disposed of, and plea bargaining can be of benefit to defendants, in jeopardy of a more severe sentence, as well as to the people represented by the prosecutor's office. Typically, the defendant agrees to plead guilty to some crime of lesser severity than the crime specified at the arraignment. In return, a judge agrees to a specified punishment and accepts the guilty plea on that basis. Once a judge has accepted a guilty plea, he or she cannot refuse to carry through the bargain that induced the plea.[51]

Preliminary Hearing

A **preliminary hearing** is an evidentiary proceeding after a felony accusation, done before a magistrate or judge, to determine whether there is probable cause that the specified felony has been committed by the accused. The district attorney will call witnesses and present evidence in support of the charges. The accused need not and usually does not present any evidence, because he or she is presumed innocent. However, most defendants' attorneys take advantage of the opportunity and cross-examine prosecution witnesses at length in order to learn as much as possible about the case. If the district attorney fails to prove a corpus delicti, the judge or magistrate will dismiss the charges immediately.

In some states, a preliminary hearing is not conducted after an indictment, on the theory that there already has been an evidentiary hearing. This rule is subject to serious constitutional question, because the grand jury is a one-sided proceeding with no judge or magistrate present. Preliminary hearings are not conducted in misdemeanor cases.

After the preliminary hearing, assuming the prosecution has presented enough evidence to justify a trial, the matter will be set for a jury or non-jury trial, to determine the accused's guilt or innocence.

Figure 4–1 presents the typical steps in a criminal prosecution.

What Are the Constitutional Rights of an Accused?

The legislative branch of government decides what activities are criminal and therefore prohibited. Commission of a proscribed act is a crime. Of course, the legislative branch of government has no power to prohibit that which the Constitution protects, such as publication of opinions critical of the government.

The executive branch of government, in turn, has the responsibility of arresting persons reasonably thought to have committed criminal acts.

The judicial branch has the responsibility of conducting trials for the accused. In the process, it is conceivable that the executive branch or the judicial branch could treat those accused of crimes in an unfair manner, thereby increasing the

FIGURE 4-1 Typical Steps in a Criminal Prosecution

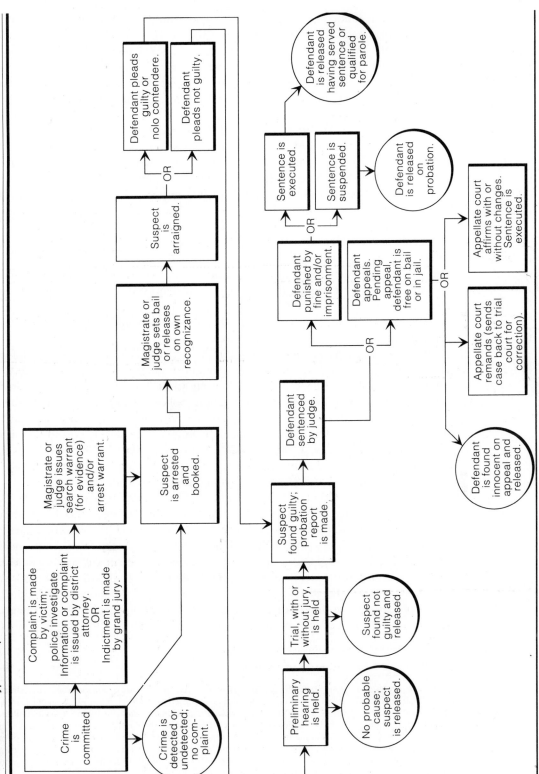

possibility that innocent persons may be convicted. To minimize this possibility, certain fundamental rights are guaranteed by the U.S. Constitution, as well as by state constitutions, to every person suspected of involvement in criminal activity.

State constitutions are free to be more stringent in guaranteeing these rights than the U.S. Constitution. In these more stringent states, those who are accused of a crime enjoy expanded rights, further protecting them from unreasonable prosecutorial activities.*

There is a right to be free from unreasonable searches and seizures, as described in a prior section. When the police (who must act with probable cause that a crime has been committed) detain or arrest anyone as a suspect in criminal activity, the person should be informed (1) of the right to remain silent, (2) that anything said can and will be used against him or her in a court of law, (3) that he or she is entitled to the presence and aid of a lawyer during questioning, and (4) that if he or she cannot afford to hire counsel, one will be provided free of charge.[52] These **Miranda warnings** technically are not constitutional rights; rather, they are procedural safeguards imposed by the courts to preserve the integrity of the judicial system.[53] Therefore, if the arresting officer fails to inform the arrestee of these rights, the court may subsequently reject as evidence anything said by the defendant that is of an incriminating nature, such as a confession. Rejection of such evidence by the court may result in the case's dismissal if there is no other evidence sufficient to convict.

Miranda warnings are required prior to custodial (while in custody) interrogation, but not before general investigatory questioning. The warnings relate to all offenses, regardless of their gravity, when an arrest is contemplated (e.g., driving under the influence). During an investigation, police can detain persons for a reasonable time for some reasonable purpose without making any arrest. (For example, detention for an hour to obtain a drug-sniffing dog is considered a reasonable time. See *U.S.* v. *Campbell,* 627 F.Supp. 320 [Alaska, 1985] aff'd 810 F.2d 206 [1987].) In petty misdemeanor cases or infractions [e.g., traffic violations], no arrest is contemplated and *Miranda* warnings are inapplicable.

The accused is entitled to "due process" in all procedures following arrest. Bail, for example, is designed to avoid punishing an arrestee, who is presumed innocent pending trial. Bail, instead of release on one's own recognizance, may be required when the presence of the defendant at the trial otherwise would not be ensured. There is a right to a speedy trial unless the defendant waives time and permits a later trial date. (For example, the time limit in California is 60 days from arraignment (Calif. Penal Code Sec. 1382). But most defendants "waive time" to better prepare their defense, or even simply to stall as long as possible.) There is a right to be informed of the specific charges pending.

---

* Persons accused of crime in California long have enjoyed broader state constitutional and statutory protections than have been available to defendants accused of federal offenses. However, in June 1990, voters adopted Proposition 115, the *Crime Victims' Justice Reform* initiative, which literally equalizes state and federal law. Affected are many criminal procedure laws, such as instigating criminal charges, selecting jurors, conducting pre-trial hearings, and even federalizing the definitions of such diverse matters as "cruel and unusual punishment" and the right to privacy. We predict that considerable litigation will be necessary to determine the full scope and applicability of this novel command by the people to lessen the protective rights of the accused.

During trial the defendant is entitled to an impartial jury and judge, and is presumed innocent unless and until found guilty. The state, representing the people, always has the burden of proof to convict "beyond a reasonable doubt and to a moral certainty." The defendant is entitled to be present in court in ordinary clothing* and is entitled to confront and cross-examine adverse witnesses, including informants†. A defendant has a right to conduct his or her own defense, but must be able and willing to abide by rules of procedure and courtroom protocol. The Fifth Amendment provides that "no person shall . . . be compelled in any criminal case to be a witness against himself. . . ." This right is known as the *privilege against self-incrimination*. Accordingly, a defendant need not take the witness stand and testify in the proceeding; the prosecution must prove its case beyond a reasonable doubt and to a moral certainty without the use of defendant's testimony.

In trying to meet its burden of proof, the prosecution cannot suppress evidence favorable to an accused.[54] Furthermore, an involuntary confession made out of court is not admissible as evidence against the defendant, and a confession is involuntary if obtained by any form of compulsion, including false promises. (Interestingly, the Fifth Amendment does not prevent police from requiring a defendant to participate in a lineup, even repeating certain words that were uttered by a guilty person; to submit to samples of handwriting; to submit to fingerprinting; or to submit to photographing.) A defendant is entitled to subpoena defense witnesses and to have a "fair" trial, generally in a place where publicity about the case has not unreasonably tainted the proceedings, which must be open to the public.‡ Defendants may waive many of these rights, if desired.

An accused may not be placed twice in jeopardy for the same offense, but one wrongful act (such as rape) may be grounds for both criminal proceedings and a civil lawsuit for battery. One criminal activity can involve violation of several statutory provisions and consequently result in several different crimes and punishments. Recall the Darwin Britcher case discussed earlier in the chapter, where three crimes were committed in one accident while he was driving under the influence. The constitutional safeguard against double jeopardy protects against a second prosecution following acquittal or conviction, and against multiple punishments for the same offense.[55]

A defendant cannot be convicted for violation of an *ex post facto law* (i.e., an act that was not a crime when committed but was later prohibited by statute).

---

* A defendant cannot be compelled to be tried in jail attire because it insinuates the defendant has been arrested not only on the charge being tried but also on other charges for which he or she is being incarcerated. The presumption of innocence requires the garb of innocence.

† A defendant is entitled to confront informants who are *witnesses* to the crime charged, not mere tipsters [*Bradford* v. *State*, 361 S.E.2d 838 (Georgia 1987)]. Also, a defendant charged with child abuse may not have the right to confront the victim in open court [*Maryland* v. *Craig*, ___U.S.___, 110 S.Ct. 3157 (1990).

‡ Giovanni Vigliotto, dubbed the "Sicilian Seducer" for his conviction of marrying and defrauding between 82 and 105 women, received national publicity (talk shows, made-for-TV movies, and even the Guinness Book of World Records) prior to his 1983 conviction in Arizona and sentence of 34 years in prison without possibility of parole. Defense attttorneys appealing the conviction contend it is the worst case of pre-trial publicity ever, a comedy of errors.

Finally, a defendant who is convicted may not receive a sentence that is so disproportionate to the offense involved as to be fairly characterized as "cruel and unusual." This constitutional protection is discussed later in a separate section in this chapter.

Is Lack of Mental Capacity a Defense?

An *insane* person is not legally responsible for criminal conduct. The rationale is that our society's collective conscience does not allow punishment where it cannot impose moral blame. Nonetheless, an insane person may be committed for an indefinite period to a hospital for the insane, an approach that satisfies society's need for protection and its duty to assist the ill.

The historical difficulty with the defense of **insanity** has to do with a satisfactory definition by which a jury is able to assess the conduct of the accused. In California, an insanity defense is available if the jury, in a separate trial for that purpose, determines that the defendant, by a preponderance of the evidence, was incapable (1) of knowing or understanding the nature and quality of the act, or (2) of distinguishing right from wrong at the time of commission of the act.[56] In New York, a defendant is not criminally responsible if he or she lacked substantial capacity to know or appreciate (1) the nature and consequences of the act, or (2) that such conduct was wrong.

Juries are accustomed to determining facts. Did the gun belong to the defendant or not? But when it comes to determining the sanity of the defendant, the jury must determine an opinion. Insanity is only an *opinion* expressed by psychiatrists until the jury says it is a *fact*. It is extremely difficult to determine that a certain state of mind is a fact, and its importance is questionable if the basic goal of society is to incarcerate defendants until they no longer are a threat to society. Some argue that all perpetrators of heinous crimes are "insane."

Insanity need not be permanent, because some mental diseases or defects may be cured. Thus the defense of "temporary insanity" is possible, whereby the accused is innocent of crime and, being sane after the act, need not be confined in a mental hospital.

Insanity is to be distinguished from **diminished capacity,** which involves a different mental state. Some crimes are defined to require a specific intent on the part of the defendant. For example, capital murder requires the specific intent to kill. If by reasons of delusion, narcotics, alcohol, or even a sexual rage the defendant's mental capacity is diminished to the extent there is no specific intent to kill, there can be no capital murder. The crime may be reduced to manslaughter because of the defendant's diminished capacity.[57] This defense has been eliminated by constitutional amendment in California.

It is possible that an accused who was sane at the time of the alleged crime, has become insane. Insanity at the time of trial is not a defense to a crime committed during a prior time of sanity. However, a trial cannot proceed until the defendant is sane because a "fair" trial, as guaranteed by our Constitution, contemplates a rational defendant who can understand the charges against him or her and assist in his or her defense. Neither can a prison sentence be served nor an execution be administered to an insane convict. In general terms, insanity suspends judicial proceedings as long as it continues. However, the defendant may be committed to a state institution for the insane until sanity is regained, at which time the criminal proceedings may resume.

What Is Entrapment?

A defendant cannot be convicted of committing a crime if the government, acting through its law enforcement personnel, induced the criminal act. The defense of **entrapment** is an affirmative defense that must be proven by the defendant by a preponderance of the evidence (not beyond a reasonable doubt). However, the defense is very narrow, limited in scope, and usually unsuccessful. It applies only when the conduct of the law enforcement agent was likely to induce a normally law-abiding person to commit the offense. The question is not whether the defendant personally was induced; the standard is the objective law-abiding person.[58] There is no entrapment when undercover agents are merely negotiating the price of and buying illegal drugs from the defendant.[59]

Joe Shapiro, operating on Whidbey Island, Washington, negotiated with Richard Russell and others for the purchase of homemade methamphetamine, or "speed." Russell needed the very scarce but legal chemical phenyl-2-propanone to prepare the drug, and this was supplied by Shapiro. A month after the batch was prepared and delivered, Russell was advised that Shapiro was an employee of the Federal Bureau of Narcotics. Arrest and trial followed in due course. Had Russell been constitutionally entrapped?

No. Entrapment occurs only if the government agent implants the criminal design or idea in the mind of the defendant. The U.S. Supreme Court held that Russell had a predisposition to commit the crime and that the mere affording of opportunity by Shapiro was not entrapment.[60]

What Is the Statute of Limitations for Crime?

A statute of limitations is a legislative determination that legal proceedings in connection with various types of civil and criminal acts may not be commenced beyond specified periods of time. Accordingly, it may be a valid defense for the defendant. The purpose of such statutes is not to shield defendants from the law; it is to prevent stale prosecutions in which witnesses' memories may have faded, and so a "fair" trial would be exceedingly difficult, if not impossible, to obtain. Criminal courts in metropolitan areas are already overcrowded. Moreover, witnesses and principals may move, get sick, or die; evidence may be obscured or lost. Society is better served if wrongdoers resume normal, productive, law-abiding lives, without the psychological burden of possible arrest endlessly hanging over their heads.

The period of time specified in a statute of limitations commences upon commission or discovery of the offense. An accusatory pleading (indictment, information, or complaint) must be filed within the period prescribed. The statute is suspended, or "tolled," by the defendant's absence from the state; this eliminates flight as a possible method of avoiding prosecution. And there is no statute of limitations for certain serious crimes, such as murder.* Although the limitation periods vary, for misdemeanors they usually are one year; for most felonies, they usually are three years. If the crime is either a misdemeanor or a felony, depending on the sentence ultimately to be imposed, the limitation period is typically three years.

What Is the Punishment of Convicted Persons?

Imprisonment and imposition of a fine are two basic forms of punishment. Either or both may be ordered, depending on what the statutory law requires and what a judge (and in some cases, a jury) decides. Misdemeanants are confined in county jails, and felons are incarcerated in state prisons. Offenders guilty of federal crimes are incarcerated in federal penitentiaries.

The death penalty is unique among all sentences in its irrevocability and rejection of rehabilitation as a possible outcome. It is highly controversial, and therefore is discussed later in this chapter in greater detail.

For Misdemeanors

Ripley Offenbach tried to shoplift a pair of jeans from a department store. He was caught, entered a plea of guilty in the municipal court, and was sentenced to 60 days in jail. While confined, can Ripley simply loaf, eat nourishing food, and in some jails watch television?

No. County jail prisoners can be made to work on public roads and trails or in other jobs for the benefit of the public. Some counties have road camps for such purposes. However, commitment to such a camp, called the "farm," is selective and Ripley may or may not be selected by jail officials. In any event, a prisoner is entitled to be fed, receive medical care, and kept from physical abuse by prisoners or guards. In some states, under work furlough programs a prisoner in a county

---

* For example, in 1983 Mary Jane Dudley Maxwell Pugh Hall (Smith) was charged with and convicted of the shooting murder of her husband, Donald Pugh, in 1970 [*Hall (Smith)* v. *Commonwealth,* 383 S.E.2d 18 (Virginia 1989)].

jail may work at regular outside employment during working hours and remain in confinement at all other times, or confinement may be served on weekends only. Assignments to the "farm" for work are made by the sheriff or other designated agency, whereas work furlough may be ordered by the sentencing judge. Under such a program, the sheriff collects the misdemeanant's earnings; withholds the cost of board, personal expenses, and administration; and may, by order of the court, have to pay the surplus, if any, to appropriate dependents.

In Illinois, misdemeanors are divided into classes A, B and C, for which maximum sentences are 1 year, 6 months, and 30 days, respectively.[61] Most other states simply have a maximum of 1 year in jail; the judge specifies the exact time in accordance with circumstances surrounding the case.

Punishments can be tailored for a specific defendant and the circumstances surrounding his or her crime by offering probation with conditions in lieu of time in jail. Conditions may involve community work, for example. In Florida, four crab poachers agreed to parade around town for four Saturdays wearing signs that said, "It is a felony punishable by five years in prison and/or a $5,000 fine to molest crab pots. I know because I molested one."*

Commonly, a county jail sentence imposed by the court may be shortened for good conduct—for example, ten days off for each month of such behavior. Additional time off may be granted for satisfactory completion of work assignments and for blood donations made to a blood bank.

For Felonies

In most states, the legislative branch of government establishes either specified periods of confinement or minimum–maximum ranges for specified offenses. For example, in Illinois second degree murder warrants a sentence between 4 and 15 years,[62] and in California rape warrants a sentence of 3, 6, or 8 years, depending on whether certain enhancements existed (these were reviewed in the earlier section concerning rape).

A specified minimum sentence is automatically increased when certain aggravating circumstances are present. Statutes specify increased or enhanced penalties for crimes if, for example: (1) the defendant has a prior conviction, (2) a weapon was used during the commission of the crime, (3) great bodily harm was inflicted, or (4) a particular class of victim was involved (e.g., a police officer). A three- or four-time felon faces the impact of a **recidivist** (repeat offender) statute (as detailed in an upcoming section concerning cruel and unusual punishment). Prior arrests not resulting in a conviction may not be used against an accused during trial or as a basis of enhancement of a sentence.

Some states follow the *former* federal system and prescribe **indeterminate sentences** that authorize penologists to tailor the actual time served to the individual criminal.

A record 627,402 men and women were in federal and state prisons on December 31, 1988, according to the Justice Department. States with the most

---

* The defendants agreed to the unique punishment to avoid prosecution in a deferred prosecution agreement (*San Francisco Chronicle,* June 15, 1989).

rapidly growing prison populations on a percentage basis are Rhode Island, Colorado, New Hampshire, Michigan, and California. Women made up 32,691 of the total.[63] Clearly, an increasing number of convicted defendants are being incarcerated.

For federal crimes, the U.S. Sentencing Commission (discussed earlier in this chapter) has prepared a Sentencing Table. The vertical axis is divided into 43 units, each corresponding to a level of offense seriousness. The horizontal axis contains six columns, each denoting a more extensive criminal history record. Judges base their sentence on the guideline corresponding to the intersection of the defendant's crime and record. Under these rules, all persons convicted of a felony will serve some time in prison (including white-collar crime defendants). Although these sentencing guidelines have been mired in constitutional law litigation since their inception in 1984, the U.S. Supreme Court ruled in 1989 that all aspects of the Sentencing Reform Act of 1984 are constitutional. The act is currently being implemented throughout the federal court system.[64] This law has necessitated extensive construction of new prisons.

In addition to fines and imprisonment, some professional persons convicted of crimes involving moral turpitude may suffer additional penalties, such as loss of professional license or employment. Teachers may lose their positions if convicted of criminal sexual misconduct, on the basis of being unfit to teach because of a lack of moral principles.[65] Likewise, a license to practice law may be suspended or revoked for conviction of a crime involving moral turpitude. Refer to the last chapter in this textbook for details about disciplining attorneys. Loss of professional license or position is not a substitute for a fine or imprisonment; it is an additional penalty that a professional person may suffer as the result of committing a crime.

What Are Parole, Probation, and Clemency?

Either a felon in a state prison or a misdemeanant in a county jail may be paroled. *Parole* suspends a sentence after incarceration has begun, as distinct from **probation,** which suspends the sentence before incarceration. Parole is decided by officials designated under legislative authority; probation is granted by a judge. The liberty of a parolee is conditional and may be suspended or revoked unilaterally for violation of conditions specified, such as avoiding certain company (e.g., former gang members) or activities (e.g., carrying a gun). The U.S. Sentencing Commission has eliminated parole in federal cases.

The purpose of probation is to aid in rehabilitation. After conviction and before sentencing, a probation officer will, at the court's discretion, thoroughly examine the defendant's background and circumstances. A recommendation to grant or deny probation will be made to the court before sentencing. There is no absolute right to probation; it is a matter of discretionary decision for the judge. There are two types of probation: formal and informal. Once formal probation has been granted, a probation officer will continually supervise the defendant. If informal probation is granted, the defendant will be "on his or her honor" to comply with the conditions of his or her release. Probation may depend on many events, such as compliance with all laws, search for gainful employment, restitution or return of stolen property or its value, abstention from using intoxicants, and submission to periodic tests for drug use.

In many states, the privilege of probation is limited by statutes. Thus probation cannot be granted to a defendant in California who was armed with a deadly weapon during commission of forcible rape, murder, kidnapping, escape, or train-wrecking, nor is probation possible for a defendant who has two prior felonies.

When probation is granted, either the sentence is suspended pending successful completion of probation or there is no imposition of any sentence at all during the period of probation. In either case, probation will be revoked if the defendant violates its terms or conditions. The original sentence may then become operative. However, revocation of probation may occur only after a hearing has been conducted to establish the fact of the violation.

A defendant has the right to refuse probation and accept the sentence in its place, but this seldom happens.

In addition, there are three kinds of **executive clemency: reprieve** (delay in execution of judgment), **commutation** (reduction of punishment), and **pardon** (release from punishment with restoration of all rights and privileges, e.g., voting rights). Governors of states possess the power of clemency over state criminals; the President possesses this power over persons guilty of federal crimes.

When Is Punishment Cruel and Unusual?

The Eighth Amendment to the U.S. Constitution prohibits government from inflicting "**cruel and unusual**" punishment on those convicted of crimes. Punishment can be cruel and unusual in either of four ways: (1) the sentence can be totally disproportionate to the offense, (2) the prisoner may be subjected to inherently cruel abuse, (3) the method of punishment may be unacceptable to society, or (4) the punishment may be inflicted arbitrarily.

Defendant Rummel was sentenced to life imprisonment under the Texas *recidivist statute.** Defendant was guilty of committing three felonies over a period of some 15 years, as follows: (1) fraudulently using a credit card to obtain $80 worth of goods, for which a sentence of three years was imposed; (2) passing a forged check for $28.36, for which a sentence of 4 years was imposed; and (3) obtaining $120.75 by false pretenses, the third felony, for which a sentence of life imprisonment was required under the recidivist statute. Under Texas law a defendant may receive parole within 12 years if he

---

* Almost all states have recidivist statutes that enhance statutory penalties to life imprisonment in the case of repeat offenders (recidivists). The purpose is to deter repeat offenders and to segregate persons who repeat crimes from the rest of society for long periods.

or she earns maximum good-time credit, and if the parole board and governor approve. Defendant Rummel contended his penalty for the third crime was so disproportionate to the crime as to violate the Eighth Amendment prohibition against cruel and unusual punishment. He appealed to the U.S. Supreme Court. What should have been the result?

The Court upheld Rummel's sentence by a 5–4 split decision.[66] The Court noted that although the monetary crimes did not amount to much money, the single crime of obtaining $120.75 by false pretenses is a felony in 35 states. Further, his single crime of passing a forged check of $28.36 would be theoretically punishable by some imprisonment in 49 states. On the other hand, only Texas, West Virginia, and Washington have such severe recidivist statutes. Many states require conviction of four felonies; some of the states require that at least one of the convictions have involved violence. Some states provide for discretionary, not mandatory, life sentences. However, one state, Mississippi, has eliminated the possibility of parole from sentences under its recidivist statute. Other comparisons reveal considerable differences in penalties among the states. For example, in Idaho theft of $100 will earn the offender a fine or a short term in jail, whereas in Nevada the penalty could be a sentence of 10 years in jail. The Texas system in effect assumes that all three-time offenders deserve the same punishment, whether they commit three separate murders or cash bad checks on three separate occasions.

Prison officials may properly use force (e.g., tear gassing, clubbing, or even shooting) in defense of themselves or other persons. On the other hand, corporal punishment (physical injury) is constitutionally prohibited. The remedy for an aggrieved prisoner remains generally inadequate: The abused prisoner presumably can obtain a writ of **habeas corpus** (Latin: you have the body), which is a procedure prompting a court hearing, or may sue under the *Civil Rights Act* or in common law tort.

Richard Black, a prisoner, heard someone whom he believed to be a guard yell "Stop that man!" Black thereupon chased a fellow inmate who had just struck another inmate with a pipe. Black shortly stopped chasing, and was placed in punitive segregation for 18 months for "running in the yard." Is that punishment "cruel and unusual?"

Yes.[67] Prison guards admitted someone yelled "Stop that man!" and that Black could have believed it to be a guard, even though it was not yelled by a prison official. Such punishment, without a prior hearing of any kind, violates the Eighth Amendment.

Critics insist that **capital punishment** is not a deterrent to crime, is "cruel and unusual," and "degrades and dehumanizes" all who participate in its administration. Statistics also suggest that most persons sentenced to die in recent years have been poor, male, and members of minority groups. This later argument was especially persuasive in the decision by the U.S. Supreme Court limiting capital punishment. It held that a state may not leave the decision whether to impose capital punishment on a particular defendant to the unguided discretion of a jury.[68]

If a state wants to authorize the death penalty, it has a constitutional responsibility to tailor it and apply that state's law in a manner that avoids any arbitrary and capricious infliction of that sentence. In other words, if a statutory procedure specifies the factors to be weighed and the procedures to be followed in deciding when to impose capital punishment, or specifies a mandatory death penalty for specified crimes, then capital punishment is constitutional.[69]

To sentence death when the crime is "outrageously or wantonly vile, horrible, and inhumane," is too vague, because virtually all homicides fit that description.[70] Also inadequate are the words "especially heinous, atrocious, or cruel."[71] However, when "cruel" is defined to mean that the defendant intentionally inflicted extreme pain or torture on the victim, above and beyond the pain necessarily accompanying the victim's death, there is sufficient clarity of standard to justify imposition of the death penalty.[72]

Illinois authorizes the death penalty when a defendant, 18 years or older, murders a peace officer or fireman on duty, a prison guard, or multiple victims; commits murder during the hijacking of an airplane or public vehicle; murders pursuant to a contract for hire; or murders someone to prevent testimony in any criminal case.[73]

A murder defendant with an IQ between 50 and 63, with a "mental age" (the ability to learn) of a 6-year-old child, and with the social maturity (the ability to function in the world) of a 9- or 10-year-old was sentenced to death by a Texas jury. Does this sentence violate the prohibition against "cruel and unusual" punishment?

No. The U.S. Supreme Court held that the defendant's ability was not so disproportionate to the degree of personal culpability as to violate the Eighth Amendment's prohibition against "cruel and unusual" punishment or even punishment of "idiots" or "lunatics."[74]

A 17-year-old male robbed a gas station in Kentucky, raped and sodomized a station attendant, and finally shot her to death so she could not identify him. In another unrelated case in Missouri, a 16-year-old male robbed a convenience store and repeatedly stabbed the store's owner, leaving her to die. State courts in both cases imposed the death penalty. Is it "cruel and unusual" punishment to sentence a minor to death?

No. Evolving standards of decency are best reflected by the statutes adopted by state legislatures, which presumably mirror the will of the people. Of the 37 states whose laws permit capital punishment, 15 decline to impose it on 16-year-old offenders and 12 decline to impose it on 17-year-old offenders. This does not establish the degree of national concensus sufficient to declare the death penalty cruel and unusual punishment when applied to minors.[75]

The death penalty is unique from all other forms of criminal punishment; unique in its rejection of rehabilitation as a fundamental purpose of our criminal system, unique in its total irrevocability, and unique in its conflict with our society's concept of humane treatment of each other. On the other hand, are there reasonable alternatives for those few cases where death is adjudged? Is life imprisonment without possibility of parole and perhaps pardon actually more cruel than death?

Can a Defendant's Record Be Cleared?

State legislatures provide for the sealing (erasing) of certain criminal records as an aid to rehabilitation of defendants who have "learned their lesson." Usually, where the sentence is probation and the defendant has successfully completed all the requirements of probation, the court will, upon motion, vacate the plea or finding of guilt and dismiss the accusation or information. Thus most disabilities arising in connection with the conviction are legally erased. However, the conviction will still stand and be counted as a prior offense.

A defendant who was under 21 at the time of conviction for a misdemeanor may, upon completion of the sentence or probation, obtain an order of the court sealing all records pertaining to the conviction. Although the records are officially sealed in this manner, some applications for professional licensure inquire whether or not records exist and have been sealed, and, if so, what circumstance surrounded the crime. Otherwise, the defendant can answer questions as if the crime never occurred. Some types of misdemeanor records or infractions typically cannot be sealed, such as those pertaining to vehicle code violations, those involving registration as a sex offender, and those involving specified drug offenses.

What Should You Do If Arrested?

A person placed under arrest, whether innocent or guilty, would be well advised to comply with the following suggestions (in the absence of more specific legal advice):

1. Do not strike an officer or resist arrest. If the officer is abusive, get his or her badge number and (if possible) name. Be attentive and try to remember the specifics of the abuse involved.
2. Do not resist the officer searching you (patting down your body) and your car.
3. Do cooperate with fingerprinting and booking procedures. Even if these procedures are personally offensive, such as a strip search, no good can come from physical resistance. If given the choice between certain sobriety tests, be sure you understand your state's penalty for refusing all such tests before making that decision.
4. Do request (if not offered) the right to make a telephone call and use it to contact someone (parent, relative, friend) who can get a lawyer or assistance in

posting bail and taking you home. If you cannot afford a lawyer, tell that to the magistrate or judge before whom you will be required to appear. You can request release on your own recognizance, and the magistrate or judge will make that decision promptly.

5. Do not respond to detailed questions beyond such harmless basics as name, address, and telephone number—until and unless you are advised to by your attorney. You cannot be penalized for remaining silent. As some attorneys advise, "Put a zipper on your mouth."

6. When applicable, do immediately mention to the arresting officer any physical condition requiring medication, such as multiple sclerosis, epilepsy, or diabetes.

7. Be frank and honest in explaining in confidence to your attorney exactly what happened. Counsel is bound by law to respect this confidence, and will be better able to represent you if in possession of all the facts surrounding the incident. Your attorney cannot be compelled to reveal your conversation, even if it involves a confession.

Case 4

PENNSYLVANIA v. MUNIZ

U.S. Supreme Court, 493 U.S.___, 110 S.CT. 2638 (1990)

An officer stopped to investigate a car parked on the shoulder of a highway. When asked if he needed assistance, Inocencio Muniz replied that he had stopped so he could urinate. The officer smelled alcohol and noticed that Muniz's eyes were glazed and bloodshot. The officer directed Muniz to remain parked until his condition improved. Muniz agreed. But as the officer was returning to his vehicle, Muniz drove off. Muniz was then pursued, pulled over, and asked to perform standard roadside sobriety tests. Muniz volunteered that he did poorly because he had been drinking. The officer then arrested Muniz and took him to the station where he was advised that the booking procedures were being videotaped. Muniz was asked his name, address, height, weight, eye color, date of birth, and current age. Muniz answered the seven questions. The booking officer then asked, "When you turned six years old, do you remember what the date was?" He responded, "No, I don't." Muniz then *was asked to repeat the sobriety tests. He did poorly. Finally, Muniz was asked to submit to a breathalyzer test. Muniz refused the test. For the first time Muniz was then advised of his Miranda rights. The arresting officer's testimony and the videotapes were used as evidence in the non-jury trial that resulted in Muniz's being convicted of driving while intoxicated.*

Justice Brennan (for the majority) . . . The Self-Incrimination Clause of the Fifth Amendment (previously held applicable to the states through the Fourteenth Amendment) provides that no "person . . . shall be compelled in any criminal case to be a witness against himself. . . ." The privilege protects an accused only from being compelled to testify against himself, or otherwise provide the state with evidence of a testimonial or communicative nature. . . . Any verbal statements that were . . . testimonial in nature and elicited during custodial interrogation should have been suppressed (i.e., excluded from evidence).

(Justice Brennan then recited precedents that have held varieties of *physical* conduct to be outside the scope of the Fifth Amendment, e.g., fingerprinting, photography, body measurement, writing or speaking for identification only, and taking a blood sample, and concluded that any slurring of speech or other evidence of lack of muscular coordination revealed by Muniz's responses therefore constituted non-testimonial evidence.) We agree . . . that Muniz's answers to the first seven questions are . . . admissible because the questions fall within a "routine booking question" exception from *Miranda* . . . .

In contrast, the sixth birthday question . . . required a testimonial response. Muniz was left with the choice of incriminating himself by admitting that he did not then know the date of his sixth birthday, or answering untruthfully by reporting a date that he did not then believe to be accurate. . . . The content of his truthful answer supported an inference that his mental faculties were impaired. . . . Therefore his response should have been suppressed. (The case was remanded to the trial court.)

Chief Justice Rehnquist (with whom Justice White, Justice Blackmun, and Justice Stevens join, concurring in part and dissenting in part) The sixth birthday question here was an effort on the part of the police to check how well Muniz was able to do a simple mathematical exercise. . . . If the police may require Muniz to use his body in order to demonstrate the level of his physical coordination, there is no reason why they should not be able to require him to speak or write in order to determine his mental coordination.

On appeal his conviction in the Court of Common Pleas was overturned by the Superior court on the grounds the Miranda *warning should have preceded the taking of testimonial evidence during booking procedures. The Pennsylvania Supreme Court declined to review the case, but the United States Supreme Court granted* certiorari *(Latin: to be informed of). (Certiorari is the process by which the U.S. Supreme Court may consider an appeal from the highest court of a state when a federal question is presented.)*

QUESTIONS AND PROBLEMS

1. Tunnel owned the Pines motel in Kilgore, Texas, and used it as a place of prostitution. Russell King, the local Justice of the Peace, was a frequent customer at the Pines. Tunnell reimbursed King for all sums spent for services at the motel in exchange for which King protected "his girls" from prosecution. Tunnell was convicted by jury trial of, among other crimes, bribery of a public official. Part of Tunnell's sentence was forfeiture of the Pines motel. On appeal Tunnell contended that free sexual favors for an official is not bribery because such favors are not a benefit "reasonably regarded as economic gain." He also contended that forfeiture of the motel was cruel and unusual punishment. What should the result be on appeal? *U.S.* v. *Tunnell,* 667 F.2d 1182 (1982).

2. Which of the following court sentences do you believe should constitute "cruel and unusual" punishment as proscribed by the Eighth Amendment: (1) a 10-year prison sentence for two obscene telephone calls, (2) a 10–20 year sentence for statutory rape, (3) the death penalty for forcible rape of an adult woman, and (4) a 12-year sentence for possession and distribution of heroin? Can you make an argument both in favor of and against each of these sentences?

3. What is the difference between a statute prohibiting the use of a drug and a statute prohibiting addiction to the same drug? Should one be a felony and the other a misdemeanor (or no crime at all)?

4. C damaged a parked police car because B threatened to kill him if he did not. Is C guilty of a crime? A prisoner testified that he escaped from prison, not because he wanted freedom, but rather to escape physical abuse. Should this be a legal defense to the crime of escape? What is the similarity between these hypothetical cases?

5. Under RICO, an accused's funds can be confiscated prior to trial, even though some of those funds are necessary for attorney fees. Can you reconcile this law with the constitutional presumption of innocence? Does it make any difference that all defendants are entitled to free counsel if they are unable to pay for one of their own choosing?

6. Suppose a state statute provided: "Persons who loiter or wander on streets must identify themselves, with credible and reliable identification, and account for their presence. Violation of this provision is a misdemeanor." Can you think of any reasons why this law might be unconstitutional?

7. Attorney Robert Bokuniewicz held funds belonging to his elderly client, Rose Harnett. Gradually he wrongfully and secretly spent the money because he was unable to find work as an attorney while his friends and family enjoyed considerable success. Finally the funds were demanded by Rose Harnett's daughter's attorney. At this meeting Bokuniewicz delivered a cashier's check, payable to himself, for $176,000 as evidence that he was good for the money, but said he needed additional time to liquidate assets he had purchased for Harnett. In truth the cashier's check had been prepared by the bank in the amount of $176. Mysteriously the three zeros had been added by alteration. Bokuniewicz was convicted of forgery and sentenced to the maximum of 5 years in prison. On appeal he contended that he cannot be convicted of forgery because he received nothing of value in return for the altered check. What should be the result of appeal? *Illinois* v. *Bokuniewicz,* 513 N.E.2d 138 (Illinois, 1987).

8. D, who trained dogs to fight, tied his pit bull "Willy" in his back yard to protect some 200 marijuana plants he was growing. A young child who lived next door wandered into D's yard and was killed in a vicious attack by the dog. The jury was instructed to decide if the appropriate crime was (1) murder in the second degree, (2) voluntary manslaughter, or (3) involuntary manslaughter. Which do you believe is the correct charge and what is your rationale?

9. A woman who gave birth to her second cocaine-dependent child was charged with the crime of child abuse for her use of cocaine during pregnancy. Can you identify her defense to this accusation?

10. Suppose the prosecutor desires a jury trial in a certain criminal case but the defendant desires trial before a judge sitting without a jury. Will a jury be empaneled? What impact do you think jury trials have on the administration of our legal system?

FURTHER READING

1. For a review of the pro and con arguments of the constitutionality of state laws that prohibit homosexual activity between consenting adults in private (sodomy statutes), see the majority and dissenting arguments presented in *Bowers* v. *Hardwick,* 478 U.S. 186 (1986).

2. Forer, Lois, *Criminals and Victims*. New York: Norton, 1980. Perceptive analyses of how crime impacts society, together with proposed reforms.

3. Gillespie, Cynthia, *Justifiable Homicide*. Columbus, OH: Ohio State University Press, 1989. A well-researched account of "justifiable homicide" cases involving battered women.

4. *Rummel* v. *Estelle,* 445 U.S. 263, 100 S.Ct. 1133 (1980). An exhaustive historical review of the prohibition against cruel and unusual punishment.

5. Schar, Edwin, *Crimes without Victims*. Englewood Cliffs, NJ: Prentice-Hall, 1965; Kiester,

Crimes with No Victims. New York: Alliance for a Safer New York, 1972; and Geis, Gilbert, *Not the Law's Business?* National Institute of Mental Health, 1972. General information and specific recommendations about crimes without victims.

6. Schulz, "Officer, What's the Charge?": An Analysis of Confession Law in Light of Colorado v. Spring. 30 *Arizona Law Review* 551, 1988. An update on the "Miranda" rule.

7. "Special Symposium on Victim's Rights," 11 *Pepperdine Law Review* 1 et. seq., 1984. A history of victims' rights under the law.

8. Turow, S. *The Burden of Proof.* New York: Farrar, Straus, Giroux, 1990.

9. Uhlman & Walker, "He Takes Some of My Time; I Take Some of His: An Analysis of Judicial Sentencing Patterns in Jury Cases," 14 *Law & Society Review* 323, 1980. Examples of federal sentencing disparities when defendants demand jury trials.

10. White, Welsh, *The Death Penalty in the Eighties.* Ann Arbor, MI: University of Michigan Press, 1987. An examination of the modern system of capital punishment.

NOTES

1. *San Francisco Chronicle,* June 23, 1990.

2. *People* v. *Pena,* 197 Cal.Rptr. 264 (1983). See also *Commonwealth* v. *Martin,* 341 N.E.2d 885 (Massachusetts, 1976).

3. *People* v. *Jones,* 407 N.E.2d 1121 (Illinois, 1980).

4. *State* v. *Pyle,* 532 P.2d 1309 (Kansas, 1975).

5. *People* v. *Municipal Court,* 151 Cal.Rptr. 861 (1979).

6. Illinois Code of Corrections, § 1005-8-1.

7. 17 Cal.Jur. III, § 71.

8. Illinois Code of Corrections, § 1005-5-3.2.

9. See, for example, California Penal Code, § 187.

10. *Roe* v. *Wade,* 410 U.S. 113 (1973); *Webster* v. *Reproductive Health Services,* 492 U.S. ___, 109 S.Ct. 3040 (1989).

11. *People* v. *Martinez,* 238 Cal.Rptr. 265 (1987).

12. *State* v. *Tesack,* 383 S.E.2d 54 (West Virginia, 1989).

13. *People* v. *Caldwell,* 203 Cal.Rptr. 433 (1984); *People* v. *Aurelio R.,* 212 Cal.Rptr. 868 (1985).

14. See, for example, *Commonwealth ex. rel. Smith* v. *Myers,* 261 A.2d 550 (Pennsylvania, 1970); *Alvarez* v. *Dist. Ct. for Denver,* 525 P.2d 1131 (Colorado, 1974); *People* v. *Wood,* 167 N.E.2d 736 (New York, 1960); *State* v. *Harrison,* 564 P.2d 1321 (New Mexico, 1977).

15. *Enmund* v. *Florida,* 458 U.S. 782, 102 S.Ct. 3368 (1982).

16. *Tison* v. *Arizona,* 481 U.S. 137, 107 S.Ct. 1676 (1987).

17. *People* v. *Aureli R.,* 212 Cal.Rptr. 868 (1985).

18. *People* v. *Hernandez,* 215 Cal. Rptr. 166 (1985).

19. *People* v. *Rosenkrantz,* 244 Cal.Rptr. 403 (1988).

20. *Commonwealth* v. *Britcher,* 563 A.2d 502 (Pennsylvania, 1989).

21. *People* v. *Watson,* 179 Cal.Rptr. 43 (1981).

22. *Time,* May 22, 1989, p. 104.

23. *San Francisco Chronicle,* July 15, 1989.

24. California Penal Code, §§ 261 et. seq., §§ 12022.5 et. seq., and §§ 667.6 et. seq.

25. Florida Crimes Code, § 794.011(3).

26. *Coker* v. *Georgia,* 433 U.S. 584, 97 S.Ct. 2861 (1977).

27. *Hall* v. *McKenzie,* 537 F.2d 1232 (1976).

28. *People* v. *Vela,* 218 Cal.Rptr. 161 (1985); *Battle* v. *State,* 414 A.2d 1266 (Maryland, 1980); *State* v. *Way,* 254 S.E.2d 760 (North Carolina, 1979).

29. New York Penal Code, §§ 130.25 and 130.30.

30. *People* v. *Hernandez,* 39 Cal.Rptr. 361 (1964), presently codified in Penal Code, § 261.5.

31. *U.S.* v. *Brooks,* 841 F.2d 268 (1988); *State* v. *Randolph,* 528 P.2d 1008 (Washington, 1974); and *Goodrow* v. *Perrin,* 403 A.2d 864 (New Hampshire, 1979).

32. California Penal Code, § 261.5.

33. Florida Crimes Code, § 794.011(2).

34. *People* v. *Alday,* 110 Cal.Rptr. 617 (1973).

35. See 31 Am.Jur.2d, *Extortion, Blackmail, and Threats,* § 1.

36. *People* v. *Lopez,* 222 Cal.Rptr. 101 (1986). Calif. Penal Code, §§ 203 and 204.

37. *People* v. *Valdez,* 220 Cal.Rptr. 538 (1985).

38. California Health & Safety Code, §§ 11,550 and 11,351.

39. Florida Crimes Code, § 893.13.

40. Florida Crimes Code, § 800.02.

41. *People* v. *John V.,* 213 Cal.Rptr. 503 (1985).

42. *Chaplinsky* v. *State of New Hampshire,* 315 U.S. 568, 62 S.Ct. 766 (1942).

43. *Time,* August 21, 1989; *The Wall Street Journal,* August 2, 1988.

44. *People* v. *Gleghorn,* 238 Cal.Rptr. 82 (1987).

45. *United States* v. *Leon,* 468 U.S. 897, 104 S.Ct. 3405 (1984); *United States* v. *Peltier,* 422 U.S. 531, 95 S.Ct. 2313 (1975).

46. *California* v. *Greenwood & Van Houten,* 486 U.S. 35, 108 S.Ct. 1625 (1988).

47. *United States* v. *Rodriquez,* 592 F.2d 553 (1979); *United States* v. *Ramsey,* 431 U.S. 606, 97 S.Ct. 1972 (1977); *United States* v. *Olcott,* 568 F.2d 1173 (1978).

48. New York Criminal Procedure Law, § 510.30.

49. 18 U.S.C. § 3142(d).

50. A federal judge set bail for Adnan Khashoggi, who was awaiting trial on fraud charges for his business dealings on behalf of the late and exiled Philippine President Ferdinand Marcos, at $10 million. Khashoggi also was required to wear an electronic bracelet around his ankle or wrist so authorities could monitor his whereabouts before the trial (*San Francisco Chronicle,* August 12, 1989). Both Khashoggi and his co-defendant Imelda Marcos subsequently were acquitted.

51. *United States* v. *Blackwell,* 694 F.2d 1325 (1982).

52. *Miranda* v. *Arizona,* 384 U.S. 436, 86 S.Ct. 1602 (1966).

53. *Rhode Island* v. *Innis,* 446 U.S. 291, 100 S.Ct. 1682 (1980). For an update on the famous Miranda rule, see 30 *Arizona Law Review* 551 (1988). Between 1971 and 1989, the Supreme Court has rendered opinions in some 30 Miranda cases. In only five did a Miranda violation vitiate the conviction (*National Law Journal,* February 20, 1989).

54. *Brady* v. *Maryland,* 373 U.S. 83, 83 S.Ct. 1194 (1963).

55. *N. Carolina* v. *Pearce,* 395 U.S. 711, 89 S.Ct. 2072 (1969).

56. California Penal Code, § 25(b).

57. *People* v. *Segal,* 429 N.E.2d 107 (New York, 1981).

58. *People* v. *Barraza,* 153 Cal.Rptr. 459 (1979).

59. *People* v. *Slatton,* 219 Cal.Rptr. 70 (1985); *People* v. *Kelley,* 205 Cal.Rptr. 382 (1984).

60. *United States* v. *Russell,* 411 U.S. 423, 93 S.Ct. 1637 (1973).

61. Illinois Code of Corrections, § 1005-5-3.2.

62. Illinois Code of Corrections, § 1005-8-1.

63. *San Francisco Chronicle,* September 15, 1989.

64. *United States* v. *Mistretta,* 488 U.S. ___, 109 S.Ct. 647 (1989).

65. In *Pettit* v. *State Board of Education,* 109 Cal.Rptr. 665 (1973), the defendant engaged in oral copulation with three men, not including her then-present husband, in a semi-public "Swinger's Club" party attended by 20 people. She lost her elementary school life diploma (permanent license to teach). In *Morrison* v. *State Board of Education,* 82 Cal.Rptr. 175 (1969), a teacher committed a non-criminal homosexual act. The court reinstated the teacher's secondary school life diploma for lack of a causal connection between the act and the ability to teach.

66. *Rummel* v. *Estelle,* 445 U.S. 263, 100 S.Ct. 1133 (1980).

67. *Black* v. *Brown,* 524 F.Supp. 856 (1981).

68. *Furman* v. *Georgia,* 408 U.S. 238, 92 S.Ct. 2726 (1972).

69. *Gregg* v. *Georgia,* 428 U.S. 153, 96 S.Ct. 2909 (1976).

70. *Godfrey* v. *Georgia,* 446 U.S. 420, 100 S.Ct. 1759 (1980).

71. *Maynard* v. *Cartwright,* ___U.S.___, 108 S.Ct. 1853 (1988).

72. *State* v. *Breton,* 562 A.2d 1060 (Connecticut 1989).

73. Illinois Criminal Code, § 9-1.

74. *Penry* v. *Lynaugh*, 492 U.S. ___, 109 S.Ct. 2934 (1989).

75. *Stanford* v. *Kentucky* and *Wilkins* v. *Missouri*, 492 U.S. ___, 109 S.Ct. 2969 (1989).

Torts: Private Wrongs

We live in a crowded, heavily urbanized, heterogeneous society. Our environment is scientifically oriented, highly mechanized, and technologically advanced. We enjoy independence and freedom of action. Nevertheless, because of the increasingly specialized nature of our work, we depend on others for most goods and services. This requires cooperative effort and frequent interaction with others, but these contacts are not always positive and productive. Sometimes persons are hurt and property is damaged because of careless or malicious behavior. There are troublesome confrontations and opportunities for abuse and exploitation. Disputes arise, which in our civilized society we are committed to resolve peacefully under law. When negotiation and other methods of dispute resolution do not provide an acceptable solution, the aggrieved person may sue. Thus we are a litigious society, in part because of the complexity of modern life and the inevitability of friction in our relations with each other.

The Litigious Environment

Consider a few of the sources of that friction with resulting occasions for litigation.

● We have approximately 188 million autos, motorcycles, trucks, and buses on our highways. They are driven by some 164 million licensed drivers. With these figures in mind, it is understandable that almost 21 million motor vehicle accidents occurred in 1987.
● In 1989, 117 million persons (16 years old or over) were gainfully employed (while 6.7 million were unemployed). They produced a gross national product (GNP) of goods and services valued at $4,880,600,000,000. Unfortunately, in the process many workers were killed or injured. In 1989, the toll was 10,600 deaths, and 1.8 million on-the-job injuries.[1]

- The impressive GNP included a disturbing number of defective products and faulty services that injured countless persons, including many customers, patients, and clients.
- Costly accidents happen even within expertly managed air, land, and sea public transport companies. The cause is often human failure in the design, maintenance, or operation of equipment.
- In interpersonal relations between strangers, and even among friends and family members, misunderstandings often degenerate into harmful acts that injure persons and destroy property.

The multiple and diverse private controversies range in importance from the trivial to the profound. Most are overlooked or are settled amicably through direct negotiation or with the assistance of others. But whatever the seriousness of the disputes, they may be resolved by legal action in accordance with the law of torts.

What Is a Tort? What Are Its Basic Types?

A **tort** is a private wrong, committed by one person (the **tortfeasor**), that injures another's (the *victim*) person or property, for which the law allows the legal remedy of monetary damages. Note that sometimes two or more persons, called **joint tortfeasors,** are liable for the particular injury to one or more victims. Torts are classified in these categories:

- Negligent
- Intentional
- Absolute liability
- Strict liability

Negligent behavior, in a word, means carelessness. By failing to act as a reasonable, careful person would act under the same or similar circumstances, the tortfeasor inadvertently causes an injury that was foreseeable.

In contrast, with **intentional torts** the tortfeasor intends the wrongful act that injures the victim. As you might expect, most crimes are also torts because the criminal act injures the victim. Thus the state may prosecute the wrongdoer in a criminal action for the public wrong to society, while the individual victim may sue in a civil action for the private wrong. Understandably, most torts are not crimes because most tortfeasors do not act with *mens rea* (Latin: guilty mind), meaning criminal intent.

The third basic type of tort, **absolute liability,** arises under certain circumstances where the victim need not prove that the defendant acted negligently or was guilty of an intentional tort. Thus, as a matter of enlightened public policy, a worker who is injured on the job is generally entitled to workers' compensation payments without trial and even if his or her own negligence caused or contributed to the accident. The fourth basic type of tort, **strict liability,** is most frequently found in product liability cases. The manufacturer as well as commercial middlemen (wholesalers, retailers) may be liable to a user who is injured because of a defect in the way the product was designed or made. It does not help the defendant to disclaim all possible liability at the time of sale; nor does it help the defendant to prove that all warranties have expired, or had been expressly excluded. (Warranties are discussed at greater length in Chapter 6.) The courts of many states simply hold that there is a duty to make products reasonably safe for use.

What Is the Tort of Negligence?

Everyone has a duty, imposed by law, to behave with due care as a reasonable, prudent person would under the same or similar circumstances. If one fails to do so, and thus injures another's person or property, the victim may sue and recover damages from the wrongdoer because of the wrongdoer's negligence. The duty of care every person owes to all others is judged by the flexible and variable, yet objectively definable, standard of a hypothetical **reasonable person.** Determinants of duty include the foreseeability of harm to the plaintiff, the proximity or closeness between the act and the injury, and the moral blameworthiness of the defendant. Also relevant are the public policy of preventing future harm; the financial burden on the defendant and the community in imposing the duty; and the availability, cost, and prevalence of insurance for the risk involved.[2]

Additionally, elements of negligence include whether the defendant **breached the duty** by failing to comply with the required standard of conduct, and whether that breach was the legal, proximate cause of injury to the plaintiff. Whether the defendant's conduct breached this duty, and if so, what monetary damages should be awarded, are generally questions of fact for the *trier of fact*. In a given case this would be the jury if one is used, or the judge if there is no jury.

Ida Nino was a member of a ski class for beginners, taking instructions in Aspen, Colorado. Her group was standing on the left side of the run. One by one, the student skiers would proceed across to the right side. Donald Hight, skiing down the mountainside, came over a mogul (hump) and crashed into the group, knocking down three girls. Ida was seriously injured and sued Don, contending he had been negligent. Is her suit sustainable in court even though the event was admittedly a regrettable accident?

Yes. An **accident** is a sudden, unexpected, unintended happening that causes injury or death, and/or loss of property. It may occur under circumstances where nobody is at fault, as in an earthquake or natural landslide. In most accidents, one or more of the parties involved was at fault because of what they did or failed to do. In skiing, the custom is that the uphill skier generally has the better vantage point and resulting control, and hence has the obligation to avoid the downhill skier at the lower level. This custom may be presented to the jury to help convince them that Donald was negligent in failing to look, see, and avoid the group of beginners below. Note that the ski instructor as well as the student skiers may also have been negligent. Such negligence could reduce or eliminate their claim for damages. Contributory negligence is discussed later in this chapter.

Violation of a Statute

In some jurisdictions, if one injures another as a consequence of violating a statute, such act is *prima facie* (Latin: on first appearance) evidence of negligence. However, the evidence is rebuttable; it may be refuted by other evidence that serves to disprove that first impression. In other states, it is **negligence per se** (Latin: by itself) and conclusive, provided causation is proved.

An interesting contrast in the impact of statutes is found in good samaritan laws, which most states have enacted. These laws shield doctors and others from liability to an injured person when they stop and render emergency aid. Of course, they are expected to use reasonable care under the circumstances and may not carelessly worsen the condition of anyone in distress. This happened, for example, when the U.S. Coast Guard temporarily abandoned a search for a fisherman who died on a life raft five days after his boat had sunk. The U.S.C.G. had negligently fouled up their own rescue message transmission.[3]

According to the **Restatement of the Law,*** "A child of tender years is not required to conform to the standard of behaviour which is reasonable to expect of an adult, but his (her) conduct is to be judged by the standard of behaviour to be expected from a child of like age, intelligence and experience. . . . It is impossible to fix the definite age at which children are capable of negligence."[4] However some courts, as in Michigan, hold that a child under the age of 7, simply is incapable of negligence.[5]

Causation: Actual and Proximate

Common sense and elementary justice tell us that one should not be liable for conduct that causes injury to other persons unless there is a logical cause-effect relationship between the defendant's negligent act (or failure to act) and the plaintiff's injury. In simple fact situations, this principle is easy to apply. But when a series of events and persons are involved—as is often the case—the problem often has no solution that can satisfy all parties.

What if two independent forces cause the injury? For example, suppose both A and B carelessly build separate campfires near C's cabin. A forest fire results,

---

* The *Restatement of the Law* (of Torts, Contracts, etc.) consists of a series of authoritative volumes written by legal scholars of the American Law Institute. In clear language, they state the principal rules of existing law in the designated areas, with numerous practical examples of their application. The Restatements identify trends in the law and present suggestions for desirable changes. Judges often cite the Restatements in their opinions.

which destroys C's home. Even if neither campfire alone could have produced that result, both A and B would be liable under the *substantial factor test,* since both contributed substantially to the destruction. The same would be true if *either* fire alone would have been sufficient to destroy the cabin.

In fairness to the defendant, his or her action must be not only the **actual cause,** but also the **proximate cause** (sometimes referred to as the *legal cause).* Theoretically—and facetiously—we might trace all events of human history in an unbroken chain of events to Adam and Eve. Practically and justly, the result (the injury to the plaintiff) must not be unreasonably remote from the cause (the negligent act of the defendant). The proximate cause is the true cause ". . . which, in a natural and continuous sequence, unbroken by any efficient intervening cause, produces injury, and without which the result would not have occurred."[6] This judicial legalese may be clarified by the following hypothetical case.

Brent Starr was testing the power of his new sportscar on a clear highway in good weather. When he reached 90 MPH, he lost control and the car crashed through a fence and into a high-voltage electricity pole. This caused a short circuit and power failure throughout the city of Barclay, 100 miles away. Among the many persons affected were the staff and doctors in General Hospital. Just as the power went out, surgeon Ramona Ramirez was making a critical incision near patient Albert Johnson's heart during open-heart surgery. As a result of the darkness and loss of power to essential equipment, she had to stop abruptly. The machines supplying vital oxygen and pumping blood went silent. Within minutes Albert Johnson was dead. Is Brent Starr liable for Albert's death?

No. One can truthfully say that Brent's wrongful conduct was the actual cause of Albert's death—but for Brent's folly, Albert would not have died when he did. But Brent's act was not the proximate, legal cause because it was so indirect and remote from the death.

Note that Brent would be liable for the damage to the fence and to the high-voltage electricity pole. It is also possible that General Hospital could be found guilty of negligence, and therefore liable, for failing to have a standby emergency electric power source available. (This is indeed standard practice in well-run hospitals, because power failures are not uncommon.)

Brent Starr's car, after ramming the pole, caromed into the brush nearby, striking and killing Tom Sneed, who was hunting doves. Brent did not know that Tom was hunting in that place. Is Brent liable for Tom's death?

Yes. Here Brent's wrongful conduct was the actual and also the proximate or legal cause of the death. The negligent act was direct and close, not remote, in time and place to the death.

Foreseeability: Essential for Negligence

Thus causation, both actual and proximate, must be proved to hold a defendant liable for negligence. However, in addition the plaintiff must prove **foreseeability:**

"The ability to see or know in advance . . . that harm or injury is a likely result of acts or omissions."[7] If and only if a reasonably prudent person, under similar circumstances, could and would have foreseen the likelihood of injury from the defendant's conduct to any person in the situation of the plaintiff does the defendant have a **duty** to exercise reasonable care to avoid such conduct.

Without foreseeability, there is no duty to act or refrain from action. Without duty, there can be no negligence. Without negligence, there can be no fault. Without fault, there can be no liability, regardless of the extent of the injury. William Prosser and Page Keeton, leading authorities on torts, unequivocally state: "The question of foreseeability is not an element of causation and does not arise until the issue of causation has been determined."[8] Another legal scholar, Leon Green, properly points out that "Causation is a neutral issue, blind to right and wrong . . . but in absence of causal relation plaintiff has no case, and all other inquiries become moot."[9] After all, the linkage of cause and effect in any series of events may be coldly analyzed and *objectively* determined. Thereafter one may inquire into whether any involved person (e.g., the defendant) *subjectively* could have and should have foreseen any of the described events or injurious effects.

Returning to Brent Starr's predicament in the preceding example, he could and should have foreseen that a person, such as Tom Sneed, might be in the bushes near the highway, perhaps hiking, hunting, resting, or bird-watching. He could not have foreseen the tragic sequence of events in the hospital, nor could he have foreseen countless other resulting events at great distances from the scene of the crash, in areas served with electricity by the power line.

Rather bored, Bill Brown was legally driving down a street where homes were mixed in with several small factories and warehouses. There was litter scattered about, including a fairly large, dilapidated cardboard carton near the gutter in the road ahead. On the spur of the moment, Bill decided to try to push the carton off the street with his bumper or simply flatten it. This he proceeded to do, only to dicover to his dismay and horror that the carton concealed a child. Kathy Wellington, age three, had been walking on the curb, holding the carton over her head. She had evidently stumbled into the street, and the carton covered her completely. Her death was mercifully sudden. Kathy's parents now seek to hold Brown liable. Will they prevail?

No. Although Bill's conduct was the actual and proximate cause of Kathy's death, he is not liable. While it is foreseeable that a pedestrian might be in the vicinity, it is not foreseeable that a tiny person would be inside an old cardboard carton in the street. (Note that if the carton had been neat and new, one might have guessed that it could have fallen off a truck. If it had contained merchandise, a jury might have found Bill negligent in his conduct and liable for the destruction of the goods, because in that location the presence of such contents might have been deemed to have been reasonably foreseeable.)

What Are Defenses to Negligence?

Under certain circumstances, a defendant who might otherwise be liable because of his or her negligence can avoid payment of all or some of the damage by proving that the plaintiff had done one of the following:

1. Assumed the risk

2. Was him- or herself negligent and therefore entitled to no damages under the doctrine of contributory negligence

3. Was him- or herself negligent (in a growing number of states) and so, under the doctrine of comparative negligence, is entitled only to reduced damages, if any

Assumption of Risk

Before the adoption of workers' compensation laws (discussed later in this chapter), employees who were injured on the job were often denied any damages because the employer could prove that they had voluntarily **assumed the risk** of injury in a dangerous task. This defense on the part of employers has declined in importance for a variety of reasons, including the fact that it can no longer be asserted against workers' claims for job-related injuries. Moreover, it is generally contrary to public policy to permit anyone to agree (in a contract) to absolve or excuse others from liability for their gross negligence or willful misconduct. Statutes often provide that when one leaves a car in a parking garage together with the keys, and an attendant moves the car, the garage may be liable for damages to the vehicle while being moved, despite exculpatory language on the parking receipt.

Nevertheless, a plaintiff who knows and appreciates a given risk may assume it, thereby absolving the defendant of liability if injury results. In sports especially, the hazards may be serious for both spectators and participants, yet both may assume the risks of reasonable hazards of such games as baseball, basketball, football, and hockey. But, for example, a baseball fan does not assume the risk of being hit by a stray baseball thrown by a pitcher who is warming up in a bullpen that has no protective screening. (This happened to a Chicago Cubs fan in the 1960s.)[10] In another case, a spectator recovered $18,700 in damages for his injury from a basketball thrown into the stands during a Harlem Globe Trotters game.[11]

In contact sports, participants assume the risk of injuries that are common and expected, even when an opponent is violating a rule of the game (e.g., when a jockey carelessly changes lanes during a horse race—a violation of a foul riding rule). But this does not give the contestants a carte blanche waiver of all violations of the rules.[12] Occasionally, a player intentionally injures an opponent; such risk is not assumable. This is exemplified by a case where the plaintiff was injured in a professional football game. After a play was ended, an opposing player approached the plaintiff from behind and intentionally hit him in the neck.[13]

Contributory and Comparative Negligence

Under the doctrine of **contributory negligence,** if two persons are involved in an accident and both are negligent, neither can recover any damages. This is so even if one party "contributed" almost all of the negligence. The identification and allocation of the percentages of negligence is a question for the trier of fact. Not infrequently, a jury will temper strict application of the rule with compassion and common sense, and simply overlook minimal amounts of negligence by an otherwise deserving plaintiff. Moreover, the contributory negligence of a plaintiff is no defense for a defendant who was guilty of willful and wanton misconduct (i.e., done either intentionally or with reckless disregard for the plaintiff's safety).

This harsh rule originated in England and was commonly applied in the United States during the 1800s, when railroads were first introduced. "Establishment-oriented" courts were interested in helping the new industry, and they applied the doctrine as a matter of law to collisions at grade crossings. The doctrine survived into the twentieth century and frequently blocked recovery damages in automobile accident cases (where it is not unusual to find at least some negligence on the part of both drivers).

Alyce Anderson had to push the brake pedal close to the floor of her car and pump it to stop the vehicle. She planned to have the faulty brakes fixed the very next day, but that morning Jim Cook made a negligent left turn in front of Alyce's oncoming car at the entrance to campus. She tried to stop, but could not because of the defective brakes. In the ensuing collision both Alyce and Jim were injured. They sued each other. Who should have won?

Neither, if the injury occurred in a state where contributory negligence is a defense. Jim was contributorily negligent in making his left turn; Alyce was contributorily negligent in driving with defective brakes.

Is the failure to use an automobile seat belt or shoulder harness (or airbag that inflates upon impact) evidence of contributory negligence? The issue is somewhat confused. Belts generally reduce the severity of injury, but in some cases can cause internal injury. However, there is no documented proof that any person has died in a fiery accident because he or she could not unbuckle the seat belt. Indeed, the crash victim, if belted, is more likely to be conscious and better able to escape. If in the driver's seat, he or she is more likely to minimize further damage by maintaining better control of the car. Most states have mandated by statute the installation of seat belts, but not all require their use. Moreover, there is really no logical connection between a collision and the failure to use a seat belt. Accordingly, most jurisdictions, including those of such populous states as Florida, New York, and Texas, have ruled that failure to use a seat belt does not constitute contributory negligence.[14] In California[15] and Illinois,[16] such failure is contributory negligence that may reduce damages only if expert testimony proves how much less the injuries would have been had the belt been used. The question should gradually become moot in the decades after 1990, because by federal order autos sold after September of that year must be equipped with air bags or automatic seat belts.

Most states have adopted the rule of **comparative negligence** as a more rational rule—it is considered to be more in accord with common sense and more conducive to justice. Under this rule, a plaintiff who is negligent may nevertheless recover damages from a defendant who is more negligent. Damages allowed are simply reduced in proportion to the amount of negligence attributable to the plaintiff. In other words, liability for damages is allocated to the parties in proportion to the fault each contributed to causing the injury, as determined by the trier of fact.

T. Ray Vitesse was driving his heavy-duty pick-up truck on a residential street in the dusk, about an hour after sunset. He was coming home from a party where he'd had several alcoholic drinks. He later claimed he was not drunk, although he had forgotten to turn his headlights on. It was raining heavily at the time, and he felt mellow and refreshed as the raindrops splashed on his face through an open window. "Just cruising along" at only ten miles over the posted speed limit (of 25 MPH), his reverie suddenly ended as he crashed into the left side of Art Aritroso's sedan. Art was backing out of his driveway, but had failed to look both ways and hadn't turned his lights on until he was in the street. T. Ray suffered no injuries and his truck required no repairs, but Art's sedan was extensively damaged and he was badly injured. Art sued and the jury decided that his negligence constituted 25 percent of the total. Art's damages total $100,000. How much is he entitled to under the comparative negligence rule?

It depends on the state. In some states, the total damages recognized are reduced by the amount of the plaintiff's negligence, as long as it is not as great as the defendant's. Under this process, Art would get $75,000 (100 percent − 25 percent = 75 percent). He would have received $51,000 if his negligence had been 49 percent (100 percent − 49 percent = 51 percent), but nothing if it had been 50 percent or higher. (This is the case in Wisconsin, one of the first states to adopt the rule.) Other states permit recovery if the plaintiff's negligence is not greater than the defendant's. Thus Art would have received $50,000 if his negligence had been as much as 50 percent, but nothing if it had been 51 percent or more. (Remember, the jury decided that his negligence was 25 percent.) Finally, in a number of states, under the "pure" comparative negligence rule, contributory negligence never bars recovery. Damages are reduced in proportion to the amount of the plaintiff's negligence. Thus, Art would recover $75,000. Even if his negligence had been 99 percent, he would nevertheless have received $1,000 (100 percent − 99 percent = 1 percent).

Further Examples of Negligence

Professional Malpractice

Few areas of legal conflict have engendered as much heated debate as **malpractice.** Malpractice is professional misconduct. It could be, but seldom is, intentional or criminal. Usually it is negligence; a failure to use that degree of care, learning, and skill ordinarily possessed and applied by the average prudent member of the profession in the same or similar locality. Thus a general practitioner in a small town is not expected to have the skills or facilities of a group of specialists in a large city.

Physicians and surgeons have been the prime targets of plaintiffs, but dentists, lawyers, accountants, architects, and engineers have comparable professional duties to those they serve, and are increasingly being sued. Lawsuits have also been brought against other similar public-service types, such as pharmacists, chiropractors, insurance and real estate agents, and investment advisers.

A physician is required to make a proper examination of every patient accepted for treatment. The volume of malpractice claims has caused sharp increases in premiums for malpractice insurance, a cost passed along to patients in higher fees. Some doctors have left the field or narrowed their specializations (obstetricians are a notable example); some other doctors have associated themselves with health maintenance organizations (HMOs), where they have readily available consultants and easier access to analytical laboratories and expensive diagnostic equipment, along with ample liability insurance. The following highlight illustrates the growing problem of medical malpractice suits.

Medical Malpractice Suits—Tip of an Iceberg?

It is possible that the scope of medical malpractice is much greater than suggested by the current volume of cases in that area. In March, 1990, Harvard University researchers reported results of a four-year state-funded study of medical malpractice in hospitals located in New York state. The research team analyzed 31,429 medical records of patients in 51 private, non-profit, and government hospitals for the year of 1984. Among the disturbing findings:

1. There were 1,133 "adverse events," ranging from patients falling down to infections caused by surgery.

2. Twenty-five percent of the adverse events could be traced to negligence, yet only one lawsuit was filed for every 9.6 cases of detected negligence.

3. If figures are extrapolated to the entire total of 2.7 million patients who were hospitalized in New York in 1984, 3.7 percent or nearly 99,000 patients experienced injury because of their medical treatment, and as many as 7,000 died as a result of negligent care.

Commenting on the study, Sidney Wolfe, director of the Washington-based Health Research Group (consumer advocates), said the study suggests that nationally some 90,000 patients die annually because of medical malpractice inside hospitals.*

The range of legal challenges doctors now face is illustrated by this series of California cases where medical practitioners were found liable:

● One doctor failed to inoculate for mumps a physically disabled infant, who later became blind from complications of that disease.

● Two defendant doctors knew their patient was diabetic and was carrying a deceased fetus that was to be surgically removed within 18 hours. They were negligent in directing her to drive immediately to the hospital for preliminary laboratory tests. She lost control of the car due to a diabetic seizure and struck the plaintiff. The doctors should have warned her not to drive in her irrational and uncontrolled diabetic condition which was also complicated by the missed spontaneous abortion.

● A doctor has breached his duty to inform a patient of the risks she was incurring by refusing to undergo a pap smear test he had recommended. (The PST permits early detection and treatment of cervical cancer, a disease which proved fatal in this case). Under certain circumstances it is a question for the trier of fact

---

* SOURCE: Ron Winslow, *Wall Street Journal,* Mar. 1, 1990, pg. B.4. Reprinted by permission.

whether a doctor is responsible for informing a patient of all material consequences of a particular procedure or treatment.
● One doctor failed to tell prospective parents of the risk that their child would be born with physical or mental defects. (In such cases the doctor can be liable to the parents as well as to the child, if the baby is born defective.) The court in this case noted that ". . . a plaintiff-child in a wrongful life action may not recover **general damages** for being born impaired as opposed to not being born at all. . . ."[17]

The debate over tort reform has shifted back and forth between courts and legislatures. California, for example, has placed a limit of $250,000 on awards of general damages in medical malpractice cases. This has survived constitutional challenge in court. In Texas, on the other hand, the Supreme Court struck down a cap of $500,000 because it found no relationship between the rise in malpractice insurance rates and the damage limit. The Supreme Court of Kansas also invalidated damage award limits and went further—it rejected a statute requiring that payments to plaintiffs for future losses be made in the less-costly form of annuities rather than in lump sums.

Possessor of Land as Defendant

The ownership or possession of real estate creates duties and imposes burdens. One burden is the ongoing possibility of a lawsuit because of any failure to exercise due care in maintaining the premises—urban or rural—in a reasonably safe condition for others. Most courts define the duties of care in terms of the type of person protected, namely trespasser, licensee, and invitee. Thus, uniquely, liability is based on the defendant's conduct but also varies radically with the status of the plaintiff.

Trespassers on Real Property   Adult trespassers to real property are uninvited, generally unexpected, and unwanted. To them minimal duty is owed—the owner (or occupier) must not set traps or spring guns to thwart or hurt trespassers or burglars, nor otherwise intentionally harm them. A landowner need not warn of dangerous natural conditions, but if trespassers are known to be on the premises there is a duty to warn of man-made risks they are not likely to discover (e.g., an attack guard dog).

It was the first day of the summer holiday. Jimmy Parker and Tom Rouble, both 10 years old, rode their bicycles into the country. They spotted an unattended tractor near the road, on the farm of Jensen Dairy, Inc. Tom said: "Let's see if we can start it!" Within minutes they were over the fence and fiddling with the controls of the machine. The engine started and in a sudden forward lurch, Jimmy was thrown off and broke his arm. On his behalf, Jimmy's parents sued the Jensen Dairy for damages. Who should have won?

Jimmy and his parents. Young children are an exception in the rules for trespassers. When they trespass because of natural curiosity about an **attractive nuisance** and are injured, the owner is liable. Attractive nuisances that are highly dangerous to children have included a fall by a 7-year-old girl from the second floor of a house under construction, an abandoned, burned-out semi-trailer with melted remnants of red tail lights that fell on an 8-year-old boy, and an open sewer drain where a 19-month-old child was found drowned.[18]

In deciding whether the attractive nuisance doctrine applies, courts consider (1) whether the defendant knew or should have known of the likelihood of trespassing children, and of the unreasonable risk of death or serious injury to them from an artificial (i.e., man-made) condition; (2) whether the children, because of their youth, do not realize the risk involved; and (3) whether the benefit of maintaining the condition, coupled with the burden or cost of eliminating the hazard, are slight compared to the risk to the children.

Licensees   A **licensee** enters the property and remains there with the implied or express permission or consent of the owner or possessor for the *visitor's convenience or benefit*. Generally, the occupier of land owes the licensee a duty of reasonable care, but has no duty to inspect premises for dangerous conditions that are not obvious. However, once dangers are known, they must be repaired or the licensee must be warned.

Social guests, U.S. Postal Service employees, public utility employees (e.g., meter readers), and building and health inspectors are licensees. Even policemen and firemen are licensees under the *fireman's rule*. Probably the vast majority of fires are caused by negligence; yet once started, they also threaten the property of neighbors. Thus public policy generally bars suits by firefighters for injuries suffered in performing their work. But, of course, the owner is duty bound to warn the firefighters of any hidden hazards he or she is aware of, if there is an opportunity to do so. Courts are divided on whether the owner is liable to the firefighter injured in a fire caused by the owner's wanton and willful misconduct (e.g., arson).

Invitees   An **invitee** enters the land or building after invitation or with the consent (implied or express) of the owner *for a business purpose benefiting the owner (or both parties)*. Shoppers and customers in retail stores, and patrons of restaurants, hotels, theaters, and amusement parks are all invitees. To them, the owner owes a high duty of care for their safety. He or she must routinely inspect for dangerous conditions, and either correct them or clearly warn the invitees.

Viola Taffat was walking in the properly maintained aisle of a supermarket, wearing her new high-heel pumps for the first time. Suddenly her left ankle twisted, and she tumbled to the floor. As she fell, she grasped at an empty shopping cart nearby, and it came down on her head. The impact broke her dentures and caused a painful, unsightly gash in her face. She sues the owner of the supermarket for damages. Is there liability?

No. Viola was an invitee, but the market is not an insurer of her safety. The accident resulted from her inability to use high-heel shoes safely. To recover damages she would have to prove (1) that the premises were in a dangerously defective condition; (2) that this condition was the result of the market owner's conduct, or that it existed long enough for him or her to learn about and correct it; and (3) that the usual rules of causation were satisfied (see the discussion of causation discussed earlier in this chapter). It is interesting to note that the California Supreme Court has abolished the traditional triple classification of trespasser-licensee-invitee status as the basis for liability. It has simply substituted the familiar duty to exercise the care of ". . . a reasonable man* in view of the probability of injury to others . . . although the plaintiff's status . . . may . . . have some bearing on the question of liability. . . ."[19]

What Is an Intentional Tort?

It has been said that the wiles of humans are infinite. In many situations, men, women, and children are motivated by greed, anger, revenge, lust, a perverted sense of humor, a distorted sense of justice, a craving for costly drugs, or a desperate quest for a quick "solution" to poverty or unemployment. So impelled, they purposely engage in anti-social conduct when they know or should know it may harm others. Deliberate conduct that is regarded by law as wrong and that causes injury to the person or property of another is an *intentional tort*. It clearly differs from negligence, which is careless, wrongful conduct. In many cases, the tort is so objectionable and offensive to society that it is termed a *crime,* and as such it is punishable by fine, imprisonment, or even death. Because most persons do not deliberately commit acts that have a high probability of injury to others, intentional torts are encountered much less frequently than negligent torts. Nevertheless, they are many in number and varied in type. Nine of the most significant are described below, in alphabetical order.

Assault and Battery

Assault is an intentional threat or attempt that places a person in fear or simple apprehension of an immediate harmful or offensive touching.

Lon Shark was arguing loudly with "Spike" Flack over a debt. Finally Spike said: "Listen, Buster, I've paid you off. Get lost!" He turned his back and started to walk away. Without uttering a word, Lon grabbed a baseball bat from the ground and swung violently at Spike's head, but missed. Oblivious of the act, Spike got into his truck and drove away. Was Lon guilty of the tort of assault?

No, because Spike, his intended target, was not aware of the deadly attempt. (Note that Lon could be found guilty of the *crime* of assault, which does not require the victim's apprehension. For a more complete discussion of this, see Chapter 4.)

A *battery* is the harmful or offensive touching of another person without justification, consent, or excuse. A successful hook to the jaw of someone you don't like is a classic example of a battery. A hook that misses because the victim saw it

---

* The court referred to "a reasonable *man*," using the term in its generic sense to cover women as well, and also children who have reached the age of reason.

coming and dodged in time is an assault. An assault often precedes, but is not an essential element of, a battery.

As part of a medical experiment, employees of the University of Chicago (in cooperation with drug manufacturer Eli Lilly & Co.) caused the drug diethylstilbestrol (DES) to be administered at its Lying-In Hospital to some pregnant patients without their knowledge. The drug was designed to prevent miscarriages. Subsequently, more than a thousand of the women alleged that their female children had suffered an increased propensity for cancer as a side effect of the drug. Were the women victims of actionable batteries?

Yes. Batteries occurred because the women did not consent to the experiment.[20] Certainly the hospital personnel intended no harm; quite the contrary. Nevertheless, it was a tort because the act of administering the drug was intentional. Note that even if the drug had no harmful effects, indeed even if it had had beneficial effects, there would have been batteries. Such touching without prior permission would be offensive because, in the words of the Restatement of the Law of Torts, ". . . it offends a reasonable sense of personal dignity."[21]

In medical practice, before administering experimental drugs, performing a surgical operation, or providing other treatment, doctors must obtain the **informed consent** of their patients. The patient must be told what risks are involved and what available alternatives exist. The consent need not be in writing and may be implied from conduct. However, doctors and hospitals are increasingly concerned about malpractice suits and usually do insist on written consent for any surgery. In cases of true emergency, when consent cannot be obtained, it is not required.

One is required to tolerate the close proximity of other persons in crowded public places. Thus, for example, bodily contact with strangers—which may be unpleasant and offensive to some sensitive individuals—is quite legal when necessary or inadvertent, as in buses and trains during rush hours, even though similar touching would be actionable battery at other times of the day.

Bad Faith in Payment of Legitimate Claims

Bad faith is the opposite of good faith in behavior. It involves dishonest intention, resulting in the defrauding or deceiving of another. Typically, there is a deliberate failure to fulfill some duty or contractual obligation, prompted by immoral purpose, with sinister execution. The tort of bad faith in actions against insurance companies, for example, generally involves either of two scenarios:

1. The insurance company (or carrier) provides protection for its customer (or insured) against claims made by persons injured by the insured (e.g., in an auto accident). The carrier investigates and usually pays the claim. Sometimes the carrier resists, and lets a court decide the amount of damages due (if any). What if the carrier refuses an offer by the plaintiff to settle for $100,000, the policy limit, and the court subsequently awards damages of $200,000? The insured must pay the extra $100,000 since the carrier, under its insurance policy, had to pay only $100,000. If the carrier acted in bad faith in refusing to settle, some courts would hold it liable for the full award.

2. The carrier, acting in bad faith, unreasonably delays payment of a legitimate claim for a loss suffered by the insured. "Bad faith" in this context may reflect the carrier's neglect or refusal to comply with contract terms. The reason may be a furtive plan to retain imputed interest on delayed payments, a desire to gamble on a less-costly award by a jury even when the claim is just and fair, or an attempt to induce a needy claimant to settle for less because he or she can't afford to wait or to litigate.

Normally, the only damages collectible for breach of a contract are compensatory. They are designed to do no more than make good the loss suffered. But if an intentional tort such as bad faith conduct is involved, the court may award punitive damages in addition to compensatory damages to punish and make an example of the wrongdoer. Courts in some states reason that insurance contracts contain an implied-in-law duty of good faith and fair dealing. This includes an obligation to accept a good faith settlement within the limits of the policy. Bad faith is a violation of that implied duty and gives rise to the tort action. Under the indicated circumstances, a plaintiff may therefore elect to sue under the tort theory.[22]

Conversion of Another's Personal Property

Any unauthorized taking of the personal property of another and wrongfully exercising rights of ownership is the tort of **conversion.** It can involve taking such things as (1) a house trailer, (2) stock certificates sold by a broker without authorization, (3) architectural plans for a residence, even though the building is in public view, and (4) the rerecording and sale of recorded musical performances owned by the plaintiff record manufacturer.[23]

Glen Glennie finds a valuable single reflex camera in a leather case under a bench at Disney World in Orlando, Florida. A business card inside has the name, address, and phone number of Daniel Daze, with the words "Reward for Return." Glennie recalls the ditty "Finders Keepers, Losers Weepers" from his childhood and decides to keep the camera. Has he committed a crime or a tort?

Both. Glennie has committed the crime of larceny, just as robbers and burglars do. Like them, he is also guilty of the tort of conversion. Unfortunately for Daze, the crime and tort will probably go undetected and unpunished. The finder is a constructive bailee of the goods. (A *bailee* is a person to whom goods are entrusted, for use, storage, or other purposes. The bailee has temporary possession, coupled with a duty to return or dispose of the goods in accordance with the trust. For example, Hertz, as bailor, may "rent" a car to you, as bailee.) As a bailee, Glennie should make a reasonable effort to find the owner, usually with the assistance of the local police. If no one claims the item within a reasonable time, the finder gets it to keep. In any conversion, whether crime or tort, the victim may sue for damages equal to the fair market value of the property. In effect it becomes a forced purchase. If there is no market value but high sentimental value, as with photos or certain heirlooms, the court may take that into account and will specify a reasonable value.

A brief, temporary, and unauthorized interference with the personal property rights of another is termed a **trespass to chattel.** The owner is entitled to damages for the limited loss of possession and any actual harm to the property. But the wrongdoer is not compelled to pay the full market value. An example is the deliberate scratching of a parked automobile (which is a tort and the crime of malicious mischief). Repainting is costly and time consuming, but such tortfeasors are usually juvenile "hit and run" types who are not likely to be caught.

Defamation

Defamation is a lie, either oral (called *slander*) or written (called *libel*), which tends to harm the reputation of the victim. It reduces the goodwill and respect a person has previously enjoyed, and subjects her or him to ridicule and contempt, and possibly hatred by others. The critical element is the effect on third parties, people in the community. Thus there can be no civil defamation without *publication,* which means communication to at least one third party. Accordingly, if one person lies about another to his or her face in private, or sends him or her a defamatory letter which only the victim reads, there is no civil defamation. (Note that this could be criminal defamation, because an unpublished lie can provoke a breach of the peace, as, for example, if the victim reacts violently by battering the defamer.) If the letter is dictated to a secretary and then delivered to the victim, there has been publication.

The furor caused by defamation is better understood when one realizes that a person's reputation or good name is usually a delicate mental image in the minds of other persons in the community. It is a priceless possession available to both poor and rich, taking years to develop. Yet it is very fragile and can be shattered in seconds by one false statement (or damaging *true* statement, but that would *not* be actionable defamation). Defamation has been likened to cutting open a down-filled pillow in a violent windstorm. To fully restore the good reputation, through denial by the victim and retraction by the tortfeasor, is like gathering up all of the thousands of tiny feathers that have scattered far and wide in the storm—practically impossible.

Slander   Slander is a false spoken or transitory gesture about the victim. To collect, the plaintiff must prove actual monetary loss, technically called *special damages* (discussed later in this chapter). However, certain types of slander are so obviously harmful to reputation that special damages are presumed to exist, and need not be proved. Such cases of *slander per se,* defamatory as a matter of law, exist whenever the defendant falsely publishes that the plaintiff (1) has committed a crime punishable by imprisonment; (2) has an existing venereal disease or other loathsome and communicable disease; (3) is unfit for his or her lawful business, trade, profession, or office (public or private); or (4) is guilty of serious sexual misconduct.[24]

Not every false statement about another person is actionable, even though it may contain vituperative, derogatory, or disparaging terms.

In the presence of other persons, Marjorie Taylor, a high school teacher, told Monty Standby, her principal, that he was ". . . plain stupid . . . not qualified . . . a disgrace to the profession . . ." and ". . . just like Lee Harvey Oswald . . . and Jack Ruby." Principal Monty sued. Who should have won?

Principal Monty won a jury verdict of $75,775 at the trial level. But judgment was reversed on appeal because Marjorie's language was not sufficiently defamatory to be slanderous.[25]

Libel   **Libel** is false written or printed communication. As such, it is in a more durable form than slander and tends to have a stronger, longer-lasting impact. Accordingly, the victim may recover general damages without prior proof of actual, out-of-pocket special damages, such as lost wages.

The Privilege to Defame Others   Public policy requires that certain persons be permitted and encouraged to express their ideas without restraint or fear of lawsuits for defamation. In our republic or representative democracy, legislative, executive, and judicial officers are encouraged to speak out for the common good. Legislators during legislative proceedings; judges, lawyers, jurors, and witnesses during judicial proceedings; top officials of the executive branch (notably the President and Vice President, Cabinet members, and major department heads); as well as high-level officials of administrative agencies, acting in the official performance of their duties, have an **absolute privilege** to say anything, even if it is false, malicious, or self-serving. The media (newspapers, magazines, and radio and television stations) have an absolute privilege in quoting the identified officials verbatim. Understandably, there is an absolute privilege between husband and wife for communications concerning third persons and for parents in expressing opinions to their children about romantic partners.

A qualified or **conditional privilege** exists for creditors who may, in good faith, exchange defamatory information about debtors whose creditworthiness is a mutual concern. A similar conditional privilege exists between employers with reference to qualifications of past and prospective employees. The privilege is qualified or conditional in the sense that the employer must act in good faith and without negligence. But note that the statements must be well founded. Nevertheless, many employers prudently refuse to express any opinion about the quality of performance of former employees, because of a fear of lawsuits claiming defamation. Even when one is vindicated, legal defense is costly.

Special Status of Newspapers   A very important expansion of the right of newspapers to print libelous materials was made by the U.S. Supreme Court in 1964, in a famous case involving the *New York Times*. The court held that the common law of libel is superseded in part by the First and Fourteenth Amendments to the U.S. Constitution, with reference to articles about public officials or public figures.[26] In effect, it gives the media a measure of the absolute privilege enjoyed by government officials as previously noted. The *New York*

Times rule bars public officials or public figures from recovering for defamatory falsehoods unless they can prove the statement was made with actual malice. *Actual malice,* here, means that it was made with prior knowledge that it was false, or with reckless disregard of whether it was true or false. Moreover, the defamation must be proved by clear and convincing evidence, which is more than the preponderance of evidence standard usually required in civil cases. Significantly, a number of state courts have applied the rule and extended it to non-media defendants as well.

Some 22 years later, in a 1986 case involving the *Philadelphia Inquirer,* the U.S. Supreme Court reinforced free speech–free press protection of the media. It held that under the U.S. Constitution, when a newspaper publishes speech of public concern about a *private figure,* the plaintiff bears ". . . the burden of showing falsity as well as fault, before recovering damages." Generally, if a newspaper defames someone who is a private rather than public figure, prompt retraction and apology are mitigating circumstances that may affect the award of punitive damages. The U.S. Supreme Court, to encourage freedom of expression, has ruled that punitive damages may not be awarded to private defamation plaintiffs in actions against media defendants (e.g., newspapers, and radio and TV stations) without proof of actual malice. The paper remains liable only for actual monetary **special damages,** and these are likely to be modest. However, in 1990, the Supreme Court imposed a new restraint on the press. It held that statements of opinion, as well as statements of facts, can be libelous. In the words of the court, saying "In my opinion Jones is a liar" is the same thing as saying "Jones is a liar."[27]

False Imprisonment and False Arrest

False imprisonment is the wrongful restraint of the physical liberty of another. It involves detention of the victim and restraint of his or her freedom of movement. There must be confinement within a given area, large or small, by means of physical barriers and/or physical force or threatened force. Generally the victim must be aware of the confinement, but it may be for no longer than the time required to recognize the fact. **False arrest** by an officer with legal authority (or even by one who pretends to have such authority) is a variety of false imprisonment.

Because of the prevalence of self-service in stores where merchandise is openly displayed, the crime of shoplifting reportedly costs merchants (and ultimately consumers) billions of dollars annually. The exact figure is unknown largely because some inventory shortages are also caused by employee pilferage. Attempts to reduce these losses through closer surveillance and the employment of plain-clothes private security personnel have brought about more arrests and charges of false imprisonment. Legislatures and police are generally sympathetic to the plight of the storeowners.

To help protect affected business firms, legislatures in many states have enacted laws that establish the *Shopkeeper's Privilege.* These statutes permit a retail merchant or authorized employee to detain a person if there are reasonable grounds to believe that the suspect has shoplifted. To reduce the number of law-suits and charges of abuse of privilege, prudent store security people use minimum restraint and promptly summon official police to conduct the search and make an arrest, if justified. As a further precaution, security people usually wait until the suspect has left the store and therefore cannot claim "I'm still shopping" when detained.

Fraud

Fraud is a tort most frequently committed in sales of goods or services. It is also called **deceit.** For fraud, the following elements must be present:

1. A false representation (i.e., a lie);
2. of a factual matter (not personal opinion, unless the opinion is that of an expert on the subject);
3. that is material (i.e., important enough to affect the decision of the intended victim);
4. known by the wrongdoer to be false, or made with reckless indifference as to its truth;
5. made with intent to induce action by the victim, who is unaware of its falsity;
6. and acting reasonably, the victim does justifiably rely on the lie in his or her decision; and
7. is injured as a result.

In a simple, often-repeated type of case, a seller of a used car may misrepresent the mileage,* the times and frequency of servicing and of overhaul, the number and identity of previous owners, or the number and nature of accidents, if any, in which the vehicle has been involved. A knowledgeable car buff might not be misled, but many amateurs would buy in trusting reliance and, if victimized, could therefore sue for damages.

Fraud may also occur under unusual circumstances, as the following cases indicate.

Peter Roberts, an 18-year-old Sears sales clerk, invented a quick-release socket wrench in his spare time. He applied for and received a patent in 1965. Thereafter, Sears negotiated to buy Peter's patent rights. He was told that (1) the invention was "not new," (2) the production cost would be 40¢ to 50¢ per wrench (Sears knew it would be only 20¢), and (3) it would sell only to the extent promoted and, hence, it was worth only $10,000. Peter agreed to accept a 2¢ royalty up to a maximum of $10,000. Within days Sears was manufacturing 44,000 of Peter's wrenches per week. A half million wrenches were sold in nine months. By 1975 more than 19 million wrenches had been sold for a net profit of more than $44 million, according to court records. Was Sears guilty of the tort of fraud?

Yes! A jury awarded Peter $1 million in damages. The U.S. Court of Appeals affirmed and also authorized Peter to rescind (set aside) his contract and sue Sears

---

* In a gross example of this offense, Chrysler Corporation was fined $7.6 million by a federal district court judge for selling thirty previously damaged vehicles as new cars, and for odometer violations. Chrysler had previously entered a plea of no contest to the criminal charges. The fine supplemented an earlier settlement of more than $16 million in a civil suit. Records showed that between 1949 and 1986, Chrysler personnel had disconnected the odometers on about 60,000 new cars that were driven for periods of one day to five weeks by Chrysler executives before being placed on sale as brand new. In the thirty specially noted cases, the cars had been damaged while being driven by the executives, and repaired before sale as new. Reported in the *San Francisco Chronicle,* August 11, 1990.

for breach of his patent. In 1982, a federal jury awarded Peter $5 million, and the judge increased this to $8.2 million, on the grounds that the infringement was willful. In 1983, this decision was overturned by the Court of Appeals, which ordered a new trial. In September 1989, 25 years after receiving his patent, Peter and his attorney finally again confronted Sears in court. This time the trial was in its fifth day when the litigants reached a settlement agreement. At the time a Sears spokesperson said that a term of the settlement was that neither side could comment on it.[28]

Soldier Steven Melandris, a truck driver in Korea, met and married Jung Ja, who was illiterate. Returning to the United States, their marriage was dominated by a quest for financial security. Steven worked as a baggage handler for United Airlines in Colorado; Jung Ja managed their money. They lived meagerly in order to save some $60,000, which they invested in United's stock. Steven met John Barron, an account executive for Merrill Lynch, Pierce Fenner & Smith, Inc. (a major securities firm), who prompted Steven to forge his wife's name to get access to the family money held as stock and to invest it in commodity options. Barron told Steven there would be an "assured gain" and "no possibility" of any loss. However, soon $30,000 was gone. Jung Ja sustained permanent emotional injury, which allegedly ". . . destroyed her ability to function as a human being. . . . She rejected this world and lives only in anticipation of life after death." May Jung Ja recover damages for fraud?

Yes. A six-person jury awarded compensatory damages of $1,030,000, plus punitive damages of $3,000,000. When denying a motion for new trial, the judge commented, "This is not a case of a lost investment; it is the tragedy of a lost life."[29]

Not all **misrepresentations** are tortious. A person commits no tort when he or she innocently does not know the information is false, but mistakenly tells you that a dog he or she is selling you is two years old when in fact it is five. Generally, you have the option of rescinding the contract (by returning the dog and getting your money back), or renegotiating the sale price. Of course, a professional veterinarian seller who knows or should know the true age could be guilty of fraud under these circumstances.

Opinions of quality in advertisements and sales talks ("the finest car on the road," "enjoy the pleasure of the best in international travel," "the best in cordless telephone just got better") are actual examples of customary commercial "puffing" and are not actionable. Social fibs likewise are not actionable (e.g., "I'll be there at 5 P.M.." and the person doesn't arrive until 6 P.M., or not at all.).

Invasion of Privacy

Most states recognize the right of **privacy** either by means of common law case decisions or by appropriate statutes. The Restatement of Torts recognizes four broad categories of invasion that may justify the award of damages:
1. Unreasonable intrusion on the seclusion of another
2. Appropriation of the other's name or likeness
3. Unreasonable publicity given to the other's private life
4. Publicity that unreasonably places the other in a false light before the public.[30]

In one famous case, consumer advocate Ralph Nader's privacy was violated by General Motors Corporation after he had criticized their automobiles. GMC employed persons who threatened him, tapped his telephone, and attempted to entice him with women—all in a futile effort to silence him.[31] In another notable case, television talk-show host Johnny Carson blocked the use of the phrase "Here's Johnny" by a corporation engaged in renting and selling portable toilets.[32] But generally public personages, such as sports and entertainment stars, cannot claim a right of privacy in their public image, performance, or duties. Usually they need, want, and solicit publicity to advance their careers; thus, in effect, waiving customary rights of privacy.

All states, as well as the federal government, have enacted laws that supplement the tort of invasion of privacy. These include legislation concerning the wrongful opening of mail, electronic eavesdropping and telephone wiretappings, and disclosure of income taxes paid and welfare payments received.

Interference with an Economically Advantageous Relationship

The Texaco-Pennzoil legal drama of 1984–88 involved an extreme example of what some authors call a "contort": a contract tainted by a tort, and therefore subject to possible punitive as well as normal compensatory damages in the event of breach. This is known as the tort of **interference with an economically advantageous relationship.** Generally, there must be a contract in existence between two parties, and the defendant must induce one of the parties to breach the contract. Thus a computer software manufacturer might wrongfully induce a talented software designer to breach a fixed term employment contract with the plaintiff and join the defendant's staff at a higher salary. This must be distinguished from the common case where an employee has the right to quit *at will,* and does so in order to join another company. This move may be encouraged by legitimate advertising and other forms of solicitation, such as the promise of higher income and greater responsibilities.

In the Texaco-Pennzoil case, the tort was committed when Texaco prevented the performance or full execution of the terms of a binding "agreement in principle" between Pennzoil and Getty. Although there was no formal written contract between Pennzoil and Getty, they had been engaged in a serious business relationship with a reasonable expectation of successful completion. This unprecedented drama involving a judgment in billions of dollars is traced chronologically in the following highlight.

The Legal Battle between Texaco and Pennzoil

It was a battle of giant oil companies in which the stakes were measured in billions of dollars.

• *January 4, 1984:* Getty Oil Company, rich in undeveloped oil and gas reserves, announces it has accepted, "in principle," an agreement for a leveraged buyout by Pennzoil Company that would give Pennzoil 43 percent of Getty. Price: $110 per share of Getty stock (plus a $5 stub, payable later).

- *January 5, 1984:* Texaco, Inc. agrees to buy the same Getty Oil property for a price of $9.98 billion, at $125 per share.
- *November 19, 1984:* A jury in Houston, Texas, awards Pennzoil $7.53 billion in compensatory damages and $3 billion in punitive damages in a suit against Texaco. There was no formal written contract between Pennzoil and Getty, as is generally required for valid sales of this type (see Chapter 6 discussion of the Statute of Frauds). However, Pennzoil successfully argued that a news release, written by Getty personnel but issued by both companies, had announced "an agreement in principle" on the terms of a four-page Memorandum of Agreement. This memorandum had been signed by the CEO of Pennzoil and by parties who controlled a majority of the Getty shares. This evidence, coupled with handshakes and other indicia, constituted a binding agreement under Texas law, and Texaco had acted tortiously in interfering with that contract. Texaco lawyers had unsuccessfully contended that under New York law, until a formal contract existed, Texaco was free to become involved as it did by offering the higher price.
- *February 12, 1987:* The intermediate Court of Appeals of Texas affirms the judgment, but reduces the punitive damages to $1 billion.
- *April 17, 1987:* Texaco files for bankruptcy in a Chapter 11 proceeding, thus avoiding an immediate need to post a $12 billion bond while it files further appeals.
- *November 6, 1987:* The Texas Supreme Court affirms the judgment. Texaco plans an appeal to the U.S. Supreme Court.
- *July 20, 1987:* Pennzoil offers to settle for $4.1 billion. Texaco reputedly counteroffers to pay $2 billion.
- *December 25, 1987:* Pennzoil agrees to accept Texaco's final settlement offer of $3 billion, with these provisos:

    1. Getty Oil is to be absolved of any legal liability.
    2. Texaco shareholders are to approve the plan and agree to give up the right to sue Texaco officers and directors for malfeasance. (Three billion dollars was about 20 percent of Texaco's net worth, and three times the net worth of Pennzoil.)

- *March 25, 1988:* Reorganized Texaco emerges from Chapter 11 bankruptcy.

Source: Facts on File, references to Texaco in issues for indicated dates in 1984, 1987 and 1988, (New York City, N.Y., Facts on File, Inc.) See also *Texaco Inc.* v. *Pennzoil Co.,* 728 S.W.2d 768 (Texas, 1987). Reprinted with permission *Facts on File Inc.,* New York.

Employees, acting collectively, may legally interfere with the commercial expectations of their employers by a lawful strike (see Chapter 9). Note also that employers may compete with each other, vigorously but fairly, for business in the open market. This is true even when the practice drives some competitors into bankruptcy as customers flock to the aggressive firm that offers a better deal (in quantity, price, service, delivery, credit, etc.).

Outrageous Conduct

Some intentional, or reckless, conduct is so extreme and outrageous that it causes severe emotional distress. There is no physical touching of the plaintiff (as in a battery), nor apprehension of an immediate harmful or offensive touching (as in assault). Because of the absence of physical harm, such claims have formerly been rejected. They are easy to make, yet difficult to disprove. Nevertheless, most courts now hold that in a proper case such injury is real and compensable.

To be actionable, the wrongful conduct must be <u>describable as atrocious, utterly intolerable in today's society, and exceeding the bounds of all decency.</u> Courts have found liability where (1) to facilitate the arrest of a mentally ill woman, law enforcement officers falsely told her that her husband and child had been badly hurt and were hospitalized; and (2) after a cursory examination, a physician refused to further assist a 10-month-old child who had been seriously injured in an auto accident and brought to his office late at night. The mother, also injured, and the child were compelled to wait outside in subfreezing weather while someone came to get them.[33]

Mark Goldfarb, a student at Tennessee State University, was attending Professor Baker's class when an unidentified assailant surreptitiously entered the room and threw a pie that hit Baker. The professor immediately, but erroneously, accused Mark of the offense. The next day Professor Baker barred Mark from the classroom and had him ejected from the building, still believing he was the culprit. Mark suffered emotional distress, especially because he was an ex-prisoner attempting personal rehabilitation; the accusation of law-lessness was particularly offensive to him. Mark sued the professor for the tort of outrageous conduct. Will he prevail?

No. The conduct was not actionable because the professor acted under provocation, and his conduct, although wrong, was the product of the sudden, unjustified, and humiliating attack.[34] This type of reflexive encounter is simply one of life's frictions and irritations for which there is no legal remedy.

Some states continue to recognize the very similar tort of **intentional infliction of mental distress.** One who intentionally acts in a manner that reasonably may be expected to cause severe mental distress to another is liable to the victim. This tort arises when creditors, often with the assistance of collection agencies, pursue debtors in an especially aggressive manner. The problem became so acute that in 1977 Congress enacted the **Fair Debt Collection Practice Act.** It prohibits abusive tactics such as threats of violence or use of obscene language, harassing telephone calls, and publication of "shame" lists. In communicating with third parties to learn the location of a debtor, one may not even state that he or she owes a debt. Abused debtors may seek damages of up to $1,000 plus court costs and reasonable attorney fees. The act does not apply to creditors who do their own collecting, but in a proper case they may instead be subject to claims for outrageous conduct.

When Is Civil Tort Liability Absolute?

As a matter of public policy, the tortfeasor is absolutely liable in a limited number of tort cases. The victimized plaintiff need not prove intent or negligence; in such instances the defendant is liable even if not at fault. This is true, for example, in the comparatively rare cases where the defendant keeps a wild animal, with dangerous propensities, that injures someone. Circus and carnival elephants, lions, and tigers may have been trained or tamed, but they remain wild. In contrast, some wild animals—such as deer, oxen, and monkeys—are excluded if they have been domesticated to live peaceably in the service of humans. Nevertheless, the owner of domestic animals, including dogs, is absolutely liable for injuries they inflict if the owner knew of their dangerous propensities. Thus a guard dog, known to be vicious, is not entitled to a first "free bite."

Of course the owner of an ordinary dog or cat not believed to be abnormally dangerous would be liable if he or she directed the animal to harm another, or negligently failed to prevent the harm. Animal behavior is often unpredictable and uncontrollable, and it is difficult to prove prior knowledge of viciousness. Therefore, some 30 states have enacted statutes that impose strict liability on owners of dogs that injure others, or specify that negligence need not be proved (e.g., as in roving dog cases and when leash laws are violated).

Certain activities are generally deemed to be so hazardous as to justify imposition of absolute liability on the responsible actor. Examples of such ultrahazardous activities are fumigating buildings with poisonous gasses and blasting with explosives in populated areas. Operating a nuclear reactor is regarded by many persons as an ultrahazardous activity. To date, there has been no Chernobyl-type disaster with loss of life in the United States. Nevertheless, Congress has responded to the potential threat with the Price-Anderson Act of 1957, which placed a liability limit on the nuclear power industry of $710 million in damages, with any additional claims to be paid by the federal government. The limit was raised in 1988 to $7.1 billion, and extended to cover university research reactors, nuclear weapons plants, and nuclear waste repositories.

Workers' Compensation

A much more important category of absolute liability is that imposed on employers when a worker is injured or killed on the job. In all states workers' compensation insurance laws now cover most employees, although farm or agriculture workers and domestic servants in homes are still excluded in some states. Under **workers' compensation,** workers receive (1) all medical treatment necessary to cure or provide relief from effects of employment-caused injuries or illness, (3) temporary or permanent disability payments, (3) vocational rehabilitation and retraining benefits when unable to return to the former job, and (4) legal assistance without charge. The benefit payments are not lavish (e.g., after many years, the weekly maximum in California rose from $224 to $266 in 1990 and then to $336 in 1991). Under some circumstances, this may be supplemented by Social Security disability payments, but together the benefits may not exceed 80 percent of the worker's average current earnings before disablement. The maximum death benefit is $95,000, with a $1,500 burial allowance. The payments are reasonably certain. Circumstances under which recovery would be denied are when the injury was the result of voluntary intoxication on the job, was intentionally self-inflicted, or the injured worker was the aggressor in a fight.

Generally, workers' compensation is the exclusive remedy available against the employer in covered businesses.* This is a major improvement over the old common law rules, which permitted the worker to sue his or her employer—a costly and seldom prudent thing to do. For starters, the worker could be fired, if still alive. Thereafter, in court, the employer could avoid liability by proving (1) the worker knew the hazards involved and assumed the risk (perhaps in exchange for a higher wage), (2) the worker was guilty of contributory negligence, or (3) a co-worker's negligence caused the accident. It is important to note that even under workers' compensation rules, a third party who caused the injury may be liable. Thus coworkers may still be liable for intentional attacks or willful and wanton negligence. Also, workers injured by defective equipment may sue the manufacturer responsible in a strict liability action. (Strict liability is discussed in the next section.)

It was a glorious spring day as Willie Jon Fisher climbed to his workstation 125 feet above the bay. As a steelworker, he was paid premium wages for assuming the risk of his hazardous job on the new Silver Gate Bridge. In a burst of youthful exuberance, he removed his hard hat, waived to his pal Don Jones 20 feet above, and danced a quick jig on the beam where he stood. Jones shouted, "Simmer down and get to work!" and then playfully tossed a short section of scrap cable at Fisher. The cable struck Willie's head and he fell, hitting a cross beam before the safety net caught his unconscious body. His injuries were permanent and he never returned to the job. Is his employer liable in any way?

Yes. Any covered employee injured on the job is entitled to benefits under the state's workers' compensation law. Years ago, before the enactment of workers compensation laws, Fisher's employer could have successfully used all three of the old common law defenses of assumption of risk, contributory negligence, and negligence of an associate worker. Today, none of these defenses is admissible.

Pressures to speed up production have accounted for more accidents on the job in recent years. Increasing numbers of workers have filed successful claims for mental stress and for strain injuries caused by repetitive hand motions. Many workers complain about aching wrists and sore fingers incurred in garment factories, meat packing plants, post offices with letter sorting machines, newspaper offices with video display terminals, and supermarkets with bar-code scanners at check-out counters. Health care and workers' compensation costs for workplace injuries and death exceeded $42 billion in 1986, according to the National Safety Council. Employers complain because premiums have risen more than twice as fast as the rate of inflation, and workers complain that benefit payments are too low.[35] Fortunately, insurance premiums are a deductible business expense for

---

* An uncommon exception would be when the employer fraudulently conceals a hazardous working condition, such as the presence of asbestos particles. In such a case, substantial damages may be claimed by the injured worker in a separate action. [See, e.g. *Johns-Manville Products Corp.* v. *Contra Costa Superior Court,* 27 Cal.3d 465, 612 P.2d 948, (1980)].

employers, and they can pass the cost along to their customers. On the receiving end, no federal income tax is assessed on workers' compensation insurance benefits (although Social Security disability payments may be subject to income tax).

What Is the Tort of Strict Liability for Defective Products?

Every year, millions of consumers are injured and thousands are killed by familiar products used in daily life. Usually there is nothing wrong with the product, but the user has been careless or has failed to follow instructions for proper use and maintenance. Examples include trucks and automobiles; power boats; skis, bats, hardballs, and other sports equipment; guns and firecrackers; knives; and patent and prescription medicines. The most innocent-appearing and useful product may in fact be lethal. For example, a child's pajamas may be made of highly inflammable chemical fabric, a sleek sedan may have a steering mechanism prone to failure, and a wonder drug that prevents miscarriages may cause cancer in any female child born to the patient.

Under common law rules, a person injured by a defective product may recover damages by proving that the product was negligently made. The negligence may be in the design, a lack of safety features, faulty materials or manufacture, or a failure to explain proper use and maintenance. Proving negligence in such cases is usually extremely difficult and costly, and often practically impossible. The suspect product may be made with thousands of interrelated component parts; these may have been assembled many years before, in a factory located thousands of miles away, possibly in a foreign land.

An injured plaintiff might also allege a breach of a contractual warranty (see Chapter 6). However, there might be no warranties or they may have expired, or recovery may be barred by a failure to give proper prompt notice of the breach. Moreover, warranties often provide for no more than repair or replacement of the product if defective, or at best for a refund of the purchase price.

In 1962, the California Supreme Court provided a solution by defining the new tort of strict liability for the manufacturer when a defective product is sold that injures a user. In this case, the product involved was an ingenious multipurpose power tool that could be used as a saw, a drill, and a wood lathe. It was purchased by the plaintiff's wife in 1955. In 1957, the plaintiff bought the attachments necessary to use it as a lathe to turn a large piece of wood. He had worked on a piece of wood several times without difficulty when it suddenly flew out of the machine and hit his forehead, causing a serious injury. Experts testified that an inadequate set of screws had been used by the manufacturer to hold parts of the machine together, and the machine's normal vibration caused the screws to be loosened and brought about the accident. The court stated that "A manufacturer is strictly liable in tort when an article he places on the market, knowing that it is to be used without inspection for defects, proves to have a defect that causes injury to a human being."[36]

In adopting the rule, the Restatement of Torts expanded the concept to include "injuries to any user or consumer or to his property," but qualified it by providing that the seller must be "engaged in the business of selling such a product . . . in a defective condition unreasonably dangerous to the user or consumer . . ." and that it ". . . is expected to and does reach the user or consumer without substantial change in the condition in which it is sold."[37] Many other jurisdictions, including such populous states as Illinois, Pennsylvania, and Texas, have adopted the rule. Contributory negligence of the plaintiff does not defeat his or her case. However some states, using comparative negligence, allow a reduction in damages. In some jurisdictions, if the product was produced in accordance with the then-existing state of the art, the injury-causing design is not considered a defect.

The rule of strict liability for defective products shifts the burden of resulting injuries from the user to the manufacturer. Middlemen such as wholesalers and retailers are also held responsible, as they are better equipped to pursue the manufacturer. The manufacturer may purchase added insurance, which becomes a routine cost of production. But in any case, producers of products can pass along added costs to all customers in the form of slightly higher prices. Manufacturers are encouraged, moreover, to be more careful in product design, pre-sale testing, inspection, quality control in production, post-sale follow-up of performance, and prompt recall and repair when defects are disclosed. In recent years many automobile models have been recalled for appropriate modifications to forestall costly strict liability litigation.

The following is a selection from a list of litigation groups of the Association of Trial Lawyers of America (ATLA), from the 1989 meeting of this influential organization. It suggests the range of areas and products that are currently subjects of strict product liability investigation and/or litigation:

- Accutane (an anti-acne drug linked to birth defects)
- Agent Orange (an herbicide used to defoliate jungles in the Vietnam War and suspected of causing cancer and genetic damage in soldiers exposed to it and their offspring)
- All-terrain vehicles
- Bendectin and Teratogens (chemicals linked to birth defects)
- BIC lighters
- Chymopapain (a drug used to treat herniated disks)
- Dalkon shield (contraceptive device associated with inflammatory disease and spontaneous abortion in users; removed from the market in 1974)
- DES (a drug used to prevent miscarriages but discontinued because of increased risk of cancer in women who had fetal exposure)
- HALCION(a drug used as a sleep-inducing medicine)
- IUDs (a birth control device)
- Motorcycle crashworthiness
- Silastic gel breast implants
- Tobacco products
- Transmissions
- Yugos[38]

What Are Compensatory Damages?

The word *damage* is often used to mean the *loss* caused by an injury. Perhaps just as often it is used to mean the *injury* itself (to a person, his or her property, or his or her rights). In the law, however, the plural version of the word—*damages*—means the *money awarded* by a court to a plaintiff in a civil action for loss and/or injury caused by a defendant's wrongful conduct. Damages may be awarded for a breach of contract, to put the plaintiff in the position he or she would have been in had the contract been performed as promised (see Chapter 6). They may also be awarded to a plaintiff because of a tort, for example an injury suffered in an accident caused by the defendant's negligence. The money received reimburses the plaintiff for medical bills (of doctors and hospital), property loss (a "totalled" car), lost wages, and/or future "lost" income that cannot be earned because of the plaintiff's injuries. Damages also are designed to compensate for physical impairment (e.g., spinal injury or broken arm), mental anguish, and/or pain and suffering (both present and prospective, because they are expected to continue into the indefinite future).

Fines imposed against criminals as punishment go to the state. Damages awarded against tortfeasors in civil actions go to the plaintiff. If two or more tortfeasors are responsible for a given injury, each is fully liable to pay the entire judgment, but of course the plaintiff is entitled to only one full recovery. In many states, a tortfeasor who pays all or more than his or her share of the damages is not entitled to any contribution or partial reimbursement from the others; a growing number of states, however, have abolished this archaic and unfair common law rule and permit contribution. Some (e.g., California and Wisconsin) divide the damages equally, while others (e.g., Iowa and New York) divide according to degree or percentage of the total fault. In cases where many manufacturers produce a harmful drug (e.g., 300 companies made DES) and the plaintiff cannot identify the maker of the medication he or she used, courts in California and New York have held that all manufacturers must pay the damages according to their share of the national market (in DES cases, during the year the plaintiff's mother took the drug). This is true even if a given manufacturer can prove it did not supply the particular prescription.

Special Damages

Compensatory damages are also called *actual damages,* because they consist of money awarded to the plaintiff for real (i.e., actual) loss or injury. Compensatory damages may consist of *special damages* and *general damages*. Special damages are often called *out-of-pocket costs,* because they can be specified and precisely measured in money. Common examples are the cost of a 5-day or 50-day stay in a hospital and the cost of repairing a car that was rear-ended. In awarding special damages for anticipated future losses, a jury may award the present value of such future sums, using an appropriate discount interest rate. The plaintiff gets a sum of money that, if invested at the selected interest (discount) rate, will grow over the years to precisely the amount that had been determined to be the total future monetary loss. Since World War II, inflation has caused a continuing decline in the purchasing power of the dollar. This fact of life may also be taken into consideration in calculating future expenses resulting from the injury. Special damages are the actual result of the particular loss or injury; they flow from it naturally and proximately because of the unique combination of circumstances in any given case.

General Damages

General damages, the second kind of compensatory damages, are also the actual and proximate result of the particular loss or injury. However, they flow from it without reference to any unique combination of circumstances; thus, they compensate for other than out-of-pocket monetary losses suffered. A prime example is compensation for pain and suffering, and mental distress caused by physical injuries (e.g., internal injuries to bones, soft-tissue, and vital organs; bruises, lacerations, and permanent disfigurement; or shock, fright, shame, and humiliation).

In certain cases, a plaintiff may recover special and general damages for personal loss suffered as the result of harm done by the defendant to a *third* party, such as a spouse or child. For example, a spouse may recover for loss of **consortium** with the injured or deceased mate. *Consortium* includes companionship, affection, and sexual relations. Damages for consortium are not recoverable by unmarried persons, regardless of the intimacy or duration of the relationship.

In early common law, if a victim died because of someone's tortious conduct, the death terminated all claims for damages. Today, however, **wrongful death statutes** compensate immediate dependent relatives for loss of companionship and financial support resulting from the death. The award may be as high as millions of dollars, such as when the victim was a highly paid executive with a surviving spouse and children. On the other hand, the death of a single person, with no children or other dependents, could result in no cause of action. However, some states have *survivor statutes* that provide that a decedent's cause of action survives the death. It is owned by the decedent's estate, rather than by the surviving dependents (if any). Damages recovered by the estate are then distributed in accordance with the decedent's last will or by intestate distribution (see Chapter 14).

What Are Punitive or Exemplary Damages?

In certain cases, the civil law resembles the criminal law in sanctions imposed. It punishes especially blameworthy wrongdoers who intentionally hurt other persons. It does this by awarding **punitive or exemplary damages** to the victim, in addition to compensatory damages. The purpose is not to enrich the plaintiff, who has already been fully compensated for his loss or injury; rather, the purpose is to punish and make an example of the wrongdoer in order to deter him or her and others from a repetition of the offense. This is so similar to the fines levied against criminals that many critics contend that all punitive damage awards should be paid to the state. Depriving plaintiffs of such "windfall profits" would presumably discourage litigation that may sometimes be motivated by questionable greed rather than justifiable need of the client and counsel.

Punitive damages are never awarded in breach of contract cases, unless they involve an intentional tort by the defendant, such as fraud or bad faith. In California, which has been a leader in this area, a more conservative Supreme Court has recently sharply limited insurance bad faith actions formerly permitted under a controversial earlier ruling. The new ruling holds that third parties have no right to sue insurance companies that fail to promptly pay plaintiffs' legitimate claims against insured policyholders. The insurer may, in good faith, decline to pay what it considers to be an excessive settlement on a claim of questionable validity.[39] In an even farther-reaching case, the California court also severely restricted the amount of damages that can be recovered by permanent workers who correctly allege that they have been fired without just cause. Such workers can no longer demand punitive tort damages, but must settle for lower compensatory damages which is all that is generally recoverable by the worker for the employer's breach of the employment contract.[40]

XYA Corporation, a California manufacturer of metal parts, sold many items to the U.S. Defense Department. Jonah Robinson, an honest XYA inspector, objected to a confidential company policy of using substandard imported steel. It was cheaper than domestic steel but did not comply with the government contract specifications. Jonah was reassigned to a desk job and told to "keep your trap shut or you're out." Nevertheless, he reported the quality problem to a government auditor. XYA fired him and denied his allegations. Tests of the metal by an independent laboratory proved him right. He sued XYA. What damages should Jonah have recovered?

Full compensatory damages plus substantial punitive damages. Firing "whistle blowers" such as Jonah is in violation of public policy and continues to justify the award of punitive damages, even in California, for the tort of wrongful termination of an employment contract.

Generally, punitive damages are available in cases of intentional tort, such as assault and battery, defamation, and fraud. They may also be awarded (1) in product liability cases, but only where the defendant acted despicably with willful and conscious disregard of the rights and safety of others; (2) in premises liability cases, where a tenant of an apartment building is the victim of criminal attack when the landlord knew of the danger of such attacks yet failed to take corrective action (e.g., by excluding unauthorized persons or preventing their access); and (3) where the defendant consumes alcohol to the point of intoxication when he or she plans to later operate a motor vehicle, and thereby harms another.[41]

Generally, punitive damages may not be awarded in the absence of compensatory damages. However, a victim who has suffered no actual loss or injury may recover **nominal general damages** (usually 6¢ or $1), so that punitive damages may then be assessed against the wrongdoer. An example would be a "Peeping Tom" whose prurient gaze caused no monetary loss to the plaintiff. The victim recovers nominal damages to support an added award of punitive damages.

In determining the proper amount of punitive damages, the nature and gravity of the offense are considered, as well as the defendant's ability to pay and the amount of compensatory damages awarded. Damage awards that are grossly inflated as a result of prejudice against large corporations, or passion, are typically substantially reduced or even rejected on appeal.

In a widely publicized case in 1989, a Los Angeles jury awarded the male lover of actor Rock Hudson $14.5 million in compensatory damages and $7.25 million in punitive damages, in an action against the estate of the deceased star. The jury found that Hudson, who died of AIDS, was guilty of conspiring with his personal secretary to keep the fatal affliction secret so that the plaintiff would continue his sexual relationship with the movie star. Is the damage award justified?

Yes. The trial judge reduced the compensatory damages to $5 million and the punitive damages to $500,000, saying he would order a new trial on damages if the plaintiff refused to accept the reductions.[42] When statutes authorize the trebling of damages, as in civil RICO (Racketeer Influenced and Corrupt Organizations Act) cases (see Chapter 4), and civil cases involving violations of federal anti-trust laws, additional sums for punitive damages cannot be awarded.

What Are Some Barriers to Recovery of Damages?

A person with a perfectly good cause of action may never recover any money if (1) he or she rests on his or her rights and is barred from suing by an applicable statute of limitations, or (2) he or she obtains a judgment but is unable to collect from a judgment-proof defendant.

Statutes of Limitation

Statutes of limitation "wipe the slate clean" after specified periods of time have elapsed without the filing of a lawsuit. They are legislative enactments that specify the limited periods of time during which the victim must formally initiate his or her action for legal relief, or, in the case of a crime, during which the government must prosecute the accused. (Chapter 4 discusses at greater length statutes of limitations for crimes.)

It is psychologically counterproductive and ethically questionable to keep a potential civil lawsuit or criminal indictment hovering over a wrongdoer indefinitely, like a Sword of Damocles. It discourages personal reform and tends to limit the individual's peace of mind as well as his or her social and economic productivity. Moreover, the country's judicial system is already crowded with current cases, and difficulties in determining the truth are multiplied by the passage of time, as evidence is lost or destroyed, memories fade, and parties and witnesses move or die.

Torts In most jurisdictions, an action to recover damages for tortious injury must be commenced within one (1) year from the date of commission of the negligent tort. The period is generally the same for intentional torts, except for fraud. The defrauded victim may not even be aware of the injury until much later, and so the time limit is usually three (3) years from time of discovery of the fraud. In 1989, New York's top Court of Appeals upheld the constitutionality of a 1986 statute that effectively extended the limit in cases involving injury by five toxic substances, including (most notably) DES. Regardless of how long ago the exposure to the substances occurred, the victim has a year in which to sue, starting with the date when the resulting injury was recognized. Generally in medical and legal malpractice actions, the statutory time does not begin to run until the plaintiff becomes aware of the injury suffered. Statutes of limitation are tolled and "the clock stops" while the defendant is out of the jurisdiction and during a plaintiff's minority. It is noteworthy that the statutory time limit for breach of contract (see Chapter 6) is typically two (2) years for oral contracts and four (4) years for written contracts and credit accounts. With crimes, the statutory periods of limitation reflect the gravity of the offenses. For felonies, three (3) years from the date of commission is typical; for misdemeanors, one (1) year. For murder, there is no limit.

Judgment-Proof Defendants

Winning a lawsuit does not ensure collection of damages. Even if found liable, the defendant may be **judgment-proof,** which means that he or she lacks sufficient liability insurance (if any) or other resources to pay (see Chapter 3). However, a judgment survives for years, and may be renewed or extended. Meanwhile it continues to grow, because the legal rate of interest (e.g., 10 percent annually in California) is added until the judgment is paid. Future earnings and other assets the debtor acquires (e.g., through gifts or by inheritance) during the life of the judgment may be levied on by the unsatisfied judgment creditor. A *levy* is a process whereby a court official confiscates assets of a judgment debtor to satisfy the judgment. The creditor has to first locate the debtor and identify the property.

Socially irresponsible debtors often "skip," sometimes leaving the city, state, and/or country and providing no forwarding address. The difficulty the FBI has in tracking down "most wanted" criminals suggests the cost and practical impossibility of locating and collecting money from a determined "skip." Finally, a judgment debtor may discharge most of his or her debts by going through bankruptcy (see Chapter 7), or may die leaving few or no assets for creditors.

Case 5

RUSSELL-VAUGHN FORD, INC. ET AL v. E. W. ROUSE

Alabama Supreme Court, 208 So.2d. 371 (1968)

Plaintiff Rouse visited the defendant's automobile salesroom and discussed trading his Falcon in on a new Ford. A salesman offered to make the trade for his old car plus $1,900. Rouse left and returned with his wife and children but made no deal. The following

night, when Rouse came back with a friend, defendant salesman Harris asked for the keys to the Falcon. Rouse gave him the keys, and then, along with his friend and defendant salesman Parker, looked at the new cars. In negotiations which followed, salesman Parker *offered to trade a new Ford for the Falcon plus $2,400. Rouse declined and asked for the return of his keys. Both Harris and Parker said they did not know where the keys were. Rouse then asked several people who appeared to be employees (including the manager and mechanics) as well as others in the building, to no avail. Several mechanics and salesmen were sitting around on cars, laughing at him. Rouse finally called the police. Shortly after the arrival of an officer, salesman Parker threw the keys to Rouse saying they ". . . just wanted to see him cry for a while." Rouse sued the dealership and the salesmen, claiming conversion of his Falcon and conspiracy to convert the automobile. The jury returned a verdict in favor of Rouse for $5,000. The trial court denied a motion for a new trial and the defendants appealed.*

Simpson, Justice. It is argued that the conversion if at all, is a conversion of the keys to the automobile, not of the automobile itself. It is further contended that there was not under the case here presented a conversion at all. We are not persuaded that the law of Alabama supports this proposition. The conversion may consist, not only in appropriation of the property to one's own use, but in its destruction, *or in exercising dominion over it in exclusion or defiance of plaintiff's right* [emphasis added] . . . .

A remarkable admission . . . was elicited by the plaintiff in examining one of the witnesses for the defense. It seems that . . . it is a rather usual practice in the automobile business to "lose keys" to cars belonging to potential customers. We see nothing in our cases which requires in a conversion case that the plaintiff prove that the defendant appropriated the property to his own use; rather, . . . it is enough that he show that the defendant exercised dominion over it in exclusion or defiance of the right of the plaintiff . . . .

Further, appellants argue that there was no conversion since the plaintiff could have called his wife at home, who had another set of keys and thereby gained the ability to move his automobile. We find nothing in our cases which would require the plaintiff to exhaust all possible means of gaining possession of a chattel which is withheld from him by the defendant, after demanding its return. On the contrary, it is the refusal, without legal excuse, to deliver a chattel, which constitutes a conversion . . . .

It is next argued by appellants that the amount of the verdict is excessive . . . . If the conversion was committed in known violation of the law and of plaintiff's rights with circumstances of insult, or contumely, or malice, punitive damages were recoverable in the discretion of the jury.

Judgment for plaintiff Rouse affirmed. The evidence justified the jury's conclusion as to the facts, and the punitive damages were recoverable in the discretion of the jury.

QUESTIONS AND PROBLEMS

1. a. It has been said that the government in our secularized society actually prescribes standards and rules of ethical conduct through the laws of torts, crimes, contracts. How is this so?
b. Does the law require that everyone be a good samaritan and go to the aid of neighbors in distress or in need?

2. Tort law has a considerable influence on the conduct of individuals and businesses.

a. What impact does strict product liability have on manufacturers of products that are potentially dangerous if defective?
b. What impact has the expansion of tort liability had on sales of insurance policies? On premiums charged for the policies?
c. What is the impact of laws that authorize punitive damages in certain cases, upon the incidence of intentional torts?

3. Nick Dekker went into the Black Oak Restaurant for dinner. When leaving, he mistakenly took George Walton's hat from the coat rack and walked out the door. Walton observed the incident, ran outside, and yelled "Stop thief!" just as Dekker was driving out of the parking lot. Walton jumped into his own car and gave pursuit. He overtook a car driven by a man who looked like Dekker, although it was really Ferdinand Sinzant. Walton pulled alongside and forced Sinzant onto the shoulder of the road by easing his car along the front left side of Sinzant's car. When the cars stopped, Walton leaped out and smashed Sinzant in the mouth, knocking him unconscious. He put Sinzant into his car and drove back to the restaurant, where he phoned the police. When the squad car arrived, Sinzant regained consciousness, and Walton said, "Arrest this man, he's a thief!" The police refused to make the arrest because they had not observed any crime. However, they advised Walton that if he made a citizen's arrest, they would book Sinzant. Walton thereupon placed Sinzant under arrest. Meanwhile, Harry Hightower was injured when his car ran into and badly damaged the left rear of Sinzant's car, which was protruding slightly into the street with its lights out. At the time of the accident, Hightower was under the influence of marijuana. What torts have occurred?

4. For years the U.S. Surgeon General and the American Medical Association have urged the public to refrain from smoking tobacco products. They allege that scientific evidence indicates that smoking can cause lung cancer and other ailments. The tobacco industry claims that the causal connection is not clearly established, if only because not all smokers are similarly affected. But in response to Federal pressure, tobacco manufacturers print warnings of the possible risks of smoking on packages of tobacco products, as well as in advertisements. Nevertheless, many heavy smokers and their heirs have filed numerous liability suits against tobacco manufacturers, claiming injuries. Are these actions futile gestures, unwarranted by the facts?

5. George Nesselrode and two business associates boarded a chartered Beech airplane that was built by defendant Beech Aircraft Corp., and owned, operated and maintained by defendant Executive Beechcraft, Inc. Within three minutes after take-off the plane crashed, killing the pilot and his passengers. Evidently the disaster was caused by improper installation of the right and left elevator trim tab actuators by Executive mechanics. These parts are critical in controlling the upward and downward movement of the plane. Airplane industry standards require that such replacement parts be designed with "work or no go" features. This means that the parts are designed so as to prevent incorrect installation. The Beech parts did not comply with the industry standard and could be—and in this case were—interchanged or reversed during installation. The parts so designed by defendant Beech were "visually identical but functionally distinct" and different. Therefore the plaintiffs sued, alleging strict product tort liability. They contended that the actuators, as designed, were sold in a defective and unsafe condition. The jury agreed and returned a verdict of $1,500,000 against Beech Aircraft and Executive. The defendants appeal (N.B. The pilot was assessed 0% of the fault and accordingly was not involved in the appeal). How should the appellate court rule? [(*Nesselrode et al* v. *Executive Beechcraft, Inc., Beech Aircraft Corp., et al,* 707 S.W.2d 371, Mo.banc, 1986)].

6. In mass torts (e.g., asbestos, Dalkon shield, and Agent Orange) where there may be hundreds or thousands and possibly millions of victims and potential plaintiffs, it is practically impossible for the courts to handle the resulting cases individually. What can be done to provide just remedies for all?

7. John Ryan, age 3, was playing in the backyard of his neighbor, Jerry Preston, age 8. Jerry ran over John's hand with a power mower and cut it severely. John's mother was a guest in the Preston home at the time of the accident. John, acting through a guardian ad litem (a guardian appointed by the court to sue on behalf of the ward), sued his mother for negligence in supervising him, her own son. He asked for $500,000 damages. No doubt John's mother has ample liability insurance, and so the real target of the suit is the insurance company. Although John could sue in his own name after becoming an adult, proof of fault would be difficult if not impossible because of the passage of time.

a. Who should win?

b. Is Jerry responsible for his own negligence? Are Jerry's parents responsible for Jerry's negligence?

c. Could John lose his case because of the doctrine of contributory negligence?

8. Barton was testing a new $750 ten-speed racing bike on a paved country roadway open only to joggers, hikers, and bicyclists. The speed limit of 15 MPH was posted at many points and a bright yellow line divided the path, permitting safe traffic both ways. At one place, at a curve in the road, Barton was riding at about 20 MPH. Suddenly another rider, Darcy, approached from the opposite direction. Riding at about 5 MPH and intently watching a group of quail along the trail on the right, Darcy rode over the yellow line and bumped into Barton. As a result Barton lost control, swerving off the path and into some trees. The bike was totalled and Barton was injured. Is Darcy liable?

9. Gramling, an expert in the use of explosives, obtained a city permit to level a ten-story building in the center of town by implosion. The explosives were carefully placed throughout the structure so that it would collapse inwardly and leave a heap of rubble on the site. Unfortunately, for unknown reasons, one charge on the third floor caused fragments of brick, concrete, and glass to fly outward. As a result, extensive and costly damage was done to plate glass in nearby buildings and to parked automobiles in the vicinity. There were also personal injuries. Is Gramling liable, even though he acted with a city permit and there was no evidence or claim of negligence? *yes –*   *p 174*

10. a. Identify the tort that corresponds to each of the following crimes:

Rape : *Assault y battery · intentional*
Robbery : *conversion*
Murder : *assault y battery ,*
Manslaughter by vehicle : *negligence*
Child abuse : *assault/battery*
Burglary : *conversion*
Petty theft : *conversion*

b. What amount of punitive damages do you believe would be appropriate for each of the intentional torts that correspond to the above crimes, assuming that you or a member of your family were the victim/plaintiff? Assuming you were the tortfeasor/defendant?

FURTHER READING

1. Couric, Emily, *The Trial Lawyers: The Nation's Top Litigators Tell How They Win.* New York: St. Martin Press, 1988. Fascinating glimpses into the strategies and tactics of champions of conflict in the courts.

2. Huber, Peter W., *Liability: The Legal Revolution & Its Consequences.* New York: Basic Books, 1988. Scathing study of how certain activist judges and legal reformers have greatly expanded the concept of product liability in recent decades.

3. Prosser, William L., and Keeton, Page, *Torts,* 5th ed. St. Paul, MN: West, 1984. A classic handbook used by generations of students and practitioners of the law.

4. Shannon, James, *Texaco & the $10 Billion Jury.* Englewood Cliffs, NJ: Prentice-Hall, 1988. A detailed story of the dispute that generated the highest damage award in history.

5. *Trends in Tort Litigation: The Story behind the Statistics.* Santa Monica, CA: Rand Corporation, 1988. Examination of the expansion of tort litigation with rising judgments for damages in three fields: (1) routine personal injury (auto accidents), (2) high-stakes personal injury (product liability, malpractice, and business torts), and (3) mass latent-injury (asbestos, Dalkon shield).

NOTES

1. *Statistical Abstract of the United States, 1989,* Tables No. 1029, 1040, 1017, 624, 690, 684; (U.S. Government Printing Office, 1990).

2. *Thompson* v. *County of Alameda,* 614 P.2d 728 (California, 1980).

3. *U.S.* v. *De Vane,* 306 F.2d 182 (1962).

4. *Restatement of the Law of Torts,* American Law Institute, Washington D.C., § 283, (St. Paul, MN, American Law Institute Publishers, 1934).

5. *Baker* v. *Alt,* 132 N.W.2d 614 (Michigan, 1965).

6. *Wisniewski* v. *Great Atlantic & Pacific Tea Co.,* 323 A.2d 744 (Pennsylvania, 1974).

7. Black, Henry Campbell et. al., *Black's Law Dictionary,* 5th ed. (St. Paul, MN: West Publishing Co., 1979), p. 584.

8. Prosser, William, & Page Keeton, *Prosser and Keeton on Torts,* §43, 5th ed. (St. Paul, MN: West Publishing Co., 1979).

9. Green, Leon, "The Causal Relation Issue in Negligence Law," 60 *Michigan Law Review* 543 (1962). See also *Weirum* v. *RKO General, Inc.,* 539 P.2d 36 (California, 1975).

10. *Maytnier* v. *Rush,* 225 N.E.2d 83 (Illinois, 1967).

11. *McFatridge* v. *Harlem Globe Trotters,* 365 P.2d 918 (New Mexico, 1961).

12. *Turcotte* v. *Fell,* 502 N.E.2d 964 (New York, 1986).

13. *Hackbart* v. *Cincinnati Bengals,* 601 F.2d 516 (Colorado, 1979).

14. *Brown* v. *Kendrick,* 192 So.2d 49 (Florida, 1966); *Abrams* v. *Woods,* 64 Misc.2d 1093 (New York, 1970); and *Mercer* v. *Band,* 484 S.W.2d 117 (Texas, 1972).

15. *Franklin* v. *Gibson,* 188 Cal.Rptr. 23 (1982).

16. *Yocco* v. *Barris,* 305 N.E.2d 584 (Illinois, 1973).

17. *Kite* v. *Campbell,* 191 Cal.Rptr. 363 (1983); *Myers* v. *Quesenberry,* 193 Cal.Rptr. 733 (1983); *Truman* v. *Thomas,* 165 Cal.Rptr. 308 (1980); and *Turpin* v. *Sortini,* 187 Cal.Rptr. 337 (1982).

18. *Chase* v. *Luce,* 58 N.W.2d 565 (Minnesota, 1953); *Selby* v. *Tolbert,* 249 P.2d 498 (New Mexico, 1952); and *Hooks* v. *City of Detroit,* 187 N.W.2d 901 (Michigan, 1971).

19. *Rowland* v. *Christian,* 443 P.2d 561 (California, 1968).

20. *Mink* v. *University of Chicago and Eli Lilly & Co.,* 460 F.Supp. 713 (1978).

21. Restatement of the Law of Torts, §19 .

22. *Ledingham* v. *Blue Cross Plan for Hospital Care,* 330 N.E.2d 540 (Illinois, 1975); and *Grand Sheet Metal Products Co.* v. *Protection Mutual Insurance Co.,* 375 A.2d 428 (Connecticut, 1977).

23. *Matthew* v. *Page,* 354 So.2d 458 (Florida, 1978); *North Carolina National Bank* v. *McCarley & Co., Inc.,* 239 S.E.2d 583, (North Carolina, 1977); *Masterson* v. *McCroskie,* 573 P.2d 547 (Colorado, 1978); and *A.M. Records, Inc.* v. *Heilman,* 142 Cal.Rptr. 390 (1977).

24. Restatement of the Law of Torts, 2d §§ 570–575.

25. *Stanley* v. *Taylor,* 278 N.E.2d 824 (Illinois, 1972).

26. *New York Times* v. *Sullivan,* 84 S.Ct. 710, (1964); and *Philadelphia Newspapers, Inc.* v. *Hepps,* 106 S.Ct. 1558 (1986).

27. *Gertz* v. *Robert Welch, Inc.,* 94 S.Ct. 2997, (1974); and *Milkovich* v. *Lorain Journal Co.,* USSC 89–645 (1990).

28. *Roberts* v. *Sears, Roebuck & Co.,* 573 F.2d 976 (1978); and *San Francisco Chronicle,* September 18, 1989, p. A5.

29. *Malandris* v. *Merrill Lynch, Pierce, Fenner & Smith, Inc.,* 447 F.Supp. 543 (1977).

30. Restatement of the Law of Torts, 2d §§ 652 A–E.

31. *Nader* v. *General Motors Corporation,* 298 N.Y.S.2d 137 (1969).

32. *Carson* v. *Here's Johnny Portable Toilets,* 698 F.2d 831 (1983).

33. *Savage* v. *Boies,* 272 P.2d 349 (Arizona, 1954); and *Rockhill* v. *Pollard,* 485 P.2d 28 (Oregon, 1971).

34. *Goldfarb* v. *Baker,* 547 S.W.2d 567 (Tennessee, 1977).

35. *The Wall Street Journal,* p. B2, June 16, 1989, and p. 1, June 22, 1989.

36. *Greenman* v. *Yuba Power Products, Inc.,* 377 P.2d 897 (California, 1962).

37. Restatement of the Law of Torts, 2d § 402 A.

38. *The National Law Journal,* p. 19, July 24, 1989.

39. *Royal Globe Insurance Co.* v. *Superior Court,* 592 P.2d 329 (California, 1979), overturned by *Moradi-Shalal* v. *Firemen's Fund Insurance Companies,* 250 Cal.Rptr. 116 (1988).

40. *Foley* v. *Interactive Data Corp.,* 765 P.2d 373 (California, 1988).

41. *Grimshaw V. Ford Motor Co.,* 174 Cal.Rptr. 348 (1981); *Penner* v. *Falk,* 200 Cal.Rptr. 661 (1984); and *Taylor* v. *Superior Court,* 157 Cal.Rptr. 693 (1979).

42. *San Francisco Chronicle,* p. A6, April 8, 1989, and p. A3, April 22, 1989.

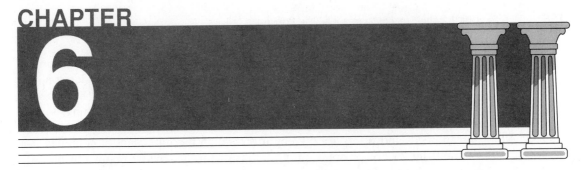

Contracts: Enforceable Agreements

A **contract** has been defined simply as ". . . an agreement to do or not to do a certain thing."[1] The authoritative Restatement of Contracts expands the definition to say it is ". . . a promise, or a set of promises for the breach of which the law gives a remedy, or the performance of which the law in some way recognizes as a duty."[2] Contracts are the intelligent response to a felt human need to get things done with the cooperation of other human beings. They reflect the fact that in our technologically advanced civilization, marked by specialization and division of labor, with individuals highly dependent on each other, "No man is an island, entire of itself."[3]

An Overview of the Promises We Live By

It is true that governmental statutes and court decisions prescribe the rules for the creation, performance, and enforcement of contracts. But contracts are generally entered into privately, between private parties. Government agencies—local, state, and federal—are not directly involved unless the government is itself a party to the contract. Of course, this happens often in our time of big government. Collectively, government is the nation's biggest employer, always under contract. It is the biggest buyer of goods and services, all under contract.

The Ubiquitous Contract

Contracts are legally binding links between producers and consumers throughout the world. They are the promises that are exchanged (and generally faithfully kept) to do the myriad things that get the world's work done. Literally billions of contracts are made and performed every day, often facilitated by the use of a common medium of exchange (money or, increasingly, credit).

Consider some ramifications of contracts in operation. Many millions of workers are employed under oral or written contracts. They work under contracts at every stage of production and distribution of goods and services. Each person contributes to the total effort that provides all of us with food, clothing, shelter, transportation, utilities, and entertainment. The seemingly limitless range of human needs and wants are thereby met through the fulfillment of contracts. The vast and incredibly complex public infrastructure of roads, highways, airports, harbors, schools, libraries, museums, fire and police departments, and sewage and refuse treatment and disposal systems has been constructed and is maintained by means of contracts. With relatively few exceptions, these binding agreements are performed without litigation. Were any substantial fraction of all contracts disputed, the country's court system would be overwhelmed and rendered inoperative. This is a tribute to the fundamental integrity and intelligence of most people. They act with enlightened self-interest, serving the needs of others while gaining benefits of the contracts for themselves.

Examine the book you are reading—the paper, the ink, and the printing. Identify, if you can, the contracts involved in cutting trees, grinding them into pulp, and transforming the pulp—with the aid of water and chemicals and heavy machinery—into rolls or sheets of paper. Don't overlook all the workers involved at each step, and the contracts they make each day. Recognize the various transportation and communication facilities utilized from start to finish. Take any of the above contract leads and pursue it to its sources; for example, the mining of minerals to produce the steel for the saws, trucks, ships, and other machinery. It is literally impossible to identify all the contracts that were involved, directly and indirectly, in placing this book at your disposal. One can convincingly argue that all human activity in our civilized, interdependent society has been implemented by an incredibly complex yet efficient network of contracts.

How Are Contracts Classified?

Generally just two parties are involved in a given contract, but there may be multiple parties when appropriate. One person (and a "person" could be a corporation or partnership) termed the **offeror** or **promisor** makes an offer to a second person (termed the **offeree,** or **promisee).** In effect, each party promises to do (or in some cases, promises *not* to do) something that the other party wants to have done (or not have done). Generally, no special words need be used. With a few exceptions (discussed later in this chapter), the contract may be oral, written, or implied from conduct and/or from some custom or usage of the particular trade, or the agreement may result from a combination of these methods of expression.

For better understanding, contracts may be classified as to method of expression, parties bound, legal effect, and extent of performance.

Method of Expression

Any person capable of reading this sentence has probably been a party to countless contracts. The agreements may have been **express,** when made in words spoken or written, or they may have been **implied in fact,** when manifested in conduct or body language (e.g., an arm waved at a vendor in a stadium during a football game, followed by the toss of a coin and a return toss of a bag of roasted peanuts).

Sometimes promises are enforced even when no true contract exists. This is done to avoid the unjust enrichment of one party who has received benefits from another under certain circumstances. The result is a contract **implied in law,** or *quasi-contract.*

 A surgeon stops her car at the scene of an automobile collision. She gives needed emergency aid to an unconscious victim of the accident. There was no agreement, yet the doctor has a legitimate claim in quasi-contract for the reasonable value of her services. In contrast, a passerby with some knowledge of first aid who performed similar services is not entitled to any payment. Such an act would be that of a voluntary good samaritan, not of a professional who is customarily paid for such services.

Generally, the parties to a contract can use any language they please. In some cases, however, statutes prescribe the terms and exact language. Examples are negotiable instruments such as bank checks and promissory notes. These special types are called **formal contracts;** other types of contracts are called **simple,** whether they are oral or written.

Parties Bound

In most contracts, both parties make legally binding promises. Their agreements are **bilateral contracts.** For example, D, a professional dog catcher, agrees to try to find A's dog during a 24-hour period in exchange for A's promise to pay $50. If D looks for the dog as promised, she is entitled to collect the $50 whether or not she succeeds in her search. In contrast, a **unilateral contract** is actually a potential agreement. One party makes a promise or offer to induce some completed *act* by another party. For example, A promises to pay $50 to anyone who will find and return his dog, dead or alive. No one is legally obliged to join in the search, nor is A obliged to pay unless the requested act is done and the dog is returned.

 In May 1927, Charles A. ("Lucky") Lindbergh became the first person to fly across the Atlantic Ocean solo and non-stop from New York to Paris, using a single-engine monoplane, "The Spirit of St. Louis." Lindbergh was responding to a unilateral contract offer made by a St. Louis businessman to pay $25,000 to the first person(s) to perform the feat. After he was aloft and on his way (a substantial effort to perform), the offer could not be revoked or cancelled. Once the offeree has clearly started to perform, the offeree has a reasonable time to complete the act, even though not legally obliged to finish.

Legal Effect

If a contract complies with all five (and sometimes the additional sixth) essential elements as described in the next section, it is a **valid contract.** Sometimes the attempt to create a contract may be totally ineffective, and so there is no contract. A futile or improper effort is nevertheless loosely termed a **void contract.** An example would be an agreement to commit a crime or a tort. Sometimes an essential element of a valid contract is missing, and a party to the contract has the power to perform or withdraw without liability. Such contract is said to be **voidable.** For example, a minor (under age 18) may generally invalidate or avoid a contract even if freely and intentionally made. A parent or guardian may also take such action on the minor's behalf.

Finally, some contracts are valid yet **unenforceable.** A proper contract claim for money or performance may have become stale and unenforceable because of the statute of limitations. For example, a creditor may have a right to be paid the balance due on a retail store credit account. The typical statute of limitations requires that such creditors sue within four years of the due date, otherwise collection is barred. Courts overloaded with current cases need not accept stale matters; evidence may have been lost, and witnesses may have forgotten facts, moved, or died.

Extent of Performance

If a contract has been fully performed by both parties, it is an **executed contract.** If something remains to be done by either or both parties, it is an **executory contract.** Often sales contracts for goods, such as automobiles, are coupled with warranties as to performance for specified periods of time or extent of use (e.g. a warranty for three years or 30,000 miles, whichever comes first). Although the basic contract may be executed, obligations created by the warranty remain for the specified time. Also, as noted in Chapter 5, if the user is injured by some defect in the product, the manufacturer may be strictly liable in tort for damages whether or not the warranty period has expired.

What Are the Requisites of a Valid Contract?

There are five requisites for a valid contract: **competent parties** who make a *mutual agreement* with *genuine assent* supported by *reciprocal consideration* and which is *legal in formation and execution.* Sometimes a sixth requirement exists when the contract must be *in the form prescribed by law.* Let us examine each requisite.

Competent Parties

The first essential for validity is that the parties who contract have *legal capacity* to do so. The law generally expects that human beings will act as rational animals with freedom of will or of choice among alternative courses of action. Thus the apparent agreement of a party may be negated by (1) infancy or minority (under age 18 in most states), (2) incapacitating mental illness, or (3) incapacitating intoxi-

TABLE 6–1   General Patterns of Effects of Incapacity on Agreements (caveat: in some states variations exist in definitions and effects)

Contracting Party	Valid contract	Voidable contract	Void agreements *(An agreement which is automatically void.)*
Minor	*All* contracts, if married *All* contracts, if emancipated* In California, *all* court-approved contracts to perform as an actor, actress, or professional athlete (not more than 50 percent of the net earnings are set aside for the minor; balance goes to parents, agents, etc.) Contract to enlist in armed service	*Most* contracts To avoid liability, any goods received must be returned if still available Some states (e.g., California) do not require a full refund even if goods cannot be returned, and even if minor lied about age; in most states the minor may disaffirm the contract, but is liable for any depreciation and wear and tear or use The contract may be ratified or avoided within a reasonable time after person reaches majority age	*Some* contracts; e.g., a contract to name an agent or a contract to dispose of real property
Mentally-ill person	*All* contracts, if person is merely neurotic *All* contracts made during a lucid interval of full sanity	*All* contracts made when person is entirely without understanding Any goods received must be returned, unless they are no longer available and other party acted in bad faith	*All* contracts, if person has been judicially declared insane and a guardian has been appointed
Intoxicated person	*All* contracts made if the person is sober enough to understand the nature of the contract (even if he or she would not have made the contract if sober)	*All* contracts made when person is too intoxicated to understand the nature of the contract Avoidance, to be effective, must be prompt after regaining sobriety and learning of the agreement	*All* contracts, if person has been judicially declared a victim of habitual intoxication and a guardian has been appointed

* Living separate from consenting parents and managing own financial affairs

cation. Although most persons have full capacity (i.e., legal qualification or power) to contract, a large number do not. The law denies them the rights that flow from contracting, primarily to protect them from the burdensome duties of performance in foolish or improvident agreements. The restrictive denial also serves to protect them from possible exploitation by unscrupulous persons who might take unfair advantage of their ignorance, naivete, or incapacity.* In all three basic types of incapacity, the contract made is usually *voidable,* but only at the option of the incompetent person (or parent or guardian in control). The agreement is sometimes but seldom absolutely *void.* It is occasionally valid. Table 6–1 illustrates the parallel status of minors, the mentally ill, and intoxicated persons.

---

* In a few instances, the restriction is a form of punishment (as where prisoners are barred from most contract activity) or national defense (as where enemies in times of war are barred from contracting with American citizens).

Exception for Necessaries   An agreement to purchase goods or services that are **necessaries** is enforceable as a **quasi-contract.** In such a case no valid contract exists, but a contractual remedy of reasonable compensatory damages is allowed to prevent unjust enrichment of the person who received the necessaries. Only the fair price would have to be paid, which might not be the bargained-for price. Necessaries include such things as food, clothing, shelter, and medical care appropriate to the person's station in life. They must be truly needed, yet not be available from or not provided by the parent or guardian of the incompetent.

Many business firms aggressively promote sales of cars, audiovisual electronic equipment, and other unnecessary items to minors, especially teenagers. They do this knowing that most of the purchases will not be returned even when the legal right to do so exists. To many teenagers, nothing is more precious than the freedom and independence provided by their very own car. Such persons are not likely to return cars, or indeed any other deeply coveted products, and demand refunds. Moreover, such items are usually acquired with parental knowledge and approval, and often with parental financial assistance. For big-ticket items, prudent retailers often require parental acknowledgement or approval and financial responsibility (e.g., by cosigning a promissory note or security agreement).

Mutual Agreement

The second essential of a valid contract is self-evident: The parties must come to a *mutual agreement*. There must be an *offer* by one and an *acceptance* by the other. There must be an agreement of the parties to the same thing (in Latin, a *consensus ad idem*). Thus, speaking quaintly, many lay-persons and even some courts say there must be a "meeting of the minds." Strictly speaking, this is not true. The law requires external or objective manifestation, in words or actions, of willingness to deal. Internal, subjective thoughts remain secret. Before, during, and after an agreement of any complexity is entered, the parties will seldom disclose the full content of their mental thinking about the terms of the contract.

The Offer   For a valid offer, the person making the offer (called the *offeror*) must intend to make a business agreement, a contract. The offer must not be made in obvious jest or in panicky fear. An invitation to a social engagement or date is not a legal offer. If accepted, it may be cancelled by either party without legal liability. Likewise, most advertisements are not legal offers to sell; they are invitations to the world to come in and make offers to buy. Thus, under contract law an advertiser generally cannot be compelled to sell goods on the terms stated in an ad. Of course, if the ad is deliberately false or misleading, the advertiser may be liable for a criminal act.

The offer must be *reasonably definite and certain*. In a case of dispute, a court must be able to determine what the parties agreed to do. Many common contracts are considered sufficiently definite and certain even though important terms are left unsettled. An example is a contract where one is hired to work and the duration of the employment is not stated. Also, contracts for the professional services of a doctor, dentist, lawyer, or accountant are often made without clear knowledge of the full scope of the time and effort that will be needed, and so no fixed fee is given. In these situations, when the price is finally set it must be reasonable in light of all the circumstances. When such uncertainty is troubling or unacceptable, one can insist on a specific figure or an hourly rate, stated in advance. To cover contingencies, error is likely to be on the side of charging too much rather than too little.

Finally, the offer must be communicated to the person to whom it is made (called the *offeree*). Only the offeree or an authorized agent of the offeree may accept. In daily life, the parties to contracts usually identify themselves more precisely than as offeror–offeree. They may be known as student–university, seller–buyer, doctor–patient, employer–employee, lawyer–client, landlord–tenant, bailor–bailee, and so forth.

The Acceptance   To create a contract, the offeree must accept the offer by making a positive response to the offeror. General rules of contract law require that the **acceptance** be a timely, responsive, and unequivocal affirmation of a desire to enter into the contract on the terms of the offer. It also must be communicated to the offeror or to the offeror's authorized agent. The rules of acceptance for contracts involving the sale of goods (i.e., essentially movable and tangible things, other than money) under the Uniform Commercial Code* are more flexible as to what constitutes an acceptance. For all types of transactions the courts will look for a timely response showing that the offeree wishes to be contractually bound.

Under the UCC, an offer to make a contract for the sale of goods is ". . . construed as inviting acceptance in any manner and by any medium reasonable in the circumstances."[4] Generally, unless otherwise specified, the offeree may accept by the same or faster means than were used by the offeror. Today many communications of offers and acceptances are made by telephone, fax (facsimile transmission) machines, or overnight express delivery services. When an offer is made by mail, the offeror impliedly authorizes the offeree to respond by mail, unless otherwise specified. The acceptance is effective, and a contract arises, when the acceptance is properly posted (i.e., placed in the custody of the U.S. Postal Service with the correct address and proper postage), even if the letter of acceptance is lost in transit. Similarly, if Western Union telegram service or private overnight express delivery services are used, the acceptance is effective when the offeree gives the document to the delivery service.

How Long Does an Offer Last?   An offer, once made, does not last forever. It is ended by the *lapse of time,* if specified (e.g., "Let me know before Friday the 27th"). If no time is stated, then it ends after a reasonable time—an elastic concept that varies with the circumstances (e.g., a broker's offer to sell fresh strawberries may be good for a few hours; an offer made in June to sell loads of firewood may be good for several months).

---

* The Uniform Commercial Code (UCC) is a comprehensive codification of rules that govern a wide range of commercial activity. The fields covered, with their assigned Article numbers, are (1) General Provisions, (2) Sale of Goods, (3) Commercial Paper, (4) Bank Deposits and Collections, (5) Letters of Credit, (6) Bulk Transfers, (7) Warehouse Receipts, Bills of Lading, and Other Documents of Title, (8) Investment Securities, and (9) Secured Transactions; Sales of Accounts and Chattel Paper. The UCC has been adopted by every state, the District of Columbia, and the Virgin Islands. Louisiana—influenced by its French civil law origins—has adopted only Articles 1, 3, 4, and 5. Other states have also excluded or modified particular rules. Note that general contract law and not the UCC applies to the sale of real property (land and things permanently attached to land); service, employment, and insurance contracts; and contracts for sale of intangibles, such as copyrights.

As noted above, when an offer is made by mail, a contract exists when the acceptance is *properly posted*. In sharp contrast, although the offeror may notify the offeree at any time that the offer is revoked, such revocation is generally effective only when the offeree receives it. If this were not so, the offeree could never be sure that an offer received in the mail was still open to acceptance. Nevertheless, in at least one state (California) revocation of an offer is effective when properly posted (Cal. Civil Code 1583), provided this is done before acceptance by the offeree.

If a week was originally specified "to let you think it over," the offeror may nevertheless generally revoke the offer, without liability before acceptance. To avoid such possibility, the offeree may pay the offeror to keep the offer open for an agreed length of time by entering into an **option contract.***** Now the offeree–optionee knows he or she has the agreed-on option time to reflect. He or she might look at alternatives, or use the time to arrange financing. If the offeree–optionee decides to accept the original offer, any money he or she paid for the option might be applied to the purchase price, if so agreed. If he or she rejects the offer, the offeror simply keeps that money as compensation.

The parties may haggle over the terms of the contract. In doing so, an unequivocal *rejection* of the offer by the offeree would end it. The rejection may take effect immediately, if made during oral negotiations; if mailed, it is effective only when received. Similarly, a *counteroffer* would end it.[†] Noncommittal words such as "Your price sounds too rich for my diet, but let me sleep on that offer" would have no effect. Understandably, death or insanity of either party, or destruction of the subject matter, ends the offer.

Genuine Assent

The third essential of a valid contract is that the agreement be made with the **genuine assent** or real consent of both parties. Assent is negated when either party acts under *duress* or because of *undue influence*. Assent, although given, is also fatally flawed if it resulted from *fraud* or certain types of *mistakes*.

Duress   Duress is an unusual occurrence in contract law. It happens when one party is prevented from exercising judgment and free will by some wrongful act or threat of the other party. It could result from threat of imprisonment (e.g., "I'll keep you locked up until you sign this contract!") or of physical injury to the other party or to a close relative or friend (e.g., "Sign here or I'll bash you so hard you'll never sign anything ever again!"). A threat of criminal prosecution would be duress; not so the comparatively common threat of civil suit to collect a debt. Why

---

* A merchant, unlike a casual seller of goods, may make a binding *firm offer* to keep the offer open for a stated time up to three months. It is not essential that the offeree pay for such a right, but the agreement must be in writing and signed by the merchant offeror. *Uniform Commercial Code* 2-205.*
† It is interesting to note that between merchants, an acceptance may be valid and binding on both parties ". . . even though it states terms additional to or different from those offered or agreed upon. . . ." However, this provision of the U.C.C. 2-207 is subject to a number of conditions that effectively maintain the offeror's control and ability to require that acceptance comply with his or her terms if there is to be a contract. UCC 2-207.

the difference? The first is a form of extortion or menace; the second is the voicing of a legal right to sue for money owed.

Undue Influence   Although peaceful and more subtle than duress, **undue influence** has the same effect: depriving a party of freedom of will. It is accomplished by wrongful persuasion and persistent pressure. Typically the wrongdoer asserts his or her position or authority, or exploits the victim's misplaced confidence in the wrongdoer's apparent good faith and wisdom.

A suspicion of undue influence exists when parties are in a confidential or fiduciary relationship. Examples include that of parent and child, husband and wife, client and lawyer, guardian and ward, and principal and agent. Because one party relies so heavily on the other, the law requires the utmost good faith, scrupulous honesty and full disclosure in dealings between such parties. To overcome a presumption of undue influence, the dominant party should make a full disclosure of all relevant facts; insist that the other party get the advice of qualified, independent counsel; and make only honest, fair contracts.

Fraud   Fraud is (1) *false representation,* a lie (2) *of a material* (important) (3) *fact* (generally not a personal opinion, unless an expert is expressing it) (4) *known to be false* (or made with reckless indifference as to its truth, or made with blameworthy ignorance of its falsity), (5) made with intent to deceive the victim and induce the victim to contract; (6) the victim is deceived and contracts in reliance on the lie and (7) the victim is thereby injured.

Peter Pride, proprietor of "Cars You're Proud To Own," sold a used car to Gene Gentille, a first-car buyer. Peter, who knew otherwise, said the car had had only one previous owner (actually, there had been two); had never been in an accident (in fact, a rear fender section, the trunk, and a bumper had been replaced after a collision); had the original paint (the car had been repainted after the accident); had only 52,000 miles and that the engine had been overhauled (in fact, the odometer had been turned back from 66,000 miles and the engine had been given only a tune-up); and had new tires (they looked new to a neophyte but were actually retreads). Peter claimed the car was really worth $10,000 but since he was trying to reduce his inventory, he'd let Gene "steal it" for only $7,500. Gullible Gene believed him, and relying on Peter's sales pitch, bought the car for the asking price. He soon learned that in its actual condition, it was worth no more than $2,500. Is Peter Pride guilty of fraud? If so, what can Gene do?

---

because of fraud

bad faith

Yes, Peter is guilty of fraud. He made a series of misrepresentations of fact, known to be false, intending to deceive Gene and to induce him to buy. Gene was deceived, and acting in reliance on the lies bought the car to his injury. Gene has several options. Under the UCC, he could *rescind* (cancel or undo) the contract, return the car, and demand a full refund of his $7,500. In addition, he could sue for compensatory and punitive (or exemplary) damages (see Chapter 5). In a minority of states his compensatory damages would be the *out-of-pocket loss* suffered (i.e., the difference in value between what he gave—$7,500—and the value of what he got—$2,500—or a net $5,000). In most states, his compensatory damages under the **benefits-of-the-bargain rule** would be the difference between the value of what he received ($2,500) and the value of performance as misrepresented by the defendant Peter ($10,000), or a net $7,500. In either case, in most states Gene could also sue for punitive damages in addition to the compensatory damages because of Peter's intentional tort of fraud. Here the jury might award as much as $50,000 or more.

Mutual Mistake   When both parties have an erroneous idea or understanding about some fact that is an important element of the contract, there is a **mutual or bilateral mistake** that generally renders their agreement void, or voidable by either party.

A famous old English case* involved a contract for 125 bales of cotton to arrive on the ship *Peerless* from Bombay, India. Unfortunately, the buyer reasonably thought of a ship named *Peerless* scheduled to sail in October. The seller reasonably thought of another ship also named *Peerless,* but scheduled to sail from Bombay in December. Was there a contract?

No. Acting in good faith, the parties referred to different ships, sailing at significantly different times. The mutual mistake of fact rendered the agreement void. Note that different opinions as to *value* (e.g., of a parcel of land, a jewel, or a share of stock) or *expectations* of future value do not affect the validity of the contract. Likewise, a **unilateral mistake** (by one party) about value, expectations, or the applicability of a statute generally does not affect the contract. However, suppose one party is mistaken or errs in submitting a bid on a construction job. The other party recognizes the obvious error but says nothing, and quickly signs the contract. A court of equity would permit the mistaken party to withdraw without liability.

Reciprocal Consideration

The fourth requisite of a valid contract is the presence of *reciprocal consideration*. **Consideration**, in this context, simply means the value given in exchange for a promise or an act. The parties "bargain for," that is, freely negotiate, an exchange of promises and/or acts whereby each party ultimately enjoys some legal benefit and each suffers some legal detriment. Each party gives; each party receives. What is given and received must have value; generally it need not be equal or adequate by any other person's standards of valuation. Thus a promise of a gift is not legally enforceable because the donor is promised nothing of legal value in return. To say "Gee, thanks!" or "I love you!" is not legal consideration.

Recalling that in a bilateral contract each party is both promisor and promisee, study the following explanation of consideration provided by the Restatement of Contracts. Consideration may be (1) a return promise (e.g., to pay money or to give some service or property), (2) an act other than a promise (as in unilateral

---

* *Raffles v. Wichelhaus,* 159 Eng.Rep. 375 (1864).

(C refraining from action such as collecting debt due)

contracts), (3) a forbearance (where one party refrains from doing what he or she has a legal right to do), or (4) the creation, modification, or destruction of a legal relationship (where, e.g., the parties agree to become associated as business partners).

Consideration is the sweetener that induces both parties to perform as promised. It conforms to the natural and customary human tendency to expect to receive something in exchange for something given, unless a gift is intended (or a tax is imposed?!). Thus, in so-called illusory agreements there is no reciprocal consideration and therefore no contract. Examples would be where the parties "agree to agree," or when a supplier agrees to sell all goods of a given type that the buyer "may want," which may actually be none at all. This is distinguishable from a deal where the seller agrees to sell and the buyer agrees to buy all of the specified type of goods that the buyer may actually and measurably need or require during a stated period of time.

Similarly, there is no consideration when the promisor is already bound to do the act (e.g., when a police officer, for a promised fee, agrees to try to apprehend a burglar), or when some past consideration is involved (e.g., when A rescues B from drowning and *subsequently* B promises to pay A $5,000).

Under some special circumstances consideration is not required, as a matter of public policy. An illustration would be a pledge or charitable subscription of $10,000 to a church or nonprofit hospital or school. The pledge states that it is for the purpose of erecting a library building, and it is made, in part, to induce others to contribute. Such a promise is legally binding in most states, even if the donor gets no valuable consideration in return. Of course the charity must act in reliance on the pledge, for example, by contracting for construction of the new facility. Likewise, no consideration need be given by a creditor for a new promise by a debtor to pay a debt that had been barred from enforcement by bankruptcy (discussed later in this chapter) or by the statute of limitations.

D debtor borrows $500 from C creditor. She gives C a promissory note in which she promises to pay to the order of C the $500 with yearly interest of 7 percent one year from the date. A year passes, and no payment is made. Four more years (the statutory period of limitations for written contracts) pass, and still no payment is made. C has thereby lost the legal right to compel payment through court action. A year later, D has pangs of conscience and sends C a letter apologizing and promising to pay the note in full. This promise revives the debt, even though C gave no new consideration. A partial payment, identified as such by the debtor, would also revive the debt. C now has four more years in which to seek payment.

Legality in Formation and Execution

As the fifth, and in most cases, the final requisite for validity, the contract must be legal in its formation and in its proposed execution. Generally, an agreement may fail to qualify either because it is (1) contrary to some statute, or (2) contrary to public policy (i.e., prevailing community standards as to what is contrary to the public good or commonweal).

Violation of Statutes   The gangland expression "There's a contract out on him" refers to an agreement to kill a designated victim. Such agreement is obviously illegal and void. The same summary condemnation would apply to any agreement to commit a tort. Not so clear is the legal status of agreements (1) to gamble or conduct lotteries, (2) to practice a trade or profession without a license, (3) to engage in profit-seeking business on Sundays, and (4) to charge interest rates that might be usurious. Consider the confusing status of these practices.

1. Traditionally, gambling agreements, lotteries, and games of chance have been illegal when they involved three elements: some payment by the gambler, for a chance, to win some prize. However, many states now have certain legal forms of gambling. Pressure to raise public revenues in recent years led to this legalization (and according to some observers, highly regressive form of taxation). Critics object to such activity as economically wasteful (unless one regards the dubious entertainment effect a valuable product). They say that the gullible and the ignorant thereby squander money that would be better spent for necessaries, and that gambling promoters cynically pander to greed and unfounded hope by falsely suggesting that "you, too, can get rich quick" despite astronomical odds against such a result.[5]

2. Many professions and trades require a license to practice. Traditionally, the legitimate objective of such licensing laws has been to protect the public against unqualified practitioners. Too often, the dominant objective has been to limit entry in order to reduce competition in service and price. Nevertheless, contracts made by an unlicensed person are generally unenforceable; he or she cannot collect for services rendered. However, when the true objective of the licensing is to raise government revenues, failure to obtain a license does *not* render the contracts of the parties unenforceable or void. This would be true of a license required of all profit-making business firms in a city.

3. In some states, strong support continues for traditional observance of the Sabbath as a day of rest and worship as mandated by the **Mosaic Code.*** Accordingly, **"blue laws"**† restrict the right to make or perform various contracts on Sundays. When such laws have been challenged as a violation of the First Amendment respecting establishment of religion, the U.S. Supreme Court has refused to interfere. Such observance is justified for needed rest and relaxation; any day of the week could be designated for the purpose.

4. Most states regulate the maximum rates of interest that may be charged for certain loans of money. *Usury* is the practice of charging excessively high rates on loans. Today most states maintain some control over how much interest may be charged, but, for example, they allow rates as high as 30 percent a year on loans of no more than a few hundred dollars made by pawnbrokers and small loan

---

* The Ten Commandments, or Decalogue, and the other precepts spoken by God to Israel, delivered to Moses on Mount Sinai. *The Bible* Ex. 20; 24:12,34. Deut. 5. (King James version).

† *"Blue laws"* originally referred to strict rules in colonial New England that outlawed such practices as working, dancing, and drinking intoxicating liquors on Sundays. The term now refers to statutes that regulate commercial activities and amusements on Sundays. In contrast, "blue sky laws" regulate the sale of stocks and bonds, and are designed to prevent fraudulent sale of securities worth no more than patches of blue sky.

companies. The extra interest charge is justified by the higher unit cost of processing such loans, and by a higher risk of defaults by borrowers. The availability of such loans also helps to keep the borrowers out of the clutches of loan sharks who may charge 100 percent a year, or more. Civil sanctions for usury vary among the states. In some states, the usurer is barred from collecting either principal or interest; in others, only the principal is payable; and/or additional variations exist. But observers suggest that many violations are unreported, often because of ignorance or fear of violent retaliation.

The purchase of goods on credit, subject to a carrying charge (some states call it **interest**) on the unpaid balance, has not been considered usury because there is no direct loan of money. However, as this practice has become very widespread, legal limits are now often imposed on the percentage rate that may be imposed. The typical carrying charge (or "interest rate") approaches 20 percent a year. This is a heavy levy, in light of the fact that the ordinary saver seldom earns as much as 8 percent in a bank savings account. The prudent alternative to much consumer borrowing, or buying on time, is to defer purchases (e.g., of a car) and to save the money that would otherwise go to scheduled payments. In a savings account the money saved would earn interest, which when added to the principal would provide cash for a better product later. Note that the **Federal Consumer Protection Act of 1968** (often referred to as the *Truth in Lending Law*) requires a full disclosure of the terms of contracts for sales on credit or for loans. But it does not set any ceiling at the federal level on the rate of interest that may be charged.[6]

2 USC §1606

Violations of Public Policy   Some agreements are obviously contrary to public policy and therefore illegal and void. The list includes attempts to obstruct justice in court by bribing jurors, paying a witness to lie under oath (this is the crime of **subornation of perjury**), or paying a witness more than the modest legal fee prescribed by statute. (Note that experts may be engaged by counsel for both the plaintiff and the defendant, to study and render their opinions about facts of the case. Often they are called on to testify during the trial. Such expert witnesses may legitimately receive fees for their services far in excess of payments made to other witnesses.) Also included in attempts to obstruct justice is paying bribes to influence legislators, administrators, and judges. Banned also, by the Foreign Corrupt Practices Act, are bribes to obtain contracts with foreign governments.[7]

Lobbying, properly practiced, is vital to the democratic process of legislation. Lobbyists outnumber legislators in Congress and in most state houses. They are usually employed under contracts with special interest groups to persuade legislators (and sometimes administrators) to vote in a certain way on legislation. Their title of "lobbyist" is derived from the fact that they frequently meet senators and representatives in the corridors or lobbies of the capitol buildings. To many persons, "lobbyist" is a term of opprobrium, no doubt because the practice of lobbying has too often in the past been corrupted by bribery or veiled purchases of favors. Nevertheless, lobbyists serve a useful purpose in providing important information on the pros and cons of present and proposed legislation. Any person may lobby on his or her own behalf; however, federal and state statutes generally require that persons who lobby for other individuals or groups must register, identify their clients, and disclose the source and amounts of payments received and dispensed.

Agreements that restrict trade and competition are generally illegal. Nevertheless, as a matter of public policy, certain market restraints are allowed when a business is sold. The seller may agree not to compete anywhere within a prescribed geographical area for a definite time, provided the restraints are reasonable under the circumstances. A shoe retailer selling her business might appropriately agree not to open a competing business anywhere in a sparsely populated county for perhaps two years; a seller of a company manufacturing heavy-duty earth-moving machines headed by a brilliant inventor whose unique products are sold worldwide, might properly agree not to open a competing business anywhere for three or more years. Thus the buyer properly gets the benefit of the price paid for the **goodwill*** value of the going concern.

What Is the Effect of Illegality?   An illegal agreement is void, and courts will normally not aid either party to the transaction. Exceptions are made and damages in tort or other relief may be awarded (1) when the violated law is intended to protect one of the parties (this is true, for example, when one party is the victim of usury), (2) when the parties are not equally blameworthy (e.g., when one party is the victim of fraud in illegal securities dealing, or when one party acts under duress or undue influence), and (3) when one of the parties repents and withdraws before the time set for performance (as in illegal wagers over the outcome of a boxing match).

Form Prescribed by Law

Finally, some important types of contracts must be in the **form prescribed by law** to be enforceable. Such contracts may be deficient in form, yet otherwise be valid. Thus if the party who is entitled to raise the issue of form does not object, the contract may be routinely performed (executed) by both parties. After the contract is performed the question of proper form is usually moot (no longer open to argument).

What Is the Statute of Frauds and Perjuries?   By statute, certain specialized contracts must contain prescribed language. This is true of fire and homeowner insurance policies. It is also true of contracts for loans and for sales of goods on credit under the Truth in Lending Act. But the most important legislation governing form in contracts was originated in 1677 in the English **Statute of Frauds and Perjuries.**[8] In essence this statute provided that certain designated important contracts, to be enforceable in court, must (1) be in writing, and (2) be signed by the party against whom enforcement is sought, or by his or her agent. Note that no problem as to form arises if the party *seeking* to enforce the contract has not signed. Such party could simply and promptly sign the document if the other party points out the lack of a signature.

---

* *Goodwill* is the valuable intangible asset of a business that is developed over a prolonged period of time through successful contractual relations with satisfied customers and suppliers. Thus, an established business with goodwill normally enjoys higher profits than a new business of the same size but lacking such goodwill.

The English statute is the original model for many versions adopted in most American states, all designed to prevent parties from fraudulently misrepresenting the actual terms of their agreements.

Writing important agreements encourages more careful draftsmanship and thus reduces potential misunderstandings and costly litigation. The requirement of a signature permits free and open negotiation without fear of unintended or premature commitment. Breaches of contracts and spiteful law suits can be discouraged by including a sentence requiring the losing party, in case of litigation, to pay all court costs and reasonable attorney fees of the winner. Better still, the written contract can provide for arbitration or some other specified alternative method of dispute resolution (see Chapter 3). Although the Statute of Frauds should encourage careful draftsmanship, any writing satisfies the requirement if it sufficiently expresses the agreement. Of course, it must be signed by the party against whom enforcement is sought. The writing could consist of a memorandum or letter(s), for example.

The following rules will be better understood if certain technical words are first defined. Under the UCC, a **sale** "consists in the passing of title from the seller to the buyer for a price" [UCC 2-106(1)]. The person who has *title* owns the property. The word **property** has a double meaning. It usually means the thing that is owned; in a strict legal sense, however, *property* means the rights of the owner to possess, use, and dispose of that thing.

Property is broadly classified as real or personal. **Real property** is the land and things "permanently attached" to the land, such as buildings. It includes rights to air space above the land, to water on the surface, and to the materials below the surface (e.g., oil, gas, and minerals). **Personal property** includes all movable property other than land. Both real and personal property appear in tangible (or corporeal) and intangible (or incorporeal) forms. Examples of tangible real property are the ground or land, and buildings erected on the land. An example of *intangible real property* is an easement, which is a right to use the land owned by another person (e.g., as a right of way). Examples of *intangible personal property* are the copyright of this book, the design patent on your watch, and the goodwill enjoyed by owners of McDonald's fast-food restaurants.

What Contracts Must Comply With the Statute of Frauds? a. *A Contract for the Sale of Land or an Interest Therein*. Some states, such as California, also require a lease for more than one year to be in writing. Thus a month-to-month lease, or a lease of as long as one year, is valid even if oral. Under what is called the *equal dignities rule,* the real estate broker's employment agreement (sometimes called a *listing*) to search for a purchaser of real property must also be in writing and properly signed.

b. *A Contract for the Sale of Tangible Goods for the Price of $500 or More.* Under the UCC, *goods* ". . . means all things . . . which are movable . . . other than the money in which the price is to be paid, investment securities . . . and things in action" (which are rights to recover personal property or money by means of a trial or other judicial proceeding).

Certain important exceptions are made to the above rule by the Uniform Commercial Code. The UCC provides that an oral contract for goods priced at

$500 or more is nevertheless enforceable ". . . if the goods are to be specially manufactured for the buyer and are not suitable for sale to others in the ordinary course of the seller's business." An example would be a unique and elaborate cabinet made with costly imported woods to hold a variety of audiovisual equipment, complete with a wet bar and built-in refrigerator. Before notice of repudiation of the contract is received, the seller must have ". . . made either a substantial beginning of their manufacture, or commitments for their procurement." Furthermore, the buyer is bound ". . . with respect to goods for which payment has been made and accepted or which have been received and accepted." Finally, the buyer is bound who ". . . admits in his [her] pleading, testimony, or otherwise in court that a contract for sale was made."[9] The contract in such case would be enforceable, but only for the quantity of goods admitted.

Here again the UCC provides a special rule for merchants. Assume that between merchants a writing in confirmation of the sales contract and sufficient *against the sender* (who has signed) is received within a reasonable time, and the recipient has reason to know its contents. This will satisfy the requirement of a signed writing *against the recipient (even though he or she has not signed)*, unless written notice of objection to its contents is given by the recipient to the sender within ten days after it has been received.

c. *A Contract That Is Not to Be Performed, and Cannot Possibly Be Performed, Within One Year From the Date of The Agreement.*   In calculating the time the law ignores fractions of days, including any fraction of the date of the agreement. Thus an oral contract for one year, to begin tomorrow, is enforceable. If it is to begin two or more days hence, it must be in writing and signed.

Other agreements that are governed by various statutes of frauds include those to make a will, those made in consideration of marriage (e.g., "if you will marry my daughter, I will give you a dowry of $100,000"—note that the contract to marry may be and usually is oral); and those to pay the debt of another person (e.g., "Sell her the goods—if she does not pay you, I will").

The Uniform Commercial Code requirement of a signed, written contract also applies to contracts for the sale of kinds of personal property not otherwise covered, in an amount or value beyond $5,000.[10] This provision does not apply to contracts for the sale of goods, securities, or security agreements, all of which are covered separately.[11]

How Can Third Parties Become Directly Involved in a Contract?

Third Party Donee and Creditor Beneficiaries

Most bilateral and unilateral contracts directly involve only the two original contracting parties. However, from the very inception of their agreement, one party may name and provide for a **third party beneficiary.** For example, a parent in a contract for ordinary life insurance may name a child as a beneficiary of the policy. The child has paid nothing and therefore qualifies as a *donee beneficiary*. As such, the child may enforce the contract and collect the proceeds of the policy upon the death of the parent. On the other hand, the third party may be a *creditor beneficiary*.

When Nikkel sold his gift and novelty shop to Oddeon, there were accounts payable (money owed to creditors) on the books with a total of $12,000 owed to five suppliers. Oddeon agreed to pay the balance due as part of the purchase price of the shop. Thus the five suppliers were third party creditor beneficiaries in the sales contract and they have legal claims under the contract against Oddeon.

An *incidental beneficiary* is a person who benefits from a contract but is not named and has no legally enforceable rights or duties under the contract. An example would be the benefit that people enjoy when the government builds a road under contract, or when private developers build a shopping center. Probably everyone has been an incidental beneficiary in many contracts.

Assignment of Contract Rights and Delegation of Duties

After a contract has been made, the original parties generally may assign their contractual rights, and/or delegate their contractual duties to others. Unless properly released from the duties, the parties remain liable for full performance. In special situations, as where they involve uniquely personal services, the duties may not be delegated. Thus, without consent of the other party, a surgeon may not transfer an accepted duty of performing an operation. Likewise, unless otherwise agreed, one may not transfer rights to personal services. A transfer of rights may not be made if it could materially increase the burden of performance on the other party to the contract. Thus you cannot transfer your fire insurance policy to someone who buys your house, nor your automobile insurance to someone who buys your car. Indeed, such contracts specifically prohibit assignment to another party.

Nevertheless, valid transfers of contractual rights and duties occur with many variations. A common example that often involves multiple transfers is a contract for the construction of a private residence.

On June 1, 1992 Able Construction Company, a general contractor, agrees to build and sell a particular house to Baker on land it owns, for a contract price of $100,000. Promised delivery date is on or before November 1, 1992. Able and a small crew of his employees prepare the site and lay the foundation. In separate contracts, on and after June 8, 1992, Able *delegates* all other construction work to independent contractors who are specialists in their fields (carpentry, plumbing, electrical work, painting, and so forth) for various prices. Able remains liable to Baker for the completed job as promised. On July 1, 1992, Baker learns that she is to be promoted and transferred by her employer to another city. Therefore she sells the house to a friend, Newcomer, on August 10, 1992. She does this by assigning her rights and delegating her duties in the project to Newcomer. These contracts are graphically portrayed in Figure 6–1.

FIGURE 6–1   Example of Contract with Subsequent Delegation of Duties and Assignment of Rights

		June 1, 1992	
ORIGINAL CONTRACT	ABLE CONSTRUCTION CO.	⟶ 🏠 ⟶ ⟵ $100,000 ⟶	BAKER
	Able agrees to construct house on lot.		Baker agrees to pay price of $100,000.
		JUNE 8, 1992 *(and other dates)*	
SUBCONTRACTS	ABLE CONSTRUCTION CO.	⟶ various $ amounts ⟶ ⟵ various labor and material	VARIOUS SUBCONTRACTORS (e.g., Charles & Co., carpenters; Peter & Co., plumbers; Edward & Co., electricians; Paul & Co., painters; et al).
	In series of separate contracts, Able *delegates* duties to independent subcontractors.		Various specified construction subcontractors agree to do work required to build house, supplying necessary materials.
		August 10, 1992	
DELEGATION OF DUTIES AND ASSIGNMENT OF RIGHTS	BAKER ⟶ 🏠 ➞ NEWCOMER Assigns to Newcomer her right to the house and delegates to Newcomer her duty to pay ABLE $100,000.		NEWCOMER
	Baker *delegates* to Newcomer duty of paying $100,000 to Able (Baker remains contingently liable and must pay if Newcomer fails to do so). Concurrently, Baker *assigns* to Newcomer her right to the finished house.		Newcomer agrees to pay $100,000 to Able because this gives her the right to take possession of the house when finished.

Note that Able might have assigned the right to part or all of the $100,000 price to a bank for a construction loan. Also, both Baker and Newcomer could have negotiated separate loan contracts with the house as security, to finance the purchase (see Chapter 13). Note, too, that Baker might have asked Newcomer to pay more or less than $100,000, but the parties agreed to the transfer at the original price.

How Are Contracts Discharged?

The customary and usual way of discharging contracts is by **performance.** The reciprocal rights and duties of the parties are legally terminated when the parties have done what they've promised to do. Sometimes the performance is not precisely as promised, but the minor deviation may be a good faith oversight or failure. In the house construction example, assume the paint used was the proper quality and color but the wrong brand, or the garage door may have been a half foot wider than specified. The buyer must still perform by paying for such **substantial**

usually written into contract

performance by the general contractor, but may deduct an appropriate amount because of any deficiency in the builder's performance. The buyer need not pay extra for any improvements "volunteered" by the builder. Often businesspersons as well as ultimate consumers will accept an alternative or a variation of a promised performance simply because the deviation is not significant or does not reduce the value of consideration received. To insist on absolute compliance may end a mutually beneficial relationship.

Rather than engage in costly and acrimonious arguments and litigation, a party may *waive (give up) or renounce legal contract rights.* For example, an employer may do so when an employee under a year's contract quits without just cause after a month or two. Occasionally a party will agree to accept some substitute for the original promised consideration.

Defft, a dentist, never refused to treat a patient who could not promptly pay for the service. When the charges for dental care of Gartner, an unemployed gardener, and his wife reached $600, they offered to redo Defft's lawn and trim all the trees and bushes on his lot in full payment or satisfaction of the debt. Defft agreed. This was an executory *accord.* When the work was completed, the debt was discharged by *accord and satisfaction.*

new contract

In the hypothetical house construction, buyer Baker's contractual obligation might have been discharged if Able, the general contractor, agreed with Baker and Newcomer to a **novation,** which would allow Newcomer to be substituted for Baker in the contract. The bank that loaned the construction money to Baker undoubtedly required her to sign a promissory note agreeing to pay. Had the bank deliberately marked the note "Cancelled" or destroyed it—a very unlikely possibility—the debt would have been discharged by *cancellation.* Similarly, any deliberate important change in a promissory note or other written contract by a party to the contract is a **material alteration,** and discharges the contractual obligation of the other party.

When there is a *material (important)* **breach,** or failure or refusal to perform a contract, the victim may *cancel* the contract with no liability and sue for damages. The right to sue, if utilized successfully, may be superseded by a *judgment* of the court. This, too, serves to discharge the contract, but by *operation of law.* Other means of discharging a contract by operation of law include (1) *subsequent illegality*—as when the Eighteenth Amendment prohibited ". . . manufacture, sale, or transportation of intoxicating liquors;"[12] (2) *bankruptcy* (the debts are not extinguished, but they cannot be enforced unless reaffirmed by the debtor with approval by the court); (3) *running of the statute of limitations* (again, the debts are not extinguished, but they cannot be enforced unless reaffirmed by the debtor); (4) *literal impossibility* (as where a contract requires personal service and the individual dies); and (5) *commercial impracticability under UCC 2-215,* where ". . . performance as agreed has been made impracticable by the occurrence of a contingency the non-occurrence of which was a basic assumption on which the contract was made."[13] Outbreak of war, surprise discovery of solid granite throughout much of the anticipated site of an underground garage and a major earthquake are examples of circumstances in which performance might be excused because it has become commercially impracticable.

Circumstances can be such that both parties "want out." In such a case, a *voluntary* **rescission** is mutually agreed on. Anything already received is returned, and the status quo ante is restored.

What Remedies Are Available for Breach of Contract?

Vigorous contract activity is essential to a healthy economy. Through its laws, society seeks to encourage people to enter contracts and to perform as promised. Failure to do so is not conducive to goodwill and continued relations. But a breach of contract is not a crime and, except in unusual circumstances (e.g., when there is a breach of covenant of good faith and fair dealing), it is not a tort. In a sense, contracting parties can usually regard a breach as a possible alternative to performance; it is surely not morally reprehensible if the victim of the breach is promptly made whole and provided with money or some alternative performance that offsets any loss suffered.

If litigation becomes necessary, the defaulting party is generally obliged by a court to pay *compensatory damages,* sufficient to place the victim in essentially the same economic position or condition that would have resulted from performance of the contract. Only if the agreement was corrupted by a related tort, such as fraud, would punitive damages be awarded.

Armond agreed to sell his used Harley-Davidson motorcycle to Bushnell for $4,500. When Armond changed his mind and refused to complete the deal, Bushnell promptly bought a comparable model for $5,200 from Caldwell. Armond is liable to Bushnell for $700 in compensatory damages. If Bushnell was lucky enough to find a similar model priced at $4,000, she could still sue for *token or nominal damages* (typically 6¢ or $1). Armond would also be liable for court costs, but not for Bushnell's attorney's fees, unless that was provided for in the original sales contract.

Sometimes the parties to a contract specify in advance what the damages shall be in case of breach. Such **liquidated damage** clauses are often used in contracts for the construction of public buildings or commercial structures where damages are difficult to determine and prove. Courts will enforce such terms as long as the damages are not in fact penalties. They must be reasonable in the light of the anticipated or actual injury or harm caused by the breach.

When Metropolitan College contracted for its new classroom buildings (price $4 million), the general contractor promised to have it ready for occupancy two years thereafter, when the fall semester would begin on August 28. A liquidated damages clause called for the payment of $150 per schoolday (Monday through Saturday) of delay in completion beyond the promised date of August 28. Losses incurred would include rental costs for temporary portable buildings and the monetary value of burdens imposed on students, faculty, and staff from overcrowding and required reassignments. Therefore this clause would be enforceable.

In some cases where money damages are inadequate, courts provide an *equitable, non-monetary remedy*. For example, since every parcel of land is unique, a buyer of land can compel delivery of possession by the owner who promised to sell. So too with unique works of art—in 1989, an unidentified Japanese bidder at an auction agreed to pay $45.9 million for "Pierrot's Wedding," a masterpiece from Pablo Picasso's famed "blue period." Under U.S. law, a seller who refuses to deliver such a painting could be compelled to do so by a buyer who obtains a *specific performance decree* from a court of equity.[14] Of course, if the painting has already been sold to another person who, unaware of the prior contract, bought in good faith and received good title, the victimized buyer would have to be satisfied with a money judgment. When appropriate, courts of equity also order *injunctions*.

The talented and temperamental opera star Matilda Nocallara contracted—a full year in advance—to perform at a gala concert in New York City, promoted by Joy Jordane. A month before the schedule date, Nocallara told Jordane that she was "indisposed" and planned instead to make "a less strenuous television appearance" that week in Los Angeles. Jordane obtained a *negative injunction* from a court of equity, forbidding her to perform in Los Angeles on the day of the scheduled concert. (The court would not directly compel her appearance in New York because that would smack of involuntary servitude and be difficult to enforce.) In addition, the court would award Jordane dollar damages if Nocallara failed to keep her New York commitment.

What Special Protection Is Provided for Individual Consumer Contracts?

All persons are consumers. The most common consumer contracts are sales (purchase) agreements. Often purchases are made on credit, involving separate contracts to permit payment over extended periods of time. Sellers (i.e., manufacturers, wholesalers, and retailers) are generally more knowledgeable about their products and services than are most consumers. Moreover, sellers are more likely to have the assistance of attorneys in drafting contracts. Consequently the agreements made are often **contracts of adhesion,** favoring the sellers; the buyers must accept them as written (i.e., adhere to and be bound by the terms as specified by the sellers) or not get the goods. To tell the consumer "**Caveat emptor**—let the buyer beware" is no help when the buyer lacks the knowledge needed to evaluate the goods (be they simple clothing or complex electronic gear).

Over the years (dating back at least to 1906, when the federal Pure Food and Drug Act was enacted) government at all levels has been involved in protecting consumers against unfair practices of a comparatively small group of unethical businesspersons and firms that are always present somewhere in the marketplace. In the 1960s and 1970s, a group of important federal consumer protection bills were added. Although abuses continue, three broad categories of legislation (before-sale laws, during-sale laws, and after-sale laws) have given meaningful "teeth"—such as fines and prison terms—to the admonition "**Caveat venditor**—let the seller beware."

Before-Sale Laws

Before-sale laws regulate the design, composition, and production of products for sale. They embrace such elements as quality, safety, purity, description, and packaging. For example, the National Highway Traffic Safety Administration has ordered automobile manufacturers to gradually achieve an average fuel economy of 26 miles per gallon in vehicles they sell. The drop in gasoline prices in the 1980s encouraged many consumers to shift to larger, less fuel-efficient cars. Automakers have therefore persuaded the NHTSA to postpone enforcement of the fuel economy goal.

Since 1972, the *Consumer Product Safety Commission* has been charged with overseeing the safety of all consumer products other than autos, trucks, airplanes, boats, food, drugs, and cosmetics (which are the concern of other federal agencies). In 1989, for example, more than 250 toys and over 100 children's products were targets of recalls or corrective action orders by the CPSC.

During-Sale Laws

During-sale laws regulate truth in advertising, extension of credit, and contract terms and language. The Federal Trade Commission, created under the Federal Trade Commission Act of 1914, was originally primarily concerned with enforcement of the federal anti-trust laws (i.e., the Sherman Anti-trust Act of 1890 and the Clayton Act of 1914). The FTC sought to prevent among business corporations unfair methods of competition that could lead to monopolies. More recently, the FTC has also been active as the principal federal agency regulating advertising.

Listerine Antiseptic mouthwash has been marketed since 1879, and its formula has never been changed. Since its introduction, it has been represented as being beneficial for colds. Advertising of this claim began in 1921. In 1972, the FTC issued a complaint charging Warner-Lambert Company (the manufacturer) with violation of the Federal Trade Commission Act by misrepresenting the efficacy of Listerine against the common cold. The prolonged legal battle finally ended in 1977, when the U.S. Court of Appeals upheld an FTC order to Warner-Lambert ". . . to cease and desist from advertising that . . . Listerine . . . prevents, cures, or alleviates the common cold." Further, the company was ordered to publish corrective advertisements stating that "Listerine will not help prevent colds or sore throats or lessen their severity."[15]

The most important section of the *Consumer Credit Protection Act* of 1968 is known as the *Truth in Lending Act,* which requires a full disclosure of the comparative costs of buying goods for cash or on credit. On credit sales and loans of money, the creditor must disclose in writing and in advance of signing the total dollar finance charge and the effective annual percentage rate (APR) of the interest or finance charge. Sellers may not mislead gullible customers, for example, by quoting a credit cost of "only 1.5 percent a month." They must disclose that the equivalent interest cost per year is 18 percent. The act also provides for a three-day "cooling off" period when a consumer agrees to borrow on the security of a second mortgage on a home. Under the law, the borrower may rescind and get back any money delivered to the creditor as long as he or she does it within the three days. The act places no limit on the rate or amount of interest or carrying charge, although some consumer advocates think it should.

Antonio and Rosita Mendez bought a new house. As part of the purchase price they signed a promissory note for $45,000, secured by a first mortgage on the property. The next day they decided they could not afford the high monthly payments. May they rescind?

No. The cooling-off rule of the Truth in Lending Act does not apply to first mortgages (or first deeds) on homes, because such credit has not generally been the basis for exploitation of unsophisticated homeowners in need of funds, and the interest rates have been reasonable. The three-day cooling off period is a narrow exception that allows a party to escape a contract acceptance. Unfortunately, many consumers have heard of a "three day rule" and think it applies to all consumer contracts. It does not.

Traditionally, *garnishment* (attachment of the salary or wages of a defaulting debtor) has been a principal remedy for unpaid creditors. To use this remedy the creditor gets a court order directing the debtor's employer to pay a certain portion of the employee's wages directly to the creditor until the judgment is paid in full. Sometimes employers used to fire workers who got into such financial trouble. Under the federal Consumer Credit Protection Act, normally the amount garnished may not exceed (1) 25 percent of the worker's weekly take-home pay, or (2) $60, or the amount by which the take-home pay exceeds 30 times the federal minimum wage, whichever is less. An employer may not discharge an employee simply because wages have been garnished for any one indebtedness.

The federal **Credit Card Act of 1970** controls certain practices of credit card companies. A consumer must apply for a credit card; it may not be thrust on the consumer without such request and consent. Moreover, the cardholder's liability for *unauthorized use* of the card by a thief or dishonest finder is limited to a maximum of $50 per card. And even this limited liability for up to a maximum of $50 can be imposed only if:

1. The cardholder requested and received the credit card, or signed or used it, or authorized another person to do so.
2. The card issuer provided a self-addressed, prestamped notification to be mailed by the cardholder in the event of loss or theft of the card.
3. The card issuer gave adequate notice of the $50 liability.
4. The card issuer provided positive means of identification (for example, signature or photo of the cardholder on the card).
5. The unauthorized use took place before the cardholder notified the issuer that such use might take place.

The **Fair Credit Reporting Act of 1970** gives consumers the right to check and correct for accurate credit information about themselves that may be on file with credit reporting services, such as the Retailers Credit Association (RCA).

The **Equal Credit Opportunity Act of 1976** forbids discrimination in extension of credit because of sex, marital status, race, or color, as well as religion, national origin, or advanced age; because the applicants get all or part of their income from a public assistance welfare program; or because the applicant has in good faith exercised a right under the Consumer Credit Protection Act.

After-Sale Laws

After-sale laws regulate credit billings, methods of debt collection, and warranties.

The **Fair Credit Billing Act of 1974** is a response to the tyranny of the computer, which sometimes electronically disgorges invoices that may be erroneous. The consumer who believes an accounting error has been made by the issuer of a credit card may notify the creditor in writing within 60 days of mailing. The creditor (or issuer of the card) must investigate and respond promptly, normally within 30 days of receipt. Within 90 days the creditor must either eliminate the error or explain why it believes the bill was correct. After notification, the creditor is temporarily barred from pressing for payment or reporting to a credit bureau, although statements may continue to be sent. The consumer is legally obligated to pay any part of the bill not in dispute. If the creditor admits an error, there can be no finance charges on the disputed amount. The creditor must submit a correct written notice of what is owed, and the consumer must be given the usual time to pay before any finance charges or late-payment charges may be assessed. If it turns out that there was no error, the consumer has to pay finance charges on the disputed amount and make up any payments missed. The debtor who is not satisfied with the creditor's explanation is allowed a minimum of 10 days after receiving the explanation in which to protest. Thereafter, whether or not such protest was made, the creditor may sue or use other collection procedures. If there was a second protest, however, the creditor who notified credit bureaus and other creditors must mention the dispute and inform the debtor of the identity of the addressees.

Failure to comply with the stated rules makes the finance charges and first $50 of the disputed amount uncollectible, even if later events prove there was no error.

The Fair Debt Collection Practices Act of 1977 outlaws a variety of unreasonably harsh tactics used in the past by overly aggressive debt collectors. Banned are late night and early morning telephone calls, the use of obscene and abusive language, threats to notify employers, false representation as police or official government agents, harassment with repeated phone calls, and similar unsavory behavior. Nothing in the law prevents creditors from using legitimate methods and conventional legal remedies to collect overdue debts (see Chapter 5).

What Warranty Protection Do You Have as a Consumer?

A **warranty** is an assurance given by the seller of goods concerning the quality or performance of a product. Some warranties are *implied* by law and exist even if nothing is said about them; other warranties are *express* and may be oral, but are usually stated in the written contract.

Merchants (professional sellers who deal in the goods) as well as *casual sellers* (such as ordinary laypersons disposing of things owned) normally are held by law to make these three **implied warranties** when they sell a product:

1. Warranty of title (that the seller has the title to the goods as claimed and the right to transfer or sell them)

2. Warranty against encumbrances (that the goods delivered will be free of liens or encumbrances—creditors' claims—of which the buyer is not aware at the time of contracting)

3. Warranty of fitness for a particular purpose (that if the buyer indicates the purpose for which the goods are needed and then relies on the seller's selection, the goods will be reasonably fit for the intended stated purpose)

When Peggy Butler visited Mac's Sport Shack, she told the salesperson that she was planning a backpack trip into the Great Smoky Mountains. Butler insisted on being out-fitted with "Pathfinder" brand mocassin boots and a "Kozy" brand sleeping bag. After several days in the wilderness, using this gear, she realized that neither product fit her needs. Her ankles were swollen and she caught pneumonia. Is Mac's Sport Shack liable on a breach of warranty of fitness for particular purpose?

No. The warranty is not given when the buyer insists on a particular brand, as here. Possibly Butler could hold the manufacturers liable if they had made express warranties as to the goods and these warranties were breached.

In addition to these three implied warranties, either a merchant or a casual seller may explicitly make the following **express warranties:**

• *Warranty of conformity to description, sample, or model*—all goods supplied must conform to the sample or model shown at the time of the sale, or to the specifications provided.

• *Warranty of conformity to seller's statement or promise*—the seller who openly states or writes a factual assertion about the goods is bound by that assertion.

Merchant sellers alone make two additional implied warranties:

• **Warranty against infringement**—the goods sold are delivered free of any rightful claim of a third party under patent, copyright, or other legal protection.*

• **Warranty of merchantability**—this is an extremely important warranty, promising that the goods are fit for the ordinary purposes for which such goods are used. Thus, a rocking chair (or stereo or toaster or umbrella) should function as such and last a reasonable length of time (which might be many years) under ordinary use.

---

* Usually the patent holder proceeds against the patent infringer rather than against the ultimate consumer. Thus, for example, in November, 1990, Judge David A. Mazone of the federal District Court in Boston ruled that Eastman Kodak Company must pay the Polaroid Corporation $909.4 million for infringing seven of Polaroid's instant photography patents. Polaroid had demanded $12 billion.

Official comments to the UCC state that contracts for sale by merchants of used or second-hand goods involve ". . . only such obligation as is appropriate to such goods. . ." Although "such obligation" includes an implied warranty of merchantability, the price, age, and condition of the goods at the time of the sale are considered in determining the scope of the warranty. Obviously, such a warranty may be of little value to the buyer, especially if the goods are worn out or in poor condition.

Typical language in an express warranty given by a representative manufacturer of consumer goods states that the product is warranted ". . . against any defects due to faulty materials or workmanship for a one-year period after the original date of consumer purchase." In fairness to manufacturers, it should be noted that a warranty extended beyond the stated short period can be very costly to service. Buyers who neglect their possessions and fail to follow recommended maintenance schedules take unfair advantage of warranties. Yet all buyers pay for the added protection that most do not need, because the added cost is distributed over the price in all sales. A better alternative is available from some manufacturers who provide "extended warranty protection" for an extended period of time only to those buyers who pay an additional charge.

May a Seller Disclaim All Warranties that Otherwise Protect the Consumer?

Yes. A seller may generally **disclaim** (limit or negate) all warranties. Fortunately, because of competitive pressure, this seldom happens. To exclude the implied warranty of merchantability, the seller must conspicuously mention *merchantability* in the disclaimer or notice of exclusion. A statement that the goods are sold "as is" or "with all faults" also serves to exclude all implied warranties. However, the UCC provides that consequential damages may *not* be limited or excluded if the exclusion is **unconscionable** (i.e., against public policy). Limitation of such damages ". . . for injury to the person in case of consumer goods is prima facie unconscionable. . . ."[16]

Formerly, sellers were often shielded from liability by legal requirements of **privity,** meaning that the plaintiff buyer seeking to enforce a warranty must be the party who contracted with the defendant seller. Thus a consumer might sue a retailer who sold the defective product to him or her, but not the much wealthier manufacturer who made it. Most states have modified or rejected this archaic doctrine and hold all merchants or manufacturers in the chain of distribution liable for any breach. The Uniform Commercial Code has extended the warranty protection beyond the buyer to include all members of the buyer's family or household and any of the buyer's guests, where they might reasonably be expected to use such goods and where the defective goods cause physical injury.[17] But in most states, innocent bystanders and others who are injured by a defective product must seek recovery on some other basis, such as strict product liability of manufacturers and middlemen in a tort action.

While trying to persuade Marjorie Ayers to buy an expensive electric typewriter, Leon Cannon said that all parts were guaranteed and would be replaced without any charge if found defective within five years. The written purchase contract that Ayers later signed spoke of only a one-year warranty against defects in materials and workmanship. Moreover, it said that the customer would have to pay for half of the usual labor charge. Which terms really govern?

The one-year warranty terms govern—unless the buyer can satisfy a judge that she was the victim of mistake, fraud, or illegality or that the written contract was incomplete. This is the result of the **parol evidence rule,** which presumes that the contracting parties have included all previous desired oral or written understandings in the final, integrated written agreement. Thus it is not enough for a consumer to get all important contracts in writing; one should also make sure that the writing includes all desired terms and oral assurances; and that they are stated correctly and completely, including a clear statement of warranty protection.

The federal Magnuson-Moss Warranty Act of 1975, to help protect ultimate consumers of personal, family, or household goods, has added the concepts of *full* and *limited* warranties.[18] Under the act no one is required to give a warranty, but the seller who elects to give a *full warranty* for consumer goods costing $15 or more agrees to fix the product within a reasonable time and without charge if it proves to be defective. If it cannot be fixed or if a reasonable number of attempts to fix it prove unsuccessful, the buyer has the choice of a full cash refund or a free replacement. Some states have added *lemon laws,* which clarify and strengthen this rule. No time limit may be placed on a full warranty, but if an otherwise full warranty has a time limit, it may be described (e.g., as a "full five-year warranty"). Any warranty that does not provide full protection must be labeled a *limited warranty* by the seller. A warranty would be limited if, for example, the buyer had to pay any fee or transportation charge in order to utilize it. Implied warranties (e.g., of title or of merchantability) may not be disclaimed if any written warranty is given, but they may be defined and limited.

What Can You Do if You Are Overwhelmed by Debts?

Several alternatives are available to an individual consumer who is overwhelmed by debts and cannot make payments on contracts or other obligations (e.g., judgments in accident cases) as they come due:

1. Contact your creditors and explain your predicament. Try to obtain a *voluntary extension of time,* or *refinance* (pay debts with the proceeds of a new loan). If possible, do this before you are in default.

2. Allow selected *secured creditors* to repossess items purchased under security agreements and that you know you can get along without. Be aware of possible **deficiency judgments,** where you give up the goods and still owe a balance.

3. Obtain a **composition of creditors.** This may be done by a credit counselor who gets the limited available money from you and distributes it to all claimants under a plan whereby the creditors allow additional time and reduce the debts in amount.

4. Apply for a *state wage earner receivership*. This is available in some states, such as Ohio. A court-appointed trustee collects all nonexempt wages of the debtor and distributes them pro rata to all creditors. Repossessions and wage garnishments are prohibited while the plan is in effect.

5. Apply for *adjustment of debts as a debtor under Chapter 13* of the federal **bankruptcy** law.[19] Any person (or sole proprietor of a business) with regular income (this could even include public welfare money or earnings from a business) may apply. Secured debts of the individual may not exceed $350,000, and unsecured debts may not exceed $100,000. The action must be voluntary; one cannot be forced into this proceeding. With a few limited exceptions, when the debtor files the necessary petition there is an automatic *stay* or termination of all collection proceedings by creditors. The debtor retains possession of all assets, and submits a plan for orderly repayment of all outstanding debts within three years (unless the court approves an extension up to a total of five years). The plan may include *modification and reduction* of the rights (to full payment) of both unsecured and secured creditors (other than a claim secured only by a security interest in real property that is the debtor's principal residence). Secured creditors are entitled only to the current market value of the collateral that secures their claims.

A court-appointed trustee gets and distributes earnings and income required for the plan. After completion of payments under the plan, all debts are discharged except (a) certain long-term debts "on which the last payment is due after the date on which the final payment under the plan is due,"[20] and (b) alimony, child support, and maintenance payments.* The plan is approved by the bankruptcy judge, provided the creditors are to receive more under the plan than they would have received under a liquidation of the debtor's assets in a **Chapter 7** proceeding (as discussed below). **Chapter 13** goes significantly further than Chapter 7 in *discharging obligations,* as explained later in the chapter. Moreover, unlike ordinary Chapter 7 bankruptcy (where the procedure may not be repeated for another six years), there is no time limit for a possible second Chapter 13 proceeding.

6. If you cannot qualify for Chapter 13 proceedings or don't want to wait for up to three to five years before discharge, go *bankrupt in a conventional Chapter 7 proceeding*. This type of bankruptcy may be *voluntary* on the part of the debtor, or *involuntary*† and forced by a designated number of creditors,‡ when the debtor

---

* Section 523 of the bankruptcy law at 11 U.S.C. lists as non-dischargeable, *inter alia, among other things* "(5) Debts owing by the bankrupt debtor to a spouse, former spouse, or child of the debtor, for alimony to, maintenance for, or support of both spouse or child, in connection with a separation agreement, divorce decree, or property settlement agreement". *

† There can be no involuntary proceeding against a farmer (who could be a giant agribusiness corporation), provided at least 80 percent of the gross income comes from farming operations, or against a corporation that is not a moneyed business or commercial corporation (e.g., a nonprofit private school).

‡ If there are *fewer than 12* creditors, excluding employees or insiders, any creditor whose unsecured claim is at least $5,000 may sign the petition. If the creditor holds security for the claim, only the amount of the claim in excess of the value of the security is considered. If there are *12 or more* creditors, at least three whose unsecured claims total $5,000 or more must sign the involuntary petition.

is generally not paying debts as they come due (or when within 120 days of filing the petition a custodian was appointed or took possession of the debtor's property). Here your creditors are entitled to claim all of your assets, excluding only certain exempt property. The court-appointed trustee *liquidates* (converts into cash) *your assets* and uses the proceeds to pay the administrative costs of the proceeding, then certain priority claimants, then the other creditors. It is not uncommon for unsecured creditors to receive no more than 5 or 10 cents for every dollar claimed. This explains why so few bankruptcies are involuntary. A further deterrent is the fact that if the involuntary bankruptcy petition was filed in bad faith, the court may award punitive damages to the debtor.

Voluntary bankruptcies, on the other hand, are encouraged by a fairly generous allowance of *exemptions* of property that the debtor may retain. The code specifies certain exemptions under federal law; individual states generally specify their own lists of exemptions. The particular state by law may bar a debtor from using the federal exemptions, but in California and many other states a debtor may choose the one that is more favorable. If a debtor owns a home, federal law allows retention of an equity of up to $7,500 as exempt from execution. Some states offer more (e.g., in California the figure is $30,000 for a single person, $45,000 for a husband and wife, and $75,000 if either spouse is over 65 or disabled and unable to engage in gainful employment). Federal law allows a $400 miscellaneous or "grubstake" exemption, to which may be added the unused portion, up to $3,750, of the $7,500 homestead exemption. Other federal exemptions include a debtor's interest of up to $1,200 in one motor vehicle; up to $200 in each of any particular item of household furnishings, wearing apparel, appliances, animals, crops, and musical instruments held primarily for personal, family, or house use of the debtor or of a dependent, up to an aggregate total of $4,000; up to an aggregate of $500 in jewelry; and up to an aggregate of $750 in implements, professional books, or tools of the trade of the debtor or a dependent. Also exempt is any unmatured life insurance contract (other than credit life); rights to receive social security, veteran's benefits, or disability, illness, or unemployment benefits; alimony, support, or separate maintenance; and payments under a stock bonus, pension, or profit-sharing annuity.[21]

Clearly, bankruptcy does not strip the debtor naked; rather, the idea is to provide overburdened debtors with a fresh economic start in life. However, *not all debts are discharged* or wiped out by bankruptcy. The debtor remains liable, after discharge under Chapter 7, for certain taxes and money due because of a fraudulent return or willful attempt to evade a tax; for money, property or credit obtained by false pretenses or fraud; for any debts that were not listed in the bankruptcy petition; for fraud or defalcation while acting in a fiduciary capacity; for embezzlement, or larceny; for alimony, maintenance, or child support; for willful or malicious injury to a person or property (not mere negligence); for educational loans made, insured, or guaranteed by the government, or made under any program funded by the government or a nonprofit institution unless (1) such loan first became due more than five years before the filing of the petition, or (2) if excepting such debts from discharge will impose an undue hardship on the debtor and the debtor's dependents; and for damages caused by drunken driving. Any loan or cash advance in excess of $1,000 obtained by the use of a credit card, and any revolving line of credit obtained within 20 days of filing a bankruptcy petition are presumed to be nondischargeable. Likewise, a debtor's purchase of more than $500 in luxury goods or services on credit from a single creditor within 40 days of filing a petition is presumed to be nondischargeable. These presumptions may be rebutted by the debtor, but that is unlikely under the given conditions.[22]

Case 6

ACHIM ZELLER v. FIRST NATIONAL BANK AND TRUST COMPANY of EVANSTON et al

Illinois Supreme Court, 398 N.E. 2d 148 (Illinois, 1979)

Plaintiff A. Zeller alleged a breach of contract to sell him real estate property. The property was held in trust by the defendant First National Bank and Trust Company for an estate. The estate was represented by the defendant law firm of Tenney and Bentley.

On December 23, 1977, defendant attorney Austin L. Wyman, Jr., a member of the law firm, wrote a letter to plaintiff Zeller, stating that he had been instructed by his principal to offer the building to Zeller for $240,000. After receipt of the letter, Zeller instructed his attorney, Roger Jamma, to communicate a counter-offer of $230,000. On January 10, 1978, Jamma sent Wyman a written counter-offer of $230,000, suggesting various interest and loan terms. On the same day, Jamma phoned Wyman and discussed the deal. Wyman testified that Jamma informed him that the counter-offer had been mailed. Both agreed that Wyman said he believed his letter of December 23 was no longer effective, and would not be honored since the owner was entertaining offers in excess of $240,000.

Jamma then informed Zeller of his conversation with Wyman. Zeller directed him to accept the original offer of $240,000. Jamma promptly sent Wyman a telegram purporting to accept the original offer of December 23. The telegram was delivered on January 10, 1978, prior to receipt of the written counter-offer. The

defendant trustee bank refused to convey the property to Zeller and so he sued in equity. In count I he asked for specific performance of the contract. In count II he sought damages from Wyman and his law firm for offering to sell property that they allegedly had no authority to convey. The trial court entered summary judgment in favor of all of the defendants and dismissed both counts of the complaint.

McNamara, Justice.   It is elementary that for a contract to exist, there must be an offer and acceptance. Moreover, to create a binding contract, an acceptance must comply strictly with the terms of the offer. An acceptance requesting modification or containing terms which vary from those offered constitutes a rejection of the original offer, and becomes a counterproposal which must be accepted by the original offeror before a valid contract is formed.

In a telephone conversation with Wyman on January 10, 1978, plaintiff's attorney discussed the counter-offer of $230,000. This counter-offer, containing terms varying from the original offer, operated as a rejection and terminated plaintiff's power to accept Wyman's offer. Once having rejected Wyman's offer, plaintiff could not revive the offer by later telegraphing acceptance.

Plaintiff urges, however, that the counter-offer which was disclosed in the telephone conversation had no legal significance because it was oral rather than written. We do not agree. It is clear that the language of an offer may govern the mode of acceptance required. Where an offer requires a written acceptance, no other mode of acceptance may be used. Since the offer in the present case did not require acceptance or other communications regarding the sale to be in writing, verbal communication of the counter-offer was an effective rejection. Thus, contrary to plaintiff's contention, it is not determinative that the subsequent written acceptance arrived prior to the written counter-offer. In view of plaintiff's rejection prior to acceptance, no binding contract was created.

The contract under which the plaintiff sought relief in both counts of his complaint was never properly formed. Therefore the trial court correctly entered summary judgment in favor of the defendants.

For the reasons stated, the judgment of the trial court was affirmed.

QUESTIONS AND PROBLEMS

1. (a) What are the five, and sometimes six, elements that are said to be essential for a valid contract?   *p. 194*

(b) In which of the six elements does the law permit performance or execution at the option of one of the parties who might have legally withdrawn without liability? Explain.

2. Is breaching a contract comparable in legal effect to committing a tort or committing a crime? If not, how do they differ?   *no*

3. Identify three contracts you have experienced or observed. Select one that is expressed in writing, one expressed orally, and one implied in fact from conduct. Classify each as to parties bound, legal effect, and extent of performance.

4. In what circumstances under contract law might an automobile or truck be legally considered "necessary" and appropriate to a minor's station in life?

5. As a matter of public policy in the United States, the law generally frowns on monopolies; contracts to monopolize trade are illegal. Nevertheless, both federal and state governments grant monopolistic rights to privately owned public utilities (e.g., gas, electric, and water supply corporations). Can you justify this inconsistency?

6. Androw orally agrees to work on Brock's farm in the Matanuska Valley near Fairbanks, Alaska. Under their contract, Androw will remain through two growing seasons, for a period of 15 months. Compensation will be room and board plus $100 paid each month and $30,000 paid at the end of the 15-month term. All goes well for six months, through the first harvest. Then Brock, because of domestic difficulties, sells the farm and fires Androw. What legal remedy, if any, does Androw have?

7. After graduating from high school in June, Brighton worked for one year before seeking admission to the state university. He was accepted, and so in July he paid $100 as a good faith deposit to hold a year's lease on an apartment near the campus (the lease would commence in September). To his chagrin, when he arrived in time for the first week of class the landlord said, "Sorry, here's your $100. I've rented the whole building to a fraternity." Does Brighton have a cause of action against the landlord? Against the fraternity?   *Breach of contract*

8. Kay Kirk had paid the outstanding balance on her Master Card credit card, and had made no further purchases with the card for three months. Then she was shocked when a statement arrived in her mail showing assorted charges on the card for a total of $2,700. She quickly checked her wallet and found her card.

    a. Must she pay the $2,700?

    b. Must she pay $50?

9. When Tom Trouster loaned Bob Barrow $100, he asked for an IOU. Barrow took a business card from his wallet and scribbled these words on its back: "I.O.U., old pal Bob, one hundred bucks," signed and dated it, and gave it to Trouster.

    a. Is the card a valid promissory note?

    b. Is the card an enforceable written contract?

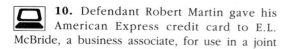 **10.** Defendant Robert Martin gave his American Express credit card to E.L. McBride, a business associate, for use in a joint business venture. Martin claimed he orally authorized McBride to charge up to $500 on the card. He also testified that he had previously sent a letter to plaintiff American Express asking them not to allow total charges on his account to exceed $1,000. McBride had returned the card to Martin and then disappeared. But McBride had actually charged approximately $5,300 to Martin's card. Under the Truth in Lending Act is Martin liable for $50 or $5,300? [*Martin* v. *American Express, Inc.,* 361 So. 2d 597, (Alabama, 1978)].

FURTHER READING

Calamari, John D., and Joseph M. Perillo, *Calamari and Perillo's Hornbook on Contracts,* 3rd ed. St. Paul, MN: West Publishing Co., 1987. Readable survey by two Fordham University professors of law that has guided many professional students safely through the rocks and shoals of contract law.

Friedman, Jane M., *Contract Remedies,* St. Paul, MN: West Publishing Co., 1981. Another volume in the excellent "Nutshell Series." It explores in clear language the variety of possible breaches of contractual duties and related available remedies.

Restatement of the Law Second, Contracts, 2nd ed. American Law Institute Publishers, St. Paul, MN: 1981. Especially helpful because of numerous practical hypothetical applications used to explain a broad range of technical rules.

Schaber, Gordon, and Claude D. Rohwer, *Contracts in a Nutshell.* St. Paul, MN: West Publishing Co., 1984. In the appropriate words of the authors, both experts in the field from the McGeorge School of Law, "this is . . . a good overview and an accurate general analysis of the more frequently encountered problems of contract law."

NOTES

1. California Civil Code § 1549.

2. *Restatement of the Law of Contracts, 2d,* Sect. 1, (St. Paul, MN: American Law Institute Publishers) 1981.

3. Donne, John, *Devotions Upon Emergent Occasions,* No. 17, 1624.

4. *Uniform Commercial Code* (hereafter referred to as (UCC) (St. Paul, MN: American Law Institute Publishers) 1987, 2-206 (1) (a); also *Restatement,* Section 30.

5. In 1988, the director of the California Lottery (Chon Guttierez) said the odds of winning the "big prize" in Lotto were 13.9 million to 1. *San Francisco Chronicle,* March 24, 1988.

6. Consumer Credit Protection Act of 1968, 15 USC § 1601 et. seq.

7. Foreign Corrupt Practices Act of 1977, 2 USC § 241 et seq.

8. Statute of Frauds and Perjuries, 29 Carolus II, C. 30.

9. UCC 2-201.

10. UCC 1-206(1).

11. UCC 2-201, 8-319, and 9-203.

12. U.S. Constitution, Eighteenth Amendment, ratified January 16, 1919; repealed by Twenty-fifth Amendment, December 5, 1933.

13. UCC 2-615.

14. *San Francisco Chronicle,* December 1, 1989

15. *Warner-Lambert Co.* v. *Federal Trade Commission,* 562 F.2d 749, District of Columbia (1977). It is interesting to note that Listerine is currently legitimately advertised as a mouthwash that inhibits plaque on teeth, a fact that has been accepted by the American Dental Association.

16. UCC 2-719(3).

17. UCC 2-318.

18. Magnuson-Moss Consumer Product Warranty and Guaranty Act, 15 U.S.C. 2301 et seq.

19. Bankruptcy Reform Act of 1978 and Bankruptcy Amendments and Federal Judgeship Act of 1984, 11 U.S.C. § 101 et seq.

20. Ibid. 1322 (b) (5).

21. Ibid. 522.

22. Ibid. 523.

CHAPTER 7

Administrative Law

Because of the complexities of modern life, the federal legislative branch cannot provide all the laws that are necessary or desirable. Furthermore, many technical matters requiring regulation are beyond the understanding of most legislators, given the limited time usually available to consider the multiplicity of pressing issues. For example, how can one person be expected to cast intelligent votes during a legislative session when thousands of bills (proposed laws) are under consideration? They may include such diverse matters as maximum speed and minimum altitude limitations for commercial aircraft, limitations on the chemical composition of fertilizers and insecticides, salary requirements and job standards of thousands of civil service employees, limitations on bullfrog hunting, and proper safety equipment standards for two-wheel and three-wheel recreational vehicles.

Obviously, the legislative branch must delegate some of its powers in order to cope with the volume and detailed specialization of problems requiring legal solutions. Most delegations of congressional powers are made to administrative agencies. Federal agencies include the Civil Aeronautics Board, National Labor Relations Board, Federal Maritime Commission, and the Internal Revenue Service.

Because of the need to get the work of government done with greater efficiency than it would be done by only Congress, some of these agencies combine legislative, executive, and judicial powers into one body. Although subject to judicial review, their rules and rulings are seldom overturned by the courts. The administrators have been selected as experts in the specialized fields, and the legislature has delegated to them powers to make rules (legislate), administer an enforce the rules (execute), and investigate and resolve violations of the rules (adjudicate).

Critics of government complain about high and still-rising taxes. They denounce heavy spending for defense, welfare programs, foreign aid, farm price support, or salaries and pensions for government employees and veterans. But their harshest criticism seems to be reserved for the administrative agencies. Why, the individual entrepreneur protests, should these noisy bureaucrats demand voluminous reports;

inspect my plant; condemn and confiscate my goods; tell me what to make and what to charge; and investigate, prosecute, and punish me without any jury trial? All at a high cost to the government, to me, and to society (because I usually manage to pass along these avoidable costs to my customers in the form of higher prices).

Not surprisingly, administrative agencies also attract very enthusiastic supporters. Consumer advocates cheer them on. Political scientists acclaim them as a logical evolutionary accommodation of our tripartite government to new needs of government control. Legislators, sensitive to public opinion, acknowledge that there seems to be no acceptable alternative. No doubt this mixed reaction is to be expected because administrative agencies reach out into the work-a-day world and regulate the production of goods and services, which is essentially a private effort in our capitalistic society. Not only do the rules imposed by administrative agencies often dictate how, when, and where things are done, but they significantly affect the profits realized by producers, and the price and quality of goods and services received by consumers.

Administrative Agencies

The rise of administrative bodies probably has been the most significant legal trend of the last century and perhaps more values are affected by their decisions than by those of all the courts. . . .[1]

Administrative agencies (bureaucracies) make and enforce rules (laws) for the implementation of public policy. For example, Congress sets the rates at which a person's income is taxed, but the Internal Revenue Service (an administrative agency) has the duty to collect the tax.

Administrative bureaucracies have multiplied since the 1930s, and so has administrative law. Today, government—a creation of law and a prolific creator of new law—extends its influence and control over a wide and still expanding range of human activities. The impact is usually positive, as when government provides schools, libraries, parks, museums, highways, financial aid, and food and shelter for the poor. Often the impact is neutral (in terms of direct effect on most persons), as when government provides a military umbrella or when it generates volumes of statistical data. Sometimes the impact is negative, as when officials in high office become involved in dishonest and greedy schemes or when police treat arrestees with brutality.

What Is Administrative Law?

Over a period of several months in 1988, three deaths occurred in a steel mill owned by USX Corp. The people died by being burned, crushed, and suffocated. The Occupational Safety and Health Administration (OSHA)—an administrative arm of the U.S. Department of Labor—was asked to investigate. After a finding of safety violations, OSHA recommended fines of $7.3 million.[2] Does OSHA have the power to assess and collect these fines?

Yes. It has the power to do both within very broad guidelines established by Congress. Can it do so without USX having an opportunity to contest OSHA's findings? (In other words, does USX have an opportunity to have a fact-finding hearing before an administrative law judge?) Yes. At the hearing, USX pleaded guilty to the violations and promised to rectify the problem and follow the recommendations of OSHA. The negotiated plea resulted in a much-reduced fine. Critics of such plea-bargaining* are answered by OSHA's declaration that it does not necessarily want violators punished; rather, it wants the safety problems corrected. OSHA's job is to make the workplace safer, not to raise money. In USX's case, an anonymous spokesperson for OSHA said if all violations were satisfactorily corrected, in all likelihood USX would have to pay a fine of only $700,000 to $1,000,000.

Administrative law consists of general rules and detailed regulations, as well as specific rulings, orders, and decisions, all made by administrative agencies. At the federal level, there are powerful administrative agencies such as the Federal Trade Commission (FTC), Interstate Commerce Commission (ICC), and Federal Reserve Board (FRB), which operate independently of the traditional government departments. But even within the traditional departments there are numerous bureaus, offices, or divisions that possess authority to make administrative law (e.g., the Internal Revenue Service (IRS) of the Treasury Department). Although no statistics are available, observers point out that the sheer volume of law generated by administrative agencies exceeds the volume produced by both the legislatures and courts combined.

Why Has Administrative Law Expanded So Rapidly?

 On May 25, 1979, an American Airlines DC-10 jet crashed on takeoff at Chicago's O'Hare International Airport after its left engine and pylon dropped onto the runway. 275 persons aboard were killed, as well as three persons on the ground. The Federal Aviation Administration (FAA), aided by investigators from the National Transportation Safety Board, immediately began exhaustive studies of other DC-10s to determine, if possible, the cause of the disaster. Could the FAA order all 138 U.S.-registered DC-10s to be grounded, while urging foreign carriers to ground their collective fleet of 142 DC-10s?[3]

Yes, even though the loss in revenues for the affected U.S. airlines would approximate $2.5 million a day. The grounding was ordered on June 6, 1979, and

---

* Plea-bargaining is to agree to plead guilty to a crime on the promise of leniency in sentencing, or to agree to plead guilty to a lesser crime to avoid paying the penalty of a more serious crime. The plea-bargain removes the need for expensive and prolonged trials.

lasted 38 days. It was lifted after the FAA determined that the disaster was caused by a crack in the aft bulkhead of the engine support pylon, and after it issued orders (1) to the manufacturer, McDonnell Douglas, to redesign the pylons; (2) to the airlines to end the maintenance procedure (of removing pylon and wing engine together as a unit instead of separately) thought to have weakened the pylons, and to begin more stringent maintenance inspections; and (3) to manufacturers and airlines to cooperate more closely with FAA engineers and inspectors in certifying the fitness of aircraft to fly. The DC-10 case illustrates the need for safety regulation by government in commercial air travel. It is reassuring to note that such travel has enjoyed a remarkably good record of safety.

Some kinds of administrative law can be traced to the earliest days of the republic. For example, in the aftermath of the Revolutionary War, veterans submitted claims for benefits that had been authorized by Congress. To have Congress or the courts review and rule on each application would have been cumbersome and costly, so the authority to evaluate claims was delegated to a special office, which has evolved into today's giant Veterans Administration (VA). Under President Ronald Reagan, the Veterans Administration became a cabinet-level office.

The first major independent administrative agency was the Interstate Commerce Commission (ICC), created in 1887 to end the abuses common in the railroad industry at the time; frenzied financing, discrimination in rates among shippers and geographical areas, widely varying levels of service, cutthroat competition, and exploitive rate structures. The ICC brought order and uniformity of service at reasonable rates, but ultimately also restrained open competition within the industry and between railroads and other transporters, such as truckers.

A surge of interest in government regulation occurred under the New Deal of President Franklin D. Roosevelt in the early 1930s. It was an attempt to retain free enterprise while rejecting government ownership and control of production, which some demanded. The Securities and Exchange Commission (SEC), Federal Communications Commission (FCC), and National Labor Relations Board (NLRB) came into being at that time.

Another wave of new agencies came in the 1960s, and again in the early 1970s, in response to demands for effective government action to end racial and sex discrimination in employment, protect the consumer from exploitation, clean the air and water of pollution, and give workers a safe and healthful job environment. New agencies included the Equal Employment Opportunities Commission (EEOC), Consumer Product Safety Commission (CPSC), Environmental Protection Agency (EPA), and Occupational Safety and Health Administration (OSHA).

What Are the Leading Areas Where Administrative Law Prevails?

There are several broad areas where the administrative process of lawmaking and enforcement has become important. Every regulatory agency was created in response to a specific need. Although critics abound, hardly anyone proposes abolition of all government regulation and control. The net result is a rejection of *laissez-faire* (French: let alone) capitalism and the substitution of a mixed economy in which government and private business are closely interrelated.

Routine, Repetitive Problems

Certain types of simple questions (which could theoretically be decided by legislatures or courts) are better resolved by specialized agencies. For example, does an applicant qualify for social security and, if so, for how much? This problem arises literally millions of times each year, and, when decided, requires continued administrative action to follow up with orderly benefit payments until properly terminated. The Social Security Administration (created in 1935)[4] is appropriately in charge, acting under broad guidelines prescribed by the Congress with approval of the president.

Utilities

Certain utilities are more efficient when operated as monopolies. However, the public interest requires protection through an agency that determines levels of service and prescribes allowable rates. This is the province of the Federal Power Commission (1930)[5] and of state public utility commissions, which regulate electricity, gas, telephone, and water suppliers.

"The Iron Fist of Administrative Law" was the catchy title of a campus lecture. In the debate that followed, Tom Dowter argued that the power and impact of administrative agencies was grossly exaggerated. "Listen," he said, "The PUB (Public Utilities Commission) grants a license to the highest responsible bidder, and then lets nature take its course. They're bureaucrats without a bite." "Not so," rebutted Cy Klopps. "They've got to review and OK every rate boost; they keep the utilities in business with a fair return on their investment, but no more. And they can even order rebates. Seldom do courts bandy about such big, I mean really *big* figures." Who is closer to the truth?

Cy Klopps, without a doubt. In an unusual but revealing single day in 1980, the Public Utilities Commission of California made three monumental orders. One compelled refunds to customers totaling $381 million by Pacific Telephone Company and $111 million by General Telephone Company, over a two-year period. The refunds were expected to amount to 3.3 times a typical customer's local telephone bill. On the same day, the PUC granted permission to the Pacific Gas and Electric Company to increase its annual electricity rates by $455 million and its gas rates by $336 million, in order to recover soaring fuel costs. These increases would add a total of about $7.71 to the monthly gas and electric bills of a typical homeowner. The allowed boost was $449 million less than PG&E had requested. (However, about two months later the PUC gave PG&E an additional boost of $1.2 billion in annual rate increases because of higher fuel costs.)

The telephone refunds were the results of a ten-year battle between the agency and the companies, following the enactment of the Federal Tax Reform Act of 1969. Under that law, companies were permitted certain tax deductions (through accelerated depreciation and investment tax credits) and could retain these savings, in effect, as tax-free loans from the government for service improvements. Attorneys for the cities of San Francisco, Los Angeles, and San Diego appealed to the California Supreme Court, which ordered Pacific Telephone to give its customers the benefit of at least part of the tax savings through rate reductions. The PUC implemented this court decision in 1974, and the U.S. Supreme Court denied a hearing, in effect upholding the PUC. As of this writing, litigation between the companies and the Internal Revenue Service continues before the U.S. Tax Court to resolve questions of the companies' eligibility for accelerated tax-depreciation allowances. Telephone companies throughout the country, including 22 other subsidiaries of the American Telephone and Telegraph Company, could theoretically be faced with a tax liability of up to $10 billion, according to some estimates.[6]

Finance

Some areas of finance greatly affect the economy and hence Americans' general welfare; yet, if left alone, they tend to be abused by incompetents and by unscrupulous and greedy manipulators. What is the government's response to this problem? The Securities and Exchange Commission (1934)[7] regulates organized securities markets and the securities traded there; the Commodity Futures Trading Commission (1974)[8] does a similar job to prevent fraud and abuse on commodity exchanges; and the Federal Reserve Board (1913)[9] regulates most of the nation's banks and helps to set important national policies on extension of credit and supply of money in an effort to control inflation without causing a serious recession or depression.

Transportation

According to economists, a transportation network is second only to education as a prerequisite for a productive society. Yet the technical complexities involved in such a system are beyond the range of skill and knowledge possessed by legislators or judges; regulators must have specialized technical education, and typically make lifetime careers in the field.

The Interstate Commerce Commission (1887)[10] regulates interstate railroads, common carrier truckers, and some waterway carriers as to levels of service and rates. The Federal Maritime Commission (1936)[11] regulates ocean-going U.S. ships. The Civil Aeronautics Board (1938)[12] did the same for airlines, although it has recently given air carriers considerable freedom in route selection, level of service, and rate making. An initial spurt in traffic and profits caused by fare cuts was followed by setbacks and losses when higher fuel prices forced boosts in fares. Confusing policy decisions to avoid duplication of regulation and legislation, passed by Congress in 1978, called for abolition of the CAB in 1985. CAB's functions and duties were then transferred to the Department of Transportation.

Closely related to the CAB is the Federal Aviation Administration (1958),[13] which regulates the manufacture of airplanes by certifying airworthiness, and which also licenses pilots. Also involved in transportation regulation is the National Highway Traffic Safety Administration (1970),[14] which regulates quality and design in the manufacture of motor vehicles and tires in the interest of safety.

Beginning in 1978, Ford Motor Company representatives were scheduled to appear before a hearing officer of the National Highway Traffic Safety Administration in Washington, D.C. Pinto and Bobcat owners, as well as company officials, were to testify as to the safety of these subcompact cars because of the alleged increased hazard of fire and explosions from rear-end collisions due to the location of the cars' gasoline tanks. Ford announced a recall of about 1.5 million models of the cars that had been built in 1971 to 1976, to modify the gasoline tanks. At a unit cost of $20 to $30 a car, the total cost of the repairs to the company exceeded $45 million. The changes, Ford said, would "reduce significantly" the risk of fires if the cars were hit from the rear. The NHTSA hearing was accordingly cancelled.[15]

Mass recall efforts, such as Ford's, are never totally successful. Not all owners or users of the defective product receive the notice; of those who do, not all respond as requested. Thus the manufacturer remains potentially liable, both before and after the recall, for injuries caused by defects in products. Significantly, Ford has been involved as defendant in a number of civil tort cases arising out of accidents with Pintos. In one unusual aftermath of such a case, the Ford Motor Company was charged with negligent homicide in the deaths of three women whose Pinto was struck from behind by a van and then burst into flames. Never before had an American corporation been prosecuted on criminal charges in a product defects case. After a ten-week trial ending March 13, 1979, the 12-person jury in Winimac, Indiana, found Ford innocent. An expert on accident reconstruction had testified that the closing speed of the van reached 50 miles per hour; and Ford's main contention was that even full-size cars could not have withstood the impact of the van without spilling large amounts of fuel.

Employment Practices

The complexities of fair employment practices have led to the establishment of the National Labor Relations Board (1935),[16] which supervises union representation elections and policies relations between union and management to prevent unfair practices by either. The **Equal Employment Opportunity Commission** (1972)[17] investigates and resolves complaints of discrimination filed by employees, generally based on color, race, or sex, but also on religion, national origin, or advanced age. In 1974, the Pension and Welfare Programs Office of the Labor Department was established to enforce the new Employee Retirement Income Security Act (ERISA),[18] which governs the integrity and fairness of private pension plans that supplement social security.

Communications

Available channels for wireless communication of radio and television messages, as well as personal messages, are strictly limited. The Federal Communications Commission (1934)[19] regulates such communications and thus maintains order where otherwise there would be chaos. The FCC also oversees interstate telephone and telegraph rates and service. The problems of the FCC are becoming aggravated as foreign countries expand their broadcast facilities. Efforts to allocate available transmission channels among the countries of the world by international agreement have so far been unsuccessful. International agreements have alleviated some of the problems by using intercontinental satellite transmissions.

Free Enterprise

Maintenance of an open market with true freedom of enterprise remains an ongoing problem. The temptation to collaborate with competitors to allocate markets and fix prices has been irresistible for many leading corporations. The Federal Trade Commission (1914)[20] shares watchdog duties with the Anti-trust Division of the Justice Department in enforcing the nation's laws against price fixing, monopolistic mergers, and other various unfair trade practices.

In 1983, the Superior Court Trial Lawyers Association of Washington, D.C. (SCTLA) went out on strike for higher wages. SCTLA members are counselors in the criminal area (i.e., criminal lawyers) in private practice. They are registered with the court to show that they are available to accept cases assigned by the court to represent indigent defendants. During the month-long boycott (strike), SCTLA members withheld their services from the court to dramatize the need for higher salaries (higher hourly rates) in order to ensure continued quality of service and a sufficient number of high-caliber lawyers to represent the increasing number of indigent cases.

After an investigation, the Federal Trade Commission held a hearing in which the boycott by SCTLA was ruled illegal, and barred any future, similar action on the part of the lawyers. SCTLA appealed. A federal appeals court ordered the FTC to reconsider its decision and determine if SCTLA had sufficient control of the market to make its boycott anticompetitive. The FTC appealed to the Supreme Court of the United States. Should the Supreme Court have forced a reconsideration of the order of the FTC?

No. The Supreme Court said: "The social justification[s] proffered for (this) restraint of trade . . . do not make it any less unlawful." The Court here applies the toughest anti-trust rule, the *per se* (in itself) rule. This means that the Court recognizes that some business activities, such as price-fixing, are so anticompetitive that they are automatically (per se) prohibited. Thus these activities do not require proof that conspirators (in this case, SCTLA members) had a motive or power to control the market. The Supreme Court overturned the appeals court order and ruled that the SCTLA strike was inherently illegal and that evidence of power to control the market was not required.[21]

Energy

The United States is one of many nations that is energy dependent. Since OPEC began its concerted program of escalating petroleum prices through quotas established by its members*, energy—its production, conservation and use—has

---

* Recently, OPEC's monopoly over world oil prices had failed because particularly oil-rich members such as Kuwait were ignoring established quotas and were overproducing, driving prices down for all the members. In order to control a larger share of the Middle Eastern oil market, Iraq invaded Kuwait. Kuwait and Iraq together represent well over 50% of the Middle East's oil reserves. The United Nations and the United States have responded by condemning Iraq's actions and have set up a military blockade.

become a matter of national survival. The Federal Power Commission (1930)[22] had previously regulated interstate transmission and sale of gas and electricity, but the major burden of responding to newly perceived needs in this area has fallen on the Federal Energy Regulatory Commission (1973)[23] of the Department of Energy, together with the Federal Energy Administration of that department. Also involved is the Nuclear Regulatory Commission (1973),[24] which licenses and supervises nuclear power plants.

The Nuclear Regulatory Commission (NRC) itself was subject to investigation by at least six separate federal, state, and private groups after a frightening accident in March 1979 that caused an emergency shutdown of the Three Mile Island, Pennsylvania, nuclear power plant. A comprehensive study was made by a special 12-member presidential commission headed by John Kemeny, president of Dartmouth College. The commission made 44 recommendations, including one to abolish the five-member NRC and replace it with an independent agency headed by a chief administrator with the power to act quickly. It did not call for a shutdown of existing nuclear plants, which at this writing have about 13 percent of the country's total present capacity to generate electric power. (That percentage is not expected to rise in the near future because additional U.S. nuclear plants are not currently being built and activated, although expansion is underway in Europe and other parts of the world.) However, the NRC has recommended that future nuclear power plants not be built near major population centers and that operating licenses be issued only after the states concerned have adopted emergency evacuation plans approved by the Federal Emergency Management Agency.[25]

Here again the courts have bowed to the expertise of administrators. A request had been made prior to the Three Mile Island accident to shut down all of the nation's nuclear power plants, although no member of the general public had been injured in more than 25 years of nuclear plant operation. The NRC refused, and on appeal to the U.S. Supreme Court the justices upheld the commission, refusing without comment to disturb their decision.[26]

Environmentalists who object to nuclear power persuaded a lower court to decree that the Nuclear Regulatory Commission had to reconsider its decision to grant an operating license to the Vermont Yankee Nuclear Power Corporation. The court held that the NRC was not adequately considering the dangers of nuclear-fuel reprocessing and nuclear waste management. The NRC appealed to the U.S. Supreme Court, claiming that the lower court had no power to interfere in the administrative process. Could the lower court legally interfere?

No. The courts do not have power to prescribe procedures that regulatory agencies must follow; at most, they may analyze whether the agency followed its own procedures and gathered sufficient evidence to support its actions. "Congress has made a choice to at least try nuclear energy, establishing a reasonable review process in which the courts are to play only a limited role," said the Supreme Court. A change, if any, must come from Congress. The courts should not attempt "to impose upon the agency [their] own notion of which procedures are best or most likely to further some vague, undefined public good."[27]

On March 24, 1989, Exxon's tanker *Valdez* struck a reef in Prince William Sound in the Gulf of Alaska and spilled 11 million gallons of crude oil into the area. Three weeks later the crude covered the beaches and island shores, killing birds and threatening the lucrative fishing industry.

Immediately the National Oceanic and Atmospheric Administration (NOAA) and the U.S. Coast Guard organized for the cleanup. The federal government chose Coast Guard Vice Admiral Clyde Robbins to coordinate the cleanup responses of the state, federal, and industry agencies. By September 1989, the cleanup ceased. The cost to Exxon was over one billion dollars. Still to be assessed are fines and penalties. Federal and state agencies have been authorized to prepare a damage assessment and claim reimbursement from Exxon for the destruction to the environment.[28]

Other Areas

The foregoing discussion touches on the leading independent federal administrative agencies, but it is far from complete. Excluded, for example, are numerous federal offices or departments with administrative powers, as well as even more numerous state agencies and offices that make and apply administrative law. For example, licensed trade and professional occupations are usually supervised by administrative bodies at the state level. So too are hospitals, nursing homes, and retirement facilities. When state legislatures made employers absolutely liable for injuries to workers suffered on the job under workers' compensation, they created special administration commissions to conduct the necessary hearings and make the required determination of injuries and of benefits payable.

At the local level too, zoning decisions, variances from established standards, and environmental impact reports are all under the surveillance and control of agencies with powers to make administrative law.

P. R. E. Voyance was a visionary investor in land. He often quoted the late Will Rogers: "Invest in land; they ain't making any more of it." "Pree," as his friends called him, predicted that the city would expand mostly to the flat farmlands on the east. Accordingly, over a period of 30 years he acquired a block of 2,000 acres, which by then was intersected by two super highways. Pree planned a major shopping center on one side of the main road, with an "edge" of three-story apartments and condominiums, and then a large area of single-family dwellings. On the other side of the main road, he planned an industrial park for light industry, to be served by truck, train, and helicopter. The time seemed ripe for development. May Voyance go ahead with his ambitious project?

Not necessarily. Most large cities and counties have administrative bodies, such as zoning commissions and planning boards, which draft master plans for real estate development. Exercising the police power of government, they may unilaterally decide that certain areas shall remain agricultural and others shall become residential, commercial, or industrial. Their decisions must be arrived at reasonably and after public hearings; but in the final analysis their judgment as experts prevails, even though they may disappoint many and enrich a few. Haphazard development is economically wasteful and socially objectionable. Voyance must yield to the opinion of the administrators as to appropriate land use.

How Is Administrative Law Applied?

Congress enacts legislation establishing the administrative agency and broadly defining its powers. Agency staff members are selected for their expertise in the field. Indeed, a common criticism is that talent moves from industry to agency, and vice versa, and that true independence of action is necessarily compromised. In reality, the interests of the public and industry are not diametrically opposed, and few major scandals of conflict of interest have developed. Administrative law is a combination of rules and regulations, fact-finding hearings, investigation, prosecution, implementation, and the other tasks that make up the duties of administrative agencies.

Regulations and Rulemaking

The power that administrative agencies possess—to pass rules and regulations—is not an inherent power of the executive branch of government. Instead, the power is created by the legislature as a delegation of their responsibility to legislate. In other words, Congress creates the agency and the agency creates the laws. Such delegations are lawful provided they are not overly broad and include adequate guidelines in the enabling statute. The legislature thus recognizes the complexity of detailed government regulation of the subject activity and the necessity that persons who create that law are experts in the field they regulate.

On the basis of its own investigations, the agency establishes standards and detailed rules. Under the federal Administrative Procedure Act (1946)[29] and similar legislation in many states, administrative agencies generally provide advance notice of intended new rules and give interested parties an opportunity to attend public hearings on the subject. If adopted, the rules are published in the **Federal Register.** Such rules, once appropriately adopted, have the same force of law as a statute passed by the legislature. In specific cases an administrative agency reaches decisions or makes rulings that apply to others in the field, under the doctrine of stare decisis.

Due process must be observed in hearings on new rules as well as in hearings on individual cases. In the latter cases, the hearing examiner or judge has the powers of a regular judge in the conduct of a trial, and both the agency and the defendant may be represented by counsel. There is no jury, and greater flexibility is permitted in the admission of evidence. The hearing examiner's decision includes findings of fact and of law, conclusions, and exceptions taken by the opposition. The agency has persuasive powers and may impose civil sanctions, suspension, cancellation or denial of licenses, confiscation of contraband, and other penalties. Any criminal sanctions require a conventional court trial.

Hearings or Administrative Adjudication

A few administrative agencies make policy by hearing and resolving individual disputes. The National Labor Relations Board is one such agency. The Labor Management Relations Act, as amended, is a detailed statute and rather than add additional regulations, the board and appointed hearing officers hear disputes under that act. The records of these proceedings are kept much in the manner of court proceedings. They form the basis of future rulings by the board and its hearing officers, as does the doctrine of stare decisis in the courts.

Other agencies provide hearings as an alternative to a court hearing, when the agency's action would deny a person some license, right, entitlement, or privilege.

Kelly and others were New York City residents receiving Aid to Families with Dependent Children (AFDC) welfare benefits. The New York City Social Service agency terminated these benefits. The agency told Kelly and those in the same situation that they could request informal review meetings and a formal hearing subsequent to the terminations. Does Kelly have a right to a hearing *before the AFDC benefits are terminated?*

Yes. The U.S. Supreme Court held that where benefits are a matter of statutory entitlement, the importance to the recipient must be weighed against the state's interest in efficient and expedient processes. In the case of welfare benefits that provide food, clothing, and shelter, a pre-termination hearing is a due process right to which Kelly is entitled.[30] The right to a hearing is an application of the due process clause of the Fourteenth Amendment, which requires that no state shall "deprive any person of life, liberty or property without due process of law. . . . "

Since the *Goldberg* v. *Kelly* opinion discussed above, the scope of due process a person can expect when facing negative government action has involved a quest for a fair balance between the nature of the individual's interest and the government's interest. That is: (1) does it involve a right or something less than a right, and (2) what is the nature of the government's interest (e.g., is this a proper and prudent use of government funds). A critical preliminary issue is what procedures might be employed to achieve a fair balance of interests.

Closely related to the question of whether a person can expect an evidentiary hearing before being the victim of negative governmental action is the issue of what type of hearing it must be. As stated by one commentator, "The fundamental policy problem of the administrative process is how to design a system of checks which will minimize the risks of bureaucratic arbitrariness and overreaching, while preserving for the agencies the flexibility they need to act effectively."[31]

At both the federal and state levels statutes provide for hearings and often define their nature, while allowing procedures that are not constitutionally required. The learned Judge Henry Friendly[32] has identified 11 attributes of a fair hearing that may or may not be constitutionally required, depending on the interests protected. With some editorial license, Judge Friendly's list is reproduced here, with a brief discussion of each item:

Judge Friendly's list.

1. *An unbiased tribunal.* In a court proceeding, such a tribunal would be a judge and/or jury without a prior opinion on the matter. In the usual administrative hearing, an agency employee who was not party to the original decision is considered sufficient. Should a trained neutral be required?

2. *Notice of the proposed action and the grounds for the action.* In a judicial process a complaint is the minimum grounds required. The notice expected for most administrative action is less specific to the kinds and number of charges, but there *must* be notice to the affected person.

3. *An opportunity to present reasons why the proposed action should not be taken.* Fundamental to all fair processes is an opportunity to tell and prove your view of the facts.

4. *The right to call witnesses.* This attribute is often allowed, but not always. In most court proceedings and even in arbitrations you not only can call witnesses, you can compel their attendance by subpoena. This is sometimes, but not always, true in administrative hearings.

5. *To know the evidence against you.* This right is self-explanatory and expected, but there are exceptions (e.g., as in prison disciplinary hearings, where such information may cost an adverse witness his or her life).

6. *To have a decision based on evidence presented at the hearing.* If the decision is based on information presented at the hearing, then one has the opportunity to rebut it. If the finder of fact makes a decision on facts learned outside the hearing, the claimant is denied a fair opportunity to contest the information. This right is almost always required.

7. *Counsel.* An important right: the right to legal or other qualified representation. But consider this: Does it mean counsel is allowed, or is it like a criminal matter where if you cannot afford counsel one will be appointed for you? Most administrative hearings allow counsel, but will not pay for it.

8. *Making of a record.* If a record is not available, how can an unfair hearing be contested? Trial courts provide records, and some (but not all) administrative hearings also do so. But what form does this record take—written, audiocassette-recorded, or videotaped?

9. *Statement of reasons for the decision.* This is an important attribute if the matter is to be appealed. If the reasons for the decision are inappropriate, they can be contested, but if they aren't given, they cannot be challenged. A statement of reasons for the decision is usually a part of the administrative hearing process.

10. *Public attendance.* Such attendance is based on the general belief that the activities of government officials should be open to the public to protect individuals from possible abuse of government power. This is often allowed, usually because of a statutory requirement rather than a court finding based on a constitutional right.

11. *Judicial review.* Court processes provide the right to an appeal; in administrative hearings appeal is also usually allowed, but the practical experience is that courts very seldom overturn administrative rulings or actions. Usually, the only chance for a successful appeal is one that is made within the agency. The best basis for an appeal of an agency action to a court is that the procedure was not fair, rather than that the result was incorrect. Courts are the experts on procedure, but they defer to the experts on the facts.

Investigations and Administrative Actions

The traditional work of an administrative agency is to execute its administrative task. That may involve investigation, prosecution, negotiation, and any number of other administrative activities. In recent years the Supreme Court has held that administrative agencies, like the police, must comply with the search and seizure provisions of the Fourth Amendment. The Fourth Amendment requires a warrant before a search can be legally conducted.[33] (There are some exceptions—e.g., inspections of nuclear reactors at utility plants.) Requirements for administrative warrants are somewhat less demanding than for criminal warrants, but the Fourth Amendment protection against unreasonable governmental intrusion still applies.

Government agencies are also subject to various information acts. Such laws are often in conflict with each other, as some prohibit the release of information (e.g., privacy acts) while under certain circumstances others mandate its release upon request (e.g., Freedom of Information Act).

Moreover, the original enabling legislation as well as all rulings of administrative agencies are subject to judicial review. Generally, the individual seeking administrative relief or challenging an administrative ruling must "exhaust available administrative remedies" before resorting to the regular courts. Prescribed review procedures are always available within the agencies. As noted earlier, the courts normally do not overrule agency decisions because the agencies are recognized as the experts in the field. However, arbitrary or capricious actions by agencies, or conflicts with the basic law, will evoke a response from the courts.

The Port Authority of New York and New Jersey is an administrative agency; its duties include the operation of the John F. Kennedy International Airport in New York. When British and French airlines sought landing rights at the airport for their supersonic Concorde jet transports, residents in the vicinity of the airport protested because of an anticipated increase of noise. The Port Authority procrastinated in developing noise standards, but meanwhile banned the planes. A federal district court overruled the Port Authority. The U.S. Court of Appeals overruled the district court, saying the Port Authority has the power to ban the flights but must exercise it in a reasonable and nondiscriminatory way. It ordered the district court to conduct a hearing to determine whether the 13-month delay by the Port Authority in making reasonable noise regulations constituted unfair discrimination against the British and French airlines and an undue burden on commerce. Meanwhile, it ordered the Port Authority to permit Concorde flights to begin forthwith. The Port Authority appealed to the U.S. Supreme Court for a stay of the order, stopping or holding it in abeyance. Should the Supreme Court have upheld the administrative agency under these circumstances?

No. The application for stay was denied, and Concorde flights began. Administrative agencies must act reasonably or the courts can override their decisions, as here.[34]

The legislature also may reenter the picture by amending the basic legislation or by reducing agency appropriations. For example, over the years directors of the Internal Revenue Service have been rebuffed in requests for money to expand audits of income tax returns. No doubt legislators agree that more stringent enforcement would generate much more revenue than it would cost, but would also be politically disastrous.

In the same vein, in the late 1970s strong lobbying efforts were made to Congress by the funeral, life insurance, and breakfast cereal industries to restrain reform efforts by the Federal Trade Commission. The Federal Trade Commission was seeking to require (1) that undertakers quote prices of component parts of a funeral service in detail and before contracting, (2) that they refrain from offering grieving relatives only the most expensive services available, (3) that they disclose to customers that expensive embalming is not necessary, (4) that life insurance companies disclose the effective rate of return on savings to policyholders who buy "whole life" policies (which include a savings element), and (5) that manufacturers of sugar-coated cereals (which are of low nutritional value and cause tooth decay) terminate their heavy television advertising of such products to children.

Congress responded in May 1980 with legislation that authorized Congress to veto any rule adopted by the FTC. This legislation was an extraordinary invasion of the agency's traditional independence. On the specific troubled points: Congress permitted FTC regulation of the funeral home industry but limited the scope to such matters as full disclosure of prices; it allowed the FTC to study the insurance industry, but only if requested by a majority vote of the House or Senate Commerce Committee; and it specified that advertising to children may be controlled, but only if proved to be deceptive, and not simply "unfair" as before.[35]

Similar resistance and resentment by regulated companies has generated congressional support for restraint on the activities of the Occupational Safety and Health Administration. Congress has prohibited OSHA from inspecting businesses with ten or fewer employees, so long as they are in industries with good safety records. This prohibition had the effect of excluding 1.5 million shops with 5 million employees. Earlier, the Supreme Court ruled that employers may refuse to admit OSHA inspectors unless they have search warrants.[36] In another case, the Supreme Court held for the opponents and affirmed a lower court ruling that requires the government to weigh the benefits of its regulations against their costs.[37] The case involves a proposed OSHA regulation limiting exposure of workers to benzene by reducing it to the "lowest feasible level." OSHA contends that exposure may cause leukemia (a form of cancer).

Although Congress finds it necessary to delegate much legislative authority to agencies, at the same time it has attempted to maintain control over decisions arising from these agencies.

In an unrelated matter, in the early 1980s the Supreme Court considered the constitutionality of the legislative veto* in the case of *Immigration and Naturalization Service* v. *Chadha.*[38] The statute in question permitted one house of the national legislature to veto decisions made by the Immigration and Naturalization Service (INS) Commissioner on deportation appeals. The Court ruled that all legislative vetoes were unconstitutional because the exercise of the veto was in essence the making of law in a manner that did not allow it to be presented to the President for a signature or veto before it becomes law.

The importance of the decision in Chadha appears to be far-reaching, as noted in this statement from a leading constitutional law text:

> In Chadha, the Court majority evidently chose to view the veto as a legislative act subject to the requirements of Article I [in the U.S. Constitution]. In adopting this

---

* Legislative veto is a legislative device whereby Congress passes laws broadly and incorporates a provision allowing for congressional review of the executive branch's implementation of the law. The legislative veto permits Congress to delegate general legislative authority and then take it away without executive approval.

approach, the Court not only invalidated the INS veto provision actually before it but rendered some two hundred similar statutory provisions presumptively unconstitutional. Thus the Chadha case can be viewed as the most sweeping exercise of judicial review in Supreme Court history.[39]

As of this writing, the full impact of *Chadha* is yet to be felt among the regulatory agencies and the general public.

A broad public sentiment against high taxes and unnecessary government regulation is part of the support claimed for a current proposal to exempt 90 percent of all businesses from OSHA inspections. The agency would presumably concentrate its limited resources on the most hazardous workplaces. Organized labor has opposed the cutback. Nevertheless, the need to reduce federal expenditures to comply with the requirements of a balanced budget by 1992 will keep public support high with respect to reduced intrusion by OSHA into most businesses. (Most economists, however, predict that President George Bush will withdraw his opposition to new taxes—"Read my lips!"—because of the savings and loan bailout cost and the need for increased military spending in the Middle East.)

The criticism of OSHA operations is not found in other regulated industries. In the field of air transport, as noted earlier, some deregulation by the Civil Aeronautics Board permitted airlines to reduce their rates. Although this initially boosted traffic and profits, when rising fuel and labor costs forced higher rates air travel dropped sharply and many lines suffered losses. Moreover, consumers complained that needed service was no longer available at the smaller cities that are "feeders" for main trunk lines.

The Interstate Commerce Commission has relaxed controls on railroad rates and mergers and on trucking rates. Although railroads have welcomed the opportunity to compete more freely with trucks, spokespersons of trucking trade associations have resisted decontrol. Here the argument is that small carriers and shippers need the government-mandated rates and regulations to protect them against the rigors of open competition from larger companies. This view, of course, contradicts a fundamental tenet of the free market philosophy that competition rewards the most efficient and is best for the great mass of consumers even though some weak producers are eliminated.

In the 1980s, under the two-term administration of President Ronald Reagan, there was a systematic cutback in regulation by governmental agencies. The motto, "Get governments off our backs" has had great popular support among the business community large and small. The popular crusade to deregulate industrial America has had a major impact on the economy. Reagan, in the hands of "supply side" economic "gurus," created what has become known as the "Reagan Revolution". However, re-regulation could be the "revolution of the 90s"—the Bush administration seems to be pumping new life into the deflated regulatory agencies.

According to a recent article in the *San Francisco Chronicle*, there is evidence that re-regulation is returning under President George Bush: (1) new restrictions on thrift institutions as part of the "bail-out"* package; (2) new concern about

---

* The U.S. government is obligated to bail out or salvage savings and loan associations that have become insolvent, often through bad management practices, risky loan portfolios, and, in some cases, fraud. Bail out involves paying depositors their insured savings balances, selling off foreclosed properties, and installing new management.

over-consolidation in airline companies; (3) new pressure on auto manufacturers from the Transportation Department to make safer cars, and from the Environmental Protection Agency to make cars that run on less-polluting fuels; and (4) new scrutiny of the trucking industry by the Occupational Health and Safety Administration.[40]

Despite recent trends, most authorities believe that re-regulation is still a long way off.

> There still is a term *deregulation movement,* but the term should be interpreted broadly. For example, while we've deregulated the airlines and the telephone industry, we still have a long way to go in such areas as foreign trade and agriculture.[41]

Re-regulation might be beginning, but after a decade of deregulation, there will be great resistance to return to a more regulated and structured society and economy.

Case 7

WYMAN v. JAMES

U.S. Supreme Court, 400 U.S. 309, 91 S.CT. 381 (1971)

Under New York state statutes and rules and regulations prescribed by Congress for assistance, the Aid to Families with Dependent Children (AFDC) program requires home visits. Mrs. James, over a period of time, refused to permit the caseworker assigned her family to enter her home. Do home visits, as required by law, fall within the Fourth Amendment's proscription against unreasonable searches and seizures?

Justice Blackmun (delivering the opinion of the Court, saying in part:) When a case involves a home and some type of official intrusion into that home, as this case appears to do, an immediate and natural reaction is one of concern about Fourth Amendment rights and the protection which that Amendment is intended to afford. Its emphasis indeed is upon one of the most precious aspects of personal security in the home. "The right of the people to be secure in their persons, houses, papers, and effects. . . . This Court has characterized that right as "basic to our free society." And over the years the Court consistently has been most protective of the privacy of the dwelling.

This natural and quite proper protective attitude, however, is not a factor in this case, for the seemingly obvious and simple reason that we are not concerned here with any search by the New York social service agency in the Fourth Amendment meaning of that term. It is true that the governing statute and regulations appear to make mandatory the initial home visit and the subsequent periodic "contacts" (which may include home visits) for the inception and continuance of aid. It is also true that the caseworker's posture in the home visit is perhaps, in a sense, both rehabilitative and investigative. But this latter aspect, we think, is given too broad a character and far more emphasis than it deserves if it is equated with a search in the traditional criminal law context. We note, too, that the visitation in itself is not forced or compelled, and that the beneficiary's denial of permission is not a criminal act. If consent to the visitation is withheld, no visitation takes place. The aid then never begins or merely ceases, as the case may be. There is no entry of the home and there is no search.

If, however, we were to assume that a case-worker's home visit, before or subsequent to the beneficiary's initial qualification for benefits, somehow (perhaps because the average beneficiary might feel she is in no position to refuse consent to the visit), and despite its interview nature, does possess some of the characteristics of a search in the traditional sense, we nevertheless conclude that the visit not fall within the Fourth Amendment's proscription. This is because it does not descend to the level of unreasonableness. It is unreasonableness which is the Fourth Amendment's standard.

There are a number of factors which compel us to conclude that the home visit proposed for Mrs. James is not unreasonable:

1. The public's interest in this particular segment of the area of assistance to the unfortunate is protection and aid for the dependent child whose family requires such aid for that child. The focus is on the child and, further, it is on the child who is dependent. There is no more worthy object of the public's concern. The dependent child's needs are paramount, and only with hesitancy would we relegate those needs, in the scale of comparative values, to a position secondary to what the mother claims as her rights.

2. The agency, with tax funds provided from federal as well as from state sources, is fulfilling a public trust. The State, working through its qualified welfare agency, has appropriate and paramount interest and concern in seeing and assuring that the intended and proper objects of that tax-produced assistance are the ones who benefit from the aid it dispenses. Surely it is not unreasonable, in the Fourth Amendment sense

or in any other sense of that term, that the State have at its command a gentle means, of limited extent and of practical and considerate application, of achieving that assurance.

3. One who dispenses purely private charity naturally has an interest in and expects to know how his charitable funds are utilized and put to work. The public, when it is the provider, rightly expects the same. It might well expect more, because of the trust aspect of public funds, and the recipient, as well as the caseworker, has not only an interest but an obligation.

4. The emphasis of the New York statutes and regulations is upon the home, upon "close (contact)" with the beneficiary, upon restoring the aid recipient "to a condition of self-support," and upon the relief of his distress. The federal emphasis is no different. . . . And it is concerned about any possible exploitation of the child. . . .

. . .

7. Mrs. James, in fact, on this record presents no specific complaint of any unreasonable intrusion of her home and nothing which supports an inference that the desired home visit had as its purpose the obtaining of information as to criminal activity. She complains of no proposed visitation at an awkward or retirement hour. She suggests no forcible entry. She refers to no snooping. She describes no impolite or reprehensible conduct of any kind. She alleges only, in general and nonspecific terms, that on previous visits and, on information and belief, on visitation at the home of other aid recipients, "questions concerning personal relationships, beliefs and behavior are raised and pressed which are unnecessary for a determination of continuing eligibility." Paradoxically, this same complaint could be made of a conference held elsewhere than in the home, and yet this is what is sought by Mrs. James. The same complaint could be made of the census taker's questions. . . . What Mrs. James appears to want from the agency which provides her and her infant son with the necessities for life is the right to receive those necessities upon her own informational terms, to utilize the Fourth Amendment as a wedge for imposing those terms and to avoid questions of any kind.

8. We are not persuaded, as Mrs. James would have us be, that all information pertinent to the issue of eligibility can be obtained by the agency through an interview at a place other than the home, or, as the District Court majority suggested, by examining a lease or a birth certificate, or by periodic medical examinations, or by interviews with school personnel. Although these secondary sources might be helpful, they would not always assure verification of actual residence or of actual physical presence in the home, which are requisites for AFDC benefits, or of impending medical needs. And, of course, little children, such as Maurice James, are not yet registered in school.

9. The visit is not one by police or uniformed authority. It is made by a caseworker of some training whose primary objective is, or should be, the welfare, not the prosecution, of the aid recipient for whom the worker has profound responsibility. As has already been stressed, the program concerns dependent children and the needy families of those children. It does not deal with crime or with the actual or suspected perpetrators of crime. The caseworker is not a sleuth but rather, we trust, is a friend in need.

10. The home visit is not a criminal investigation, does not equate with a criminal investigation, and despite the announced fears of Mrs. James and those who would join her, is not in aid of any criminal proceeding. If the visitation serves to discourage misrepresentation or fraud, such a byproduct of that visit does not impress upon the visit itself a dominant criminal investigative aspect. And if the visit should, by chance, lead to the discovery of fraud and a criminal prosecution should follow, then, even assuming that the evidence discovered upon the home visitation is admissible, an issue upon which we express no opinion, that is a routine and expected fact of life and a consequence no greater than that which necessarily ensues upon any other discovery by a citizen of criminal conduct. . . .

It seems to us that the situation is akin to that where an Internal Revenue Service agent, in making a routine civil audit of a taxpayer's income tax return, asks that the taxpayer produce for the agent's review some proof of a deduction the taxpayer has asserted to his benefit in the computation of his tax. If the taxpayer refuses, there is, absent fraud, only a disallowance of the claimed deduction and a consequent additional tax. The taxpayer is fully within his "rights" in refusing to produce the proof, but in maintaining and asserting those rights a tax detriment results and it is a detriment of the taxpayer's own making. So here Mrs. James has the "right" to refuse the home visit, but a consequence in the form of cessation of aid, similar to the taxpayer's resultant additional tax, flows from that refusal. The choice is entirely hers, and nothing of constitutional magnitude is involved. . . .

The Court in a six to three decision reversed and remanded with directions to enter a judgment of dismissal. Mrs. James' Fourth Amendment rights were not violated.

QUESTIONS AND PROBLEMS

1. The rules of X State University provide that students must not engage in disruption of class activities. If they do so, they are subject to expulsion. Rules of the college provide that before expulsion can occur, the students are entitled to a conference with the Dean of Students. Jim is a student who has been accused of obstructing the administration of the school by engaging in a sit-in demonstration. He asserts that he is entitled to more procedural protection than the rules afford him.

a. The college says that Jim enrolled in the school and therefore has waived any further protections than those granted him in the rules and regulations. Is this position well taken? *no*

b. Jim asserts that he is entitled to have his lawyer present during any procedures designed to expel him. Is this position reasonable? *no*

c. Jim states that he has the right to cross-examine the witnesses against him. Is he correct? *no*

d. Jim maintains that the Dean of Students is biased against him because of statements the Dean has made to the effect that Jim is a menace and should be removed from the school. Is Jim's objection allowable? *no - classic appointh by one disgruntled ?*

e. Would it make any difference to Jim if the school in question was a private university rather than a public one? Restrict your answer to the right to a hearing and the general nature of such a hearing.

2. In 1970 Congress passed the Occupational Safety and Health Act (OSHA) to improve the safety and working conditions of employees in the private sector. Among the power assigned to OSHA was adjudication. Atlas Roofing Co., Inc. which was fined for unsafe workings, claims that OSHA's adjudicatory powers which imposed the fine are unconstitutional and a violation of the *Seventh Amendment*. Is the claim valid? [*Atlas Roofing Co., Inc.* v. *Occupational Safety and Health Commission,* 430 U.S. 442, 97 S.Ct. 1261, (1977).]

3. In violation of Federal Aviation regulations, a pilot used as a runway (for takeoff and landing) an airport strip intended solely for taxiing airplanes on the ground. The illegal use of the runway caused the plane to fly within 10 to 60 feet of persons, vehicles, and buildings on the ground. The National Transportation Safety Board (NTSB) suspended the pilot's license for 180 days. He appealed to the courts. Decide this case.

4. As a general rule, administrative searches of businesses require a warrant. A liquor store owner was inspected by Alcohol, Tobacco and Firearms officials without a warrant. The liquor store owner claimed that the officers conducted a search in violation of his Fourth Amendment rights. Is this a valid claim? [*Donovan* v. *Dewey,* (1981), 452, U.S. 594, 101 S.Ct. 2534]

5. States are permitted some regulation as to who may get an abortion and under what conditions. One of the arguments used in the defense of a right to an abortion is that a woman has an absolute right to control her body, to the exclusion of all other rights. Does this same argument justify the decriminalization of prostitution? Of suicide? Why? (Note that state law generally applies to prostitution and suicide.)

6. Henri Simone is a rugged individualist who built a business with a large annual sales volume from a modest beginning in his garage. He thinks it is his constitutional right and management prerogative to hire, control, and fire employees as he pleases. Is his opinion in accord with the law?

7. Under the Fifth Amendment at the federal level and the Fourteenth Amendment at the state level, government may not deprive any person of life, liberty, or property without due process of law. Oshida, who runs a small greeting-card printing company, argues that both amendments are violated by laws that require her to keep costly records at her own expense in order to withhold and pay state and federal income taxes for her employees. She makes the same complaint about a series of other reports that government agencies require her to submit regularly or sporadically, at substantial cost to her, especially since the information is simply "compiled, published, filed, and forgotten." May she justifiably refuse to comply with such government demands?

8. Railway Express Agency, a company doing business in and licensed by the state of New York, sold advertising space to be placed on the side of its vans and trucks. The city of New York passed a "traffic safety" ordinance prohibiting advertising on the sides of all vehicles except to advertise the company to which the vehicle belongs. Railway Express sued and lost. Railway Express appealed to the Supreme Court of the United States on the grounds of undue interference into its commercial activities. Is this claim constitutional? [*Railway Express Agency* v. *New York,* 336 U.S. 106, 69 S.Ct. 463, (1949)]

9. Which government is best equipped to regulate and control the environment—federal or state? Why? Did the Exxon *Valdez* oil spill influence your answer? Why?

10. The Equal Employment Opportunity Commission sought to enforce the Age Discrimination in Employment Act against the state of Wyoming. A state employee was involuntarily removed from his job as a game warden. Was the game warden's firing a proper use of Wyoming's control over its employees? [*Equal Employment Opportunity Commission* v. *Wyoming,* 460 U.S. 226, 103 S.Ct. 1054 (1983)]

FURTHER READING

1. Burns, J., J. Peltason and T. Cronin. *Government by the People.* Englewood Cliffs, NJ: Prentice-Hall, 1989. This is (has been) the most popular textbook on *American* and *state* government that is in print.

2. Dye, T., and H. Zeigler, *The Irony of Democracy.* Monterey, CA: Brooks/Cole, 1990. A popular analytical treatise of American governments and their bureaucracies, with an excellent treatment of the role of the media in elections.

3. Gellhorn, W. and C. Boyer, *Administrative Law and Process.* St. Paul, MN: West Publishing Co., 1981.

4. Marshall, B., *A Workable Government.* New York: Norton, 1987. A work written for the bicentennial celebration of the writing of the U.S. Constitution. After 200 years it is still "working" and proof that those who wrote it planned well.

5. McDonald, F., *Novus Ordo Seclorum.* Lawrence, KS: University of Kansas, 1985. A fine historian's account of the founding of our constitutional republic.

6. Stephens, O. and J. Schleb, *American Constitutional Law.* New York: Harcourt Brace Jovanovich, 1988. A popular, up-to-date textbook on constitutional law, written especially for undergraduate students.

NOTES

1. U.S. Supreme Court Justice Jackson, *FTC* v. *Rubberoid Co.,* 343 U.S. 470, 72 S.Ct. 800, (1952).

2. "When Fines Collapse," 74 *National Law Journal,* Dec. 4, 1989, p. 1, 40–41.

3. *Facts on File,* Transportation, p. 420 (1979) New York City.

4. 42 USCA 301 et seq.

5. 16 USCA 791 et seq.

6. *The Wall Street Journal,* February 14, 1980, p. 2, and April 30, 1980, p. 6; *San Francisco Chronicle,* February 14, 1980, p. 1.

7. 15 USCA 77 et seq.

8. 7 USCA 221 et seq.

9. 12 USCA 221 et seq.

10. 49 USCA 1 et seq.

11. 46 USCA 861 et seq.

12. 49 USCA 1301 et seq.

13. 14 USCA 81 et seq.; 49 USCA 1711 et seq.

14. 23 USCA 404 et seq.

15. *The Wall Street Journal,* June 12, 1978, p. 2.

16. 29 USCA 151 et seq.

17. 42 USCA 2000 et seq.

18. 5 USCA 5108 et seq.

19. 15 USCA 21 et seq.

20. 15 USCA 761 et seq.

21. *The Wall Street Journal,* January 23, 1990, p. B8.

22. 16 USCA 791 et seq.

23. 15 USCA 761 et seq.

24. 42 USCA 2011 et seq.

25. *Report of the President's Commission on the Accident of Three Mile Island* (Washington, D.C.: Government Printing Office, 1979).

26. *Honicker* v. *U.S. Nuclear Regulatory Commission,* 441 U.S. 906, 99 S.Ct. 1995 (1979), memorandum decision.

27. *Vermont Yankee Nuclear Power Corporation* v. *Natural Resources Defense Council, Inc.,* 435 U.S. 519, 98 S.Ct. 1197 (1978).

28. "Alaska's Big Spill," *National Geographic,* January 1990, p. 5–42.

29. Administrative Procedure Act (1946). 5 USCA 551 et seq.

30. *Goldbert* v. *Kelly,* 397 U.S. 254, 90 S.Ct. 1011 (1970).

31. Gellhorn, W., and Clark Byse, *Administrative Law* (New York: Foundation Press, 1987).

32. Friendly, H., "Some Kind of Hearing," 123 *University of Pennsylvania Law Review* 1267 (1975).

33. *Marshall* v. *Barlow's Inc.,* 436 U.S. 307, 98 S.Ct. 1816 (1978).

34. *Port Authority of New York and New Jersey et al.* v. *British Airways et al.,* 434 U.S. 899, 98 S.Ct. 291 (1977), memorandum decision.

35. *The Wall Street Journal,* May 21, 1980, p. A18.

36. *Marshall* v. *Barlow's Inc.,* 436 U.S. 307, 98 S.Ct. 1816 (1978).

37. *American Petroleum Institute* v. *Secretary of Labor,* 448 U.S. 607, 100 S.Ct. 2844 (1979).

38. *Immigration and Naturalization Services* v. *Chadha,* 462 U.S. 919, 103 S.Ct. 2764 (1983).

39. Stephens, O., and J. Schleb, *American Constitutional Law* (New York: Harcourt, Brace, Jovanovich, 1988), p. 232–233.

40. *San Francisco Chronicle,* January 2, 1990, p. C1.

41. Statement by noted economist Milton Friedman, *ibid.* p. C6.

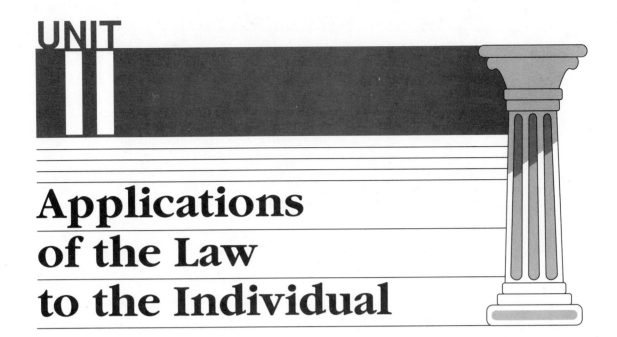

UNIT II

Applications of the Law to the Individual

8

Family Law

Family law governs the legal relations of the basic social unit, the family. For the most part, the applicable rules and principles have been established by the legislative branches of state governments—there is no federal marriage or divorce law. As a family member, however, a person may become involved in a matter involving federal jurisdiction. For example, if American citizen Bruce Brown, husband and father, was caught at Nogales, Arizona, entering the United States with contraband, such as marijuana, he would be involved in a federal crime. But the question of how Brown's absence from the family, if he was jailed, would affect his marriage and his duty to support his children would be determined by principles of family law in the state of his residence. In addition, there are federal laws designed to protect the family when issues raised involve more than one state. For example, the Child Abuse Prevention and Treatment Act of 1984 encourages states to adopt remedial statutes; the Omnibus Budget Reconciliation Act of 1981 provides for interception of income tax refunds payable to parents who are delinquent in their support obligations; and the Parental Kidnapping Act of 1984 provides special penalties for child "snatching" parents. You will find wide variations in family law from state to state, because legislative viewpoints differ on the very sensitive and important principles applicable to the family.

Most principles of family law are found in civil law. But some are found in criminal law also, because certain conduct involving family members is so objectionable that society, through legislation, expresses its disapproval by imposing criminal penalties. Child abuse and spouse beating are examples of such conduct.

Criminal and civil statutes have been enacted principally to protect and enhance marriage and the family. Criminal laws designed to protect the family include those that proscribe adultery, bigamy, seduction accomplished by false promise of marriage, and incest. Incest is cohabitation (i.e., living together as husband and wife) or sexual intercourse between a man and a woman who are so closely related to each other that marriage is forbidden by law. Examples of civil laws relating to the family declare that there is a reciprocal obligation of support binding both spouses during marriage; and that on termination of the marriage, courts may distribute the family property equitably (in accordance with applicable state law) and define the continuing rights and duties of family members.

What Is Marriage?

Marriage is a status entered by means of a contract that is enforceable by courts. When the status is created, the law grants enforceable rights to the parties, but also imposes various mutual obligations. Such official governance of the relationship is justified because marriage is recognized as the essential foundation of healthy families and therefore of a healthy, viable society.

Statutes regulate the lawful creation of marriage. All jurisdictions prohibit the marriage of persons of the same sex. In most states, a minimum age of 18 years is prescribed for marriage. Parental consent is required for the marriage of minors, but in special situations (e.g., pregnancy out of wedlock), some state courts are authorized to approve marriages of underage persons. All states prohibit marriage between members of the immediate family (ascendants–descendants, i.e., parent and child) and siblings (brothers and sisters). Most prohibit uncle/niece or aunt/nephew marriages, and some extend the prohibition to first cousins. A few continue to proscribe matrimony for certain relationships of affinity (e.g., step-father/stepdaughter). Statutes typically require that a person entering marriage be of sound mind—not be insane, an idiot, an imbecile, or a lunatic—although doctors have difficulty diagnosing mental illness, and there is confusion as to what such terms mean in law. Most states require a health examination showing freedom from certain venereal diseases as a pre-condition for issuance of a marriage license. Solemnization is generally required by either a civil (justice of the peace or judge) or religious (minister, priest, rabbi, or the like) authority.

Common-Law Marriage

In 14 states, a **common-law marriage** may arise when a man and a woman continue to live together as husband and wife but without legal formalities (health examination, license, and solemnization). For a common-law marriage to exist, parties who are legally permitted to marry must cohabit and create the public impression that a marriage exists, and they must intend that it exist.[1] Once the common-law marriage is created, it is treated in the laws the same as all other marriages. The vast majority of states do not permit this method of establishing a marriage; however, Article IV, Section 1 of the U.S. Constitution provides: *"Full faith and credit shall be given in each state to the public acts, records, and judicial proceedings of every other state."* New York and California, for example, do not permit common-law marriages, but they must recognize as valid a common-law marriage that previously was created in Ohio or Texas.

The "Marvin Marriage"

Michelle Triola met noted actor Lee Marvin during the filming of *Ship of Fools.* The couple soon moved into the same household. Thereafter Lee divorced his estranged wife, Betty, but in 1970 left Michelle to marry his childhood sweetheart, Pamela. Michelle sued for a share of Lee's considerable earnings as well as compensation for the earnings she allegedly sacrificed for Lee's sake in giving up her career as a singer. What should have been the result?

Michelle ultimately lost her case. But the celebrated trial between Michelle Triola and Lee Marvin exemplified a trend in some segments of our society whereby persons choose to live together in a continuing relationship without the formality of marriage. The historical attitude of the courts had been to give no protection to either party of a so-called **meretricious** (based on pretense of marriage) relationship. Thus, on separation neither "pseudo-spouse" could obtain a share of the other's earnings or accumulated wealth or receive payments for continued support. Any contract that purported to create property or support rights in another in exchange for participation in a meretricious relationship was void as against public policy.

Departing from tradition, the California Supreme Court held that adults who live together and engage in sexual relations are, nonetheless, competent to *contract* to pool (i.e., combine) earnings or to keep each one's earnings and other property separate. The court stated that such an agreement may be express, implied (inferred from conduct), or may be based on "some other tacit understanding." However, the contract may not be based on the exchange of sexual favors.[2] The California Supreme Court remanded the *Marvin* case to the trial court to determine if such an agreement existed between Triola and Marvin. The trial court rejected Michelle's contention that a contract existed, but awarded her $104,000 for rehabilitative compensation. That award subsequently was reversed on a second appeal and Michelle ultimately received nothing.

A rash of similar lawsuits followed in California, setting a trend for courts in other states to grant relief to "discarded" companions when existence of a contract could be proved. Legislatures have remained reluctant to enact protective laws for cohabiting persons. In effect, some courts have discarded public policy objections and recognized the economic value of the pseudo-spouse as a homemaker. Courts in many states now protect cohabitants by awarding division of property or payment of support through enforcement of an express (written or oral) or implied (inferred) agreement.[3] Homosexual couples receive Marvin-type relief in some jurisdictions.[4] On the other hand, some states continue to deny all relief to cohabitants on the grounds of public policy.[5]

What Are the Legal Consequences of Marriage?

Obligation of Support

The marital relationship implies a continuing and mutual obligation of support. Support includes food, shelter, clothing, medicine, and usually a wide range of consumer goods, all appropriate to the family's wealth and established standard of living.[6] Management of the family budget is left to the wise judgment of the spouses.[7] Courts seldom become involved in support disputes unless the marriages in question are in the process of dissolution or divorce.

Robert Hamilton became crippled and unable to work. His wife, Sally, a trained legal secretary, had been serving as housewife and homemaker. Sally declared that she would not
seek gainful employment to support her husband and would henceforth terminate the
marriage. Is Sally required to go to work to support Robert if the marriage remains intact?
If it is terminated?

Yes, Sally will be required to apply her earning skills in support of her husband
whether or not the marriage remains intact. Also, in this hypothetical case, she
could be required to use property owned in her name for his support. The specific criteria often used by courts in setting the amount of required support following termination of the marriage are reviewed later in this chapter.

Property Rights

Common-Law Jurisdictions (Most States)   Under original common-law theory,
title to all property owned by a woman was automatically vested in her husband
upon marriage. During marriage, the wife owned no property. Marriage created
one entity: the husband. A creditor who successfully sued the wife received a
judgment against the husband, and thereby reached all the family's non-exempt
assets.

Rejecting the original common-law theory, 41 common-law states have adopted
some form of the Uniform Marriage and Divorce Act, which created the distinction
between separate and marital property. **Separate property** is all property
acquired before marriage or during marriage by gift or inheritance. The husband
and wife are "partners" in the **marital property** earned during marriage. How
marital property is handled during divorce is explained later in this chapter; but
during marriage, there is uncertainty of the extent to which creditors of one
spouse can reach the entire nonexempt marital property. A uniform law has been
proposed, called the Uniform Marital Property Act, which would subject all of the
marital property to the creditors of either spouse.[8] However, only Wisconsin has
adopted the act as of this writing. Courts in Maine have ruled, in the absence of
any statute, that all of the marital property can be reached by creditors of either
spouse, and that rule appears to be the new trend.[9] But until the trend becomes
established, courts in many states may continue to rule that creditors of one
spouse can only reach marital property held in that spouse's name. This pre-trend
law holds that property rights generally are based on who owns title. Creditors
can only reach property held in the name of the debtor—the title owner possesses
all incidents of ownership. Spouses, in essence, are treated as strangers with
respect to the other spouse's property.

Community Property Jurisdictions.*   **Community property** is all property
acquired by the husband or the wife during marriage other than by gift or inheritance. The respective earnings of husband and wife during marriage are owned

---

* Community property states are Arizona, California, Idaho, Louisiana, Nevada, New Mexico, Texas,
Washington, and Wisconsin.

equally when received. Upon dissolution of the marriage, accumulated earnings (as with all other community properties) are divided equally between the spouses, because the ownership of community property is equal.

As stated earlier, separate property, on the other hand, is property either brought into the marriage or acquired during marriage by gift or inheritance. Separate property retains its character so long as separate, independent records are kept. For example, cash kept in a separate savings account will retain its separate property classification. **Commingling** of separate property and community property occurs when the two are so combined that they cannot be traced back to their original status. In such cases, the separate property has become *transmuted* into community property and lost its former identity. An example is cash brought into the marriage and subsequently combined in the family checking account with monthly community earnings. The status of property as separate or community can be altered by an agreement between the spouses.

Because both spouses own an undivided one-half interest in the community property, neither spouse can defeat the other spouse's ownership rights by giving it away without consent.

In Seattle, Washington, George Marichol was enamored of his secretary, Vickie Evans, and gave her a Jaguar XJS purchased with earnings from his accounting business. When his wife, Betty, learned of the gift, she insisted that the car be taken from Vickie. Can this legally be done?

Yes. Whenever either spouse gives away community property without the other's consent, the injured spouse can request the court to set aside the transfer of property and order the property returned to the community. However, if the automobile was "given" to the secretary in exchange for services legitimately rendered, then the "gift" would be in the nature of a bonus or wage and would not be set aside. Realistically, in the above hypothetical example, the marriage probably would have deteriorated to the extent that Betty would pursue a dissolution (divorce) rather than continue the marriage following a lawsuit to restore an improper gift to the community. Upon any divorce, the court, in dividing the community property equally, would give Betty "credit" for her one-half value of the XJS.

Unpaid creditors who obtain a judgment against either the husband or wife can reach all non-exempt community property to satisfy their claims. Property declared "exempt" by statute cannot be taken from anyone by any creditor. *Necessaries of life* (personal clothes, food, medicine, etc.) are an example of exempt property. Accordingly, for example, if a husband wrongfully punches a mail carrier and severely injures the carrier's eyesight, the victim can receive payment of his judgment from the accumulated earnings of the defendant's wife, or from any other non-exempt community property. Of course, the husband's separate property would be liable for his torts or personal debts incurred before or during his marriage; his wife's separate property would not. Reciprocally, the wife's separate property would be liable for her torts or other debts; her husband's separate property would not. However, a spouse's earnings during marriage may be diverted from the marriage and taken to satisfy premarital debts.

One spouse is not responsible for the crimes or torts of the other, and a spouse's separate property is immune from fines or judgments against the other. Indirectly, of course, the innocent spouse is hurt if a fine is paid from community property or if, as a result of confinement, community property is not earned. Marriage does not shield one's separate property from his or her own creditors.

What Laws Govern Parenthood?

Prenatal Laws

Perhaps the most controversial issue in family law is the question of **abortion.** Under the leading and much-publicized case of *Roe* v. *Wade*,[10] a pregnant female (married or single), in consultation with her physician, has an unqualified, absolute right to have an abortion during the first trimester (three months) of her pregnancy. This right cannot be vetoed by the natural father, a parent, or a husband. During the second trimester the right continues, but the abortion procedures may be regulated by the state, if it chooses, in ways that are related to maternal health (e.g., hospitalization). During the final trimester and when the fetus has become viable (capable of life independent of its mother), the state may, if it chooses, prohibit abortion unless it is necessary for the health or preservation of the life of the mother. In the more recent *Webster* case, the U.S. Supreme Court held that a state *may* withhold the use of public employees and facilities to perform or assist abortions that are not necessary to save the mother's life.[11] Also, while *Roe* held that there is a compelling state interest in protecting a fetus (through regulation) once it has become viable, in *Webster* the court held that a state may regulate abortion *before* the fetus is viable by requiring medical tests to determine if the point of viability has occurred. Even more recently, the U.S. Supreme Court has ruled in two similar cases—(1) an Ohio law requiring an unmarried minor to notify at least one parent of her intended abortion, and (2) a Minnesota law requiring an unmarried minor to notify both parents—that both are constitutional.[12] In both states a procedure to bypass parental notification is provided if the female chooses to obtain a judge's order.

Legitimacy

A **legitimate** child enjoys rights, and sometimes duties, of support; possesses rights of inheritance; and typically carries the father's surname. Such a child is the issue of his or her natural, married parents. Historically, an illegitimate child was a child born of an unmarried mother or born of an adulterous, incestuous, or bigamous relationship. Statutes today are inclusive and tend to resolve any doubt in favor of legitimacy. For example, children conceived within a specified time of marriage, or born within a specified time after divorce (or death), are presumed to be legitimate. Likewise, children born of a married woman are presumed to be legitimate; that is, fathered by the woman's husband.

The presumption of legitimacy is difficult to overcome and usually will depend on the husband's showing of impotency or on a blood-typing analysis that conclusively proves that the husband could *not* be the child's father. With modern blood-typing techniques and analyses, experts can determine whether or not it was biologically possible for a suspect to be the natural father. Such tests also can show a high probability that a specific man is the father. Every state (except South Dakota) now has statutes providing for the admissibility of specified genetic tests in paternity cases.[13]

The basic handicaps of an illegitimate child are financial. Such person does not inherit as an heir of the father (although he or she does inherit as an heir of the mother) whose relationship has not been determined by court. Moreover, the father has no legal duty to support the child during minority unless he agrees to do so, or unless a court establishes the fact that he is the father and orders him to do so. There is a trend to equalize the rights of illegitimate and legitimate children. This trend reflects the facts that increasing numbers of children are born out of wedlock and that such children are innocent of any wrongdoing. Thus the U.S. Supreme Court has held that states may not discriminate against illegitimate children and must require that natural fathers support both their legitimate and illegitimate children,[14] nor may a state create a right of action in favor of legitimate children for the wrongful death of a parent and exclude illegitimate children from the benefit of such a right.[15] Also, illegitimate children may not be excluded from sharing equally with other children in the recovery of workers' compensation benefits for the death of their parent.[16]

Gomez v Perez 1973

The scope of the problem of support by the fathers of illegitimate children is revealed by national statistics. Between 1985 and 1988, the rate for white out-of-wedlock conception increased to 33 percent of all first births; for black first-time mothers, the rate rose to 79 percent; and for hispanic women bearing first children, to 42 percent. Single mothers are likely to be poor, and without the assistance of the father's earnings, probably will need financial help from public agencies.[17]

Custody of a child conceived out of wedlock remains with the mother so long as she is a suitable person. Otherwise, custody may be awarded to another suitable person, including the natural father.

Some states have adopted statutes that permit the illegitimate child with ascertained **paternity** to inherit from his or her father. In the absence of such a statute, the illegitimate child will inherit only from his or her mother.

In some states, an illegitimate child automatically becomes "legitimated" upon the subsequent marriage of the child's parents. Other states require the father's acknowledgement (sometimes in writing) of the child's status to give the child inheritance rights as an heir. And some states have equalized the rights of legitimate and illegitimate children in all respects, including inheritance.

Legal rights for nonmarital offspring have little meaning unless the natural father becomes identified. The fact of birth obviously identifies the mother. The mother or child may bring a civil paternity action to establish the child's natural parentage. A male who is accused in a paternity action has a right to trial by jury. Usually the mother's testimony is admitted to show the requisite act of intercourse. Proof that an unmarried mother had sexual intercourse with other men during the period of possible conception is admissible; however, testimony concerning the mother's sexual activities before or after the time of possible conception may not be considered by the jury.[18] If the mother prevails and paternity is established, the judgment will include an order of periodic support and reimbursement of medical costs, expenses of pregnancy, and her attorney fees. Once paternity is established, all states authorize their courts to order the payment of support because of state interest (welfare authorities may have the burden of support if the natural father is not held responsible). A few states also confer inheritance rights on a child "legitimized" by a paternity proceeding. But even then, any child may be completely disinherited by the will or his or her parent. (See Chapter 14 for a more complete discussion of inheritance and disinheritance.)

Surrogate Mother Contracts

To obtain a biologically related child, a husband and wife may desire to artificially inseminate a contracting **surrogate mother,** who agrees to carry the fetus until birth and then relinquish her parental rights to the biological father. The natural father's infertile wife then adopts the child.

In 1985, William Stern and Mary Beth Whitehead entered into a surrogacy contract. It stated that Stern's wife, Elizabeth, was infertile, that they wanted a child, and that Ms. Whitehead was willing to provide that child as the mother with Mr. Stern as the father. The contract provided that through artificial insemination using Mr. Stern's sperm, Ms. Whitehead would become pregnant, carry the child to term, bear it, deliver it to the Sterns, and thereafter do whatever was necessary to terminate her maternal rights so that Ms. Stern could thereafter adopt the child. Mr. Stern agreed to pay $10,000 to Ms. Whitehead.

On March 27, 1986, Baby M was born; on March 30 she was delivered to the Sterns. Later that day Ms. Whitehead underwent an emotional crisis; she was deeply disturbed, disconsolate, and stricken with unbearable sadness. She had to have her child. Fearing she may commit suicide, the Sterns returned Baby M in exchange for Ms. Whitehead's promise to return her child in one week. The struggle over custody then began in the courts and Melissa (Baby M) was returned to the Sterns pending final outcome of the litigation. Ms. Whitehead was permitted limited visitation. The trial court ruled in favor of the Sterns, and Ms. Whitehead appealed. What should have been the result?

The Supreme Court of New Jersey held that the surrogacy contract conflicted with the state's adoption laws, especially by calling for the payment of money, and by providing for the irrevocable agreement of the natural mother to terminate her parental rights in aid of the adoption. Also, the contract's basic premise that the natural parents can decide in advance of birth which one is to have custody of the child, conflicts with the law that the child's best interests shall determine custody. Therefore, the court reasoned, the contract was void and unenforceable. The court then decided that custody with the Sterns was in the best interests of Melissa, regardless of the invalidity of the contract. Ms. Whitehead was awarded visitation rights.[19]

Legal issues presented in such cases concern validity of the underlying contracts, forfeiture of parental rights by surrogate mothers, assurance of adoption by wives of the natural fathers, the best interests of the children, inheritance rights following the intestate death of either of the biological parents, and commercialization of the whole process.

In addition to the legal issues, there is a fundamental social question: Is surrogacy a worthwhile solution to the problem of female infertility? Or is it a "forced" baby sale, exploitive of poor women? Suggestions for further reading on this difficult issue are presented at the end of this chapter.

Parental Rights and Liabilities

Freedom from governmental intrusion into family affairs is a fundamental value in our society. Parents have a constitutional right to autonomy in rearing their children, and the state cannot interfere except under "clear and convincing" proof of severe child abuse or abandonment.[20] In general, parents have the right to custody of their children and are free to raise them as they see fit. However, intrusion by the state in family business is becoming more frequent. Out-of-wedlock births have contributed to a growing number of single-parent families, often requiring the intrusion of public assistance. The state also must intrude when a serious need arises, for example, to avoid serious harm from drug addiction, venereal disease, or pregnancy. Finally, the state now intrudes in the once exclusive area of parental control through official acceptance of teenagers' decisions with regard to abortion and contraception.

Unfortunately, children sometimes are forced to live without adequate or even any parental supervision, and may be abandoned, turn delinquent, or even become incorrigible. Legislatures have created juvenile court systems to protect minor children and the public. Children are not under the jurisdiction of juvenile court laws simply because they are **minors** (under age 18); juvenile courts become involved only when necessary. For example, minor children who are in need of proper parental care or who are destitute (with no home and without the necessaries of life) are within the jurisdiction of the juvenile court system. They can be made "dependents" of the court, which then can make any of a wide variety of possible orders for their care, supervision, custody, and support. A dependent child may be taken from the custody of its parents and, for example, be placed in a foster home, or the home of a relative, or any other arrangement in the best interests of the child.

Minor children who commit crimes also are subject to the jurisdiction of juvenile courts. Because juveniles may be confined, they are entitled to many constitutional protections. For example, a minor in juvenile court has the right to representation by an attorney (without charge, if the minor is indigent) and cannot be compelled to be a witness against him- or herself. The burden of proof is the same as in criminal cases generally, that is, "beyond a reasonable doubt." However, no right to trial by jury exists in juvenile court, nor is there a right to bail (although prehearing release is common).

Ordinarily, juvenile court hearings are not open to the public. If the accused person is found to have committed the charged offense, the court will declare the minor a *ward* of the court. Juvenile courts can make various orders, such as probation; fines; and commitments to juvenile homes, ranches, camps, or to special jails for youthful offenders.

Under specified conditions (usually the passage of a number of years) juvenile courts will officially seal all records pertaining to a minor's case. The minor then officially has no criminal record and will not be handicapped in the future when seeking employment.

Not all juvenile offenders are processed by juvenile court. The circumstances of some youthful offenders, and the severity of their alleged crimes (such as homicide, armed robbery, or rape) may lead the juvenile court to reject jurisdiction, thereby making the minor stand trial as an adult, facing all the usual criminal procedures and penalties.

In keeping with the policy of parental autonomy, children historically could not sue their parents for personal injuries caused by parental negligence. Such immunity was considered necessary to preserve family harmony. An exception to parental immunity was customary for intentional torts committed by parents. Most states now permit negligence actions by children against their parents.[21] In these cases, the parents' insurance company may be expected to pay any judgment in favor of the child against the parent, so family harmony is essentially unaffected.

As a general common-law rule, parents are not liable for torts their children commit that cause injury to third persons. However, nearly half the states have statutes creating parental liability up to certain specified limited amounts, often as high as $10,000 or thereabouts, for their children's torts.[22] Many states create parental liability for malicious mischief when their children damage school or other public property.

State statutes impose the obligation on parents to support their children until majority, or until any earlier emancipation when the minor child may become self-supporting. However, some states provide for postminority (over age 18) support by order of the divorce court or by statute.* Even when postminority support is not required, states will enforce marital agreements that call for such support. The general purpose of postminority child support is to pay for college education.

In most states, child support is a joint obligation, although it may be apportioned between the parents according to their respective financial circumstances.

A parent may intentionally disinherit his or her child completely, even if the child is a dependent minor of tender years. This rule of *absolute testamentary freedom* originated in the common law. Obviously most parents do choose to provide for their children by will. Although parents have no duty to include their children in their wills, statutes commonly provide that if a parent fails to make appropriate gifts while alive, doesn't expressly exclude the child from the will, or neglects to leave some token for the child in the will, the child takes a statutory share of the estate as though there were no will. The purpose of such statutes is to protect children who have been inadvertently overlooked by their parents when preparing his or her will (called pretermitted heirs). Thus a parent must expressly disinherit a child if such is the intent (see Chapter 14).

Sexual Abuse of Children

Sexual abuse of a child is a serious felony that is difficult to detect, often occurring in complete privacy. The victimized child may be the only witness and may be reluctant or unable to testify adequately. Forced testimony by a child in

---

* New Hampshire, New York, Pennsylvania, New Jersey, California, Colorado, Washington, Iowa, Indiana, Oregon, Illinois, Mississippi, South Carolina and Missouri.

open court may result in the child suffering serious emotional distress that may adversely affect both the child and the usefulness of the information obtained. The scope of the problem is staggering, with an estimated 100,000 to 300,000 cases each year.[23]

Nearly all of the states have adopted statutes designed to protect child witnesses. To balance the protections of the child with the rights of the accused, various techniques are evolving to obtain testimony from involved children outside the presence of the person allegedly involved in abusive conduct. For example, out-of-court statements (hearsay evidence) made privately by children to mental health or child protection professionals, who often use anatomically correct dolls, sometimes can be used in court.* This procedure assists many children who are unable to recall, report, or evaluate events accurately. (Critics, however, point out that some experts, with the best of intentions, may come to faulty conclusions based on interpretations of the manner in which children manipulate dolls.) The protective procedures include closed-circuit testimony from a private room, videotaping of such out-of-court testimony, and exceptions to the hearsay rule of evidence that otherwise would exclude from the trial incriminating out-of-court statements. But some of these protective laws may clash with the Sixth Amendment to the U.S. Constitution.

The Sixth Amendment grants an accused the right to confront all witnesses, and thus the U.S. Supreme Court has *denied* the use of a screen in court to shield a child from visual contact while testifying.[24] But one exception to the right to eye-to-eye confrontation between the accused and a child witness testifying in court has been approved by the U.S. Supreme Court: A 5–4 majority of justices held that the Sixth Amendment does not invariably require face-to-face confrontation between a defendant and an adverse witness. It concluded that public policy, including the interest in protecting child witnesses from trauma, can justify an exception to the normal "preference" for face-to-face confrontation. The court upheld a Maryland statutory scheme permitting a child to testify from outside the courtroom via closed-circuit television.[25]

Note that protection of the child from confrontation with the accused is a different problem than closing the trial to the public and press. Court proceedings almost always are open to the public; however, under appropriate circumstances, a judge can close the courtroom to protect a child from serious emotional injury.

As you may recall from Chapter 4, proof of guilt in criminal cases must be "beyond a reasonable doubt." Such a high standard of proof is not easily met with testimony that is incomplete, inconsistent, or even contradictory. The age and maturity of a child can make prosecution especially difficult in sexual abuse cases, even when eye-to-eye confrontation between the child and the defendant is not permitted. The best example of the difficulties in determining the guilt or innocence of the accused is the notorious *McMartin* case (the longest and costliest criminal trial in U.S. history), in which the defendants were found not guilty of molesting numerous children who had been under the defendants' care in a

---

* Admission into evidence of such hearsay evidence is proper only when the "totality of circumstances" surrounding the testimony render the witness particularly worthy of belief. Out-of-court hearsay was ruled not admissible where the doctor conducted an interview without a videotape, asked leading questions, and had a preconceived idea of what the child should be disclosing (*Idaho* v. *Wright,* ___ U.S. ___, 110 S.Ct. 3139 (1990).

preschool. However, the jury in the three-year trial deadlocked on certain charges against one defendant, and a retrial limited to those charges again resulted in a hung jury. The acquitted defendants in that case have filed a civil suit against the local city and county, alleging their civil rights were violated and that they lost ownership of their preschool, which was given to defense attorneys as fees.[26] Clearly emotions are very high and consequences are very serious with regard to everyone involved in such difficult and complex litigation.

In civil law divorce and child custody proceedings, more relaxed procedures and reduced standards of proof are applicable. For example, there is no right to trial by jury in divorce or custody matters. Civil remedies also are quite different than criminal penalties for sexual abuse of a child. For example, jail is the probable result of a criminal conviction for child abuse, while a court order that all child visitation be supervised is one possible result of a civil proceeding.

The social and legal aspects of child abuse, both in its criminal and civil aspects, are rapidly evolving, and few conclusions can accurately be drawn at the time of this writing. At the end of this chapter, we have provided additional readings on this important subject.

How May Marriage Be Terminated?

As there is a need for marriage, so is there a need for **divorce.** In response to that need, legislatures have traditionally provided for divorce for an "innocent" spouse from a "guilty" spouse. The "fault" basis of divorce, in some form or other, is in effect in some states. However, all states also provide for some variety of **"no-fault" grounds for divorce.**[27]

In response to widespread disenchantment with fault systems of divorce, many states have adopted some variety of no-fault divorce exclusively. A pure no-fault system of divorce would amount to unilateral divorce on demand, which remains an unacceptable alternative. Therefore, the prevalent no-fault system requires proof of two elements: a breakdown of the marriage, and the objective fact of physical separation of the spouses for some specified period of time, such as six months. This separation period offers the added benefit of preventing overly hasty divorces. Some states have also retained the fault basis of divorce in order to provide immediate relief in severe cases or to justify unequal distributions of marital property. Distributions of property and rights to spousal support following divorce are covered separately later in this chapter. A *breakdown* is established by testimony that the marriage is irretrievably broken because of the attitude of one or both spouses, or a long-continued physical separation without a resumption of cohabitation. Following appropriate evidence of a breakdown, divorce is then provided for by law.

Annulment

Annulment is a declaration by a court that a purported marriage does not exist and never existed because of some defect existing at the time of the marriage ceremony.

Examples of such serious defects that could exist at the inception of marriage are incest, bigamy, mental incapacity, physical incapacity to consummate the marriage, insanity, or consent resulting from fraud, dare, or drunkenness.

When a defective marriage exists only the innocent victim is given the option to annul, and he or she must do so promptly upon discovery of the defect. False statements that one is pregnant or that one will attempt to have a child will justify an annulment. Less significant false statements, for example, that one is rich or that one is a virgin, will not justify an annulment.

Even though a marriage is annulled, a child conceived prior to the annulment is legally a legitimate child of the marriage.

"Bed and Board," Separate Maintenance, or Legal Separation

Many states provide for a partial termination of marriage. Divorce from **"bed and board"** allows the spouses to live apart without fixing desertion on one or the other. Support obligations are established and property is divided by the court. However, the couple is not divorced. The remedy is appropriate where the spouses (1) do not intend to remarry, (2) desire a complete settlement of their economic affairs, (3) want to preserve entitlements under certain public laws (e.g., social security), and (4) are opposed to divorce on religious grounds. **Separate maintenance** and *separation* are very similar to "bed and board" and provide the same benefits to the couple, except that property division normally is not adjudicated.

What Are a Spouse's Rights and Duties Upon Termination of Marriage?

Maintenance or Alimony

Upon termination of the marriage by divorce (often called **dissolution**), the question of *maintenance* (often called **alimony** or *support*) may be established by the court in both dollars-per-month and duration of payments. Rehabilitative or *limited-term* alimony terminates at the end of a specified time period, during which the recipient seeks education, training, or experience to become self-supporting.[28] *Permanent* alimony or maintenance is indefinite in duration. Many couples who divorce arrive at a mutual agreement as to maintenance and thereby avoid the time, expense, and uncertainty of a court's decision. (Note that such marital agreements are subject to approval by the court.) But if the former spouses cannot agree, the judge, sitting as a court of equity and hence without a jury, will consider all relevant factors and make the award.

In 1979, the Supreme Court "de-sexed" alimony and held that gender-based alimony statutes were unconstitutional.[29] Texas remains the only state that does not provide for alimony upon divorce. Alimony is required from either spouse if the other is in genuine need. One is in need, for example, if he or she cannot be self-supporting or if there is a child whose situation precludes employment by the parent with custody. Generally, marital fault is not a factor in determining whether or not alimony should be awarded, although a few states specifically consider fault.*

The amount of alimony is related to the needs of the spouse receiving it and the ability of the other to pay. The following factors are considered by courts in setting alimony:

- The length of the marriage
- The age, health, education, and station in life of the parties
- Their occupations, vocational skills, and employability
- Their needs and opportunities for future income
- Contributions of each in acquiring or maintaining marital property (including noneconomic contributions)
- The need of a custodial parent to occupy the marital home
- Any tax consequences involved

The obligation of permanent alimony ends with the death of either spouse. (Some believe it contributes to an early demise!) Also, remarriage of the spouse receiving alimony automatically terminates the duty to pay.

In the 1970s, the push for equality between the sexes resulted in a shift of state laws from permanent to rehabilitative alimony. But regardless of notions of equality, the reality often is that some women, especially those in their 40s or 50s, can not go back to school, become doctors or lawyers, and compete with their former husbands in earning capacity. As a result, such displaced homemakers often suffer a severe drop in their standard of living following divorce. Many such women lack job skills or even knowledge about the changing workplace. Moreover, they often face sex and age discrimination. For these reasons the trend is now to limit the concept of rehabilitative alimony. Courts in Ohio, Maryland, Louisiana, and Florida have begun to require permanent, rather than limited-time, alimony awards. State laws in New York and Pennsylvania permit courts to award permanent alimony.[30] Contrary opinions remain that alimony should not be a "perpetual pension" or that permanent alimony ought to be awarded to older women in marriages of long duration, but not to younger women who are capable of becoming self-supporting.

When circumstances change, alimony may be modified (even terminated) by petition to the court, which retains continuing jurisdiction until alimony is finally terminated. All relevant factors are considered by the court when hearing a petition to modify.[31] Often the changing factors relate to changes in the relative financial conditions of the former spouses. For example, a former husband can be reluctant to support his ex-wife while she is living with another man. Generally, cohabitation with another person is not solely a basis for terminating alimony;[32] however, some states do provide for modification or termination of alimony under such circumstances.[33] These laws are equally operative if a former wife is paying support to her ex-husband.

---

* Connecticut, Florida, Michigan, Missouri, New Hampshire, North Dakota, Pennsylvania, Rhode Island, South Dakota, and Tennessee take fault into consideration in setting alimony. Marital fault is a bar to an award of alimony in Alabama, Georgia, Idaho, Louisiana, North Carolina, South Carolina, Virginia, Washington, and West Virginia.

Dennis Hall agreed to a divorce settlement in which his wife received the home, furnishings, and vehicle, totaling more than $100,000 in value, plus alimony of $15,000 annually. Three years later he petitioned the court to terminate alimony due to changed circumstances. One Robert Jones, who was sharing Hall's former home with his former wife, contributed nothing toward rent or maintenance, and engaged in sexual intercourse with her. The trial court terminated the alimony because Hall should not be compelled to "support his divorced wife and her paramour in idleness and fornication." What should have been the result on appeal?

The judgment was reversed. Alimony may not be utilized as a club to regulate an ex-spouse's sex life. On the other hand, the court did remand the case to the trial court for a reduction in alimony.[34]

Property Division in "Equitable Distribution" States

Forty-one common-law states authorize courts to equitably distribute property upon divorce, either in the form of property division or maintenance. The *doctrine of* **equitable distribution** awards a marital interest in any property in which the spouse has made a material economic contribution toward its acquisition, regardless of which spouse holds legal title. The economic contributions of both spouses during the marriage are compared to the marital assets that are available at the time of divorce.

In many states, the nonmonetary contributions of a homemaker are considered to be the equivalent of the wage earner's monetary contributions. The starting point in making an equitable distribution is a presumption that equality is equity: an equal division is the most just.

Sam's premarital house appreciated in value during his marriage with Sally. On the advice of his attorney, Sally agreed to quitclaim deed all her right, title, and interest, if any, in the house to Sam for a payment of $10. Did Sally lose her marital interest in the house?

No. The court ruled that all increase in value of a premarital house is a marital asset if the nonowner spouse takes an active role in its upkeep and management. The court will not uphold an unconscionable agreement.[35]

The trend is to minimize relative fault of the spouses as a factor in property division.[36] However, many states consider *economic fault* (e.g., dissipation of marital assets pending divorce) in making an equitable division.[37] The criteria used in most states in making an equitable distribution of marital property between the spouses are comparable to the factors (previously listed) that are relied on in setting alimony awards. Payments received for food stamps, aid to families with dependent children (AFDC), and child support payments are not considered income to the recipient parent and therefore are not included as a factor in dividing marital property.[38]

Property Division in "Community Property" States

As stated earlier in this chapter, *community property* is all property acquired by the husband or the wife during marriage other than by gift or inheritance. In nine states, all of the community property is subject to the jurisdiction of the court upon dissolution of the marriage. But it must be distributed equally, because each spouse is the "owner" of an undivided one-half interest in all the community property. Upon divorce, the court allocates the net value of the one-half interest to each spouse. If the community property cannot be physically distributed in equal portions, it may be sold and the cash proceeds divided, or a promissory note may be made from one spouse to the other to equalize the values received from an unequal physical distribution. (A physical distribution of assets is called a distribution *in kind*.)

In some community property states (e.g., Washington and Texas), the court may divide the marital property in any manner it deems "just and equitable," not necessarily equally.[39] An unequal distribution of community property may act as a substitute for alimony, which is not available under Texas law.

All property either brought into the marriage, or acquired by gift or inheritance, is *separate property* (mentioned earlier in the chapter). Separate property remains separate, and its earnings are separate if proper records are kept.

In 27 states, separate property is not subject to distribution by the court upon divorce. In 16 states, all property of the parties is subject to distribution. In seven states, a combination of all marital property plus some nonmarital property is subject to distribution. These three categories and their respective states are listed in Table 8–1.

TABLE 8–1   Character of property a court may distribute between divorcing spouses, and states where applicable

Both community and separate property	Community property only	Hybrid system involving both community and separate property
Connecticut	Alabama	Alaska
Hawaii	Arizona	Arkansas
Indiana	California	Iowa
Kansas	Colorado	Minnesota
Massachusetts	Delaware	Nevada
Michigan	District of Columbia	New Mexico
Montana	Florida	Wisconsin
New Hampshire	Georgia	
North Dakota	Idaho	
Ohio	Illinois	
Oregon	Kentucky	
South Dakota	Louisiana	
Utah	Maine	
Vermont	Maryland	
Washington	Mississippi	
Wyoming	Missouri	
	Nebraska	
	New Jersey	
	New York	
	North Carolina	
	Oklahoma	
	Pennsylvania	
	Rhode Island	
	South Carolina	
	Tennessee	
	Texas	
	Virginia	
	West Virginia	

Uncertainty exists in the law as to how an advanced degree, such as a Master's in Business Administration (MBA), or a professional license, such as a license to practice medicine, should be treated upon divorce. Are degrees and licenses marital or community property, the value of which should be equitably distributed, or divided, upon divorce? Suppose one spouse has sacrificed her education to "put her husband through medical school." Upon divorce that immediately follows graduation, should the wife be awarded half of the degree or license? If so, how should it be valued? In New York, it has been held that a husband's medical license is marital property under the state's equitable distribution law.[40] In North Carolina, professional degrees and licenses are separate property, but their value is taken into consideration in dividing marital property.[41] In Kentucky, a professional degree or license is considered in determining the standard of living to be maintained in setting alimony.[42] But it has been widely held that college degrees and professional licenses are property rights that are not capable of being owned by a community (in marriage) and are not subject to distribution upon divorce.[43] In some states, restitutional alimony may be awarded to reimburse one spouse for contributions made to the other in earning a professional degree.[44]

Child Custody and Support

Court awards of child custody and visitation rights are always based on the best interests of the child. Generally, parents are sensitive to their child's needs, and so they amicably agree on custody and visitation. In such instances, courts normally comply with the parents' joint request. However, when both parents demand custody or argue about visitation rights, the court must determine the best interests of the child and make appropriate orders. Forty-four states have adopted some form of the Uniform Marriage and Divorce Act, which specifies criteria for determining custody arrangements in the best interests of the child. These criteria typically include the wishes of the parents and the child; the child's adjustment to his or her home, school, and community; and the mental and physical health of all individuals involved. Although courts consider the wishes of the child, they weigh their importance by the age and maturity of the child. It is not appropriate to ask a child in open court which parent he or she chooses to live with, because custody does not turn on the temporary desires of a child.[45] (1988 Newberry v Newberry)

Children may be most affected by divorce, and no doubt are the least able to protect their own rights, especially since the court receives most of its information about finances and emotional trauma from the parents. For this reason, one theory holds that children ought to be independently represented by their own attorney. On the other hand, a contrary theory holds that the illusions of power created by one's own attorney might be inimical to children's emotional well-being. Courts have the power to appoint a special **guardian ad litem** (Latin: for the purpose of the suit) to protect the interests of the child. In Alaska and Wisconsin, courts have directed such guardians to vigorously advocate for the children in custody disputes.[46]

The granting of meaningful visitation opportunities may be expected to temper the impact of a change in custody, unless visitation is used by a vindictive spouse as a weapon to prolong the agonies of divorce for all concerned. In such situations the court may prohibit visitation or strictly limit its terms.

When divorced parents reside in different communities, split custody—where one parent has custody during summer, the other during the school year—may be an effective alternative.

Joint custody has become the most widespread choice of courts in the 1980s. In keeping with the trend, most state legislatures have expressed a preference for joint custody in their statutory guidelines. The theory is that ideally children need two actively involved parents in their lives. However, experience has demonstrated that children are not best served when joint custody is awarded to parents who continue their bitterness and disagreements after the divorce. In keeping with this experience, California now has neither a preference nor a presumption for joint custody awards. This policy is expected to be followed in many states that still have a presumption favoring joint custody orders.[47]

Virtually everyone agrees that a mutually acceptable custody and visitation arrangement is the best method of minimizing the traumatic experience of divorce on children. Through mediation, parents sometimes can reach agreements that otherwise might be impossible. The assistance of a professional and neutral third party can be a valuable catalyst to a mutually acceptable custody and visitation arrangement. Studies indicate that children of mediated divorces appear to adjust better and their parents appear to retain less hostility.[48] California has adopted mandatory mediation proceedings that are applicable whenever child custody is in dispute.[49] Critics of mediation contend that professional mediators tend to push for agreements because they may measure their professional success and personal esteem by the number of "successful" outcomes they bring about. Further, husband and wife may not have equal bargaining power, and one may give away some of his or her rights in reaching an agreement. This inequality may be especially significant where full disclosure of financial matters is not enforced as rigorously as it is in court proceedings, where formal discovery procedures are available.

In addition to custody orders, the court granting a divorce must make orders providing for the future support of minor children. More than 40 states have enacted statutory guidelines to assist courts in setting child support amounts. For example, these guidelines include the necessity for day care expenses.

Collection of child support payments is a far more difficult problem than setting their monthly amounts. When the parent who is delinquent in making child support payments (the *obligor*) resides nearby, in the same state as the child, the custodial parent has several options in collecting monthly child support payments. Legal procedures (often called the *levy of a writ of execution*) are provided for taking the delinquent father's assets, including bank accounts and real property. However, portions of all of a debtor's assets are exempt from execution and cannot be taken. Legal procedures necessary to obtain relief by writ of execution can become so complex as to be ineffective, especially when the debtor does not have substantial assets. If the delinquent obligor is employed, a wage assignment is an alternative. Under this legal mechanism, a portion of the obligor's wages are withheld from weekly or monthly earnings and are forwarded to the custodial parent.

A judgment ordering the payment of child support also can be enforced by contempt proceedings when the failure to support is wilful. Theoretically, an obligor who has the ability to pay the ordered child support but purposefully fails to do so can be jailed for contempt, that is, violating the court's order. However, courts are reluctant to jail an employable parent. Jail precludes employment and contributes to an already crowded correction system. On the other hand, the threat of jail or a short sentence for contempt of court may act as a catalyst in encouraging a delinquent obligor to make the required child support payments.

When the parent who is delinquent in making child support payments resides out of state, another difficult problem exists. How can the custodial parent enforce the payment of child support from a former spouse who resides in another state? To alleviate this problem, most states have adopted the Uniform Reciprocal Enforcement of Support Act of 1968, called URESA. Under this special law, the prosecutor in the local state (residence of the custodial parent) will cause a formal legal proceeding to be initiated in the foreign state (residence of the delinquent obligor), which will be prosecuted in the foreign state by the local prosecutor there. The court in the foreign state will enter a support order there, and enforce it under that state's laws (including the issuance of a writ of execution or contempt of court proceedings, if appropriate). Monies collected in the foreign state are forwarded to the custodial parent.

If the failure to make support payments is a crime,* the foreign court can extradite (return) the delinquent obligor to the local state for criminal prosecution.

When court-ordered child support payments become delinquent, they do not disappear; rather, they accumulate and may be collected at any time in the future, in the same manner that other money judgments are collected, such as by levy of writ of execution to take assets or portions of wages of the debtor. Nor are they discharged (eliminated) if the delinquent obligor successfully petitions for bankruptcy.

Even with existing legal remedies that are available to enforce child support (and alimony) payments, collection remains a serious problem in most states in the United States. It is widely acknowledged that in most cases custodial parents actually receive only inadequate child support. Almost always the father is the delinquent obligor, and even though the allocation of his earnings between a former family and a second-marriage family can be a very sensitive issue, the law declares that children should not be made to suffer from lack of adequate necessaries and support. The sensitivity of this issue was dramatized when a group of second wives, distressed by the impact of support payments from their husbands to their former families, staged an organized protest against new enforcement procedures recently enacted in Wisconsin. The new procedure protested as unfair is automatic withholding of support payments from the obligor's paycheck. It has proven a very effective means of ensuring child support payments in Wisconsin.[50]

May Family Law Be Modified by Private Contract?

Prenuptial Agreements

A marital contract made before marriage is called an **antenuptial,** *premarital,* or *prenuptial agreement.* Premarital agreements should be in writing to be enforced,

---

* The willful (deliberate) failure to supply necessaries of life to a child, without any excuse, is a crime. Failure to make such provision when the parent is financially unable to do so is not a crime.

and some states require that they be witnessed by a third person or notary public. They are increasingly popular as more and more persons prudently seek to establish and fix, before their nuptials, property division and/or support payments in the event that the marriage ends in divorce. Especially when either spouse has a disproportionately large estate of separate property, the premarital agreement can help to resolve future potential misunderstandings without costly litigation.

In response to this need, some 15 states have adopted some version of the 1983 Uniform Premarital Agreement Act.* Theoretically, premarital agreements can deal with (1) property and support rights during and after marriage, (2) the personal rights and obligations of the spouses during marriage, or (3) the education, care, and rearing of children. But the most common subjects of marital agreements are property divisions and support rights upon death or divorce.

In most states, *upon death of a spouse,* the surviving spouse has an elective right to choose between inheriting under the decedent's will or rejecting the inheritance and taking instead a portion of the decedent's estate as provided for by statute. Premarital agreements may alter this portion. On the other hand, this election is not available in community property states because the surviving spouse is protected through ownership of one-half of the community property. This ownership interest also can be altered by premarital agreement. Even states that do not permit contracts that alter the incidents of divorce do permit contracts that alter property distributions upon death of one spouse.

Upon divorce, premarital agreements can alter court determinations concerning both property division and continuing support (alimony or maintenance). However, antenuptial agreements are void, as a matter of law, to the extent that they adversely affect the rights of minor children. Agreements affecting custody, care, or education of minor children can be valid, but are subject to approval by the court. The court will void agreements if they adversely affect the children's best interests. Although about one-half of the states authorize premarital agreements that alter the legal incidents of divorce, some will not enforce agreements affecting support (alimony, maintenance, or child support).

Arlene, a talented and promising young actress, had received her first multi-million dollar contract to act the lead in a major movie production. She also was contemplating marriage to Bud, her off-again, on-again childhood sweetheart, who was a professional boxer with a low earning potential. Arlene decided to confer with an attorney concerning preparation of a premarital agreement. What might such a contract accomplish?

If Arlene and Bud lived in a community property state and did not have a premarital agreement, Bud would be the "owner" of one-half of Arlene's accumulated earnings after the marriage and would be entitled to his one-half of all community property acquired with her earnings upon any future divorce. A contract could provide that all of Arlene's earnings would remain her separate property, and that,

---

* Arkansas, California, Colorado, Hawaii, Kansas, Maine, Montana, New Jersey, North Carolina, North Dakota, Oregon, Rhode Island, South Dakota, Virginia, and Texas.

in this case, upon divorce, Bud would be entitled to a cash payment of $100,000. In an equitable distribution state, Arlene and Bud also could agree that $100,000 would be distributed to Bud upon any future divorce. In some states, Arlene and Bud could agree that, upon any divorce, Arlene would pay alimony to Bud in some specified amount for some specified time. Courts, however, would not enforce such a promise attempting to set support payments unless it was fair.

Antenuptial agreements can be updated during the marriage to reflect the desires of the spouses as their circumstances change from time to time.

As distinguished from antenuptial agreements, contracts made during marriage are called simply *marital contracts,* or *separation agreements* if they are entered while contemplating a forthcoming divorce. Marital contracts are intended to resolve the same sorts of future problems as antenuptial agreements, and receive comparable enforcement by the courts.

Courts will not enforce marital contracts of any kind that are unconscionable (unjust, unfair, or excessive). Preceding marriage, there often is unequal bargaining power between the prospective spouses, and the opportunity for overreaching (taking unfair advantage) may be available. Contracts signed immediately before the marriage ceremony are suspect and may be voided by the court. Similarly, a contract that is prepared by the attorney of only one of the parties is suspect; it should at least be reviewed and approved by counsel of the other party before signing. Courts' reluctance to automatically enforce all premarital agreements reflects a judicial tradition of protection of women from exploitation.

It is customary for each spouse to receive independent legal advice before signing a premarital agreement. Legal representation minimizes the possibility of unfair overreaching, and a possible subsequent declaration of invalidity by a court. This procedure also increases the likelihood that all assets will be disclosed, and taken into consideration, before the contract is signed. Because there is a public policy against divorce, courts will not enforce prenuptial agreements that are unconscionable or that promote divorce. A prenuptial agreement drafted so as to absolve a breadwinner from *all* obligations after divorce would, no doubt, be declared unconscionable and therefore would be unenforceable.

At the time of this writing the most celebrated attempt to set aside a premarital agreement, on the grounds that it is unconscionable, involves the pending Donald and Ivana Trump divorce case in New York. Although their agreement had been modified from time to time during the marriage, Ivana contends that she is entitled to an equitable distribution from her husband Donald instead of the $25 million provided for her in their updated antenuptial agreement. Donald's net assets have been publicly valued at $1.7 billion. We cannot predict whether or not a considerable monetary disparity in a marital agreement might be held unconscionable by the courts of New York.

As a general rule, courts are more likely to enforce premarital agreements that affect property rights than those that affect support rights.

Separation Agreements

As noted above, a marital contract made during marriage but when a divorce or dissolution is being contemplated or occurring is called a **separation agreement.** These agreements are enforceable if each spouse fully discloses to the other all financial information, and if the agreement's provisions are not unconscionable. Public policy favors private settlement of disputes, and courts will usually approve separation agreements as a part of the divorce proceedings. Parties to separation agreements should obtain legal counsel before signing, because ramifications of such contracts are not readily apparent to or understood by a layperson. For example, will payments from one spouse be taxable income to the other? Will agreed-on support payments be subject to future modification by the court in case of changed circumstances (e.g., an unanticipated disability)? What would be the effect of a bankruptcy on the contractual obligations? Will the support provisions be enforceable by contempt powers of the court (or a court's ability to jail a party who disobeys a proper order, such as to pay support)? What effect will a subsequent marriage of either spouse have on the earlier separation agreement? The answers to these questions, as well as many others, may differ based on the needs and desires of the separating spouses and the law of the particular state. Accordingly, couples usually require the services of a qualified attorney to achieve desired results that are fair to both parties.

Cohabitation Agreements

Unmarried persons who live together as husband and wife may desire to protect their respective financial interests by entering into a **cohabitation agreement**. The first obstacle facing such a couple is the long-standing refusal of courts to enforce any contract purporting to exchange property for sexual favors.*

Mary orally agreed to "quit her job and be available to travel" in exchange for a man's promise to "take care of her for the rest of her life." Is the agreement enforceable?

Yes. The contract services do not necessarily include sexual favors.[51] In some states the agreement would fail because it is oral and extends far into the future. In still other states the contract could be interpreted as including sexual favors and therefore be violative of public policy.

Michele, 20, orally promised to "account to" Charles, 80, "all of her waking moments; to be at his beck and call . . . as he should desire," for which services he would pay her $1,000 a month for the rest of her life. Is this contract enforceable?

This contract would not be enforceable in most states because it is oral at the same time that it extends indefinitely into the future, and/or because it is against public policy. Public policy will not condone a contract that impliedly calls for the exchange of sexual favors.[52]

---

* There are, however, exceptions where states have rejected the illegal consideration (sexual favors) doctrine. See, for example, *Latham v. Latham*, 547 P.2d 144 (Oregon, 1976), and *Cook v. Cook*, 691 P.2d 664 (Arizona, 1984).

The preceding examples demonstrate the difficulties in establishing consistent laws for the enforcement of cohabitation agreements. Cohabitation agreements that do not contemplate the exchange of property for sexual favors are enforceable in most states, whether express (written or oral) or implied.

To increase the probability of enforcement of such an agreement, the parties would be well-advised to obtain legal counsel for each party, fully disclose their respective financial resources, provide for a reasonable distribution of their property, and express it all in writing.

Case 8

BECHTOL v. BECHTOL

Ohio Supreme Court, 550 N.E.2d 178 (1990)

Joseph and Nancy Bechtol were married in 1980. Their son Joseph Patrick was born in 1981. Divorce proceedings were begun in 1986 and Nancy was awarded temporary custody. Joseph testified at trial that he had decreased his use of alcohol since the early days of the marriage. Nancy testified that she was a recovering alcoholic, and that she had not had a drink since 1985. During the marriage, Nancy did not work outside the home and was the primary caregiver to Joseph Patrick. Joseph has spent much time with his son after the breakup.

A court-appointed psychologist testified that either the mother or father was capable of being the custodial parent, but in a "close call" he preferred custody be granted to Joseph.

The court awarded custody to Joseph and ordered Nancy to pay child support. Nancy was awarded $3,600 in alimony payable in 12 monthly installments of $300. Both Nancy and Joseph appealed to the Ohio Supreme Court.

Justice Wright In any determination of [custody], the trial court must consider all relevant factors, including but not limited to those enumerated in [the applicable Ohio statute]: (1) The wishes of the child's parents; (2) the wishes of the child . . . if he is eleven years of age or older; (3) the child's interaction and interrelationship with his parents, siblings and any other person who may significantly affect the child's best interest; (4) the child's adjustment to his home, school and community; and (5) the mental and physical health of all persons involved in the situation. [Where, as here] a permanent award of custody is supported by a substantial amount of credible and competent evidence, such an award will not be reversed as being against the weight of the evidence by a reviewing court. [Quoting from a prior case, the court continued] In proceedings involving the custody and welfare of children the power of the trial court to exercise discretion is peculiarly important. The knowledge obtained through contact with and observation of the parties and through independent investigation cannot be conveyed to a reviewing court by the printed record.

The judgment is affirmed.

QUESTIONS AND PROBLEMS

1. Family law is in a state of change because of rapidly evolving social patterns. For example, there is an emergence of informal marriage (cohabitation with contract) alongside formal marriage (ceremonial or statutory). Both varieties of relationships often are terminated by choice, creating special legal consequences. Based on your general understanding, compare the implications of both types of relationships on the following criteria:
  a. Federal and state income taxes
  b. Selection and use of surname
  c. Child support obligations
  d. Credit extension
  e. Expense of creating or ending the relationship
  f. Mutual support obligations
  g. Vicarious tort liability
  h. Recovery for lost consortium or wrongful death *a statutory right*
  i. Privilege not to testify against one another
  j Immunities for sex crimes
  k. Division of assets upon death or termination of relationship
  l. Inheritance rights when there is no will
  m. Costs and coverage of insurance
  n. Social security benefits
  o. Privacy in business matters upon termination of marriage
  p. Workers' compensation benefits

2. It has been said that divorce is "the great American tragedy." Among measures suggested to reduce the divorce rate are higher age requirements for marriage; computerized analysis of personalities and backgrounds of prospective spouses; a longer mandatory waiting period after a marriage license is obtained; mandatory "marriage license training" (including instruction in the financial, social, psychological, and sexual aspects of marriage); trial marriage for a probationary period; and government-sponsored day-care centers for infants and preschool children, to free working mothers from the burdens of child care. What do you think should be done, if anything?

3. Which of the following promises are enforceable if contained in an antenuptial agreement?
  a. Wife waives any claim for support upon any future divorce.
  b. Husband agrees to raise children in a specified religion.
  c. Both agree to a specified variety of sexual activities with a specified frequency.
  d. Husband agrees to transfer certain valuable property to wife immediately upon marriage.
  e. Wife agrees that husband may have custody of the children, if any, upon any future divorce.

4. What legal rights may accrue to a woman who lives with a man to whom she is not married for 13 years in your state? Does it make any difference if she had received an oral promise of future support?

5. Parents are legally obliged to support their minor children. Should adult children who are financially able to do so be obliged to support their elderly parents if indigent? State laws vary on this issue. What are they in your state? What should they be?

6. A child born during the marriage of his or her mother is generally presumed to be legitimate under the law. Should this presumption be rebuttable by evidence that a possible father, who is not the mother's husband, resembled the child? Would your answer be different if the husband was determined to be impotent, or simply traveling out of state during the time of possible conception?

7. What legal problems can you think of that might arise if a surrogate mother changed her mind immediately following birth, and therefore refused to release her child to the natural father, as she had contracted to do?

8. Under what circumstances do you believe courts should award permanent alimony upon a marriage's dissolution or divorce? Does permanent alimony encourage or discourage the recipient from remarrying? Can you think of specific examples of circumstances that would justify modifying (increasing, decreasing, or terminating) an award of alimony that had been in effect for several previous years?

9. Courts in some states enforce oral agreements between unmarried cohabiting persons that provide for division of assets, or support payments, following their permanent separation. What pros and cons of this policy can you identify?

10. If one spouse puts the other spouse through medical school by working and delaying his or her own formal education, and if divorce occurs soon after the doctor completes residency, how might a court's judgment take these factors into consideration?

FURTHER READING

1. Alsdorf, James and Phyllis, *Battered into Submission: The Tragedy of Wife Abuse in the Christian Home.* Downers Grove, Illinois: InterVarsity Press, (1989).

2. Bottomley, Anne, *The Cohabitation Handbook: A Woman's Guide to the Law.* London: Pluto Press, 1984.

3. Bruch, Carol S., "Cohabitation in the Common Law Countries a Decade after Marvin: Settled In or Moving Ahead?" 22 *University of California, Davis Law Review* 717 (1989). An overview of the international impact of the *Marvin* case.

4. Connie, Jon, *Father's Rights: The Sourcebook for Dealing with the Child Support System.* New York: Walker (1989).

5. Field, Martha A., *Surrogate Motherhood: The Legal and Human Issues.* Cambridge, MA: Harvard University Press, 1989. This is a comprehensive work exploring all the issues involved in surrogate motherhood. Also see: D'Aversa, Carmina, "The Right of Abortion in Surrogate Motherhood Arrangements." 7 *Northern Illinois University Law Review* 1 (1987); Eaton, Thomas A., "Comparative Responses to Surrogate Motherhood." 65 *Nebraska Law Review* 686 (1986); and "Litigation, Legislation and Limelight: Obstacles to Commercial Surrogate Mother Arrangements." 72 *Iowa Law Review* 415 (1987).

6. Houlgate, Lawrence D., *Family and State: The Philosophy of Family Law.* New Jersey: Rowman & Littlefield, (1988).

7. Jaff, Jennifer, "Wedding Bell Blues: The Position of Unmarried People in American Law." 30 *Arizona Law Review* 207 (1988). A thorough essay on how the law discriminates against unmarried people, and whether or not the traditional family should be a preferred model.

8. Mason, Mary A., *The Equality Trap.* New York: Simon & Schuster, (1988).

9. Simpkins, Mark A., *What Every Woman Should Know about Child Support: Getting It!* Port Washington, N.Y.: Ashley, (1985).

10. Wallerstein, Judith S., *Second Chances: Men, Women and Children a Decade after Divorce.* New York: Ticknor & Fields, (1989).

NOTES

1. Texas Family Code Annotated, § 1.91.

2. *Marvin* v. *Marvin,* 134 Cal.Rptr. 185 (1976).

3. *Levar* v. *Elkins,* 604 P.2d 602 (Alaska, 1980); *Carroll* v. *Lee,* 712 P.2d 923 (Arizona, 1986); *Boland* v. *Catalano,* 521 A.2d 142 (Connecticut, 1987); *Donovan* v. *Scuderi,* 443 A.2d 121 (Maryland, 1981); *Eaton* v. *Johnson,* 681 P.2d 606 (Kansas, 1984); *Hierholzer* v. *Sardy,* 340 N.W.2d 91 (Michigan, 1983); *Hay* v. *Hay,* 678 P.2d 672 (Nevada, 1984); *Morone* v. *Morone,* 413 N.E.2d 1154 (New York, 1980); and *Watts* v. *Watts,* 405 N.W.2d 303 (Wisconsin, 1987).

4. See *Whorton* v. *Dilingham,* 248 Cal.Rptr. 405 (1988); and *Small* v. *Harper,* 638 S.W.2d 24 (Texas, 1982).

5. *Hewitt* v. *Hewitt,* 394 N.E.2d 1204 (Illinois, 1979).

6. In California, for example, Civil Code §242 provides that: "Every individual shall support his or her spouse and child, and shall support his or her parent when in need." See also Code of Virginia, §20-61.

7. In California, for example, Civil Code § 5125 provides that: ". . . either spouse has the management and control of the community personal property." See also Iowa Code Annotated, § 597.14.

8. See "Creditors and Debtors under the Uniform Marital Property Act," 69 *Minnesota Law Review* 111 (1984), for an excellent review of the law in common-law jurisdictions.

9. Checkoway, R., "Marital Property and Creditor's Rights," 4 *Maine Bar Journal* 254 (1989).

10. *Roe* v. *Wade,* 410 U.S. 113, 93 S.Ct. 705 (1973).

11. *Webster* v. *Reproductive Health Services,* 492 U.S. ___, 109 S.Ct. 3040 (1989).

12. *Ohio* v. *Akron Center for Reproductive Health,* ___ U.S. __; 110 S.Ct. 39 (1990).; and *Hodgson* v. *Minnesota,* ___U.S.___, 110 S.Ct. 2926 (1990).

13. Kaye and Kanwischer, "Admissibility of Genetic Testing in Paternity Litigation: A Survey of State Statutes," 22 *Family Law Quarterly* 109 (1988).

14. *Gomez* v. *Perez,* 409 U.S. 535, 93 S.Ct. 872 (1973).

15. *Levy* v. *Louisiana,* 391 U.S. 678, 88 S.Ct. 1509 (1968).

16. *Weber* v. *Aetna Casualty,* 406 U.S. 164, 92 S.Ct. 1400 (1972).

17. *San Francisco Chronicle,* June 22, 1989.

18. *Fults* v. *Superior Court of Sonoma County,* 152 Cal.Rptr. 210 (1979).

19. In re *Baby M,* 525 A.2d 1128, reversed at 537 A.2d 1227 (1988).

20. *Wisconsin* v. *Yoder,* 406 U.S. 205 (1972); and *Santosky* v. *Kramer,* 455 U.S. 745 (1982).

21. *Goller* v. *White,* 122 N.W.2d 193 (Michigan, 1963); and *Gibson* v. *Gibson,* 92 Cal.Rptr. 288 (1971).

22. California Civil Code § 1714.1; and California Education Code §§ 10,606 and 28,801.

23. *San Francisco Chronicle,* January 17, 1990.

24. *Coy* v. *Iowa,* ___ U.S. ___, 108 S.Ct. 2798 (1988).

25. *Maryland* v. *Craig,* ___U.S.___, 110 S.Ct. 3157 (1990).

26. *San Francisco Chronicle,* January 20, 1990, *Time,* August 6, 1990, p. 28.

27. "Family Law in the Fifty States: An Overview," 20 *Family Law Quarterly* 460 (1987).

28. *Hanson* v. *Hanson,* 404 N.W.2d 460 (North Dakota, 1987).

29. *Orr* v. *Orr,* 440 U.S. 268, 99 S.Ct. 1102 (1979).

30. *The Wall Street Journal,* October 31, 1988.

31. *Murphy* v. *Murphy,* 470 S.2d 1297 (Alabama, 1985).

32. *Bliss* v. *Bliss,* 488 N.E.2d 90 (New York, 1985).

33. Alabama, California, Georgia, Illinois, Louisiana, Maryland, New York, Ohio, Pennsylvania, Tennessee, and Utah permit modification in such cases. 23 *Family Law Quarterly* 546 (1990).

34. *Hall* v. *Hall,* 323 N.E.2d 541 (Illinois, 1975). In 1983 Illinois adopted §510(b) of its Marriage and Dissolution Act, which terminates alimony if the former spouse cohabits with another person.

35. *Burgess* v. *Burgess,* 710 P.2d 417 (Alaska, 1985).

36. *Aster* v. *Gross,* 371 S.E.2d 833 (Virginia 1988); but see *Pommerenke* v. *Pommerenke,* 372 S.E.2d 630 (Virginia 1988) where the court approved less than ten percent of the assets to an adulterous wife.

37. *Smith* v. *Smith,* 331 S.E.2d 682 (North Carolina, 1985).

38. *Bradley* v. *Bradley,* 336 S.E.2d 658 (North Carolina, 1985).

39. Texas Family Code Annotated, § 3.63.

40. *O'Brien* v. *O'Brien,* 489 N.E.2d 712 (New York, 1985).

41. *Dorton* v. *Dorton,* 336 S.E.2d 415 (North Carolina, 1986).

42. *Lovett* v. *Lovett,* 688 S.W.2d 329 (Kentucky 1985).

43. *In re Marriage of Aufmuth,* 152 Cal.Rptr. 668 (1979); *In re Marriage of Washburn,* 677 P.2d 152 (Washington, 1984); and *In re Marriage of Lundberg,* 318 N.W.2d 918 (Wisconsin, 1982).

44. *In re Francis,* 442 N.W.2d 59 (Iowa 1989); and *Wilson* v. *Wilson,* 434 N.W.2d 742 (South Dakota, 1989).

45. *Newberry* v. *Newberry,* 745 S.W.2d 796 (Missouri, 1988).

46. *Veazey* v. *Veazey,* 560 P.2d 382 (Alaska, 1977); and *DeMontigny* v. *DeMontigny,* 233 N.W.2d 463 (Wisconsin 1975).

47. *San Francisco Chronicle,* September 2, 1988.

48. Pacquin, "Protecting the Interests of Children in Divorce Proceedings," 26 *Journal of Family Law* 303 (1987–88).

49. California Civil Code, § 4607.

50. *The Wall Street Journal,* July 29, 1988.

51. *Mullen* v. *Suchko,* 421 A.2d 310 (Pennsylvania, 1980).

52. See *Roth* v. *Patino,* 80 N.E.2d 673 (New York, 1984); and *Rubenstein* v. *Kleven,* 261 F.2d 921 (1958).

Employee Rights and Duties

Most readers are familiar with the biblical story of Adam and Eve in the garden of Eden. Recall that the aftermath of the temptation and fall was banishment under a mandate that included these prophetic words: "With sweat on your brow shall you eat your bread."[1]

Whether or not one accepts the biblical account as literal truth, it is evident that human beings live in a finite, often hostile environment. It sustains them only as the result of considerable, continuing, usually tiring, and sometimes oppressive personal labor, both physical and mental. "Employee" is the legal status of most adults, who spend a substantial portion of their waking hours engaged in gainful employment, coupled with the often boring routine of getting to and from their places of work. In addition, people spend countless hours working in and around their homes producing goods and services (albeit not for pay).

How Are Workers Legally Classified?

The world of work has been a prime concern of lawmakers over the centuries. Rules enforceable in court govern the relationship in some detail for the many who are employees, as well as for the comparatively few who are self-employed or who personally employ others. In exchange for pay, an employee agrees to work for another, the employer. The employer has the power and the legal right to direct and control the employee's conduct on the job.

Sometimes employees are authorized to deal with third parties and make binding contracts with them on behalf of their employers. Legally, such employees are **agents** acting for their employers, who are called **principals.** Acts of agents, when done within the scope of the authority received from their principals, legally bind the principals. This rule applies to contracts that agents make for their principals. Under the doctrine of **respondeat superior** (Latin: let the master answer), it even applies to torts agents commit within the scope of their employment. Agents are obligated by a fiduciary duty of utmost good faith and loyalty to their principals. This means they must place the principal's interest ahead of their own. They must keep the principal informed of relevant facts they learn, and make no secret profits nor collect fees or gratuities from third parties without the consent of the principal. (Agency is discussed more fully in Chapter 10.)

Finally, workers may be legally classified as **independent contractors.** Such workers contract with various employers to do specific jobs, but retain control over how their work is to be done. The "Yellow Pages" of telephone directories list many such independent contractors, from accountants to locksmiths to word processing specialists. Many operate sizeable firms, and employ their own staffs of ordinary employees and agents. What is their appeal? Usually they are experts in their specialized fields, and they perform jobs (such as painting houses) that are required only occasionally by the persons who employ them. An employer who hires independent contractors is relieved of the burdens of hiring and maintaining such specialists in a permanent work force. Eliminated also are troublesome and costly chores of recordkeeping, payment of wages and workers' compensation insurance premiums, and the provision of fringe benefits such as medical insurance. However, as noted below, the relationship can be misused.

In 1989, the General Accounting Office estimated that the U.S. government was losing between $1.6 billion and $8 billion annually because some employers failed to withhold taxes from paychecks of ordinary employees who were improperly classified as independent contractors. Construction companies were major offenders. Legally, when the employer controls the location, the hours, and the quality of the work, the individuals are in fact ordinary employees, and the employer must withhold and transmit their income and social security taxes.[2]

A Changing Picture: Who Works, and Where?

In George Washington's time, approximately 90 percent of all Americans could be classified as farmers. In 1988, our total population of 246,329,000 included a civilian labor force of almost 122 million workers. Of that number, only 4,951,000 lived on farms and just 2,954,000 worked as farmers. Thus our agricultural revolution has enabled 1.2% of our population to produce more than enough food to feed the nation.[3] The industrial and agricultural revolutions of the last hundred or so years shifted most people into urban areas, where manufacturing and various service activities expanded. In more recent times, continued mechanization, automation, and robotization, aided by computers, have sharply reduced the need for factory workers and miners. The dramatic realignments are reflected in a 1989 Gallup poll that showed that only 15 percent of all employees work in factories, and another 11 percent in construction or outdoor activities. Service jobs dominate with 32 percent working in offices, and 13 percent in restaurants, stores, or retail outlets. Some 15 percent work in schools or medical facilities; the remaining 14 percent work in a variety of other places, including a small percentage in agriculture.[4]

Expanded Role of Women

During the past three decades, women—who constitute the majority of our society—have taken a greatly expanded role in the country's work force. Census Bureau figures tell us that in 1960, just under 35 percent of the nation's women (14 years old and older) were gainfully employed. By 1988, the figure (for women 16 years and older) had jumped to almost 56 percent.[5] There had been temporary bulges in such employment when women helped win the production battles of World War I and II, but more permanent shifts have followed, encouraged by changed attitudes, continued mechanization and simplification of household chores, a trend toward smaller families, and legal protection against traditional gender discrimination. Although the civil rights movement has been primarily an effort by black citizens to gain legal equality, women generally have also been beneficiaries of the resulting remedial legislation. A notable failure for women, however, was the unsuccessful campaign between 1972 and 1982 to add an Equal Rights Amendment to the Constitution. That measure provided that "Equality of rights under the law shall not be denied or abridged by the United States or by any state on account of sex." Ratification required approval by 38 states; only 35 did so before the deadline. But presumably most essential rights are already ensured; today there are very few bona fide occupational qualifications that might justify exclusive selection of an employee of a particular sex (or color, or religion), and the concept of equal pay for equal work is gaining in acceptance.

How Does the Law Affect Workers and the Workplace?

Legislation and court decisions affect or control answers to a wide range of questions concerning employment.

- *Who* may work? Labor of persons under 18 is limited and strictly regulated under federal and state laws. Thus persons aged 16 or 17 are barred from hazardous work, including driving motor vehicles, mining, logging, and wrecking. Persons aged 14 or 15 may work in office or sales jobs, and in retail, food service, and gasoline service, but not during school hours. Under specified conditions persons of any age may deliver newspapers; act in movies, theater, radio, or TV, and work on any farm owned or operated by their parents. Other regulations are prescribed by the Secretary of Labor.[6] Many laws are designed to prevent discrimination in hiring, training, promoting, and dismissing employees simply because of their race, color, sex, national origin, religion, or advanced age (40 to 70).[7]
- *What* work may be done? By statute, scores of occupations, from commercial aviator to X-ray technician, are open only to persons with prescribed education and experience, often capped by qualifying examinations and continuing formal education.

- *When* may the work be done? Generally, one day in each week must be set aside for rest and recreation. Traditionally, Sunday has been so designated. Legal provision of this day of rest has been upheld by the U.S. Supreme Court as a valid state exercise of the police power in the interest of public health and general welfare. (Reasonable exceptions to Sunday closing laws permit sale of commodities necessary for health and recreation. This does not violate the equal protection or due process clauses of the Fourteenth Amendment.)[8] Annual vacations of one week or longer are not mandated by law but are generally provided as a fringe benefit. Most states, by legislative enactment or executive proclamation, observe some ten federal holidays that are legally designated by the President and Congress specifically for the District of Columbia and for federal employees. Many states add one or more local legal holidays of their own.

- *Where* may the work be done? Extensive legislation and administrative regulations prescribe minimal acceptable environmental conditions in workplaces.[9] Some 25 states (including California, Florida, Illinois, Michigan, New York, and Pennsylvania) have **right-to-know laws.** These require disclosure to workers of information about any hazardous chemical substances they are likely to be exposed to on the job.

- *How* may the work be done? For example, the Occupational Safety and Health Administration (OSHA) has outlawed tasks involving repetitive hand, arm, and wrist motions that cause crippling injuries from tendonitis. In 1987, I.B.P., Inc., a Nebraska meat packer, was fined $3.1 million for requiring employees to do such work when ways of reducing the risk were available. In 1990, the California state Division of Occupational Safety and Health responded to a complaint of the Newspaper Guild, a union of editorial employees. The employees had suffered similar tendonitis injuries from repeated work at video display terminals. Under an agreement with Cal–OSHA, the newspaper involved (the *Fresno Bee*) agreed to spend $750,000 in corrective action for new furniture, adjustable chairs, support tables, and special training sessions.[10]

- The *number of consecutive hours one may work* in certain occupations is also regulated by law. For example, regulations control the maximum number of hours that bus drivers and airline pilots can be on duty without time off for sleep.

- *How much* must be paid for labor? At both the federal and state levels minimum wage laws have been in effect since the Great Depression. They are coupled with regulations of the maximum hours of work that employers may demand without the payment of "time and a half" for overtime.[11]

- *Do workers have the legal right to unionize?* Federal and state laws guarantee to workers the right to organize into unions of their own choice, and require employers to bargain collectively with the representatives of such unions over wages, hours, and a broad spectrum of conditions of employment.[12]

The law's concern with the employment process is pervasive. It precedes hiring, applies during employment, continues through dismissal, and extends into retirement. An expensive, legally mandated public education system provides life-long learning opportunities that facilitate useful employment. Without proper knowledge and skills one is likely to be underemployed or unemployed throughout one's life. Legal involvement continues when jobs are lost because of an economic recession, and public funds pay unemployment compensation.[13] A permanent worker who is dismissed without just cause may sue for damages under developing tort law. (The tort of wrongful discharge is discussed more fully later in this chapter.)

Economic Safety Nets

In every state society intervenes when a worker is hurt or killed on the job by providing for compensation or death benefits under applicable workers' compensation laws (see Chapter 6.) The worker who is permanently disabled, on or off the job, may qualify for social security disability payments, as may the worker's dependents. Eventually the worker who routinely retires qualifies for retirement benefit payments, and dependent survivors of a deceased worker may qualify for survivors' benefits under social security.[14] If a private employer has voluntarily provided a private pension to supplement social security retirement payments, the worker is again protected by the federal **Employee Retirement Income Security Act** (ERISA), which regulates such plans. Under ERISA, the Pensions Benefit Guaranty Corporation (PBGC) was created to ensure the financial soundness of about 100,000 plans for some 40 million workers and retirees in the private sector. Needed reserves come from insurance premiums paid by the participating private employers.[15]

In 1986, the LTV Corporation, a Dallas-based steel and aerospace company, filed for bankruptcy. It used a Chapter 11 proceeding (as discussed in Chapter 6), which permitted LTV to reorganize and continue operating with reduced debts. At that time, its private pension plan for its 100,000 workers had about $2.3 billion in liabilities for promised benefits. PBGC promptly declared these LTV pension plans terminated and assumed responsibility for paying the pensions. However, by 1987 LTV had negotiated a new pension plan with its unions, leaving the PGBC burdened with the heavy deficit of LTV's prior plans. The PBGC objected, saying the new plan required the use of the insurance fund to pay retirees the same pensions they would normally have received if the termination had never occurred. When the PBGC ordered LTV to resume responsibility for administering and financing the original plans, it refused. Lower federal courts upheld the refusal, saying the order was "arbitrary and capricious." The PBGC appealed to the U.S. Supreme Court. How should the Court have ruled?

The U.S. Supreme Court agreed with the PBGC. Justice Henry Blackmun, writing for the majority of 8 (only Justice John Paul Stevens dissented), stated the law gives the PBGC ". . . the power to restore terminated plans in any case in which the PBGC determines such action to be appropriate and consistent with its duties." The PBGC authority, he noted ". . . is not contrary to clear congressional intent and is based on a permissible construction . . ." of the 1974 Employment Retirement Income Security Act.[16] (See Chapter 7 for a discussion of the potent powers of administrative agencies.)

Government attorneys had warned that the PBGC could face a crisis similar to the one confronting the Federal Savings and Loan Insurance Corporation (FSLIC) since 1987. If the PBGC were barred from ordering financially able companies to restore their private employee pension plans, the resulting financial burden could climb into billions of dollars beyond its insurance reserves.

As of this writing, LTV insists that it cannot afford the restored pension plans. The Supreme Court ruling, in effect, makes a corporation's pension plan liability a debt that cannot be transferred to the PBGC while the corporation continues to operate after a Chapter 11 bankruptcy reorganization. Financially troubled corporations that have failed to fund their private pension plans adequately with appropriate assets could thus be forced to liquidate in Chapter 7 bankruptcies if and when they cannot pay their debts as the debts come due.

Individual Pension Plans

If a private employer does not provide a supplemental pension plan, the federal Internal Revenue Code allows qualified individual workers to set aside a certain percentage of earned income, tax-free until retirement, in **individual retirement accounts** (IRAs). Some employers contribute to their employees' IRA accounts under what are called **simplified employee pension plans** (SEP plans). Under *401(k) plans,* companies with profit sharing or stock bonus plans may contribute cash to a trust account for their employees. Required funds may also be obtained by means of appropriate salary reduction or by foregoing a salary increase. Self-employed persons may establish **Keogh retirement plans**, which serve the same purpose.[17]

Does Every Person Have a Constitutional Right to Work for Pay?

No. The U.S. Constitution does not recognize any right to work for pay. In 1946, however, Congress enacted the **Employment Act,** which committed the federal government to achieving full employment through "all practical means" for those able, willing, and seeking to work. These means included a job-finding program under the leadership of the U.S. Training and Employment Service; gathering and interpreting economic data and advising the President and Congress via the Council of Economic Advisers, using the weapons of taxation and spending; and regulating the availability of money and credit through actions of the Federal Reserve Board of Governors.[*]

We have never achieved 100 percent employment. The reasons are numerous. For example, some jobs are seasonal, as in professional sports and farming. Also, every year thousands of high school and college graduates attempt to enter into and must be absorbed by the full-time job market. Additionally, the supply and demand for products and services are in a constant state of flux in our competitive business world. And some persons are simply unemployable.

---

[*] Controls available to the Federal Reserve Board of Governors include (1) Changing the discount rate (interest) charged to member banks when they exchange promissory notes for cash. A lower rate releases more money into the economy. (2) Buying or selling U.S. government securities. Buying them from member banks releases more money into the economy. (3) Increasing or decreasing the reserves that member banks must maintain. Lowering the reserves releases more money into the economy.

Laura Lanier was pleased and honored when she was discharged from the U.S. Army, but now she needed a job in the private sector and could not find one. She heard that her state had enacted a "right-to-work" law, and so she went to a state employment office, described her skills as a truck driver, and demanded a job. "It's my legal right," she said. Must she be employed?

No. *Right-to-work laws,* which have been enacted in 20 states, in no way guarantee every able and willing person a job.* The term was coined to gain voter support for legislation that outlaws union shops (which are discussed later in this chapter). Many believe such laws are actually designed to weaken unions rather than to protect jobs or an authentic right to work. In states with right-to-work laws, a worker is not obligated to join a union or to pay dues to get or to keep a job. Note, however, that even in states without such laws, most workers do not belong to unions. In the situation described above, Lanier, as a veteran, may legally be given preferential treatment in competition with non-veterans for federal civil service jobs. (Many states and local governments allow some such bonus.) Thus 5 points may be added to the veteran's score on qualifying tests for federal jobs, and 10 points if the applicant has a service-connected disability and was disabled while in uniform.

Disappointed in her quest for civilian employment after leaving the Army, Laura Lanier enrolled as a student in a private business school. Within a year she was qualified as a computer operator, and she was hired by a wholesale hardware supply house for work using a computer in its inventory control department. Her performance and output soon equaled that of several male computer operators who had been with the company for periods ranging from three to ten years. All of the men were paid more than Laura. Was this a violation of federal equal pay legislation?

Equal Pay For Equal Work

The federal **Equal Pay Act of 1963** specifically prohibited wage discrimination on the basis of sex for equal work in jobs that require equal skill, effort, and responsibility and that are performed under similar working conditions. However, the law permits inequality in pay on the basis of (1) seniority, (2) merit, (3) quality or quantity of production, or (4) any factor other than sex (e.g., a shift differential; a higher rate maintained for an employee reassigned to a lower-rate job because of "exigencies of the employer's needs"; a training program; or higher sales commissions because of higher profits on goods sold). The employer must, however, act in good faith without unlawful discrimination in assignment and evaluation of work. Thus, in Laura's case, there was no violation if the pay differentials were based on seniority.

---

* These states had right-to-work laws in 1990: Alabama, Arizona, Arkansas, Florida, Georgia, Iowa, Kansas, Louisiana, Mississippi, Nebraska, Nevada, North Carolina, North Dakota, South Carolina, South Dakota, Tennessee, Texas, Utah, Virginia, and Wyoming.

Unfortunately for women—and for the country—employment practices over many decades have placed most women employees in positions of less responsibility and lower wages than those held by most men. This condition tends to be maintained by the practice of some women who accept less-demanding part-time employment in order to work concurrently as homemakers and care-givers (of children or elderly relatives). In past decades, women also often left gainful employment after marrying. Years later they may seek to re-enter the job market as full-time employees but are at a further disadvantage because others have outpaced them in seniority and experience.

Continued advancement in the ongoing campaign to equalize employment opportunities for women (as well as for minority members of both sexes) will probably require additional years during which women (and minority members) qualify through formal education and experience for the better and the best jobs. It will also require continued enforcement of existing equal employment opportunity legislation. Major employers have been compelled by legal action to pay millions of dollars in retroactive wage adjustments for past discrimination. Publicity given to prominent cases alerts other employers to the importance of complying with the law. Any person who believes that he or she has been victimized may file a complaint with the federal Equal Employment Opportunity Commission at one of its regional offices. Although more burdensome for the employee, a private action may also be brought. The aggrieved individual may even rely on the federal Civil Rights Act of 1866, a post-Civil War law that forbids employment discrimination on account of race or color.[18]

It is a grim fact that women, who constitute the majority in our nation, as a class of workers earn less than men. Thus the Census Bureau reports that in 1987, all wives who worked (full time or part time) earned $13,245 on average, compared to $29,154 earned by husbands who worked. The married women who worked full time (slightly more than half of the total) average $18,929, or only 57 percent of the income of $33,005 received by their male counterparts working full time.

Happily, the income picture is gradually improving for women. After adjustments for inflation, between 1981 and 1987 the earnings of working wives had risen 23 percent compared to 12 percent for working husbands. Among couples with both spouses working, wives earned more than their mates in roughly one of every five marriages. Highlighting the value of higher education, working couples with college degrees earned an average of $59,750 in 1987, which was more than double the $28,000 earned by couples with only high school diplomas.[19]

Comparable Worth in the Future—The Outlook for Women

For a variety of reasons, certain jobs tend to be held mostly by women—and most of these jobs pay less than most jobs held by men. Presently, when different pay scales are based on differences in work performed, there is no unlawful discrimination. However, under the theory of **comparable worth,** jobs that have equal social and economic value should be paid equally. Thus the services of a registered nurse who helps to keep you alive are worth at least as much as those of a licensed electrician who helps to provide light and power in your hospital room. The problem is that it is extremely difficult to measure with precision and fairness all the elements and variables that should determine the dollar value of different jobs at different times in different places. Presumably, the economic forces of supply and demand should automatically decide the question. Realistically, this function of the free market is distorted by such factors as traditional attitudes, long-established seniority rights, union pressures, government licensing regulations, a willingness or ability to make a commitment to long-term, full-time, career-type employment.

In 1986 the state of Washington pioneered with legislation that has narrowed the gap between average wages of men and women employees doing work of comparable worth from 20 percent to 5 percent. The program is to be re-evaluated in 1992. The Canadian province of Ontario passed a law in 1987 designed to introduce comparable worth standards by 1990 (or later) to both government units and private companies with at least 10 employees. It requires employers to define job classes by grouping positions with similar qualifications and duties that are recruited and paid in similar ways. Jobs are ranked in terms of skill, effort, responsibility, and working conditions. For each female-dominated class (60 percent or more), the employer must seek a comparably rated male class. If the women are paid less, they must get a raise.

What Is the Minimum Wage for All Employees?

The minimum wage under the federal Wages and Hours Act had been frozen since 1981 at $3.35 when it was boosted to $3.80 in April 1990 for all workers who are at least 20 years old. It was scheduled to rise to $4.25 in April 1991. Persons under 20 may be hired for 90 days at 85 percent of the full rate but for no less than $3.25 an hour. The teenager may subsequently be hired by another employer for an additional 90 days at the sub-minimum rate, as long as that employer provides on-the-job training. Otherwise, the new employer must pay the teen the minimum wage.

What Other Types of Discrimination Are Barred by Law?

Employees in G. R. Coleman's machine shop in a small New England town accurately reflected the social makeup of the community. All were white, Anglo-American, protestant, male, and highly skilled. Coleman was proud of his business and its products, and he ascribed much of its success to the homogeneity of the work force. He therefore refused to hire Samara Fuguady when she applied for work in the mechanical drafting department. A native of southern Egypt, she was a naturalized American citizen, had extremely dark skin, and was a practicing Muslim. Samara had excellent references culled from ten years of experience. "It's not that I'm prejudiced," Coleman said, "but your presence would be disruptive and no one would be happy—least of all you." Is Coleman within his legal rights in refusing to hire Samara?

No. The Equal Pay Act of 1963 was followed a year later by the **Civil Rights Act of 1964.** Title VII of that very important act made it unlawful for an employer "to fail or refuse to hire or to discharge any individual, or otherwise to discriminate against any individual, with respect to compensation, terms, conditions, or privileges of employment because of such individual's race, color, religion, sex, or national origin."[20] All employers with 15 or more employees, engaged in interstate commerce, are subject to this act. A similar proscription applies to employment agencies and labor unions.[21]

Under the act, discrimination in pay and other employment practices are permitted only if in conformance with a bona fide (1) seniority system; (2) merit system; (3) system that measures earnings by quantity or quality of production; or (4) system that is based on the results of a professionally developed ability test (not designed or intended to discriminate on any of the barred bases); provided that the test is job-related in that persons who do well on the test do well on the job, and vice versa.

Some 115 female flight attendants brought a class action against Pan American World Airways, Inc., in 1984. The women had been suspended, denied promotion, or fired for being overweight. The airline had used different tables of heights and weights, classifying men under the heading of "large frames" and women under "medium frames." The resulting difference between the two sexes was 11 pounds for a person 5'7" tall. Did the corporation's standards discriminate illegally against women?

Yes. The Federal district court in San Francisco found the weight standards discriminatory against the female employees, while reserving the issue of damages for later determination. Pan American began an appeal, but dropped it in 1989. Without admitting bias, it agreed to pay the attendants $2.35 million. It also adopted a more flexible weight policy with a new "large frame" category for women. Under it, a 5'7" woman of medium frame should weigh 139 pounds; for a 5'7" woman with a large frame, the acceptable weight could be as much as 150 pounds. Moreover, the attendant could add up to three pounds upon reaching the age of 35, and again at ages 45 and 55.[22]

The following case illustrates how the well-intended protection of one group can hurt another.

Johnson Controls, Inc., of Milwaukee, produces batteries. The manufacturing process exposes workers to levels of airborne lead considered harmful to a fetus and may result in the birth of a defective baby. In 1982, Johnson instituted a program banning women from all jobs in the division where the airborne lead level was 25 micrograms per cubic meter or higher, unless they presented a doctor's certificate of sterility. It also barred women from jobs where the lead level was below 25 micrograms if the jobs could lead to promotion to more dangerous areas. Female employees working in the lead division were transferred to other divisions without loss of pay or seniority. The United Auto Workers union claimed this was illegal sex discrimination, and filed a complaint with the Equal Employment Opportunity Commission on behalf of seven involuntarily transferred women (and one man who had been denied transfer to a lower lead-level division because women got priority in transfers). A federal civil rights suit followed, and the district judge awarded summary judgment to Johnson without trial, although a 1982 amendment to Title VII (the Pregnancy Discrimination Act) declared that ". . . women affected by pregnancy or childbirth . . . shall be treated the same for all employment related purposes . . . as other persons not so affected but similar in their ability or inability to work." The UAW appealed. How should the appellate court have ruled?

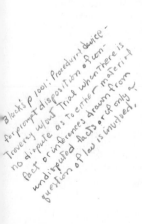

The Court of Appeals, in a seven to four ruling, upheld the trial court. Despite what appears to be a clearly contra position stated by Congress, the appellate court declared that ". . . the physical differences between the human sexes creates a distinction between men and women that accords with our previous recognition that Title VII permits distinctions based upon the real sex-based differences between men and women, especially those related to childbirth." If generally applied, the ruling could bar as many as 20 million women from employment in workplaces where similar toxic chemical exposure exists. As of this writing, the case is before the U.S. Supreme Court. Proponents argue that the patent discrimination is a business necessity: to provide a safe work environment and to avoid potential liabiity for lawsuits. Being male, they say, is a bona fide occupational qualification (BFOQ) reasonably required for normal operation of that particular business and a valid exception to Title VII.[23]

Role of the EEOC

Important amendments to the Civil Rights Act of 1964 were made by Congress in the **Equal Employment Opportunity Act of 1972.** For the first time, the federal Equal Employment Opportunity Commission (EEOC) was given power to institute civil actions in court to eliminate violations of the law. Formerly, it had to rely on informal methods such as conferences and conciliation, which an employer could ignore. The individual victim seldom was willing or financially able to take the grievance to court. Today the EEOC may do so, but its record has not been impressive. In 1989, one critic noted that the EEOC had a backlog of about 53,000 cases and reported that it had found "reasonable cause" for the workers' complaints in fewer than 3 percent of the cases it had closed.[24]

Harry Rockwell lost his job with the Majestic Admiral Products Corporation when he was 45 years old. A friend told him about a similar job that had just become available in the Crescent Moon Company because of the death of the incumbent. When Rockwell applied, the personnel manager said, "You are eminently qualified for the assignment, except that you're too old. We're looking for a bright young college graduate with maybe five years of experience. We want him or her to grow with the company." Does Rockwell have any legal recourse?

Yes. Three years after the Civil Rights Act became law, Congress passed the **Age Discrimination in Employment Act of 1967,** which applies to persons between 40 and 70 years of age.[25] It makes it unlawful for an employer in interstate commerce to fail or refuse to hire, to discharge any individual, or otherwise to discriminate against persons with respect to compensation, term, conditions, or privileges of employment, because of age. This law also applies to employment agencies and unions. It permits discrimination when age is a bona fide occupational qualification, and it recognizes the propriety of disciplining or even discharging a person for good cause. Enforcement of this law has been difficult and less than satisfactory. Realistically, sophisticated employers are not likely to tell a job applicant "You're too old." Moreover, they can often find other bases for

An amendment of Title VII of Civil Rights Act of 1964

refusal to employ the more mature worker—including "overqualification" for the available job. Recall, however, that the developing tort law of wrongful dismissal may protect permanent employees against arbitrary discharge without good cause.

Almost all states have enacted their own laws barring employment discrimination on the basis of race, sex, religion, national origin, and advanced age. Holdout states not following the federal example are Alabama, Arkansas, Georgia (except as to age), Mississippi, and Virginia. Most states call for equal pay for equal work, and also follow the federal model of protecting the employment rights of handicapped persons.

What Is Meant by Affirmative Action in Employment Practices?

Because of many years of discrimination in employment against women and minorities, government administrators and judges have made special efforts to provide them with more opportunities for gainful employment. By threatening to terminate lucrative supply and research contracts, federal government departments have pressured employers to adopt *affirmative action programs*. Essentially, these require positive efforts to hire and promote minorities and women, in percentages roughly equal to their representation in the neighboring communities (sometimes referred to as the "potential applicant pool"). This has sometimes caused **reverse discrimination** against qualified non-minority male employees and male applicants. The presumption, however, is that such persons are better able to fend for themselves in the job market; they can look for and find suitable employment where there are no federal contracts that might require affirmative corrective action.

The Acme Electronics Company, a Texas-based corporation, had operated for the past ten years in a city near the international border where many citizens of Mexican ancestry resided. After a preliminary screening of applicants for an important job in its computer center, Adam Ramirez (a Mexican-American) and Richard Ellis (an Anglo-American) were the final contenders. Both were university graduates and appeared to be qualified or qualifiable with a minimal amount of training. Ellis, however, had five extra years of experience. He was highly recommended by his previous employer. Most of Acme's contracts were with the federal government and almost all of its employees were white males. Whom should Acme hire?

To protect its federal supply contracts, Acme should hire Ramirez. Some legal experts question the constitutionality of affirmative action. Efficiency experts insist that employment and promotion should be based on merit. Opponents of affirmative action say that the Civil Rights Act of 1964 calls for neutrality, with no discrimination for or against anyone. Proponents argue that with neutrality, corrective action might take a generation or longer, and that is too long.

The U.S. Supreme Court has unanimously held that it is a violation of the Civil Rights Act of 1964 for an employer to require a high school diploma and a passing score on a general intelligence test for employment or promotion when neither can be demonstrably related to job performance.[26] This tends to open the door to minority members who often lack the benefit of high school education but are willing and capable workers. Moreover, the Court held that employment and personnel management practices, procedures, or tests neutral on their face and even neutral in terms of intent, cannot be maintained if they operate to "freeze" the status quo of prior discriminatory employment practices. Thus disparate hiring of relatively few women or minorities is illegal unless truly *necessitated* by lawful business purposes or requirements.

The Court did not say that present employees must be fired to make way for women and minorities, but in a subsequent case in 1979, the Supreme Court did give its stamp of approval to a private, voluntary arrangement negotiated by the Kaiser Aluminum and Chemical Co. with the United Steelworkers Union. This program set up a skilled craft-training program with half the slots arbitrarily reserved for blacks and half for whites. At the time, although there was a 30 percent black population in the geographical area of the plant, fewer than 2 percent of the skilled craftworkers were black. Brian Weber, a white, had been passed over for skilled craft training and had challenged the company and union plan as discriminatory. He lost.[27] The Court's approval of this private, voluntary, affirmative action plan to correct manifest racial imbalance automatically legitimized some 175,000 similar plans already in existence at that time, and others that were added later. Moreover, one effect was to shield such employers from charges that the plans impliedly admitted prior bias for which they could be sued.

A New Direction in Affirmative Action

In January and June of 1989, the U.S. Supreme Court issued four major decisions that sent tremors through the ranks of ardent civil rights advocates. Subsequently in a public speech, Justice Thurgood Marshall, the first and only black member of the Court, asserted that 35 years after the Court had ended the era of legal segregation with its decision in *Brown* v. *Board of Education of Topeka*,[28] "We have come full circle." The decisions, he argued ". . . put at risk not only the civil rights of minorities, but the civil rights of all citizens," and he urged civil rights lawyers to look beyond the U.S. Supreme Court to state legislatures and Congress for assistance.[29]

Others welcomed the dramatic changes. Senator Orrin Hatch, a senior member of the Senate Judiciary Committee, said that those who oppose the Court's decisions actually support ". . . equality of results and reverse discrimination instead of equality of opportunity and color blindness."[30]

The decisions merit close study. They are presented here in chronological order:

1. *City of Richmond* v. *Crosson.* By a vote of six to three the Court declared that Richmond, Virginia had violated the Fourteenth Amendment's "equal protection of the laws" clause in 1983 with a statutory plan. The plan required that 30 percent of the amount of every construction contract awarded by the city must go to minority-owned subcontractors. This is a **racial quota.** The Court ruled that state and local governments may adopt affirmative action measures only to correct well-documented examples of past discrimination, but racial quotas that specify how many minority members must be hired are generally outlawed. Although not explicitly stated, the decision appears to be applicable not only to construction contracts, but also to other affirmative action programs, as in school employment. As the law may not discriminate against racial minorities, it may not discriminate against the racial majority. Surprisingly, the Court held that under appropriate circumstances, the federal government alone could impose quotas because it, alone, has the power to enforce the Fourteenth Amendment. In the following year (1990), the Court reinforced this position. It upheld the Federal Communications Commission (FCC) affirmative action policy of giving preference to minorities* seeking licenses to operate radio and television stations. The decision was the first time the Court endorsed an affirmative action program designed not to rectify past discrimination but to encourage future opportunity. Nevertheless, speaking for the minority in the five to four decision, Justice Anthony Kennedy said he ". . . cannot agree with the Court that the Constitution permits the government to discriminate among its citizens on the basis of race in order to serve interests so trivial as 'broadcast diversity.' "[31]

2. *Ward's Cove Packing Co., Inc.* v. *Atonio.* By a vote of five to four, the Court held that canneries operating in remote areas of Alaska during the summer salmon run may legitimately have an imbalanced work force in which most skilled jobs are held by white workers, while nonwhite workers hold most unskilled jobs. It overruled the Court of Appeals, which had held that the imbalance created a prima facie case of illegal discrimination against the employees. In effect, the employer with racially imbalanced work forces would otherwise be forced " . . . to engage in the expensive and time-consuming task of defending the business necessity . . . " of its hiring method. In the alternative, the employers would have ". . . to adopt racial quotas . . . a result that Congress expressly rejected in drafting Title VII." The Court imposed a heavy treble burden on the complaining worker to first compare the proportion of the plaintiff's racial group in the employed work force with the *qualified* members of that group in the pool available to the employer. Second, the complaining worker must prove existence of a specific illegal employment practice alleged to be responsible for the disparity. The defendant *employer* need merely prove business justification for its practices. Finally, the plaintiff (worker) ". . . bears the burden of disproving an employer's assertion that the adverse employment action or practice was based solely on a legitimate neutral consideration." In this case the employers said that most higher-paying jobs required skill and experience that it is difficult for non-white workers to acquire because they come for the seasonal work from remote regions of the state. Thus, although the statistical evidence established a disparate impact, there was not sufficient proof that the employer had intentionally discriminated.[32] 1989

---

* Minorities were identified by the FCC as black, Hispanic-surnamed, American Eskimo, Aleut, American Indian, and persons of Asiatic-American extraction. In 1986, these minorities made up at least 20 percent of the nation. However, they owned only 2.1 percent of the more than 11,000 American radio and TV stations.

3. *Martin* v. *Wilks*. By a vote of five to four the Court considered a controversial affirmative action lawsuit involving employment of firefighters. The white plaintiffs had not been parties to a prior law suit that had ended in a consent decree, but that decree affected them and they deemed it objectionable. The lower court decree had approved an affirmative action plan that gave special preferences to minorities and women in the hiring and promoting of firefighters. Although the Supreme Court did not condemn the plan, it ruled that the ". . . decree between one group of employees and their employer cannot possibly settle . . . the conflicting claims of another group of employees who do not join in the agreement . . . . [A] person cannot be deprived of his legal rights in a proceeding to which he is not a party."[33]

4. *Patterson* v. *McClean Credit Union*. In a five to four vote, the Court ruled that the Civil Rights Act of 1866 may not be invoked to sue over alleged on-the-job sexual harassment. The Civil War-era law was enacted to implement the Thirteenth Amendment, which abolished slavery. It applies only to the making and enforcement of contracts. Thus it forbids an employer to refuse to hire a person because of race or sex, because in effect that would be a refusal to contract. However, it does not extend to wrongful conduct of an employer after the contract is made. The 1866 law permits lawsuits to remedy some forms of private discrimination (e.g., it has been properly used to prevent a private school from refusing to admit blacks), but a worker who claims sexual harassment (in this case, a black woman bank teller claimed harrassment, refusal to promote, and wrongful dismissal) may sue under Title VII of the Civil Rights Act of 1964.[34] Civil rights advocates object, however, arguing that such an alternative involves a burdensome delay. The EEOC would have to first review the claim, and, as noted earlier, it has been unequal to its work load.

These four cases appear to signal a new trend in the thinking of the nation's highest court with reference to affirmative action employment rights of women and minorities.

However, upon the recommendation of Justice Marshall, Congress responded with a proposed Civil Rights Act of 1990. President George Bush vetoed the bill because it would allegedly force employers to use hiring quotas for women and for minorities to avoid job discrimination suits. The House had approved the bill by a vote of 272 to 154, and the Senate by a vote of 65 to 34, but both votes fall short of the two-thirds margin needed to override a veto. Hence the issue remains unresolved for the foreseeable future.

In July, 1990, President Bush signed into law another landmark civil rights law, hailed as a declaration of independence for some 43 million disabled Americans. The **Americans With Disabilities Act of 1990** applies to both the public and private sectors, and goes well beyond existing protective legislation at the state and federal levels. (Federal contractors and recipients of federal funds have been subject to similar restrictions since 1973).

Under the Act, a disability is any physical or mental impairment that ". . . substantially limits a major life activity." It applies to practices in employment, public and private accommodations, transportation and telecommunications facilities. Because of its scope and the anticipated costly economic impact, the law will be phased in gradually. Thus, regardless of the number of employees, business firms and other establishments must improve access for the disabled within 18 months if "readily achievable" without "undue hardship." This hardship could involve the nature and cost of the accommodation in comparison to overall size of the firm and its financial resources. The actual application of such modifying terms will probably have to be clarified through litigation. Within 2 years, employers with 25 or more full-time employees, and within 4 years employers with 15 or more employees may not discriminate in employment of the handicapped who are capable of performing the essential functions of the job. Note that the Act does not require employment of anyone who is unqualified for the job, nor does it require preferential treatment for the handicapped.

What Are Your Basic Duties as an Employee?

 Two weeks after being employed as a deckhand on Plato Parnasi's 180-foot yacht, the *Invincible,* Jake Morgan refused to obey an order of the Chief Mate Ben Blight to swing over the side on a rope ladder and scrape and repaint a rusted section of the hull. Morgan argued that nothing had been said about such dirty and potentially dangerous duties when he was hired. Moreover, he said, "I'm too tired. Why don't you do it?" May he be fired without recourse?

Yes. Scraping and painting are customary duties of deckhands. This was reasonably implied, if not explicitly expressed, in their employment agreement. The agreement could have been expressed in words (spoken or written) or implied from conduct of the parties, or from customs of people in that occupation. Also, being too tired during working hours is no excuse for refusal to do a job. An employee is duty bound to obey reasonable orders and to comply with reasonable rules. However, one cannot be required to do anything that is illegal, immoral, or contrary to public policy, nor can one be compelled to do work not covered by the employment contract. Thus, if Morgan had been hired as a steward or engine room mechanic, he could properly refuse to do the scraping and painting of the hull.

The Supreme Court has decided, however, that a worker may refuse to do a job that appears to be unreasonably dangerous. The specific task in question involved walking on angle-iron frames of a wire mesh screen suspended about 20 feet above the shop floor, to remove objects that had dropped onto the screen from overhead conveyor belts. Only ten days before, a coworker had fallen to his death while doing similar work. The U.S. Labor Department supported the worker's position, claiming authority under OSHA (the Occupational Safety and Health Act), which seeks to guarantee a hazard-free working environment for employees.[35] 1980

An employee is not a slave, nor an indentured servant bound to remain for a prescribed time. One has the *power* to quit at any time; simply leave the job. But there is no legal *right* to quit when to do so breaches a contract in which one has promised to work for a specific period of time. An employee who quits without good cause before the contract ends may be liable in damages. However, employers seldom sue their rank and file employees. A lawsuit would be costly, it would be resented by other employees, and any sizable judgment obtained would probably be uncollectible. The implied or expressed duration of the contract is usually short, perhaps a month or a year. But of course it may be extended by formal or informal renewals into permanent employment, which could last until retirement.

Many employment contracts are entered into informally, for an indefinite or open-ended period of time, with no detailed agreement as to the rights and duties of the parties. Traditionally such employment is **at will,** with both parties free to terminate the relationship at any time without liability (other than payment by the employer for services rendered to date, or sometimes to the end of the pay period). Indeed, employees under such contracts continue to have the right to quit at will without liability. However, as noted in Chapter 5, in a number of states the employer may be held liable for the tort of **wrongful discharge** of a permanent employee, unless the firing was for good cause (e.g., insubordination of the worker, or lack of business or bankruptcy for the employer). To the chagrin of many employers who wish to avoid such liability, a worker who started in a contract of employment at will may gradually become a permanent employee with the simple passage of time. As a result, many employers now explicitly state that employment is at will and may be terminated at any time by either party without liability. They take this precaution in oral and in written contracts as well as in employee handbooks.

Nevertheless, courts and legislators throughout the country continue to grapple with the difficult issue of wrongful discharge. At stake is the propriety and viability of extending to many workers something comparable to the security now enjoyed by tenured faculty in the employ of colleges and universities. Certainly the employer and the employee can explicitly agree on the duration of the intended employment, but in the past probably the vast majority of employment contracts have failed to address this matter, or they have confused or contradicted it as the actual employment continued over many years.

Three rules appear to be emerging in courts that have been confronted with the problem:

1. As a matter of public policy, the employer is guilty of a tort and vulnerable to a claim for substantial damages if the employee is fired for refusing to follow company orders to commit perjury or another illegal act.

2. The employer may also be liable in tort when an employee is fired in violation of the covenant (promise) implied in every contract to perform all promises in good faith (i.e., with honesty) and fair dealing.   *emerging trend*

3. The employer is at least guilty of a simple breach of contract if the employee is fired in violation of an *express* contractual agreement of continued employment. More often this would be the case when the court finds an *implied* contractual agreement not to fire unless there is good cause to do so. The implied agreement may be evidenced by favorable job evaluations over a long period of time, especially when accompanied by promotions and salary boosts.[36]

A highly valued employee who quits during the specified term of a written contract to take a better-paying job elsewhere cannot be compelled to return to his or her job. But a court of equity might grant the first employer a **negative**

injunction barring the employee from working for anyone else during the contract term. To defy the court order would mean citation for contempt and a possible fine, as well as a judgment for damages. The second employer might also be guilty of the tort of interference with a contract or an economically advantageous situation. (See Chapter 5 for a more detailed discussion of the issue.)

Every employee is duty bound to use reasonable skill in performing assigned work, to perform it conscientiously (i.e., to do "an honest day's work for an honest day's wages"), and to do nothing contrary to the interests of the employer. For example, one may not sabotage equipment, steal supplies, or sell company secrets to competitors.

Ed Block was a stationary engineer in charge of a battery of boilers at the Metropole Chemical Works. Safety valves would prevent a major explosion, but the equipment could be seriously damaged even if the fail-safe devices worked perfectly. All controls had to be closely monitored and regulated. One day Block's wife left him after a prolonged argument over their son, who had been arrested on a narcotics possession charge. Perhaps understandably, but not excusably, Block had consumed a large bottle of bourbon before he went to work on the swing shift. Within an hour he was sound asleep at the control panel. The boilers soon overheated and shut down automatically. Repairs would cost at least $5,000, to say nothing of the cost of disrupted production and spoiled goods in process, worth perhaps another $50,000. Is Block liable for the loss?

Yes. Theoretically, an employee may be charged with the cost of the employer's products he or she spoils or the value of equipment damaged either intentionally or through negligence. Practically, most employers seldom go beyond dismissing the errant employee. They absorb such spoilage costs as part of the price of doing business, and pass them along to consumers in higher prices for finished products. Insurance sometimes helps cover the costs.

could sue on basis of negligence (handwritten margin note)

What Are Your Basic Rights as an Employee?

Every employee is entitled to compensation for services as agreed on with the employer. If no figure is specified, the prevailing or customary wage applies, or whatever would be reasonable under the circumstances. Sometimes, as in many sales jobs, pay in the form of commissions is related to particular performance, such as a specified percentage of all sales made. A common variation is a contract that calls for payment of a minimum base salary or "draw," to be offset by commissions earned. Any excess commissions are retained by the employee. State laws commonly require payment every two weeks, or sometimes weekly.

In any event, the employee does not receive all of the earnings. Legally, the employer must withhold federal income taxes (and, in some states, state income taxes) and social security taxes, and pay them directly to appropriate government agencies. By agreement with the employee, deductions are also common for such purposes as buying insurance, government savings bonds, or company stock; paying off company credit union loans; paying union dues (called the **check off**); or putting money into savings accounts.

If wages are not paid, an employee has the right to sue for money owed. Special legislation in most states and under federal bankruptcy laws gives the employee a preference or priority over other creditors of the employer.

Compensation? Reimbursement? Indemnity?

Darleen Gorski was employed as a sales engineer by the Apogee Corporation at a salary of $2,000 a month plus a commission of 5 percent of all net sales made in excess of a minimum specified at the beginning of each year. The company supplied her with a car and agreed to pay all expenses of its operation and maintenance. (Apogee had so many agents on the road that it set aside the equivalent of premiums on automobile insurance and was thus self-insured.) At the end of the first month, Gorski submitted an itemized bill of $409 for gas and oil and $1,175 to cover the cost of replacing wheels and tires and a tape deck that had been stolen. Were the items claimed by Gorski collectible as part of her compensation?

No. Although Gorski was entitled to both sums, technically the $409 was *reimbursement* for expenses properly incurred, and the $1,175 was **indemnification** for a loss suffered. Neither is *compensation* for services rendered; neither is includable in taxable income.

Working Conditions

Every employee is entitled to reasonably safe working conditions. The federal Occupational Safety and Health Act of 1970 broadly requires the employer in interstate commerce to furnish employment and a place of employment that are free from recognized hazards that cause or are likely to cause death or serious physical harm. The law extends to such diverse items as equipment, protective clothing, vapor and noise levels, and in-plant health facilities. It provides for inspections, investigations, issuance of citations, judicial review, and penalties for violations. All states have a variety of similar local regulations governing production in intrastate commerce.

Fringe Benefits

An employee has no constitutional right to fringe benefits, but legislation, competition, and union pressure have made them an integral part of most employment contracts. Such benefits are provided in addition to the regular wage or salary. Social security, no doubt the most important fringe benefit, is mandated by the Social Security Act of 1935. Financed by taxes paid by both employers and employees, the massive social security program provides benefits to some 40 million persons, a growing number which includes retirees (who generally start receiving pensions at the age of 65), dependent survivors of insured persons, and qualified disabled workers and disabled dependents. It also encompasses the Medicare program of health benefits for qualified retirees. Many private

* In corporate law, in practice by which corporations pay expenses of officers named as defendants in litigation relating to corporate affairs.

employers supplement social security retirement benefits with their own pension, stock purchase, and profit sharing plans. Some provide a simplified employee pension plan (SEP), whereby they contribute to the employee's Individual Retirement Account (IRA). Vacations and holidays with pay, and medical and dental insurance are very valuable fringe benefits for most employed persons. A variety of less significant benefits are offered by some employers. These include life insurance; legal aid plans; sick leave; pre-natal, child, and elder care; maternity and paternity leave; adoption assistance; social, recreational, physical fitness, and continuing education programs; and employer-assisted housing. The dollar value of fringe benefits often equals as much as 20 to 30 percent of the monetary wages paid. The appeal of fringe benefits is enhanced by the fact that most are tax-free to the employees and tax-deductible as business expenses to the employers.

Employee Stock Ownership Plans (ESOPs)

A relatively new fringe benefit could significantly affect the traditional dichotomy that many persons perceive between the interests of capital and labor—the **Employee Stock Ownership Plan (ESOP).** The basic concept of employees acquiring stock in the company that employs them is not new. For example, for decades Sears, Roebuck & Co. has encouraged and helped its employees to buy Sears stock. It is a promising way of sharing the wealth, building employee loyalty, and stimulating the productivity—much needed as international competition intensifies. The concept gained new prominence under a provision of the federal Tax Reduction Act of 1975, which gives special tax benefits to participating employers. A subsidy is given to the company's ESOP, a trust that buys company stock. The company invests the money received for the stock in new plants and equipment, and after seven years the stock can be distributed to the employees. Under a variation, the ESOP borrows money to buy company stock. The company guarantees the loan and agrees to pay it off. As the loan is paid off, shares are allocated to employees in proportion to their pay. Workers who quit or retire may take their allocation of shares, to hold or sell them. Unions have been wary of the idea because it could divide worker loyalty, employers have been indifferent, some sociologists and economists see a contradiction in the idea of a worker's capitalism, and employees themselves generally prefer immediate benefits and fear the risks of stock ownership with its fluctuating value and returns. In any event, ESOPs have recently enjoyed a spurt in popularity as a management technique to ward off unfriendly takeovers by corporate raiders. The National Center for Employee Ownership estimated that 10,000 plans were in effect in 1989, with some 10 million worker-owners participating. Among leading corporations with ESOPs are Avis, Procter & Gamble, ITT, J.C. Penney, 3M, Anheuser-Busch, and Lockheed.

A New Employer Duty to "Warn"

Following a long established practice in western European countries, the federal WARN Act **(Worker Adjustment and Retraining Notification Act)** took effect early in 1989[37]. Generally, it requires managers of fairly large business enterprises*

---

* Covered by the act is any business enterprise that employs at any single site at least 100 full-time employees, or 100 or more employees (full-time or part-time) who, in the aggregate, work at least 4,000 hours a week.

to give employees at least 60 days' advance notice before either a *plant closing**
or a *mass layoff*.† Certain exceptions are permitted. For example, if the closing or
layoff is due to **business circumstances** that were not reasonably foreseeable,
the notice must be given only as soon as the **closing or layoff** becomes reasonably foreseeable.

Have Workers Always Had the Right
to Join with Coworkers in Unions?

No. The history of relations between labor and capital, or between workers and
professional management hired by the owners of capital, is long and stormy. In
1806, a group of Philadelphia boot and shoemakers (called *cordwainers*) who
joined together were found guilty of common law criminal conspiracy and were
fined.[38] In another classic case about 35 years later, *Commonwealth* v. *Hunt,* the
Supreme Court of Massachusetts rejected the idea that a combination of workers
was criminal simply because of their concerted action. The proper test, the court
said, was the purpose of the combination; if intended "to induce all those engaged
in the same occupation to become members," it was not unlawful. "Such an association might be used to afford each other assistance in time of poverty, sickness,
or distress; or to raise their intellectual, moral, and social condition, or to make
improvement in their art; or for other proper purposes."[39] 1842

Nevertheless, **unions** continued to be harassed by court action instituted by
employers who resisted any erosion of their decision-making power. For example,
the federal Sherman Anti-Trust Act of 1890 was enacted to protect trade and commerce against unlawful restraints and monopolies of business firms, but was also
applied by courts to unions. Injunctions were often used to restrain concerted
labor activity such as picketing (patrolling outside a business location to
encourage workers to join the union, to gain recognition from the employer, or to
gain sympathy and support from third parties during a strike). But the pendulum
eventually did swing in the opposite direction to favor labor and union organization. Peaceful picketing, for example was recognized by the Supreme Court in
1940 as a form of free speech protected by the First Amendment. However, in
1988, the Court upheld a local law that banned picketing in front of any particular

---

* *Plant closing* means the permanent or temporary shutdown of a single site of employment, or one
or more operating units within a single site, if it will result in an employment loss at that site during
any 30-day period for 50 or more full-time employees. A *full-time employee* is one who works an
average of 20 or more hours a week, and has worked at least 6 months in the preceding 12-month
period. An *employment loss* includes termination, a layoff for more than 6 months, or a loss of at least
half of the employee's working hours for six consecutive months.

† A *mass layoff* is a reduction in the work force that, during any 30-day period, causes one-third of
the employees or 50 employees (whichever is less) to be terminated, laid off for more than 6 months,
or to lose at least half of their working hours for 6 consecutive months. If at least 500 employees are
affected by the mass layoff, notice is required regardless of the percentage of the employees who are
affected.

or private home. (Nevertheless, marching through a residential neighborhood or in front of an entire block of homes is not prohibited.)[40]

The New Deal in Labor-Management Relations

During the Great Depression (1929–1939), many new socioeconomic laws were enacted as part of the New Deal of President Franklin D. Roosevelt. In the labor field, two important laws survived challenges to their constitutionality:

- The **Anti-Injunction Act of 1932** (popularly known as the Norris-La Guardia Act, after its prime movers) regulates the issuance of injunctions by the federal courts in labor disputes.[41] Together with the Clayton Act of 1914, it effectively exempts unions from prosecution as monopolistic trusts or conspiracies in restraint of trade. Norris-La Guardia also outlaws **yellow dog contracts,** under which an employee—as a condition of employment—agrees never to join a union.
- The **National Labor Relations Act of 1935** *(Wagner Act)* recognizes the right of employees to form, join, or assist unions, and to bargain collectively with employers through representatives of their own choosing.[42] The act listed and outlawed five unfair labor practices of employers, including most notably inter-ference with employees in their right to form unions and firing an employee for filing charges under the act.

Antonio Mondalli and Jack Smith were the two youngest and toughest workers at the Iceberg Cold Storage and Ice Company. When their request for a wage boost to match community levels was denied, they started to persuade other workers in the plant to join them in forming a local union, or to affiliate with the Teamsters Union. When Artemus Finley, owner-manager of Iceberg, heard of the talk, he promptly fired Mondalli and Smith. Do they have any recourse under the law?

Yes. They can file a complaint with the nearest office of the National Labor Relations Board. For intrastate businesses, in some states they could apply to a comparable state board. In either case, the board could order their reinstatement with back pay.

The Pendulum Swings Back

Some critics claimed that in applying the Wagner Act, the National Labor Relations Board favored the revitalized unions unfairly. And so the pendulum eventually swung back with two new laws that restrained unions (but did not deprive them of their basic rights). The **Labor-Management Relations Act of 1947 (Taft-Hartley Act)**[43] amended the Wagner Act and added a list of unfair labor practices of unions, including, most notably, coercion of employees in their right to join or to refuse to join a union. It outlawed the **closed shop,** which mandated that one must belong to the union before getting a job, and it banned **secondary boy-cotts,** in which pressure is brought by striking workers against neutral third parties who supply or buy from the affected employer. For example, workers on strike at a furniture factory may not legally picket the independent retail stores that sell the furniture.

Farm workers are not covered by this act. Cesar Chavez and his striking United Farmworkers have therefore been able to utilize the secondary boycott by picketing stores that handle grapes and lettuce from non-unionized farms. This apparent advantage of farm workers is more than offset by the fact that employers are not legally obliged to recognize the farmworker unions or to bargain collectively with them. However, California has pioneered with a state law granting to farmworkers the rights to organize and bargain collectively. Significantly, in 1988 the U.S. Supreme Court partially revived the secondary boycott weapon for all unions. It permitted a union to pass out handbills urging shoppers and others at a shopping center not to patronize any of some 85 stores, even though the stores were not involved in the dispute. The dispute arose when De Bartolo hired Wilson to build a store in the mall. Wilson, in turn, hired the H.J. High Construction Company to work on the project. High had provoked the union's ire because it allegedly was paying substandard wages. The Court held that Congress had not intended ". . . to proscribe peaceful handbilling, unaccompanied by picketing, urging a consumer boycott of a neutral employer."[44]

Legal Injunctions

The Taft-Hartley Act reintroduced the injunction against strikes, but made it available only at the request of the National Labor Relations Board or of the President, in case of disputes that endanger the national health and welfare. After an *80-day* **cooling off period** in such cases, during which time the issues are investigated and reported on by a public board, the strike may resume—to be ended possibly by government seizure and operation under an act of Congress. This extreme option is very seldom utilized. Courts may also issue injunctions against illegal strikes or lockouts and illegal activity in connection with either, such as mass picketing in a strike or violence in a lockout. A number of cases in recent years have involved illegal strikes by government employees such as firefighters, police, and teachers. Feelings have been intense and court orders to return to work have been defied. In the case of an illegal strike of air traffic controllers in 1981, then-President Ronald Reagan ordered dismissal of some 11,000 strikers, and their temporary replacement by U.S. Air Force controllers. Permanent civilian replacements were then hired and trained; few of the striking controllers were rehired.

 Loren Hilton was a rugged individualist and as a matter of principle he opposed joining any mutual help organization. He was also a highly skilled toolmaker. Some time after he was hired by Advanced Avionics Corporation, the company signed an agreement with the toolmakers union that called for a union shop. Must Hilton now join the union if he wants to keep his job?

Yes. In a **union shop** an employee must join the union within 30 days after being hired. It is legal under the Taft-Hartley Act, although as noted before, some states have enacted "right-to-work" laws that outlaw this limited approach to union security and stability. Employers who accept the union shop reason that if they have to deal with a union, it may as well include all workers in the bargaining unit. There is likely to be less internal discord; the union leaders feel more secure and are less likely to make outrageous demands or promises to justify their existence. Also, since the union provides benefits, the members understandably believe all workers should share the costs; thus those who do not join the union are regarded contemptuously as freeloaders.

A variation of the union shop is the **agency shop,** in which all employees in the bargaining unit (non-members as well as members) support the union by paying union dues as a condition of employment. Non-members simply designate the union as their agent to conduct negotiations with the employer and to conclude employment contracts on their behalf. Many public-employee labor unions have agency-shop agreements that apply to non-members. The union may not use any of such agency-shop dues for activities not directly related to collective bargaining.

The **Labor-Management Reporting and Disclosure Act of 1959 (Landrum-Griffin Act)** is sometimes called the bill of rights of union members, because it guarantees their right to participate in union affairs, protects their freedom to speak up in union meetings, and requires that they be kept informed about the union's financial condition.[45]

Raul Keroupian had joined the union at his plant shortly before the day of the meeting at which officers were to be selected. When nominations were made from the floor, someone moved to elect the entire incumbent slate by acclamation. Keroupian swallowed nervously, then stood up, and said "I don't think we can do that; it would be illegal." There were hoots and cat calls from the back of the room. Was he correct?

Yes. Among other things, the Landrum-Griffin Act prescribes that every local labor organization must elect its officers at least once every three years by secret ballot among the members in good standing.

Do Most Workers Belong to Unions?

No. In 1988, within our nation's total force of 101.4 million employed wage and salary workers, only 17 million,* or 16.8%, were union members.[46]

Unofficial estimates show a further drop since then.* Comparatively few professional workers, government employees, and white-collar workers belong to

---

* The total was 19.2 million workers who were members of a labor union or an employee association similar to a union, as well as workers who report no union affiliation but whose jobs are covered by a union or an employee association contract.

unions. Moreover, many union members are employed in open shops where union membership is not required as a condition of getting or keeping a job, or in firms where no union is recognized as the representative of all employees.

Although a union had been selected by a majority of the workers in his department, Virgil Redman refused to join. There was no union shop agreement, and he insisted on making his own "deal with the boss." "After all," he said, "I've been doing it that way for more than 30 years. We're both satisfied. I don't intend to stop now." May Redman make his own contract with his employer governing his compensation and other terms of employment?

No. When a union is designated as the bargaining representative for workers in a given unit, it represents all workers in that unit, including non-members. This is true even when only a bare majority of eligible workers participated in the representation election, and consequently only a minority of the total eligible workers voted for the union. The same phenomenon can be found in political elections and campus elections when there is a light turnout.

Thus simple numerical totals of union membership are misleading; they may reflect lethargy rather than ardent support. On the other hand, they may underestimate the true scope of union influence. Unions are very strong in certain key industries: steel, aerospace, automobiles, coal mining, transportation, printing, and construction. A major strike in any one of these could have serious repercussions throughout the economy. Moreover, the wages and conditions set forth in union contracts tend to become models for other labor contracts. And unions may exert pressure on legislatures through lobbying efforts made possible by their unity and access to large sums of money from the dues of many members.

Do Most Workers Engage in Strikes?

No. Most workers are not unionized, and strikes are normally called by unions. A **strike** is a concerted refusal by employees to perform the services for which they were hired. Strikers do not quit permanently; they consider themselves employees and plan to return to their old jobs when the strike ends. By then, they hope that their employer will have acceded to all or some of their demands. The strike is the ultimate weapon of unions, just as the ultimate weapon of employers is the **lockout**—a shutdown of operations in response to union activity or demands. Neither is used casually or frequently, although the strike is much more common.

Figures compiled by the Bureau of Labor Statistics of the U.S. Department of Labor show that since 1960 we have had as many as 3,305,000 workers involved

---

* It is ironic that while unions were in decline in this country during the 1980s (See Lipset, *Unions in Transition—Entering the Second Century,* San Francisco: Institute for Contemporary Studies, 1986), the Solidarity union movement came into being in Poland. The union's leader, Lech Walesa, won the Nobel Peace Price in 1983 and spoke before a joint session of Congress in 1989. The example of the Poles became a historical model for other nations that had been behind the "Iron Curtain." They too asserted a significant measure of independence with more democratic rule.

in strikes during a given year. Nevertheless, during that span of years, never did the estimated working time lost exceed half of 1 percent of all working time. In 1988, for example, there were only 40 work stoppages. They involved only 118,000 workers and .02 percent of estimated working time.[47] Moreover, production was often expanded by other firms to take up the slack, or by the affected firm itself after settlement was reached.

Such statistics do not reflect the full impact of a labor strike, however. They do not show the indirect or secondary effect on other companies that are forced to cut back or even shut down because markets or sources of needed supplies are cut off. Nor do they reflect the inconvenience and added cost or deprivation imposed on the disputants as well as on innocent third parties. A strike of a major automobile manufacturer that buys component parts from thousands of suppliers and ships autos to hundreds of dealers quickly sends shock waves throughout the nation's economy. Layoffs in the main plant are followed by cutbacks in satellite shops and dealerships.

Society accepts these costs, even as it accepts the costs of competition that sometimes forces business firms to close at great loss to investors and other dependent parties. **Compulsory arbitration** of labor disputes might eliminate strikes, but most people reject the idea of having a third party (or panel) make decisions on the issues, which will then be binding as a matter of law. Some disputants are not eager even to utilize a government or private **conciliation and mediation service,** in which a neutral party uses reason, advice, and persuasion to bring labor and management together in a voluntary settlement.

Once labor and management agree on the terms of an employment contract, it is common practice to include a clause requiring arbitration of disputes that may arise over the interpretation and operation of the detailed provisions of the contract. For example, a worker may claim that his or her duties qualify him or her for a higher-paying wage classification, or a worker may charge a supervisor with unfair discrimination against him or her if the employee is assigned dangerous or unpleasant tasks.

What Kinds of Strikes Are There?

Pat McGillicuddy was unhappy with the wages, hours, work schedule, plant rules, heating and lighting of the work room, fringe benefits (there were none), and supervision at his place of employment. One day, after weeks of grumbling and complaining to his coworkers, he got up from his work bench, put on his coat and hat, and shouted so that all in the large room could hear: "I strike!" Then he walked out the door and started to picket in front of the building. Was he on strike?

No, because there was no union ordering the strike nor combined action by a group of workers. It is Pat's individual protest, and his employer can take Pat's action to mean that he has quit and thus can be replaced.

When there is a union and it orders all members to walk out in an **economic strike** (over wages, hours, or conditions of employment), the employer may legally hire **strike-breakers** as permanent replacements. After the strike is over, however, if the jobs again become available, the employer must rehire the strikers, provided they have not taken substantially equivalent permanent jobs elsewhere. On the other hand, when the strike is an **unfair labor practice strike** prompted by one or more unfair labor practices of the employer, the striking workers retain full rights to their jobs and must be restored to them when the strike ends. Moreover, the offending employer must pay back wages to the strikers.

The Snug Fit Shoe Corporation had a three-year contract with its production workers under a collective bargaining agreement. The union vote approving the contract had been very close, and initial dissatisfaction had gradually turned into outspoken protest. After 16 months, the workers defied their leaders and announced through a spokesperson: "We're on strike. To prevent strikebreakers from taking our jobs, we're going to stay right here in the plant." A sitdown had begun. Friends and relatives brought the strikers sleeping bags and food for a long stay. Was the strike legal?

No. **Sitdown strikes,** in which workers retain possession of the employers' property, are illegal.[48] Moreover, this was a **wildcat strike** in violation of the contract and of the union's own rules. As such, it constituted an unfair labor practice on the part of the workers and the employer could hire permanent replacements for the strikers, who could be evicted by the police and be subject to punishment. Sometimes workers of one employer walk out when workers of another employer go on strike or are locked out. This is a **sympathy strike** and obviously is more serious than the common union labor practice of refusing to cross a picket line. It is a variation of an economic strike and the employer may treat it as such.

Case 9

MERITOR SAVINGS BANK, FSB v. MECHELLE VINSON

U.S. Supreme Court, 477 U.S. 57, 106 S.Ct. 2399 (1986)

Mechelle Vinson, a female employee, brought a sexual harassment suit against the Meritor Savings Bank and Sidney Taylor, its vice president and her supervisor. It was undisputed that during her four years at the bank, she had been promoted to assistant branch manager based on merit alone. In September 1978, she took sick leave; on November 1, 1978, the bank discharged her for excessive use of that leave. She then sued the bank and Taylor, seeking

injunctive relief, compensatory and punitive damages, and attorney's fees. She alleged that Taylor had constantly subjected her to sexual harassment in violation of Title VII of the Civil Rights Act. More specifically, shortly after being hired by Taylor, he invited her to dinner and during the meal suggested they go to a motel to have sexual relations. At first she refused, but eventually agreed out of fear of losing her job. Subsequently over the next several years they had intercourse "some 40 or 50 times," and he forcibly raped her on several occasions. He also fondled her in front of other employees. These activities ended after 1977 when she started going with a steady boyfriend. Because she was afraid of Taylor, she never reported his acts to his supervisors and never used the bank's formal complaint procedure. Taylor denied her allegations and the bank claimed it was ignorant of the alleged conduct, which it never approved or consented to. The district court found that if the alleged sexual relationship existed, it was a voluntary one and there was no violation of Title VII. The Court of Appeals reversed. It identified two types of sexual harassment: (1) harassment that involves conditioning of employment benefits on sexual favors, and (2) harassment that, while not affecting economic benefits, creates a hostile or offensive working environment. Since Vinson's grievance was clearly of the hostile environment type, and the district court had not considered whether such violation occurred, a remand was necessary. Moreover, if ". . . Taylor made Vinson's toleration of sexual harassment a condition of her employment, her voluntariness had no materiality whatsoever." As to the bank's liability, the Court of Appeals held that a supervisor is an agent of his or her employer for Title VII purposes. The employer is absolutely liable for sexual harassment practiced by supervisors, whether or not it knew or should have known of the conduct. Therefore, the Court of Appeals reversed the judgment of the district court and remanded the case for further proceedings. The U.S. Supreme Court intervened and granted certiorari (Latin: to be informed) of an order to bring the case before the Supreme Court.

Chief Justice Rehnquist   First, the language of Title VII is not limited to "economic" or "tangible" discrimination. The phrase "terms, conditions or privileges of employment" evinces a congressional intent "to strike at the entire spectrum of disparate treatment of men and women" in employment . . . .

Second, in 1980 the EEOC issued Guidelines specifying that "sexual harassment," as there

defined, is a form of sex discrimination prohibited by Title VII . . . . The EEOC Guidelines fully support the view that harassment leading to noneconomic injury can violate Title VII. . . . They describe the kinds of workplace conduct that may be actionable under Title VII. These include "unwelcome sexual advances, requests for sexual favors, and other verbal or physical conduct of a sexual nature" . . . whether or not it is directly linked to the grant or denial of an economic quid pro quo, where "such conduct has the purpose or effect of unreasonably interfering with an individual's work performance or creating an intimidating, hostile, or offensive working environment." . . .

Since the Guidelines were issued, courts have uniformly held, and we agree, that a plaintiff may establish a violation of Title VII by proving that discrimination based on sex has created a hostile or abusive work environment. . . .

Allegations in this case—which include not only pervasive harassment but also criminal conduct of the most serious nature—are plainly sufficient to state a claim for "hostile environment" sexual harassment . . . .

The fact that sex-related conduct was "voluntary," in the sense that the complainant was not forced to participate against her will, is not a defense to a sexual harassment suit brought under Title VII. The gravamen of any sexual harassment claim is that the alleged sexual advances were "unwelcome." . . .

We decline the parties' invitation to issue a definitive rule on employer liability, but we do agree with the EEOC that Congress wanted courts to look at agency principles for guidance in this area. While such common-law principles may not be transferable in all their particulars to Title VII, Congress' decision to define "employer" to include any "agent" of an employer, surely evinces an intent to place some limits on the acts of employees for which employers under Title VII are to be held responsible. For this reason, we hold that the Court of Appeals erred in concluding that employers are always automatically liable for sexual harassment by their supervisors. . . . For the same reason, absence of notice to an employer does not necessarily insulate that employer from liability. . . .

Finally, we reject petitioner's view that the mere existence of a grievance procedure and a policy against discrimination, coupled with respondent's failure to invoke that procedure, must insulate petitioner from liability. . . . The bank's grievance procedure apparently required an employee to complain first to her supervisor, in this case Taylor. Since Taylor was the alleged perpetrator, it is not altogether surprising that respondent failed to invoke the procedure and report her grievance to him.

We do not know at this stage whether Taylor made any sexual advances toward respondent at all, let alone whether those advances were unwelcome, whether they were sufficiently pervasive to constitute a condition of employment, or whether they were "so pervasive and so long continuing . . . that the employer must have become conscious of (them)." . . .

The judgment of the Court of Appeals reversing the judgment of the District Court is affirmed, and the case is remanded for further proceedings consistent with this opinion.

QUESTIONS AND PROBLEMS

1. Problems abound in the area of employment. The following questions indicate some of the more difficult and challenging ones. What are your suggestions for answers and solutions?

a. Do minimum wage laws discourage employment of young persons, especially the unskilled, and thus encourage idleness and crime? Should the minimum wage laws be eliminated or modified for minors and young adults?

b. Subtle illegal discrimination because of sex, color, religion, age, and national origin still exists in many places. How can it be further reduced or eliminated? How can victims of discrimination facilitate that elimination?

c. Should the federal government be the employer of last resort for those who cannot find jobs in the private sector? What meaningful work could such persons do?

d. Are current workers' compensation benefits for job-related injuries and deaths reasonable? What do they encompass in your state?

e. Should workers be encouraged to buy shares of stock in the corporations that employ them, under ESOPs or other plans?

f. Should all states enact "right-to-work" laws?

g. Should labor strikes and management lockouts be forbidden, and labor-management disputes be settled by compulsory arbitration?

h. Are unions obsolescent or obsolete? If not, why, when, where, and how should union membership be encouraged?

i. Should comparable worth laws be enacted at the federal and state levels? Would women be the only beneficiaries of such legislation?

j. Since people live longer now than when the Social Security Act was enacted in 1935, should the normal retirement age be advanced from 65 to 70?

k. Should racial and other special-interest or minority quotas for employment and educational (e.g., college admission) opportunities be legalized?

2. After a strike was legally called, Phil Thornbush joined co-workers on "picket duty" at their place of work, an intrastate business. There was no violence and only two picketers at a given time marched in front of the plant, day and night. Thornbush and his partner were arrested and convicted under a state statute that made loitering and picketing a misdemeanor. They appealed, claiming the state violated their federal constitutional right to free speech. Should the convictions be reversed?

3. In question 2 above, after the arrest almost all of the striking employees, as well as scores of sympathizers, gathered at the plant entrance. A strikebreaker's car was overturned and burned; rocks were thrown into plant windows. Police were called and order was restored, but the plant manager feared a recurrence in the future. What defensive legal steps might she take?

4. The technicians at television station KTVE went out on strike in a dispute over the terms of a proposed contract. The strike dragged on for weeks. Ordinary picketing seemed to be ineffective, and so some of the strikers prepared and distributed 5,000 handbills, which in sharp language disparaged the quality of KTVE programs. The employer fired those responsible for the printing and distribution. As an employer, was KTVE guilty of an unfair labor practice?

5. Victor Fusee was employed by a small daily newspaper with a circulation of about 10,000. All of the papers were sold locally except for less than 2 percent, which were regularly sold out of the state. Fusee claimed he was protected by the federal Fair Labor Standards Act (Wage and Hour Law) and was therefore entitled to time-and-a-half wages for all overtime he worked. The publisher insisted that he was engaged in intrastate, not interstate, commerce and so could not be bound by federal law. Who is right?

6. Ann Hopkins, C.P.A., managed the Washington, D.C., office of Price Waterhouse. She had brought in more business than any of the other 87 candidates for the position, yet was denied partner status in the firm. Some partners evidently thought she was "too macho," too aggressive, and said she sometimes used profanity. A supervisor had suggested that she should ". . . walk . . . talk . . . [and] dress more femininely . . . [and] wear make-up. . . ." She sued her employer, charging illegal "sex stereotyping." Should Ann win her case?

7. At the Argosy Department Store, Joe Boccacci is the stationary engineer in charge of the heating and air conditioning equipment. His formal education ended with a diploma from a technical high school. He is a member of a union and earns $40,000 a year. Janet Stanton is the store's personnel manager, and a college graduate. Her salary is $25,000. Joe and Janet are the same age, and both have been with the company five years. Does the disparity in compensation mean that Argosy is violating the Equal Pay Act?

8. Agender, an agent employed by Prontotype, Inc., was driving his own car and rushing to an important luncheon meeting scheduled with a prospective customer. He saw the amber light in the signal ahead, but to stop and wait would delay him at least four minutes, and he was already late. So he pushed the accelerator down, even though the light had changed to red, and raced ahead at 50 MPH through the intersection—*almost*. Before he got across, his car collided with Thirpar's truck,

which had legally entered on the far right side. Thirpar was injured and the truck was demolished.

   a. Is Agender's employer, the principal Prontotype, liable?

   b. Would the employer be liable if Agender was an ordinary employee?

   c. Would the employer be liable if Agender was an independent contractor?

   d. Would your answer be different in *a, b,* and *c* above if Agender was violating not only the speed limit but also Prontotype's explicit orders not to go faster than 35 MPH in town?

   e. Is Agender personally liable to Thirpar?

   f. Is Agender personally liable to Prontotype?

9. A was a skilled salesperson hired by B Company under a combined fixed-salary and commission plan. Through energetic efforts, A developed the designated number I sales territory and made $105,000 in commissions in the first year, in addition to her $10,000 base salary. In the second year, A earned the base salary plus $179,000 in commissions while continuing to service all the accounts. Then the sales manager transferred A to territory number II, where B company sales were minimal. Although her base salary was doubled to $20,000, no commission was to be paid to A on sales to A's old accounts in territory number I. "Those accounts will be institutionalized;" A was told, "we'll service them with our regular office staff." Greatly upset, A objected. Can A legally compel B Company to continue to pay commissions on accounts she developed in territory number I?

10. S. G. Borello & Sons, Inc., was a commercial cucumber grower in California. The company hired 50 migrant laborers to harvest their crop, under agreements (written in English and Spanish) that designated each signatory worker as a "Share Farmer" who agreed to furnish him- or herself (and his or her family) as a self-employed independent contractor. As such, each was paid for "production" of picked cucumbers, not for labor, the details of which each controlled in the fields. The state deputy labor commissioner challenged this designation, and issued a stop order/penalty assessment against Borello for failure to secure workers' compensation coverage for the workers as ordinary employees. Borello appealed to the State Supreme Court. Who should win?

FURTHER READING

1. *The Developing Labor Law,* 2d ed. Washington, D.C.: Bureau of National Affairs, Inc., 1988. More than 300 members of the American Bar Association's Committee on the development of the law under the National Labor Relations Act contributed to this scholarly analysis of the basic labor-management law.

2. Hunt, James, *The Law of the Work Place—Rights of Employers and Employees,* 2d ed. Washington, D.C.: Bureau of National Affairs, Inc., 1988. A practical and useful handbook that succinctly discusses the impact of federal regulations on the worker and the workplace.

3. Leslie, Douglas L., *Labor Law in a Nutshell,* 2d ed. St. Paul, MN: West Publishing Co., 1986. Excellent discussion of the highlights of the Wagner, Taft-Hartley, and Landrum-Griffin Acts.

Written by an expert, in language understandable by the layperson.

4. Lipset, Seymour M., *Unions in Transition—Entering the Second Century*. San Francisco: Institute For Contemporary Studies, 1986. Nineteen experts contributed essays on the future of labor unions that were ". . . once considered a pillar of the Western industrial democracies . . . " yet are ". . . today unarguably in crisis."

5. Player, Mack A., *Federal Law of Employment Discrimination in a Nutshell,* 2d ed. St. Paul, MN: West Publishing Co., 1981. A worthy companion to the Leslie work, it covers the major federal civil rights laws and has a helpful discussion of the Rehabilitation Act of 1973, which is designed to protect the rights of handicapped persons.

NOTES

1. The Bible, Genesis 3:19

2. Posner, Paul L., Associate Director, General Accounting Office, quoted in *Insight Magazine,* June 12, 1989, p. 24.

3. *Statistical Abstract of the United States 1990 The National Data Book* (Washington, DC: U.S. Department of Commerce, Bureau of the Census, Barbara Everett Bryant, Director, 1990), Tables No. 12, 629, 1098.

4. Kohut, A. and L. Destafano., quoted in *San Francisco Chronicle,* September 4, 1989.

5. *Statistical Abstract of the United States 1990,* op. cit. Table 635.

6. Fair Labor Standards Act of 1938, 29 USC 201 et seq. (a.k.a. Wages and Hours Act). There is similar legislation in many states governing intrastate commerce.

7. Civil Rights Act of 1964 (notably Title VII), 42 USC 2000a et seq. (a.k.a. Fair Employment Practices Law). There is similar legislation in most states governing intrastate commerce.

8. *McGowan* v. *Maryland,* 81 S.Ct. 1101 (1961); and *Braunfeld* v. *Brown,* 81 S.Ct. 1144 (1961).

9. Occupational Safety and Health Act of 1970, 29 USC 651 et seq.

10. *San Francisco Chronicle,* May 12, 1987, p. A-56, and June 23, 1990, p. A7.

11. Fair Labor Standards Act of 1938, 29 USC 201 et seq.

12. National Labor Relations Act of 1935, 29 USC 151 et seq. (a.k.a. Wagner Act); and National Labor-Management Relations Act of 1947, 29 USC 141 et seq. (a.k.a. Taft-Hartley Act).

13. Social Security Act of 1935, 42 USC 301 et seq.

14. Ibid.

15. Employee Retirement Income Security Act (ERISA), 29 USC 1001 et seq.

16. *Pensions Benefit Guaranty Corporation* v. *The LTV Corporation,* U.S. S.Ct., *Case #89–390.* Decided June 18, 1990. Tentative citation 110 S.Ct. 2668 (1990).

17. *J.K. Lasser's Your 1990 Income Tax* (Prepared by the J.K. Lasser Institute, New York, Simon & Schuster, Inc., New York: 1989).

18. Civil Rights Act of 1866, 42 USC 1981 et seq.

19. *Earnings of Married Couple Families, 1987:* (Washington, DC: U.S. Bureau of the Census, 1989); *The Wall Street Journal,* July 26, 1989, p. A-12; and *San Francisco Chronicle,* July 26, 1989, p. A-5.

20. Civil Rights Act of 1964, 42 USC 703 (a) (1).

21. Ibid, Section 703 (b) and (c).

22. *Independent Union of Flight Attendants* v. *Pan American World Airways, Inc.,* Case #84-4600, Federal District Court, San Francisco, November 27, 1989. This is a decision in a federal trial court where generally no opinions are written or published.

23. *International Union, United Automobile, Aerospace and Agricultural Implement Workers of America, UAW, et al.* v. *Johnson Controls, Inc.,* 680 F.Supp. 309 (E. D. Wisconsin, 1988). Also *International Union v. Johnson Controls,* U.S.S.Ct., Case No. 89-1215 (1990).

24. Jost, Kenneth, *"Precedent, Race, and the Court,"* *California Lawyer,* January 1989. In this article, EEOC Chairman Clarence Thomas blames the backlog on "budget problems."

25. Age Discrimination In Employment Act of 1967, an Amendment of Title VII of the Civil Rights Act of 1964.

26. *Griggs* v. *Duke Power Co.,* 91 S.Ct. 849 (1971).

27. *United Steelworkers of America* v. *Weber,* 99 S.Ct. 2721 (1979).

28. *Brown* v. *Board of Education of Topeka,* 74 S.Ct. 686 (1954).

29. *San Francisco Chronicle,* September 9, 1989, p. A7.

30. *The Wall Street Journal,* September 18, 1989, p. A18.

31. *City of Richmond* v. *J.A. Grosson Company,* 109 S.Ct. 706 (1989); and *Astroline Communications Co.* v. *Shurberg Broadcasting* and *Metro Broadcasting Inc.* v. FCC, USSC 89–453 and 89–700 (1990).

32. *Ward's Cove Packing Company, Inc.* v. *Atonio,* 109 S.Ct. 2115 (1989).

33. *Martin* v. *Wilks,* 109 S.Ct. 2180 (1989).

34. *Patterson* v. *McLean Credit Union,* 109 S.Ct. 2363 (1989).

35. *Whirlpool Corporation* v. *Marshall, Secretary of Labor,* 100 S.Ct. 883 (1980).

36. *Palmer, Floyd J., and Patrick H. Hicks,* "Wrongful Termination and the Foley Decision," Sacramento, CA: *Docket,* Sacramento County Bar Association, June, 1989, p. 10. Note: In *Foley* v. *Interactive Data Corporation,* 765 P.2d 373 (1988), the California Supreme Court ruled that *punitive* damages are not available for breach of the covenant of good faith and fair dealing.

37. Worker Adjustment and Retraining Notification Act of 1988, 29 U.S.C. 2101–2109.

38. *Commonwealth* v. *Pullis* (Philadelphia Cordwainers Case), Philadelphia Mayor's Court, 3 Commons and Gilmore (1806).

39. *Commonwealth* v. *Hunt,* 45 Mass. (4 Met.) 111, 38 Am.Dec. 346 (1842).

40. *Thornhill* v. *Alabama,* 60 S.Ct. 736 (1940); and *Frisby* v. *Shultz,* 108 S.Ct. 2495 (1988).

41. Anti-Injunction Act of 1932, 29 USC 101 et seq.

42. National Labor Relations Act of 1935, op. cit.

43. National Labor-Management Relations Act of 1947, op. cit.

44. California Agricultural Labor Relations Act of 1975, Labor Code, Sec.1140 et seq.; *E.J. DeBartolo Corp.* v. *Florida Gulf Coast Building and Construction Trade Council & NLRB,* 108 S.Ct. 1392 (1988).

45. Labor-Management Reporting and Disclosure Act of 1959, 29 USC 401 et seq.

46. *Statistical Abstract of The United States 1990,* op.cit., Table No. 689.

47. Ibid., Table No. 683.

48. *NLRB* v. *Fansteel Metallurgical Corporation,* 59 S.Ct. 490 (1939).

CHAPTER 10

Law and the Small Business

How big can a small business be and still be considered "small" by the United States government? When Congress created the Small Business Administration (SBA) in 1953, it used a definition of "small business" that embraced more than 99 percent of all U.S. firms.[1] Including firms of self-employed individuals, small businesses employ almost 60 percent of the nation's work force and account for some 40 percent of the gross national product.* That means that fewer than 1 percent of truly "big" business firms—such as American Telephone and Telegraph Company (AT&T), International Business Machines (IBM), and General Motors Corporation (GM)—employ 40 percent of the entire work force and produce 60 percent of the total goods and services.

New small firms, according to the SBA, account for 2 out of 3 new jobs created annually.[2] The sheer number of small firms provides diversity, variety, and competition that translates into new jobs. The start-up effort and the ongoing struggle to survive and to succeed undoubtedly encourage creativity. Small businesses, according to a National Science Foundation study, have generated more innovations per research and development dollar than large businesses. Large businesses are often burdened with heavy fixed costs of overhead and expensive, time-consuming internal review and approval procedures before they can sell a new product.[3]

Clearly, both large and small business firms are vital to the economic health of the nation. Large corporations depend heavily on small businesses for the supply of component parts and the provision of various services. Moreover, the giant firms rely on thousands of small wholesale and retail firms to distribute their products and to service them once they have reached the ultimate consumers. Small business firms offer more appropriate employment opportunities for young would-be entrepreneurs, thus providing suitable models and hands-on experience that best prepare individuals to strike out on their own after some years of such employment.

---

* The gross national product (GNP) is the value of all goods and services produced by the nation during a stated period. It was approximately $5 trillion in 1989.

Accordingly, in this chapter we emphasize the legal environment of the small business firm. We first examine the law of agency, because a business cannot be conducted in the legal format of a partnership or corporation without the use of agents. Sole proprietors also use agents. We then study the legal structure of the principal forms of business firms, both small and large, and compare their advantages and disadvantages. We review essential legal steps that must be taken to begin operation of a small business, regardless of its legal format. Finally, we philosophize about the "publics" or constituencies that have legitimate claims on the output and profits of the business firm.

What Is Agency?

Agency is described in technical language by the authoritative *Restatement of Agency* as ".... the fiduciary relation which results from the manifestation of consent by one person to another that the other shall act on his behalf and subject to his control, and consent by the other so to act."[4] Let us translate that legalese into understandable parts:

1. Agency is a relationship between two persons, the *principal,* or employer who wants to get something done, and the *agent*, or employee who is authorized by the principal to do the specified job.

2. The relationship is always *consensual*. Both principal and agent must expressly or impliedly consent to the relationship. For example, as a favor Juanita acts as Lou's agent to purchase tickets to the big game. Lou reimburses Juanita for the price paid, but gives her no more than a "thank you" for her services. Had Juanita bought the tickets without Lou's consent, he would have no obligation to pay. The relationship is also usually *contractual,* meaning that both parties give and both receive consideration (see Chapter 7). For example, under an employment contract, Craig serves as Molly's agent (sales representative) in the Chicago territory. Craig makes contracts on Molly's behalf and binds her to perform. She pays him a salary and/or commission for his services.

3. The agent represents and acts on behalf of the principal in dealings with third parties. The resulting contract is legally binding on the principal, provided the agent acted within the scope of his or her authority as given by the principal. Usually the agent is not bound to the third part under the contract.

4. An agent who acts beyond the scope of his or her authority is personally liable to the third party. If in doubt as to the nature and scope of the agent's authority, the third party should check directly with the true or alleged principal, asking: (a) Is he/she your agent, and (b) What is your agent's authority (e.g., to sell? to buy? etc.).

5. The agent, in effect, walks in the shoes of the principal, even when out of the principal's presence. The principal has the continuing right to control the agent, but while alone, the agent may make a foolish contract or commit a tort (e.g., drive a company car negligently and injure someone) and the principal is nevertheless liable under the doctrine of respondeat superior (Latin: let the superior answer). The employer is liable to third parties for injuries caused by the negligence of employees while acting within the scope of their employment. Note that even if the agent violates explicit orders, the principal would be liable to affected innocent third parties (e.g., the agent sells goods below a minimum price set by the principal; grants credit in violation of stated company policy; or drives a company car on a business call at excessive speed, contravening express orders to obey all traffic laws).

6. An official notice (e.g., legal summons and complaint) given to a duly authorized agent is legally deemed to be a notice to the principal. Also, the agent is duty bound to perform as promised and to use reasonable care (which could be appropriate skilled care, as when the agent is a lawyer or real estate broker).

7. Agency is a fiduciary relationship in which the agent must act in scrupulous good faith and honesty toward the principal, always placing the interests of the principal first. He or she must be loyal, never serving two adverse parties (e.g., the buyer and the seller in a transaction) at the same time, unless both are fully informed and consent. Of course, an agent may be employed by a group of associated principals. Also, an attorney at law may be employed by two or more persons to prepare a partnership agreement. The clients must give their informed consent, and the attorney must treat them with impartiality and balanced fairness. The agent must account to the principal for all receipts and disbursements, and never keep a secret profit.

Creation of the Agency Relationship

Generally, no special formalities are required for the creation of the agency relationship. Exceptions exist under the Statute of Frauds when the agency cannot be performed within one year, and when a real estate broker is hired as an agent to sell a parcel of land (see Chapters 6 and 13). Practically speaking, any agreement that will entail much time, money, or detail should be in writing for the guidance and protection of both parties.

Under certain unusual circumstances a principal may subsequently ratify and be bound by acts of the agent (or even acts of a non-agent) that were done beyond the scope of any authority given by the principal. Also, in some cases a principal may be estopped (legally barred) from denying that an impostor was indeed his or her agent. This could happen if the principal simply stood by, without protesting, when such an imposter acted as an authorized agent in dealing with a third party who was present.

Why Is Agency Essential for Partnerships and Corporations?

Tom Riser had financed his way through four years of college by buying and selling cars and trucks, one at a time. He was handy with tools, and so he would buy an old vehicle and use it for his own transport needs while fixing it up, and then resell the vehicle for a profit. After graduation, he decided to expand this work into a full-time occupation, which would require more time, space, labor and money. He consulted an attorney, who suggested either a partnership or a corporation. "You've been a sole proprietor," the attorney said. "Now you'll have to rely on agency law." Is this so?

One or more carefully chosen partners could give Tom the help he needs in labor and capital. But when two (or more) persons associate as general partners, under law they impliedly authorize each other to conduct business through contracts that will bind all partners. Thus, in legal effect, the partners are agents of each other and principals of each other in relations with third parties outside their partnership. Internally the partners may agree to limit or expand the agency authority. One partner may be authorized, exclusively, to do all the necessary buying; the other may be authorized, exclusively, to do all the selling. However, third parties who are unaware of such limitations may generally assume that the partners have equal powers, and that both partners may bind the firm in sales and purchases.

If, instead, Tom decides to incorporate, all business will be done by the corporation, which is considered a legal person by the law. It is an entity distinct from its shareholding owner or owners. Accordingly, a corporation can acquire, possess, and dispose of property in its own name; it can hire, control, and fire employees; and do all other things necessary to run the business. But a corporation is not a human person; it can act only through human agents, who make contracts with third parties on behalf of the corporation. Of course, corporate officers may also hire persons as ordinary employees and as independent contractors to do other work that does not involve making of contracts with third parties for the corporation. (see Chapter 9).

May Anyone Legally Start any Business?

Theoretically, yes; practically, no. Licenses and financial qualifications are required for certain business ventures. Under the law, exclusive licenses are given in fields where unlimited competition would be impracticable or wasteful—for example, radio and television, public utilities, and transportation. Can you image a street with two (or more) competing sets of electric and telephone poles? Typically in such cases, to get and keep the necessary license (which may ensure a virtual monopoly), the business firm must provide a certain level of service and charge rates or prices prescribed by law.

To help protect the public, the law requires business firms in certain fields to demonstrate minimum financial responsibility before they open. Banks, savings and loan associations, and insurance companies must first obtain prescribed, substantial amounts of capital. The recent scandalous wave of failures among federally insured savings and loan associations (more than 700 became insolvent) led to a federal government bailout beginning in 1989 under the direction of a new administrative agency, the Resolution Trust Corporation. Many people share the blame for this fiasco; for decades American taxpayers will share the cost. The final bailout cost is expected to exceed $200 billion, and may reach as much as $500 billion.

As noted in Chapters 9 and 15, in some occupational fields (such as law and medicine) the entrepreneur must attain technical or professional competence through formal schooling and then further demonstrate it through examination and, increasingly, maintain it through continuing education programs. In general, however, all fields are open to all persons in our free enterprise system. Anyone may attempt to enter even those fields that require certain qualifications. Usually the principal obstacles to going into business for oneself are not legal, but economic and psychological.

An **entrepreneur** needs capital: to buy supplies and equipment; to rent or buy suitable space; to hire employees; to finance production, advertising, and sales; and to extend credit to customers. A blend of personal qualities is also needed for success: intelligence, energy, ambition, initiative, the courage to take risks, foresight, industriousness, perserverance, and good luck—qualities that do not often come together in one person. If the success is to be enduring and free from the threat of possible legal sanction and disturbing socioeconomic pressures (discussed later in this chapter), the entrepreneur must also act with integrity and in a socially responsible manner.

Another economic deterrent to going into business for oneself is the likelihood of failure. According to the Small Business Administration, the majority of small businesses fail in their first year. A staggering 95 out of 100 fail within their first five years. The causes of failure are many, but the most common one cited by observers is simple incompetence or mismanagement. Mismanagement can usually be minimized by careful formal study (e.g., of accounting, marketing, and communications) and by informal learning on the job in the employ of a successful entrepreneur. Learning "the ropes" in the employ of a going concern is a time-tested, acceptable, and prudent prelude to going into business for oneself. A mutually beneficial variation is to buy an interest in your employer's firm, either as a shareholder (if it is a corporation) or as a partner (if it is a partnership or sole proprietorship). Frequently the sole owner needs and wants a responsible buyer to purchase the business upon his or her retirement or death, and employees may be the best prospects.

Failure may cause not only loss of your time and money (and often that of others), but also an embarrassing retreat and disposal of the business assets piecemeal or as a unit. Selling the business in haste and under compulsion often involves the loss of part or all of what the owner has invested. Failure does not necessarily nor usually entail formal bankruptcy proceedings. (See Chapter 6 for a discussion of bankruptcy). Failure is often caused by avoidable mistakes resulting from the lack of a carefully thought-out, realistic plan of action updated from time to time. "Fail" is probably an unduly harsh label for many of the business firms that close down. A firm may sell out or liquidate with little or no loss of capital. Sometimes the proprietor gets bored or weary or decides to move, maybe even starting a new firm at a new location. Perhaps a business was intended to last only a limited time (e.g., during a county fair, or a vacation period, or until the proprietor retires). Firms may merge, or sole proprietors of going concerns may opt to work for others,. And, sadly, sometimes the proprietor may become seriously ill or die.

Succeeding in a business of one's own is difficult. Profits, the excess of revenues (or receipts) over costs (or expenses), are not automatic. They typically require bringing capital, labor, materials, and machines together. These ingredients must be combined and coordinated efficiently to produce and market a saleable good or service. The output must be priced competitively. It must be advertised and sold. Major hurdles remain in billing and receiving payment (perhaps after a delay because of credit extension). After sales there may be returns, adjustments, and servicing problems. Federal, state, and local governments may take as much as 40 percent or more of your income in taxes. Fortunately, prices may be adjusted upward to include the income taxes, which is feasible because most competitors in any given field are similarly situated. The ultimate consumer who gets the primary benefit of the goods thus indirectly pays the tax just as he or she pays for labor, materials, and other costs involved in the production and sale of goods and services.

Entrepreneurs like to maximize their profits, an elusive concept probably meaning "make greater." But successful entrepreneus are usually willing to settle for a reasonable return on invested capital, together with a reasonable salary for their personal services. Even such modest success generally requires that the firm consistently identify and cater to consumer needs and wants. The customer is not "king;" however, customers "vote with their dollars," and collectively they decide the fate of every business. Honest value is generally recognized and rewarded with customer patronage.

What Legal Forms of Business Organization Are Available?

 Paul Ward and Carla Kane had been friends since their college days. Within ten years after graduation, each had saved almost $50,000. They knew they could borrow another $50,000 from close relatives. They had several trustworthy and competent friends who might be interested in joining them in a business venture if invited. Carla had been employed for several years as a tennis instructor at the local country club. Over a four-year period, Paul had worked most of the jobs in the largest sporting goods shop in town, and for the past year he had served as assistant manager for the owner-manager. Now Carla and Paul considered starting a private fitness center of their own, coupled with a sports store offering a selective line of equipment. It was to be located in a rapidly growing suburb. What legal form of business organization should they use?

They could use any of a number of possible forms of business organization recognized by law. Most important in terms of popularity and volume of business are the sole proprietorship, the partnership, and the corporation.

Sole Proprietorship

Either Paul or Carla could elect to "go it alone" and become the sole owner of the business. He or she would own all assets, be responsible without limit for all liabilities or debts, make all important decisions, be entitled to all profits, and suffer all losses. If both Paul and Carla worked in the **sole proprietorship,** by necessity one would be an employee. In all likelihood the sole proprietor's hours would be very long, and the business problems would go wherever the owner went. Income from the business would be regarded as ordinary personal income and would be taxed as such (up to 33 percent at the top federal level). Of course, Paul and Carla might become a married couple. Then, if one spouse owned and operated the business as a matter of legal record, the other would enjoy property rights in it as a result of their matrimonial relationship. (See Chapter 8 for a discussion of the effect of matrimony on property rights.)

Partnership   *Limited partnership p 316*

Together or in company with one or more other persons, Carla and Paul could form a partnership—"... an association of two or more persons to carry on as co-owners a business for profit."[5] Although the partners might contribute unequal amounts of capital and spend unequal amounts of time at work, they would share the profits and losses equally unless they agree to some other plan of distribution.

Partners who put up most of the capital may insist on getting most of the profits, and the other partners may go along with such demand. Partners may also agree that one will assume a larger than equal share of future possible losses. Outside creditors, however, are not bound by such an internal agreement of the partners. To the outside world, the partners remain jointly and severally liable without limit for the debts of the business. If the business should fail, creditors would first seek payment from the firm. If available firm assets proved to be insufficient, the creditors could sue any or all of the partners for the balance due, invading their personal fortunes or estates. Any partner compelled to pay could go to court to force the other partners to share the loss equally or as previously agreed. Obviously, a partner who lacked financial resources might be judgment-proof (i.e., insolvent, or protected by statutes that shield wages and property). This possibility suggests that at the outset one should try to select partners who are financially responsible and able to share fairly in any loss suffered. Every partner chosen should also be competent, because all may have to share in or assume the full burden of losses caused by the foolish decisions of any one partner. Certainly, partners chosen should be honest, trustworthy, industrious, and compatible. Although not required by law, it is highly desirable that the partners' agreement be in writing and signed. Moreover, wisdom and prudence deem that it be prepared by qualified legal counsel.

When a partner retires from the business (with or without good cause), goes insane, or dies, the partnership is *dissolved.* Upon dissolution, the partners legally cease to be associated in carrying on the business. Unless arrangements are promptly made to continue the business a **winding-up period** follows, during which assets are sold, debts paid, and partners' investments returned. After the winding-up, the partnership is *terminated.* With a little sensible advance planning, however, the losses inevitable in such hasty forced sales can be avoided. The partners simply make a **continuation agreement** that permits the surviving partner (or partners) to keep the firm's assets intact while paying an agreed amount to the retired partner (or to the heirs of the deceased partner). Such payment can be made over a period of years in a manner fair to all.

Another possibility is to have the partners enter into a **buy and sell agreement** *or contract,* funded by life insurance. For example, partner A buys a policy of life insurance on partner B's life, and agrees to buy out B's interest in the firm over a prescribed period of time if B dies first. The insurance proceeds would help pay the bill. Reciprocally, Partner B buys a life insurance policy on A's life and agrees to buy A's interest if A dies first. In a variation of this plan, the partnership may pay the premiums on life insurance for all of the partners as a business expense. The firm is designated as beneficiary. When a partner dies, the proceeds are used to help retire the deceased partner's interest (i.e., by paying the heirs).

As noted previously, unless otherwise agreed, each partner is an agent of the other partner or partners; each may enter into contracts for the firm with third parties and all partners are bound. Because of this great power and its related potential for abuse, no partner may join the firm unless unanimously approved by existing partners or an alternative plan had been previously adopted unanimously. Likewise, all partners must agree on modifications in their partnership agreement and on fundamental changes in company objectives and operations. Ordinary business decisions (such as setting policies on purchasing, pricing, or warranties) are made by a majority. If there are disagreements, a majority vote resolves them. Individual partners may make routine decisions for the firm (such as buying, selling, hiring, and firing), always acting within the policies established by the majority. Deadlocks in voting are possible when there is an even number of partners. In such deadlocks, the firm falters and may have to be dissolved. This possibility suggests again that at the outset one should select partners who are competent and trustworthy (their decisions will bind you) and compatible (you will have to get along together and agree on many matters).

Income Taxes   Income taxes are not levied on partnership income, although the firm must file an informational tax return. Each partner's share of income, whether distributed or not, is taxable as part of that person's individual personal income. This tax status could be disadvantageous if the partner already enjoys a sizable income from other sources. It might be preferable to let the money remain to work in the business, as is possible in a corporation. A corporation, after paying its income tax on net profits, may enable its shareholders to avoid paying personal income tax on those profits by not distributing them as dividends. In effect, earnings retained in the corporation (by decision of its board of directors) are added investments of capital.

Corporation

In a typical **corporation,** stockholders who own shares in the business elect three or more **directors,** who are legally responsible for the proper management of the business. The directors select *officers* (president, vice president, secretary, and treasurer), who actively control and manage the day-to-day affairs of the company, usually with the assistance of hired workers.[6] (See Figure 10–1.)

Acting separately, or together, Paul and Carla could form a small **close** or **closely held corporation,** in which one of them could be the sole stockholder and director as well as president or chief executive officer. As owner of all the stock, he or she could find other cooperative directors and other officers, if so desired. In some states, incorporators obtain a **charter,** or a permit to do business, from the state. In most states, incorporators prepare and file **articles of incorporation** with a designated state office. Figure 10-2 on page 314 is a sample distributed by the Secretary of State of California. It is a model that meets minimum statutory requirements in that state. Articles of incorporation generally state the name and purpose(s) of the firm, identify its first managing directors, describe its capital structure (i.e., what kind(s) of shares of **stock** representing ownership of the corporation are to be

FIGURE 10–1   Organization of a Typical Small-Business Corporation

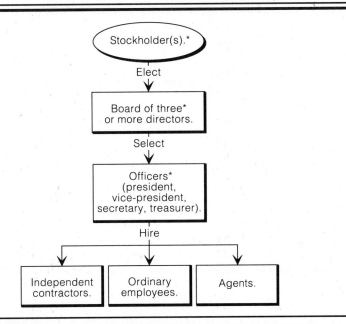

*Note that the corporation could be organized and operated with only one, or with many more, stockholders, directors, and officers.

issued), and give its principal address. For a small business, incorporating and obtaining permission from the state to sell stock to a limited number of investors are routine matters. Nevertheless, these are important tasks that generally should be done with the assistance of qualified legal counsel.

Under the **Model Business Corporation Act,** a corporation "... may be organized ... for any lawful purpose or purposes except for the purpose of banking or insurance."[7] Special laws govern the formation of banks and insurance companies because of the need to provide added protection for lenders/savers and insured persons. The powers of the corporation as specified in the articles of incorporation may be stated with great precision, or they may be identified very broadly, as, for example, "... to have and to exercise all powers necessary or convenient to effect its purpose."[8] In California, Washington, and some other states, one person may be the sole promoter who gets the idea for the business and translates it into action. He or she could then become sole incorporator, stockholder, director, officer, and employee. In a sense such a person is a sole proprietor with the legal status of a corporation.

Although the corporation is a legal entity and is liable without limit for its debts, the **stockholders** (investors) basically can lose no more than they paid for their shares.* Of course the amount of the shareholder's investment in the business

* In rare cases, stockholders buy shares of stock at a discount, or below the par value (printed on the face of the share). If the corporation later fails financially, creditors may insist that those stockholders pay the balance of the value. Some corporations, such as banks, make their stock *assessable*—the corporation directors may later call on the stockholders to pay an additional sum or assessment up to a predetermined maximum. In some states, shareholders of small corporations may be personally liable for employee wages.

FIGURE 10–2   Sample Articles of Incorporation

ARTICLES OF INCORPORATION

I

The name of this corporation is _____

II

The purpose of this corporation is to engage in any lawful act or activity for which a corporation may be organized under the General Corporation Law other than the banking business, the trust company business or the practice of a profession permitted to be incorporated by the Corporations Code.

III

The name and address in the State of this corporation's initial agent for service of process is:

Name _____

Street Address _____

City _____ State _____ Zip _____

IV

This corporation is authorized to issue only one class of shares of stock; and the total number of shares which this corporation is authorized to issue is:

_____

_____

_____
(Signature of incorporator)
_____
(Typed name of incorporator)

increases whenever the directors retain and reinvest earnings, a very common practice. This **limited liability** feature of the corporate form of organization appeals to many persons, and so corporations are able to raise large amounts of capital for the mass production and distribution of goods, so critical in our economy. Paradoxically, a banker may refuse to lend money to a close corporation unless its officers guarantee the loan, agreeing to be personally liable in full. Thus the advantage of limited liability may be lost in the small corporation owned by just one or a few individuals.

Unlike the partnership, a corporation lives on when stockholders die or when its shares are bought, sold, or transferred by gift in life or by inheritance upon death. The corporation is an artificial but legal person in the eyes of the law, and so it may last indefinitely, into perpetuity. The business may fail and the corporation may "die" (be dissolved) if it is seriously mismanaged or if a key official (possibly the sole stockholder and chief executive officer) dies. Generally, however, the fact that it is an entity, separate from its owners and officers, permits it to endure, and facilitates the easy transfer of shares of stock. This aspect appeals to investors, but again most persons are understandably reluctant to buy shares in closely held corporations. They properly fear failure of the business and they recognize the possibility that dominant owners who are also officers may pay high salaries to themselves and declare low or no dividends to shareholders.

Income Taxes   It has been said (probably in desperation if not with justification) that the United States Internal Revenue Code, which governs the calculation and collection of income taxes, is the longest, most complicated, and most difficult-to-understand code of laws in the history of the world. This is especially true of provisions applicable to business firms, and to individuals who invest in income-producing property. Accordingly, most business firms are compelled to employ qualified accountants, tax specialists, and tax lawyers for advice and assistance in financial planning as well as in the preparation of tax returns. As of 1990 the taxable income of corporations was subject to federal tax as follows:

Cumulative Total of Taxable Income	Segment	Tax Rate	Tax	Cumulative Total Tax
$150,000	So much that does not exceed $50,000	15%	$7,500	$ 7,500
75,000	$50,000 but doesn't exceed $75,000	25%	6,250	13,750
100,000	So much as exceeds $75,000 (and so on)	34%	8,500	22,250

An additional 5 percent tax, up to $11,750, is imposed on corporate taxable income over $100,000.[9] In addition, in most states corporate income is also subject to the state's income tax.

"Double Taxation"   If the earnings are distributed in **dividends,** the receipts are subject to a second federal tax (up to 33 percent) on the personal income of each stockholder, and in most states, also to a state tax on personal income. As already noted, to avoid these additional levies corporate directors may decide to declare no dividends, retaining all or most of the earnings and reinvesting them in the business.*

Stock Splits and Stock Dividends   To keep stockholders happy when no cash dividends are declared, the directors may **split** the existing stock, giving, for example, two shares for each one owned. Since there is no cash distribution, the new shares are not taxable. Because the earnings were retained to be used in the business, the company should be earning more and the aggregate of shares should be worth more than before. The shareholder who wants to take a portion of the profits in cash can sell some of his or her stock.

The excess over what was paid for the stock and what it sold for is **capital gain,** which is taxable as ordinary income.† The split may also be designed to bring the stock price within *trading range,* a lower level that is more appealing to investors and speculators. For example, an investor owns one share of XYZ Corporation common stock with a market price of $100. The XYZ board of directors orders a four-for-one stock split. Each old share is exchanged for four new shares. The market price of each new share quickly moves to perhaps $28. Thus the market value of the investor's stock holding has gone up from $100 for one share formerly held to $112 for four new shares now held.

As an alternative, the corporation's directors could declare a **stock dividend** by issuing, for example, one new share for each share owned. The net effect is essentially the same as in a stock split, but technically the stock dividend involves a bookkeeping transfer from the "retained earnings account" to the "capital stock account." Thus, legally, such transferred and permanently capitalized earnings are no longer available for the payment of cash dividends. In contrast, after a stock split the directors could still legally use any balance in the retained earnings account to pay a cash dividend. Having such retained earnings balance may result in pressure from stockholders for a cash dividend or in pressure from employees for a wage boost. Yet there may be little cash available because it has been invested in equipment and other assets.

Limited partnership.   In this cross between a partnership and a corporation (which must be formed in strict compliance with applicable statutes), at least one

---

* Most corporations are allowed to accumulate earnings up to $250,000 (less any accumulated earnings of the preceding taxable year) without incurring liability for a special added tax of 28 percent. For personal service corporations, the maximum of such permitted accumulation is $100,000. In a U.S. Senate explanation of the 1988 Technical and Miscellaneous Revenue Act, P.L. 100-647, 11-10-88, a personal service corporation is described as one ". . . that meets both a functional test and an ownership test. The functional test is met if substantially all activities of the corporation are the performance of services in the field or fields of health, law, engineering, architecture, accounting, actuarial science, performing arts, and consulting. The ownership test is met if substantially all (i.e. 95 percent) of the value of the outstanding stock in the corporation is owned, directly or indirectly, by employees performing services for the corporation in connection with the qualified services performed by the corporation, retired individuals who performed such services for the corporation, or its predecessor(s), the estate of such individual, or any other person who acquired stock by reason of the death of such an employee (for the two-year period beginning with the death of such employee)."
† At the time of this writing (1990), Congress is considering some reduction in the tax on capital gains, to encourage savings. The resulting investments in new plant and equipment would presumably result in more jobs and higher production levels.

partner must be a general partner with unlimited liability for firm debts.[10] However, if the business fails, the **limited partner(s),** like a corporate share-holder, stand to lose no more out of pocket than he or she invested. The limited partner is not individually liable for firm debts. To preserve this privileged status, however, the limited partner may not participate in management of the firm, nor act as its agent. Some states do permit limited partners to vote on some important matters, such as admission of new partners. If this is so, why not simply lend money to the firm? Because the interest returned would be a set amount, with the rate limited by usury laws, and the loan could be paid off, thus ending the investor's involvement. In contrast, as a limited partner, one is a co-owner and may share in profits that theoretically can increase without limit.

Is a Corporation Ever Regarded as a Partnership for Tax Purposes?

 Max Rogarous started his mobile-home construction business as a sole proprietorship. He built the first unit in his garage. As the business prospered, he added a partner and later incorporated the company in order to raise more capital by selling stock to seven wealthy friends. All nine owners are now in the upper tax brackets and quite unhappy with their tax status. The firm pays the maximum federal and state corporation income taxes on most of its income. When cash dividends are declared, each owner has to pay whopping federal and state personal income taxes on money received. Can they end this multiple taxation?

Yes. They could change the firm back to a partnership. But none of the other owners wants the burdens of sharing in management with Rogarous and his hired assistants. All fear the unlimited liability of general partners for firm debts. They are also concerned about the inevitable dissolution when a partner withdraws or dies, even though prior arrangements could be made to continue the business.

Therefore, they elect to be treated as an **S corporation,*** as permitted by the Internal Revenue Code. The company retains its corporate status but is considered a partnership for federal income tax purposes. No federal corporation tax is paid; all income is shared by the stockholders according to their proportional ownership of common stock. As in a partnership, the income is regarded as taxable income only to the stockholders, whether or not it is distributed to them or retained within the business. The S corporation simply files an information tax return.

To qualify as an S corporation certain conditions must be met, including the following:

1. It may have no more than 35 stockholders. They must be individuals, estates of individuals, or certain trusts. However, a husband and wife are regarded as one stockholder. All stockholders must give written consent to change to S corporation status.

---

* Formerly called a *subchapter S corporation* after the applicable Internal Revenue Code section.

2. It may have outstanding only one class of stock (e.g., common, which may consist of both voting and nonvoting shares. It may not consist of common and preferred stock.)

3. It may not include any nonresident alien stockholders. All shareholders must be citizens or residents of the United States.

What Happens if the Corporate Form Is Used to Perpetrate a Fraud on Creditors?

 With minimal capital of his own, Irving Tuttle went heavily into debt to organize a corporation. He then went even deeper by borrowing funds and using trade credit. He proceeded to use the firm's assets to pay inordinately high salaries to himself and to his wife and to incur lavish business entertainment and travel expenses. Then he filed for bankruptcy for the corporation. Soon after, he organized a second corporation in which he and his wife owned most of the stock. When they tried to use the same routine as before but with different lenders and suppliers, some of his corporate creditors blocked the second discharge in bankruptcy. They sued the couple and sought payment from their personal assets. Will the creditors succeed?

Yes, in all likelihood. A court "tears aside the corporate veil" and holds the owner (or owners) liable without limit as sole proprietor (or partners) when the corporation has been organized to perpetrate a fraud on creditors. Such piercing of the corporate veil is a long-recognized exception to the principle that a corporation is a legal entity separate from its owners and alone liable for its own debts.

There is, of course, nothing illegal or immoral about paying reasonable salaries to family members or incurring reasonable business expenses, nor is it illegal or unethical to incorporate in order to obtain the advantage of limited liability for stockholders with no fraudulent intent. Note also that prospective suppliers can sell on COD (cash on delivery) terms. They can request financial statements and other relevant information from the corporation or from credit rating agencies such as Dun & Bradstreet, Inc. Then they can refuse to extend credit if the management is suspect or if corporate assets and earning power appear to be inadequate to meet all debts as they become due.

Sometimes before starting a risky business venture a sole proprietor or partner will transfer certain assets to a spouse or other relatives. If the transfer is made before the risky business begins and before debts or liabilities are incurred, subsequent creditors of the business (sole proprietorship or partnership) cannot reach the previously transferred assets to get paid. Before extending credit, they should check on the assets and liabilities of the prospective debtor and possibly require special security. To meet this requirement, the proprietor or partner may need to persuade the relative(s) to return the assets or to co-sign promissory notes. Such return or co-signing negates the attempt to shield the assets from seizure by unpaid creditors.

TABLE 10–1   Rating Legal Types of Small Business Organizations

Characteristics	Sole Proprietorship	Partnership General	Partnership Limited	Small Corporation
1. Ease of starting	1	2	2	3
2. Cost of starting	1	2	2	3
3. Access to capital	4	2	3	1
4. Ease of transferring interest in firm	3	4	2	1
5. Independence:	1	2	2	3
Sole control	1	2	4	3 (1 if close corporation with
Receipt of all profits	1	2	2	3 one owner of stock)
6. Privacy	1	2	2	3
7. Duration or potential life	3	2	2	1 (3 if close corporation with one of owner stock)
8. Liability of owner for debts of firm	2	3	1	1 (3 if owner guarantees debts)
9. Income tax burden on firm	1	1	1	2 (1 if it is an S corporation or retains and reinvests earnings)
10. Credit rating	2	1	2	3 (1 if owner(s) guarantee(s) debts)
11. Potential for growth	3	2	2	1
12. Division of labor and access to specialists	3	2	2	1
13. Availability of incentive plans and company-paid fringe benefits (pensions, profit-sharing plans, group life insurance, health insurance)	2*	2*	2*	1†
14. Ease of termination	1	2	3	4

Note: 1—normally most favorable to owner(s); 4—normally least favorable to owner(s).

* May utilize federal Keogh plan for tax-free accumulation of retirement benefits.

† May be expense to corporation and not taxable income to recipient. Income may be deferred until retirement when total personal income is down and therefore applicable tax rate is lower.

What are the Comparative Advantages and Disadvantages of the Leading Forms of Business Organization?

In Table 10–1 the principal forms of small business organization are rated from 1 (best) to 4 (worst),—from the owner's viewpoint—in regard to several basic characteristics.

How Does the Law Affect the Ongoing Operations of Your Business?

When Mrs. Polly Gerber started making canned fruit and jam preserves in her kitchen, she never dreamed that neighbors would beg her to sell them some of the products of her hobby. But they did, and she did. Within three years she rented a factory building and started producing in quantity, employing 57 persons and selling in every state. She was a sole proprietor and a rugged individualist. She insisted that as long as she paid her property tax and income taxes, Uncle Sam and all "government snoopers" would have to "keep their cotton picking hands off her business." Is she right?

No. If she has not already discovered the truth, she soon will. The long arm of government legal regulation will reach into many corners of her business, telling her what she must do and may not do:

1. Obtain a local business license.

2. Comply with local, state, and federal health and food purity regulations governing the sanitary conditions in the factory and the quality of the output.

3. Comply with federal laws regulating the packages and the disclosure of contents on the labels.

4. Comply with safety and health requirements for the benefit of her employees under state and federal occupational safety laws.

5. Pay at least minimum wages, limit work to maximum prescribed hours, and pay premium wages for overtime.

6. Recognize the right of workers to organize into a union or unions of their own choosing. If a majority join, she must bargain in good faith with them over wages, hours, and conditions of employment.

7. Pay workers' compensation insurance premiums to compensate workers who may be hurt on the job.

8. Not discriminate in hiring or promoting workers on the basis of race, sex, color, religion, national origin, advanced age or physical or mental disability.

9. Contribute FICA (Federal Insurance Contributions Act) taxes to provide unemployment, disability, retirement, and survivors' benefits for the workers and their families. Withhold and transmit to state and federal taxing authorities income taxes due from employees.

10. Not violate anti-trust laws, engage in unfair trade practices, or discriminate among customers in pricing (in violation of the Robinson-Patman Act and other legislation).

11. Comply with the corporation code of the state and with federal and possibly state regulations governing the issuance of securities (if she decides to incorporate).

12. Make good the express and implied warranties on products sold, if breached. She may also be liable to anyone who is injured if a product sold proves to be defective on the basis of negligence or strict product liability (see Chapter 5).

13. Comply with regulations on fuel use to reduce pollution of the air, and with regulations on waste disposal to reduce pollution of the soil and water.

14. Be careful not to make false or misleading statements in any advertisements.

15. Comply with the laws of contracts, agency, commercial paper, bailment, torts, and all other fields, where applicable.

16. Pay damages to third parties injured negligently by any of her employees in the course of their employment.

What Is Franchising?

 As Don Powers and Janet Zinda drove down the main street of Hometown, U.S.A., Don said: "Count the retail stores that are locally owned and run and those that belong to national corporations based in New York, Chicago, or other large business centers." The casual survey disclosed that many were owned by out-of-town corporations: K mart, Macy's, Sears, Wal-Mart, and J.C. Penney. Some were local. But a fairly large number were hard to classify because Don and Janet had seen them in other cities they had visited around the country, and yet they knew the stores were owned by local businesspersons: McDonald's Hamburgers, Colonel Sanders Kentucky Fried Chicken, A&W, Ace Hardware, Century 21, Chevron (Standard) Gasoline, Howard Johnson's, Motel 6, and TravelLodge. How can these business firms be classified?

As **franchises.** Under a contract with a corporation headquartered elsewhere, a local person obtains the right to use the name of the national firm and to enjoy its established goodwill. The national corporation, as **franchisor,** typically provides assistance in selecting a location; in building, furnishing, and stocking the place; in bookkeeping; and in other details of operation. In exchange, the **franchisee** is usually required to make a substantial cash contribution to build and/or furnish the outlet, and to provide necessary working capital (i.e., funds for wages, utilities, supplies, and inventory). The franchisee pays an initial fee and an annual percentage of its gross (total) or net revenues. The franchisee also agrees to comply with established standards of operation and product quality. The franchisee is usually required to buy needed supplies and inventory items from the parent company. The contractual arrangement is known as *franchising*.

A carefully chosen franchise is one way to minimize the risks involved in going into business for oneself. The most common cause of business failure is mismanagement; the franchisor helps to anticipate and forestall this problem.

Because some franchisors are unscrupulous and dishonest, they have been subjected to special legal controls at both the national and state levels. A Uniform Franchising Disclosure Law went into effect in 1979 under the administration of the **Federal Trade Commission.** Under it, the franchisor must provide the franchisee with a disclosure statement at least ten days before the contract is signed. Although there is no screening of ideas for their economic merit, the franchisor is prohibited from misrepresenting the nature and value of the franchise and from misrepresenting records of profitability. The franchisor must disclose its financial condition, history of litigation, the background of its management, and the truth about the failure record of its franchises. More than half of the states have regulations of their own that supplement the FTC rules. Nevertheless, the prospective franchisee should carefully evaluate the business potential of an outlet where planned and should have an attorney and an accountant review all documents presented by the franchisor.

Who Can You Call on for Assistance and Advice if You Go Into Business for Yourself?

Individual entrepreneurs need not stand alone to confront the countless problems encountered in finance, production, marketing, personnel, and information systems while transforming their dreams into a profit-making business reality. At the outset, and as legal problems arise, such venturesome persons should consult a qualified attorney who specializes in business law, as well as a banker. For assistance in setting up books of accounts and in preparing necessary tax returns, a qualified accountant (preferably a certified public accountant) is a must. Entrepreneurs would do well to consult the nearest office of the federal **Small Business Administration** for the names of local retired business managers who are members of SCORE (discussed in the next section); to obtain valuable advice; and sometimes for financial assistance. They may need a reliable real estate agent when buying or leasing real estate, and a good insurance agent to help select appropriate liability coverage. For any extensive advertising they will need an advertising agent. Sometimes a business management consultant can prove useful. Most lines of business have trade associations with publications, conventions, and seminars, all of which can be invaluable sources of useful information and advice. Always ready and eager to provide assistance are suppliers and would-be suppliers of inventory and equipment.

In the final analysis, however, these expert specialists can do no more than advise and assist the entrepreneurs who, as the prime movers, must decide and do. They must manage the business, plan ahead, set up a suitable internal organization, staff it with qualified help, direct and supervise activities, and exercise adequate follow up and control to make sure that things get done according to plan. Overall, they must coordinate the work of assistants in accomplishing the mission of the firm, be it production or distribution of goods or services at the retail or wholesale level or some combination thereof. They will probably find that there is a direct correlation between rewards received and effort expended over days, weeks, months, and years of hard work. (Refer to the Suggestions for Further Reading section at the end of this chapter, where some extremely useful reference materials are listed.)

What Are Some of the Legal Steps
You Must Take to Start a Business?

Details of your plan of action will vary depending on the nature of the business, its legal structure, its initial size, its employees, and its location (state and city); but certain basic legal steps are fairly uniform in all new business ventures.

Assume that you have established a proper foundation for your bold move into the world of competitive business. You have already learned much about general business management and operation through reading, observing, taking formal courses, and learning on the job in your field of choice. You have considered many alternative types of small business that appear to be interesting and promising. You have evaluated your own qualifications for the job ahead, and perhaps you have discussed the possibilities with one or more potential associates. Very early in your program, you have consulted the nearest office of the federal Small Business Administration (SBA) for information and advice, including ideas about financing assistance. You have certainly taken full advantage of the free advice available on a person-to-person basis from one or more members of SCORE, the **Service Core of Retired Executives.** (The SBA has enlisted some 13,000 experienced business managers in SCORE. They can be found at 750 locations nationwide and are ready to provide expert counseling and training, without charge, to new small business owners.)

You have tallied up your financial resources, and have spoken seriously with potential sources of the money and credit you expect to need immediately and in the foreseeable future. You soberly estimate the start-up costs, in human effort as well as related time and money. Long before you get to "D-day," you have selected and consulted a banker, a lawyer, and an accountant, all familiar with small business ventures and all willing to work with you for reasonable fees in the mutual hope of a continuing productive and profitable relationship. Having selected the desired legal form of organization, your lawyer has attended to the related legal formalities. Let us assume that you are an entrepreneur and have decided to start out as a sole proprietor. Now what?

1. *Select a name for your business.* You may do business under your own name. But if you use a **fictitious name** (e.g., "Tick Tock Tacos,") or even call it your own taco shop (e.g., "Mary Stein's Tacos"), you are required to register it with your County Clerk and publish your registration. You would first consult the Fictitious Name Indices in the Clerk's office to avoid a charge of unfair competition and any lawsuit that might follow the use of another's proprietary name.

2. *Register with the local tax collector and pay the annual registration fee.* Many local governments impose a flat fee (or tax) for those who do business in the community. Failure to pay (and in some places, to prominently post a Business Tax Registration Certificate) could eventually lead to a penalty and back charges.

3. *Obtain any required local license.* In large cities most businesses are required to have a license or permit to operate, coupled with the payment of specified fees. Restaurants and laundries are subject to review by the local health department. Street vendors, taxicab services, and places of entertainment may require clearance from the police department. Lacking a license may lead to a summary order to close.

4. *Obtain the necessary city permits for any new building construction or alteration.* An application to do extensive work usually must include detailed drawings signed by a licensed architect or engineer. Be sure the project complies with any applicable zoning laws. Your building contractor will probably handle these tasks, and your attorney might review these documents as well as any other major contracts you enter into.

5. *Obtain a seller's permit* from the state tax office if your state imposes a sales tax, as many now do.

6. *Obtain any required state license(s)* to engage in the particular business or activity. In California, for example, more than 40 different state bureaus or offices issue licenses for specific businesses. Recall also that some professions require prior completion of specified formal schooling and the subsequent passing of oral or written examinations. Engaging in these businesses without a license is a misdemeanor.

7. *Register with the state employment department* for employee recruitment and placement.

8. *Obtain a policy of workers' compensation insurance* from any private insurance company that issues such policies (or, in some cases, from a state agency). Such insurance is required if your business has even one employee other than yourself, so that employees can be compensated in case of on-the-job injuries or illnesses (see Chapter 9).

9. a. If you hire one or more employees, you must also *notify the state income tax department and arrange to withhold taxes.* Then you must transmit to the state office, on a quarterly basis, the withheld portion of each employee's wages to pay the applicable personal income tax.

    b. *Pay the tax or premium to provide state unemployment insurance* for each employee.

    c. In a few states (including California, the most populous state) you must *pay premiums to the state for disability insurance,* which covers each employee for injuries or illnesses suffered *off* the job.

10. *Obtain an employer identification number (EIN) from the Internal Revenue Service, as well as a taxpayer identification number (TIN).* The latter can be your EIN or your social security number (SSN). You will be required to file a business income tax return as an individual. (Partnerships and S corporations file informational returns; their owners are taxed as individuals. Corporations file returns and pay taxes on their net taxable income).

    a. As a sole proprietor, you will be required to pay *your own social security tax* (self-employment tax). The 1990 rate is 15.3 percent on net self-employment income up to $48,000. However, a deduction is allowed for one-half of this tax on the Form 1040 Individual Return.

    b. If you have any employees, you will be required to *withhold income tax from each employee's wages* or salary, *as well as the social security tax* (known as the FICA, which stands for **Federal Insurance Contributions Act).** In addition, you will have to pay the employer's equal portion of the total social security tax for each employee.*

Social Responsibility and Enlightened Self-Interest of Business Managers

Business managers and legislators are increasingly concerned with ethical conduct: to do what is right and fair in all dealings with others. Newspaper accounts of white-collar crimes (see Chapter 4) provide all too frequent reminders that some businesspersons are willing to violate the law to "make a buck." Simple reflection on the scope of legitimate business activity behind our country's gross national product (some *$5 trillion* a year) is reassuring evidence of general business integrity and intelligence. Most business is conducted ethically, and most managers act in a socially responsible manner. In essence, this means that in conducting their business, managers recognize and respect the rights and interests of a number of readily identifiable groups in our society. The basic groups (or *publics* or *constituencies,* as they are sometimes called) are (1) the owner(s), (2)

---

* Note that if you produce or sell certain products such as alcoholic beverages, tobacco products, or guns, you may have to pay specific excise taxes on all sales made and comply with other special regulations.

FIGURE 10–3 The Wheel of Progressive Business Production and Distribution of Goods and Services*

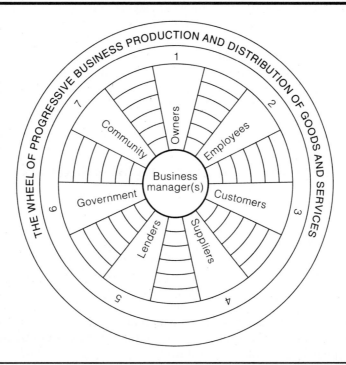

THE WHEEL OF PROGRESSIVE BUSINESS PRODUCTION AND DISTRIBUTION OF GOODS AND SERVICES

1 Owners
2 Employees
3 Customers
4 Suppliers
5 Lenders
6 Government
7 Community

Business manager(s)

* A graphic representation of the constituencies toward whom business managers have significant responsibilities.

the employee(s), and (3) the customer(s). Four other significant constituencies also look to business managers for definable benefits. These secondary groups are (4) the lenders of capital, (5) the suppliers of needed goods and services, (6) the government in its many branches, and (7) the overall community. Figure 10–3 illustrates the relationship between the managers who control the business firm and their constituencies. Note that managers are placed at the hub, the nerve center of the enterprise. More so than anyone else, top managers are uniquely positioned to behave in a socially responsible manner. They possess the necessary power and control over resources while engaging in the task of producing and distributing the bulk of our nation's gross national product.

The exact relationship between a given business firm and its constituencies depends on many variables, including notably the size, location, and economic condition of the firm. While each constituency retains its identity, its actual composition will change over the years as individual members come and go.

It is important to understand that all seven constituencies provide business firms with services and a variety of solid benefits that collectively (and in some cases selectively) are essential for their success and survival. It is equally important to understand the concomitant and related justification for the demands and expectations of the seven constituencies. Frequently this drama is reflected in contracts, with valuable consideration flowing between the firm and the constituency. Obvious examples are the exchange of labor for a wage or salary by employees, and the exchange of money for goods and services by customers. Not so clear is the exchange of taxes paid for public services provided by the government. Even more remote is the link between the overall quality of the operation of the business on the one hand, and on the other hand the total environment and human and natural resources essential for the firm's success, which are routinely provided by the community.

In the paragraphs below the three primary constituencies are discussed in terms of their contributions to the enterprise and their negative or even punitive responses if managers fail to satisfy reasonable (and sometimes unreasonable) expectations of the constituencies. Circumstances related to the four secondary constituencies are also briefly presented.

Three Primary Constituencies of Business Managers

1. _Owners' expectations._ Because they contribute the risk capital, the owners are primary claimants to the fruits of the enterprise. They stand to lose their investment if the firm fails. If it succeeds, they are entitled to a fair return on their equity. If feasible, the return should be generous, or even bountiful if that is possible without hurting other constituencies.

Possible negative responses (if the owners' legitimate expectations are not met): In a corporation, the owners might vote to change the top management and the directors, or they might sell their stock. In a sole proprietorship or partnership, there should be a serious reevaluation of the firm's tactics and strategy. If the condition continues beyond a reasonable time (which could be months or years) the firm would probably be dissolved.

2. _Employees' expectations._ The employees, who include all hired managers, are also primary claimants. In truth, permanent workers may devote to the company the bulk of their waking hours for 40 or 50 years. They are surely entitled to fair compensation, a living wage that should at least be competitive with what is paid by other companies in the area. Fair compensation includes reasonable and comparable fringe benefits. The job should be secure, with no wrongful dismissal (see Chapter 5). When justified, there should be even-handed transfers and opportunities for training and promotion. When financially practicable, there should be private retirement benefits to supplement social security. The work environment should be clean, safe, healthful, and as pleasant as reasonably possible.

Possible negative responses: Lackadaisical work habits, tardiness, absenteeism, low morale, occasional sabotage and pilferage, and complaints to OSHA, steps by employees to unionize, production slowdowns, strikes, and departure to work for other companies, thereby imposing resulting costs of hiring and training on the former employer.

3. _Customers' expectations:_ Customers (past, present, and future) are entitled to honest, safe products and services of acceptable quality, at fair, competitive prices. They should be available on reasonable credit terms if required or desired. Related services should be courteous, prompt, efficient, and effective. The company should make an ongoing, positive effort to improve the quality, design, and performance of its products and services.

Possible negative responses: Returns of merchandise and demands for adjustments, replacements or refunds; repeated complaints; unfavorable publicity to relatives, friends, and associates; and occasional costly lawsuits for injuries caused by defective products. Ultimately, but often immediately and usually without any complaint, dissatisfied customers vote with their dollars by simply shopping elsewhere.

Four Secondary Constituencies of Business Managers

1. The *suppliers* provide diverse goods and services, including essential inventories of goods for resale. Most suppliers also often help finance the business by extending trade credit. Trade credit is a revolving type that must be paid off regularly, but in a true sense it becomes part of the permanent working capital because the firm's balance sheet always shows a substantial amount in accounts payable. If not paid promptly, trade creditors shift to cash-on-delivery (COD) sales, which limit the size and growth of the firm. For slow-pay and no-pay debtors, creditors report the faulty performance to credit rating bureaus, which further restricts available credit. Disgruntled creditors can sue debtors. They can force the defaulting business into bankruptcy.

2. *Lenders*. Lenders include bond holders for long-term loans, note holders for middle-term loans, and banks for short-term loans. The money they lend is sometimes referred to as the "lifeblood" of the business. Lenders who are not promptly paid interest and principal when they are due can sue for payment and execute against the debtor's assets. When defaulted notes or bonds are secured by mortgages, creditors can foreclose and seize the collateral. Collateral could consist of the firm's plant, store, or warehouse. In secured transactions for trucks, for example, creditors can simply repossess the equipment. Again, involuntary bankruptcy proceedings are also a possibility.

3. *Government*. Federal, state, and local government agencies provide countless services and assistance to business firms. These benefits run the gamut from security against potential foreign foes and domestic criminals to free or subsidized transportation networks and free public education for the work force. Taxes must be paid or liens can be imposed and enforced through seizure and sale of assets. Local government officials can be less than totally cooperative in providing road construction, waste disposal, and other services requested by recalcitrant business firms. Desired zoning changes and land use permits can be delayed and possibly refused. The government can impose extraordinary requirements that business products be safe and that the firm's facilities be environmentally acceptable and in compliance with stringent noise, air, water, and ground pollution controls.

4. *The community*. The business is expected to be a good neighbor in every sense of the word. All of the identified constituencies, as well as other definable groups and individuals, are members of the total community, which sustains business firms and is reciprocally sustained by those firms. The community includes the immediate neighborhood where business is conducted, but it properly extends to the entire city, the state, the region, the country, and the world. Business is expected to do more than contribute labor and money to charities of its choice, or to the local Community Chest campaign; for example, a business that carelessly pollutes the air with illegal emissions of noxious smoke and fumes can cause acid rainfall hundreds of miles away. Chemical pesticides and fertilizers produced and misused on one continent drain into ocean waters that enclose all continents. Clear-cutting by lumber companies of virgin timber in regions as far apart as Brazil and the states of Washington and Oregon may disturb the ecological balance of nature that is vital for all nations. The release of ozone-depleting chlorofluoro-carbons (CFCs) used in air conditioners and refrigerator compressors is thought to be causing a global warming effect, which could have disastrous effects on ocean water levels throughout the world. International conferences on the CFC problem have called for corrective and preventive action throughout the world during the next decade and beyond, but the problem is uniquely one that faces individual business firms that are called on to take the initiative with appropriate action.

The local community reasonably expects its business firms to operate efficiently and properly. The community expects that current and future generations of citizens will be gainfully employed by these firms. Citizens want to take justifiable pride in their factories and stores and in the products and services they produce and distribute. Managers who neglect, deny, or callously defy such local expectations at the very least provoke a reaction of negative public opinion, often spearheaded by the local communications media (press, radio, TV). Stronger community reactions can include costly litigation, repressive legislation, and possible decline and failure of the offending business firms.

Case 10

WILLIAM MINTON, ET AL v. MAUDE CAVANEY AS EXECUTOR

California Supreme Court, 15 Cal Rptr. 641, 364 P.2d 473 (1961)

Pall aside corporate veil

The Seminole Hot Springs Corporation operated a leased swimming pool, open to the public. After the plaintiffs' daughter drowned in the pool, the plaintiffs sued Seminole and won a judgment of $10,000 for her wrongful death. This judgment was not paid. Therefore the plaintiffs sued defendant William M. Cavaney, an attorney at law who was a director and secretary/treasurer of Seminole, to hold him personally liable for the unsatisfied judgment against the corporation. Subsequently Cavaney died and his widow, executrix of his estate, was substituted as defendant. Evidence introduced at the trial disclosed that about five months after the drowning, Seminole officers applied to the commissioner of corporations to issue three shares of stock, including one share to Cavaney, but none was ever issued. In an earlier legal document Cavaney stated that "[I]nsofar as I know, this corporation has no

assets of any kind or character." The trial court entered judgment against Cavaney's estate for $10,000 and the defendant appealed.

Justice Traynor for the Supreme Court of California The figurative terminology "alter ego" and "disregard of the corporate entity" is generally used to refer to the various situations that are an abuse of the corporate privilege. The equitable owners of a corporation, for example, are personally liable when they treat the assets of the corporation as their own and add or withdraw capital from the corporation at will; or when they provide inadequate capitalization and actively participate in the conduct of corporate affairs.

In the instant case the evidence is undisputed that there was no attempt to provide adequate capitalization. Seminole never had any substantial assets. It leased the pool that it operated, and the lease was forfeited for failure to pay the rent. Its capital was "trifling compared with the business to be done and the risks of loss." The evidence is also undisputed that Cavaney was not only the secretary and treasurer of the corporation but was also a director. The evidence that Cavaney was to receive one-third of the shares to be issued supports an inference that he was an equitable owner . . . and the evidence that for a time the records of the corporation were kept in Cavaney's office supports an inference that he actively participated in the conduct of the business.

There is no merit in defendant's contentions that the "alter ego" doctrine applies only to contractual debts and not to tort claims; that plaintiffs' cause of action abated when Cavaney died . . . or that the judgment in the action against the corporation bars plaintiffs from bringing the present action.

[However] in this action to hold defendant personally liable upon the judgment against Seminole, plaintiffs did not allege or present any evidence on the issue of Seminole's negligence or on the amount of damages sustained by plaintiffs. They relied solely on the judgment against Seminole. Defendant correctly contends that Cavaney or his estate cannot be held liable for the debts of Seminole without an opportunity to relitigate these issues. Cavaney was not a party to the action against the corporation and the judgment in that action is therefore not binding upon him . . . .

For reasons stated, the judgment was reversed. To prevail against Cavaney's estate, another lawsuit must be filed in which the evidence of the Seminole Corporation's negligence and the amount of damages sustained by the plaintiffs must be presented.

QUESTIONS AND PROBLEMS

1. Problems abound in the area of small business. The following questions identify some of the more difficult and challenging ones. What are your suggestions for answers and solutions?

a. Liability insurance has become a major cost for many small business firms. Can you suggest equitable ways of reducing the threat of lawsuits and the resulting potential burden of damage awards?

b. Increasingly, demands are made for employers to provide comprehensive medical and dental insurance for their workers. Many small business firms claim the cost would be prohibitive. Can you suggest a fair solution?

c. Current capital gains taxes do not reward investment in new plant and equipment by small business firms. What could Congress do about the capital gains tax rate (currently the same as for other income)?

2. Is the sole proprietor truly his or her "own boss?" If not, why not? To whom must such a proprietor answer to, cater to, and satisfy?

3. a. The editors of *Small Business Success* conducted a survey of more than 100 California business owners. They asked "What is the key to business success? (1) Business knowledge, (2) market awareness, (3) hands on management, (4) sufficient capital, or (5) hard work." What would your answer be? (List the keys in order of importance.) Why?

b. The editors also asked "Which is the largest potential trouble spot?" (1) Too much growth, (2) too little growth, (3) too fast growth, (4) too slow growth, and (5) sporadic growth. What would your answer be? (List in order of importance.) Why?

4. a. What are the distinguishing characteristics of (1) ordinary employees, (2) agents, and (3) independent contractors?

b. Generally speaking, which of the above is likely to involve the least out-of-pocket expenditure for the employer in the short term? In the long term?

5. a. Sandra Synick, a classmate, insists "The purpose of business, big or small, is to maximize profits!" Do you agree? Explain why or why not.
b. Frank Filosoffer, another classmate, says "Business, big or small, has many purposes. The wise manager knows this and acts accordingly." Do you agree? Explain why or why not.

6. Arden and Barden are about to start a business of their own. They debate whether to become partners or to incorporate. Barden pushes for incorporation. "Most new businesses fail. We don't expect to, but we might. As partners we'll both be liable without limit for debts of the firm. As owners of the stock of a small corporation we'll limit our liability to the cost of the stock." Is Barden right? What might increase Barden's and Arden's liability even if they do incorporate?

7. Ever since Bennett had to pay his first income tax, he's been obsessed with what he calls the "crushing burden of confiscatory levies," referring to taxes on business enterprises.
a. Are all legal forms of business organization subject to the same income taxes? Explain.
b. Are there legitimate ways by which Bennett can minimize taxes on his business? How?
c. Can he legally avoid payment of any income taxes?

8. a. Should the corporation income tax be abolished, as some economists have suggested? Why or why not?
b. Has the corporation income tax, in practical effect, already been abolished for some corporations?

c. Would such abolition of corporation income taxes help to place all small corporations on a "level field" of competition with sole proprietorships and partnerships?

9. Hannah Hitachi has an uncanny talent for identifying land on the outskirts of town that is ripe for development. She has made a fortune building shopping centers and apartment houses, but is too busy to do more than invest $100,000 as a limited partner in Ken Kurosawa's limited partnership, which operates supermarkets featuring fresh fruits and vegetables. After much pleading by Kurosawa, Hannah agreed to review the plans for ten new locations. She approved seven and gave convincing reasons for dropping three. Is Hitachi a limited partner?

10. Edward Tuttle operated a successful barbershop for more than ten years in a small Minnesota town. Cassius Buck the town banker and a man of considerable wealth started a competing barber shop. He provided the business services at prices lower than Tuttle and indeed at prices which insured Tuttle's business would not profit. He disparaged the services of Tuttle and told Tuttle's customers that continuing their patronage of Tuttle would place them in Buck's displeasure. Tuttle lost a considerable amount of business and sued Buck for his losses. Is the competition described lawful? *Tuttle* v. *Buck,* 119 N.W. 946 (Minnesota, 1909).

FURTHER READING

1. Elster, Robert J., ed., *Small Business Sourcebook,* 2nd ed. Detroit, MI: International Thomson Publishing, Inc., Gale Research Company, 1987. Ideal companion for the Ryans book; comes in two volumes, along with supplements published in 1987 and 1989. This is an annotated guide to "live and print" sources of information and assistance for 181 specific types of small business. The 1989 Supplement adds 11 brief profiles of unusual ventures. The businesses range alphabetically from "accounting tax preparation service" to "word processing service." There is detailed information about each type, including such matters as "primary associations" (i.e., trade societies), "sources of supply," "trade periodicals," and "trade shows and conventions."

2. Ryans, Cynthia and Paul Wasserman, *Small Business: Information Sourcebook*. Phoenix AR: Onyx Press, 1987. A comprehensive collection of titles of books, with succinct descriptions of their contents, on some 40 topics of concern to any person who is seriously thinking of starting and operating a small business. Topics range from "Accounting" to "Women in Business." A Core Library is included with listings of Bibliographies and Indexes, Data Bases, Directories, and Periodicals.

3. *SBA—Building Excellence in Enterprise*. Washington, DC: U.S. Small Business Administration, 1989. This booklet will introduce you to the Small Business Administration and its program. Dozens of publications useful to the small business entrepreneur are available free or for a nominal charge from the SBA.

4. *A Tribute to Small Business—America's Growth Industry*. San Francisco: Pacific Bell Directory, 1987. The final report of the White House Conference on Small Business held in Washington, D.C., in 1986. Sixty detailed policy recommendations were voted on by more than 1,700 active small business entrepreneurs from the entire country. As the report says: "An impressive agenda for the future of the U.S. economy."

5. Walters, Cathy, *Small Business Success*. Pacific Bell Directory, 101 Spear St. (Rm. 429), San Francisco, Ca., 94105. Excellent annual publication written to help the small business entrepreneur start and succeed. Articles in the 1988 edition include "Winning Ideas for Small Business Success," and "Young Entrepreneurs: The Promise and Perseverence of Youth."

NOTES

1. Small Business Administration Act, 15 USC 631, amended most recently by Small Business Administration Reauthorization and Amendment Act of 1988, Public Law 100-59.

2. *SBA Building Excellence in Enterprise,* U.S. Small Business Administration, (Washington, DC: U.S. Small Business Administration, 1989). Currently, to qualify for a loan as a small business, size standard eligibility is based on the *average number of employees* for the preceding 12 months *or* on *sales volume* averaged over a three year period. More precisely, the general size standards are: *Manufacturing:* Maximum number of employees may range from 500 to 1,500, depending on the type of product manufactured; *Wholesaling:* Maximum number of employees may not exceed 100; *Service:* Annual receipts may not exceed $3.5 to $14.5 million, depending on the industry; *Retailing:* Annual receipts may not exceed $3.5 to $13.5 million, depending on the industry; *Construction:* General construction annual receipts may not exceed $9.5 to $17 million, depending on the industry; *Special trade construction:* Annual receipts may not exceed $7 million; *Agriculture:* Annual receipts may not exceed $0.5 to $3.5 million, depending on the industry. (SBA Office of Public Communications, OPC-6, May, 1989).

3. Walters, Cathy, ed., *Small Business Success* San Francisco, CA: Pacific Bell Directory, 1988.

4. *Restatement of the Law, Agency* 2d §1.

5. The Uniform Partnership Act, §6(1). The UPA has been adopted in all states except Georgia and Louisiana. It has also been adopted in the District of Columbia and the Virgin Islands.

6. The Model Business Corporation Act (1950) was drafted by a committee of the American Bar Association, the largest national organization of lawyers. The Revised Model Business Corporation Act, published in 1979, included substantial changes. The current act has not been adopted verbatim by any state, but most states have included portions of the act in their own corporation codes.

7. Model Business Corporation Act, §3.

8. Ibid. §4(q).

9. *Tax Guide for Small Business,* Publication 334, Department of the Treasury, Internal Revenue Service for tax year 1989 (page 1). A free copy may be obtained from the *Forms Distribution Center* in your area. This is a very informative and authoritative guide to income, excise, and employment taxes for sole proprietorships, partnerships, and corporations. The companion free book for use in preparing income tax returns for individuals is *Your Federal Income Tax,* Publication 17, available from the same source. Both are updated annually.

10. Either the Uniform Limited Partnership Act or the Revised Limited Partnership Act has been adopted in all states (and the District of Columbia and the Virgin Islands) except Louisiana.

10. Either the Uniform Limited Partnership Act or the Revised Limited Partnership Act has been adopted in all states (and the District of Columbia and the Virgin Islands) except Louisiana.

11

Owning and Operating Motor Vehicles

How people transport themselves and their products from one location to another is a major concern in all societies. Whether people can do this is one way in which developed and undeveloped third world countries are distinguishable. Public policy issues arising from transportation questions will compete with other major issues pressing for attention into the 21st century. Where shall we live relative to where we work? How are goods best distributed in a worldwide market? What are the costs of different transportation systems? How much environmental harm is caused by pollution and how can it be minimized? Is it economically feasible to provide growing and emerging metropolitan areas with efficient mass transportation systems?

In considering legal questions about transportation, our primary focus will be on the automobile. Note that law applicable to automobiles usually also applies to other types of motor vehicles. Automobiles are the most valuable item of personal property owned by most Americans, and by others who live in industrialized countries of the world. No other mass-produced, mass-distributed products are more costly than automobiles, trucks, and mobile motorized variations. Few appeal as much to both the young and the old. Few are as intricate in design and construction, with various interdependent control systems and thousands of parts. Few are as frequently used for pleasure and profit and yet also essential in industry and commerce. But automobiles generate countless legal problems. They are expensive to acquire, insure, and maintain. They are heavily taxed in purchase, ownership, and operation. They are a prime target for thieves and incredibly useful for criminal activities, dangerous to the life and limb of users and other persons, and a major corruptor of clean air and quiet in our communities.

Motor vehicles have generated a diverse galaxy of satellite industries and support facilities: from factories for parts to more than four million miles of streets and highways in this country alone. Motor vehicles have a profound effect on the way cities are built; on where subdivisions, shopping centers, and factories are located; even on the way troops are moved and hence how wars are fought.

Few human-made objects have had as extensive and intensive an impact on the law. Registration of more than 188 million vehicles and licensing of more than 164 million drivers are monumental, recurring tasks mandated by statute. Comprehensive vehicle codes govern drivers. Administrative agencies regulate vehicle manufacturers, with particular emphasis on safety and fuel consumption. Other administrative agencies evaluate the environmental impact of new building construction to anticipate the effect on traffic flow and volume. Executive and legislative branches of the government, especially at the federal level, continue to struggle with the problem of maintaining a fuel supply for a nation on wheels. Collectively, millions of workers manufacture the vehicles, fuel them, service them, use them as tools, and ultimately dispose of them as scrap—a sizeable problem in itself.

Contracts permeate this economic, political, social, and cultural phenomenon. Torts involving motor vehicles crowd court dockets in heavily populated areas because of traffic accidents, usually caused by negligence of the drivers. In rapidly rising numbers, plaintiffs seek recovery for injuries caused by alleged defects in the design or manufacture of the vehicles. A new emphasis on safety and fear of such lawsuits has led to recalls by all automakers to correct potentially or demonstrably hazardous conditions in vehicles.

Motor vehicles are highly coveted by thieves; in 1987, more than 1.25 million were stolen,[1] and one of every 44 registered motor vehicles was stolen and/or vandalized.[2] Moreover, motor vehicles facilitate ready access and quick escape for countless crimes of a more serious nature against persons and property.

No human contrivance—not even war—has killed or wounded more Americans than motor vehicles. In 1988 34.2 million motor vehicle accidents occurred causing 49,000 deaths, 5.5 million injuries, and $89 billion in economic losses (wages; legal, medical, hospital, and funeral expenses; insurance administration costs; and property damages). The Insurance Institute estimates that more than 2 million persons have died and about 200 million have been injured in the last 50 years. These figures are seen in their appalling reality when compared to the number of Americans killed in World War I (53,513), in World War II (292,131), and in Vietnam (47,192).* It is easy to see why ownership and operation of motor vehicles is a matter of prime economic, social, and political concern, the subject of a large body of law, and the cause of much litigation.

There is no body of law called motor vehicle law. However, areas of law already discussed, such as contracts, torts, and crimes, have application to motor vehicles. We will also introduce personal property law as it relates to motor vehicles. The application of all these different areas of law to one type of personal property highlights both the rules and the importance of this type of property.

Owning a Motor Vehicle

An automobile is a form of property, **personal property,** in the law called a **chattel.** Personal property is property that can be moved without undue difficulty.

---

* World Almanac and Book of Facts (N.Y.: Newspaper Enterprise Association, Inc.) 1980, p. 333.

Property that cannot be moved is real property, land, and things affixed (permanently attached) to the land. Personal property can be owned in many ways. It can be created as you would create a painting. It can be given. It can be bought, traded for, and found. A discussion of all the various methods of acquiring personal property is beyond the scope of this text. However, because of the importance of vehicles, some issues of ownership of personal property will be reviewed.

Persons become owners of motor vehicles in the same manner as other forms of personal property, although few of us are skilled enough to make a motor vehicle. The most common method of acquiring title to a motor vehicle is by purchase, although a growing number of individuals and businesses lease their autos and trucks. Technically, "leases" are *bailments* for use, with a separate body of applicable law. A bailment is a temporary right of possession of the goods of another.

Is a Special Contract Required to Purchase a Motor Vehicle?

No. The sale of a motor vehicle is an ordinary contractual transaction subject to the law of contracts relating to personal property (see Chapter 6). While the purchase contract is not unique, a few observations are helpful. The contract involves a sale of goods and is subject to sales law provisions of the Uniform Commercial Code (see Chapter 6). Sales law relaxes some of the strict rules of contract formation and performance, and the law of motor vehicles sales is largely uniform throughout the states.

Motor vehicles usually cost more than $500, and if so the *statute of frauds* applies to the purchase. Accordingly, there must be a writing signed by the party to be obligated as evidence of the contract. This requirement is usually met with a standard form contract prepared by the commercial seller. Standard form agreements are called *contracts of adhesion.* Language in these contracts is strictly interpreted in favor of the buyer if it is ambiguous. Nevertheless, the buyer should be aware that the contract will be written to protect the interests of the seller.

Bill Clark was concerned about whether there was sufficient storage space in the trunk of his new car. The salesperson, Frank, assured him there was adequate room in the trunk for luggage for a family of four. Frank also said "If there isn't enough room, bring the car back and we will install a luggage rack." Bill signed a standard form automobile purchase contract, which did not include any reference to the luggage rack. A few months later, Bill, unable to load four suitcases in the trunk, returned to the dealership expecting a new luggage rack. Will Bill have a legally enforceable right to the luggage rack?

Bill's claim will be thwarted by the *parol evidence rule.* This rule holds that when parties have adopted a writing (or writings) as the final and complete expression of their agreement, the contract is integrated. If a contract is integrated, neither party may introduce as evidence any prior or contemporaneous oral or written materials to add to or modify the written contract. The lesson is, if important promises are made to you (e.g., warranties and credit terms), be sure they are included as part of the written contract.

In motor vehicle sales transactions, there are standard sales customs, and techniques. A complete discussion of the mini-culture of "list price," "5 percent over invoice," and "clearance sales" are beyond the scope of this text. However, buyers are well advised to consult reliable references for help in selecting the appropriate vehicle, and for information on negotiating the best deal.[3]

What Warranties Are Provided in the Purchase of a New Motor Vehicle

The seller of a new motor vehicle transfers title to the goods with several *implied warranties*. Recall that implied warranties are warranties that arise in every transaction of a particular type unless specifically disclaimed. The most important sale of goods warranties are usually the *warranty of title* and the *warranty of merchantability*. The warranty of title is a promise to the buyer that the seller possesses good title to the motor vehicle and is transferring good title to the buyer. The warranty of merchantability refers to the quality of the personal property, and is a promise that the vehicle is of usual and ordinary quality—it is fit for its ordinary and intended use. Given the value of a motor vehicle and its intended use, the implied warranty of merchantability is very extensive.

When Margo Orange bought her new automobile, she expected 100,000 or more miles of carefree motoring. She carefully maintained and serviced her vehicle. The written warranty from the dealer said, "This warranty is in lieu of and excludes all other warranties, express or implied, including the warranty of merchantability." The warranty covered defects in materials or workmanship "for one year of 12,000 miles, whichever occurs first." Did Margo lose anything when she received this warranty?

Yes and no, the above is a *disclaimer* sufficient to limit but not totally eliminate the implied warranty of merchantability. A disclaimer is a specific statement indicating a particular warranty does not exist or which limits its duration. Total exclusion of an implied warranty of merchantability requires legally acceptable language of disclaimer. The most common methods of total disclaimer for an implied warranty of merchantability in a consumer transaction are (1) use of the terms **as is** or "with all faults," or (2) a statement that no warranty, including that of merchantability, exists. The federal Magnuson-Moss Act allows sellers of consumer goods to limit but not eliminate warranties if a limited express warranty is given. All motor vehicle manufacturers provide express warranties and the implied warranty of merchantability is often limited with the express warranty provision in the sales contract.* The extent of the express warranty, both as to scope of coverage and length of coverage, is a very important issue when determining which motor vehicle to buy and how much to pay.

---

* Some states have also passed laws that limit a seller's ability to disclaim implied warranties.

Extended warranties are commonly offered by motor vehicle dealers. These warranties typically extend the time and expand the coverage provided by manufacturer warranties. These policies can be purchased from other companies in addition to the original dealership and often at more favorable prices. Before deciding whether to purchase an extended warranty, one should become an informed consumer by studying the need for the product and the different available extended warranties and prices. There are substantial differences in price, scope, and length of coverage, and possible restrictions on who may service the vehicle.

See p. 13

A manufacturer providing a written warranty is required to comply with the **Magnuson-Moss Warranty Act** (see Chapter 6) and applicable state laws. The Magnuson-Moss Act does not require a warranty, but it governs express warranties if they are given. The Federal Trade Commission is empowered to enforce many Magnuson-Moss Act provisions. The Magnuson-Moss Act also provides a federal cause of action against business firms who fail to honor their written warranty.

What is a Lemon Law?

Margo Orange was very happy when she selected her new convertible Magetoes Seven from Hal Worthingpound AutoWorld. She drove it off the lot and headed toward Slim's Health Club to show it off. Two blocks from the dealership the engine died. The car needed to be towed back to AutoWorld. A very angry Orange was not mollified when the sales representative said "We'll be happy to repair or replace that cracked engine block." Orange snapped back; "I expect to get a new and different Magetoes Seven. I am one Orange who won't be satisfied with a lemon." Will Orange get a new car or must she allow the repair or replacement of the engine block?

The legal issue is did the dealership perform its contractual obligations when it delivered the vehicle. If the delivery is legally sufficient, AutoWorld need only honor the warranty. This usually requires either a repair or replacement of the defective part. If the delivery is insufficient, AutoWorld must replace the defective car with a new car.

A buyer has a right to inspect goods before accepting them and becoming obligated to pay the purchase price. What is considered an appropriate inspection depends on the circumstances and the nature of the goods. In this situation, although Orange received and took possession of the vehicle, no normal inspection would have shown that the engine had a cracked block. Since she discovered the vehicle was nonconforming almost immediately after receipt, she can return it because she had never really accepted it. Orange did indeed get a lemon[4] (sour deal) and she has a legal right to a full refund or a new vehicle under the UCC.[5] There are additional UCC rights that may also be claimed to assist a buyer when there is a major contract breach by the seller. Perhaps even if Orange accepted the vehicle, she could revoke her acceptance and have the same rights (or replacement or full refund) as if she had rejected it initially. It is necessary that she revoke within a reasonable time after she discovered or should have discovered the reason for revocation, and before there is any substantial change in the condition of the goods (not caused by their own defects).[6]

Most situations are not as clear as to what constitutes an insufficient delivery of acceptable goods by the seller and reasonable inspection by the buyer. Thirty states[7] have passed so-called **lemon laws** to provide protection for angry consumers who are dissatisfied with extensive warranty work and instead want a new car or their money back. A typical lemon law provides that if a car is a lemon, the dealer must refund to the customer the purchase price of the car, plus sales tax, registration, and license fees, minus a reasonable allowance for use.[8] The problem, of course, is to define **a lemon** with sufficient precision and to enforce consumers' rights in a fair and prompt manner. A common definition of a lemon states that it is "a major problem not fixed in four attempts, or a car out of service for repairs for a cumulative total of 30 calendar days during the covered period"[9] (usually a year or the period of warranty). Most lemon laws allow for the use of ADR methods, such as arbitration, to assist in the resolution of the dispute (see Chapter 3). There is considerable frustration among buyers and sellers in implementing typical lemon law statutes.[10]

What Are Automobile Recalls?

"On December 13, 1984 the attendants at Spring Mall Cars in Springfield, Virginia started the engines in a number of new cars to keep their batteries charged. While left idling, seven 1984 Ford Escorts caught fire."[11] A month later, Marguerite Rorie of Washington, D.C. watched her idling 1985 Escort catch fire in her driveway.[12]

After the sale of a motor vehicle, manufacturers have a continuing obligation to ensure vehicle safety. Under federal law they are required to notify consumers and the National Highway Traffic Safety Administration (NHTSA) of safety defects and how they propose to cure the defects. Since 1966 more than 88 million vehicles have been recalled.[13] Recalls can be voluntary or mandated by the NHTSA. The Ford Escorts in the above example have not been recalled and Ford Motor Company has denied a problem exists. Complaints about the 1984–85 Escorts have been the subject of an investigation by NHTSA since 1986. (The investigation has not been complete at the date of this writing.)[14]

Does the Law Require That Motor Vehicles Be Registered?

The government requires that ownership of most types of motor vehicles be registered and that formal documents of ownership be properly executed. Similar requirements do not exist for most other types of personal property, such as stereos and backpacks.

Advantages of Registration   Registration provides a method by which a state can ensure automobile owner compliance with safety and environmental requirements. To be registered, the vehicle must comply with minimal safety and pollution standards governing brakes, lights, and exhaust emissions. Registration of ownership also ensures orderly transfer of title. By requiring presentation and release of the certificate of ownership signed by the seller, the buyer has a better possibility of receiving good title and becoming the true owner. If the car is stolen, the certificate of ownership and registration facilitates identification and restitution to the rightful owner. If a vehicle is involved in an accident in which property is damaged and/or a person is injured or killed, vehicle license numbers help trace the party responsible and facilitate follow-up measures. The issuance and renewal of the certificate of registration also serves as a convenient means of raising tax revenues for a variety of purposes, including highway construction and maintenance. Annual motor vehicle registration lists also aid selection of jury panels and the collection of unpaid traffic fines.

Licensing and Registration Procedures   States issue two certificates to the owners of motor vehicles: a certificate of ownership, or title, showing who owns the vehicle; and a certificate of registration, permitting operation of the vehicle on the highways of the state. License plates, or annual renewal taxes, are also issued in conjunction with the certificate of registration.

A motor vehicle is licensed in the state where it is usually driven. When you move to another state, your vehicle registration generally remains valid for a limited period of time (30 to 90 days) before a local vehicle license is required. Special laws also govern the vehicle and driver when traveling in foreign countries; these laws should be reviewed with a knowledgeable travel agent before departure.

Many counties and cities require the registration and periodic licensing of bicycles. The money generated from this is commonly used to maintain records that facilitate recovery and return of stolen bikes.

Kitty Horrigan was carefully riding her new imported English motorcycle along a city street when Stuart Guarino negligently lost control of his automobile and crashed into her. Guarino now claims Horrigan was guilty of contributory negligence because she failed to register her motorcycle as required by law. Is it considered negligence to drive an unlicensed motor vehicle on a public road?

In Relation to Accidents   No. Horrigan's failure to register her motorcycle had nothing to do with the accident, and will not prevent her from recovering damages for her injuries.[15] However, failure to transfer title to a new **owner** when delivering possession of a motor vehicle may leave the original owner liable to third parties injured by the motor vehicle in a later accident. Some states provide that the registered owner is liable (usually limited liability) for damage caused by the negligence of any authorized user of the vehicle.*

---

* California, Connecticut, Florida, Idaho, Iowa, Massachusetts, Michigan, Minnesota, New York, North Carolina, Rhode Island, Tennessee, and the District of Columbia.

It is common for a certificate of ownership of a newly purchased vehicle to list two owners: a **registered owner** and a **legal owner.** Most automobiles are purchased on credit and the lender retains a security interest in the vehicle. The purchaser-borrower is the registered owner (also called the **equitable owner**), with an ownership interest in the vehicle to the extent that the loan is paid. Persons who refer to their equity in a vehicle mean the difference between the automobile's market value and the amount still owed to the lender. The lender (or creditor), having advanced the purchase money or sold the car on credit, retains a security interest in the vehicle and remains the legal owner until the loan is paid in full. A legal owner is generally not responsible for the manner in which the equitable owner uses or misuses the vehicle. The legal owner is primarily concerned with timely payment. For protection in the event that the car is damaged or stolen, the lender (legal owner) will require the equitable owner to carry adequate collision and comprehensive automobile insurance. The former covers damages to the vehicle by collision; the latter covers damages to or theft of the vehicle by vandals. Prudent owners also carry liability insurance to protect the owner-insured against liability for injuries to others. But lenders (legal owners) are only interested in protecting the value of their collateral, increasing the probability the loan will be repaid in full.

Because the registered owner has potential tort liability, it is very important to comply with state law and change registration upon the transfer of the vehicle. State requirements for a valid registration transfer vary. It is common to require both a signed transfer of a certificate of ownership ("pink slip") and a notification to the department of motor vehicles requesting a change in the registered owner of the vehicle. The seller should file the notice of change of ownership, transferring all tort liabilities to the buyer along with the ownership.

Why Must Drivers Be Licensed?

Kathy Jarens' license to drive had been revoked for proper cause. (She had been convicted of speeding on three occasions within 18 months.) She resented this interference with her freedom of movement and decided to drive anyway—but with extra care to avoid any trouble. As luck would have it, while driving safely and in compliance with the rules of the road, another motorist negligently ran a red light and rammed into her car. Will her lack of a driver's license have any effect on civil and criminal court proceedings?

No and yes. Unless there is some cause-and-effect relationship between the lack of the driver's license and the accident-caused injury, the lack of license is immaterial. It is not by itself proof of negligence, and thus Kathy's rights in a civil action for damages resulting from the accident are not affected by her lack of a driver's license. However, she would be guilty in a criminal proceeding for the offense of driving without a license, and for this she could be fined and/or jailed.

It has been said that driving a car is like aiming a two-ton weapon. This is painfully true when the driver is careless, intoxicated, or otherwise unfit to drive. Legally, motor vehicles are not considered inherently dangerous instrumentalities as are explosives and wild animals. Ordinary people can safely drive them, and drivers are not held to extraordinary standards of care.[16] Nevertheless, for their own safety and the safety of others, prospective drivers are required to demonstrate at least minimal ability to drive in traffic and minimal knowledge of the rules of the road.

Driving is a privilege, not a constitutionally protected right. As such, driving is subject to reasonable regulation by government as an exercise of government police power.[17] A license to drive may be suspended or revoked for violating rules of the road, or even for inability to demonstrate financial responsibility after an accident. Increasingly, computers are used to track convictions for moving traffic offenses. Demerit points may be assigned, and a person's license suspended or revoked for accumulating too many points too quickly. An accident may count as one point; reckless or drunken driving, two points; causing property damage by hit-and-run, two points; and a total of four points in one year may cause suspension of the license. Auto insurance companies have access to such information and routinely charge higher premiums or may cancel coverage after one or more moving violations. The individual must then purchase a minimum coverage policy at a premium price under an assigned risk program (in which all insurance companies are required to participate). A habitual offender may be jailed and may lose his or her license to drive for years.

Computer tracking has become the comeuppance in some states for drivers who blithely and brazenly collect dozens of parking tickets and never pay fines imposed. The department that renews vehicle registrations is kept informed by computer and simply withholds new license plates or tags until all fines are paid.

Generally, any competent adult may qualify for a driver's license upon passing a written test, a driving test, and a vision test. A minor of proper age (typically 16) may also qualify, but often must, in addition to the requirements for an adult, complete a driver education and/or driver training course. Most states also require that parents sign and verify the minor's application and consent to responsibility for any civil liability incurred by the minor while driving on a highway.

Fortunately for parents, their liability is typically limited to amounts prescribed by the state's financial responsibility laws (e.g., $15,000 for injury or death, payable to any one person, and $30,000 payable to any number of persons, plus $5,000 for property damage as the result of any one accident for which their minor child is found to be legally responsible).[18] Insurance may be mandated by statute; if not, prudence and compassionate concern for the rights of others who may be injured by a child's negligence would dictate that a parent purchase at least the minimum coverage.

Parental liability for a child's torts related to motor vehicles deviates from the general rule. Parents generally are not vicariously responsible for a child's torts unless the act of the child was committed at a parent's command or in the course of a parent's business. In recent years, some states have extended the motor vehicle exception to include limited liability of parents for the willful misconduct of minor children.[19] Even in states where statutes create this parental liability, the minor tortfeasor is likewise liable. Realistically, however, the minor usually lacks the financial resources to pay the injured victim. Moreover, in cases of negligence the minor could ultimately escape a heavy judgment by bankruptcy, unless the accident was caused by drunken driving (see Chapter 6 for a discussion of bankruptcy).

Driving a Motor Vehicle

What Standard of Care Does the Law Prescribe for Drivers?

The standard of care necessary when operating a motor vehicle is one example of the rules of negligence discussed in Chapter 5. The duty to act as a reasonable person requires that you, whether on or off the highway, refrain from injuring another. The question always is, were you as careful as a hypothetical reasonable person would have been under all circumstances surrounding the event? This broad duty may be violated negligently or willfully. Comparatively few people injure others willfully, with deliberate intent to harm. Such conduct could be criminal, and could result in a civil action for punitive damages as well as compensatory damages. In one case, the court said:

> Here there is testimony from which the jury could find that defendant saw plaintiff 196 feet away in the paved portion of the roadway, and neither slowed nor sounded his horn. There is also the testimony that defendant's car swerved toward plaintiff immediately before the impact. Thus the evidence could support a jury finding that defendant was guilty of willful or wanton misconduct.[20]

From time to time, most of us are careless. We fail to exercise reasonable care. We do not behave as an ordinary and prudent man, woman, or child of comparable age should behave under the same or similar circumstances. If someone is injured as a result of our negligence, we are generally liable.

It is possible, of course, that persons are injured while we are acting without negligence or willful intent to harm. Then there is no legal liability. Such an injury could happen in a pure accident, a casualty that is sudden, unexpected, unforeseeable, and unplanned—perhaps the result of an unknown cause or the unpredictable result of a known cause. There is no liability, for example, when an injury results from a natural calamity (a violent storm) or from the victim's own carelessness (when a person, walking and reading a paper, steps off a curb into a stream of traffic and is the victim of a sudden injury or even death).

Robby Drexhage was driving on a freeway with his girlfriend, Karen, at his side, bragging to her about his car and about himself as a "hot driver." Suddenly, without notice to her or signal to other drivers, he accelerated within seconds to 95 mph. Visible ahead, moving at different speeds in three lanes, were about a dozen other vehicles. Robby rapidly passed them all, weaving skillfully from outside to inside lanes and back again. There were no highway patrol officers in sight, he was not arrested, and he did not cause an accident. Has he breached any legal duty?

Yes. He breached his general duty to drive as an ordinary prudent person exercising reasonable care for the safety of the lives and property of others. He did not respect the rights of his date and all others on the highway. He breached specific duties to drive within the speed limits, to refrain from weaving in and out of traffic lanes, and to signal before changing lanes. Most breaches of duty that are crimes go unpunished; fortunately, most such breaches do not cause injury to others.

Must Drivers Stop at Accident Scenes?

Gus Shikel, an expert in first aid, was driving along a lonely country road when he came upon the scene of a one-car accident. The wrecked vehicle had collided with a utility pole. Inside were two adults and a child, all unconscious or in shock. One was bleeding profusely. Not wanting to get involved, Shikel drove on. Was he legally obliged to stop and render aid?

Not in most states. The victims were strangers to whom he legally owed no duty. Generally, the law does not require one to be a **Good Samaritan.** If Shikel had in any way caused or contributed to the accident (as by drifting across the center line and forcing the oncoming driver into defensive maneuvers that resulted in the crash), he would be obligated to stop and would be criminally and civilly responsible if he failed to do so.

In any event, if he does stop—and one hopes that he would—and renders first aid, he must do so with reasonable care. Conceivably if one stops and renders aid, injured persons could sue the Good Samaritan if he or she failed to exercise reasonable care and aggravated their injuries. Such lawsuits are extremely rare and recovery rarer still. Moreover, most states have specially enacted statutes to shield the volunteer. North Carolina has a typical statute, stating that no person shall be liable for damages for injuries or death claimed to result from the rendering of first aid or emergency health care treatment when the circumstances require prompt decisions and actions, and when the necessity is ". . . so reasonably apparent that any delay . . . would seriously worsen the physical condition or endanger the life . . . " of the patient.[21]

Immunity is not given when the act is determined to be gross negligence, wanton conduct, or intentional wrongdoing. Nor does the statute relieve persons of liability for damages ". . . while rendering health care services in the normal and ordinary course of a business or profession."[22]

Does a Traffic Citation Prove Civil Liability for an Accident?

Kevin Harper was driving on the wrong side of a two-lane highway when he was involved in a head-on collision with Lisa Bowden. Lisa was proceeding legally in the opposite direction. Kevin was cited by the state patrol for violation of the vehicle code. Is he guilty of negligence per se because he was apparently violating a statute at the time?

Probably. *Negligence per se* (Latin: of itself) means proof of the act establishes the duty. Violation of a statute raises a *prima facie* (Latin: at first sight) presumption or inference of negligence. If the plaintiff proves that the statute was violated and no contrary evidence is introduced by the defendant, it is concluded that the defendant was negligent. Violation of the statute must bear some relationship to the accident and be the proximate cause of the accident. For instance, violation of a statute requiring the driver to be licensed would not bear any relationship to Kevin's accident and would not be its proximate cause. However, violation of a statute established to protect against driving the wrong way down a road and injuring others driving on the proper side of the road would be negligence per se. That very type of harm occurred and it appears Kevin is liable.

Although difficult, a presumption of negligence can be rebutted by proof of excuse or justification. It is possible that Kevin diverted his car because of conditions beyond his control (such as an object in the road, an unforeseeable failure of his steering mechanism, a sudden heart attack that he could not have anticipated, or an illegal action by another car squeezing by on his right side).

Are Owners Liable for the Negligence of Other Drivers?

Clearly an owner-driver is liable for injuries to others caused by his or her own negligent driving. Under the principle of **vicarious liability** (liability for another), the owner may also be liable when someone else is the driver, if:

1. The driver is the employee or agent of the owner, and is acting within the scope of his or her employment. (In most states, the owner is not liable for the negligence of another driver who is not the owner's agent.)

2. The owner is negligent in lending or giving the car to someone who the owner knows or should know is not qualified to drive.

3. The owner lends a car that the owner knows or should know is an unsafe vehicle.

4. In a number of states, owners are responsible when a member of their immediate family or household drive and a third party is injured because of the negligence of the driver. (This is called the "family purpose doctrine.")*

5. In about 50 percent of the states, parents or guardians who sign a minor's application for a driver's license become liable for damage caused by the minor's negligent operation of the vehicle. As discussed earlier, there typically are dollar limits to the amount of this liability.

6. Many different variations and combinations of state statutes provide for liability when an owner permits another to use the vehicle. In six states, owners are liable if they have furnished a car to a minor who negligently injures a third party.[23] In another 12 states, owners are liable if they permit anyone to use the vehicle who negligently injures a third party.[24] As noted earlier, there often are limits on liability under these statutes.

If the driver is an employee of the owner and is acting within the scope of employment, the owner-employer is liable without limit under the doctrine of *respondeat superior.* The driver is always liable without limit for his or her own torts. Either defendant, but more likely the employee, may be judgment-proof. The purchase of insurance to protect injured parties is critical.

---

* Arizona, Colorado, Connecticut, Georgia, Kentucky, Michigan, Minnesota, Nebraska, Nevada, New Jersey, New Mexico, North Carolina, North Dakota, Oregon, South Carolina, Tennessee, Washington, West Virginia, and the District of Columbia.

Karl Mellon parked his car in the street and ran into the post office to mail a parcel. In his haste, he forgot to remove the ignition key. When he returned the car was gone. Later the police reported that his stolen car had been in a collision with a motorcycle, injuring its rider, Joanna Denton. Denton later sued Mellon. Is he liable?

No. Although leaving the key in an unattended car is negligent and, in some states, a violation of a statute, the owner has no duty to protect the public from unexpected and illegal activities of thieves. The theft and negligent use of stolen property is an intervening and supervening act. A contrary argument can be advanced that Karl's carelessness created a danger and a result that was very predictable,[25] but most states have rejected an extension of liability to a careless owner when third parties are injured by the thief.

Luella Wilson, a 91-year-old Vermont grandmother, enjoyed her own home, friends, and family and had more than $500,000 in the bank. She loaned her grand-nephew, Willard Stuart money to buy a car. After a night of drug and alcohol use he was involved in a serious accident. A passenger in his car, Mark Vince, was paralyzed from the waist down and lost a leg. Stuart had no driver's license, no assets, and no automobile insurance. The victim sued Luella, alleging that she knew Willard did not have a license and used drugs and that she was therefore negligent in loaning him the money to buy the car. She did not appear at the trial because she was ill. What verdict?

The jury held for the plaintiff against Luella Wilson in the amount of $950,000.[26] This case of negligent lending attracted considerable attention and was appealed. The Vermont Supreme Court did not reverse the trial court verdict, but did order a new trial to determine whether Luella's liability should be shared by the automobile dealership and the salesperson who sold Willard the car.[27] At the new trial the parties reached an out-of-court settlement, with the plaintiff apparently dismissing his claim against Luella.[28] The out-of-court settlement relieved Luella of her liability but it did not change the rule of law in this case, which found liability for a person other than a driver in a case of negligent entrustment (loan of the car).

A more common extension of liability to persons who neither own nor were driving the car involved in an accident has been in so-called dramshop statute cases. **Dramshop statutes** are state laws that make it a crime for a tavern proprietor or employee to serve intoxicants to an obviously inebriated patron. Injured victims of accidents caused by drunk patrons have in some states successfully sued the bars and restaurants when it could be proved that a dramshop statute had been violated.[29] A few states have allowed suits against social hosts of parties where intoxicating beverages or drugs were served and guests shortly afterward were involved in automobile accidents.[30] Wisdom and prudence dictate: If you drink, don't drive. Avoid the problem by designating drivers who do *not* drink alcoholic beverages or take any mood-altering substances.

Are Drivers Liable for Injuries to Guests in Their Cars?

Generally, yes. A driver has a responsibility not only to persons outside the vehicle but also to passengers inside the vehicle. The duty is that of ordinary and usual care for the safety of others. Issues of comparative negligence and assumption of the risk must also be considered when appropriate. Ten years ago drivers were usually not liable to **guest** passengers for injuries caused by ordinary negligence, because of special protective statutes called **guest statutes.** Today there are only nine states with guest statutes.[31] Proponents of guest statutes argue that when the drivers are insured, there can be collusion in staged accidents to defraud insurance companies. Even in the absence of fraud, a negligent driver who is a relative of the guest might receive dollar damages and indirectly profit from his or her own wrong. Guest statutes also prevent possible fraudulent claims by guests who may be the only witnesses to a single-car accident. Texas courts have upheld the Texas guest statute, holding that the legislature is justified in seeking to prevent possible fraudulent claims against insurers.[32] Moreover, a guest is a passenger as a result of his or her own voluntary choice, and normally can get out at will.

As social views have changed, most states have abolished guest statutes. California, for example, was among the leaders in permitting lawsuits and recovery of damages by any guest of the driver.[33] The rationale was that the recovery will probably come from an insurance company, and if you buy insurance to compensate strangers whom you might injure you probably would want to have the same protection for relatives and friends who are your guests. Of course, drivers who do not have insurance are personally liable to their passengers. Seventeen states have repealed their guest statutes since the California lead and permit guests to sue.*

Even when a state has a guest statute, liability exists when the plaintiff can prove that death or injury resulted from intoxication or willful misconduct of the driver. Thus Willard Stuart, who was high on drugs and alcohol, was not protected from the lawsuit by a guest statute. He was, however, judgment-proof, which led the injured plaintiff to seek other possible defendants who were not judgment-proof.

Is It Illegal to Drive Under the Influence of Liquor or Drugs?

"Drunk drivers kill almost 25,000 people annually, more than are murdered each year."[34] That shocking statistic introduces the important subject of persons who **drive under the influence** (DUI) of mind-altering chemicals. Excessive drinking of alcoholic beverages is the major cause of accidents on the highways, and is an ingredient in most fatal accidents. In addition, DUI has been identified as the crime most often committed by otherwise law-abiding persons. "The vast majority of Americans occasionally drive after drinking. Alcoholics who have access to a car habitually drive after drinking."[35]

---

* Arkansas, Colorado, Connecticut, Florida, Idaho, Iowa, Kansas, Michigan, Montana, New Mexico, North Dakota, Ohio, Oregon, South Dakota, Virginia, Washington, and Wyoming.

During the past decade several organizations have been established to protect the rights of persons who are victims of such criminal activity. These organizations—all elements of a resolute social movement—include MADD (Mothers Against Drunk Driving), RID (Remove Intoxicated Drivers), and SADD (Students Against Drunk Driving). They have had a significant effect on public attitudes and laws concerning driving under the influence. In the past ten years, 30 states joined the other 20 establishing 21 as the age for legally drinking alcohol,[36] reversing a prior trend lowering the legal drinking age. The penalties for DUI have increased with longer and more certain sentences, license revocations, and larger fines. The percentage of drugs in the blood system necessary to classify a person as DUI has been lowered in most states.

Lawrence Harberson and several friends were at Lawrence's apartment celebrating the end of the school year. Beer was flowing freely. Harberson, a 260-pound star tackle on the college football team, had finished his first 12-ounce can when he opened a second. Waving the can, he jumped into his car and burned tire rubber as he drove off to pick up his girlfriend at the airport. En route he was stopped by a highway patrol officer for exceeding the posted speed limit by 20 MPH. Is he also guilty of driving under the influence of alcohol?

Probably not, although he could be required to demonstrate his sobriety. One beer is not likely to intoxicate a 260-pound person (see Table 11–1). However, he could be cited for carrying an open container of an alcoholic beverage in his car.

TABLE 11–1 How Many Drinks Does It Take?

To approximate your blood-alcohol concentration, determine your weight category and find the number of drinks you expect to consume in two hours. An average drink is 1-1/4 ounces of 80-proof liquor, a 12-ounce can of beer or 4 ounces of wine.

Your weight	Number of drinks							
90 - 109 lbs.	1	2	3	4	5	6	7	8
110 -129 lbs.	1	2	3	4	5	6	7	8
130 - 149 lbs.	1	2	3	4	5	6	7	8
150 - 169 lbs.	1	2	3	4	5	6	7	8
170 - 189 lbs.	1	2	3	4	5	6	7	8
190 - 209 lbs.	1	2	3	4	5	6	7	8
210 - 229 lbs.	1	2	3	4	5	6	7	8
230 lbs & up.	1	2	3	4	5	6	7	8

☐ (.01% - .04%) May be DUI ▨ (.05% - .07%) Likely DUI ■ (.08% - up) Definitely DUI

SOURCE: California Highway Patrol

Understandably, police officers are vigorous in enforcing laws against driving while drunk or under the influence of drugs that may interfere with normal control of a vehicle. When stopped under suspicion of intoxication, the driver is required to submit to a **field sobriety test**—a preliminary test at the scene, where one may be asked to walk a straight line, to stand on one foot, or to perform some other similar act. A person who appears intoxicated may be taken to a police station and asked for a sample of breath, blood, or urine, to be analyzed for alcoholic content.

Refusal—by exercising your constitutional right against self-incrimination—may cause forfeiture of your license to drive. Every person who accepts a license to drive implicitly consents to sobriety tests upon police suspicion, with probable cause, of the driver's intoxication. The driver is entitled to a proper warning of the law's effect and is entitled to an administrative hearing on the matter before the license is revoked.

There is a presumption that if the blood alcohol content is .10 percent or more (in some states such as California the standard is .08 percent), the individual is intoxicated and legally incapable of properly operating a motor vehicle. In some states, this presumption is rebuttable by proof that the defendant had adequate control of his or her faculties; in other states, driving with a blood content level at or above the stated percentage is a violation of law.

Criminal penalties for driving under the influence can be severe. In a representative state, a jail sentence of from two days to six months is imposed if one is convicted two or more times for drunk driving within five years; a judge who fails to send the defendant to jail must write a formal opinion justifying this action. A fine of from $500 to $2,000 is also assessed. Under certain circumstances, the vehicle may be impounded. In addition, automobile insurance premiums will rise. A study of the effect of a single DUI on insurance costs found increases as high as $2,030 per year for three years in Baltimore, Maryland.[37] Multiple DUIs lead to cancellation of insurance by the carrier.

Must Owners Maintain Their Vehicles in Good Repair?

Yes. One appellate court stated this generally applicable duty in the following words:

> Generally speaking, it is the duty of one driving a motor vehicle along a public highway to see that it is properly equipped so that it may be at all times controlled to the end that it be not a menace to the safety of others or of their property. The law requires that such a vehicle be equipped with brakes adequate to its quick stopping when necessary for the safety of its occupants or of others, and it is equally essential that it be maintained in such a condition as to mechanical efficiency and fuel supply that it may not become a menace to, or an obstruction of, other traffic by stopping on the road. But if the person in charge of such vehicle has done all that can be reasonably expected of a person of ordinary prudence to see that his vehicle is in proper condition, and an unforeseen failure of a part of his equipment occurs, it does not necessarily follow that he must be deemed guilty of negligence as a matter of law.[38]

Indeed, not only would the driver not be liable for injuries suffered by others from an unforeseeable mechanical failure of his or her automobile, but, if he or she is injured, he or she might recover damages from the manufacturer or a middleman on the theory of strict product liability. The driver need prove that the defendant placed the product (automobile or component part thereof) on the market, knowing that it was to be used without inspection for defects by the consumer. The driver additionally must show that he or she was injured as a result of a defect in the design or manufacture of the product while he or she was properly using it, and that he or she was unaware that such defect made the product unsafe for its intended use.

When Alberta Ayers stopped for a cup of coffee at the Moonlight Cafe, she complained that she had a "short pedal" on the hydraulic brakes of her heavy-duty truck. She had to pump the pedal to get a braking response. Nevertheless, after her coffee break she proceeded up the mountain road. On her way down, the brakes did not hold and she lost control. The truck careened over the side of the road and landed 200 feet below. Was the manufacturer of the truck or brakes liable?

No. Even if the brakes were defective in design or manufacture, Ayers knew of the condition and was negligent by returning to the highway, especially in the mountains without a checkup and adjustment or repair.

Both federal and state government assist owners by prescribing a variety of safety standards for motor vehicles.[39] Not only are manufacturers required to manufacture motor vehicles meeting minimum safety standards, but in recent years many states (both through courts and legislatures) have increased the responsibilities of drivers for their own safety.[40] The most common personal safety example is the required use of safety belts. With respect to motorcycles, it is the requirement that protective headgear be worn while driving. Such statutory requirements exist in a growing number of states.

A non-owner driver of a vehicle is generally not responsible for the vehicle's condition, except for obvious and/or known dangers that create an unreasonable risk of harm to the driver or others. Examples of such dangers include missing headlights or brakes in obvious need of repair.

Are There Special Laws for Rented Vehicles?

When you rent an automobile, you contract for the use rather than the ownership of personal property. The legal term for this relationship is a **bailment,** which is a temporary right of possession of the goods of another. The rental car company is a **bailor,** and the renter a **bailee.** Although bailment law has very well-defined rights and duties, the most important determinant of the relationship is the language of the rental agreement., Although laws relating to rental car bailments vary significantly among the states, two rules are uniform. The first is that the bailor has a right to the return of the car in the same condition in which it was rented, minus ordinary wear and tear. The bailee is responsible for harm to the car even if it was not the bailee's fault. Rental companies suggest special collision insurance (collision damage waivers) to cover this risk. As this insurance is extremely costly (rental companies make a sizeable profit on this add-on fee), many states have restricted rental car company practices in promoting this special coverage.[41] If you have collision insurance on your own automobile, your policy typically will cover this risk (minus the deductible) on any rental car (however, check your policy to determine your specific coverage).

The second uniform rule is that the rental car company has a duty to provide a vehicle that is safe to use and in good driving condition. A bailee has rights in contract and in tort if harmed by a breach of this duty.

Are There Special Laws Involving Common Carriers?

A **common carrier** of passengers is one who agrees to transport for payment all persons applying for passage, assuming there is available space and no legal excuse for refusal.[42] Railroads, airlines, subway systems, bus lines, and taxicabs are all classified as common carriers. Common carriers are required to be licensed and are regulated by federal and sometimes state agencies. Regulations usually cover routes, safety measures, operating methods, rates, passenger contracts and treatment, and luggage handling. At the heart of the relationship are two legal concepts: (1) specific obligations or duties to passengers created by a contract of transport, and (2) general duties imposed as a matter of public policy. These general duties are independent of private contract and arise from the carrier's position as a public utility.[43] We will discuss common carrier legal duties for passenger safety and baggage care.

Mark Oglesby and Mark Finken, both seventh graders, were riding on the Milwaukee County bus system. A group of about 20 youths boarded the bus, some through the windows. The youths demanded money of Finken and, when he refused, beat him. Oglesby and Finken fled. During the entire event the bus driver, although watching in her rearview mirror, made no attempt to intervene or protect the passengers. Did the bus driver breach a duty owed Oglesby and Finken?

Yes. Common carriers are responsible for the safety of their passengers. Because common carriers are open to everyone, the public reasonably expects to be safe. Although the carriers are not insurers of the passengers' safety, the duty of care is either high or the highest duty of care.[44] This duty includes inspection of equipment, safe means of access and departure, use of protective restraints such as seat belts in airlines and possibly even in buses,[45] and protection from fellow passengers.[46] In the above case the court stated, "It was reasonable to infer . . . that the assault would not have occurred had the driver ordered the youths off the bus for their rowdiness, warned them, or notified them she was summoning the police."[47]

A common carrier is also responsible for the safe transport and return of a passenger's baggage, as covered by that passenger's ticket or fare. If there is no extraordinary excuse (such as confiscation of the baggage by police), the carrier is responsible for loss or damage to the baggage, without proof of fault. Statutes regulating baggage transport typically provide that although liability may not be eliminated, it may be limited by contract to certain defined amounts. Such partial disclaimers are allowed as long as the passenger is given the right to have the monetary limit raised after paying an additional fee. As baggage transport contracts generally include a disclaimer, it behooves the passenger to protect valuable goods through a suitable declaration of higher value and paying the additional fee.

What is the Financial Responsibility Law?

Both Jill Searle and Bob Ranney drove their cars to college in Nashville. Rushing to their 8:00 A.M. classes, they collided at the campus entrance. The resulting traffic jam caused almost half of the student body to miss the first class. Many regarded the event as a festive occasion, because no one was hurt. But damage to each car exceeded $500. Searle and Ranney notified their respective insurance companies and relaxed in the thought that both had adequate coverage. Have they forgotten anything important?

Yes. Tennessee, like most other states, has a **financial responsibility law.** About one-half the states demand certainty of financial responsibility and thus require *compulsory automobile insurance.* The other states do not absolutely require insurance but instead require proof of financial responsibility from drivers who have been involved in an accident. Under financial responsibility statutes, after any accident that causes more than a specified modest amount of property damage (such as $500) or in which someone is injured (no matter how slightly) or killed, each driver involved, regardless of fault, must report the accident to a designated state agency within 15 days. A driver who does not have the prescribed minimum amount of automobile insurance coverage is required to post a cash deposit or equivalent bond (up to $60,000) unless the other driver provides a written release from liability. These procedures and requirements apply even for one not at fault, because there could be a disputed question of fact to be resolved in court, possibly years in the future.

Failure to report an accident of the defined severity (e.g., $500 damage, injury, or death) can mean suspension or revocation of one's driver's license. This can be disastrous for someone who must use a car to commute to work or school. Failure to prove financial responsibility can mean suspension until proof is presented. With employment and normal life so dependent on driving, prudence suggests carrying at least the minimum insurance coverage. The minimum financial responsibility requirements vary among the states, but a common required amount is $25,000 for injury to or death of any one person in any one accident, $50,000 for injury to or death of more than one person, and $10,000 for property damage.[48] Insurance salespersons and brokers should know your state's minimum coverage requirement.

Financial responsibility requirements, as the name suggests, are designed to provide some assurance that persons who use the highways and negligently injure others will pay resulting claims. Obviously, damages awarded by a court may far exceed the statutory responsibility limits. Ironically, since financial responsibility need not be demonstrated until after an accident has occurred, there is no guarantee that any particular driver is complying with the law. Indeed, socially irresponsible persons who violate the rights of others with impunity are the least likely to buy the needed insurance. Even states that require motor vehicle insurance are left with many liability issues unresolved. The minimum coverage required is typically low, unregistered automobiles are still driven, and unlicensed drivers still drive. Many states have both financial responsibility requirements and compulsory insurance, and other states have either a financial responsibility requirement or compulsory insurance.

Negligently backing his car and house trailer across a mountain road, Malcolm Maclede caused a major accident in which three persons were seriously injured and two $17,000 automobiles were wrecked. Medical expenses alone exceeded $70,000 within a year, and one victim had to be confined to a bed apparently for the rest of her life. All three were adults with families, and none could work for a year or longer. Maclede had the minimum insurance coverage required by the financial responsibility law. Is Malcolm guilty of a crime? Will he lose all his assets in civil litigation? Can he escape punishment through bankruptcy?

He is not guilty of a crime because he was not criminally negligent. If he had been intoxicated he would face manslaughter and possibly even murder charges (see Chapter 4 for examples). He will, no doubt, lose all of his assets not otherwise subject to creditors' claims, unless he is very wealthy. He can escape his civil liability through bankruptcy, but all his non-exempt assets could be seized. **Exempt assets** are assets that every debtor is permitted to keep, such as an automobile, personal clothes and effects, and a homestead. The moral is that all drivers should carry adequate public liability coverage for bodily injuries to others as a matter of prudent self-interest as well as of social justice and concern for other human beings.

Purchasing Automobile Insurance

An owner of a car needs to protect its value against losses that may arise from, for example, a collision, vandalism, or a theft. A car owner and driver also needs to be protected against the far greater losses that could arise from injury to oneself, or others, as a result of an auto accident.

The typical family **automobile insurance** policy covers the named insured (and spouse, if any) and residents of the same household (including children even when they are temporarily away from home, as when attending a distant school). The policy also covers other persons when they are using the vehicle with the permission of the named insured. Persons in the household other than the named insured cannot give permission to others to use the family car with continuing coverage by the policy. When an insured person drives another owner's car with permission, the driver's policy provides additional supplementary coverage if the owner's policy is insufficient to cover a valid claim or judgment.

What Types of Automobile Insurance Are Available?

When Tosh Takimota celebrated his 20th birthday, his parents gave him his first new car. "Remember," his father said, "you won't be driving one horse, you'll be driving 100 of them. That can be worse than a stampede. So before you use these keys, let's see our insurance agent and make sure you're adequately covered." What sort of insurance coverage does Tosh need?

Tosh needs all four basic types of automobile insurance—liability, medical payments, uninsured motorist, and physical damage—to meet the hazards caused by motor vehicles and those who drive them.

Liability Insurance   A policy of liability insurance will cover bodily injury (also called **personal liability** or PL insurance) and **property damage** (also called PD insurance) losses occurring as the result of the negligence of the insured or other covered drivers. If your state requires insurance this is the coverage required, because it compensates others who are injured by the negligence of the insured. The PL coverage pays claims against the insured for losses resulting from the injury or death of the victim(s). The PD coverage pays claims resulting from damage to the car or other property of the victim(s). This coverage is provided in most states with a single liability limit, such as $50,000. Some policies are still written with "split limits," such as $10,000/$20,000/$5,000 (that is, in any one accident the company pays up to $10,000 for injury or death to any one person or $20,000 to all persons, and $5,000 for property damage).

Medical Payments Insurance   **Medical payments insurance** covers medical and funeral expenses incurred by the insured and family members of the insured's household as a result of an automobile accident. Usually this protection is extended to guests who are injured while occupying the insured's automobile. Payments are made without reference to fault. If the named insured or family members are injured by a motor vehicle while they are pedestrians, or if they are injured while occupying another motor vehicle, they will still be protected by this coverage.

If a person already has adequate health insurance, this additional coverage may be unnecessary. Of course, guests in the insured's car may not have health insurance, and for their sake this comparatively inexpensive coverage should be considered.

Stranded in downtown Atlanta without his wallet, which had been picked from his pocket, Dean Labordee desperately needed to get to the airport for a return flight to Detroit. (His airline ticket was safely tucked in his breast pocket.) Frantically, he "hot wired" the first idle car he came upon, an Oldsmobile owned by Thad Turner, and headed for the airport. Labordee had been drinking, and within a block he crashed into a telephone pole. Before it was all over, his medical payments totaled $8,789. Will Thad Turner's medical payments policy (limit $10,000) have to cover Labordee's loss?

No. In order for Turner's medical payments insurance to apply, he must have given the driver, Labordee, permission to use his vehicle. Labordee did not have Turner's permission; he had stolen Turner's car. His own medical payments coverage is inapplicable, and so is the rest of his automobile insurance policy because as a thief he was using a vehicle without a reasonable belief of permission. However, if Labordee also carried ordinary health insurance, his medical expenses would be covered.

Pedro Perez was at the wheel of his car, patiently waiting for the traffic light to turn green. Suddenly he heard and felt a horrendous crash from the rear. He was wearing a shoulder harness, but his head and chest were snapped in a violent whiplash. Although conscious, he was dazed and could not identify the hit-and-run driver and car that had rear-ended his car, made a U-turn, and sped off. What type of automobile insurance protects Perez in this situation?

Uninsured Motorist Insurance   Perez can recover his medical expenses (and in about one-half the states, his property damage) under **uninsured motorist insurance.** At a relatively low cost, this policy typically pays between $15,000 and $25,000 for bodily injury suffered by the insured as a result of being struck by a hit-and-run driver who escapes without being identified, or by an identified but uninsured or judgment-proof driver who is at fault. Some states require uninsured motorist insurance to be included in all PL/PD policies.

Physical Damage Coverage   Two types of insurance are available to pay for damages to your own automobile: collision and comprehensive. **Collision** pays for damage to the insured's motor vehicle caused by a collision, no matter who is at fault. If the other party was at fault, your insurance company may pay the claim and then seek reimbursement from the wrongdoer by right of **subrogation.** The right of subrogation allows an insurance company to succeed to the insured's rights against a wrongdoer.

Comprehensive, also called _other-than-collision loss,_ protects against any losses to the insured's vehicle except those that aren't caused by collision. Comprehensive applies if the vehicle is stolen, vandalized, or otherwise damaged (as by fire, earthquake, flood, or sandstorm). The policy does not pay for loss caused by theft of personal effects (e.g., clothing, cameras, or luggage) left in the vehicle or for the theft of radio or stereo equipment, which usually requires separate coverage.

Who Are Protected by Automobile Insurance?

Sally and Ben McFarland have a teenage daughter, Karen. All drive the family car. Are all covered by the couple's automobile policy?

Yes, if the insurance company is properly informed that everyone drives the family car. As all family members are likely to be significant drivers, the insurance company has a right to notice of who drives in the family in order to properly assess their risk and charge the appropriate insurance premium (cost to the owner). With respect to an owned automobile identified in a policy, the following persons are normally insured:

1. The named insured and spouse, if residing in the same household.
2. Declared residents of the same household. (This applies even if the person is temporarily away from home; for example, if Karen goes to school in another state.)
3. Other persons who use the automobile with the permission of the named insured. This coverage is provided to nonresident drivers who infrequently drive the insured vehicle.
4. Other persons who might be liable because of negligence by the insured. This could be the employer of the insured, if Sally or Ben got into an accident while on company business.

Under most policies, if you sell your car and buy another, your automobile coverage continues for at least 30 days, or at most until the next policy anniversary date. Thus, you are fully protected in case you are in an accident during the short transition period. However, the company should be notified promptly so it can make the necessary changes in your policy, including an adjustment in the premium.

While on vacation in Glacier National Park, Nelson Salbeck borrowed a four-wheel drive vehicle from some friends and took off on a cross-country trip. Does his automobile insurance policy cover him while he drives the borrowed vehicle?

Yes, Salbeck and relatives who reside in his household are all covered when they drive non-owned passenger automobiles with the permission of the vehicle's owner. A *non-owned automobile* is defined as an automobile or trailer not owned by, or furnished for, the regular use of the named insured. Of course, insurance carried by the owner of the vehicle would provide the basic coverage and Salbeck's insurer would only pay amounts in excess of the owner's policy limits.

When Nelson Salbeck came home, he learned that his adult son, Jack, who still lived with his parents, had bought a new car with a manual gearshift and had insured it in his own name. Nelson asked if he might try it out; Jack said yes, and Nelson took off. He had an accident in which the car was damaged, and both a pedestrian and Nelson were injured, all because of his negligence in shifting gears. Did Nelson's insurance cover him?

No. Technically, the son's car is not non-owned, since it is owned by a resident relative, the son. However, since Nelson drove with his son's permission, the son's policy will cover the accident. Unfortunately, this might be much less coverage than Nelson considers adequate—he is vulnerable to a sizable claim for damages by the pedestrian. An exception to the above rule exists if Nelson borrows his son's car while his own is being serviced or repaired. The son's car would be considered a *temporary substitute automobile,* and both policies would cover the loss.

Aaron Dittmar bought a trailer for camping trips, and hooked a light trail motorcycle to the rear of the trailer. Are these vehicles covered by Dittmar's automobile insurance policy?

The trailer is covered, without an added premium, for PL and PD only if it is designed for use with a private passenger automobile and is not used for business or commercial purposes. Motorcycles, dune buggies, all-terrain vehicles (ATVs), mopeds, motor homes, and other similar vehicles are generally excluded from coverage unless specially added to your policy. Of course, individual policies may be written directly for a motorcycle or other vehicle.

A policy effective within the United States generally does not cover the insured in other countries unless specially endorsed in exchange for an extra premium. Most U.S. policies apply to travel while in Canada, but U.S. drivers need to carry proof of insurance coverage while driving there. Most U.S. insurance is not considered sufficient in Mexico. Before driving in Mexico, a driver should purchase a policy covering Mexican travel. Such policies are sold in both countries. It is extremely important that you review your automobile liability and property damage coverage with your insurance agent before you leave to travel by car in foreign countries. If you do not and you have an accident while driving abroad, you could be burdened with a non-covered judgment and might even be jailed pending trial because of lack of local insurance to cover possible damages.

What Is No-Fault Insurance?

No-fault is a type of insurance requiring each driver to look to his or her own insurance carrier for reimbursement of losses after an accident. Under no-fault, every driver is required to buy insurance. After an accident, each company pays the physical injuries damages suffered by its insured up to some prescribed limit, regardless of fault. The label "no-fault" means the insured will be paid even if he or she caused the accident. There are different versions of no-fault insurance, but in its purest conceptual form neither party may sue the other, nor may the insurance companies sue by right of **subrogation** after making payment. With pure no-fault, the insured may not recover any damages for pain and suffering. If there is a dispute as to the proper amount of damages to be paid, an administrator decides after a hearing. Each party collects from his or her own company for medical or funeral expenses and lost wages (usually for a limited time), both for themselves and for other occupants of the car.

No-fault insurance replaces the typical method of establishing responsibility for wrongs related to automobile accidents. It replaces the tort fault system and thus it is a system itself. The closest existing parallel is workers' compensation insurance, which replaced the fault system for most work-related injuries. All the states that have adopted no-fault systems have implemented modified versions of the pure concept. For instance, in a modified plan if an accidental death, permanent injury, or disfigurement results, or if medical expenses exceed a specified minimum (such as $2,500 or $5,000, or 90 days of disability), it is called the "threshold for suit." When the "threshold" is met, the general prohibition against suits is waived. If it is then proved that the other party's negligence caused the accident, a larger sum may be recovered, including all special damages (for medical expenses, loss of wages, or destruction of property), and payment of general damages for pain, suffering, and disfigurement.

Massachusetts pioneered no-fault in 1971, and about one-half of the states have followed with a variety of no-fault plans. Some states have adopted plans and then abandoned them.* Other states, such as California, have considered the idea during every legislative session for more than 15 years without adopting the system.† At the federal level, repeated unsuccessful efforts have been made to enact a comprehensive national plan, excluding only those states that have acceptable equivalent plans.

Individuals who are not satisfied with recovery schedules under no-fault can, of course, buy additional health or medical payments, accident, and disability insurance coverage for themselves. Most no-fault plans exclude property damage, and so drivers should continue to buy such protection, both comprehensive and collision.

Arguments for No-Fault   Most Americans drive or ride in automobiles and thus repeatedly risk injury. Auto accidents are complicated events: facts are elusive and subject to distortion because of faulty observations and fallible memories as well as "elastic consciences." Negligence is difficult to establish, and a little contributory negligence on the part of the plaintiff may bar any recovery in some states, even when the defendant was overwhelmingly at fault.

Courts in heavily populated areas are crowded with cases involving claims arising out of automobile accidents. Court delays may induce injured persons (perhaps hospitalized, out of work, and in desperate need of money) to accept less than a fair amount for their injuries from insurance company claim adjusters, and to waive their legal rights to a trial. Insurers tend to overpay small claims (to avoid costly litigation) and to overresist legitimate large claims. Only about one-half of the claims involving automobile accidents are settled within six months. The more serious the claim, and thus the more needy the claimant, the longer it takes to resolve the claim.

A typical contingency fee in an accident case is 25 percent of any recovery after the suit has been filed; 30 percent if the case goes to trial; 40 percent if the defendant appeals. No fee is charged nor personal expenses of the attorney reimbursed if the plaintiff loses; however, the losing plaintiff is supposed to pay the court costs including jury fees, costs of discovery, and charges made by private investigators, amounts that can be substantial.

An analysis made by the Auto Club Insurance Association showed that 48 cents of the insurance premium dollar went to injured parties, while 32 cents were spent

---

* Both Nevada and Pennsylvania have repealed their no-fault plans. An Illinois plan was declared unconstitutional by the Illinois Supreme Court.
† An initiative before California voters to establish no-fault was defeated at the polls on November 8, 1988.

on court costs and legal fees in states with the traditional fault system. Under the Michigan no-fault system, 73 cents went to injured victims and 4 cents to court costs and legal fees.[49] Elimination of costly litigation and some economies in marketing policies should reduce costs to drivers. Possible overall reduction of payments to injured persons would also reduce costs.

Arguments against No-Fault Many trial lawyers and other concerned citizens, including some consumer advocates, object to no-fault plans, the primary reason being that such plans deny most accident victims their right to "a day in court," with the related opportunity for full compensation for injuries suffered. As in workers' compensation insurance, the damages prescribed on the no-fault scale may be grossly inadequate, and nothing is paid for the pain and suffering and emotional distress caused by the wrongdoer's negligence. In less serious accidents, many drivers are already covered by other health and collision insurance. **Disability insurance** and workers' compensation insurance at least partially indemnify others injured in auto accidents. Moreover, anyone can already buy collision and comprehensive insurance for property damage to one's own vehicle. These types of coverage are similar to no-fault insurance for the policyholder, although the subrogated insurer may sue and recover from the other driver if at fault.

Although a major argument in favor of no-fault is that it will reduce the cost of insurance premiums, the converse has been true. In states adopting no-fault insurance plans, premiums have risen despite the promise of more affordable policies to the consumers. As more persons receive benefit payments, even when they have been guilty of negligence, insurance rates go up.

Many insurance companies favor no-fault because it removes decision making from juries composed of sympathetic peers of the injured and turn it over to paid, dispassionate professionals who act in the combined roles of judge, jury and advocate. The assurance of payment and freedom from suit could encourage carelessness, although violations of vehicle codes would still be punishable by the state.

Allegedly, exorbitant legal fees could be subjected to statutory limits. Already, if a minor is the successful plaintiff, the court decides what is a fair fee. Moreover, the fee received in one victorious suit enables the lawyer to represent clients in other, losing suits. Court delays are more likely caused by the increased number of criminal actions; the part of the system in difficulty should be the part reformed. Furthermore, delays do not exist equally in all states.

Can Automobile Insurance Premiums be Minimized?

Tim and Jane Quinn are both graduate students, working at multiple jobs to support themselves and their infant child. Every dollar is important in the family budget. They wonder how they can economize on insurance for the car they are buying. They know that if either of them negligently injures or kills another person while driving, they would be hardpressed to pay a judgment that could be for hundreds of thousands of dollars. Even if they could clear themselves of such a judgment by bankruptcy, they do not want to hurt others and have no hope of making good the loss. Also, they do not want a discharge in bankruptcy on their credit records. What automobile insurance should they buy?

The Quinns have limited freedom of choice if they are buying the car on credit. A lender seller will insist that the buyers carry collision and comprehensive insurance until they are paid in full. Because of the Quinns' fear of incurring a huge debt in damages, they decide to add bodily injury and property damage liability coverage to their automobile insurance package. Most states require this liability insurance. They find that they can substantially increase the amount from a basic 10/20/5 to 100/300/50 for perhaps only 40 percent higher premiums. This "bargain rate" for the larger amount of coverage is economical for insurance companies because most claims are for small amounts. Yet, it is also better for the policyholder, because the big risk is a financially devastating judgment.

In three to five years, when the car is paid for, the Quinns can drop the expensive collision and comprehensive coverage, because even total destruction of the car would not be a catastrophic loss. At the very least, they should contract for the *maximum* **deductible.** Thus, they would pay, perhaps, the first $500 cost of any damage to the car. The premiums would then be lower. Indeed, if a loss were to occur, it would be wiser to make no claim unless the damage were to exceed the deductible, for the company would probably raise the premium the year following the claim. After a series of small claims, some companies cancel policies at renewal time. In some states statutes or administrative bodies limit the companies' right to raise premiums or cancel policies.

The Quinns can also save on automobile insurance now by driving carefully and avoiding moving violation citations, which lead to rate increases and cancellations. An insurance company may legally refuse to insure an applicant for any reason related to the hazard insured against: a bad driving record because of accidents that are the fault of the driver, moving traffic violations, employment in a line of work with an unfavorable loss experience (high insurance risk work such as bartending, barbering, acting, or soldiering) physical or mental handicaps, or a reputation of being a deadbeat (slow-pay or no-pay debtor).

A person who cannot otherwise get insurance may qualify for a risk assignment policy. Most insurance companies supply policies on a risk assignment basis as a condition of state law for handling other, less risky business. Under risk assignment plans, companies may be required to accept the unwanted business on a rotating basis in proportion to the volume of policies voluntarily sold in the state by each firm. The plans usually provide minimal coverage.

Companies often offer significant discounts to young men and women who have successfully completed approved driver education courses. Insurance company records show those who have received such training are less likely to be involved in accidents. Some companies give discounts to drivers who do not drink or smoke, who travel very little and do not commute to work, or who drive compact cars. Young drivers may qualify for discounts if they are superior students on the scholastic honor roll or maintain a "B" average. Insurance companies have evidence that such persons have fewer accidents, and so the rate discrimination is legal.

As a Driver, What Should You Do if Involved in an Accident?

The following suggestions are made to help protect your legal rights in the event that you have an accident while driving a car. More important, they help to protect human lives, including your own.

1. If your car is not stopped by the accident, park it in a safe place, immediately ahead of the accident area and preferably off the highway. To hit and run is a serious criminal offense and morally wrong. Clear the other vehicle involved out of the way of oncoming traffic, if safe and practicable. If possible, post someone to warn oncoming vehicles, place warning flares, or do both. If you hit an unattended car or damage other property, leave your name, address, telephone number, and automobile license number on a note inside the car or under the windshield wiper.

2. Provide first aid to anyone injured if you are qualified to do so. Do not move anyone unless absolutely necessary, lest you aggravate injuries.

3. Call, or have someone call, for an ambulance, if appropriate. As soon as is practicable, you should see a doctor if you have been injured. This is important because some serious injuries are not immediately apparent. There may be a delayed reaction by your body; early consultation with your doctor is very important.

4. Call, or have someone call, the highway patrol or local police when anyone is injured or killed, or property damage is substantial. Get the name or number of the officer who investigates the accident. Although the officer's name will be on the police report, you will not receive this report for some days. Persons protecting your interests (e.g., your insurance company or your attorney) will want to immediately begin their investigation of the accident.

5. Even before the police arrive, write down (or have someone else write down) the vehicle license numbers, names, addresses, and phone numbers of all witnesses (they might leave the scene after a few minutes) and of the driver and occupants of the other vehicle. Ask for the name of the other driver's insurance company.

6. Do not admit responsibility for the accident. Any such admission of fault would be later held against you in court. Right after an accident is not the time to make dramatic conclusions, especially since they may be erroneous.

7. Always notify your insurance company if the other party may have been injured or has suffered property damage.

8. As soon after the accident as possible, write down the full details of what happened immediately before, at the time of, and immediately after the accident. A map or sketch of the scene may help. Note the weather and road conditions, time, speed estimates, and skid marks. If you can, get pictures of the cars and any skid marks.

9. If the accident was serious, contact your attorney as soon as possible. If you do not have one, find one. (Methods of attorney selection are discussed in Chapter 15.) The attorney may have a professional photographer take pictures of the scene, including skid marks, aided by your memorandum of the event.

10. Notify the appropriate government agency, using its pre-printed forms, to comply with the state's financial responsibility law.

11. If an insurance claims adjuster for the other driver contacts you, refer such person to your attorney. If you have no attorney, be careful not to admit any fault to the adjuster, who openly or with concealed equipment may be recording every word you say. Do not make any settlement until you are reasonably certain of the full extent of your damages—that is, until you have been released by your doctor or have received some clear indication of the medical outlook for your case, and have received legal advice. Remember, if you are an innocent victim of another driver's negligence, you may be entitled to damages sufficient to cover (a) medical and hospital expenses, incurred and prospective; (b) damage to property (car, clothing); (c) loss of wages, actual and prospective; and (d) payment for pain, suffering, and disfigurement. When the amounts are substantial you are usually well advised to retain an attorney. Even after the attorney's fee, you will probably receive a sum larger than the best direct offer of an insurance claims adjuster.

12. You will probably want to have your car repaired if it has been damaged. The insurance company will often ask for two written estimates to be obtained by you from reliable repair shops, and the company will indemnify you (i.e., make good your loss in cash or pay the bill for repairs) on the basis of the lower estimate. However, if it appears that a defect in your vehicle caused the accident, consult your attorney before you have anything done to the car. The attorney may arrange to have an expert examine the suspect parts and preserve them as evidence to establish strict product liability.

Case 11

BELL v. BURSON

U.S. Supreme Court, 402 U.S. 535, 91 S.Ct. 1586 (1971)

The petitioner was a traveling clergyman whose ministry required that he travel by car to three different rural Georgia communities. One Sunday, a 5-year-old child rode a bicycle into the side of the petitioner's automobile. Her parents filed an accident report claiming damages of $5,000. The petitioner did not carry automobile insurance. Georgia's Motor Vehicle Safety and Responsibility Act provides that "the motor vehicle registration and driver's license of an uninsured motorist involved in an accident shall be suspended unless he posts security to cover the amount of damages claimed by aggrieved parties in reports of the accident." Although the state provided for an administrative hearing before suspension of the license, drivers were restricted to issues of involvement and insurance. The petitioner was not allowed to offer proof that the accident was not his fault to avoid suspension. He was given 30 days to comply with the statute or suffer suspension.

Mr. Justice Brennan delivered the opinion of the Supreme Court of United States: If the statute barred the issuance of licenses to all motorists who did not carry liability insurance or who did not post security, the statute would not, under our cases, violate the Fourteenth Amendment. It does follow, however, that the amendment also permits the Georgia statutory scheme where not all motorists, but rather only motorists involved in accidents, are required to post security under penalty of loss of the licenses. Once licenses are issued, as in petitioner's case, their continued possession may become essential in the pursuit of a livelihood. Suspension of issued licenses thus involves state action that adjudicates important interests of the licensees. In such cases the licenses are not to be taken away without that procedural due process required by the Fourteenth Amendment. This is but an application of the general proposition that relevant constitutional restraints limit state power to terminate an entitlement whether the entitlement is denominated a "right" or a "privilege."

We turn then to the nature of the procedural due process which must be afforded the licensee on the question of his fault or liability for the accident. A procedural rule that may satisfy due process in one context may not necessarily satisfy procedural due process in every case. Thus, procedures adequate to determine a welfare claim may not suffice to try a felony charge. Clearly, however, the inquiry into fault or liability requisite to afford the licensee due process need not take the form of a full adjudication of the question of liability. Since the only purpose of the provisions before us is to obtain security from which to pay any judgments against the licensee resulting from the accident, we hold that procedural due process will be satisfied by an inquiry limited to the determination whether there is a reasonable possibility of judgment in the amounts claimed being rendered against the licensee.

The State argues that the licensee's interest in avoiding the suspension of his license is outweighed by countervailing governmental interests and therefore that this procedural due process need not be afforded him. We disagree. In cases where there is no reasonable possibility of a judgment being rendered against a licensee, Georgia's interest in protecting a claimant from the possibility of an unrecoverable judgment is not, within the context of the State's fault-oriented scheme, a justification for denying the process due its citizens. Nor is additional expense occasioned by the expanded hearing sufficient to withstand the constitutional requirement.

The hearing required by the Due Process Clause must be "meaningful," and "appropriate to the nature of the case." It is a proposition which hardly seems to need explication that a hearing which excludes consideration of an element essential to the decision whether licenses of the nature here involved shall be suspended does not meet this standard.

. . . [I]t is fundamental that except in emergency situations (and this is not one) due process requires that when a State seeks to terminate an interest such as that here involved, it must afford "notice and opportunity for hearing appropriate to the nature of the case" before the termination becomes effective.

We hold, then, that under Georgia's statutory scheme, before the State may deprive petitioner of his driver's license and vehicle registration it must provide a forum for the determination of the question whether there is a reasonable possibility of judgment being rendered against him as a result of the accident . . . .

Reversed and remanded.

QUESTIONS AND PROBLEMS

1. Scott had not quite mastered the stick shift in his new four-wheel drive truck. While parking in a shopping center lot he shifted into forward when he wanted reverse. With a sickening crunch, his truck rammed into the side of a new limousine, causing $5,000 in damages. His own vehicle needs $2,000 in repairs. Scott purchased his car with a loan from Schools Credit Union. Since he had repaid only 25 percent of the loan, the Schools Credit Union was listed as the legal owner of the truck. Who is <u>liable</u> for the damages to the limousine?

2. Darryl Galloway is 14 years old, but he has been driving autos, trucks, and all-terrain vehicles on his family's 300 acre cattle ranch for more than five years without a driver's license. Sometimes he drove on a neighbor's land and sometimes on nearby U.S. forest service land. Are he or are his parents guilty of violating the state's vehicle code?

3. A driver was seated behind the steering wheel when her car stopped in the fast lane of the highway. The car started drifting backwards, its transmission in neutral, while the driver was trying to start the car. Officers tried without success to find out what she had been doing. A field sobriety test showed probable cause for a breath test, which she failed with a .13 reading. What criminal offenses might the driver face, if any? [*People* v. *Garcia,* 262 Cal.Rptr. 915 (1989)] *DWI*

4. As Alyse Brooks was easing from her tight parking space in the three-story "Park Yourself" garage, she creased the side of the neighboring vehicle, a 1975 Pinto, with her front bumper. She stopped, looked, and left, thinking it was an old car not even worth spending the $100 it would take for repairs. Has Brooks violated any law? *Under 100?*
Affirmative duty to stop & leave note ext/or private
property

5. David was the proud purchaser of a new Yamaha motorcycle from Anderson Vehicle Sales with a six-month limited warranty. About 2½ months and 3,115 miles after its purchase, a tapping noise in the engine caused David to bring the cycle in for repairs. The seller agreed the repairs were under warranty, but through mis-diagnosis, a wait for parts, and another wait for additional parts, the cycle remained in the shop for two months. At that time David informed Anderson Vehicle Sales the limited warranty was inadequate and he was exercising his right to revoke under the UCC. Three and a half months after repairs began the cycle was as good as new. Could David revoke his acceptance and demand his purchase price be returned? [*Kelynack* v. *Yamaha Motor Corporation,* 394 N.W.2d 17 (Michigan, 1986)]

6. Following an extra-inning night baseball game, won by the San Francisco Giants, thousands of fans were pouring onto the local highways where visibility was poor due to fog. On the main highway, 37 vehicles smashed into each other in a massive chain collision. If it is established that Douglas Burham, driver of the second car in line, was at fault because he rear-ended the first car, is he liable for damages to all the other damaged vehicles?

7. Dunning borrowed Brady's car with his permission. Due to carelessness in making a U-turn,

Dunning was involved in a collision. The driver of the other vehicle was faultless, and neither his person nor his heavy-duty truck suffered damage. Brady's car needed $1,500 worth of body work. Both Dunning and Brady have collision insurance coverage, each providing for a $250 deductible. Which policy, if either, will pay for Brady's loss?

8. Joann liked Ford Grenadas so well that she purchased a used one three years' newer than her previous Grenada. Within three days the car needed valve work, relocation of the radiator, and various other repairs. O'Neal Ford agreed to make these repairs under a limited guarantee that appeared in the contract of sale. Joann sent a letter revoking acceptance under rights provided by the UCC and requested a return of her payments. Can a buyer revoke acceptance of a used car under the UCC? Does the fact that she was given a limited warranty prohibit her claim of revocation? [*O'Neal Ford, Inc.* v. *Earley,* 681 S.W.2d 414 (Arkansas, 1985)]

9. You intend to drive your automobile into a foreign country for a four-month vacation. What legal issues regarding the car's use should you consider prior to your trip?

10. Parthworthy owned the Old Eagle Tavern, located with a beautiful view overlooking Deadman Canyon. One Saturday night the bartender, Tran Ong, was serving Craig Hamada "Long Island Iced Teas" (an especially potent alcoholic drink) from 8 P.M. until 2 A.M. Tran knew his friend would have to drive some 15 miles to get home. Craig left for home at 2 A.M., after "one more for the road," and had gone only two miles before crashing into an oncoming car driven by Shelia. Shelia was killed; the relaxed Craig was uninjured. Shelia's mother brought a wrongful death action against Craig Hamada, Tran Ong, Parthworthy, and the Old Eagle Tavern. Discuss.

FURTHER READING

1. Annual Auto Issue, *Consumer Reports,* every April. This issue is devoted to rating new and old cars, identifying marketing practices, and other

topical issues related to automobiles. Don't buy a car without this or some other helpful guidebook.

2. "Auto Insurance," *Consumer Reports,* October 1988. Every three or four years, the Consumers Union reports on auto insurance. This specific review includes a very clear discussion on auto insurance and ratings of most insurance companies.

3. Lewis and Goldstein eds. *The Automobile and American Culture.* Ann Arbor: University of Michigan, 1983. "Scholarly and popular" short essays on America's "love affair" with the automobile.

4. Nader, R. *Unsafe at Any Speed.* New York: Grossman Publishers, 1965. This book about automobile safety is credited with launching the modern consumer era and the career of Ralph Nader as a leading consumer advocate.

NOTES

1. *National Underwriter,* October 3, 1988, p. 29

2. Ibid.

3. Every April, *Consumer Reports* publishes an issue devoted to how to select and buy new and used cars.

4. A "lemon" has been defined as "something or someone that proves to be unsatisfactory or undesirable: *DUD FAILURE . . ."* [*John* v. *John Deere Co.,* 306 N.W.2d 231 (South Dakota, 1981)].

5. UCC § 2-601, 2-602, & 2-607.

6. UCC § 2-608(1)(b) & (2).

7. *Consumer Protection Reporting Service* (Owings Mills, Maryland: National Law Publishing Co.) 1986, p. 94.

8. For examples of lemon laws see California Civil Code § 1793.2, Florida General Statute § 42-179, and New York General Business Law § 198-a.

9. "A Twist of Lemon," *Consumer Reports,* April 1985, p. 192.

10. Ibid.

11. "A Breakdown in Auto Safety," *Consumer Reports,* February 1989, p. 84.

12. Ibid.

13. Blomquist, G., *The Regulation of Motor Vehicle and Traffic Safety* (Boston: Kluwer Academic Publishers, 1988), p. 21.

14. "A Breakdown in Auto Safety," p. 84.

15. *Shimoda* v. *Bundy,* 142 P. 109 (California, 1914).

16. *McNear* v. *Pacific Greyhound Lines,* 146 P.2d 34 (California, 1944).

17. *Lee* v. *State,* 358 P.2d 765 (Kansas, 1961).

18. For instance, see California Vehicle Code, § 17709, for 15/30/5 liability amounts.

19. See, for example, California Civil Code § 1714.1.

20. *Lovett* v. *Hitchcock,* 14 Cal.Rptr. 117 (1961).

21. North Carolina General Statute § 90-21.14.

22. Ibid.

23. Delaware, Idaho, Kansas, Maine, Pennsylvania, and Utah.

24. See note 13.

25. See *Ney* v. *Yellow Cab Co.,* 117 N.E.2d 74 (Illinois, 1954), and *Hergenrether* v. *East,* 39 Cal.Rptr. 4 (1964).

26. *Sacramento Bee,* October 30, 1989.

27. *Vince* v. *Wilson,* 561 A.2d 103 (Vermont, 1989).

28. *Sacramento Bee,* February 21, 1990.

29. *Wanna* v. *Miller,* 136 N.W.2d 563 (North Dakota, 1965).

30. *Coulter* v. *Superior Court,* 145 Cal.Rptr. 534 (1978). This case along with California's Dramshop liability was abrogated by statute. See California's Business and Professions Code § 25602 & Civil Code § 1714 (C).

31. Vaughan, E., *Fundamentals of Risk and Insurance* (New York: Wiley), 1989, p. 515. Delaware, Georgia, Illinois, Indiana, Nebraska, Nevada, South Carolina, Texas, and Utah.

32. *Tisko* v. *Harrison,* 500 S.W.2d 565 (Texas, 1973).

33. *Brown* v. *Merlo,* 506 P.2d 212 (California, 1973).

34. Foley, *Stop DWI: Successful Community Responses to Drunk Driving,* (Lexington, MA: Lexington Books, 1986), p. 1.

35. Ibid.

36. McAllister, "The Drunken Driving Crackdown: Is It Working?" 74 *American Bar Association Journal* 52 (September 1988).

37. "What a DUI Costs," *Aide Magazine,* August 1988, p. 10.

38. *Rath* v. *Bankston,* 281 P. 1081 (California, 1929).

39. National Traffic and Motor Vehicle Safety Act of 1966, Title 15 § 1381 et seq.

40. "The Seat Belt Defense," 35 *Am. Jur. Trials* 349, (Rochester, New York: *Legal Encyclopedia of American Jurisprudence Trials,* Lawyer Co-operative Publishing Co. and Bancroft-Whitney Co., San Francisco) 1987.

41. California Business and Professions Code § 22325.

42. *Rathbun* v. *Ocean Accident & Guarantee Corporation,* 132 N.E. 754 (Illinois, 1921).

43. *McNeill* v. *Durham C. R. Co.,* 47 S.E. 765 (North Carolina, 1904).

44. *Kasanof* v. *Embry-Riddle Co.,* 26 So.2d 889 (Florida, 1946).

45. A California jury held a bus company negligent for failure to equip buses with safety belts [*Greyhound Lines* v. *Superior Court,* 83 Cal.Rptr. 343 (1970)].

46. *Lopez* v. *Southern California Rapid Transit District,* 221 Cal.Rptr. 840 (1985).

47. *Finken by Gutknecht* v. *Milwaukee County,* 353 N.W.2d 827 (Wisconsin, 1984).

48. *Insurance Facts* (New York: Insurance Information Institute, 1987), p. 104.

49. "Auto Insurance," *Consumer Reports,* October 1988, p. 625.

CHAPTER 12

Renters and Landlords

For one reason or another, millions of adult Americans do not own the dwellings in which they live. Lack of funds to buy is usually the primary restraint, although personal preference influences many. These people, called **tenants**, rent their living quarters.

The future is not bright for renters. Inflation continues to dramatically increase the cost both of new construction and of operating and maintaining rental dwellings; the resulting upward push on rents is obvious.

At the same time, demand for owner-occupied housing is increasing significantly, largely because of the evolution of the post-World War II "Baby-boom" children into parents and buyers in the housing marketplace. Many young renters in areas in and around large cities who desire to buy their first homes are unable to qualify as purchasers because of escalating home prices. These reluctant renters contribute to overall low vacancy rates and higher rents. One result of this inordinate demand for owner-occupied housing has been the recent trend to convert apartment units into condominiums, thereby further reducing the number of apartments available for rent. As the housing shortage intensifies, rents escalate and the clamor for government remedial action increases. Some local governments have responded with rent controls; others have enacted laws restricting condominium conversions. Government-subsidized apartment building programs are demanded in populous areas, while some frightened communities curtail their rental housing supply by passing growth limitation laws because growth impacts their lifestyles and requires expanded public services that are partially financed by higher taxes.

Unfortunately, the relationship between tenants and their **landlords** often is characterized by misunderstanding, controversy, and ill will. Many of the legal problems experienced by these parties may be anticipated simply from the nature of the relationship. Landlords desire to pick and choose selectively from among tenant applicants who, in turn, rely on civil rights for protection against discrimination.

Once in occupancy, tenants do not have any compelling economic incentive to maintain the rented premises. They have no proprietary interest in the properties;

all monetary benefits go to the landlords. On the other hand, landlords have an incentive to maintain their rental premises only if their expenditures are covered by rental receipts. Rising maintenance costs, taxes, and utility charges promote rent increases, which can be onerous for the poor and create hostility even among tenants who are able to pay. Moreover, tenants are often considered to be in a lower social position because they rent. This erosion of self-esteem is heightened by the insecurity caused by landlords' continuing power of eviction.

The law governing the landlord-tenant relationship evolved from archaic concepts that related to an agrarian, feudal society. Those concepts are largely irrelevant to the relationship as it is or as reformers think it should be in our urbanized, egalitarian democracy. For example, a lease of a dwelling historically had been considered primarily a conveyance of a property interest, not a contract with reciprocal rights and duties. Accordingly, the landlord owed no continuing duty of maintenance because the tenant was in exclusive possession of the "property." This is an application of the rule of *caveat emptor* (Latin: let the buyer beware) to tenants.

But there is a new trend emerging as legislatures and courts increasingly approach the relationship of landlords and tenants in a more enlightened manner. For example, most states now consider a lease to be primarily a contract with reciprocal rights and duties; thus, a landlord now may be required by law to repair and maintain the rented premises. In some states legislatures have adopted comprehensive schemes that have replaced or modified ancient common law rules. In California, a leader in tenant reform, the following laws illustrate a significant departure from the common law:

- The landlord must maintain the premises in a habitable (reasonably livable) condition, unless the tenant agrees otherwise.
- If the landlord fails to maintain the property, the tenant, under specified conditions, may do so—spending up to one month's rent—which then may be deducted from the next rent installment.
- The landlord cannot evict a tenant in retaliation for exercising any tenant right; if such an attempt is made, the landlord may be held liable for punitive damages up to $1,000.
- Landlords must refund security deposits within two weeks of vacancy if not properly applied to harm to the premises or cleaning charges. Damages of $200 may be imposed for a failure to comply with this law. Non-refundable security deposits are illegal.
- Charges by the landlord for cleaning or damage repair, withheld from security deposits, must be itemized and explained. The landlord has the burden of proving the reasonableness of each charge if they are contested in court by the former tenant.[1]

Unfortunately, rental property reform has been slow in evolving, thereby prompting various disruptive developments: organizations of militant tenant groups, legislatively imposed rent controls, and increasing reluctance of investors and lenders to become involved in certain geographical areas, thus aggravating the shortages of rental dwellings (especially for low- and moderate-income tenants).* Another trend has been the willingness of public-interest attorneys to misuse procedural laws to further exacerbate the landlord-tenant relationship.

Hopefully, enlightened courts and legislatures will continue to bring the landlord-tenant laws of the various states into a higher degree of uniformity with progressive changes for the benefit of both parties, and of society as well. Meanwhile, prospective tenants need to bargain carefully and effectively with landlords to minimize the risk of possible future conflict and abuse.

How Does the Residential Rental Business Operate?

The landlord and tenant are involved in a business relationship. One must recognize this fact if one is to understand the applicable law. In this section we shall review the landlord's business, to clarify for renters some perplexing landlord-tenant issues. For purposes of illustration we shall focus upon the business of renting apartments, but these generalizations also apply to the business of renting most other dwellings.

The owners of an apartment complex usually are a group of private investors, or a corporation, who develop the project in order to earn a profit. Typically 75 percent or more of the entire project cost will be borrowed from a lending institution. The balance of needed funds will be provided by the owners. Apartments normally are carefully designed to meet the needs of specific market segments, for example, unmarried students (perhaps three bedrooms), senior citizens (perhaps one bedroom), or small families (perhaps two bedrooms). Future rents are estimated; this estimate influences the design and extent of amenities to be included in the project. An apartment complex anticipating young professional persons who are able to pay higher rents may provide larger rooms, extra closets, tennis courts, a jacuzzi pool, a clubhouse, and similar features. An apartment designed for persons with more modest incomes who are, consequently, able to pay only lower rents, will not have such lavish facilities. Unfortunately, many existing apartments are very old and small; they are dilapidated because of lack of maintenance, repair, and sometimes even minimal housekeeping.

After construction and during rental operations, the owner incurs significant operating expenses. The borrowed capital, with interest, must be repaid in monthly installments; property taxes, utilities, salaries for managers, supplies, insurance, maintenance and upkeep charges, and accountant and attorney fees are

---

* Many apartments are constructed especially for low-income renters in subsidy programs authorized by the U.S. Housing Act, as amended from time to time. These programs are implemented by the Department of Housing and Urban Development (HUD) which has sought to improve landlord-tenant relations in such projects through elimination of the most onerous clauses from its leases and rental agreements. For example, distraint clauses (which authorize the landlord to seize the tenant's property for unpaid rent) and exculpatory clauses (which immunize the landlord from responsibility for all injuries or losses caused by negligence) have been stricken from standard HUD forms. Even so, tenants of public housing projects still must rely on the statutes and court decisions of their respective states in determining other basic legal rights as renters.

typical operating expenses. Under inflationary pressures, operating costs continue to escalate. Total rental income ordinarily should be enough to pay these expenses and produce additional revenue to provide a reasonable return on the owner's cash investment of time and money.

An apartment that is operating successfully provides substantial economic rewards for the owner. As the financing loan is gradually paid off, the owner's equity increases. Additionally, in these times of rising construction costs, the market value of every existing apartment complex is increasing, in part because all new apartment buildings cost more to build. Clearly, though, this inflationary spiral is not prevalent throughout the country; in some areas, such as Colorado and Texas, economic growth lagged in the 1980s and real estate has been more stagnant than in growth areas such as California. When market values are rising, owners of apartments can realize a considerable profit upon sale.

Under proposed federal legislation, it may soon become possible for owners of real estate once again to enjoy lower capital gains tax rates on such profits. Under present tax law, however, profits realized upon sale of apartments are taxed at the same rates as other taxable income (not a favorable tax incentive).

A positive cash flow (total cash receipts exceed total cash expenditures) is another benefit that accrues from ownership of an apartment, and it will be totally or partially tax free. Federal and state income tax laws permit owners of apartments to depreciate their buildings for tax purposes, creating deductions from taxable income that do not require expenditures of any cash. The owner effectively and legally pretends that money was spent for expenses, and deducts such pretended expenses from taxable income.* Since taxable income is reduced by the depreciation deduction, taxes paid also are reduced. Sometimes the annual depreciation deduction from taxes is greater than the taxable income produced by the apartment; this results in a favorable "tax loss." This flow of tax-free income (money that would have been paid as taxes but for the depreciation deduction) is a major incentive for owners of apartment projects.

Note that the depreciation deduction does *not* mean that the apartment building is depreciating in value; to the contrary, most apartment buildings are appreciating over time.

Another advantage of ownership is to use equity in the apartment as collateral for new loans, the proceeds of which may be invested in other real estate projects or investments. Borrowed money is not taxed, so the owner's equity can be transferred from the apartment investment to another investment without any shrinkage from taxation; or the borrowed funds can simply be used for pleasure; either way they are tax free when received, but, of course, they must be repaid eventually, and almost always with interest.

With this brief background, it should be clear that the owner/landlord's primary concern is that total rent received be sufficient to cover all cash outlays, including periodic major expenditures to replace carpets and appliances, to repair roofs, and to repaint building exteriors. As these cash outlays rise with inflation, pressure

---

* The depreciation deduction, or pretended expenditure of cash, is not a nefarious tax evasion scheme—it is a perfectly legitimate device authorized by federal and state governments to encourage investment in real estate.

grows to raise rents proportionately. Since the renters of many modern projects also enjoy rising incomes, they are able to meet these new rent levels, and the owner's project continues to appreciate in value. (Note that the preceding overview pertains primarily to those multi-family projects that rent to more affluent segments of society.)

Millions of other dwelling units are rented by low-income persons who cannot afford any increases in their rent, which already represents a formidable portion of their total income. Landlords are reluctant to spend money on maintenance and repairs when existing rent levels cannot justify such expenditures. Consequently, some multi-family neighborhoods languish in disrepair and gradually become virtually uninhabitable. These properties do not promise owners the positive cash flow and appreciation of alternative projects that command high rents. Mainstream thinking is that laws designed to force landlords to spend money to properly maintain and repair would actually hurt low-income tenants who could not afford to pay the necessary resulting increases in rent. They would be forced to move into even more deteriorated units commanding lower rents, or even onto the street.

Typically the owner/landlord, who prefers to remain out of personal contact with tenants, hires a manager to handle the day-to-day business of the apartment—collecting rent, paying bills, maintaining the property, or employing others to perform some or all of these tasks. The on-site, or resident, manager is the person with whom the residents must deal, at least initially, in solving whatever problems arise. Unfortunately, some managers may be primarily interested in doing as little work as possible in exchange for the customary free rent and small salary. Thus tenant complaints may fall on "deaf ears" in cases where the owner/landlord is a passive investor, secure in anonymity and absent from the premises.

Owners of larger complexes frequently hire property management firms that specialize in managing apartments. These organizations supervise the resident manager, the collection of rents and payment of bills, and maintenance and repairs. They often charge a percentage of the gross rent collected for their services, which tend to be more professional than owner-supplied services.

The manager, whether an individual or a professional organization, is the owner's agent for all purposes connected with the conduct of the rental business, including the receipt of notices and complaints. It therefore is a wise policy for a tenant, when necessary, to make complaints in writing to the resident manager and retain a copy for possible future use.

The nature of the rental business obviously places the landlord and tenant in conflicting financial positions. On the one hand, the landlord is in the superior position, having business experience and the availability of professional help from attorneys and accountants. On the other hand, government regulation, modernization of applicable state laws, and enlightenment of the renting public has done much to balance the relative positions of landlord and tenant. But to bargain effectively, the tenant must be aware of what problems can be solved in advance. Unfortunately, sometimes the bargaining power is so lopsided in favor of the landlord that the tenant has little choice but to sign on the dotted line. The landlord proffers a form lease that is full of disclaimers and is often printed in difficult-to-understand legalese. It is primarily for this reason that many consumer protection laws have been created to protect tenants, as detailed later in this chapter.

What Kinds of Leases Are Available?

A **lease** transfers possession of a dwelling or apartment unit from the owner/lessor to the renter/lessee in exchange for **rent**. It usually is, and always ought to be, in written form. A *lease* contains the mutual promises of the parties. Because a lease involves both the transfer of a property interest (possession) and reciprocal agreements, it is often said to be both a conveyance and a contract.[2]

A resident's occupancy (or tenancy) commonly is called a lease if it continues for a fixed period of time (e.g., "I have a one-year lease"). On the other hand, if the tenancy is agreed to last indefinitely, usually renewing automatically from month to month, it commonly is called a **rental agreement.** (e.g., "I have a month-to-month rental agreement"). Technically, both tenancies are created by a lease and are called a *tenancy for years* and a *periodic tenancy,* respectively.

Tenancy for Years

The unique characteristic of a **tenancy for years** lease is that it is always for a stated period of time, usually one year.*

The main advantage of such a lease to the tenant/lessee is that all terms, including the amount of rent and duration of occupancy, are fixed by the lease and cannot be changed by the landlord/lessor until the lease expires. However, it is legal to include a provision in such a lease that authorizes the landlord to change the operating rules for the rental premises from time to time. For example, the hours during which a swimming pool may be used may change during the leasehold if such a provision is included in the lease.

The main advantage to the lessor of a fixed-term lease is that rental income is uninterrupted for the term of the lease; there will be no need to advertise the premises or to prepare them for another resident, or to sustain a loss through a vacancy during the lease term. A disadvantage is that the rent is locked in for the duration of the lease and cannot be increased to reflect increases in operating expenses. However, some landlords include an adjustable rent feature in their leases that limit annual increases to some percentage, say 4 percent. This protects them from a decline in their cash flow from increasing operating expenses. Tenants know they face an increase in rent each year, but at least it is limited in amount.

Periodic Tenancy

A **periodic tenancy** is commonly called a month-to-month tenancy because most landlords prefer to do business on a monthly basis rather than, for example, a

---

* Technically this variety of leasehold is called an *estate for years,* even though it terminates in a fixed period of time, often less than one year.

weekly basis. As with a tenancy for years, a month-to-month tenancy should be put in writing. As stated earlier, such a document is commonly called a rental agreement, although it is really a lease. Written agreements minimize the possibility of future misunderstandings. The unique characteristic of a month-to-month tenancy is that it continues indefinitely for successive monthly periods until properly terminated in writing, by the lessor or the lessee. The main advantage of a month-to-month tenancy to the resident is the freedom to vacate without further liability for rent upon giving relatively short notice, usually 30 days. The main advantage to the landlord is the freedom to increase the rent or to evict a "problem" tenant, upon giving the same short notice. The tenant faced with an unreasonable rent increase may choose simply to move elsewhere.

There are other methods of occupying a non-owned living unit, but they are very uncommon and don't merit inclusion here. Examples are a **tenancy at will** (indefinite occupancy at landlord's or tenant's pleasure) and **tenancy at sufferance** (unauthorized occupancy following termination of a previous tenancy).

What Laws Govern the Landlord-Tenant Relationship?

Under basic principles of contract law, landlords are generally free to rent to whomever they please on whatever terms they please. Of course, the marketplace dictates a maximum rent, which must be competitive if vacancies are to be minimized. But in addition to market forces, many metropolitan areas now have comprehensive rent control or rent stabilization laws that regulate increases of rent and criteria for eviction.*

Rent control repeatedly has been ruled constitutional over the basic contention that it really is the "taking" of private property for which the state should pay "just compensation." The constitutionality of rent control depends on the actual existence of a housing shortage and its concomitant ill effects. Under those circumstances, rent control is a rational curative measure.[3] Others who oppose rent control contend it is a disguised tax, shifting wealth from landlords to society that otherwise would be forced to subsidize renters. Still others argue that rent control results in the deterioration of rental units because artificially low rents are not sufficient to cover the increasing costs of maintenance and repairs.

Almost all rent control laws exempt new construction from its coverage to avoid the possibility of discouraging new developments. One alternative to rent control is to make direct cash subsidies (through rent vouchers or some other mechanism) to qualified low-income renters who could then pay market rental rates. This alternative would tend to shift the burden from landlords to taxpayers in general.

---

* Restrictions on eviction are necessary to prevent landlords from avoiding rent restrictions by periodically evicting tenants for no reason and then renting to new tenants at increased rates. Valid cause to evict in jurisdictions that regulate eviction would include such defaults as failure to pay rent or damage to the premises.

Other terms that the landlord is free to impose include noise limitations; parking regulations; restrictions on wall hangings, number of guests, and frequency of parties; and so on. Some landlords choose to be strict, while others are lax. These types of restrictions usually are pointed out to renters when their tenancy begins, although the laxity or strictness of enforcement by the landlord is not. The remedy available to the landlord for violation of such rules is the same as for non-payment of rent—eviction plus recovery of any monetary damages to the premises.

The power of the landlord to exclude prospective tenants is not without limitation. Although illegal for more than two decades, racial discrimination in housing still exists. This phenomenon is attributable to weak enforcement tools and efforts in the past, as well as to apparent regional preferences for segregated lifestyles by persons of different races. The Fair Housing Amendments Act of 1988[4] has been hailed as the greatest new weapon in many years to combat housing discrimination. Its primary weapons include the possible award of generous damages (no limit is specified) as well as necessary reasonable attorney fees, coupled with an overall expanded role of the federal government. New classes of persons now protected from exclusionary discrimination are children, the physically disabled, and the mentally impaired. AIDS sufferers also cannot be excluded from rental housing. (Note, however, that qualified senior citizen complexes are permitted to discriminate on the basis of age.) Protection from discrimination in housing is continued in the traditional categories of sex (gender), race, color, religion, ancestry, and national origin. Areas of historical discrimination ignored by the act are lack of wealth (minimum income restrictions); marital status (unmarried couples); family size (separate bedrooms for each child); and sexual preference (homosexual relationships). However, state civil rights or human rights laws protect some of these categories.[5] Kentucky is a leader in adopting laws requiring housing providers to disclose, in public reports, minority participation in their projects. And California long has protected against discrimination on the basis of sex (gender), sexual orientation, race, color, religion, ancestry, national origin, blindness or other physical disability, and children.[6]

Furthermore, certain potential terms of leases or rental agreements generally are declared to be against public policy and cannot be enforced by landlords. Non-refundable security deposit clauses and exculpatory clauses (explained later in this chapter) are examples. Unfortunately, a tenant may unknowingly sign rental papers that include a provision that is unenforceable; in such a case, an unknowing tenant may ignorantly submit to its consequences. For example, an unsophisticated or illiterate tenant who agrees in a written contract and believes that the security deposit is non-refundable very likely would make no effort to obtain a refund. Any unscrupulous landlord who obtained such an illegal waiver is not likely to volunteer a refund that the tenant did not seek.

Damages and Eviction

If a tenant fails to pay rent (defaults) and leaves the premises (abandonment), the landlord may sue the tenant for accrued rent and damages. Damage may include the cost of repairs for physical damage to the premises, as well as the rent the landlord would have received if the tenant had fulfilled the rental arrangement. In a month-to-month tenancy, for example, the landlord typically would be entitled by state statute to one month's notice of intention to terminate (not necessarily on the first day of the month) and would be entitled to rent for that period.

In a tenancy for years (a lease with fixed term), the landlord is entitled to receive rent for the entire unexpired portion of the lease term. However, the landlord would have to deduct from that amount any rent received, or which should have been received, from any successor tenant. In other words, the landlord is not entitled to obtain double rent from the premises, once from the tenant who abandoned and once again from a replacement tenant. Sometimes landlords will not sue for damages because their defaulting tenants "skip," leaving no forwarding address, or are without financial resources and are therefore "judgment-proof." Many rental agreements also include a provision allowing the landlord to recover attorney fees incurred in settling the matter after an abandonment.

When the tenant remains in possession after default in the payment of rent, the situation becomes more complex. The tenant may have defaulted in the payment of rent because of some personal circumstance, and remained in possession simply because there was nowhere else to go. Or, the tenant may have defaulted in rent because of what the tenant believed was just cause, such as a continuing failure of the landlord to maintain habitability (e.g., to repair the heating system). Regardless of why the tenant-in-possession defaulted in the payment of rent, the landlord will ordinarily seek to reclaim possession by evicting the tenant.

Under archaic rules of common law, a landlord could forcibly **evict** tenants who were in default and literally throw their possessions into the street. *Forcible eviction* is now prohibited in all states. Furthermore, the former self-help remedy of *peaceable eviction* is now also obsolete. Thus a landlord may no longer enter the apartment of a defaulting tenant with a master or duplicate key while the tenant is out, remove all personal property, and change the lock on the door. Although entitled to possession of the property ultimately, statutory remedies are designed to compel the landlord to respect the present possession of the tenant and to rely on what most landlords consider to be time-consuming legal remedies.[7]

All states provide for statutory remedies that enable a landlord to resolve the problem of a defaulting tenant who remains in possession. These proceedings generally are called *summary proceedings,* although different terms for the process are used in different states. (Other common titles are **unlawful detainer**, *dispossessory warrant proceedings,* and *forcible entry proceedings.*)

Uniformly, the purpose of summary proceedings is to secure possession of the premises quickly, pending any subsequent and time-consuming litigation concerning collection of unpaid rent, forfeiture of deposits, or damages. Because summary proceedings for eviction are so important—involving a person's shelter—most states (1) require a notice to precede the litigation, giving the tenant a grace period to cure the default; (2) make trial by jury available to decide disputed factual contentions, although this option imposes expenses on the tenant and landlord and practically requires hiring attorneys; (3) permit the tenant to continue his or her occupancy by paying all overdue rent and court costs even after loss of the case; and (4) give the proceedings priority of hearing time on court calendars, which are frequently crowded.[8]

Eviction, when decreed by the court, is effected by the marshall, sheriff, or other designated officer, who physically removes the tenants (if necessary) and places their personal belongings in a municipal warehouse or other designated place. Personal property may be redeemed by the tenant upon payment of storage fees and any outstanding judgment.

Although the disposition of abandoned personal property may sound unreasonably harsh at first blush, the tenant has the opportunity and responsibility to make other arrangements. In the case of valuable goods, only under exceptional circumstances are they left behind by the evicted tenant. Warehousekeepers who store belongings must be paid for their services, and usually enjoy a statutory possessory lien to help ensure payment of storage fees through sale of the goods, if necessary. Either way, the handling of such a tenant's property is unpleasant for all persons who are involved.

The typical defense to a summary proceeding for eviction is exemplified by the tenant who testifies: "Yes, I admit I did not pay the rent. But that was because the toilet does not work," or ". . . there's a big leak in the roof." This response may or may not be a proper defense to the eviction proceedings, depending on who has the duty to repair and maintain under the contractual terms of the lease or under applicable statutes. Unfortunately, most tenants are not adequately informed as to the laws of their state and do not know whether they can successfully resist eviction on the grounds that the premises are not habitable.

On the other hand, many public-interest lawyers are experts in resisting evictions, both properly and improperly. It is unethical for an attorney to stall an eviction by using legal procedures for which there is known to be no legal justification, and court-ordered sanctions can be used for enforcement.[9]

Sometimes a landlord may improperly evict a tenant without obtaining court sanction, as by taking physical possession and re-renting the property to another person; by breaking locks, then entering and removing the tenant's possessions; by failing to furnish heat or by boarding up windows in the leased premises.[10] Under such circumstances, tenants may have a good cause of action against their landlords. They may not be likely to sue, however, because of their ignorance and the costs involved.

Implied Warranty of Habitability

Under archaic principles of common law, a landlord had no continuing duty to maintain the rented premises—the duty to maintain and repair was the tenant's. Fortunately, such a duty generally has now been created in virtually all of the states by courts and legislatures.[11] This duty, called the **implied warranty of habitability,** means that the landlord guarantees that there are no concealed defects in the facilities (those that are vital to the use of the premises for residential purposes) because of faulty original construction or deterioration from age or normal usage. This warranty applies to the condition of the premises at the time the rental arrangement is made.[12]

What about necessary maintenance and repairs arising during the lease term? Under archaic common law the landlord had no duty to make any repairs, because, it was reasoned, the tenant had the exclusive possession of the premises. This rule is unfair, because many appliance breakdowns are not related to the occupancy of the unfortunate tenant who suffers from the ultimate breakdown. The parties are free to include a provision in their lease specifying who will make all repairs. Unfortunately, in part due to their unequal bargaining power, the tenant/lessee frequently agrees to make all repairs, thereby canceling any implied warranty of habitability.

As already pointed out, courts and state legislatures consistently have been abandoning these old common law rules and instead have been imposing certain duties on the landlord to maintain and repair the premises reasonably, unless otherwise agreed. In this way the common law is continually expanding, meeting new and changing circumstances. For example, in the common law there is a principle called the *covenant of quiet enjoyment*. It is a duty implied by law and declared by courts to be an incident of the landlord-tenant relationship. The historical covenant merely provides that the tenant will not be put out of possession (i.e., evicted) by any act or failure of the landlord. Some courts have extended this principle so that any substantial interference with the tenant's use of the premises is considered a violation of the implied covenant of quiet enjoyment. Thus where a clogged sewer pipe caused foul odors, where there was lack of heat, and where the landlord permitted occupants of other parts of the buildings to carry on lewd activities, courts have found a violation of the implied covenant of quiet enjoyment. It does not mean that occasional noise is prohibited. As a result of such "constructive" evictions, the tenant becomes free to abandon the premises without further responsibility for rent and may sue the landlord for wrongful eviction.

In addition to this developing private duty for landlords to maintain rental premises, most cities and towns have housing ordinances designed to protect the health, safety, and welfare of renters and the public, and to prevent the deterioration of dwellings to substandard or slum conditions. These ordinances may wreak supposed hardships on landlords, but they are constitutional exercises of police power. Typically, for example, these ordinances usually require that a flush toilet, lavatory sink, bathtub or shower, kitchen facilities, heating system, and similar essentials be in operating order.

Failure to comply with housing codes or ordinances may subject a landlord to governmental sanctions. But the landlord's obligation is to the municipality and not to the tenant who, accordingly, cannot bring an action to enforce it. The tenant is entitled to complain to the appropriate local official and wait for administrative enforcement of the housing code. Many tenants would decline this remedy out of fear of a *retaliatory eviction* (an eviction for revenge).*

Many housing codes impose reciprocal duties of cleanliness and housekeeping on the tenant, but enforcement is rare as the landlord usually is reluctant to register a complaint that will invite inspection of the premises by an official.

If the landlord fails to maintain the premises, what remedy is available to the tenant? Under such circumstances, and depending on the terms of the lease and the state statutes involved, one of the following situations exists:

---

* Most states prohibit retaliatory eviction by statute. See 47 Louisiana Law Review 1 (1986). Case law reaches the same result. See, for example, *Toms Point Apartments v. Goudzward,* 339 N.Y.S.2d 281 (New York (1972).

1. The landlord is in breach of an implied warranty of habitability or an implied covenant of quiet enjoyment (whether these are created by court decision or by statute).

2. The landlord is in violation of a term contained in the rental agreement or lease.

3. The duty to repair is on the tenant, and there is no remedy against the landlord.

If the landlord persists in violating a duty to maintain or repair, the tenant is free to declare the lease terminated and abandon the premises. This breach of duty will be a good defense for the tenant in any action the landlord may pursue seeking unpaid rent.

More likely, however, the tenant desires to remain in possession as originally agreed, and simply wants the landlord to fulfill the duty of maintaining and repairing the premises. Most states require the tenant to pay the rent and then sue for redress. Damages recoverable for breach of the contract of quiet enjoyment or the implied warranty of habitability are measured by the difference between the rental value of the premises actually received and the rental value if the premises had been as "covenanted" or "warranted." Thus the costly testimony of expert witnesses as to their opinion of these values will be necessary.

Some enlightened states have created new tenant remedies. Some permit the tenant to make necessary repairs and deduct their cost from the rent. The amount of the deduction from rent usually is limited to a maximum of one month's rent.[13] This remedy of "repair and deduct" exists in more than half of the states and is subject to various procedures and limitations. Some states have permitted abatement (temporary suspension of rent) so long as the premises remain uninhabitable.[14] In New York, under its Multiple Dwelling Law, a court may, under certain circumstances, order that rents be paid into an approved escrow (i.e., to a neutral third party) and be disbursed to pay for remedying specified defective conditions.

As previously noted, a tenant facing eviction because of a failure to pay rent may admit the charge, but seek legal justification because of the landlord's failure to maintain the premises. Where an implied warranty of habitability or an expanded covenant of quiet enjoyment exists, the answer is relevant and would constitute a valid defense to the summary proceedings for eviction. Every prospective renter should inquire as to which party will have the duty to maintain and repair. Where feasible, the tenant should negotiate to impose that burden on the landlord in the terms of the lease; otherwise the tenant should give long and careful thought to the potential financial burdens before assuming that responsibility.

As noted earlier, many real estate scholars believe that forcing landlords to repair and maintain will hurt low-income tenants who are unable to afford increases in rent levels. This thinking, however, is far from unanimous.[15]

Security Deposits

Security deposits are commonly demanded by landlords to protect them from various forms of loss that may result when a tenant/lessee defaults, or if the lease simply ends while rent is due. The legal right to return of a security deposit depends on how it is characterized by the court interpreting the documents involved. It may be considered (1) an advance payment of rent, (2) a bonus to the landlord for renting to the tenant, (3) liquidated or agreed-on damages that may later be owed to the landlord, or (4) security for the tenant's performance. The advance payment of rent, usually for the first and last months of the occupancy, serves to give the landlord security because the tenant has something to lose in the event of an abandonment. In such event, the landlord, in effect, has at his or her disposal "paid for" time during which to locate another tenant. But advance rent is rent and cannot be retained by the landlord as compensation for damage or cleaning. Sometimes a "bonus," or "key money," is paid to a landlord when desirable rental quarters are hard to find. It becomes the landlord's money and is not refundable to the tenant under any circumstances. Liquidated damages are an amount the parties agree will compensate the landlord for any damages that may actually be incurred, whether they ultimately turn out to be more or less. A security deposit is a security fund held by the landlord to be applied against any losses incurred by the landlord from any default by the tenant. Any portion of the security deposit in excess of actual damages must be refunded to the tenant; however, actual damages in excess of the deposit remain the tenant's liability.[16] Although the security deposit is the tenant's money until properly applied to damages, the landlord is not, in most jurisdictions, obligated to pay any interest on it to the tenant.

Many disputes arise in connection with the return of security deposits because of disagreement as to the condition of the premises at the beginning and end of the term. Also, there can be differences in opinion as to the meaning of **ordinary wear and tear.** Ordinary wear and tear is deterioration attributable to the passage of time and reasonable use by a tenant, not to any abuse or wrongful conduct. Over time interior paint will fade, discolor, and even crack; carpets will wear down, especially in high-traffic areas; curtains will sag, lose their shape, and discolor from the sun's rays and from oxidation; sediment in water will accumulate around gaskets and washers and cause faucets to leak; caulking around showers and tubs will discolor, crack, and ultimately leak; wood surfaces around door handles and cupboard pulls will become marred from fingers and fingernails; etc.

All of these examples are varieties of normal wear and tear, and correcting them is not the legal responsibility of the tenant. On the other hand, damage beyond ordinary wear and tear generally is the tenant's responsibility. Cigarette burns on furniture, unremovable stains on carpets, chipped porcelain in sinks, burns from fireplace embers, broken windows or light fixtures, scratched and gouged walls, and animal urine on carpeting or flooring are examples of damage.

Disagreements may arise concerning cleanliness. Dirt is not damage, nor is it ordinary wear and tear. A tenant is obligated to return the premise to the landlord as clean as they were at the beginning of the term. The landlord cannot legally retain security deposits to make the premises more clean, even if the deposit is labeled a "cleaning deposit" in the paperwork.

Generally, the landlord and tenant are free to contract as they please. However, because of their unequal bargaining power, courts will not enforce certain terms that frequently appear in landlord-tenant agreements because they are "against public policy." For example, a security deposit that is agreed to be non-refundable nonetheless must be refunded to the extent it is not applied to some proper purpose, such as the repair of damage to the apartment. Unfortunately, many tenants, through ignorance of their legal rights, permit their former landlords to wrongfully retain so-called non-refundable security deposits.

Assigning and Subletting

A lease may prohibit the future transfer of possession of the rented premises by the resident to a substitute tenant. Such a transfer is called an **assignment** or, more commonly, a **sublease.** (Technically, an assignment is the transfer of the full unexpired term of the lease, while a sublease is the transfer of less than the full term. The distinction is ignored for the purposes of this discussion.)

The lessor usually does not want another person, of unknown desirability as a tenant, to appear suddenly as a subtenant. On the other hand, a tenant who has permission to assign thereby has a practical escape route from the lease if it becomes necessary (e.g., when a change of employment occurs). A typical compromise is for the lessor to permit an assignment subject to the approval of the landlord. The approval must not be unreasonably withheld. Solid reasons to withhold approval of a prospective substitute tenant would be a poor credit record or a history of evictions from prior rental units. Following a proper assignment, the former tenant is released from liability for future rent.

Negligence and Exculpatory Clauses

Suppose a landlord negligently maintains the common areas of a multiple dwelling structure. For example, a pool is accessible to infants because of a broken gate latch, soap slickens the laundry room floor, or master keys are unaccounted for and become available to unauthorized persons or thieves. If such negligence by a landlord is the proximate cause of injury to a tenant or other person properly on the premises, the victim may recover damages from the owner.[17]

Reese Johnson was a senior citizen tenant in an apartment owned by the estate of Harris. It was located in the Detroit inner city. Returning home in the early evening, Reese reached for the doorknob when, suddenly, the door was jerked open and he was assaulted, struck, and robbed by an unidentified youth who was lurking in the poorly lighted, unlocked vestibule. Reese brought an action against the estate of Harris for negligence for failure to provide adequate lighting and locks. What should have been the result?

Reese would win in many states. Often, however, courts hold that a landlord's negligence cannot be the proximate cause of a criminal's act. This contention is supported by the concept that public safety is the business and responsibility of government, not of landlords. But many courts find liability where the criminal activity can fairly be said to be foreseeable by the landlord.[18]

Landlord Agnes Roseberry intended to replace a rain gutter over the doorway of the house she rented to Rienecker. In freezing weather, both Roseberry and Rienecker knew rain would run off the roof and freeze into ice on the doorstep. One January night Gary Borders, who had been visiting, slipped and fell on the ice that had accumulated on the doorstep to Rienecker's dwelling. Borders sued the landlord for damages for personal injury. What should have been the result?

would this? work in RI.

Borders lost, because a landlord owes no duty to social guests of tenants to repair a condition known by both the landlord and tenant to be dangerous.[19] *1975*

As stated earlier, an **exculpatory clause** is a provision in a lease or rental agreement whereby the tenant agrees that the landlord shall not be liable for negligence. At common law, through the use of exculpatory clauses, landlords could effectively escape liability for personal injuries stemming from their negligence in maintaining the premises or from physical defects in the premises. Liability could not be avoided for wilful or wanton misconduct, for such would be against public policy. Legislatures in more than one-half the states now prohibit broad exculpatory clauses; among these leaders are California, Florida, New York, Ohio, and Georgia. Nine other state legislatures have severely limited the scope of exculpatory clauses in their states; Maine, Maryland, and Michigan are within this category. Finally, in seven additional states, where legislatures have been silent, courts have ruled exculpatory clauses unenforceable as being against public policy; Alabama, Indiana, and New Jersey are within this category.[20] Therefore, we can safely conclude that the modern trend of protecting tenants from broad exculpatory clauses in leases has been fulfilled.

Lewis Crowell's father rented an apartment from the Dallas Housing Authority. The apartment contained a defective gas heater that leaked carbon monoxide. The lease contained an exculpatory clause whereby it was agreed the landlord would not be liable for any negligence. After his father's death from carbon monoxide poisoning, son Lewis brought a legal action. What should have been the result?

Lewis won. The exculpatory clause was against public policy.[21]

Maria owned a vicious dog, a doberman, which she believed was necessary for her protection, both in her apartment and while jogging. She paid additional rent each month for the privilege of keeping the dog. While the dog was exercising on the apartment lawn, it attacked and severely injured Albert East, a guest who was visiting his girlfriend who also lived in the complex. East sued the landlord for his injuries, primarily because Maria carried no personal liability insurance. What should have been the result?

East wins if the landlord knew, or should have known, of the dangerous propensity of the dog.[22] Under such circumstances, a prudent landlord should request the tenant to immediately remove the animal from the premises. If the tenant fails to act, his or her lease should be terminated by the landlord to avoid injury to others as well as personal liability. While eviction proceedings are underway, the landlord should seek the assistance of local officials and, if reasonably necessary under the circumstances, warn other tenants and others likely to be endangered, such as postal employees. The landlord is not responsible for injuries caused by tenants' pets that previously have exhibited no dangerous propensities, or are not inherently dangerous.

How Can a Renter's Problems Be Minimized?

The bargaining power of a renter is slight, especially where vacancies are scarce. Lease and rental agreement forms are commonly supplied by the prospective landlord and favor the owner's position; landlords tend to know more about the applicable laws and customs. How then may a prospective tenant minimize the risk of controversy, litigation, and victimization? Here are some suggestions:

1. Correctly estimate the economics of the transaction. In addition to the rent, the prospective tenant should determine as precisely as possible, by inquiry, all expenses that will be involved in the rental. Each utility service paid by the tenant (which may include water, gas, electricity, sewage, heating oil, garbage, and telephone) should be estimated. Increased commuting costs, if any, should be taken into consideration. Find out what penalty, if any, is levied for a tardy rent payment. Ask if rents are increased each year, and if so, by how much. Ask when the last rent increase was made. Consider asking for a longer-term lease to protect against future increases in rent, providing you are reasonably sure you won't be under pressure to move elsewhere because of a change in job or family situation. It sounds simple, but many renters make the mistake of miscalculating their total housing cost. Don't bite off more than you can chew.

2. Clarify the landlord's interpretation of the future disposition of all required security deposits. Often the landlord's forms are not sufficiently clear as to how security deposits are to be used. Ascertain how any deductions, if applicable, are to be calculated; when deposits will be refunded; what the landlord means by ordinary wear and tear; and whether full refunds will be made if there is not any damage and the premises are left as clean as when you moved in. Ask when the dwelling was last painted on the inside, who will be responsible for repainting, and when. Make thorough notes while obtaining this information. On important items, later send the landlord a memo stating your understanding of the oral agreement, and keep a copy.

3. Ask about security and prior criminal activity in the building and vicinity. Everyone expects to be safe and secure in his or her "castle." Unfortunately, some areas are more vulnerable than others to burglaries or even felonious assaults and rapes. The inquiry may prompt the installation of dead-bolt locks, window security pins, exterior lighting, or other apparatus designed to reduce the chance of such occurrences.

4. Ask about master keys and authorized entry. Most leases and rental agreements do not mention the circumstances under which the landlord may enter the rented premises in the absence of the tenant. Entry should be authorized for an emergency (e.g., a broken water pipe), but otherwise prior notice should be given to the tenant and an appointment made at a mutually convenient time and for agreed on purposes. This discussion should lead to the question of who has a master key and when the locks were last changed. It is not a major task to adjust a lock to reject prior keys. The landlord's manager or agent customarily will have a master key for emergencies, but there is no reason why the gardener's master key that fits the maintenance shop must also fit your entry door.

5. Ask who has the duty to make needed repairs within the dwelling. In far too many states, ancient common law rules prevail; that is, the tenant has the duty to make all needed repairs within the dwelling. The landlord should assume, or be imposed with, the responsibility for making all repairs occurring from normal wear and tear. The tenant should be required to make only those repairs necessitated by the tenant's negligence (e.g., carelessly allowing a spoon to lodge in a garbage disposal) or willfulness (e.g., throwing a beer bottle through a window).

6. Prepare a thorough inventory of the rented premises and their contents (see Figure 12–1). Before moving into the rented apartment or dwelling, inspect the

FIGURE 12–1   Inventory of Rented Premises and Their Condition

Room	Damage	Cleanliness
Kitchen	Chip in counter near stove burners	Dust and debris behind refrigerator
		Linoleum clean but not waxed; several cuts and loose patches
		Encrusted stains in oven and on stove top
Living room	Electrical outlet cracked	Windows spotted and streaked with dirt
	Hole in ceiling from former hanging object	Stain on carpet near front entry, about 1 foot square
	Holes in wall board from picture hangers	
	Carpet torn near entry into kitchen	

Landlord _____

Tenant _____

premises for both cleanliness and damage. List your findings room by room. Be accurate and do not exaggerate. As soon as the inventory is prepared, deliver a signed copy to the landlord (or agent) and obtain a signed copy in return. Keep your copy with your other valuable papers, for future reference. If the landlord challenges the accuracy of the information, suggest a confirming joint inspection. Sometimes color snapshots are useful, especially if the premises are furnished.

7. Occasionally everyone will be faced with extraordinary unanticipated expenses. If such compels a tardy payment of rent, advise the landlord in advance. Often, late charges will be waived in exchange for such prompt and courteous notice; indeed, your landlord-tenant relationship may even be strengthened.

8. Upon departure at term's end, compare the premises to the inventory and ask for a joint inspection with the landlord. The time to discuss the condition of the premises (for cleanliness and for damage) is the day of departure. Comparison of the premises to the previously made inventory will help to minimize misunderstandings. Usually an agreement can be made on the spot as to the ultimate disposition of the security deposit.

The foregoing suggestions have been arranged in checklist form for quick review (See Table 12-1).

In the event these suggestions do not avoid a serious misunderstanding with the landlord, the best recourse is to take the matter to the appropriate court, usually a Small Claims Court. In many states no attorney is necessary to do this, and whatever assistance is required may be obtained from a designated clerk or administrative official. All documents should be available for the court, including the notes taken at the time the lease was negotiated and the inventory prepared upon taking occupancy. This procedure is relatively inexpensive and will usually result in a satisfactory solution for the well-prepared tenant who has a valid claim. The successful tenant, depending on the state, may recover attorney fees (if they were actually paid) and double or triple the amount of deposits wrongfully retained by the landlord. Some landlords successfully avoid small claims suits by

TABLE 12-1   Checklist to Minimize Rental Problems and Disputes

Before signing a lease, find out:

Projected expenses (stay within your budget!)

- What are personal expenses connected with living in the rental unit?
- What cash is due upon moving in (e.g., prepaid rent, cleaning deposit, security deposit, telephone deposit)?
- What are the average utility rates? Are additional deposits required?

Deposits

- What is the disposition of all deposits at end of lease? Is a full refund possible?
- Is there interest paid on deposits? Are deposits held in a separate account?
- Will your landlord or manager inspect the premises with you on the day of your departure at end of the lease?

Condition of premises

- What is the condition of each room: ceiling, walls, drapes, carpet, and all doors?
- What date was the unit last painted, the drapes cleaned, and the carpets professionally shampooed? Who pays for these items If they are necessary at end of lease?
- What is the operating condition of each appliance? Check them out.
- How does your landlord define "ordinary wear and tear?" Who is expected to pay for it at the end of the lease?

TABLE 12–1 Checklist to Minimize Rental Problems and Disputes (Continued)

- How clean does the landlord expect the unit to be at the end of the lease? Tell him or her that you will prepare a room-by-room checklist for both of you.
- Are all lightbulbs new? Who must replace them? Are any exterior lights wired into the tenant's system, with the cost of electricity added to the tenant's electrical bill?
- Policy regarding alterations, pictures, bookcases, decals, adhesive shelf paper, etc.

Safety

- Under what circumstances will the landlord enter your apartment in your absence?
- Who has master keys? When were the locks last changed? Are there deadbolt locks in the entry doors?
- What security measures are in effect? Is there a roving security patrol?
- Are fire extinguishers provided in or near your prospective unit?
- How soon do police and firemen respond to a call in that area?
- What lighting exists in and around the unit at night? Are the parking areas well lit at night? You should visit the prospective unit in the middle of the night to see for yourself.
- What security problems have there been in the past? Assaults, burglaries, or thefts from cars?
- What is the policy about confidentiality of your rental application?
- Who are the neighboring tenants? Have there been any prior noise, safety, or other problems with them, or with traffic on fronting or nearby streets during rush hours?
- Are there safety pins or other devices for securing sliding glass doors?
- Are all windows equipped with screens? Are they in good condition?

Rights and responsibilities

What are the rules of the rental property regarding stereo use, swimming, pets, parking, guests, parties, laundry facilities, and the like?
- Under what circumstances may a tenant break the lease? What about a job change, flunking out of college, illness, marriage, divorce, or birth of a child?
- Does a tenant have the option to substitute another person as tenant? What are criteria for landlord's approval of a sublease, if required?
- When is the rent due? What is the delinquent rent penalty? What excuses are acceptable for late payments of rent without incurring any penalty, such as a check lost in the mail, a bank error, or an illness?
- In student housing, or other joint housing arrangements, is each of several roommates fully responsible for rent? (All occupants should sign the lease.)
- Who is responsible for repairs (e.g., roof leaks, plumbing failure, sewer drain blockage, and garbage disposal and appliance breakdowns)? Ask if there has been a history of any such problems in your prospective unit.
- Who is to be telephoned if problems arise late at night, or on Sundays or holidays?
- What is the name and address of the owner (with the understanding that you will deal directly with the manager without disturbing the owner)?
- Who pays for utilities (electricity, gas, water, sewer, and refuse disposal)?
- What are the rules concerning pets?

In case of disputes

- Will any disputes be handled by arbitration or by courts?
- Will tenant's attorney's fees be paid by the landlord if the tenant wins in a court proceeding? And vice versa?

Upon signing a lease and before moving in, do:

- Make and date written notes of your understanding of your conversations with the landlord. Carefully enumerate subjects that do not appear to be covered in your lease.
- Prepare a detailed list of any damages on the premises (e.g., chipped counters, stains, cuts or tears in the carpeting, cracks around door handles, tears or bends in screens, caulking and stains in the bathroom, stains in the drapes, stains around heating and air conditioning vents, cracks in windows, and so forth). Be thorough, because when you leave, the landlord will be.
- Prepare an inventory of all furniture and items on the premises, and the condition of each.
- Prepare a list of the cleanliness of the unit, room by room. Pay special attention to the kitchen appliances and bathroom facilities.
- Deliver a signed copy of these lists (but not your notes) to the landlord. Invite verification by personal inspection. Obtain a signed copy for your records.
- Do not be lulled into complacency by the personality of the landlord. After all, landlords change periodically, and you may be dealing with a different face when checkout time comes.

Before moving out, do:

- Make the unit as clean as it was when you moved in, or hire a professional cleaner to do so.
- Compare the original damage list to the unit's present condition. Arrange for repairs, or bargain with the landlord for an agreed on amount of deduction from deposit.
- Insist on a personal inspection of your unit by the landlord in your presence. Make notes of what is said. If possible, get the landlord to admit that the place is clean and the damage is as you indicate.
- Give your new mailing address to the landlord for your refund; ask when it can be expected.

concealing their identity and address, which makes the service of process practically impossible. Only the resident manager is known to the tenant. But a persistent tenant can obtain needed information from the local tax assessor's office or from the catalog of fictitious business names, maintained by the clerk of each county, which lists the true names of owners.

Case 12

MARINA POINT LTD. v. WOLFSON

California Supreme Court , 180 Cal.Rptr. 496 (1982)

A landlord refused to rent an apartment to any family with a minor child. The landlord contended that middle-aged persons, having worked long and hard, raised their own children, and paid both their taxes and their dues to society, have a right to spend their remaining years in a relatively quiet, peaceful, and tranquil environment of their own choice. This right is lost in the presence of children who are rowdier, noisier, more mischievous, and more boisterous than adults.

The trial court agreed, holding that the exclusionary rental policy was reasonable and not arbitrary, and therefore not barred by a state statute that prohibited arbitrary discrimination in business establishments. On appeal, a majority of the California Supreme Court reversed the trial court and held the exclusion improper.

Justice Tobriner [T]he basic rights guaranteed by [the California civil rights statute] would be drastically undermined if, as the landlord contends, a business enterprise could exclude from its premises or services entire classes of the public simply because the owner of the enterprise had some reason to believe that the class, taken as a whole, might present greater problems than other groups. Under such an approach, for example, members of entire occupations, or avocations, e.g., sailors

or motorcyclists, might find themselves excluded as a class from some places of public accommodation simply because that, as a statistical matter, members of their occupation or avocation were more likely than others to be involved in a disturbance. . . . [T]he exclusion of individuals . . . on the basis of class or group affiliation basically conflicts with the individual nature of the right afforded by the [civil rights statute] of access to such enterprises.

. . . [T]he exclusionary practice at issue in this case is clearly distinguishable from the age-limited admission policies of retirement communities or housing complexes reserved for older citizens. Such facilities are designed for the elderly and in many instances have particular appurtenances and exceptional arrangements for their specified purposes.

In the foregoing case, there was no issue concerning due process or equal protection under the U.S. Constitution because there is no state action in the apartment rental business. The rule of the Marina Point *case has been extended to apply to nonprofit homeowners' associations that attempt to restrict condominium occupancy to adults.[23] On the one hand, exclusion of children as a class is not permitted. On the other hand, however, housing accommodations exclusively for the elderly are permitted.[24]*

QUESTIONS AND PROBLEMS

1. Arlene, Sherry, and Marguerite, college students, are roommates in an apartment they leased for one year. Their rent is $450 a month. If for important reasons (e.g., illness in the family, flunking out of school, or marriage) they need to break their lease six months before its termination, may they do so? What are the consequences of breaking their lease? If only Marguerite needs to leave, and Arlene and Sherry desire to remain, what are the probable consequences?

2. What arguments can you make to support the notion that security deposits should earn interest for the tenant? Can you think of any opposing arguments?

3. How can a tenant effectively challenge the amount of money a landlord deducts from the security deposit?

4. Who, between landlord and tenant, suffers the loss for ordinary wear and tear? How many examples of ordinary wear and tear can you describe?

5. What are the pros and cons of rent control? Should rent control be on a city, state, or national basis?   *p 373*

6. Should it be illegal for a landlord to refuse to rent to an unmarried couple? Is it helpful to your answer that universities often reserve campus housing for married students? Should a landlord be required to accept the first person who asks to rent the premises?

7. Can you formulate a proposed law declaring the circumstances under which a landlord ought to be held liable for criminal acts that injure a tenant? Would your proposed rule treat criminals who also lived in the complex the same as criminals from off the street? Is there any action, under your proposed rule, that a landlord could take to obtain immunity from liability to victimized tenants?

8. What is the difference between a periodic tenancy lease and a tenancy for years lease? Which type would a prospective tenant probably prefer?

9. Assume that a landlord who was angry because a tenant's rent was unpaid entered the tenant's apartment with a master key, placed all of the tenant's possessions in a refuse disposal container, and changed the locks on the door. What would be the tenant's legal remedy?

10. What should a tenant do if a landlord wrongfully refuses to return a security deposit at the end of the lease? Would attorney services be necessary?

FURTHER READING

1. Baranov, Alvin B. *How to Evict a Tenant,* 12th edition, Paramount, California: Wolcotts 1985.

2. 54 *Brooklyn Law Review* beginning at page 1215 (1989). A comprehensive analysis in support of rent control presented in a series of comments; Epstein, Richard A. "Rent Control Revisited: One Reply to Seven Critics." 54 *Brooklyn Law Review* 1281 (1989). A thorough rejoinder advocating abolition of rent controls.

3. Faber, Stuart J. *How to Outsmart Your Landlord (if you're a tenant) or How to Outsmart Your Tenant (if you're a landlord): An Understandable Outline of Landlord-Tenant Law.* Los Angeles: Good Life Press, 1982.

4. Jones, William K. "Private Revision of Public Standards: Exculpatory Agreements in Leases." 63 *New York University Law Review* 717, 738 (1988). A complete analysis of the trend prohibiting or restricting landlords' exculpatory clauses.

5. Kushner, James A. "The Fair Housing Amendments Act of 1988: The Second Generation of Fair Housing." 42 *Vanderbilt Law Review* 1049 (1989). A comprehensive review of the history of racial discrimination in housing.

6. Schoshinski, Robert S. *American Law of Landlord and Tenants.* Rochester, New York: Lawyers Co-operative Publishing Company; San Francisco, Bancroft-Whitney Company 1980.

7. Judge Simons, dissenting in *Braschi v. Stahl Assoc. Co.,* 544 N.Y.S.2d 784 (1989). A historical summary of New York's comprehensive rent control and rent stabilization law.

8. Zeigler, Luther. "Landlord Tort Liability for Injuries Caused by Latent Defects." *Real Estate Law Journal,* vol. 14, no. 4, page 349 (1986).

NOTES

1. Calif. Civil Code § 1940 et. seq.

2. *Steel* v. *Latimer,* 521 P.2d 304 (Kansas, 1974); and *Old Town Development Company* v. *Langford,* 349 N.E.2d 744 (Indiana, 1976).

3. *Birkenfield* v. *Berkeley,* 130 Cal. Rptr 465 (1976).

4. Public Law No. 100–430, 102 Statutes 1619 (1988) amending 42 U.S.C. 3601–3619, signed by (then) President Ronald Reagan in September 1988, to become effective in March 1989.

5. The New York Court of Appeals, noting that the term family member was not specifically defined in the applicable statute, held that it included a gay life partner under the New York rent control laws. *Braschi* v. *Stahl Assoc. Co.,* 544 N.Y.S.2d 784 (1989).

6. Unruh Civil Rights Act, California Civil Code, § 51 et. seq.

7. *Floro* v. *Parker,* 205 So.2d 363 (Florida, 1968); *Jordan* v. *Talbot,* 12 Cal. Rptr 488 (1961); *Bass* v. *Boetel Co.,* 217 N.W.2d 804 (Nebraska 1974); and *Edwards* v. *C.N. Investment Co.,* 272 N.E.2d 652 (Ohio, 1971).

8. California now permits some unlawful detainer actions to be decided in its Small Claims Courts, where attorneys are prohibited. California Code of Civil Procedure, §§ 116 and 116.2.

9. California courts can order a party (or even the party's lawyer) to pay the expenses and attorney fees of the other party for actions or tactics that are frivolous or solely intended to cause delay. California Code of Civil Procedure, § 128.5. One attorney was disbarred in part due to such tactics. *Snyder* v. *State Bar,* 133 Cal.Rptr. 864 (1976).

10. See examples, cases, and notes collected in 27 ALR 3d. 924 and 33 ALR 3d. 1356.

11. Illustrative decisions that establish such a duty in residential leases are *Lemle* v. *Breeden,* 462 P.2d 470 (Hawaii, 1969); *Javins* v. *First Nat'l Realty,* 428 F.2d 1071 (1970); *Pintes* v. *Perssion,* 111 N.W.2d 409 (Wisconsin, 1961); and *Marini* v. *Ireland,* 265 A.2d 526 (New Jersey, 1970). Courts have reached the same result in New York, Illinois, New Hampshire, Iowa, Washington, and California. States that have adopted the Uniform Residential Landlord and Tenant Act (URLTA), which contains a like duty, include Alaska, Arizona, Kansas, Kentucky, Nebraska, New Mexico, Oregon, Tennessee, and Virginia.

12. In the leading case of *Becker v. IRM Corp.,* 213 Cal.Rptr. 213 (1985) the California Supreme Court held that the principle of strict liability applies to landlords. A tenant fell against an untempered, frosted glass shower door, severely breaking and lacerating his arm. The landlords were not aware the doors were made of untempered glass, and therefore were not aware of any risk to tenants. Nonetheless, the court held the landlords strictly liable for the tenant's injuries.

13. See, for example, California Civil Code § 1940 et. seq.

14. *Majer Realty Corp.* v. *Glotzer,* 61 N.Y.Supp.2d 195 (1946); *Pintes* v. *Perssion,* 111 N.W.2d 409 (Wisconsin, 1961); and *Marini* v. *Ireland,* 265 A.2d 526 (New Jersey, 1970).

15. Kennedy, Duncan. "The Effect of the Warranty of Habitability on Low Income Housing: Milking and Class Violence," 15 *Florida State University Law Review* 485 (1987). An article contending that laws imposing a duty to maintain and repair will actually help low income tenants.

16. See, for example, California Civil Code § 1950.5(e); *Geiger* v. *Wallace,* 664 P.2d 846 (Kansas, 1983); and *Riding Club Apartments* v. *Sargent,* 440 N.E.2d 1368 (Ohio, 1951).

17. *Kopera* v. *Moschella* 400 F.Supp. 131 (1975) (six-year old girl drowned in pool); *Monroe Park Apts. Corp.* v.

Bennett, 232 A.2d 105 (Delaware, 1967) (injury caused by snow and ice on walkways).

18. A leading case holding a landlord liable for criminal acts of third parties injuring a tenant is *Kline* v. *1500 Mass. Ave. Apt. Corp.,* 439 F.2d 477 (1970). Security measures had been relaxed by the landlord after the tenant moved into her apartment. Subsequently she was injured by a criminal in a common hallway. The court ruled that under those circumstances, the landlord had a duty to protect the plaintiff. Other illustrative cases finding some theory of liability include: *Kwaitkowski* v. *Superior Trading Co.,* 176 Cal.Rptr. 494 (1981) (failure to repair a defective lock and knowledge of crime in area rendered landlord liable when a tenant was raped and robbed in the lobby); *O'Hara* v. *Western Seven Trees Corp.,* 142 Cal.Rptr. 487 (1977) (landlord concealed existence of recent rapes of female tenants in the apartment complex and misrepresented security measures in effect); *Graham* v. *M & J Corp.,* 424 A.2d 103 (Washington, D.C. 1980) (failure to provide door locks in common areas); and *Carline* v. *Lewis,* 400 So.2d 1167 (Louisiana, 1981) (security guard was negligent; landlord held liable). There are numerous cases pending in various state courts as of this writing. For example, one tenant was raped by a man who broke into her apartment. The victim is suing her landlord, alleging he failed to warn her that the neighborhood was a high-crime area. In another case, a woman was looking at an apartment as a possible rental when a man wandered in off the street and raped her. She is suing the landlord for failing to protect prospective tenants. The National Apartment Association concludes that the sphere of liability for apartment owners is expanding. *The Wall Street Journal,* May 20, 1988. See also "Liability for Criminal Acts," 24 *Tulsa Law Review* 261 (1988).

19. *Borders* v. *Roseberry,* 532 P.2d 1366 (Kansas, 1975).

20. Jones, William K. "Private Revision of Public Standards: Exculpatory Agreements in Leases." 63 *New York University Law Review* 717, 738 (1988).

21. *Crowell* v. *Housing Authority,* 495 S.W.2d 887 (Texas, 1973).

22. *Uccello* v. *Laudenslayer,* 118 Cal.Rptr. 741 (1975).

23. *O'Connor* v. *Village Green Owner's Association,* 191 Cal.Rptr. 320 (1983).

24. *Taxpayers Ass'n of Weymouth Township* v. *Weymouth Township,* 364 A.2d 1016 (New Jersey, 1976).

13

Home Ownership

Most people want to own their own home. The desire is so prevalent it often is called The American Dream. This dream has become a reality for about half the U.S. population, but has remained out of reach for the rest. It is no secret that in many parts of the country the values of homes have skyrocketed in recent years, pushing their prices increasingly beyond the reach of many. Of course there are renters who could afford to own their homes but choose to rent for personal reasons, such as freedom from the responsibilities of home ownership. Nonetheless, most renters would probably prefer to own their own homes.

There are pros and cons to owning a home, some of which are completely subjective—benefits to some and liabilities to others. Gardening, for example, may be one person's delight and another's agony. In general, the principal expected benefit from home ownership is economic in nature. There is a potential that the value of the home will increase. This potential has consistently become such a reality in many parts of the country that some people, no doubt, regard it as a certainty. If well selected and properly maintained, a home is more likely to appreciate in value than to depreciate, because of limited available land, rising population demographics, and increasing construction costs. There could, of course, be a general economic depression, as in 1929–1939, but this is not likely. Also, wholly unexpected events that cause widespread economic upheaval (such as the $500 billion savings and loan scandal and the Persian Gulf crisis which are impacting our nation at the time of this writing), can flatten or depress home values in the short run. However, most people would agree that home ownership is the best hedge against inflation over the long run.

Other financial benefits for owners include reducing income taxes by deducting property taxes and interest paid on mortgage loans used in buying their properties. The unpaid balance due on the mortgage notes is gradually paid, thus increasing the owner's equity in the property. This "setting aside" of principal each month is like a savings account. Also, as equities increase (through increasing values and decreasing loan balances), homeowners can use their equities as collateral for additional home equity loans, with which to finance additional wants and needs (such as automobile purchases, college tuition, or even long-awaited holidays abroad). Home-equity loans, however, may require the payment of interest at relatively high rates.

Many other benefits of home ownership satisfy human needs and wants. Typically, a house offers more spacious living accommodations in a more pleasant location than does an apartment. Consider the garage, storage space, number of rooms, outside living areas, and appliance space. Buying a home offers the advantage of selecting a neighborhood with compatible people, away from congestion, street noise, and commotion. Before making the purchase, buyers consider the quality of schools, availability of shopping and public transportation, commuting distances, security, and a host of other intangibles that contribute to an improved lifestyle as compared to that of renters choosing units in multiple-family dwellings where fewer options are available. Furthermore, ownership of a home typically enhances one's sense of security, employability, credit rating, and social and economic status in the community. It generally provides a better environment for bringing up children.

People tend to demand considerably more amenities (benefits) in a house than in a rental unit. Consequently, they pay more each month even though, as owners, they no longer contribute to the profits of a landlord. Home ownership often involves near exhaustion of liquid savings for a down payment and closing costs. The balance of the purchase price, being borrowed money, involves a long-term commitment to payment of interest and repayment of principal.

Sometimes furnishing the house may require credit purchases at high interest rates. Acquiring a home in a suburban area usually boosts the costs of commuting, including automobile insurance. For example, a no-car or one-car family renting an apartment in the inner city may be forced to become a two-car family when owning a home in the suburbs. In crowded metropolitan areas, such as the New York and San Francisco Bay areas, many persons commute 50 miles or more and often endure gridlock on highways for the privilege of living in less-crowded and more-affordable housing.

In addition to large outlays of money when the home is acquired, the monthly expenses may prove burdensome. Insurance premiums, utilities, property taxes, and repair and maintenance expenses must be paid as well as principal and interest on the mortgage loan. Most of these expenses are included in the rent of the apartment dweller—often at a lower level because the accommodations are less elaborate—and therefore are more easily budgeted.

Because of the personalities and lifestyles of the individuals involved, home ownership can become a nightmare. Consider the possible negative impact of yard work, relations with neighbors, commuting time, boredom with neighborhood routine, house maintenance, and the need or desire for mobility (the ability to move on short notice). Obviously, the decision to buy should be made with the care befitting a decision of major financial, personal, and legal consequences.

How Do You Find Available Homes?

Two general categories of homes may be available: new subdivision homes and pre-owned homes. Additionally, more affluent buyers may have the option of a custom-built home.

Developers of *subdivision homes* usually advertise heavily in local newspapers. Prospects who visit a new subdivision are usually given written data and shown furnished model homes. Typically, the subdivision developer has a real estate agent available on the premises to answer questions and handle sales. A real estate agent is a professional licensed by the state to perform services in connection with the buying and selling of real estate. (More about agents is presented later in this chapter.)

One advantage to buying a new subdivision home is that the developer/seller probably will have a financing package or prearranged loan available for qualified (in terms of creditworthiness) buyers, sometimes at very favorable interest rates. One disadvantage is that the character of the neighborhood is not set because many homes are practically new, or may not be constructed until the purchase is made.

The owner of a home available for *resale* usually hires a real estate agent to find a buyer. Such an owner is said to *list* the home with the agent. Buyers, likewise, most often will be assisted by sales agents who work under the supervision of professionals who hold broker's licenses. Large brokerage companies hire numerous sales agents in real estate offices located throughout the country.

In general, when a sale is made, the owner/seller pays the *listing* broker an agreed-on fee, called a **commission.** The commission is expressed as a percentage of the sales price received by the seller. The amount is fully negotiable between the owner and his or her employee, the listing real estate broker. Brokers pay their sales agents a portion of the commissions generated (received from sellers), in lieu of salaries. (The listing process is explained fully later in this chapter.)

The buyer does not pay any commission. In assisting buyers in selecting a home, sales agents often rely on multiple listing services that provide a data base containing most homes currently for sale in the community. Specific information about the homes for sale appearing in the multiple listing service is provided by the listing agent. Homes that fit the general requirements of the buyer may then be visited by the prospect who, with the advice of the sales agent, finally makes a selection. The most effective sales agents frequently advertise desirable properties in local newspapers to attract potential buyers to their offices.

A person who wants to build a *custom home* has to do the preliminary work of locating an available lot. Some custom home builders have lots available in subdivisions and will build a custom home provided it meets certain standards. Otherwise, the services of an architect or designer, as well as those of a building contractor and lending institution, must be obtained. Persons desiring a custom home can obtain names of possible builders from advertisements in the "yellow pages" telephone directory and local newspapers, as well as by contacting local architects and savings and loan associations for recommendations. The decision to hire a contractor to build a custom home should not be lightly or naively made.

Three other types of home ownership are growing in importance and are available in both the new and pre-owned markets: the cooperative apartment, the condominium, and the mobile home. With respect to **cooperative apartments,** a corporation is formed to acquire land and erect a multi-family building. Interested persons buy sufficient shares (of capital stock) in the corporation to obtain rights to proprietary leases that entitle them to live in one of the units and to use the common areas (such as stairs, elevators, swimming pools, and gardens). The corporation arranges for a single mortgage loan on the property and pays taxes and other costs, allocating them to the resident shareholders. Any owner of shares may sell the shares and assign the lease to someone else, who is then entitled to reside in the seller's unit. Shares offered for sale often are advertised for direct sale or submitted to sales agents in the area.

A more common variety of home is the **condominium.** Each owner of a "condo" receives a deed conveying title to a particular unit, and arranges individual financing for its purchase. Only the areas used in common are owned in common, typically by a corporation whose stock is owned by the unit owners. In some condominiums the common areas are owned as a tenancy in common (a form of co-ownership) among all the unit owners. The corporation maintains the building exteriors and common areas, and the owners share the related costs. Condominiums vary in type from townhouses with common walls, to the John Hancock skyscraper in Chicago that has commercial establishments on lower floors and residences on upper floors.

All condominiums are governed by a homeowners' association and, if applicable, a set of corporation by-laws and rules. Prudent buyers should carefully read all applicable governing rules, making certain there are no surprises (e.g., no dogs allowed in common areas) that would make their purchase undesirable.* Pre-owned condominiums are advertised individually and also offered through multiple-listing services as with single family detached residences.

The popularity of converting rental units into condominiums and cooperatives has set the stage for unscrupulous developers to gouge and literally cheat purchasers of new units. For example, in the past some developers would reserve lucrative and unfair management contracts when selling condominium units. In some parts of the country, especially Florida, these abuses became so notorious that Congress enacted a special law giving new legal remedies to buyers of condominiums and cooperatives who had been so taken advantage of.[1]

Finally, the factory-manufactured mobile home is available at prices starting near $20,000 and sometimes exceeding $85,000. Owners usually set down these homes in mobile home parks, with no expectation of moving them. Rent must be paid to the owner of the mobile home park for use of the lot on which the home is placed. Because the homes are compact and relatively economical, and include much built-in furniture, they have a special appeal for budget-minded couples, both young and old. Financing is typically available only for shorter terms than is usually available for mortgage financing of other conventionally built homes. The term may be as short as 7 years with larger down payments (as much as one-third of the purchase price) than for standard homes. Dealers of mobile homes typically advertise in both "yellow pages" telephone directories and in local newspapers.

What Factors Influence the Selection of a Particular House?

Within a price range permitted by the buyer's budget, the most important factor in selecting a particular house from those available is usually its location. Location

---

* Some states require the seller to submit copies of specified documents, such as by-laws, rules, and restrictions, to the buyer before the sale is complete to reduce the risk of unpleasant surprises later.

influences commuting time to work and shopping areas, availability of police and fire protection, utility services, refuse and sewer disposal facilities, school and house of worship districts, ambulance and medical care services, public transportation patterns, proximity to public and private recreational facilities, and whether the home is in the path of decline or growth. Specific location can indicate whether the neighborhood is deteriorating; whether surrounding properties are of comparable value; whether local traffic, noise, or commotion is excessive; whether airplanes fly low patterns overhead; whether factories with fumes, smoke, and noise are nearby; whether television reception is poor in the area; whether neighbors are likely to be compatible socially and economically; whether there are deed restrictions and zoning regulations that increase or decrease values; whether ground waters are clean; whether high-power overhead electrical cables are nearby; whether the building is in a flood plain or vulnerable to earthquakes; and so forth. Clearly, numerous questions need to be asked and answered before final decisions to buy are made.

Another significant criterion for evaluating a home is the configuration of the house itself. Does the lot drain well? Is it located on a corner? Where does the sun shine in the morning and afternoon? Is there sufficient privacy? How old is the house? Are bathrooms and kitchen up to date and functional? What is the condition of the electrical system, the plumbing, and the heating and cooling systems? Must the roof be redone? Is the house well insulated? Are the rooms adequate for storage, furniture, and appliances? A myriad of other common-sense questions should be considered. If you lack the necessary expertise to ask and answer such questions, arrange for someone who knows to help you.

Fixer-Uppers

A special category of pre-owned homes may be appealing to certain budget-minded buyers who are handy with tools. *Fixer-uppers* are properties where building and landscaping have been allowed to deteriorate to some considerable degree. These properties usually are sold through foreclosure sales and auctions by government agencies. Although the price asked for a fixer-upper may seem very attractive, prospective buyers must be very careful to ensure that no serious and prohibitively expensive structural defects exist that may make the modest price unacceptable. But houses that suffer only superficial or limited deterioration, obsolescence, and disrepair may be bargains for buyers who have the skill and the will to do most of the cleaning, painting, repairing, and planting themselves.

How Can a Lawyer Help a Person
Who Is Buying a House?

 Dave and Kathy McDaniel were in the market for a home priced around $175,000. While deciding whether to buy a pre-owned or new subdivision home, they contacted their attorney, Ms. C. Strong, for advice about available financing. What would Ms. Strong's advice likely be?

Their attorney would probably advise the McDaniels that financing is primarily an economic, not a legal, question. The most knowledgeable persons concerning the availability of loans and their terms are found in real estate brokerage firms. Additional information can be obtained from local banks, savings and loan institutions, and FHA (Federal Housing Administration) offices in large metropolitan areas. Ms. Strong might properly suggest, however, that all documents be reviewed by legal counsel before they are signed. This is especially true for any offers to purchase or owner-contractor agreements for a new custom home, if only to be sure that all of the McDaniels' rights and duties are clearly understood.

Because most questions that arise in buying homes are simple and repetitive, real estate agents develop considerable expertise and are usually qualified to assist buyers in the preparation of purchase agreements without the need for legal assistance. However, agents are primarily in the business of selling and are not qualified or authorized to render legal opinions to prospective buyers. A prudent buyer who asks questions and receives fuzzy or incomplete answers would be well advised to obtain legal assistance before signing any contracts. Fees for contract review are likely to be modest because attorneys can perform such routine services in a short time.

How Can a Buyer Finance the Purchase of a Home?

Most buyers do not have the cash to pay the entire purchase price of a home. Even if they did, they may prefer to make a relatively low cash down payment and borrow the balance of the purchase price, because they can then invest the rest of their savings elsewhere. These buyers assume that with continuing inflation, rising prices, and climbing wages or salaries, it will become progressively easier to pay off the fixed amount of the loan as time goes by.

New Financing

Several different types of loans are available to persons who desire to purchase a home. Most loans are made by savings and loan associations, banks, mortgage brokers, and mortgage bankers. *Mortgage brokers* prepare loan packages for borrowers that they send to other lenders who advance the funds and close the loan. These brokers often work with a pool of many lenders and try to find the most attractive loan terms for borrowers. *Mortgage bankers* may fund loans that they later resell for cash, which they use again as working capital. All lenders supply the information and forms necessary to apply for a mortgage loan. Usually there are loan application and sometimes appraisal fees that must be paid, even if the applicant fails to qualify for or abandons the loan.

Once loans are made (or *originated*), they are sold to buyers in the *secondary mortgage market,* which is a market of agencies and buyers interested in purchasing new loans. Selling loans gives lenders the cash with which to make additional loans. The major buyers in the secondary mortgage market are government agencies known widely by their acronyms, Fannie Mae (FNMA), Freddie Mac

(FHLMC), and Ginnie Mae (GNMA).* Since these buyers purchase home mortgages, they have the power to prescribe the terms of the loans (e.g., interest rate, length for repayment, qualifications of borrower) that the mortgages secure. They will buy only those mortgages that comply with their guidelines. These guidelines are regularly reviewed and updated to keep pace with changing market conditions.

Buying loans is one way these three agencies—FNMA, FHLMC, and GNMA—fulfill their responsibility to stabilize the mortgage-money market. For example, when money is "tight" (difficult to borrow and interest rates are climbing), these agencies will purchase loans from lenders, thereby making more cash available to them. When money is "loose" (easy to borrow and interest rates are falling), these agencies will sell loans at an attractive price, thereby taking money out of circulation. These transactions help avoid wide fluctuations in interest rates in our economy.

Conventional Loan   A *conventional loan* is one in which the terms are not directly influenced by government regulations or subsidies. If the lender is not going to sell its mortgages, the borrower qualifies for the loan on the criteria established by the private lender, usually a bank or savings and loan association. Such a lender is called a *portfolio lender,* because the loan is retained in the lender's portfolio of outstanding loans. In the event of a default by the borrower, the lender receives no relief or reimbursement from government but must look solely to the debtor and the value of the home for satisfaction of the debt. Lenders usually require a larger down payment for these loans than for loans that are partially guaranteed by an agency of the U.S. government. Most conventional loans are, however, sold in the secondary market, and then the buyer must qualify for (meet the guidelines of) either of the two largest buyers of such mortgages, Fannie Mae or Freddie Mac. If the down payment is less than 20 percent, the buyer must purchase *private mortgage insurance* (PMI) to guarantee the loan purchaser against loss in case of default by the homeowner/borrower. Thus PMI achieves the same security for the ultimate holder of the home buyer's mortgage loan as does FHA insurance.

FHA Loan   In a *Federal Housing Administration (FHA) loan,* repayment is insured by the U.S. government, and so the lender (or current mortgage holder) is not likely to lose its money. Since the loan is insured, lenders are able to accept transactions where the down payment is small and almost all of the price of the house is financed. The maximum single family home loan amount changes from time to time; at the time of this writing, it is $124,875. By insuring loans, the FHA is able to promote the government's policy of encouraging affordable housing.

VA Loan   In a *Veteran's Administration (VA) loan,* repayment is guaranteed by the U.S. government because the borrower is a qualified veteran. No down payment is required for these loans unless the price paid for the home exceeds its "reasonable value" as determined by the VA appraisal (professional estimate of

---

* Federal National Mortgage Association, Federal Home Loan Corporation, and Government National Mortgage Association, respectively.

value). In such cases, the excess must be paid in cash by the veteran. The VA does not have loan ceilings, but VA lenders adhere to guidelines set by Ginnie Mae and Fannie Mae. The VA loan limit as of this writing is $184,000.

The principal sources of all of these loans are savings and loan associations, commercial banks, and mortgage brokers who represent insurance companies, pension funds, and a variety of other organizations. The terms of loans, such as their interest rates, change from time to time. A prudent buyer will shop for a lender willing to offer the most advantageous terms. Generally borrowers seek the highest loan ratio (lowest down payment), longest loan repayment period, lowest interest rate, and lowest loan charges.

Veterans may qualify for a VA loan, or, in many states, for state assistance. In California, a direct loan is obtainable from a state agency. Although the interest rate for such loans fluctuates with the cost of money to the state, it is far below the conventional loan market rate. Oregon and Wisconsin offer their veterans a benefit in the form of a loan repayment guarantee, but not a direct loan.

Some of the factors a borrower should consider in determining which loan is best are the repayment term (the longer the better), interest rate (the lower the better), qualification requirements (the more relaxed the better), and amount of the loan (the larger the better). We have suggested what is "better" only as a guide; obviously, what is better for you will depend on your circumstances.

In types of loans where the interest rate may fluctuate (called *variable interest rate mortgages* or *VIRMs,* or *adjustable rate mortgages,* or *ARMS)* borrowers should examine carefully what limits (called *caps*) are placed on fluctuations. Caps may restrict how high the interest rate can ultimately go, how much it can increase at any one adjustment, and how often adjustments can be made. Prudent borrowers will make certain they understand the parameters of any variable interest rate loan they are considering.

Repayment Term   The longer the time span during which the loan must be repaid, the lower the monthly payment. For example, the monthly payment to **amortize** (pay off) a 10 percent loan of $100,000 over *15 years* is $1,075.* The same loan repaid over a *30-year* period requires a monthly payment of $878, which is $197 a month less. The "savings" in monthly payments are offset by the increased amount of total interest that must be paid because of the longer-term loan. For example, the purchaser of a $115,000 home who borrows $100,000 of the purchase price at 10 percent will pay $193,500 ($1,075 × 12 × 15) over 15 years, whereas the total cost would be $316,080 ($878 × 12 × 30) if the term of the $100,000 loan were 30 years. This $122,580 difference goes to pay interest because of the longer term of repayment. Sales prices of homes vary considerably throughout the U.S. The example given is intended only to demonstrate the change in loan payments when the term of the loan is extended from 15 to 30 years.

There are distinct advantages in taking a loan with a longer term:

---

* In addition to principal and interest of $1,075, the borrower also must pay property taxes and casualty insurance. Lenders often require those payments on a monthly basis, which are then held in "impound" accounts until remitted to the applicable insurance company and tax collector. Principal, interest, taxes, and insurance are often referred to by the acronym PITI.

1. The longer repayment term gives young buyers extra cash in early years while their family increases in size and cost of support.

2. The young buyer's income is probably rising, and so postponed payments will be easier to make.

3. Continuing inflation helps pay off the loan later with "cheaper" dollars.

4. Buyers might otherwise have to rely on costlier installment credit (18 percent or more a year) to buy wanted (now!) goods and services if extra cash goes into larger payments on the home.

5. The tax deduction for interest paid on the mortgage remains available over the longer term. But note that it is more profitable to pay no interest than to obtain a tax deduction for interest that is paid.

A long-term loan can, of course, be paid off much earlier if the borrower chooses to make extra principal payments each month. Most loans permit an additional payment of principal each month without penalty. The longer-term loan gives the borrower the choice, whereas a shorter-term loan requires the larger payment each month regardless of changing financial circumstances.

There are limits on the available term, typically 30 years for FHA and VA loans. Conventional lenders who sell their loans in the secondary mortgage market also are limited to 30-year terms; however, loans to 40 years are possible with portfolio lenders.

Interest Rate   *Interest* is the price of borrowing money. The higher the interest rate, the higher the monthly payment (which includes both principal and interest). For example, a real estate loan of $100,000 over 30 years at *11 percent* interest requires a monthly payment of $952. If the interest is reduced to *9 percent,* the monthly payment decreases to $805, a savings of $147 a month. Thus, the total payments under the $100,000 mortgage would be $342,720 ($952 × 12 × 30) for the 11 percent loan and only $289,800 ($805 × 12 × 30) for the 9 percent loan, a savings of $52,920. The following schedule will give you a more complete idea of monthly payments necessary to amortize (pay off) various loan amounts (payments for property taxes and insurance are not shown):

Loan Amount *(30-year loan)*	*Monthly Payment* *(9% interest)*	*Monthly Payment* *(11% interest)*
$ 50,000	$ 402.32	$ 476.17
75,000	603.48	714.25
150,000	1,206.96	1,428.51
200,000	1,609.28	1,904.68

Note that the above calculation should take into account the fact that interest payments on a home loan are tax deductible, so that your real cost of financing, after tax savings, would be different depending on your family size and personal tax bracket. Conversely, interest payments (or carrying charges) on consumer loans or credit purchases for cars, furniture, and so forth, are not tax deductible, as effective in 1991.

At the time of this writing, the national average price of housing is $137,000. But that price is an average price, and many houses sell for $60,000 or even less.

In many geographical areas in the West, the average price exceeds $225,000; and more than $175,000 in Milwaukee, Boston, Atlanta, and Seattle.[2] Sales of thousands of homes that were previously foreclosed on by distressed Savings and Loan Companies are being sold by the government-related Resolution Trust Corp. (RTC), and many believe that the supply of these houses at competitive prices will create buying opportunities for many first-time home buyers.

Increased pressures for realistic financing and monthly payments within the average budget, as well as for stability within the mortgage markets, have resulted in new variations of loans. The **variable interest rate mortgage** (VIRM) provides for an increase or decrease in interest rate depending on prevailing interest levels. Because lenders of VIRMs are protected against being locked into a low rate should prevailing rates increase, they are willing to begin the loan at an interest rate lower than is available for fixed-rate mortgages. If market interest rates decrease, the borrower is protected against being locked into a higher rate. Some borrowers worry that variable interest rates will go in one direction only—up. But even so, the rates cannot exceed a cap as determined by reference to some specified interest rate index, such as U.S. Treasury Bill rates.

To avoid the possibility that the monthly payment may become unbearably high, the loan contract can call for maintenance of the same monthly payment even when the interest rate automatically increases in step with the relevant index, simply by extending the term of the loan. Other VIRMs may maintain the same monthly payment even though its variable rate has increased, calling for a larger monthly payment. The monthly difference owed but unpaid is simply added to the unpaid balance of the loan each month; this is called *negative amortization* because the unpaid balance of principal of the loan is actually getting larger each month. VIRMs also are called *adjustable rate mortgages,* or ARMs.

Another variation is the **graduated payment mortgage,** where early payments are kept artificially low (through reduced interest rates) for young persons who are beginning their careers. But interest rates are increased later to artificially high levels (above market interest rates) when the arrearage (amount remaining unpaid) can be repaid without undue hardship. Yet another variation is the *rollover loan,* where an existing mortgage loan is periodically replaced entirely with a new loan at then-current interest rates. The borrower usually is not charged loan fees or processing costs for the new loan.

The pressure on housing supply and financing availability no doubt will prompt new government subsidy programs and private sector ingenuity. Whatever happens, the purchase of living accommodations will continue to be the most significant financial undertaking of most adults.

As is widely perceived, market interest rates are both unpredictable and variable from time to time. The rates on FHA and VA loans are regulated by the federal government and tend to be among the lowest available.

Interest rates should not be confused with loan charges, or **points,** which are one-time charges made by a lender when a loan is originated. A point is a percentage point and is computed much like any percentage commission. That is, two points on a $100,000 loan total $2,000. Points are said to be a payment designed to bring the effective or true profit of the loan in line with prevailing interest rates. Points also may generate cash for the lender to pay a loan broker's commission. Often the seller pays the points to the lender in order to avoid losing the sale, because on FHA and VA loans the buyer-borrower may not be charged more than one point, which is considered a *loan origination fee*. This limitation keeps buyers' closing costs down; but sellers, who can do so, may boost their sales prices, indirectly passing this added cost to their buyers.

Amount of Loan   The greater the amount of money that can be borrowed to purchase a home, the lower the required down payment. Lenders will loan up to a specified percentage of the **appraised value** of the home. Conventional lenders generally lend up to 90 percent of the appraised value. Thus, to purchase a home appraised at and selling for $100,000, a loan of $90,000 can be made, requiring a $10,000 down payment.* FHA loan limits are adjusted from time to time by governmental regulation, but always are more liberal than conventional loan limits. For example, in 1990, FHA permits (will insure) loans up to $124,875 with as little as 5 percent down payment. Current FHA and market data may be obtained from any real estate sales agent or lending institution.

Loan Qualification Requirements   To obtain a loan to purchase a home, a borrower must meet credit worthiness criteria set by the lender. For a conventional loan, for example, a lender may require that monthly payments of principal and interest not exceed 40 percent of the borrower's total monthly income. Spouses, or unrelated co-owners of a home, may pool their respective incomes and credit standards to qualify for a loan. For government-subsidized loans, such as FHA and VA loans, qualifications are set by administrative regulation. All of these qualifying rules use ratios comparing the borrower's anticipated monthly housing expense and total monthly obligations to monthly gross income. Qualifying criteria often change, but current requirements are readily available free of charge from offices of real estate brokerage firms, banks, and savings and loan associations.

Promissory Note   A **promissory note** evidences the loan (see Figure 13–1). It is signed by the borrower, who is called the **maker**, and delivered to the lender when the sale is completed (i.e., when escrow closes). As evidence of the debt, the note contains important information pertaining to the loan. For example, the note will contain the interest rate and any caps that may be applicable if the interest rate is of the fluctuating variety, the amount of the monthly payment, the penalty the debtor must pay if any monthly payment is tardy, and the amount of any assumption fee and any increase in interest that will be expected in the event the note is assumed by any future purchaser of the property. (An existing mortgage is "assumed" when a new purchaser of the home agrees to make its contractual monthly payments.) Also, most notes contain a provision that if litigation becomes necessary by the lender, the borrower must pay the lender's reasonable attorney fees and court costs.

Notes receivable (secured by deeds of trust, or mortgages) represent streams of future income to the lenders. As previously explained, lenders often sell their

---

* The actual cash requirements of the buyer will be somewhat higher than $10,000 because of closing costs, which are explained later in this chapter.

FIGURE 13–1   A Promissory Note

PROMISSORY NOTE
SECURED BY DEED OF TRUST

$100,000   June 1, 19__

FOR VALUE RECEIVED, I PROMISE TO PAY TO _____
(the lender/payee) _____ , OR ORDER, AT _____ (lender's
address),_____ THE PRINCIPAL SUM OF $100,000, WITH INTEREST FROM
THIS DATE UNTIL PAID AT THE RATE OF _____ PERCENT A YEAR ON THE BALANCE
REMAINING FROM TIME TO TIME UNPAID. PRINCIPAL AND INTEREST SHALL BE DUE
AND PAYABLE IN MONTHLY INSTALLMENTS OF $ _____ , OR MORE,* COM-
MENCING ON THE_____ DAY OF _____ , 19__, AND CONTINUING THERE-
AFTER UNTIL THE PRINCIPAL AND INTEREST ARE FULLY PAID.

　　UPON ANY DEFAULT IN THIS NOTE OR IN THE TERMS OF THE DEED OF TRUST
SECURING THIS LOAN, THE UNPAID PRINCIPAL AND ACCRUED INTEREST SHALL AT
ONCE BECOME DUE AND PAYABLE, WITHOUT NOTICE, AT THE OPTION OF THE
HOLDER OF THIS NOTE.

　　MAKER AGREES TO PAY ALL REASONABLE COURT COSTS AND ATTORNEY FEES
INCURRED BY PAYEE IN CONNECTION WITH THE ENFORCEMENT OF THIS NOTE.

　　IF ANY MONTHLY INSTALLMENT IS RECEIVED BY PAYEE MORE THAN 10 DAYS
AFTER ITS DUE DATE, LATE CHARGES OF____ PERCENT OF SAID PAYMENT, BEING
THE SUM OF $____ EACH PAYMENT, ALSO WILL BE DUE AND PAYABLE.

　　PRIVILEGE IS RESERVED TO MAKE ADDITIONAL PRINCIPAL PAYMENTS NOT TO
EXCEED A TOTAL OF $ ____ IN ANY 12-MONTH PERIOD DURING THE FIRST 36
MONTHS OF THIS LOAN.

                                                    _____
                                                    /s/ Maker

---

* The phrase "or more" gives the borrower the option to make additional payments of principal. Technically, if the phrase
is not included in the note, the loan is said to be "locked in," meaning that the borrower cannot make additional monthly
payments. However, most states have declared that locked in home-purchase loans are against public policy, and unenforceable; therefore lenders customarily add a provision, such as found at the bottom of this exemplar note, specifically
authorizing additional principal payments in specified amounts.

notes receivable for cash in the secondary mortgage market. The cash received
enables lenders to make new loans to new borrowers. Thus a homeowner borrowing from one institution may end up making monthly payments to a different
institution that happened to have purchased the note and mortgage. It is unlikely
homeowners would be aware of transfers of their mortgages, because monthly
payments typically are forwarded to service companies that collect payments and
then remit them to the current owners of the loan.

Collateral   The lender will not trust the borrower as the sole source for
repayment of the loan. Usually too much money is involved. The lender will want
collateral, or security, so that if the borrower defaults (fails to make the proper
monthly payments in repayment of the loan), the lender may acquire the security
(the real property), sell it, and apply the proceeds of the sale to pay off the
balance of the loan. This procedure is called **foreclosure.**

　　The customary collateral is the house and lot being purchased by the borrower.
The document that establishes the home as collateral is called a *real mortgage,* or

simply a **mortgage.** The borrower or debtor is called the mortgagor; the lender or creditor is called the mortgagee.

Very similar in purpose is the **deed of trust**, or trust deed, commonly used in some states, such as California and Missouri. It also is signed by the borrower, who is called the trustor. The lender is called the beneficiary. The trustee (usually, but not necessarily, a title insurance company) holds title to the property solely for the purpose of either returning it to the borrower when the loan is finally paid off, or (in the event of the borrower's default), transferring the title and ownership through a trustee's sale to another purchaser so that the proceeds can be given to the lender. Any excess funds received by the trustee in such a forced sale go to the original borrower/buyer who defaulted.

The effect of the mortgage and of the deed of trust are identical; the creditor may conduct a foreclosure sale and take the proceeds in satisfaction of the unpaid debt. Even in states exclusively using deeds of trust, most real estate people and homeowners refer to them as mortgages.

When the loan is completely paid off by the mortgagor, the mortgagee will return the promissory note and mortgage to the borrower who then may "burn the mortgage" or, perhaps, frame it. In the case of a deed of trust, once the loan is paid the trustee will return the title to the borrower with a deed of reconveyance. The beneficiary will return the original promissory note to the borrower.

Assumption of Existing Financing

The obligation of an existing mortgage may be transferred from the debtor (home-owner who desires to sell) to another person (a prospective buyer) who desires to become obligated to its monthly payments. This transfer of obligation is called an **assumption of mortgage**, as noted earlier.

Equity is the market value of a property minus the unpaid balance of loans outstanding (unpaid) against it. Frequently, the sellers of a home will have only a small equity in their property. In such a situation, the purchasers may not need to borrow directly; rather, they may desire to assume the loan of the sellers.

Laura Shields wanted to sell her home for $100,000. She still owed $88,000 against it as represented by a promissory note payable to the bank in monthly installments of $724, including interest at 9 percent. The note was secured by a deed of trust on the home. Mark Failor offered to buy the house by paying Laura $12,000 for her equity and by assuming her loan for the balance of the purchase price. Laura contacted her attorney, C. Strong, to find out what would happen if she accepted Mark's offer, and, at some future time, Mark failed to make his assumed monthly payment. What should Ms. Strong advise her?

Laura's attorney should advise her that when Mark assumed the bank loan, he would become a debtor of the bank. The bank could either accept him as the sole debtor and release Laura from the loan, or keep both Laura and Mark as debtors. In either case, if the bank is not paid each month on time, the trustee can sell the house at public auction and give the proceeds of the sale to the bank in satisfaction of the debt. This may not bother Laura, since she already would have received $12,000 for her equity; however, her credit rating could be adversely affected since her name would remain on the defaulted note. In addition, if the loan was federally insured (such as an FHA loan) and the sales price at foreclosure was less than the unpaid balance due on the loan, Laura could be made to pay the bank any deficiency (unpaid balance) on the loan remaining after a foreclosure sale. For this reason, most sellers whose mortgage is being assumed by a buyer request a *release of liability* from the lender at the time of the sale. A release will be given by the lender only if the assuming purchaser enjoys a satisfactory credit record, or if the loan balance is small compared to the value of the security (the house).

Some states have **anti-deficiency laws** that apply to conventional purchase-money loans. A **purchase-money loan** is any loan the proceeds of which are used by the borrower to purchase a home. Anti-deficiency laws prohibit the collection of any deficiency by the creditor following a foreclosure sale. A deficiency would arise if the proceeds of the foreclosure sale were less than the amount then owed on the defaulted loan, plus certain costs. These debtor laws date back to the Great Depression of the 1930s, when many people lost their homes and substantial equities through foreclosures and still ended up owing their lenders money. If the home is fully paid for, and a mortgage is then given for a loan, this statutory protection generally is not available. No doubt legislators believe such borrowers are not vulnerable seekers of shelter, but sophisticated borrowers for profit. For the same reason, *construction loans* for the purpose of building a house generally are not protected, nor are *refinance loans* that are taken out to replace an existing loan. Another type of unprotected loan is the home equity loan. *Home equity loans* are currently popular, whereby a homeowner borrows for miscellaneous purposes, such as travelling, paying tuition, or buying expensive consumer goods. Under present tax laws interest on home equity loans is tax deductible, whereas interest on consumer debt is not, which explains their current popularity. Note that income tax laws change frequently; professional advice should always be obtained before making financial decisions based on supposed tax consequences. Because these loans also are not protected by anti-deficiency statutes, a deficiency judgment remains a possibility if a foreclosure sale should fail to generate enough cash to pay a home equity loan off in full.

Seller's Financing

Sometimes prospective buyers do not have sufficient funds for a substantial down payment, or are unable to qualify for a new loan under then-existing qualification requirements.

Carryback Mortgage Financing   Sellers of homes that are free and clear of any loans may themselves finance, or "carry," their buyers. In this situation, the buyer usually makes a small down payment and signs a promissory note in favor of the seller. The seller, like a bank, will not be content with the mere promise of the buyer to pay the unpaid balance but will want the home as collateral. The seller will then require the buyer to execute a *carryback deed of trust* (or mortgage).

If the buyer fails to make payments when due, the trustee (or mortgagee) will sell the property in a foreclosure auction and apply the cash proceeds to satisfying the defaulted debt. This would be a purchase money mortgage (or deed of trust) and the seller could not obtain a deficiency judgment against the buyer/debtor if the proceeds of sale were inadequate to pay off the loan. The seller would simply absorb any such loss.

Creative Financing **Creative financing** is a term often used to describe any situation where a seller finances a portion of the sales price (say 30 percent), accepts cash (say, 10 percent), and transfers the existing mortgage loan (say, 60 percent) to the purchaser. This is an example of a combination carryback and assumption transaction. Institutional lenders normally will charge an assumption fee and increase the existing interest rate on the assumed loan. Generally, these modifications are not attractive to most buyers; on the other hand, it is easier to qualify to assume an existing loan than it is to qualify for a new loan.Creative financing is most popular when the real estate market is sluggish.

Contract for Deed or Installment Land Contract   As an alternative method of financing, the buyer and seller may enter into an **installment land contract,** also called a *contract for deed,* that will not require the seller to immediately convey title to the buyer. Rather, title is retained by the seller until the buyer has made monthly payments for many years. This method is used when a buyer cannot qualify for a loan and has no money for a down payment. In these circumstances, the buyer simply makes monthly payments to the seller for, say, 20 years, at which time the seller conveys title, by grant or warranty deed, to the buyer in exchange for payment of the balance of the purchase price.

From the buyer's standpoint, this is not a good method of purchasing a home, but when no other financing is available, it does solve the immediate problem. This type of transaction may be tempting to a budget-conscious buyer because closing costs can be eliminated, no legal assistance is necessary, the cost of title insurance may be avoided, and appraisal fees are dispensed with, as are lender's up-front fees (points). Even the down payment may be small. However, some of these are false savings—the seller may inflate the price of the house as compensation for the munificent terms offered to the buyer.

The buyer under a contract for deed who fails to make a monthly payment may simply be evicted, as would a defaulting tenant, and have no asset to show for the payments made. Since the buyer did not receive title, there is no need for the seller to foreclose. Simple eviction is a potent remedy for the non-paying seller. However, if payments have been made regularly for a long time, in the vast majority of states a court of equity will require the seller to recognize that the buyer has acquired some reasonable amount of equity in the property. But this remedy would require a lawsuit by the buyer, who could be out of possession of the residence pending the litigation. Following litigation, there would be a fore-closure sale; any balance received in excess of the unpaid balance on the contract would go to the defaulting buyer.[3]

Generally speaking, the parties to a land contract should be very careful, and preferably obtain legal advice, before entering such a transaction.

Lease with Option to Buy   A buyer who has inadequate funds for a down payment and who may have difficulty qualifying for a new loan may sometimes be able to purchase a home by leasing it with an option to buy. An *option to buy* gives the renter an absolute right to purchase the property at a future date at a fixed price. The renter who would like to buy now hopes to be better able financially to complete the purchase a few years in the future. A typical lease would be for five years. A portion of each month's lease payment would be credited to the purchase price. This gradual buildup of equity helps reduce or even eliminate the need for a down payment when the option is exercised. Any appreciation in the value of the residence above the agreed-on option price would benefit the buyer. Meanwhile, lease payments are made, equity is growing, and opportunity exists for the buyer to enjoy his or her future home while saving for a down payment. The seller, on the other hand, receives the advantage of delaying income taxes by delaying the sale to some future year. Tenants with an option to buy probably will be excellent residents, making improvements and caring for the property as if it was their own. The seller receives a depreciation tax deduction (similar to that received by owners of apartments, as explained in Chapter 12) and, probably, a positive cash flow. Furthermore, with a future sale in the works, a real estate commission may be avoided.

How Is an Offer to Purchase a Home Made?

An offer to purchase real property, such as a home, should be made in writing. Otherwise, under the Statute of Frauds, it is unenforceable should either party dispute its terms or even deny its existence. The offer must state essential terms, such as a description of the property, the purchase price, and financing terms. The offer is usually made on a form document called an *Agreement of Sale and Deposit Receipt*, or simply **Deposit Receipt**. This latter expression is a misnomer because, once properly signed, a deposit receipt is a binding contract between seller and buyer. Often the real estate agent, who has been hired by the sellers of the property to represent them, assists the prospective buyer in completing the offer to purchase. The signed offer to purchase is delivered by the real estate agent to the seller.

Once the offer has been formally accepted by the sellers (when they sign the purchase agreement or deposit receipt), a contract is created that is legally binding on both parties. If the buyer wrongfully fails to complete the purchase after the agreement of purchase is made, the typical form contract will authorize the seller to retain the *earnest money deposit* made with the offer, as **liquidated damages** for the breach of contract. There is no legal requirement that a buyer include a deposit with the offer, but it is a customary sign of serious intent and ability to buy, and a seller would be most unlikely to accept an offer without one. Liquidated damage is an amount of money agreed on between the contracting parties that fairly represents all losses of the innocent party if the contract is wrongfully broken. Such a provision is common and eliminates the necessity of litigation, since a solution already has been agreed on. Often the earnest money deposit (the amount usually agreed on as liquidated damages) will approximate 1 percent of the purchase price.

Personal checks and promissory notes are not money, and prudent sellers require certified checks or money orders as earnest money before accepting any offer. If the seller signed the contract and accepted a personal check that subsequently bounced (was dishonored by the buyer's bank), the buyer nonetheless would have a binding contract to purchase unless and until it was declared invalid by a court. Although the buyer would have breached the contract at the outset, it may require the time and expense of a lawsuit to rescind or otherwise terminate the buyer's rights. Meanwhile, title to the home is clouded and a substitute buyer may be unwilling to wait for the matter to be clarified.

Audra made a written, signed offer to purchase Greenacre from Sam Seller, who accepted in writing, complete with signature. Subsequently, pending close of escrow (the usual moment when ownership passes to the buyer), Sam refused to complete the transaction. Audra believed that Sam did this because he found out the property was worth more money than she had offered to pay. Audra contacted her attorney. What advice should she receive?

Audra's attorney should advise her that she has two legal remedies. In the first, she can proceed in equity and request the court to order Sam Seller to comply with the agreement. This remedy is called *specific performance* and is available when dollar damages would be inadequate. Money damages would be inadequate here because every parcel of land is considered by the courts as unique (no two parcels can be in the same place) and cannot be substituted for in the marketplace, as can, for example, an automobile.

In the alternative remedy, Audra can sue at law and request the court to assess damages against Sam in an amount equal to her out-of-pocket expenses plus the benefit of her bargain, if any. (This "benefit of the bargain" could be the difference between the price of Greenacre and its higher fair market value.)

In addition, and as a separate matter, if Sam Seller had "listed" the property with a real estate brokerage firm, he would be obligated to pay the firm a commission, even though the sale was never consummated. This is so because the broker had found, in Audra, a ready, willing, and able buyer who had signed a written offer to buy on terms originally specified by the seller. **Listing agreements,** which actually are employment contracts, typically contain language protecting real estate agents from non-payment by sellers who change their minds and withdraw their property from the market either before or after signing sales contracts. Listing agreements are explained fully later in this chapter.

What Is Title Insurance?

In some states, such as New York, attorneys perform title searches and render legal opinions regarding the quality of title to property. These opinions are called **abstracts of title**. In most states, however, title insurance companies guarantee property purchasers that they have accurately searched the public records. At the time the title insurance policy is issued, the owner is given a list of recorded documents. The accuracy of this list is guaranteed by the policy of **title insurance**. Losses arising from something in the public records that was not found by the title insurance company (and therefore not placed on the list) are insured.

In addition, standard coverage title insurance covers some losses that may arise from matters not readily ascertainable from the official records, such as forgery of a deed in the chain of title, lack of capacity of parties who are grantors (perhaps through mental incompetency), or lack of delivery of a deed to a former owner. Losses from forgery are unlikely because documents must be notarized before being recorded. Losses from lack of capacity of previous owners also are unlikely, because court judgments declaring a person incompetent (lacking in capacity) are available in official records. Nor is lack of delivery of deed a likely defect, since the law presumes delivery whenever a document, such as a deed, is recorded.

Standard title insurance is a policy of insurance whereby the owner of real property may insure against a narrow range of losses, up to the specified face amount of the policy. As noted, covered losses arise from any failure of the title insurance company to inform the insured of the existence of all pertinent documents recorded in the official records of the county. For example, if a title insurance company failed to inform a purchaser of the existence of a deed of trust that had been duly recorded in the official records, any losses from that omission suffered by that owner would be covered.

Percy Fairchild bought a property, Pancake Flat, on which to grow rice. In connection with the purchase he acquired a standard policy of title insurance. Thereafter, he began leveling the land and constructing ditches to provide for irrigation by flooding, as required in rice cultivation. He was served with a lawsuit in which his neighbor, Georgette Simpson, was plaintiff. Georgette alleged that she owned an easement across the middle of Pancake Flat because she had driven her cattle across it for years. She requested the court to enjoin the land leveling, ditching, and future irrigation of rice to protect her easement. Percy asked his lawyer to cross-complain against the title insurance company for the apparent defect in his title. Will he win?

Percy will probably lose his case with Georgette and will certainly lose his cross-complaint against the title company. Among defects in title that are not covered by title insurance are **easements** (i.e., rights to use the land of another) that are not recorded in the official records. Many easements do not appear in the public records because they are created by adjacent landowners who repeatedly use another person's land for access over many years. These *prescriptive easements* are not evidenced by any documents, and therefore do not appear in the public records. Prescriptive easements are not covered by standard title insurance, which primarily guarantees an owner that all recorded documents in the public records, as well as accrued property taxes, have been disclosed. In Georgette's case above, the court would not bar Percy from any agricultural use of Pancake Flat, but could order him to make some portion suitable for continued periodic access by Georgette's cattle.

Other exclusions from coverage in standard title insurance policies are boundary discrepancies and errors about how many acres or square feet are contained within the parcel.

Many lenders require extended coverage insurance against loss from any defect, including such unrecorded matters as the presence of tenants or adverse possessors who may assert a claim of ownership in the property. An **adverse possessor** is anyone who physically occupies and pays taxes on someone else's property for a number of years, such as five, under some color or claim of ownership. Such interlopers can be awarded ownership rights by judicial proceeding even though they never paid a cent for the property. Extended insurance costs more than standard coverage because the title insurance company must make an on-site physical inspection in addition to the customary search of the official records.

Unfortunately for home buyers, the premium charged for title insurance is a function of the sales price of the insured property, not a function of the risk of loss by the insurer. That is, the premium is calculated as a percentage of the purchase price of the home each time it sells, whether or not there is any increased risk of loss to the title insurance company. Therefore, the buyer of a new subdivision home faces a purchase price that already includes the accumulated costs of premiums for title insurance paid by the developer and the builder. The buyer must pay again for title insurance already twice paid for, all on the same lot and all, perhaps, in the same year. Should the buyer resell the home immediately, the next buyer would face another title insurance premium based on the new purchase price.

Title insurance premiums are a major part of closing costs in the sale of every home. Buyers and sellers are free to negotiate as to who will pay the title insurance premium, and are well advised to do so. It is not realistic to avoid purchasing title insurance because mortgage lenders require it as a condition to making their loans.

What Is Escrow?

To consummate the purchase of a house, many things need to be done simultaneously. At the moment title passes, the buyer wants to be certain that title insurance and fire insurance are in effect; the seller wants receipt of the sales price; the lender wants the promissory note and mortgage or deed of trust; the real estate broker wants the earned commission; and so forth. Because it would be awkward for all these persons to meet and hand some documents out with the left hand while simultaneously taking other documents in with the right, the practice of hiring a third party intermediary (called the *escrow agent,* or simply **escrow**), developed.

Title companies, escrow departments of banks, escrow companies, and sometimes real estate brokers and attorneys may act as escrow agents. The escrow agent collects the required monies and documents from all the interested persons as necessary, and then, at the **close of escrow**, disburses and distributes them to the appropriate persons. Close of escrow is execution of the contract to sell; title is conveyed to the buyer, cash is delivered to the seller, etc.

Each party interested in a real estate transaction instructs the escrow agent in writing as to what such person will put into escrow and what is expected out of it upon its close. For example, in simplified form, the seller may instruct the escrow officer: "I hand you a duly executed grant deed that you are authorized and instructed to record and deliver to the buyer upon the receipt on my behalf of $150,000, the sales price." The escrow agent who complies with all of these instructions will not be liable for any losses suffered by any of the parties.

Sometimes, pending close of escrow, the buyer and seller disagree as to how some of the money should be disbursed by the escrow officer. Facing conflicting demands, the escrow officer may file a court action called *interpleader*, deposit the contested funds with the clerk of the court, and withdraw completely, leaving the buyer and seller with the problem of settling their dispute in court. The rationale is that the escrow officer is a mere stakeholder who is obligated to follow instructions as received. When instructions conflict, the stakeholder should be allowed to withdraw. Since the escrow officer is a disinterested stakeholder, neither buyers nor sellers should rely on escrow for advice about the merits or consequences of any real estate transaction.

Closing Costs

Carol Biller was buying Henry Foster's home for $145,000. She had arranged financing of $130,000 from a savings and loan association and anticipated putting down $15,000 of her own cash. Will she be required to pay more than $15,000 into escrow?

Yes. The seller will likely have prepaid real property taxes and fire insurance premiums. Sellers don't prepay these costs to accommodate buyers. Property taxes, for example, are demanded by the tax collector only twice each year. Each payment covers portions of both taxes already due and future taxes, so some taxes are always prepaid. The same sort of allocation results with prepaid casualty insurance. The seller is entitled to be reimbursed by the buyer for prepaid taxes that are allocable to the future beyond the date of sale. In contrast, the buyer will probably pay the cost of a boundary survey if needed, termite inspection, loan fees, perhaps title insurance unless it is paid by the seller, and notary and recording fees. All of these costs make up what are commonly called **closing costs.**

It is customarily the responsibility of the seller to pay any transfer taxes, and to pay for any corrective work that is determined to be necessary because of damage, such as by termites or dry rot. However, almost all details of the purchase of a home are a matter of contract and are freely negotiable between the buyer and the seller.

The Legal Significance of Close of Escrow

Prior to close of escrow, the buyer has promised to buy, the seller has promised to sell, the lender has promised to lend, the broker has earned a commission, and so forth. All of these contractual promises are executory, that is, still to be performed. Upon the close of escrow the buyer has received title to and possession of the home and is its owner; the seller has sold, received the net purchase price, and no longer owns any interest in the property; the lender has made the loan, which the buyer has promised to repay; and the broker has received the agreed-on commission. Most of the promises have been executed or performed. The buyer, as borrower, must of course continue to make future payments on the loan as promised in the note. Although it is possible to agree that the seller will retain possession for a period subsequent to close of escrow, or that the buyer will move into the home before close of escrow, these terms are invitations to trouble. The best practice is to have a final walk-through just prior to close of escrow, and to have possession change immediately thereafter.

How Is a Home Taxed?

A home may be located within the boundaries of both a county and a city as well as within various municipal taxing districts, which may tax residents for things such as schools, colleges, flood control, mosquito abatement, air pollution control, parks, water systems, sewers, and so on. All of these needs are expressed in a combined budget, which reflects the money local governments must obtain from its residents in order to function.

Taxation of real property, including homes, is one principal method by which local governments obtain needed funds. All nonexempt properties are taxed in proportion to their value, whether they are residential, commercial, industrial, or whatever. The county assessor appraises each property at its **market value** (called **full cash value**) and declares a uniform fraction of that amount to be its **assessed value.** Some states assess at full cash value. Whether a full cash value or fractional assessment (some arbitrary portion, or fraction, of full cash value) is used has no effect on the amount of property tax paid by the homeowner. These values are listed on the assessment roll. The applicable combined budget is then divided by the total assessed value of all property to arrive at the *tax rate*—the percentage that must be applied to the assessed value of each parcel of property in the county to determine how much its share of the entire budget should be.

In this way property owners are taxed in proportion to the value of the property they own. A property worth 30 percent more than another property will be liable for 30 percent more in taxes, if both are within the same municipal taxing districts. Also, a home worth $75,000 will be liable for exactly the same amount of tax as a service station worth $75,000, if both are within the same districts.*

---

* Some states, following California's lead, have adopted property tax limitations that apply to older, but not newly sold, properties. Therefore, a home recently sold for $75,000 may be chargeable with more property tax than a home or service station worth $75,000 that has been owned a number of years by its original builder.

Owners who believe their taxes are unfairly high in comparison with similar properties may informally request a reappraisal by the assessor, or formally appeal to the specified appeals body (such as the local Board of Equalization). If unsuccessful here, one can appeal to a court, but courts generally do not overrule administrative agencies, especially on matters of taxation.

If government expenditures (initially proposed in budgets) increase, property taxes increase. If government expenditures are constant, total tax revenues are constant, regardless of whether assessed values increase or decrease.

$$\frac{\text{Total expenditures, i.e., the budget}}{\text{Assessed value, all taxable property}} = \text{Tax rate} \times \frac{\text{Your assessed Value}}{} = \frac{\text{Your tax*}}{}$$

Of course, an individual's property may be reappraised, and if its assessed value goes up, its specific tax bill will rise. Conversely, a person whose property goes down in assessed value in relationship to other properties will pay a lower tax. Increases or decreases in assessed values or tax rates have nothing to do with increased total taxes, which can occur only when government expenditures increase.

Typically, all assessed values in a county are increased annually by some percentage to reflect estimated general inflationary pressures. A constant tax rate thus is consistent with an increase in the budget, producing, in turn, higher taxes for everyone's property.

Not all real estate is subject to property taxes. Property owned by any type of governmental organization is exempt from taxation. Thus, when private property is acquired by a local government, as for a public park or school, property tax collections are reduced. If total expenditures are to be maintained, or increased, the remaining private property must contribute more to taxes assessed and collected. Federal lands and the lands under highways and streets are all exempt from taxation.

Property taxes typically are paid twice a year, in December and April, although they accrue daily. Some lenders require their borrowers to pay taxes monthly to the lender, who in turn remits them to the tax collector twice a year. The funds collected monthly are held in an impound account by the lender until disbursed to the tax collector. A small amount of interest is paid the borrower for these prepayments of taxes. The reason lenders prefer impounds is that it gives them an assurance that the homeowner has set aside enough money to pay the taxes when due.

---

* Notice that so long as all property is assessed on the same basis, whether that basis is full cash value, 25 percent of full cash value, or 10 percent of full cash value, the particular basis used in your community will not affect the amount of tax paid by any one homeowner.

What If the Seller Lied About the House?

 C.J. Thomas and his wife Joan, who in the process of selling their home, were attending an open house conducted by their agent when a prospective purchaser, Art Shab, arrived and asked several questions. Specifically, Art asked whether the neighbors ever made unusually loud noises or otherwise caused problems, and whether the house was insulated. C.J. answered that the neighbors were quiet and that yes, the building was well insulated. In truth and as C.J. knew, the neighbors were extremely boisterous and noisy, often screaming profanities in the early hours, and their children were known to break windows, empty garbage cans over neighbors' fences, and race motorcycles up and down the street. Likewise, as C.J. also knew, the house was not insulated. Art purchased the home and shortly thereafter learned the truth about the neighbors and the insulation. He contacted his attorney seeking to revoke the purchase, claiming fraud. Will he succeed?

Art will succeed if the seller (1) made a representation, (2) of a material fact, (3) knowing the statement to be false, (4) which asserted fact was reasonably relied on by the buyer, and (5) induced the buyer to consummate the purchase. The falsehood concerning the "quiet neighbors" is irrelevant because it is only a personal opinion. What is admirable to some is anathema to others. However, the presence or absence of insulation is a question of fact. If the absence of insulation would be obvious to an ordinary layperson, Art would again be out of luck—a buyer cannot close his or her eyes to the obvious and then complain after the sale. But if the presence or absence of insulation is not readily ascertainable, Art may pursue either of two remedies. He may seek to recover the cost to cure the defect as compensatory damages, and he could also seek, and might receive, an additional sum as exemplary or punitive damages because of C.J.'s intentional deception or fraud.* Alternatively, Art may rescind the purchase, giving the house back to C.J., and receive reimbursement for his down payment and other monies expended in the purchase.

Here are some examples of statements of personal opinion, often exaggerated, that a seller may make without fear of either liability for damages or a rescission:

- "This house is really worth much more."
- "This is the finest home in the area."
- "This is the best-constructed home you will ever live in."
- "Taxes will never go up in this neighborhood."
- "The value of this house will increase 5 percent per year."

If false, statements such as the following may justify a rescission or action for damages:

- "A new roof was installed on this house two years ago."
- "All excess surface water drains off during the rainy season."

---

* Some states, such as Washington, do not authorize the award of punitive damages. Punitive damages are explained more fully in Chapter 5.

- "There are no termites."
- "The foundation was not damaged by the earthquake."

A more difficult question arises when a seller, knowing of some important defect (such as a fractured foundation), simply doesn't say anything to the prospective buyer. No lies are told; important information is simply withheld. In some states, a seller has no duty to speak. The rationale is that the buyer is free to investigate and to inquire—and then the seller's answers must be truthful. But a modern trend has begun in California, where all sellers are required by statute to disclose a great deal of specific information about the property they are offering for sale. The law requires the seller to disclose, in writing and as soon as practicable before close of escrow, information that is either known to or can be ascertained by the seller. For example, one category of disclosure requires a checklist of items on the premises, such as a range, dishwasher, washer/dryer hookup, burglar alarm, and so forth. Another category of disclosure requires notice to the buyer if any of the systems or appliances are not in good working order. Yet another category requires notice of any defects or malfunctions in the roof, ceiling, floor, foundation, driveway, plumbing, sewer/septic system, etc. A final category calls for disclosure of general knowledge the seller has about any easements, absence of a building permit for any additions, a landfill under the house, settling or sliding incidents, flooding or drainage problems, zoning violations, and even neighborhood noise problems. Furthermore, both the seller's agent and any buyer's agent also must inspect the property and report to the prospective buyer any problems they observe. If the seller is negligent or dishonest in making any disclosure that later comes to the buyer's attention, a suit for money damages is authorized by statute. The sale, however, cannot be rescinded (undone).[4]

What If a Homeowner Defaults on Monthly Loan Payments?

Upon default by the buyer, the lender may simply do nothing for a while and give the homeowner extra time to pay, or the lender may start foreclosure proceedings. Both deeds of trust and mortgages contain many promises of the borrower, such as to pay property taxes as they come due, to keep casualty insurance in force, to maintain the property, and to comply with all applicable laws.

A breach of any of these promises or of the promise to make monthly payments is a default for which the lender's basic remedy is foreclosure. Most lenders choose foreclosure by private sale. Under a deed of trust, the trustee, at the request of the beneficiary (lender), begins the private **nonjudicial foreclosure** sale process by recording a document called a **notice of default** with the county recorder. The forthcoming foreclosure sale will be publicized by an advertisement in a local newspaper and a notice posted in the county courthouse.

Before the sale, the homeowner (trustor) may reinstate the loan by paying all delinquent monthly payments as well as late payment charges and the trustee's costs and fees to date. This right of **reinstatement** exists even though the borrower may have agreed in the terms of the promissory note that upon default the entire unpaid balance becomes immediately due and payable.

If the defaulting homeowner does not reinstate (or pay off) the loan, the trustee will conduct a foreclosure sale no sooner than three months (plus several weeks for advertising in the newspaper) from the date the notice of default was recorded. At the sale, the trustee will accept the highest cash bid and convey title to the successful bidder by trustee's deed. The homeowner receives advance notice of the foreclosure sale.

Proceeds of the sale go to the beneficiary to satisfy the homeowner's debt. Any excess, of course, belongs to the homeowner whose home was sold. But if there was any significant potential excess at the time of foreclosure sale, it is unlikely the loan would have been permitted to remain in default.

If the beneficiary is entitled to a deficiency judgment and seeks to obtain one, a **judicial foreclosure** is necessary. Litigation is required and the foreclosure sale is conducted under court supervision or approval. Most lenders prefer nonjudicial foreclosures by private sale because they are quicker, less expensive, and don't require the services of an attorney.

Any deficiency judgment obtained through judicial foreclosure probably would be uncollectible anyway, due to lack of funds or assets of the debtor.

In states where mortgages instead of deeds of trust are involved, only two parties are involved in the transaction: the mortgagor (borrower) and the mortgagee (lender). If the loan is defaulted, the mortgage may be enforced by judicial foreclosure. However, the mortgagor (debtor) typically has a full year after the judicial foreclosure sale during which to redeem the property by paying the balance due on the debt plus added costs and fees. No such right of redemption exists after a private foreclosure sale under a trust deed. Mortgages now typically include a *power of sale,* authorizing a nonjudicial private sale much like foreclosure under a deed of trust. This power eliminates the necessity of court proceedings and terminates the debtor's right of redemption.

Foreclosure by purchase-money mortgage creditors cannot be defeated by state *homestead* laws. Homestead laws are designed to protect the family home (including buildings and land) from subsequent creditors. (Note: homestead laws do not concern the acquisition of land by residence and cultivation from the public lands of the United States.) State homestead laws vary in many details including the scope of protection they afford homeowners.* But the purpose of all homestead laws is to protect the family's principal residence from creditors.

How Does a Homeowner Resell?

The owner of a home that is for sale usually *lists* the property with a real estate brokerage firm.

---

* For example, in California a creditor can cause a forced sale of the family home, but the first net proceeds up to $45,000 (for a married couple) go to the debtor with which a substitute home can be purchased. See California Code of Civil Procedure §§ 704 et. seq. In Florida, on the other hand, no sale can be forced during the lifetime of the debtor, or even following his or her death. See Seiden, Donna L., "An Update on the Legal Chameleon: Florida's Homestead Exemption and Restrictions." 40 *University of Florida Law Review* 919 (1988).

Rupert and Kimberly East signed a standard *exclusive listing* with Acme Real Estate for the sale of their home on specified terms. Shortly thereafter, at a social gathering, they met a couple—the Auburns—who were interested in buying a house similar to the Easts'. The Auburns came by and decided to make an offer to purchase in an amount that was satisfactory to the Easts. Rupert telephoned their agent to cancel the listing because they had found their own buyer. Their sales agent, Sam Saltsman, responded: "Fine, you may mail me a check for the 6 percent commission you owe." Do Mr. and Mrs. East owe a commission even though their sales agent did no work and did not find the buyer?

Yes. The commission is owed. Another variety of listing agreement, called an **exclusive-agency listing**, specifically authorizes owners to find their own buyer and not pay a commission. Such a listing is preferable from the seller's standpoint. Most form listings, however, are *exclusive listings,* which require payment of commission regardless of who finds a buyer, including the owner.

The contract between seller and listing brokerage is completely negotiable. It is an employment contract even though it is referred to usually as a mere "listing." The basic promises made by the property owner in a listing are (1) to authorize the broker, and any agents in his or her employ, to solicit purchasers personally, by **multiple listing** (a book of homes for sale in the area, available to and from all brokers in the area), by advertising and posting "for sale" signs on the premises, and so forth, and (2) to pay a specified commission if the broker finds a purchaser who is ready, willing, and able to purchase at the listed price or any lesser price agreed to by the seller.

The one basic promise made by the broker in the listing is to use diligence in hunting for a purchaser. Agents do not promise to find a buyer, but rather only to seek one. A listing agreement is analogous to a hunting license.

Curiously, real estate agents customarily do not promise to spend any specified amount of money on advertising, but prudent sellers can negotiate for that useful provision. Furthermore, prudent sellers will examine carefully the listing agreement form offered by the hopeful agent. Most, if not all such forms, contain many paragraphs of promises by the owner with only one small sentence containing but one promise by the agent, and that customarily is simply to use diligence in seeking a buyer. It is difficult, if not impossible, to prove in court that an incompetent agent failed to "use due diligence" in hunting for a buyer.

If the broker finds a purchaser willing to buy at a price lower than the listed price, and the owners accept the offer, they may not then refuse to pay a commission because the broker failed to find a buyer ready, willing, and able to buy at the listed price. Acceptance of the lower price effectively amends the listing (or employment contract) to provide for a commission based on the actual sales price. Indeed, the only reason to include a listing price in the listing agreement is to provide a measure of damages the agent might obtain if the seller should withdraw the residence from the market before any offer is accepted.

Before hiring a real estate broker to sell your home, you should negotiate for some, if not all, of the following provisions:

● A specified advertising budget, to be paid by the agent. Your Sunday newspaper carries many real estate advertisements, because they are effective. Make sure an ad for your house will appear there.

● The right to pay no commission if you find your own buyer. Often a potential buyer may be transferring to your workplace, or surface through recommendations of your friends and acquaintances.

● A short listing period, perhaps as few as 30 days with the understanding it will be extended in 30-day increments if the agent is satisfactorily "pushing" the property.

● A reduced commission, perhaps 5 or even 4 percent, if the property is readily salable and market conditions are good. Always calculate what percentage of your *equity* a 6 (or other) percent commission of the *sales price* represents.

● A list of all repairs thought necessary to put the house in condition for sale. Also, obtain advice with regard to what disclosures about the condition of the house you will need to make in contracting with a buyer.

● Restrictions on when agents and their prospects will be permitted to enter the house, especially if you are still residing there.

In addition to negotiation, at the same time you should fully discuss each of the following matters with prospective brokers:

● Will the house be multiple listed? If multiple listing is agreed on, it should begin immediately to quickly disclose to sales agents in the community that the property is on the market.

● How and when will the house be shown to potential buyers by all other agents? You will not want to have agents arriving at unexpected times during your daily routine.

● Obtaining a *written* estimate of the highest possible market value.

● Getting a *written* estimate of the absolutely lowest price you should consider accepting. This will be useful later when your agent begins bringing you offers to consider, and what dollar amount counteroffers you should make. There is no need to disclose to your agent the actual lowest price you would accept, or any other information that might suggest you have an urgent need to sell.

● Receiving a *written* estimate of the net cash proceeds from escrow, assuming various sales prices. This will avoid any surprises from exaggerated expectations concerning how much cash you ultimately will receive.

● Obtaining a list of all comparable homes sold in your area within the last 12 months, and identification of which ones were handled by the subject brokerage firm. Agents tend to specialize by geographic area (their "farm"), and those agents successfully working your area probably will get better results sooner than agents who customarily farm (or work) other areas.

● How will the commission be divided? If your property becomes multiple listed, the commission you pay the broker you hired may be shared with some other brokerage firm whose sales agent actually finds a buyer. The sales agents will receive approximately 50 percent of the amount received by his or her broker, so the commission you pay often is split four ways. Be aware of who receives the compensation you are paying.

● Will the seller be permitted to hold any earnest money deposit received? If not, why not? If it is deposited in an escrow or trustee account, it will be difficult for the seller to obtain if the sale is not consummated. And will the earnest money deposit be restricted to a certified check or money order? If not, why not? How will the earnest money deposit be divided if the prospective buyer defaults (backs out) before escrow closes?

● How much effort will the agent signing the listing personally expend? Will your agent accompany potential buyers or simply send them by? Will your agent qualify each and every prospect to make sure they are financially able to buy your home, or are simply "tire kickers?"

● Is an immediate termite inspection advisable? If major repairs need to be made, shouldn't you know that before signing a contract obligating you to sell? If not, why not?

● What are the current terms of financing available for a buyer of your home? Should you be offering an assumption and carryback of some of the unpaid balance? If financing is not available for the probable buyers of your home, should you consider a lease-option and make a quick deal? What do you owe your agent if you make a lease-option during the listing period?

● Is it really necessary to conduct an open house? (Many agents conduct open houses primarily to obtain listings from other persons in the neighborhood who may be considering selling.)

● Precisely what does the broker intend to do, step by step, in diligently hunting for a buyer? Where will ads be placed, and how often? Does your broker exchange referrals with other brokers nationwide? Are new employment centers opening that may provide clues about potential buyers moving into your area?

A candid discussion of the above topics with the prospective listing agent ought to illuminate many areas of potential misunderstanding. You are free to modify the terms of the proferred listing agreement in any manner agreed on. Everything is negotiable!

Selling Your Home Yourself

Some homeowners desire to sell their home without using an agent, in order to avoid paying the negotiable sales commission. If a home sells for $150,000 and there is a mortgage outstanding with an unpaid balance of $130,000, the owner's equity is $20,000. A 6 percent commission equals $9,000 (.06 × $150,000), which equals 45 percent of the owner's equity ($9,000 ÷ $20,000). For this reason, some homeowners do not hire sales agents.

Sellers who do not utilize agents are referred to as *FSBOs* ("for sale by owner," pronounced somewhat disrespectfully as "fizzbo").

Most sellers can arrange for effective advertising simply by consulting with specialists at the local newspaper. Once a buyer is obtained, all the paperwork necessary (escrow instructions) can be accomplished by the title company or escrow company that is selected to close the escrow. A formal sales contract is not essential. Once the escrow instructions are prepared and signed, they constitute a legally binding contract.

Pending preparation of the escrow instructions and before they are signed, the parties should hire an attorney to prepare a purchase agreement, if they want one. Generally it is in the seller's interest *not* to have such a contract, because the seller then can continue to receive offers that might be higher or more favorable. In short, the seller's property is not technically "off the market" until a contract is signed. Signed purchase agreements protect buyers and agents more than sellers.

Problems face FSBOs in preparing their properties for sale, in determining the highest price they might receive, in dealing face-to-face with buyers who expect to benefit from dickering about the price, in separating qualified buyers from "lookers," and in retaining confidence in their ability to handle the sale in the face of many licensed agents who may contact them attempting to obtain a listing. But the problems can be solved and the benefits to the seller can be substantial, especially in a seller's market (i.e., where the demand for homes exceeds the available supply, and properties offered for sale are promptly sold).

A FSBO can pass along some of the commission savings to his or her buyer (e.g., through price reduction, or inclusion of items of personal property), thereby making the deal especially attractive.

How May Title to Your Home Be Held?

Title may be held (1) by one person, which is termed **in severalty,** (2) by two or more persons (co-owners) as **tenants-in-common**, (3) by two or more persons (co-owners) as **joint tenants** *with right of survivorship,* or (4) by two or more persons (co-owners) as *partnership* property. About half the states permit a variation of joint tenancy between husband and wife called **tenancy by the entireties**. Nine states, (Arizona, California, Idaho, Louisiana, Nevada, New Mexico, Texas, Washington and Wisconsin) have community property, a variation of co-ownership by a married couple.

When two or more persons decide to purchase a residence, a decision must be made as to the legal form of joint ownership to be used.

Mr. and Mrs. Robert Ramirez were buying their first home. Just before close of escrow, they were advised by their real estate agent to take title in joint tenancy.* Should they do so? What alternatives should they consider?

Owning a home in joint tenancy is a common form of ownership by married couples. Upon the death of one joint tenant, transfer of ownership to the survivor is expedient because the property need not go through probate. Joint tenancy property cannot, however, be affected by a will, and may be vulnerable to death tax problems in large estates.

In some states, Mr. and Mrs. Ramirez would probably take title as tenants by the entireties, with essentially the same effect as if they were joint tenants. In any of the nine states where available, they might consider taking title as community property, so that each spouse's share could be disposed of by will, if so desired.

---

* This advice is dangerously close to constituting the unauthorized practice of law. A more prudent agent would provide his or her client with published materials generally describing the alternatives available and add that they should obtain any further advice from an attorney.

Community property ownership also offers income tax advantages to the surviving spouse when his or her highly appreciated house is sold. In one community property state, Washington, law requires that married couples own their home as community property.

If two or more unrelated persons decide to pool their resources in order to improve their quality of life by purchasing a home, they would, no doubt, prefer to retain the right to individually will their undivided interests to relatives or loved ones. They would accordingly select the tenancy-in-common form of home ownership.

Jinna Roberts and Kathy Jennings, unrelated, owned Sky-High Ranch as joint tenants. Upon learning that their respective interests would go to the survivor regardless of any will, they decided to change their ownership form. May they do so?

Yes. Jinna and Kathy can simply **deed** the property to themselves as tenants-in-common. Then both may will their respective shares or 50 percent interests. If either should die without leaving a will, the decedent's undivided one-half interest would go to her closest surviving heirs. Such surviving heirs would automatically become tenants-in-common with the surviving co-owner.

Typically, a **quitclaim deed** is used to change the way title is held. It is a deed by which the grantor, or transferor, of real estate merely gives up any claim he or she may have to the property. The grantor makes no promises or warranties to the grantee, or transferee, about the condition of the property or quality of title. The quitclaim deed is appropriate when land is transferred by gift or to clear some possible "cloud on title" that might otherwise be the basis for a later lawsuit.

In contrast to a quitclaim deed, a **warranty deed** is used for transfers of real property by sale. By its use, the grantor impliedly makes certain covenants or promises:

1. The grantor has full ownership of the exact interest being conveyed.
2. The property is free of liens or claims of third persons except as revealed.
3. The title will not be challenged by third persons.
4. The grantor will execute any further documents that may be required to perfect the grantee's title.

In states where title insurance policies provide considerable assurance that there will be no surprises found in the official records, the simple **grant deed** is commonly used. By use of the word "grant," the grantor (seller) impliedly warrants that (1) he or she has not previously conveyed the property to someone else, and (2) the estate (ownership) conveyed is free from prior encumbrances by the grantor, unless noted.

Married persons can change the form of ownership of property held as community property to tenancy-in-common or joint tenancy, or vice versa, by deed. Under some circumstances, courts have held that even though held in joint tenancy or in severalty by one spouse, the husband and wife actually intended to and did hold the property as community property. The result of such a ruling is a favorable tax advantage, in that surviving owners of community property pay considerably less income tax on any future sale than do surviving joint tenants.

 Paul Gerb made an appointment with his attorney, Sid Lifkin, to discuss an estate plan. Among other things, Paul desired that, should his wife survive him, the family residence (which was his separate property owned in severalty) would be available for her use as long as she lived. But he did not want his daughter, Melody, to get the house upon his wife's death. He felt that if he simply left the home to his wife, Melody would ultimately receive the property. Will Sid be able to solve Paul's problem?

Yes. Sid can advise Paul that the house may be left to his wife for her use only so long as she lives; thereafter, it would be automatically transferred to someone else designated by Paul in his will. A person whose interest in property lasts only as long as he or she lives is said to be a *life tenant,* the owner of a **life estate.** After Paul dies, his wife would be powerless to prevent ownership of the home from going to the person named in his will. The person who will ultimately receive the property is called a **remainderman**.

It is possible to have successive life tenancies, and tax advantages may be obtained with this type of ownership. The life tenant has all the rights and duties incident to exclusive possession of the property; however, the life tenant may not injure the interest of the remainderman by committing waste (unreasonable or destructive use of the property) or by failing to pay property taxes.

Remaindermen are free to sell their future interest to whomever they please, and its market value would be a function of both the current market value of the property and the life expectancy of the life tenant.

What Is Fire Insurance?

A private home is the costliest single asset the typical adult couple or single person is ever likely to acquire. The greatest hazard both buyer and lender face is the possibility that a fire may break out and damage or completely destroy the building and contents. To protect their respective interests, both lender and buyer generally agree that the latter shall purchase appropriate fire insurance. The insurance policy in most common use is the dwelling buildings and contents basic form. This basic policy can be supplemented by appropriate clauses called *endorsements,* and by standardized printed forms that legally prescribe, and sometimes expand, the scope of protection provided. Finally, the individual policy may be modified by additions or amendments called *riders* (usually typewritten and pasted to the policy). Essentially, the basic policy covers (1) the dwelling, together with equipment and fixtures, such as heating and air conditioning equipment, and (2) the contents, including furniture, clothing, and other household goods. Many additional coverages are available for an added premium, such as damages from a windstorm, from hail, from an explosion, or from any object falling from a plane.

You should not try to insure everything against all risks—it simply cannot be done. Besides, in the process of trying, you may become "insurance poor," with so much costly coverage against a variety of hazards that you and your dependents suffer a serious reduction in your standard of living.

How May Homeowners and Renters Protect Their Belongings?

Homeowner's insurance is available to protect against the loss of personal property (as by theft) and against personal liability for civil (tort) losses. (Tort losses were explained fully in Chapter 5.)

A renter is generally not concerned about loss caused by damage or destruction of the dwelling place, but there is a risk of fire and other perils to personal belongings, possibly including furniture. To meet this need a tenant may purchase a standard fire policy with what is known as the *tenant's personal property form.* Other tenants' policies are available to cover losses similar to homeowners' potential losses.

Case 13

U.S. v. PREMISES KNOWN AS 3639 2D STREET, N.E., MINNEAPOLIS, MINNESOTA

United States Court of Appeals, 8th Circuit, 869 F.2D 1093 (1989)

David Freeman owned a home in Minneapolis, Minnesota. On February 7, 1985, Anthony Bruzek dropped by and purchased two ounces of cocaine. Bruzek made an $1,800 down payment and left for a prearranged meeting with Stan Johnson, who wanted to buy the cocaine. When Bruzek made the sale he discovered that Stan Johnson was an undercover officer. Upon his arrest, Bruzek revealed that he had acquired the cocaine from Freeman, who then was promptly arrested. Freeman pleaded guilty to a narcotics violation and was sentenced to two years in prison.

The U.S. government then sought to acquire ownership of Freeman's home through forfeiture proceedings. The U.S. district court held that forfeiture was not appropriate because the

home was not substantially connected to illegal drug activity. On appeal, the U.S. Court of Appeals held that forefeiture of Freeman's home was valid.

Senior Circuit Judge Ross: Bruzek's affidavit showed that he had gone to Freeman's house several times and met Freeman in the garage, discussing future drug deals of larger amounts of cocaine and once receiving a couple of "lines" of cocaine for his personal use. Freeman testified that he had never before used his home to facilitate drug purchases or sales, and that the small quantities of drugs and paraphernalia in his home were for his own use. The district court concluded that the government had not shown that the house had been used in "any continuing drug business" or was "an integral part of an illegal drug operation."

We cannot agree with the district court that forfeiture of the house would be outside the spirit or intent of the law, and we find no requirement of a continuing drug business or ongoing operation. Rather, we believe that if persons make real property available as a situs [place] for an illegal drug transaction, it is forfeitable. [W]e find the proportionality between the value of the forfeitable property and the severity of the injury inflicted by its use to be irrelevant.

When forfeiture of a home occurs under the drug laws, pre-existing claims against the property (such as mortgages) are not affected, that is, they are paid from the proceeds of the forced sale. But net proceeds following sale of forfeited assets are not credited against any fine imposed on the defendant, nor are any of the net proceeds payable directly to the defendant.

QUESTIONS AND PROBLEMS

1. What is the amount of the standard real estate commission charged by brokerage firms in your community? Is the commission rate negotiable? Express the dollar amount of an average commission as a percentage of the typical amount of equity a seller might have in the home being sold.

2. What specific services are rendered to a homeowner by a licensed real estate agent who has a listing on the property?

3. What questions should you ask the seller, or the seller's agent, before you buy a house to live in?

4. Do income tax laws indirectly subsidize the private home owner? Explain, and compare the tax treatment given tenants.

5. If you were selling your home and a prospective buyer suggested use of a land contract with only a $1,000 down payment, what factors would you take into consideration?

6. If you were applying for a loan at a savings and loan association for the purpose of buying a home, which three of the following factors would be the most important to you?
  a. A relatively low interest rate.
  b. A relatively long repayment term.
  c. The right to prepay principal payments without penalty.

  d. A relatively low penalty for late payments.
  e. The right to have someone else assume your loan without an assumption fee or increase in the interest rate.
  f. The absence of any requirement that you pay the lender's attorney fees upon any default.
  g. The absence of an acceleration clause that otherwise would make the entire unpaid balance due upon any default.

7. As a prospective buyer of your first home, what disadvantages would there be in leasing with an option to buy?

8. Would you prefer to finance the purchase of your home with a fixed rate mortgage, or a variable rate mortgage that begins with an interest rate one full percentage point lower than the first alternative? Why?

9. Would you prefer to own a single-family detached home or a condominium? What are your perceptions of the advantages and disadvantages of each?

10. What is the primary reason you hope to be a homeowner in the future? If for some reason there was to be no future appreciation in residential property, would you still prefer to be a homeowner? Explain.

FURTHER READING

1. Abrams, Kathleen S. and Laurence F. *Successful Landlording*. Farmington Michigan: Structures Publishing Company 1980.

2. Barton, Stephen E. and Carol J. Silverman, *Homeownership in the Common-Interest Development*. Berkeley, Ca: Institute of Urban and Regional Development, U.C. Berkeley, 1987.

3. Burns, Leland S. *The Social and Political Importance of Home Ownership*. Los Angeles: School of Architecture and Urban Planning, U.C.L.A., 1988.

4. DeHeer, Robert. *Realty Bluebook I,* San Rafael, California: Professional Publishing Corporation 1991. Practical information relating to the business of buying and selling homes. Especially useful for future real estate sales brokers and agents.

5. Freyfogle, Eric T. "The Installment Land Contract as Lease: Habitability Protections and the Low-Income Purchaser." 62 *New York Law Review* 293 (1987). A review of the impact of the implied warranty of habitability on landlords and tenants, with an argument that the same protection should be extended to buyers under installment land contracts.

6. Karn, Valerie A., J. Kemeny, and P. Williams. *Home Ownership in the Inner City: Salvation or Despair?* Brookfield, Vermont: Gower 1985.

7. Peach, Richard W. "The Investment Returns to Homeownership." *Mortgage Banking,* vol. 49, no. 1 (October 1988).

8. Poliakoff, Gary A. *The Law of Condominium Operations*. Deerfield, Illinois: Callaghan 1988.

9. Saunders, Peter R. *A Nation of Home Owners*. Boston: Unwin Hyman, 1990.

NOTES

1. Condominium and Cooperative Abuse Relief Act, 75 U.S.C. §§ 3601–3616 (1982).

2. *San Francisco Examiner,* January 7, 1990.

3. *Skendzel* v. *Marshall,* 301 N.E.2d 641 (Indiana, 1973). A leading case on protecting the buyer under an installment land contract.

4. California Civil Code, § 1102 et. seq.

CHAPTER 14

Wills, Trusts, and Probate

Time spent planning for one's death is not pleasurable. Most of us avoid the subject as long as possible. Although the legal concerns of this chapter are usually discussed in reference to death, they do also apply to life. Preservation of a family's assets at the death of a spouse is one example where advance planning is extremely important.

As often mentioned in this book, there are times when most of us need the professional services of a lawyer. Issues raised when considering one's inevitable death may require the assistance of a qualified attorney at law.

What Is Estate Planning?

Estate planning refers to the systematic analysis of present and prospective financial assets and liabilities of an individual (or married couple), to maximize enjoyment of assets while a person lives and to minimize normal shrinkage of family wealth from death, taxes and administrative expense when he or she dies. This is a plan for the best use of your money during your life, and appropriate and effective distribution after death. *Financial planning* is a similar but more restrictive term, because it might not include arrangements for the disposition of property upon death.

Estate plans generally include the following three major objectives (and might include the fourth):

1. To provide for the economic needs of the planner while alive. (If married, the day-to-day needs of the spouse and other dependents are also a primary concern.)
2. To reflect the desires of the planner in generously providing for deserving beneficiaries or excluding any beneficiaries believed to be unworthy.

425

3. To minimize or legitimately avoid income taxes payable while the planner is alive, and those payable by beneficiaries following the planner's death. Estate and inheritance taxes (**death taxes**) also should be minimized upon death.

4. To avoid or minimize the delays, costs, and publicity of probate (the process of proving the validity of a will in court, coupled with administering the decedent's estate).

Even for persons of modest wealth and income, the importance of proper estate planning cannot be overstated. Such planning involves investment strategies, saving for the purchase of major assets, borrowing, and retirement planning. All aspects of estate planning have legal consequences, but the focus of this discussion is on elements of estate planning involving the transfer of property to others before or after death, and trusts and wills as they relate to probate.

What Tax Burdens Is the Estate Planner Trying to Reduce or Avoid?

The federal government imposes an **estate tax** based on the total value of **assets** exceeding an exempt amount. This is a progressive tax on the privilege of giving property to others upon death. Some state governments also impose estate taxes; states are, however, more likely to impose an **inheritance tax** than an estate tax. An inheritance tax is a tax on the privilege of receiving property from the estate of a decedent; it is paid by the individual recipient of a gift from a deceased person.

Inheritance tax rates vary depending on the relationship of the recipient to the decedent (spouses and close relatives pay less than friends) as well as on the value of the **bequest** (gift of personal property) or **devise** (gift of real property) received. Many states, including California and Washington, have no death taxes. It is impractical to present the schedules of state death taxes here; they vary widely and are subject to constant change. The interested reader may obtain a tax schedule from his or her state taxing office.

In 1981 and 1986, federal tax law as it relates to estate planning changed dramatically. Among the 1981 changes was the creation of a *unified estate and gift tax*.[1] This tax system combines for tax purposes the total of gifts made during the donor's life as well as any property transferred at death. Taxes are then levied on the total value of these gifts, after deduction of a *unified credit* or exemption. The credit allows a transfer totalling $600,000 in property before the individual's estate is taxed. (The exemption is really a tax credit in the amount of $192,800—the amount that would be due on an estate valued at $600,000.)[2]

Some gifts are totally exempt from tax. An individual may make annual tax-free gifts of up to $10,000 to each of any number of donees. A husband and wife may give up to $20,000 in total. An exempt gift may be given *in addition* to the $600,000 unified credit.

Once $600,000 is transferred by gift or will, the estate tax is imposed. It begins at 37 percent of the gift and increases to a maximum of 55 percent. Most modest estates may be distributed to **donees** (recipients of gifts) tax free. More substantial estates are heavily taxed, unless appropriate advance tax planning reduces this burden (see Table 14–1). Probably the most effective ways to accomplish the goal of legal tax avoidance (both income and estate) are through varieties of exempt gifts, trusts, and wills. The most common type of tax-reduction trusts are marital and generation-skipping trusts, both of which are described later in this chapter.

Some popular methods of transferring valuable property to avoid estate and gift taxes and income taxes were made less attractive by the so-called Tax Reform Act of 1986. Tax laws always affect behavior. Often government purposely encourages certain conduct through particular tax laws (e.g., home ownership is encouraged because of the deductibility from taxable income of both property taxes on the home and interest paid on real estate loans incurred to buy the home). Tax laws also stimulate the creative energies of tax advisors who seek ways to reduce tax burdens for their clients. Not all such behavior is desired by those who draft tax laws. The result is that every few years tax laws are amended to encourage some behaviors and discourage others.* It is an oft-repeated ritual.

The Tax Reform Act of 1986 focused on discouraging certain behavior. A positive result of this law is it emphasized the truism that it seldom makes sense for a person to make a financial decision for strictly tax avoidance reasons. If your tax

TABLE 14–1   Unified Federal Estate Tax Rate Schedule

Column A	Column B	Column C	Column D
Net Taxable Estate Over	Net Taxable Estate Not Over	Tax on amount in Column A	Rate of tax on Excess Over Amount in Column A Percent
0	$ 10,000	0	18%
$ 10,000	20,000	$ 1,800	20
20,000	40,000	3,800	22
40,000	60,000	8,200	24
60,000	80,000	13,000	26
80,000	100,000	18,200	28
100,000	150,000	23,800	30
150,000	250,000	38,800	32
250,000	500,000	70,800	34
500,000	750,000	155,800	37
750,000	1,000,000	248,300	39
1,000,000	1,250,000	345,800	41
1,250,000	1,500,000	448,300	43
1,500,000	2,000,000	555,800	45
2,000,000	2,500,000	780,800	49
2,500,000	3,000,000	1,025,800	53
3,000,000	infinity		55

---

* One such loophole (legal method to avoid taxes that was not planned by legislators) was the transfer of property to children through an irrevocable but temporary trust, called a Clifford Trust. The transfer was irrevocable for at least ten years, during which time the income belonged to the child and was the child's taxable income (at a much lower rate). After ten years, the property would return to the donor. The Tax Reform Act of 1986 closed this loophole by taxing income from a Clifford Trust to a child under 14 at the same rate as the donor would be taxed.

advisor suggests an idea that is not a good investment or sound decision except for tax reasons, change tax advisors. Investments made in recent years only to reduce taxes have often resulted in a lost investment and extensive tax liability.* Tax reduction or avoidance is but one of many things to consider in estate and income planning. If an investment is financially sound, changes in tax law will not ruin its value; if it is not sound, it may become worthless regardless of tax savings.

Concerning Wills

What Is a Will?

A **will** is the legal expression of a person's wishes for the disposition of his or her property, effective upon death. The author of a will is the **testator**. Recipients of gifts under the will are **beneficiaries.** The will is a conditional document; it has no present or immediate legal effect. It becomes operative if it has not been revoked before the testator's death—it "speaks upon the author's death." If the testator destroys it or supersedes it with another will, it ceases to have legal authority. This conditional nature makes a will a unique document, and adds importance to its authentication upon death of the testator. For example, what if a decedent (testator) had crossed out a copy of his or her will, marking it "canceled and revoked," but had failed to make the notation on the original? Wills are very powerful, yet tentative. The testator should take care to make clear what truly are his or her last wishes as to the deposition of his or her property.

A well-drafted will can provide many advantages:

1. Property is distributed as the testator wishes. Some beneficiaries get more, some less. Specific assets, such as family jewelry, go to specified donees (beneficiaries).

2. Gifts may be made to charities, to distant relatives, to friends, or to faithful employees.

3. The possibility of a disaster that kills both husband and wife, and possibly one or more children, can be anticipated and accommodated. Although unlikely, this is a real danger with high-speed automobiles and air travel. If not provided for, there may be multiple costly, tax-burdened probates. (Probates for each decedent may be required when couples or family members die in close succession over a period of days or weeks from injuries sustained in a common calamity.)

4. Death taxes may be avoided or reduced, by taking the *marital deduction* (deduction allowed a surviving spouse) or by creating or funding trusts.

---

* In 1989, thousands of California teachers faced loss of more than $100 million invested in limited partnerships run by Teacher's Management and Investment Corporation (TMI). For two decades profits had been made, but the Tax Reform Act of 1986 eliminated "tax shelter" advantages that had been the foundation of TMI's success (*San Francisco Chronicle*, November 21, 1989).

5. Confusion is minimized as specific property owned by the testator is identified, as are the correct names of beneficiaries. Also minimized, is the possibility of lawsuits among contending claimants, a costly drain of estate assets.

6. The testator may nominate appropriate guardian(s) for minor children and their estates. Nominations are generally honored, but the welfare of the child (or children) is the dominating concern of the court. If a natural parent survives, this problem does not arise. If there is no nomination the court makes the appointment.

7. A personal representative (**executor**) may be selected to handle the estate. Otherwise, the probate court must name an **administrator.** A statutory commission, or fee, is payable to the personal representative. In simple estates, this fee can be kept in the family; in complex estates, a bank or trust company may be designated as executor, or as co-executor with a member of the family.

8. If a will does not waive it, a **fidelity bond** is required. A fidelity bond insures against losses caused by a faithless performance of duties by the personal representative (and a guardian, if any is named). (While this provides added protection, it is an expense to the estate.)

9. The will may direct the executor to pay inheritance taxes, as well as estate taxes, from the residual property (property not specifically identified and given to a beneficiary) of the estate. Therefore, assuming sufficient assets, gifts to named beneficiaries will not be reduced by taxes.

10. The will can give funeral instructions, although this can and should also be done in a letter of "last instructions" separate from the will.

Ideally, a personal or family balance sheet, listing assets and liabilities, should accompany a will and be updated periodically. A **letter of last instructions**, as mentioned earlier, should also be prepared. This letter is not binding on the executor, but it is helpful in disclosing the location of assets and liabilities. It can indicate how the testator would like details requiring immediate attention to be handled. Note that "letters" of last instructions, or even explanations for survivors, can be prepared by the testator in many ways: in writing, on an audio recording, or even via a video recording. These instructions are not legally binding, but merely explanatory in nature.

What Types of Wills Are Valid?

Dave Decker decided to make a will entirely in his own handwriting. He was sure a person could validly make such a will. He carefully wrote on a blank sheet of paper, "I give all I own to Dora." He signed and dated the paper. As an afterthought, he took the document to his office and asked his friend, Art Bamish, to sign and date his paper as a witness for him. Is the document a valid will?

No. Although in many states a person may prepare a valid will without witnesses, in one's own handwriting, signed and dated by oneself, Dave has probably failed in his attempt. Why? Dave had a wife and daughter, both named Dora, and the probate court will be unsure to whom he intended to leave his property. The gift will fail because of the uncertainty as to who is the beneficiary under the will—the ambiguity will invalidate the will.*

Even if it was proved that Dave meant his wife Dora, the will would be modified by law because he failed to mention his daughter in the will. **Pretermitted heir statutes**, existing in most states, give to a testator's child (or grandchild if the child is dead and there is a grandchild) a statutory share of the testator's property. This share supersedes the will if the child was not otherwise provided for (as by some settlement or gift of an equal share of property to the child as an advancement while the testator still lived) or was not expressly excluded from the will. If a parent testator wishes to ignore a child in his or her will, it must be made clear that the omission was intentional. A parent may give a child little or nothing, but must do so expressly. If a child is not mentioned, the assumption is the omission was inadvertent and not intended.

Usual requirements for a will are capacity, intent, that it be in writing, a signature, attestation, and publication. Sufficient capacity exists if the testator is both an adult and of sound mind. The required intent is the purpose and free will to dispose of one's property upon death through the will. The requirement of the will's being in writing varies, as discussed later in the chapter. The will must be signed by the testator. A formal will must be witnessed (attested) by competent witnesses (having capacity without a personal interest in the will) and, in some states, declared by the testator (publication) to be a will. What is a legal will varies state by state, and strict adherence to local statutes must be followed. The general purpose of state laws governing the making of a will is to prevent fraud or mistakes in carrying out the decedent's intentions. A will that is valid where it was created continues to be valid even if a person moves to and dies in another state.

Three types of wills are generally recognized as valid: *formal* (or *witnessed*) *written wills, informal* (or *holographic unwitnessed written wills*), and *nuncupative* or *oral wills.*

Formal Witnessed Will   The **formal witnessed will** is usually prepared by a lawyer and is generally typewritten or done on a word processor. It must be signed at the end (subscribed) by the testator. The subscription must be made in the presence of two witnesses, or in their presence the testator must acknowledge it to have been previously made by him or her or under his or her direction. Four states—Maine, New Hampshire, South Carolina, and Vermont—require three witnesses. Thus, in the hypothetical case, Dave Decker failed to prepare a valid formal will because he had only one witness.

The testator must declare to the witnesses when he or she subscribes (or acknowledges) that it is his or her will, and ask that they serve as witnesses. Again Dave made a mistake, because he did not tell Art Bamish that the document was his will, nor did he sign or acknowledge his signature in Bamish's presence. Finally, witnesses must sign in the testator's presence. Some states also require they sign in the presence of each other.

---

* Once invalidated, state laws provide a *statutory will* for the testator, more formally called *statutes of succession.* Under such statutes, both wife and daughter would share in Decker's estate in a specified proportion.

Will formalities are strictly enforced by probate courts and provide added assurance of validity. After all, the testator is dead when the will "speaks," and not able to challenge fraudulent claims. If witnesses are also dead at that time and cannot supply appropriate affidavits (sworn statements in writing), their hand-writing on the will may be authenticated by other means. This complication is usually avoided by using witnesses that are younger than the testator.

The testator must be of sound mind—he or she must understand the nature of a will; the nature and extent of property owned, at least in general terms; and the nature of relationships to relatives and friends who are "the natural objects of one's bounty." The testator must be sane at execution of the will, but note that illiteracy or physical or mental infirmity caused by old age (such as senility) do not necessarily prevent making a valid will. Where there is physical or mental infirmity, it is advisable to have as one witness a medical doctor who will be able to testify that the condition did not affect the soundness of the testator's mind at the execution of the will. In most states, the testator must be an adult.

Michael Taylor signed a new will three days before he died of AIDS. The new will left most of his 3.5 million estate to a charitable trust for the decorative arts. The next largest gift was to his companion, who was to receive property worth about $400,000. His 87-year-old mother challenged the will. What should have been the result?

A San Francisco superior court jury held that Michael, in a weakened condition in the final days of his illness, was subjected to undue influence by his companion. He lacked the freedom of will necessary to express his intent and the will was declared invalid.[3]

Many will signings are videotaped to provide proof that the ritual was correctly followed and as additional proof of the demeanor of the testator. These tapes have been used effectively to counter will contests.[4]

One type of formal will is a **statutory will,** a form will with blanks to be completed by the testator. Statutory wills have been in existence only since 1983 and are currently authorized in only four states.* Introduction of such wills has proven to be very popular. In California alone, the state bar has distributed more than a half million statutory will forms in six years.[5] Statutory wills were devised to provide for the simple and usual circumstances of persons who may otherwise die **intestate** (without a will). Statutes authorizing such wills commonly provide that no changes to the form will are permitted. Although it appears that many of these wills have been created, few have been admitted to probate (accepted by the courts as an authentic and proper will). Preliminary reports show although the wills were created to be very simple, about half of them have been denied admission to probate because they were improperly completed.[6] It is too early to assess the overall usefulness of the statutory will form.

---

* The first statutory will was adopted in California in 1983, Probate Code § 6200. The other three states that have adopted such wills are Wisconsin, Michigan, and Maine.

Holographic Unwitnessed Will A **holographic will** is a variety of self-prepared will. In general, it is a will written, signed, and dated with a complete date, all entirely in the handwriting of the testator. Fewer than half the states recognize this type of will.

In most states that provide for a holographic will, requirements must be precisely followed. A major objection to the holographic will is the absence of witnesses. Probate courts are concerned, among other things, with forgery and undue influence. As these wills are not witnessed, there is little protection against forgery or undue influence. Many attempted holographic wills are held invalid because the will was partially typed (thus not entirely in the handwriting of the testator) or not dated.

A few states, such as California, have liberalized the requirements for a holographic will, allowing typed or printed provisions if the ". . . signature and the material provisions are in the handwriting of the testator."[7] Even where holographic wills are legally acceptable, preparing one is questionable. Most people are not careful communicators and may fail to express their intentions properly. They also may fail to take advantage of readily available techniques to minimize estate costs. If a person insists on proceeding without legal advice, a self-help book with a standard-form will is a better option.

> [An] individual, trying to avoid leaving anything to her daughter (a drug addict) carefully specified each piece of property in her will and which heir was to receive it. However, after writing her will, she received a large inheritance from her father. Because the inheritance was not listed in her will, under the intestacy laws of the state of Texas, the inheritance passed to her daughter—clearly not her intent. These are . . . horror stories I have come across that could have been prevented if the people involved had consulted an attorney rather than written their wills.
>
> Daniel Palmer, Attorney at Law, Texas[8]

Oral or Nuncupative Will An *oral (nuncupative) will* is of limited importance. A **nuncupative will** may be created without many of the formalities required of a formal will. It can only be created when the testator is in fear of imminent death (e.g., an accident victim with fatal injuries). Under a representative statute, two persons must hear the orally expressed intentions. One or the other must be asked by the testator at the time to bear witness that the statement was a will. One witness must reduce the statement to writing within 30 days, and the writing must be offered in court within six months after the words were spoken. Most states limit the property that a testator may dispose of in this manner to only personal property of no more than a small designated sum (usually $1,000). Because of the limitations and special requirements, nuncupative wills are not common or very important.

Thirty states recognize a *soldier's and seaman's will,* another oral or sometimes written will that does not need to conform to usual rules of execution. Persons in uniform, especially in time of war, may face great dangers of sudden death, yet they may have special difficulty in preparing a will. As with other nuncupative wills, statutes limit the amount and type of property that may be transferred to personal property valued at no more than $1,000.

What Happens to the Estate of a Person Who Dies Without Leaving a Will?

If there is no will or if a will is rejected because it is defective, the estate is distributed under state law of **intestacy** (that is, without a testament or last will). This procedure may accomplish what the decedent would have wanted. Table 14–2 shows a typical pattern of intestate distribution of property (in this case, in California).*

---

* It should be noted that California is a community property state. All community property goes to the surviving spouse if there is no will. If there is a will, the decedent may dispose of his or her 50 percent share as desired. Separate property would be distributed according to Table 14–2.

TABLE 14–2   Intestate Distribution of Property under California Law[1]

		ESTATE GOES AS INDICATED TO SURVIVNG				
Deceased	Survived by	Spouse	Parent(s)	Child(ren)	Brothers or sisters	Next of Kin
Husband or wife[2]	No descendants, parents, brothers, sisters, or their descendents	All property				
	One child	1/2		1/2[3]		
	Two or more children	1/3		2/3 (divided among them)[3]		
	Parents only	1/2	1/4 to each (or 1/2 if only one surviving)			
	Brothers and sisters only	1/2			1/2 (divided among them)[4]	
Widow, widower, single person	Parents only		1/2 to each (or all if only one surviving)			
	Brothers and sisters only				All property[4]	
	No descendants, parents, brothers, sisters, or their descendants					All property
Widow or widower	Child or children			All property (divided equally among them)[3]		

[1] California Probate Code, § 220–230.
[2] If there is no will, all community property goes to the surviving spouse.
[3] Descendants of a deceased child take his or her share.
[4] Descendants of a deceased brother or sister take his or her share.

What Are Living Wills and Durable Powers of Attorney?

Two major realities have combined to make this subject timely and of growing importance. The first is the aging of the United States population, caused by longer life expectancy for and the aging of persons born during the post-World War II "baby boom." The second is miraculous advances in medicine, sustaining lives of persons who during earlier decades would have died at a younger age. Both of these realities will continue to influence social, political, and economic policy and related law in the future. There is a growing acceptance of a document created by an individual that instructs his or her family and medical personnel as to what medical procedures to follow under specified circumstances.

The term **living will** is unfortunate—a living will has nothing to do with the transfer of property after death. A less confusing term used in many states is **directive to physicians**. No matter the name, the document is directed to a physician, communicating wishes regarding the use of life support systems in the treatment of a terminal illness. Forty states provide for living wills, but requirements vary.* Living will statutes generally require the document be executed after a patient has learned of a terminal illness. The living will must be witnessed by two or more disinterested persons, and prepared using a statutorily correct and specific form.[9] In states without specific provisions for a directive to physicians, a document may still be used in court to show the desires of the ill person if he or she is unable to testify.

A **durable power of attorney** is a more flexible document than the directive to physicians. It authorizes another person to make health care decisions for a person who becomes incapacitated. **Powers of attorney** are common legal documents allowing the creator, a principal, to empower another to act on his or her behalf. However, the use of a power of attorney for life and death decisions involving health care is something new. The durable power of attorney allows an appointed person to make decisions such as ordering the withdrawal of life support systems for another. Twelve states and the District of Columbia have statutes authorizing the durable power of attorney.[†]

Laws regarding this sensitive matter are in an early stage of development. More states will undoubtedly authorize the durable power of attorney in the next few years, although requirements for the creation and use of the document may continue to vary.[10] This document, like the directive to physicians, requires the signature of non-interested witnesses and must contain exact, approved statutory language.

Two important differences exist between the living will and the durable power of attorney: (1) the durable power of attorney can be created at any time—one need not be terminally ill, and (2) it delegates very extensive as well as critical decision-making powers to another person. Select that person carefully.

---

* The ten states that do not provide for the living will by statute are Kentucky, Massachusetts, Michigan, Nebraska, New Jersey, New York, Ohio, Pennsylvania, ~~Rhode Island,~~ and South Dakota.
† California, Idaho, Illinois, Maine, Maryland, Nevada, Oregon, Rhode Island, Texas, Utah, Vermont, Virginia, and the District of Columbia.

Concerning Probate

Is it the eccentric nature of the customers or the probate system itself that generates so much attention? I think it is a little bit of both.

Probate Judge Pat Gregory
Harris County, Texas[11]

What Is Probate?

Probate is a court proceeding where wills are proved to be valid or invalid and estates of decedents are properly distributed. Probate serves several useful purposes. For example, probate provides an orderly opportunity for unsecured creditors of the decedent to submit claims for payment or remain unpaid forever.* Note that applicable death taxes are payable whether or not there is a probate proceeding. If the court finds a valid will, it distributes the net assets (after all debts are paid) and liabilities of the decedent in accordance with the will. If there is no will, the probate court will accomplish similar tasks by complying with the state's law of intestate succession.

Can Probate be Avoided?

Probate has important disadvantages. It takes time, generally a minimum of six months, often one to two years, sometimes longer. During this time title to property is in limbo, as it is not yet transferred to the beneficiaries pending proof of the will and payment of the debts of the estate. The trauma of a loved one's death may be aggravated by the inability to use assets that the survivor(s) badly needs. In addition, the facts about the estate and its disposition become a matter of public record. If the probate is of a prominent figure, information about the estate and beneficiaries is often publicized in newspapers and on television.

Probate fees are payable to the personal representative (executor or administrator) and to the attorney who handles the estate. Sometimes the executor will be a principal or sole beneficiary and will waive probate fees to increase the inheritance. The fees are taxable as earned income. The inheritance may be tax free, depending on its size.

In California, the following percentages of the probated estate's gross value are the statutorily prescribed fees received by both the executor and the attorney:[12]

4 percent of the first	$15,000	$600
3 percent of the next	$85,000	$2,550
2 percent of the next	$900,000	$18,000
1 percent of the next	$9,000,000	$90,000
.5 percent of the next	$15,000,000	$75,000
A reasonable amount determined by the court of any amount over	$25,000,000	

---

* In a secured debt, evidenced by a mortgage or trust deed and a promissory note with the decedent's home as collateral (see Chapter 13), neither the death nor the probate affect the contractual obligation to pay.

In some states statutory fees are higher than California, in other states lower. The amount of the attorney's fee may be negotiated by the executor, and the attorney may agree to a lesser fee. The statutory fee is usually the amount paid. If unusual or extraordinary services are provided, a court may allow a higher fee. If a state does not provide for a statutory fee, the usual practice is for an attorney to bill by the hour.

Some persons try to avoid probate. With proper estate planning, the size of the probate estate may be substantially reduced. Certain types of property transfer to a new owner without the need of probate:

1. Undivided interests in property owned by the decedent in joint tenancy (or tenancy by the entireties) goes to the survivor(s) without probate under the right of survivorship.

2. In community property states, only one-half of the community property will go through probate, since the surviving spouse already owns the other half.

3. Life insurance proceeds may be paid directly to beneficiaries.

4. Certain U.S. government bonds are paid directly to the person listed on the front of the bond as POD ("paid on death").

5. Property previously transferred to an inter vivos trust (discussed later in the chapter) is not probated. *p 440 " Among the living"*

What Are the Duties of an Executor?

One day Robert Yu received the sad news of the death of his wealthy uncle, Wilbur Yu. A few days later he received some good news and some bad news. The good news: he was named a beneficiary in his uncle's will and was to receive a gift of 1,000 shares of extremely valuable common stock. The bad news (or so he regarded it): he was named executor of his uncle's will. Should he accept the appointment?

Probably yes. If he says no, the court will appoint a substitute administrator. If he says yes, an attorney he selects to handle the estate in probate court will do the legal work and will guide him in the proper performance of his duties. Both will be entitled to payment prescribed by statute, plus compensation for extraordinary expenditures (e.g., the possible costs of defending the estate against a challenge to the validity of the will). This compensation is usually adequate and even generous, at least for larger estates. Compensation is usually set by statute based on the gross value of the estate (total value of assets without regard to liabilities). Executor and attorney fees are the same for a complicated estate consisting of various business and assorted assets as they are for an estate consisting of one bank account, if the values of each estate are the same.

The duties of an executor are important. The executor generally:

1. Complies with decedent's special instructions for funeral and burial.

2. Locates and notifies witnesses to the will.

3. Notifies heirs (i.e., persons who would get the estate if there were no will) and beneficiaries named in the will, preferably meeting with them.

4. Arranges for bond, if necessary, to cover faithful performance of duties as executor.

5. Notifies the Post Office to send the decedent's mail to the executor and discontinues telephone and other services as appropriate.

6. Opens a bank account for the estate.

7. Assists the attorney in identifying creditors and arranging for payment of debts.

8. Identifies, inventories, and safeguards all probate assets. Safeguarding may require getting or maintaining adequate fire, property, and liability insurance.

9. Reviews non-probate assets (joint tenancy and trusts) for appropriate action to ensure legal transfer.

10. Offers the will for probate in court and is <u>formally appointed by the court as</u> executor. This appointment is referred to as receiving <u>*letters testamentary*</u>.

11. Reviews and takes appropriate action regarding the decedent's financial records: leases, mortgages, notes, life insurance policies, pensions, social security, stocks, bonds, savings accounts, checking accounts, etc.

12. Collects any dividends, interest, and/or rent; pays any rent, interest, insurance premiums, and other obligations.

13. Has assets appraised when advisable or required.

14. If decedent had a business, acts to continue proper operation if feasible, or to sell and liquidate if necessary.

15. Publishes statutorily required notice to creditors, reviewing claims and paying them when approved by the court.

16. Keeps detailed records of receipts (income) and disbursements (expenses and debt payments).

17. Determines cash requirements for taxes (income and estate), probate expenses, valid claims, and cash bequests, and decides which assets are to be used or liquidated for these needs.

18. With the aid of an accountant, files income tax returns (final return of decedent, tax returns for the estate while administration continues) and death taxes (inheritance and/or estate) and makes necessary payments.

19. Prepares a final estate accounting to submit to the court (listing assets, receipts, disbursements, sales with gains and losses, and a reconciliation of beginning and ending balances).

20. Transfers title to real and personal property to beneficiaries (and sometimes trustees) in accordance with the probate court decree of distribution under the will, obtaining receipts for same.

21. Obtains formal court approval of the settlement of the estate and final discharge as the executor.

What Is the Uniform Probate Code?

A *Uniform Probate Code (UPC)*[13] has been adopted in part by 16 states.* The UPC seeks to simplify and standardize will requirements and the law of probate. Under

---

* Alaska, Arizona, Colorado, Florida, Hawaii, Idaho, Kentucky, Maine, Michigan, Minnesota, Montana, Nebraska, New Mexico, North Dakota, South Carolina, Utah.

the UPC, a person must be 18 or older and of sound mind to make a will. The will must be in writing and signed by the testator (or in the testator's name by someone else in the testator's presence, by his or her direction). The will must be witnessed by two competent witnesses. They need not be present when the testator signs, but must be present later when the testator acknowledges the signature on the will. The code continues to permit holographic wills, but not nuncupative wills.[14] A major goal of the creators of any uniform code is that it be adopted by most states in order to provide uniform law throughout the country. Because of the mobility of our society, compelling arguments exist for uniformity in probate law. The goal of general acceptance of the UPC remains elusive.

Concerning Trusts

What Are Trusts?

Charles Fabor and his wife, Johanna, are very wealthy. They are also concerned that when their children Charles, Jr., and Sue inherit their shares of the family fortune, it will be spent within a short time. The children have never worked and, in the opinion of their parents, "simply do not know the value of a dollar." They are considered to be spendthrifts, even by their friends. What can the parents do to protect their children against squandering the inheritance?

A solution is the creation of a **trust**. Essentially, a trust is a separate legal entity, governed by a **trustee**, that holds property for the benefit of another, the **beneficiary**. The trust is created by a person called either the **trustor**, **settlor**, or **donor**. The legal distinctions between these terms are unimportant for our purposes. The term settlor will be used in this chapter for clarity.

A trust is created by the transfer of legal title from the settlor to the trustee to hold for the benefit of, and someday distributed to, the beneficiary, in accordance with the settlor's instructions (see Figure 14–1). How property is to be distributed is determined by the settlor and stated in the trust document. The trustee receives possession and legal title to the property for the duration of the trust, until it is distributed to the beneficiaries. Initially the beneficiary has an equitable interest in the property—a beneficial interest without the right to possess or transfer the property.

Legal requirements for a trust include appropriate mental capacity of the settlor, an intent to create a trust, proper purposes, and a transfer of property. In addition, although its being in writing is not absolutely required, it is expected, and the trust instrument should name a trustee with appropriate capacity.

What Are the Duties of the Trustee?

The trustee is a **fiduciary** to the beneficiary of the trust. The trustee owes to the beneficiary a duty of utmost care, honesty, and loyalty. The settlor may serve as

FIGURE 14–1 Distribution of a Trust

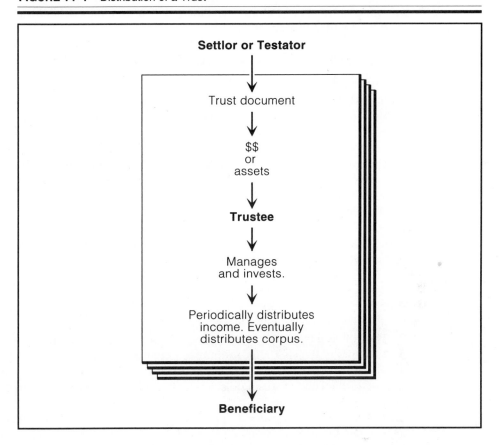

trustee, or the settlor may select a relative or trusted friend. In addition, many commercial companies (i.e. banks) offer their services as commercial trustees.

The method for determining fees for service as a trustee may be provided in the trust instrument. If not mentioned in the trust document, trustee's fees are awarded consistent with state statute or as allowed by the probate court. Trustees, like attorneys and personal representatives in probate proceedings, are entitled to extra compensation for special services and expenses, such as defending a lawsuit.

A person nominated as a trustee is free to decline. If a successor or alternate is not named in the trust document, the court will usually name a trustee. Once a trustee undertakes the responsibility of the trust, he or she cannot resign unless trust purposes are complete or a court permits. Most states require that trustees purchase a *fidelity bond* (an insurance policy for the beneficiary if the trustee violates official duties). The purchase of a fidelity bond is an expense of the trust. This bond can be, and often is, waived by the settlor in the trust document.

A trustee is duty bound to properly manage the assets of the trust, to properly account to the beneficiaries, and to invest the property prudently. As the trustee is a fiduciary, personally profiting from the trust is a conflict of interest and a violation of the fiduciary duty to the beneficiary.* The exact nature of trustee duties are specified in state statutes, but these duties may be modified or further specified by the trust document.

Irrevocable Inter Vivos Trusts

As settlors, the Fabors can create trusts while still alive. Trusts created during life are called **inter vivos** (Latin: among the living) *trusts.* If the trust is made **irrevocable** (cannot be revoked, nor can the property be returned to the settlor), income from the trust is taxable to whoever receives the annual income. This can reduce the amount of tax paid on income by shifting it to someone in a lower tax bracket. Another possibility is to keep property out of a settlor's estate at death and avoid the cost and delay of probate.[15] If the Fabors create a marital life estate trust (to be discussed later), they may also limit payment of death taxes.

The Fabors could name themselves as trustees, or they could name another person or a bank or trust company to perform the task.† As settlors, the Fabors could create a trust with provisions to become operative upon the settlor's death, including the following:

1. The children shall receive a limited amount of income from the trust as spending money, but most of their needs shall be paid for directly by the trustee (to shield such funds from possible creditors of the children).
2. The children may not give away or sell their rights in the trust.
3. Creditors of the children cannot reach the trust principal.
4. The trustee may spend part of the principal of the trust, if necessary, for the welfare of the children (using discretionary power to "invade the **corpus**" or body of the principal).
5. The trustee shall transfer 25 percent of the trust to each child when he or she attains age 30, and the balance at age 40. (Presumably, they would have matured by those ages and could safely be given the assets.) Alternatively, the parents could direct that the principal remain intact and go to the then-living grandchildren. This would eliminate a possible levy of estate taxes on the trust assets when their children die.

A major disadvantage to the irrevocable trust is it cannot be updated to meet changing circumstances. On the other hand, a will can be changed frequently to reflect new thoughts about how assets ought to be distributed upon death.

Revocable Inter Vivos Trusts

The Fabors may be reluctant to make the trust irrevocable, in case they need their money before they die. Instead, they might create a *revocable inter vivos trust.* With a **revocable trust** they can change the terms, beneficiaries, or completely

---

* Payment for duties as a trustee is obviously not considered a conflict of interest. Also, if the trustee is a beneficiary of the trust, profiting from the trust does not violate the duty of the trustee as long as the benefit is consistent with the terms of the trust.
† Professional trustees charge fees for their services, and their use may not be appropriate except in very substantial trusts.

terminate the trust at any time, regaining full control over the principal. All trust income is taxable to them as owners, however, and the value of the trust principal is taxed to their estates. The extent of death taxes might vary depending on the nature and terms of the trust. On the other hand, the trust assets will not be probated if the trust existed and was funded (i.e., property had been transferred to the trust) prior to their deaths.

What Is a Living Trust?

The term **living trust** is a popular term for a revocable inter vivos trust whose primary purpose is to avoid probate. The reasons for avoiding probate include a desire to avoid or reduce the expenses of probate and to maintain privacy in the settlement of family affairs. The living trust is usually less expensive than probate, and is private. Although one can avoid probate through the use of a living trust, a living trust will not by itself reduce death taxes.

Don and Pat Lee have a gross estate of $900,000 and a net estate (after payment of debts) of $800,000. They wish to avoid probate expenses for whichever of them is the surviving spouse. Ultimately they wish to minimize shrinkage of estate assets for their only child, Kelly. They decide to create a living trust. How will they create the living trust and will it accomplish their goals?

They will create a revocable inter vivos trust through a proper written document. All or most of their property will then be transferred into the trust. For example, if they own a home their ownership interest will be conveyed by deed to the trust. Many spouses own their home in joint tenancy. Thereafter, the trust is legal owner of the property. Other property, stocks, bonds, and pension contracts should be transferred to the trust. The transfer of real property will probably be their most complicated transfer.

The Lee's may name themselves co-trustees with the surviving spouse the successor trustee, anticipating the inevitability of death. (They might name additional successor trustees as well.) They will also name the beneficiary (or beneficiaries) to receive distributions from the trust after the death of the settlors. At the death of the first spouse, the property remains in the trust. At the death of the second spouse, the property is distributed to the named beneficiary (or beneficiaries) in compliance with the terms of the trust.

Assuming Don dies first and all their property is in the trust, Don's death would not affect the record title to the property. The trust continues to own all the Lee's property. As the title to property has not changed, there is no need to probate the property in trust. Fees for an executor and an attorney for a probate of Don's estate with a gross value of $450,000 in California would be $20,300. (See the earlier discussion about probate fees.) Probate fees with their property in the living trust upon Don's death are zero ($0). If the property was probated at the time of Pat's death (assuming that her gross estate now totals $900,000), the probate fees would be $38,300. (An assumption is made that Pat has lived within her income and the estate is larger because Pat inherited Don's property.) However, with the property in the living trust, there are only minimal fees to transfer the property to the surviving beneficiary for (or beneficiaries). The total probate fee savings, in California, could be as much as $58,600 ($20,300 + 38,300). Although the example assumes a marital living trust, a living trust would also reduce probate fees for the estate of a single person.

There are costs involved when creating the trust, when transferring title to the property into the trust, when managing the trust, and when making its final distributions. Attorney fees may be incurred at every stage. In addition, probate fees are deductible on the decedent's final income tax filing, and so the savings is overstated. These costs are probably much lower than probate fees. What the living trust does require is advance planning about fees that may be triggered upon death.

There are disadvantages to the living trust. The simple living trust discussed makes the most sense for unconditional gifts to family members. The trustee is expected to be the settlor. (In a marital living trust, both spouses are joint trustees with the surviving spouse being the successor trustee.) The trustee's duties are expected to be simple; the most important and complex of these is the distribution of the property. The trust must be kept current with title to property kept in the trust's name. That is a nuisance to many persons.

The following situations are among those that suggest extreme caution in the creation of a living trust, and in these authors' opinions the advice of an attorney is essential.

1. A minor child is among the beneficiaries. Special attention must be taken for the care of the minor child, and property should remain subject to the trust until the minor reaches majority.

2. Long-term care of a beneficiary is contemplated (e.g., a developmentally disabled child or a spouse who is mentally incapacitated). This situation contemplates a more complex trust and significant long-term responsibilities for the trustee.

3. Conditional gifts to beneficiaries are contemplated (e.g., in the Lee's case, property to Kelly if she graduates from college). This situation suggests increased responsibilities for the trustee. If the trustee has discretion, then conflict between the beneficiary and the trustee is possible.

4. The value of the estate is significant (e.g., $1,500,000) and estate taxes are to be paid. Depending on whether the estate is liquid (i.e., cash, stocks, and bonds) or not (i.e., real property, most partnership interests, or a sole proprietorship business), determining and accumulating the money to pay the death taxes may complicate the duties of the trustee.

5. You have or expect to have a substantial number of unsecured debts. One of the advantages of probate is the provision for an orderly method of paying debtors of the decedent—a living trust does not extinguish the debts of the settlor. Creditors expect to be paid, and without probate the process may be awkward. Secured property (e.g., real property with a mortgage or an automobile with a secured interest) will be transferred subject to its indebtedness. Unsecured creditors have a claim against all property of the decedent. If the amount of debt is minor, there will be little problem. If debts are significant, then careful planning to pay the debts should be made. Creditor claims complicate the trustee's duties and can cloud the title to property for beneficiaries for some time.

None of these situations make a living trust inappropriate. However, if they or other complications exist, then how these complications need be resolved should be stipulated in the trust document.

Testamentary Trusts

The Lee's instead might create **testamentary trusts**—a trust as part of their wills. Testamentary trusts are also revocable, changed or terminated by simply amending or revoking their wills anytime before death. Testamentary trusts become effective upon the death of the author of the will. Since the property is part of the decedent's estate, a testamentary trust does not avoid probate fees nor provide the privacy of inter vivos trusts.

Marital Life Estate Trusts

Don and Pat may wish to reduce federal death taxes on their estate. The living trust will not accomplish that goal. A **marital life estate trust,** also called an *A and B trust,* can, however, significantly reduce death taxes to the ultimate benefit of the beneficiaries. This trust, whether created inter vivos or by will, restricts the freedom of the surviving spouse to use the property as he or she might wish. Once the first spouse dies, the surviving spouse receives a life interest in the property, and someone else (the designated beneficiary) has a *remainder interest* (the interest remaining after the life interest). An owner of a life interest can use the property for life, but cannot convey it away by contract or will. At the death of the owner of the life interest, the owner of the remainder interest (usually a child) automatically becomes the sole owner of the property.

How does it work? Again, assume Don dies first and all property is to go to Pat. In an estate without a trust, there would be no death tax because federal law allows an unlimited amount of property to be transferred to a spouse without tax, because of the *marital deduction.*

In an estate with a trust, Don's $400,000 share of the net community property is transferred first to Pat, and then to Kelly, in the following fashion. Pat receives a right to the income from the $400,000 for the rest of her life, and Kelly has a right to the principal upon Pat's death. There are no federal death taxes because the interest to Pat is exempt as a marital transfer and the value of the interest to Kelly is less than the $600,000 estate tax exemption. At the death of the first spouse, Don, there is no federal estate death tax savings, because each spouse has an unlimited marital deduction. Depending on the state, there could be state death taxes.

At Pat's death it is quite a different story. If there were no trust, her entire net estate, valued at $800,000, would go to Kelly. As the starting tax rate after the $600,000 exemption is 37 percent, the amount of tax would be $74,000.

Net estate	$800,000
Exempt estate	600,000
Amount to be taxed	$200,000
Rate of tax	37%
Total federal estate tax	$ 74,000

If a marital life estate trust had been created, only the $400,000 solely owned by Pat is transferred at her death because the value of Don's estate had already been transferred. Remember that Kelly already had a right as remainder owner to the first $400,000 inheritance from Don, when Pat, the life beneficiary, died. Pat's death did not create the interest in the trust, it perfected it. As the $400,000 inherited from Pat is less than the amount allowed to pass tax free, there is no tax. The net tax savings to Kelly is $74,000. If Don and Pat created this type of trust as an inter vivos trust, they could protect the estate from both probate fees and federal death taxes.

There are, of course, additional costs of creating and maintaining the trusts and a loss of deductions on the decedent's final tax return. Actual predicted savings for an individual should be determined in consultation with tax and estate planning advisors. This type of trust has significant consequences to the settlors, which may make it undesirable. A person should not create a trust without competent legal and tax advice, and that admonition is particularly true for this kind of trust.

The Rule against Perpetuities

There is an old saying that you cannot take it with you. The law has not found a way to get around that fact, but instruments such as trusts and wills do the next best thing—they allow a person to control who gets his or her property and to instruct and/or restrict how that property may be used. The use of these instruments can allow a decedent to control property for generations. However, the **rule against perpetuities** applies to trusts and other legal instruments that restrict the use and free transferability of property in the future. The rule states that title in property must vest (i.e., some beneficiary must get full and unrestricted possession and ownership of the property) no later than a life or lives in being, plus 21 years, plus (in the case of a fetus) the applicable period of gestation.

The details of this rule are very complicated and beyond the scope of this text. The rule's purpose is to prevent a trust from accumulating and compounding income for perhaps ten generations, by which time a small sum may have grown to a prodigious amount. It also serves to keep assets under the control of the living rather than donors long since dead. The rule does not generally apply to charitable gifts. A gift of real property to a church, so long as no alcohol is served on the property, would not violate the rule. Such a restriction can last for hundreds of years, but a violation may lead to a reversion of the property to the donor's heirs.

Taxation of Generation-Skipping Trusts

The Tax Reform Act of 1976 created special rules to tax certain large generation-skipping transfers of wealth. Trusts are usually used for such transfers. For example, in a *generation skipping trust,* a father (first generation) creates a trust under which his daughter (second generation) receives the income while she lives. When she dies the principal goes to her child, a son (third generation). There is a death tax when the father dies, but no second tax when the daughter dies. The daughter's generation has been skipped as to estate tax liability because the daughter never received or controlled the principal. (Of course, when her child dies, any property from the trust still in his possession would be part of his estate for tax purposes.) This technique of tax avoidance is effective only for a trust that, on the death of the second generation member (the daughter in the above example), has a value of less than $1 million. Any value in excess of $1 million is taxed.[16]

What Are Some Other Uses of Trusts?

H. Pauline Amesbury dearly loves her husband, who is 15 years her senior and in his 80s. She is terminally ill and afraid that when she dies first, as is likely, he will be unable to manage the family estate alone. He might be talked into foolish investments, or worse, into remarriage to someone interested mostly in his money. What can Pauline do to protect her husband against such development?

She can create an inter vivos or testamentary trust, specifying that he gets the income and that the trustee may invade the principal if necessary for his welfare. When he dies, the property will not appear in his estate, where it would boost his estate tax. Instead, it can be distributed to the children, for example, or even held for the grandchildren. (The effect is the same as the marital life estate trust, even if only one spouse creates the trust, as long as the settlor spouse is the first to die.)

The trust instrument could name charities or other beneficiaries selected by H. Amesbury herself, or designated by Mr. Amesbury if he is given a **power of appointment.** This useful estate planning tool allows the trust to postpone deciding which child or children or other beneficiaries receive what gifts. In these ways, a trust can frustrate would-be fortune hunters who prey on wealthy and unsophisticated beneficiaries.

Sometimes trusts make sense when the beneficiary is ill, mentally retarded, or very old. A settlor may even create a trust naming himself or herself as the beneficiary, to spare him or herself the burden of managing his or her estate. One may also create a trust and name it as beneficiary of insurance policies on one's life. This arrangement is often preferable to allowing the insurance proceeds go as a lump sum to a beneficiary unequipped to handle such a sum.

A *discretionary sprinkling and accumulation trust* may be appropriate when flexibility is vital to meet the changing needs of family member's beneficiaries. The trustee is authorized to decide who among the designated beneficiaries is to receive periodic payments of income or principal or both. Beneficiaries who need more can be given more; those who need less get less. To help the trustee distribute the trust funds the trust specifies guidelines, which might include maintaining a stated standard of living or comfort and general welfare for beneficiaries and allowing special payment for educational or medical fees. Income not paid is accumulated and ultimately distributed as part of the principal.

Who May Be a Trustee and What Does a Trust Cost?

The settlor who creates a trust may serve as trustee, but unless the trust is a living trust, the settlor usually chooses a competent and trustworthy relative or friend or a commercial trust company with its staff of experts.

Fees must be paid to trustees, but the benefits may be well worth the expense. In a testamentary trust, the probate court fixes the trustee's fees. Three-fourths of one percent of the fair market value of the trust estate is commonly specified. To determine whether a fee is reasonable, the court considers the size of the estate, time required to administer it, services performed, and results achieved. In inter vivos trusts, the fees are negotiated. Common percentages are three-fourths of one percent of the fair market value of real estate and obligations secured by real estate, and three-fifths of one percent of the fair market value of other assets in the trust estate.

The percentage may be less for a very large trust (e.g., in excess of $1 million). Corporate trustees frequently charge one-tenth of one percent as an "acceptance fee" when the trust takes effect, and a one percent "distribution fee" for all amounts they distribute. Trustees, like attorneys and personal representatives in probate proceedings, are also entitled to extra compensation for special services and expenses, like defending a lawsuit.

Can Property Held in Joint Tenancy Be an Effective Way to Avoid Probate?

Joint tenancy (or the similar tenancy by the entireties between spouses in some states) is a form of ownership for two or more persons to hold real and personal property. One of the most important aspects of joint tenancy is its *survivorship feature*. If Al and Beth own a house in joint tenancy and Beth dies, Al automatically becomes the sole owner of the house without probate. The interest passes to Al even if Beth leaves a will and attempts to give her interest in the house to her mother, Sue. Surviving joint tenants automatically receive the interests of a deceased joint owner. As Al's interest is perfected at the moment of Beth's death, there is no interest in the house left to convey by will. Depending on the circumstances and desires of the co-owners, this feature is either a reason to own property in joint tenancy or a reason not to own property in this manner.

Because the ownership transfers automatically at the death of a joint tenant to the remaining tenant(s), joint tenancy property is not subject to probate. It is an effective way to avoid probate. However, like a living trust, a transfer by joint tenancy will not reduce death taxes, because the transfer itself is taxable. Other disadvantages to holding title to property in joint tenancy to avoid probate include:

1. Either joint tenant can secretly terminate the tenancy by conveying his or her interest to another person. The owner of the conveyed interest will not be a joint tenant but a tenant in common with the other joint owner(s).
2. Creditors may terminate the tenancy by claims against the interest of one of the tenants. Such a claim may require sale of the asset to satisfy the claim. Such actions can tie up and cloud title to the property, even though the creditor's claim is generally good only against the debtor's interest in the property.
3. The establishment of joint tenancy in property other than a bank account might be considered a gift. To the extent that its value exceeds $10,000 in a given year, the gift is a federal taxable event.

4. Following the death of a joint tenant, there may be adverse capital gains treatment for the surviving tenant when the property is subsequently sold. Explanation of such complex tax consequences is beyond the scope of this text. The moral is: If you are dealing with significant financial interests, seek legal and tax advice as to the most appropriate manner of joint ownership.

What Are Conservatorships and Guardianships?

 Peter White, age 78, is a millionaire who sometimes acts in a way his family considers eccentric. His son Ed has been particularly disturbed since Peter bought a large sailboat and announced his intention to sail to the South Pacific with an all-female crew. Ed contacted an attorney to inquire how he might stop his father from squandering the family fortune. Can Ed tie up his father's money?

Not unless there is more to the story. Peter appears to be capable of handling his own affairs, including his personal needs and financial resources. However, if he was physically or mentally unable to handle his affairs, his son could petition the court to declare a **conservatorship.** A responsible person would be named the conservator, to manage the assets and personal affairs of the conservatee. The conservator will make periodic reports to the court showing the business and personal transactions that have occurred. Although the conservatee is without authority to handle his or her own affairs, he or she ordinarily can still make, or modify, a last will. A conservatorship cannot and will not be declared simply to stop an eccentric person from overspending and thereby dissipating his or her estate.

An alternative procedure, called a **guardianship**, is available for those who, for many reasons, are unable to care for themselves or their estates. Usually a guardianship is created to provide for a minor whose parents are dead but an adult who is infirm may be judicially declared incompetent and placed in a guardianship. The person subject to a guardianship is called a **ward**. The person in charge of the ward's personal and financial affairs is called the **guardian.**

Under a typical guardianship statute, in order to declare one a ward, proof must show that the person is substantially unable to provide for his or her own personal needs (food, clothing, shelter, medical care). It must be proved the person is substantially unable to manage his or her financial resources. Isolated incidents of negligence or improvidence will not suffice as evidence of substantial inability. The alleged incompetent has the right to appear at the court hearing and to oppose the petition with the aid of counsel. A proposed conservatee has similar rights, and either party may call for a jury trial if provided by state law. If the petition is granted, the court monitors the activities of the person in charge, requiring periodic reports. Both guardianships and conservatorships are usually costly to the estate of the protected party.

The Principal Elements of Estate Planning

The following actions are representative of those actions one should consider in developing an estate plan. See Figure 14–2 for a useful checklist.

1. Prepare a personal or family balance sheet to show assets and liabilities. Keep accurate records of dates along with evidence of the acquisition costs of assets, including real property and its improvements (with receipts, for future tax purposes). Prepare a budget to monitor your earning, spending, saving, and investing on a monthly and annual basis.

2. Consider life insurance if appropriate for the needs of beneficiaries. (Be sure you understand the difference between term and ordinary life policies.) Select a suitable settlement option for each policy.

3. Consider creation of trusts (inter vivos or testamentary, or both). Consider using a living trust to avoid probate.

4. Both you and your spouse should prepare a will specifying the recipients of all your possessions. Prepare a will even if you use a trust to avoid probate. Let your heirs rejoice if there is insufficient property to require probate because you effectively and economically transferred your estate by other means.

5. Write a letter of or record your last instructions. Leave a version of Exhibit 14–2 explaining where important records and assets are located.

6. Consider donating your organs at death and prepare appropriate documents. Make your intentions known to others (e.g., on a card in your wallet, as such information should be immediately accessible).

7. Consider execution of a living will and/or a durable power of attorney to permit implementation of your wishes if you become terminally ill or incapacitated.

8. Consider the transfer of certain assets into joint tenancy so that they will pass to the surviving joint tenant, avoiding probate.

9. Make tax-free inter vivos gifts, to reduce the size of your estate and thus reduce the level of income taxes and death taxes that will have to be paid upon your death. A salutary side effect is to help the donees when they need the money most and not years later when unpredictable destiny forces a distribution by death.

10. Review pension plans to see how much retirement income to expect from these sources.

11. Consider investments in annuities to supplement a fixed income expected from pensions. Annuities can be created from the lump-sum proceeds of cash surrender values of life insurance policies.

12. Keep in mind the possible assistance obtainable from workers' compensation insurance, in case of accidental injury or death on the job, and from unemployment insurance, in case of forced idleness.

13. If one of your major assets is a stock in a closely held corporation, prepare and execute a buy-sell agreement coupled with qualified plans for deferred compensation through profit sharing or company pension plans.

14. If one of your major assets is a partnership, prepare and execute a suitable buy-sell agreement and arrange for life insurance or some other means of providing cash to fund the purchase.

FIGURE 14–2 Checklist for planning your estate. When a death has occurred, a major problem for survivors is finding all property and valuable papers of the deceased. Some advance planning can help your heirs. Complete this form and give copies to your spouse, a relative or a friend who might help in settling the estate, the executor of your will, and your attorney. Set aside a day each year (maybe after you have completed your annual income tax form) to update this information.

WHERE TO FIND MY IMPORTANT PAPERS

Name _____ Social Security Number _____

My valuable papers are stored in these locations (address plus where to look):
A. Residence _____
B. Safe-deposit box(es) _____
C. Other _____

Item	A	B	C	Item	A	B	C
My will (original)	___	___	___	Retirement papers	___	___	___
Powers of appointment	___	___	___	Deferred compensation; IRA papers	___	___	___
Spouse's will (original)	___	___	___	Titles and deeds	___	___	___
Location and combination of safe	___	___	___	Notes (mortgages)	___	___	___
Trust agreements				List of stored & loaned items	___	___	___
As settlor	___	___	___	(item, bailee, and address)			
As beneficiary	___	___	___	Motor vehicle ownership records	___	___	___
Life insurance policy(ies)	___	___	___	Birth certificates (yours, spouse's	___	___	___
Health insurance policy(ies)	___	___	___	and children's)			
Homeowner's insurance policy	___	___	___	Military enlistment and discharge papers	___	___	___
Motor vehicle insurance policy(ies)	___	___	___	Marriage certificate(s)	___	___	___
(including boats)				Divorce/separation records	___	___	___
Employment contract(s)	___	___	___	Contracts	___	___	___
Partnership agreement(s)	___	___	___	Important receipts*	___	___	___
List of checking, savings accounts	___	___	___	Important warranties	___	___	___
List of credit cards	___	___	___	Other	___	___	___
Brokerage account records	___	___	___		___	___	___
Stock certificates	___	___	___		___	___	___
Bonds	___	___	___				

* Including receipts for capital improvements to residence

IMPORTANT NAMES, ADDRESSES AND PHONE NUMBERS
Beneficiaries under my will (list)

_____

_____

_____

Attorney _____
Accountant _____
Insurance agent _____
Stock broker _____

Date prepared _____
People to whom copies have been given _____
1. _____
2. _____
3. _____
4. _____

15. If one of your major assets is a sole proprietorship, provide a funded plan that will provide for the continuation of the company or a liquidation under favorable circumstances.

16. Review and update your plan anytime there is a change in your personal status, or at least every few years. An outdated plan may be worse than no plan.

Case 14

AHLMAN V. WOLF

Florida District Court of Appeal, 483 So.2d 889 (1986)

Harry Ahlman filed a petition to probate the last will and a codicil of Mrs. C. W. Hand. Each had been prepared approximately two years before Mrs. Hand's death at the age of 97. Harry Ahlman and Dr. Raymond Breitbart were substantial beneficiaries under the offered will. Harry Ahlman was Mrs. Hand's social secretary and managed most of her affairs; Dr. Breitbart was her personal physician. Prior wills of Mrs. Hand had provided modest gifts to Harry Ahlman and no gift to Dr. Breitbart. Mr. Ahlman influenced Mrs. Hand's selection of a new attorney, Robert White, substituting for her previous attorneys (who were also old friends). Ahlman was present during conferences between Mrs. Hand and Mr. White while they discussed the contents of and executed the will. Ahlman was the only contact with the attorney in the drafting of codicil. Witnesses to the will were recruited by Mr. Ahlman. Mrs. Wolf, the closest living relative to Mrs. Hand, objected to Mr. Ahlman's petition, alleging the will and codicil were the product of undue influence. The trial court invalidated the will and codicil, finding that both were the product of undue influence by Ahlman and Breitbart.

Judge Baskin Under a *[In re Estate of] Carpenter* analysis, a presumption of undue influence arises when a substantial beneficiary who occupies a confidential relationship with the testator actively procures the will. In the case under consideration, the trial court found that most of the *Carpenter* criteria for determining the active procurement of the will were satisfied. While we do not necessarily agree with all of the trial court's findings, we recognize that a majority of the factors signifying active procurement were present.

[W]hen . . . circumstances give rise to a presumption of undue influence, the burden shifts to the beneficiary to come forward "with a reasonable explanation of his . . . active role in the decedent's affairs, and specifically, in the preparation of the will. . . ." Although the judgment did not address either the presumption or whether Ahlman successfully rebutted the presumption, we do not find this omission to be fatal.

The record demonstrates that Ahlman rebutted any presumption of undue influence: his active role in the decedent's affairs and in the preparation of her will are reasonably explained by his position as Mrs. Hand's social secretary. *Carpenter* requires only a minimal response to overcome the presumption. Once the presumption vanishes, the trier of fact must determine whether the preponderance of the evidence establishes the existence of undue influence:

> [Since] the facts giving rise to the presumption are themselves evidence of undue influence, those facts will remain in the case and will support a permissive inference of undue influence, depending on the credibility and weight assigned by the trial judge to the rebuttal testimony.

The evaluation of conflicting evidence is the function of the trial court. . . . We find no error in the trial court's exercise of its responsibility.

Affirmed. The will was denied admission to probate.

QUESTIONS AND PROBLEMS

1. Joe Goldstein never made a will. Now he is flat on his back in a hospital bed after being injured in a crash of his private plane. Both his arms are in casts and he has extensive internal injuries. But his mind is alert and he can talk. Realizing that the prognosis is bad, he calls for his lawyer. Can they prepare a formal, witnessed will, even though Goldstein cannot write his name?

2. When Pauline Puffington died, she left her entire estate of $3 million to a trust for the care of her 12 dogs and 14 cats. After the pets' deaths, the principal was to be paid to a designated society for the prevention of cruelty to animals. Relatives challenged the will, proving not only that she was eccentric and senile when she made it, but also that she was insane when she died. Can the will be enforced?

3. Mary Dorsett was convinced that making a will was tantamount to writing one's own death warrant. Even after she married and had given birth to twins, she did nothing to ensure the economical transfer of her estate to her family after her death. She was a hard-working dentist and had acquired an estate of $250,000 by age 30. Then she suddenly died of a heart attack. Under the state's law of intestacy, her husband received one-third of her separate property and the twins, age five, shared the balance equally. What expenses and burdens might she have avoided for her widower?

4. Richard Kalfus murdered his wife, Domenica. He pled guilty and was sentenced to prison. Domenica was survived by her husband and two infant children. She left no will. Under New Jersey's law of intestate succession, a husband is entitled to a one-third share of personal property if children also survive the deceased parent. The statute made no reference to the effect of wrongful acts by an heir. Is Richard entitled to his intestate share of Domenica's estate? [*Estate of Kalfus* v. *Kalfus,* 195 A.2d 903 (New Jersey, 1963)]

5. Harry Gordon died at the age of 83. The sole beneficiary in his will was a charitable organization. The attorney who drafted Mr. Gordon's will was the regional vice president of the organization and his practice was located in the same building as the charity. All witnesses to the will were officers of the corporation, as were the executors. The original of the will was kept in the charity's offices. The will was executed seven years before Mr. Gordon's death. Would there be a presumption of undue influence? Was undue influence present? [*Herman* v. *Kogan,* 487 So.2d 48 (Florida, 1986)]

6. Discuss some of the situations in which a directive to physician would apply. A durable power of attorney? What ethical dilemmas are created by these instruments?

7. What is the difference between a revocable and an irrevocable trust? Identify a circumstance where each would be appropriate.

8. First Virginia Bank of Tidewater was the trustee of testamentary marital trust. In the course of the bank's service as trustee, it invested $40,000 in real estate investment trusts (REITs). The investment became worthless. The beneficiaries of the trust brought suit, complaining that the bank had violated the Virginia statutory "prudent man rule," which guided trustees in careful investment of trust assets. The bank defended, alleging the settlor had granted the bank broad discretion, obviating the "prudent man rule." Language in the will authorized real estate investments and to hold or sell investments ". . . without liability of the part of the fiduciary for depreciation in the value. . . ." Can a settlor supersede a statutory standard for a trustee? Did the testator settlor do so in this case? [*Hoffman* v. *First Virginia Bank of Tidewater,* 263 S.E. 402 (Virginia, 1980)]

9. J. T. Payne executed a valid will on June 29, 1934. On April 24, 1956, a will with singed edges was offered to the probate court. Three of his children challenged the will, contending it had been revoked by the deceased. A witness at the trial testified that in July of 1934, J. T. Payne said, "I am going to get rid of this damn will right now," and he threw it on live coals in the fireplace. Payne's wife rescued the document and, with it smoking on one end, put it into her apron. No language of the will offered in probate was obliterated or obscured.

Can this be considered a valid will? [*Payne* v. *Payne,* 100 S.E.2d 450 (Georgia, 1957)]

10. Sung Fong had two strong obsessions during a long, eventful life: to become a millionaire, and to "go it alone." He never married and now, at age 90, has a net worth of more than $10 million, almost all in stocks and bonds. He has no enemies, explaining with a chuckle that he's outlived them all. He has no true friends and no known relatives. With his health failing rapidly, he's added a third goal: to pay no death tax to the government. "Not one cent," he repeats. Can you tell him how to accomplish this last strange goal?

FURTHER READING

1. Clifford, D. *Plan Your Estate.* Berkeley: Nolo Press, 1989. Excellent self-help book on the most important aspects of wills, trusts, and probate. This is useful even if you consult an attorney—it will help you understand what the attorney is doing.

2. *Nolo's Simple Will Book.* Berkeley: Nolo Press, 1989. A how-to book from how-to specialists.

3. Regan, J., *Your Legal Rights in Later Life.* Glenview, IL: Scott Foresman and Co., 1989. Helpful publication by the legal counsel for the American Association of Retired Persons (AARP).

4. *Willmaker.* Berkeley: Nolo Press & Legisoft, Inc., 1989. Computer software program to prepare your own will. An instruction manual accompanies the software. Available for most types of computers.

NOTES

1. Internal Revenue Code, 26 U.S.C. 2001.

2. Internal Revenue Code, 26 U.S.C. 2010.

3. *San Francisco Chronicle,* March 17, 1989.

4. Zickefoose, T., "Videotaped Wills: Ready for Primetime," 9 *Probate Law Journal* 139 (1989).

5. Rice, S., "Too Little too Late, California's Simple Wills Aren't Simple for the Testator or the Probate Court," 9 *California Lawyer* 36 (June 1989).

6. Ibid.

7. California Probate Code § 6111.

8. "Dear Abby," *San Francisco Chronicle,* June 19, 1989.

9. Forms and individual state requirements are available at no cost from The Society for the Right to Die, 250 West 57th Street, New York, 10107.

10. Forms and individual state requirements for the durable power of attorney are available at no cost from The Society for the Right to Die; 250 West 57th Street, New York, 10107.

11. "Probate Texas Style," *The National Law Journal,* May 22, 1989.

12. California Probate Code §§ 901 and 910.

13. Uniform Probate Code, 1974 as amended through 1987.

14. Ibid., §§ 2–502 and 2–505.

15. Internal Revenue Code, 26 U.S.C. 671–677.

16. Internal Revenue Code, 26 U.S.C. 2631 and 2601 et. seq.

CHAPTER 15

The Attorney-Client Relationship

A law firm receptionist answered the phone the morning after the firm's senior partner had passed away unexpectedly.

"Is Mr. Smith there?" asked the client on the phone.

"I'm very sorry, but Mr. Smith passed away last night," the receptionist answered.

"Is Mr. Smith there?" repeated the client.

The receptionist was perplexed. "Perhaps you didn't understand me. I'm afraid Mr. Smith passed away last night."

"Is Mr. Smith there?" asked the client again.

"Madam, do you understand what I'm saying?" said the exasperated receptionist. "Mr. Smith is dead."

"I understand perfectly," the client sighed. "I just can't hear it often enough."

(Quoted from a recent U.S. Senate confirmation hearing of a Supreme Court Justice.)

Lawyers have been targets of criticism in the guise of humor, and otherwise, throughout history. No doubt the classic quip is Shakespeare's oft-quoted line from *Henry VI:* "The first thing we do, let's kill all the lawyers." Why this thinly veiled animosity? What are attorneys-at-law? What functions do they perform in our legal system? Do they advance the cause of justice "of rendering to every man what he is due?"

An **attorney-at-law** (also called a *lawyer*) is a person authorized by law to represent clients in legal matters. Attorneys also draft documents involving legal rights and duties and give expert advice on legal questions. Countless businesses and public organizations routinely look to attorneys for such help. More than two-thirds of the adults in the United States have consulted attorneys for assistance with personal legal problems. Most of these problems involve the preparation of wills, the purchase or sale of real property, divorce or marriage dissolutions, serious personal injuries caused by other persons, consumer problems (e.g., disputes with landlords or with lenders), or difficulties with governmental agencies.[1] Every person should anticipate direct or indirect involvement with an attorney sometime in his or her life. Accordingly, one should be familiar with the legal profession, and learn how to select, retain (hire), cooperate with, and evaluate an attorney's performance.

About the Legal Profession

Who May Practice Law?

Generally, only licensed attorneys may perform legal services for clients. Most state legislatures have created state **bar associations** to regulate lawyers and the practice of law. The rules of such associations, as well as state statutes, combine with the inherent powers of the court to regulate and govern the legal profession. Each state sets its own qualifications for admission to practice law within its borders. To practice in more than one state, an attorney must have a separate license from each state.*

A candidate for a license to practice law must possess good moral character, complete certain minimum educational requirements,† pass a "bar" examination, and take an oath to support the law and conform to rules of professional conduct of that state. There is no inherent right to practice law or to represent others in court. The practice of law is considered a privilege granted to those who demonstrate fitness in intellectual attainment and moral character.[2]

Bonnie Cord and Jeffrey Blue, an unmarried couple, bought a home and resided together in a rural area of Warren County. Bonnie, an attorney licensed to practice law in Washington, D.C., applied for a license in Virginia. Duncan Gibb, judge of the circuit court of Warren County, denied her application because her living arrangement "would lower the public's opinion of the Bar as a whole." Bonnie appealed to a higher court. What should have been the result?

Bonnie won the case and her license because her conduct did not affect her fitness to practice law.[3] The same result has been reached where an applicant admitted a sexual preference for persons of the same sex.

With a few exceptions, no one is required to use an attorney to represent him or her in a legal proceeding. A party to a case before a trial court may appear **in propria persona** (Latin: in one's own person) or in *pro se* (Latin: for him or herself), that is, without the services of an attorney. Generally, it is not advisable to go to court without an attorney. A common saying, even among lawyers, is "one who serves as his own lawyer has a fool for a client!" An attorney usually uses another lawyer when he or she is a party to serious litigation. All of us, even attorneys, are emotionally involved in our own cases. Clients need unemotional, educated, and experienced counsel to analyze issues dispassionately and to argue them persuasively before judge and jury. It is important to have an independent advocate.

---

* Occasionally, an attorney will represent a client in the court of another state after receiving permission from that court. However, the host state may require the temporary association of a local attorney licensed in that state.

† The educational requirements vary depending on the state. Most states require that any person wishing to take the state bar examination must be a graduate of a law school accredited by the American Bar Association. Law school provides a graduate professional education and so virtually all law students possess a baccalaureate degree before entering law school.

A defendant in Superior Court decided to be his own lawyer, which some say was mistake number one. His second mistake was the first question he asked the victim, "Did you see my face clearly when I took your purse?"

The sentence: Two to ten years.[4]

Each federal court (e.g., U.S. Supreme Court, U.S. Court of Appeals, U.S. District Court) recognizes its own separate bar or group of attorneys permitted to practice before it. Although there are separate federal regulations, permission to practice law in the federal courts is granted to attorneys licensed in any state without requiring further education or achievement.

Government regulation of the legal profession exists because the attorney-client relationship requires technical expertise and is fiduciary in nature. A *fiduciary relationship* exists, as the attorney is in a position of trust and confidence with the client. The attorney must exercise the utmost good faith, honesty, and fairness toward that **client.**[5] Licensure is designed to protect the public by seeking to ensure that every attorney is competent, honorable, and worthy of that trust.

The close relationship and the resulting need for absolute confidence and trust has given rise to the *attorney-client privilege.* In all states, communications made by the client to the attorney are **privileged**, meaning the attorney cannot be compelled to reveal them.[6] However, the privilege does not cover all communications; for example, there is no privilege protecting communications made in the presence of others, or if the communication indicates an intent to commit a future crime. As the privilege belongs to the client, an attorney cannot refuse to testify if the client requests it.

Rule 1.6 of the American Bar Association (ABA) Rules of Professional Conduct prohibits a lawyer from revealing ". . . information relating to representation of a client unless the client consents after consultation. . . . " Several cases involving difficult situations have brought these rules to public attention.

A client (we'll call J. Doe) contacted an attorney after Doe's involvement in a fatal hit-and-run accident. Doe instructed the attorney to plea bargain with the prosecutor about criminal charges while Doe remained anonymous. The prosecutor refused to bargain without revelation of Doe's identity. The victim's family sued the attorney to force disclosure of the client's name. Can the family get Doe's real name?

No. The Florida circuit court held that the information was privileged, and the attorney was not required to disclose the client's name.[7] Attorneys understand the natural public resentment that arises with such rulings. Nevertheless, ". . . if the privilege is not maintained in 'hard' cases such as this, troubled individuals with legal problems will only dare to consult lawyers in 'easy' cases—where there is little to hide in any event."[8]

Specialization

Like a license to practice medicine, a law license is a broad grant of power. It permits an attorney to undertake a wide variety of legal tasks. Common sense for both lawyer and client suggests that a general-practice attorney should undertake only routine matters. A complex case should be referred to a specialist in the particular area of law involved. Normally, a specialist is familiar with the intricacies, procedures, and detailed rules in the specialized area. In all areas of law practice there are unwritten norms that elude understanding and discovery without repeated investigation; the specialist usually will be able to bring a legal problem to a faster, more satisfactory conclusion than an attorney not well versed in the particular area.

Attorneys may choose to specialize in any one or more areas, such as divorce law, probate and estates, criminal law, administrative law, real property law, personal injury law, small business law, and consumer law. These specialties usually correlate with the most common public needs. Other specialties include anti-trust law, labor law, tax law, bankruptcy law, patent and copyright law, international law, workers' compensation law, and water law. A client should learn the specialty of any attorney he or she consults with.

Until recent years, attorneys were prohibited from identifying themselves as specialists in all but a few areas of law (such as patent, copyright, and admiralty law). Many states (including Texas, New Mexico, Florida, and California) now allow specially educated and experienced attorneys to identify and advertise themselves as certified specialists if they have met the standards of education and experience set by the state bar. In California, for example, specialties now include: criminal law; family law; immigration and nationality law; tax law; workers' compensation law; and probate, estate planning, and trust law.

Geographical location plays a role in the type of law services available. For example, anti-trust, patent, immigration, and securities specialists are found in large metropolitan areas, while general practitioners are usually found in suburbs and rural communities. Family, criminal, and probate law attorneys are found in all communities of any substantial size.

Organizations of Attorneys

An attorney may choose to practice alone, may combine with one or more other attorneys in a law partnership, or may (in most states) conduct business in a professional corporation. Most attorneys who associate with others do so as partners. When lawyers form professional corporations, they do not gain all the attributes of other types of corporations. For example, there are generally no restrictions on who may be a shareholder (part owner) in the usual corporation. But in a professional law corporation, non-legal professionals (e.g., legal secretaries, paralegals, and investigators) are not allowed to be shareholders. In addition, although the corporate form usually protects a shareholder from all personal liability, it does not protect a shareholder in a professional corporation. To protect the public, such corporations do not shield attorney shareholders from liability for wrongful errors and omissions (malpractice) arising from the practice of law.* The primary reason why lawyers incorporate is to enjoy the tax advantages of pension and profit-sharing plans.

---

* Various statutory mechanisms provide protection for clients of professional corporations. One simply prohibits limited liability of shareholders. Another requires the professional corporation to purchase insurance against errors and omission liability—the insurance is a condition for an initial and a continuing certification to do business. A third requires all shareholders to personally guarantee all corporate obligations for malpractice as a condition for certification.

Law partnerships and corporations range in size from two to more than 1,400 attorneys.* Lawyers in large firms are typically assisted by large staffs of **paralegal aides** (persons qualified to perform a wide range of administrative and legal tasks), secretaries, investigators, and office managers. A medium-to-large law partnership normally includes attorneys qualified to provide a wide variety of specialized legal services. On the other hand, some law firms limit their entire practice to a single type of practice or litigation, for example defense of automobile injury cases. These firms are employed by automobile insurance companies to represent their customers who are involved in automobile accidents.

Prestige within the legal community is often related to the size of the firm: the larger the firm, the greater the prestige and usually the higher the fee. This phenomenon is partly the result of large, well-established firms attracting top graduates from elite law schools. Members of these firms often earn high personal incomes, serve wealthy clients, and enjoy luxurious offices. The solo practitioner, rightly or wrongly, is often found at the bottom of the image and income ladder.[9] The nature of the practice of law appears to be changing drastically. While the evolution of legal practice from solo practitioners to large firms has been going on for 60 years, the establishment of the mega-firm with offices in different cities, states, and countries is a recent innovation.

Types of law practice also create prestige, particularly among other lawyers. An example of the strong sentiments about one type of practice are expressed below in a newspaper quoting a judge (with obviously strong, but not necessarily accurate, opinions) who was contemplating his return to practice.

> When he goes back into practice, Winner said he will accept any kind of case except divorce cases. "I'll represent whores, pimps, or newspaper reporters, but I'm not going to try divorce cases," he said. "There is no end to them, and no end to the calls at home. There's also no satisfactory solution to any of them. The cause of most divorces is that there isn't enough money, and if there isn't enough money to support one family, there sure isn't enough money to support two."[10]

Public attorneys represent various local, state, and federal governments (e.g., public defenders, district attorneys, U.S. attorneys, and county counsels). Attorneys in public service are usually bound by the same rules of ethical conduct as are attorneys in the private practice of law.

Generally, free legal counsel is not available to poor people involved in civil actions. However, many communities have established legal aid offices that provide limited legal advice in civil matters and assistance to people who cannot afford an attorney. In personal injury cases, legal services are available from private attorneys on a **contingent fee** basis. The fee (a percentage of the amount recovered) is contingent on the outcome of the case. In other words, no fee is paid unless money is won for the client. Court costs are paid by the client,

---

* The largest law firm in the country has 1,400 lawyers. As do other large law firms, it has offices in several states and overseas. If current trends continue, some observers predict that law firms will continue to grow and a smaller number of firms will someday dominate much of the nation's legal work. [Gibbons; T. "Law Practice in 2001," 76 *American Bar Association Journal* 69 (January 1990)]

although the attorney might not press for payment if the case is lost. Strictly speaking, payment of court costs for the client is **maintenance,** which is maintaining, supporting, or promoting the litigation of another. Maintenance is considered unethical and improper because it encourages litigation.

The *federal Legal Services Corporation (LSC)* provides some legal assistance to the underprivileged. The Legal Services Program, created in 1964 as part of President Lyndon Johnson's "War on Poverty," was intended to assist the states in providing legal services to the poor. However, advocacy for the poor often has unpopular political ramifications and the program has been controversial. Cases brought by the LSC often name other government agencies as defendants, creating political backlash and resentment. President Ronald Reagan attempted several times to eliminate the Legal Services Corporation but was thwarted by Congress. Funding cutbacks have, however, severely curtailed the effectiveness of the LSC.[11]

Many bar associations and legal commentators urge lawyers to allocate part of their time to **pro bono publico** (Latin: for the public good) services free of charge. Many attorneys do contribute their time and effort to servicing the legal needs of the poor, but the problem of providing legal services in civil matters for the poor is vast and far from being satisfactorily resolved.

Assistance to indigent persons accused of crimes is provided without charge through state and federal public defenders' offices. A court will appoint private attorneys when public attorneys are not available. These private attorneys are paid standardized fees by the state government. Under the Sixth Amendment, free legal assistance is a constitutional right for all persons accused of crimes punishable by imprisonment, if they cannot afford to hire private legal counsel.

Some "store-front lawyers" or "law clinics" operating out of retail store-type quarters provide routine legal services at low cost. This type of law practice began in the 1970s with the relaxation of rules prohibiting advertising. They often provided representation of clients in limited areas such as family law, criminal defense, and probate matters. To lower costs, the clinics emphasize perfecting standardized legal forms and procedures for routine matters. In the last few years many of these clinics have added most other legal specialties to their offered services.

Group and *prepaid legal service plans* are designed to make legal services available at reduced cost to members of unions or other organizations, such as financial institutions. These plans are typically limited in scope but do provide low-cost assistance in routine legal matters (e.g., simple wills, document review, and warranty problems). Some attorneys object to these plans, arguing that they restrict a client's free choice of counsel and create a conflict of interest for an attorney between loyalty to the client and obligation to the group employer. However, these plans are growing in use. They have been declared constitutional by the U.S. Supreme Court and have been approved by the American Bar Association.[12]

A form of legal services that became popular in the late 1960s is the *public interest law firm.* These firms offer assistance in particular areas such as employment, minority rights, civil rights, family law, and environmental law. Public interest law firms are sometimes funded by grants from private charitable organizations. Often there are public interest firms representing both sides of controversial legal issues.

What Are Professional Ethics?

Professional rules of conduct for attorneys are established and enforced to protect the public, and to preserve and improve the reputation of the bar. A breach of these rules may lead to an attorney's being disciplined for unethical conduct. Discipline may take the form of (1) **disbarment,** (2) suspension from practice for a stated period of time, (3) probation, or (4) reproval (formal private or public censure). In 1983, the American Bar Association drastically revised its Model Code of Professional Responsibility into the current Model Rules of Professional Conduct. As of 1989, 31 states had codified the Model Rules into state law or court rules.[13] Most remaining states have adopted modified versions of the previous code.

> In the nature of law practice, however, conflicting responsibilities are encountered. Virtually all difficult ethical problems arise from conflict between a lawyer's responsibility to clients, to the legal system and to the lawyer's own interest in remaining an upright person while earning a satisfactory living. The Rules of Professional Conduct prescribe terms for resolving such conflicts. Within the framework of these Rules many difficult issues of professional discretion can arise. Such issues must be resolved through the exercise of sensitive professional and moral judgment guided by the basic principles underlying the Rules.[14]

Charging an unconscionable and exorbitant fee, stealing a client's funds, improperly soliciting employment, neglecting a client's case, and misusing a client's funds are all examples of unethical conduct directly related to the attorney's profession.[15]

Attorneys may also be disciplined for conduct involving moral turpitude (conduct contrary to justice, honesty, and good morals). Disciplinary hearings may take place even if questionable conduct does not directly relate to the attorney's ability to practice law. Perjury, failure to pay income taxes, murder, larceny, participation in business fraud, child molestation, and sale of narcotics are all examples of crimes involving moral turpitude subjecting an attorney to professional discipline, in addition to separate criminal charges and individual law suits.[16] For example, former Vice President and attorney Spiro T. Agnew was disbarred following his plea of nolo contendere ("no contest"—a special form of guilty plea) to willful tax evasion.[17]

 In March 1984 Grace Akinsanya retained [Attorney] Pineda to represent her in a real estate matter, and gave him $1,500 as an advance fee. By May 1984 Akinsanya became dissatisfied with Pineda's inaction and asked him to agree to a substitution-of-attorney. However he refused to sign a substitution of attorney form, despite the intervention of Akinsanya's new attorney, and failed to return Akinsanya's files or refund any part of the advance fee. Only after the Superior Court sanctioned him for his actions did he withdraw from the case or turn over the file.[18]

Based on the above and six other similar acts of failure to perform services for clients, attorney Pineda was suspended from the practice of law for two years and placed on probation for five years.[19]

An important distinction exists in the ethical obligations of private and public attorneys. A **private attorney** is ethically bound to zealously support and try to win the client's case. When an attorney represents a client in litigation, the attorney is usually working with the record of historical events, which lawyers refer to as facts. All doubts about the facts, as well as about legal questions, must be treated by the private attorney in the client's favor (even if the attorney does not believe them!). This is so because the private attorney in court is an advocate, not charged with the responsibility of passing judgment. The role of the attorney as advocate is one aspect of the adversary system, explained in Chapter 3. A **public attorney**, such as a prosecutor or other government lawyer, has a primary duty to see that justice is carried out, not simply to win a case. For example, a prosecutor must notify the defense of any evidence in a criminal case that obviously tends to show the defendant's innocence. Although defense counsel is not obligated in the same way, he may not destroy nor present as true any evidence that is known as false nor solicit or condone perjury in order to win a case.[20]

Attorney Tak Sharpe represented the plaintiff in an automobile accident case that was nearing trial. To encourage a compromise, Tak telephoned the defendant, Sandra Broderik, instead of calling Ms. Broderik's attorney. He told Sandra that $7,500 would be a fair settlement. Sandra responded that she would prefer to discuss the matter with her attorney. Has Tak acted unethically?

Yes.[21] Opposing counsel is not permitted to communicate directly with another attorney's client concerning a pending case. Tak should have telephoned Broderik's lawyer. The purpose of this rule is to prevent one lawyer from undermining the advice given by opposing counsel.

Questions of professional **ethics** are sometimes very complex and susceptible to misunderstanding. The attorney's job is to vigorously represent the client. For example, a criminal law attorney must attempt to persuade a judge and jury to free a client, even if he or she personally suspects that the client is guilty of the offense. This is considered ethically correct because the lawyer's duty is not to judge, and everyone is entitled to all available legal advantages. Even after a client has been convicted, the attorney will argue for probation rather than prison. A tax attorney will look vigilantly to find a loophole allowing a client to legitimately reduce or avoid tax payments. Ethically, this is proper so long as no evasion (violation of tax law) or fraudulent practice (such as forging documents) is involved. Congress often authorizes loopholes or tax shelters to encourage certain types of socially desirable investments. For example, Congress allows interest paid on home mortgages to be deducted from taxable income, reducing the income taxes paid by homeowners.

Most judges are also attorneys, and judges are subject to special rules of ethical conduct.

District Judge William Haworth, Jr., tampered with a jury list by substituting five persons in a panel (list of prospective jurors), operated a loan business from his chambers (office) using court staff and public facilities, and released a felon from jail as part of a political conspiracy to elect a candidate for district attorney. Was the judge's conduct unethical?

Yes.[22] Judge Haworth was removed from office and permanently disqualified from holding any office of public trust. In addition, his license to practice law was suspended for two years.

Judges are expected to conduct themselves in a manner that will maintain public confidence in the fairness of the judiciary. State court judges are subject to disciplinary action in accordance with state laws. State judges are often appointed by the governor; after the initial appointment, they must stand for reelection or confirmation in office after a prescribed number of years. They may be removed from office for misconduct. Methods of removal, such as impeachment, vary among the states. Federal judges are appointed by the President, confirmed by the Senate, and serve for life. They can be removed from office only by impeachment.[*]

Dealing With An Attorney

Is An Attorney Necessary?

Attorneys are called on to process a seemingly endless stream of problems for private persons, businesses, government agencies, and other organizations. Obviously, many clients consider attorneys an essential source of information, advice, and representation in a myriad of situations. Nonetheless, some legal problems are routinely resolved by persons without the assistance of an attorney. Among these are simple divorces, settlement of "fender-bender" car crash cases, simple handwritten wills, consumer purchase and sale contracts (such as "pink slip" certificates of ownership of vehicles), and real estate purchase agreements. Numerous disputes involving small sums are within the jurisdiction of the small claims court (remember, attorneys are usually excluded by law, unless they are parties in a case). Unfortunately, too often persons in genuine need of legal advice or assistance, through ignorance or neglect, fail or delay in consulting an attorney. The result is a permanent loss of a valuable legal right.

Some general guidelines may be helpful in deciding whether or not an attorney should be consulted. Do consult an attorney if the matter can be characterized in any of the following ways:

1. The matter involves the risk of losing, or the possibility of obtaining, a sum of money that seems significant to you.
2. The matter involves actual or possible physical or mental injury, suffered or threatened, that can be characterized as more than minor.
3. The matter seems very important for any other reason (e.g., a major impact on your life or that of a dependent, such as a child custody dispute).

Not every dispute or problem ought to be taken to an attorney. Indeed, elementary economics militates against such petty litigiousness. The potential impact

---

[*] Seven federal judges have been impeached and convicted, two in 1989 (U.S. District Judges Alcee L. Hastings—bribery for a lenient sentence, and Walter L. Nixon—perjury before a grand jury).

of events on one's life should be considered when considering the need for an attorney's services.

How Do You Find a "Good" Attorney?

Carefully! Time, energy, and resourcefulness spent in finding an attorney will go a long way toward a satisfactory relationship and result. Too often the presence of a serious problem that prompts the search also prompts great haste in the selection process. An exhaustive search should not be necessary in order to avoid a "bad" attorney; to the contrary, in populous areas there are a number of qualified attorneys ready, willing, and able to perform the required service. But a cavalier approach to the selection process increases the chance of retaining an attorney who may not perform as well as others equally available.

Paid Advertisements   Until recent years, lawyers were legally prohibited from advertising their services. The profession considered advertisement as unbecoming and unethical conduct. Prohibitions and distaste regarding advertising were not confined to the legal profession—many professions feel that advertising is not consistent with the conduct of a professional person. Specifically, many in the legal profession have feared that advertising will lead to extravagant and misleading claims and practices, and thus it would create rather than resolve conflict. Many attorneys also believe that advertising further tarnishes the general reputation of attorneys.*

Rules of conduct regarding publicity and advertising have been liberalized in recent years. In 1977, the U.S. Supreme Court ruled that the public had a right to information as to the availability and cost of routine legal services, and attorneys had a right to furnish that information.[23] States have formulated rules regarding advertising, although many issues are still debated. Claims about an individual attorney's competence or ability to achieve results are still considered unethical by the profession.

Initially, major firms with outstanding national reputations declined to advertise; recently, even they have begun to do it, but they avoid TV and are more likely to use simple announcements, news releases, brochures, newsletters, and advertisements in selected special audience magazines.

Most public libraries contain directories of attorneys with biographical information, including practice specialties and lists of representative clients. Information directories have been available for many years and have never been considered advertising.

Word-of-Mouth Reputation   Generally, the most reliable advertising is word of mouth. However, an attorney's reputation is more than simply "good" or "bad." Better questions to ask concerning the reputation of a particular attorney are:

---

* . . . [M]arketplace lawyer advertising, using all the sights, color, sounds, subliminal messages and not-so-hidden persuaders of commercial television, adversely affect not only the public's perception of those court officers, but also of the courts and the total judicial system." Justice Reynoldson, retired Chief Justice of the Iowa Supreme Court, "The Case against Lawyer Advertising," 75 *American Bar Association Journal* 60 (January 1989).

- What is the attorney's specialty?
- How long has the attorney been in practice?
- Does the attorney have a reputation for being a problem solver? Thorough? Expensive? Aggressive? Sincere? (Or any other quality thought to be appropriate or inappropriate for the case?)
- Do judges and attorneys generally think highly of the individual or firm?
- Is the attorney active in the community?
- Has the attorney been disciplined by the bar or been a defendant in malpractice cases?
- Is the attorney in good health?
- Does the attorney have a reputation for consuming alcohol to excess or taking harmful drugs?
- Is the attorney usually victorious in cases?
- Does the attorney make the fee arrangement clear?
- Does the attorney have a favorable reputation for keeping the client informed on case progress?

The selection of an attorney should be accompanied by some introspection by the client. Clients should consider their own attitudes, goals, and objectives, and, as dispassionately as possible, the nature of their claims. Some attorneys are "problem solvers" and others are "problem winners". A "problem solver" might complete the task in a short period of time, but the resolution may require considerable compromise on the part of the client. The "problem winner" might be victorious and provide more of what the client wanted, but may take considerably more time and require a different emotional commitment by the client. (Fewer than 5 percent of all civil cases actually go to trial, and so even "problem winners" typically compromise; they just do it later in the process.) The "problem solver" may preserve a friendly, mutually profitable relationship for the client with the other party. That is seldom possible with a "problem winner," who may have embarrassed, angered, or even humiliated the opposing party.

The reader is cautioned to not select an attorney or a firm because of some preconceived notions of how an expert attorney should look. Some eminent specialists, especially trial lawyers, are colorful characters, unique in personality and lifestyle, who may strike the prospective client as unusual. But they know how to appeal to juries and are often winners.

Probably the best source concerning the reputation of attorneys is a practicing attorney in one's community. The knowledge of one attorney about another attorney is more meaningful if they practice similar varieties of law. For example, a divorce attorney rather than an anti-trust lawyer could be a useful source concerning the professional reputation of other divorce attorneys.

Is it realistically possible to obtain good legal advice and help? We believe it is. A person in need of an attorney's services would be well advised to solicit help from several persons who might be in a position to obtain and relay information about the professional reputation of attorneys practicing in the community. Business managers, bankers, title company officers, city and county government officials, educators, merchants, stockbrokers, insurance executives, real estate personnel, and, of course, lawyers, are likely to have direct communication with and knowledge about members of the bar. They will often share their knowledge of the professional reputation of attorneys in the community. An employer is often a good source of information. Although most attorneys are listed in the Yellow Pages of the telephone directory and some even place ads, the phone book in no way ensures competence.

Meeting with the Attorney   Once a prospective client gets the name of one or two attorneys as possible selections, an office appointment may be made with each by telephone. An initial appointment of 30 minutes or so is often available without charge, or for a modest fee quoted in advance upon request. A prospective client has many questions concerning the rules of law thought to be applicable to the case. Unfortunately, there are usually a number of laws that may be applicable and the attorney, pending further study, will necessarily be noncommittal. This is to be expected, because no attorney is capable of explaining all the law concerning a matter without careful research and preparation; nor is any attorney capable of predicting with certainty the outcome of any complex case.

No commitment need be made at the first meeting; a simple "Thank you, I would like to consider the matter for a couple of days" permits a graceful departure. During the initial meeting, much can be learned from a few questions to the attorney:

- Do you frequently handle cases of this nature?
- Is this your specialty? If not, how many cases of this type have you handled?
- Will you be doing all the work or will other persons be involved?
- Would you prefer to refer my case to another attorney you know or handle it yourself?
- Would my case conflict with any of your other obligations, court calendars, or appointments?
- Would it be best to simply settle this matter now, even at a loss, rather than to be embroiled in a lengthy legal battle?
- May I have a copy of your standard retainer agreement?
- Will you provide an estimate of costs and fees for handling this matter?
- How do you keep a client informed about the progress of the matter?

Much can be learned about the prospective attorney by arriving early and observing the law office in operation. Confusion and disorganization often suggest a lower quality of service. An office cluttered with files, papers, and books justifiably does not inspire confidence. After you leave, will your file simply be part of the mess?

You should be aware that not all attorneys will appreciate being asked all the above questions. Some will interpret your inquiries as an indication that you will be a problem or malcontent client. A consumer of any service, including legal services, has a right to assure themselves that they will receive quality service. There are, however, some clients who are never satisfied no matter how well they are served. Protect your interests but use common sense.

Attorney Referral Services   In some communities, bar associations have established referral services where a person in need of legal assistance is referred to a specific attorney. Often the participating attorney will accept referrals for specific types of cases. Referrals may be made alphabetically. Participating attorneys frequently are newer members of the bar actively seeking business. They may charge reduced rates for their services. These referral services are often located in the Yellow Pages of telephone directories.

Public Defenders   As noted earlier, a defendant accused of a serious crime (i.e., a felony) has a constitutional right to be represented by a competent attorney at all stages of legal proceedings. If a defendant is indigent (unable to afford the services of a private attorney), the court will appoint an attorney, often called a **public defender,** to defend the accused free of charge. Contrary to some popularly expressed views, attorneys in public defender roles generally are very competent and zealous advocates for the defense. They are specialists. They handle a heavy case load, develop vast experience in a short time, spend much time in court, and know the judges and court staff. Since they handle many criminal matters, they know the probable results of a plea negotiation or bargain. Often records of losses reflect more the fact that they are not able to choose their clients. Public defenders by inclination fight for the underdog.

Solicitation

Occasionally, a lawyer may seek to find a client rather than wait for a client to find the lawyer. Most forms of solicitation of clients are considered unethical. Public policy frowns on efforts to promote litigation such as "ambulance chasing," where an accident victim is solicited to sign an employment agreement with an attorney. More sophisticated forms of solicitation, through a "capper" or "runner" who frequents likely places for generating legal business, are likewise unethical. Investigators, as well as nurses in emergency wards, have been used as cappers. They may receive an illegal referral fee from the attorney. Such payments frequently are made in cash to facilitate tax evasion. If solicited personally by an attorney or a capper, a prospective client should be aware that he or she is dealing with an unethical lawyer and should report the matter to the local bar association.[24]

How Do You Hire and Fire an Attorney?

An attorney in private practice is free to accept or reject employment, subject to certain general ethical obligations. The attorney has an ethical obligation to reject a frivolous case or a case in an area he or she lacks competence.*

After a prospective client locates an appropriate attorney, the employment relationship is accomplished by contract. The attorney promises to represent the client in exchange for a promise of compensation. In some instances, an attorney will require a written agreement; in others, an oral agreement is considered adequate. Many states, such as California, require that an attorney provide the client with a written contract shortly after undertaking the matter.[25] Whether or not an

---

* Filing of frivolous and defamatory litigation justifies disciplinary action. The attorney would also be subject to a civil lawsuit for malicious prosecution, although such actions are seldom successful.

agreement is required by the law, the client should request a written agreement. The agreement should be clear and fully explained to the client.

The agreement will necessarily have limitations. It cannot guarantee any particular result or any particular completion date, and will usually not detail the step-by-step procedures the attorney will ultimately take. This lack of detail is not sinister, but instead realistic. Even the most common legal problem or case may entail many unpredictable complications. The client should carefully ask questions until all ramifications of the problem or case are at least generally understood.

In offering suggestions for the employment of an attorney, we mention only generalities because of the great variety of cases and contingencies. Our comments may only be useful for the most common types of legal cases. Obviously, different questions arise when engaging an attorney in a complex business contract case. But in most situations, before signing, the prospective client should seek the following information:

1. What is the computational basis of the fee to be charged? If hourly, is the "meter" running at the same rate while junior attorneys or paralegal personnel are working on the case? How much library research is anticipated and at what rate? Will the fee statement be itemized as to hours spent and tasks accomplished? How often will the client be billed?

a. If the fee is contingent (client and attorney share in any recovery), are costs to be deducted from the award before or after computation of the attorney's share? If the case is lost, who pays for costs incurred? If the matter is settled quickly (and so the attorney's involvement is less than was anticipated), is the fee division reduced commensurately?

b. What happens if the lawyer's work increases greatly, as when a new trial is granted or an appeal must be initiated?

c. If a flat fee is charged, how will costs be paid? What does the fee include? What happens if there is an appeal? There must be a careful delineation of the work to be performed.

2. What specific important actions and events does the attorney predict will occur, and when are they most likely to happen?

3. What are the possible outcomes, good and bad? Is there any point of no return; that is, a point beyond which the client cannot practically withdraw from the matter?

4. Will there be need to refer all or any part of the case to another attorney? If so, how will the fee and work be affected and divided?

5. What will be the means (letter or telephone) and frequency of communications with the attorney or secretary? Will copies of all documents and correspondence routinely be sent to the client?

A client has the right to dismiss an attorney at any time for any reason. Difficulty may arise with respect to how much of the fee, if any, has been earned at the time of the discharge. The rule is easy to state but difficult to apply: the attorney is entitled to be paid the reasonable value of work done before discharge. In a contingent fee case, the attorney is entitled to be paid the reasonable value of the work done only when and if a recovery is obtained.

If the client discharging the attorney is unable to pay all fees the attorney has earned up to the time of discharge, a serious conflict may arise. The attorney demands payment while the client demands return of all documents (the file) connected with the case. The attorney may seek to pressure payment of accrued fees by refusing to release the file. In the absence of a statute giving the attorney the right to do so (called a *statutory* or *common-law retaining lien*), such conduct is illegal and probably unethical. However, many states do authorize such a lien.

A client may have difficulty hiring a new attorney for the case if one or more attorneys have been fired or have withdrawn. An attorney considering whether to accept such a case is usually suspicious of its merits and the client's stability.* Care should be exercised in locating the best attorney for the case at the beginning.

As a general rule, an attorney can terminate the employment relationship if there is a reasonable basis for the withdrawal. For example, the client's failure to pay the agreed-on fee is grounds for withdrawal. However, an attorney must (1) give reasonable notice to the client of intention to withdraw; (2) obtain court permission to withdraw if pleadings have been filed; (3) return the client's papers and money, where appropriate; and (4) refund any unearned fees. An attorney *must* withdraw from the employment when continued representation would require the attorney to violate a disciplinary rule. Other good reasons for withdrawal include failure of the attorney's health materially affecting his or her ability to continue, or a conflict of interest becoming apparent.

How Expensive Are Attorneys?

The amount of the attorney's fee is a matter of the attorney-client agreement. This freedom of contract is not, however, without limitation. In some instances, attorney fees are limited by statute or by the courts. Furthermore, when fee disputes arise, courts tend to give the benefit of any doubt to the client because of the usual bargaining superiority of the attorney.[26] In some states, the law presumes overreaching by the attorney if representation is begun before the fee is agreed on.[27] In such instances, the attorney is hard pressed to justify and collect the fee sought.

Although attorneys are free to charge their "going rate," the client's case may not be deliberately delayed for the purpose of coercing payment of a delinquent installment,[28] nor may an attorney charge an unconscionable or clearly excessive legal fee. The attorney is subject to discipline for making such an attempt.[29]

Important factors that normally are taken into consideration in setting an attorney's fee are:

1. The time required.
2. The degree of legal skill needed and novelty of the legal question presented.
3. The customary fee charged in the locality for similar services.

---

* Shortly after beginning their practice, many new attorneys will be approached by a potential client, who, with thick and tattered files, will spin a tale of conspiracy, malevolence, and grievous harm. Believing they have found the case that will make their reputation, the young lawyers begin their investigation. Within a short time they find out every attorney in town is already very familiar with their client.

4. The experience, reputation, and ability of the attorney.

5. The amount of money involved in the case.

6. The result obtained for the client.

7. Whether or not the case precluded the lawyer from accepting other legal work.

8. The nature and length of the attorney's relationship with the client.

9. Time constraints imposed by the client.

10. Whether the fee is certain or contingent.

Attorneys usually set their fee based on an hourly rate (e.g., $90 per hour), a flat fee (e.g., $5,000 payable in two installments), a contingency fee (e.g., 35 percent of net recovery), or a combination of these methods. The client should understand the possible conflicts created by various fee arrangements. For example, in a contingency fee arrangement, depending on how it is structured either the attorney or the client "wants" a quick settlement while the other would be better off by proceeding through trial. In a flat fee arrangement, the lawyer may have an incentive to dispose of the case as quickly as possible. An attorney paid by the hour might be tempted to overwork the case.

A variation of the fees listed above is the **retainer fee**. A retainer fee is a sum of money paid an attorney solely in exchange for a promise to remain available for the client's consultation, if needed. Legal insurance plans often involve a retainer fee. If the client calls the retained attorney, he or she will provide minor specific legal services without additional fees. If requested services are complicated or time consuming (such as conduct of a trial), additional charges are billed as "earned" fees. The rate of additional fees might be according to the retainer agreement. Many attorneys also use the word "retainer" to describe the periodic receipt of earned fees from a regular client.

A growing number of states place percentage maximums that may be charged in contingent fee contracts. In New Jersey, a maximum graduated scale is used in tort cases: from 50 percent on the first $1,000 to 10 percent of any excess over $100,000.[30] In California, a special limitation exists for medical malpractice cases, from 40 percent of the first $50,000 of recovery to 10 percent of any excess over $200,000.[31] Similar statutory limitations exist in matters processed by administrative agencies rather than by courts (e.g., veterans' benefits, social security claims, and workers' compensation cases).

In addition, a fee charged by an attorney may be set by, or subject to the approval of, the court. An example of this would be fees of attorneys appointed to represent indigents or minors. When a fee limitation is applicable (by statute or court order), the client should ask whether the fee is prescribed or is a maximum allowed by law. In many cases, the statutory fee is a maximum and the client is free to negotiate payment of a lower fee (e.g., a probate fee).

Many countries, including Great Britain, provide that attorney fees (as well as court costs) are to be paid by the loser in a case. In contrast, in the United States each party is usually responsible for their attorney fees, unless they agreed otherwise. (The loser always pays the court costs.) For example, a landlord suing a renter for past-due rent might benefit from a lease providing that the renter is to reimburse the landlord for any attorney fee expense incurred in collecting rent or enforcing the lease (this clause is commonly found in rental agreements). Many state statutes provide that if such a provision exists in the contract, it will be construed to give the victor in the legal dispute—be it the landlord or the tenant—the right to reimbursement of legal fees. So even if contract language states only that it protects the landlord, the tenant will be awarded attorney fees if he or she wins the lawsuit.[32]

Actual fees charged for legal services are difficult to compare because of the many factors used in setting fees in specific cases. Hourly fees in large cities at the time of this writing range from $60 to $400 and more. A flat fee for a simple divorce with no significant property or child custody dispute may range from $350 to $1,000; complex divorces for wealthy clients, on the other hand, may command fees in the many thousands of dollars. Contingent fees are rarely less than 25 percent of the net recovery or more than 50 percent. Astronomical fees in celebrated cases involving national corporations or prominent persons and politicians shed little light on fees charged for the routine legal problems of the ordinary consumer.

If you become involved in a dispute with your attorney and cannot settle it through direct negotiation, contact the local bar association. The local bar is probably listed in your telephone directory. Local bar associations have established procedures where disputed fees are reviewed in light of all applicable circumstances. Often a mutually satisfactory result is achieved without further legal action. Some 30 states permit arbitration of attorney fee disputes to expedite settlement of client claims.

Financing Attorney Fees   In some instances, a client may need to borrow money to pay attorney fees. A loan may be made by the creditor/attorney, a lending institution, or a third person (e.g., a relative). If the attorney finances the debt, a promissory note will be expected from the client. This arrangement may create a conflict of interest, because the attorney is both a creditor and agent of the client. An attorney may not use unreasonable collection methods; such conduct is unethical. Many attorneys are reluctant to sue a client to collect a fee (they think it would generate bad publicity) and simply demand cash in advance or refuse to extend credit to clients. An attorney may accept payment by credit card, although it is still not common. Such attorneys are subject to all laws regarding vendors and credit card users.

Financing the Client's Case   Often, as a legal case progresses, costs are incurred long before any recovery is possible. Costs in a typical personal injury case are:

1. *Court cost*—The court charges fees (e.g., $100) to cover at least some of the administrative costs of processing the paperwork connected with litigation. Other court charges are made for such diverse items as daily fees paid to jurors in a jury trial (e.g., $15) and fees of expert witnesses.
2. *Investigation*—Most attorneys do not have the time, skill, or inclination to personally inspect the accident scene, photograph it, and talk to potential witnesses. These and similar tasks might be performed by a hired professional investigator.
3. *Discovery*—Sworn testimony is taken before a court reporter, usually in the office of the attorney who made the request. The session may be audiotaped or videotaped. Discovery is often very expensive.

4. *Medical examination*—An issue in an injury case is the physical, and sometimes mental, condition of the injured victim. Before trial, one or more medical examinations will probably be made by a physician who will expect to be paid. This procedure is distinguished from medical treatment. Some physicians specialize in examination of injury victims (provide testimony in court) rather than the treatment of patients.

5. *Expert witness fees*—Court testimony from experts is often necessary. Experts, as distinguished from lay witnesses, are entitled to give a formal opinion about a matter within their expertise. Lay witnesses are allowed to testify only as to what they saw, heard, or otherwise experienced. In an automobile accident case, one or more physicians might testify as to the nature and extent of the victim's injury. An economist might testify as to the lost wages of the victim because of the injuries. A model maker may present a replica of the intersection involved, complete with model cars and signal lights. New types of experts include persons who devise computer simulations of many facets of an accident. All these experts expect to be well paid for their services.

The sum total of these expenses can be staggering—sometimes many thousands of dollars. Most of these expenses are incurred long before any recovery is awarded and received.

Ethically, an attorney is permitted to "advance" litigation costs even though the lawyer is arguably creating an investment in the outcome of the client's case. The attorney might be tempted to suggest an early settlement not because it is the client's best interest, but rather to recapture costs advanced as well as to participate in the recovery.[33] American Bar Association rules permit advances if the client is ultimately responsible for reimbursing the attorney. The requirement of reimbursement is believed to mitigate possible conflict of interest between the attorney and the client. Although the client is responsible for such costs, attorneys commonly absorb them when there is no recovery by not asking the client to pay. The attorney's duty to require reimbursement raises interesting ethical questions. For example, failure to require reimbursement might be characterized as maintenance.

If the fee is contingent and there is a recovery, litigation costs may be shared by the plaintiff and plaintiff's attorney. For example:

Recovery (in damages or settlement)	$25,000
Less net litigation costs incurred by plaintiff's lawyer, which equal total out of pocket litigation costs incurred (e.g., filing fees, investigation costs)	–3,250
Less portion of court costs recovered from unsuccessful litigant (e.g., jury fees reimbursed by defendant)	+750
Net recovery	22,500
Attorney's fee (35 percent of net recovery)	–7,875
Client's recovery	$14,625

As this computation shows, the attorney absorbs 35 percent of the litigation costs paid, and the client absorbs 65 percent (i.e., 35 percent of $25,000 equals $8750; 35 percent of $22,500 equals $7,875; the difference of $875 is 35 percent of the plaintiff's net litigation costs of $2,500).

Litigation costs may be modest in some types of cases, such as a simple divorce, while litigation costs in anti-trust cases may be hundreds of thousands or even millions of dollars in celebrated cases involving national corporations.

Inventor Charles Hall brought lawsuits against several defendants, alleging patent infringement regarding his water bed innovations. To finance the lawsuit, he syndicated interests in the possible outcome of the suits. He raised $750,000. May he finance his lawsuit in this fashion?

No. The doctrine of **champerty** forbids the financial participation in the lawsuit of another.[34] Champerty is defined as ". . . a bargain by [another] with a plaintiff or defendant for a portion of the matter involved in a suit in case of successful termination of the action, which the [other] undertakes to maintain or carry on at his own expense."[35] Society's concern is that investment in cases by outsiders encourages gambling and litigation.

What Are Common Attorney-Client Problems?

Attorneys have often assumed broad control over a lawsuit while their client remained passive. Many attorneys believe a client's participation should be limited to following the lawyer's advice to either settle or pursue the matter to conclusion. The passive client is quiescent and trusting, relying on the lawyer's professional expertise and judgment.

A modern and client-oriented view of the attorney-client relationship calls for more client participation. The client is expected to understand the progress of the case and share in the decision making. This view holds that the client is capable of evaluating the attorney's performance as the case progresses.

Any legal dispute is a marriage of the client's problem and the attorney's skills and expertise in seeking a resolution satisfactory to the client. Appropriate control of strategy and decision making is often difficult. This marriage is best reconciled when the client makes decisions regarding the merits of the case and the attorney makes decisions regarding procedure, strategy, and tactics. For example, the client alone decides whether to settle (compromise) or drop a civil case[36] and, in a criminal case, whether to demand trial by jury.[37] Realistically, many attorneys expect the client to take advice and not actively participate in case decision making. Such a view of client relations may explain why most common attorney-client problems involve communication problems.

The client, to whom the case is extremely important (perhaps even to exaggerated proportions), expects frequent communication from the attorney. This communication is reassurance that things are happening and the matter is not forgotten. For the attorney, to whom the case may be routine and just one of many, there is little need or time to increase an already burdensome paperwork load with letters to the client explaining routine developments. Communication takes time and increases the cost of the matter to the client. How can a client minimize the chance of becoming unhappy about a lack of communication from the attorney during the course of the litigation or legal matter? One strategy is for the client to raise the issue at the time the attorney is employed, by asking questions like:

● What are the steps that may be expected to take place in this case?
● Will I be informed by you or your secretary when each step is accomplished?
● May I call you or your secretary for an update from time to time?
● Will I be mailed copies of all incoming and outgoing correspondence, documentation pleadings, and briefs concerning my case?
● When will we meet next?

Common problems between an attorney and a client also include fee disputes, misunderstandings of time periods involved, and misconceptions of what is and is not possible in a legal case. Simple neglect of work and misuse of client's funds form the basis of many other client complaints; both of these practices are unethical.

What Is Legal Malpractice?

All states impose a minimum standard of care for attorneys in performance of legal services. The tort of *malpractice* occurs when an attorney fails to meet (or even at times, exceed) that standard of care and as a result the client suffers a loss. This standard of care has been described in various ways, but generally an attorney is required to possess the knowledge and skill, and to exercise the care and diligence of other attorneys in the community. Attorney specialists are held to higher standards of performance than are other attorneys. Negligence by an attorney in handling a legal matter is malpractice.

To recover damages for attorney malpractice, the client needs to hire a second attorney to pursue the case against the lawyer accused of negligence. For the dissatisfied client, this is undoubtedly not a pleasant prospect. A malpractice case must be initiated within a prescribed time, usually within one to three years from the time of the negligent act(s).

In a malpractice trial, the purported victimized client must prove that, but for the attorney's negligence, the result in the earlier matter would have been more favorable to the client. The accused attorney may deny the charge or contend, "Yes, I may have been negligent, but the result was fair, adequate, and reasonable." The client winning a malpractice case still faces the problem of collecting the judgment. Attorneys who commit serious malpractice may also be the least able to pay a sizable judgment and the least likely to have purchased adequate malpractice insurance.

Mike Kline could not decide whether to consult an attorney about the neck injury he suffered when Dorea Carson sideswiped him while he was skateboarding in a crosswalk. He had medical insurance and he expected his pain would soon stop. However, after nine months of continued distress and intermittent suffering, he consulted Attorney Jules Doe about a suit for damages. Doe assured him he had a good case and prepared a contingency fee retainer agreement, which Mike signed. Several months later (13 months after the accident), attorney Doe contacted Mike and said that after further study he concluded that Mike really did not have a good case after all, "But not to worry; I won't charge you a cent." What should Mike do?

Mike should be very suspicious and either receive a full and completely satisfactory explanation of why Doe wishes to drop the matter or consult another attorney. It is possible that Doe committed malpractice by failing to file the complaint within the statute of limitations (one to three years is a common range of time for claims for physical injury caused by tort). Once an attorney accepts a case, it is his or her obligation to comply with procedural requirements. Failure to file timely documents is the single most common act of malpractice.[38]

An attorney is not guilty of malpractice just because a case is lost. Ultimately in every case with two or more adversaries, someone loses and someone wins. A strategy decision that subsequently turns out to be disastrous is not usually malpractice. The attorneys representing Texaco in the *Pennzoil Co.* v. *Texaco, Inc.* case were considered to be among the most able attorneys in Texas, yet Texaco lost the case at trial and suffered damages of $10.53 billion[39] (see Chapter 5).

Attorney malpractice exists for a wide variety of negligent acts and omissions: failure to apply settled principles of law to the case, failure to protect the right to appeal, failure to draft pleadings (court-related documents) properly and promptly, failure to appear and defend, failure to assert all possible claims or defenses, failure to present relevant evidence, lack of diligence in prosecuting a case once initiated, and misdrafting a will. An ounce of prevention in the careful selection of an attorney is worth a pound of cure in suing for malpractice.

In fairness, the following words from a former Chief Justice of the United States Supreme Court merit attention:

> All of us have long known that there are problems in some areas of our profession which deserve and which receive criticism not only from the public but from the bar itself. The bar is the severest and most expert critic of the profession. At the same time, most citizens will acknowledge what history shows about the courageous lawyers who have been among the staunchest defenders of liberties. Virtually every advance in the cause of civil rights came at the hands of lawyers—often serving without compensation.[40]

Unauthorized Practice of Law

Practicing law without a license is a crime, just as practicing medicine or dentistry without a license is a crime. A non-lawyer providing legal advice who bills a client for the service may not use the courts to collect the fee. Contracts for legal services by a non-attorney are illegal and void. Any payment made by the client is recoverable.

All states provide for licensure in order to practice. A person who does not have, or who fails to maintain, a license to practice law is forbidden to do so. It is sometimes a difficult question whether a given act is offering legal advice or simply performing a standard business practice. In different states there are different answers. For example, in California it is a common practice for title searches to be conducted by title companies (albeit with the aid of in-house staff attorneys). In other states, independent attorneys perform this activity. Non-lawyers (such as real estate brokers) are generally permitted to complete blanks on forms that may affect legal rights. However, these must be standard forms, and legal advice may not be offered with the forms. Accountants prepare tax returns and suggest probable tax consequences, but must be careful not to interpret tax statutes, rules, or cases or render tax planning legal advice.

There is currently popular support for relaxing the historical prohibition against the unauthorized practice of law to allow some routine legal matters to be handled by legal assistants, paralegals, or legal technicians. Such work is already often performed by paralegals under the direction of lawyers. Lawyer supervision adds to the cost of such services, causing some consumers and non-lawyer providers to question whether the public is being protected or fleeced.[41] Routine matters usually include uncontested divorce pleadings, simple wills, eviction notices, simple bankruptcy filings, and probate of small estates.

The contention is that these services can be delivered to the consumer at lower cost, with higher pay for the legal service technician, by eliminating a superfluous middle person—the attorney. Opponents to the relaxation of unauthorized practice laws are concerned the dividing line between what is and what is not the practice of law will become even more confused. They are concerned that consumers do not appreciate or realize the difference in the educational preparation of legal assistants. Furthermore, it is difficult if not impossible to predetermine what is simple and routine.* A California proposal to allow legal technicians to perform specified services provides that such legal technicians be licensed after meeting education and training requirements. The California law would theoretically satisfy many objections, but it also creates a new profession.[42]

Do-it-yourself probate kits (designed to assist the personal representative-executor or administrator in necessary procedures following death) and divorce kits are not considered to be the practice of law because the information is generalized and not tailored to the needs of a single client.[43] In recent years, many self-help books in a variety of legal areas have been published.

Alternative Dispute Resolution

In Chapter 3, the use of alternative dispute resolution (ADR) techniques was introduced. The purpose of that discussion was to identify alternatives available to the court resolution of disputes. When retaining legal counsel for a civil matter, any client should discuss with the attorney the possible use of negotiation, mediation, and arbitration. The attorney's willingness to consider these alternatives may be an important factor to assist your employment decision. While we explained the main methods of ADR in Chapter 3, there are additional dispute resolution methods that have proved to be useful in some cases.

---

* Every attorney has been told by a client, "I just want a simple will," only to discover that either the client's circumstances or desires make that impossible.

Expert Fact Finding

Neutral expert fact finding is a non-binding process where an appointed third-party expert investigates or hears facts on selected issues, and makes findings of fact. Findings may assist in negotiations or even be admissible in a more formal process if the process does not immediately result in a negotiated settlement of the dispute. Fact finding may be part of a negotiation, mediation, or arbitration.

Mini-Trial

A **mini-trial** is a voluntary process where the parties, usually sizable business organizations, agree to an informal trial-like proceeding. Each side agrees to the procedural rules, to exchange information, and decides on a neutral advisor. The focal point of the process is to present the facts of the case to a special private jury. The jury is composed of high-ranking company officials, with dispute settlement authority, from the disputing organizations. As jurors, the officials learn about the dispute as it is perceived by a jury who hears both sides. Hopefully they then are better able to predict the probable or possible resolution of the conflict. Often, the well-informed key managers are able to negotiate a settlement and avoid the actual court trial.

Summary Jury Trial

The **summary jury trial** is similar to the mini-trial. It is a process for cases already in litigation that have not yet settled. Prior to trial, parties present their cases to a private mock jury. The mock jury is composed of lay citizens chosen (and employed) to mirror an expected actual jury. The presentations are abbreviated and the jury is asked to determine its probable verdict in a short period of time. After the jury verdict, the attorneys question the jurors about their decision. The process is non-binding and is used to facilitate settlement by giving insight to the lawyers as to the probable result at trial and the reaction of jurors to their case.

What Price Justice?

 The Wall Street Journal reported that Mr. Fuller rejected a settlement offer of $12,500 in his breach of contract and tort action against ten former associates. He believed he was entitled to $500,000 in punitive damages. The case went to trial. The "good news" was Mr. Fuller won a jury verdict of $25,000. The "bad news" was it took three years to resolve and he was unemployed. His single-minded concern with the case alienated friends and relatives. The case cost him $75,000 in litigation expenses. During the prolonged dispute he employed seven different lawyers, one at a time—six of them quit.[44]

Mr. Fuller won his case, so one can assume he was wronged. It is however true that if he had accepted the settlement offer he would have had a positive net recovery, rather than a $50,000 negative victory. After the "victory," he continued to be consumed by the case ". . . suspecting that the judge, defense attorney, defendants and his own attorneys had all joined in a plot against him."[45]

This news vignette concludes *Understanding the Law*, leaving you with more questions than answers, more problems than solutions. However, we trust that your ability to understand the problems and competing interests in legal disputes has improved. Mr. Fuller sought justice as he understood it, but he may have also sought vengeance. His lawsuit for damages complained of fraud in addition to breach of contract and he hoped for $500,000 in punitive damages. Convincing a jury of fraud without overwhelming evidence of wrongful intent is very difficult, and the claim of fraud invariably complicates a trial. It appears that Mr. Fuller might not have accepted such an explanation from his attorneys.

The court that heard the case was staffed by expensive professionals in an impressive but costly courthouse, to ensure a fair and impartial trial. The expense of these services by the state is generally overlooked by litigants. The plaintiff felt vindicated even though he lost money, but did he violate a social responsibility to the public? Was his pursuit of "justice at any price" at too high a price to the public?

The use of seven different attorneys by the plaintiff in the same case is unusual. The most probable explanation would not be that the attorneys were unethical, but that Mr. Fuller was unreasonable. At the trial's conclusion, the dispute was not necessarily over—the defendants were considering an appeal. Mr. Fuller's interview stated he was pursuing other aspects of the case, including complaints against the attorneys on both sides.

It is a simple truth that the shortest distance between two points is a straight line. A person aggrieved often expects that legal satisfaction is a simple matter of being given his or her deserved due. The "simple straight line" truth is not really that simple, and neither is the achievement of justice or legal satisfaction. A mountain or a canyon can make it practically impossible to travel in a straight line. A freeway crossing a straight line can make it dangerous to proceed without modifying your route. A similar problem exists in the quest for "Equal Justice Under Law."* The path to justice is seldom a straight line, even though we might wish it. The path is full of obstacles. They are, however, usually apparent, discoverable, and surmountable for travelers assisted by knowledge and expert guides.

Case 15

PEOPLE EX. REL. GOLDBERG v. GORDON

Colorado Supreme Court, 607 P.2d 995 (1980)

Betty Weirick employed attorney Robert Gordon, Jr., to perform all legal work necessary after the death of her husband, John. The only known assets of John Weirick was a home valued at $4,000; $20 in the bank; an automobile valued at $100; a pickup truck of no

---

* Words inscribed in marble above the entrance to the United States Supreme Court building in Washington, D.C.

value; and 10,000 shares of stock. All property was held in joint tenancy, with John and Betty as the joint tenants. John Weirick had executed a holographic will naming Betty his sole heir. Attorney Gordon admitted the will to probate and attempted to effect the transfer of the property through the probate proceeding. When he found out a probate proceeding was unnecessary, he demanded $400 payment before he would undertake to close the estate. (This was in addition to $561 Betty Weirick had already paid him.) After he took an attorney's lien on the shares of stock, Mrs. Weirick paid him the additional $400. He did not close the estate or communicate with or explain his conduct to his client. While trying to collect the $400 and secure a deed of trust on his client's house to secure payment, he explained that "my fee could be as much as $5,000." A formal complaint was lodged with the Supreme Court Grievance Committee. Their recommendations are included in the opinion of the court below.

The hearings committee made extensive findings and concluded that each of the allegations of the formal complaint had been proven by clear and convincing evidence. Without repeating . . . the findings and conclusions, the committee determined the issues against the respondent as follows:

(1) Respondent failed to represent competently the affairs of his client by undertaking matters which he was incompetent to handle without associating counsel competent in the matter or without preparation adequate in the circumstances;

(2) Respondent provided legal services which were totally ineffective to accomplish the desired results;

(3) Respondent provided legal services which were totally unnecessary;

(4) Respondent failed to address specific legal issues and questions in a competent and timely fashion;

(5) Respondent failed to complete legal matters commenced on behalf of his client in a timely and competent fashion;

(6) Respondent charged or attempted to charge a clearly excessive fee and wrongfully attempted to obtain security for such fee;

(7) Respondent wrongfully asserted an attorney's lien on certain documents and papers of his client.

. . . [The] lack of recognition on the part of Respondent of basic operative facts and principles of law was not sinister or fraudulent; rather it evidences a total lack of understanding of fundamental principles essential to the practice of law. At no time during his representation . . . has Respondent recognized the errors enumerated above nor the inappropriateness of his action on behalf of his clients.

. . . The Grievance Committee recommended that respondent's license to practice law be suspended for a period of three years, and that it be reinstated only upon a showing the respondent has attained a level of competence adequate to justify the reissuance of a license, including satisfaction of all requirements of the Board of Law Examiners for initial admission to the bar, including satisfactory completion of the bar examination.

A license to practice law is a proclamation to the public that the holder thereof is one to whom a member of the public may, with confidence, entrust his professional matters, with the assurance that in the performance of legal services the lawyer will perform the basic legal tasks undertaken, competently, ethically, and in accordance with the highest standards of professional conduct. The public, therefore, has every right to expect that one who has demonstrated through professional misconduct a lack of minimal professional competence required of attorneys, shall be appropriately disciplined. Respondent in this case has failed to measure up to the minimum standards of fitness to practice law.

Respondent, Robert M. Gordon, Jr., was suspended from the practice of law for three years and until further order of the court.

QUESTIONS AND PROBLEMS

1. The legal profession is in the process of change. Following are some current issues involving change that have impact on the public interest.

    a. Should attorneys who participate in formal courtroom trials be trained differently from other lawyers?

    b. Should charges of unprofessional conduct be heard by other attorneys, by non-lawyers, or by both?

    c. What limitations ought to be imposed on the rights of attorneys to advertise for and to solicit legal business?

    d. What are the advantages and disadvantages to society in permitting live televising of courtroom proceedings? How might attorneys and witnesses be affected? Should live television be allowed in both civil and criminal trials?

2. To qualify for a license to practice law, a candidate must be of "good moral character." Which—and how much—of the following types of conduct ought to disqualify a candidate from the practice of law?

    a. Excessive drinking of alcoholic beverages

    b. Cheating on income tax returns

    c. Occasional use of marijuana, cocaine, or other illegal drugs

    d. Adultery or sexual promiscuity

    e. Deliberate misuse of student loan funds, grant monies, or food stamps

    f. Dishonorable discharge from military service

3. An ad in the *Orange County Apartment News* stated, "Evictions as low as $65." Roberta Spiegel visited Landlords Professional Services (LPS), the business that placed the ad, when she needed to evict a tenant. An employee whose business card identified him as a counselor (Bill Watts), told Roberta in response to her questions that her use of a three-day eviction notice was insufficient and she would have to take another notice to the apartment. Did Bill Watts and LPS engage in the practice of law without a license? [*People* v. *Landlords Professional Services*, 264 Cal.Rptr. 548 (1989)]

4. Attorney Hippard admitted by stipulation five counts and numerous instances of misconduct between 1972 and 1975. His misconduct included borrowing money in excess of $22,000 from clients without providing security or disclosing his poor financial condition. He also misappropriated money from clients, issued checks drawn on accounts that were closed or had insufficient funds, and abandoned his clients on three separate instances. He resigned from the state bar in 1977. In 1980, Mr. Hippard filed for bankruptcy discharging his debts, including obligations owed to a number of his former clients. In 1987, Mr. Hippard petitioned the state bar for reinstatement. He provided substantial evidence of rehabilitation. He also argued that although he had not repaid his former clients, to deny restatement because of a ". . . failure to repay debts discharged by bankruptcy in the absence of a clear showing of financial ability to do so contravenes due process and violates the purpose of the bankruptcy laws." Is Mr. Hippard correct? [*Hippard* v. *State Bar of California,* 264 Cal.Rptr. 684 (1989)]

5. Contingent fee arrangements are said to make legal services available to persons who otherwise would be unable to pay; but contingent fee arrangements are also said to promote litigation unnecessarily, because potential plaintiffs (victims) have nothing to lose by suing. What do you think of these contentions?

6. The Goldfarbs were buying a home in Fairfax County, Virginia. They ran into a series of hurdles. They needed financing to buy the home, but the finance company required they secure title insurance. In order to get title insurance, the insurance company required that a search of the record of title of the property be conducted. In Virginia, that search was required by law to be conducted by an attorney. They contacted several attorneys and inquired as to the price for this service. They found out three things. First, the Fairfax Bar Association maintained a list of recommended minimum prices for common legal services. Second, most attorneys told the Goldfarbs the minimum fee on that schedule for a title search would be the fee charged. Third, although they contacted 36 attorneys, they could find no one who would perform the title search for less than that minimum fee. The Goldfarbs filed suit, alleging the fee schedule, although voluntary for attorneys, amounted to price fixing (an illegal combination in restraint of trade under Section 1 of the Sherman Anti-trust Act). What result? [*Goldfarb* v. *Virginia State Bar*, 421 U.S. 733, 95 S.Ct. 2004 (1975)]

7. In England, the loser in civil litigation must pay the victor's attorney's fees. In almost all types of cases in the United States, each litigant pays his or her own attorney's fees. What are the arguments in support of each of these positions?

8. Liability insurance is available to cover potential attorney malpractice. As with most liability insurance, the premiums charged have increased significantly in recent years. Malpractice insurance coverage for attorneys is usually not required either by law or by the Professional Rules of Conduct. As in many other liability situations, those who can most afford a major loss carry ample insurance, whereas those that have little financial ability are more likely to be without insurance. Should malpractice insurance be required as a condition for the practice of law? Discuss.

9. Mallard, an attorney admitted to practice before the U.S. District Court in the Southern District of Iowa, was selected by the U.S. Magistrate to represent indigent inmates. The inmates' suit was filed against prison officials under a federal statute that provided that federal courts may "request" an attorney to represent any person claiming poverty status. Claiming he was not competent to handle a complex matter of that kind, he filed a motion to withdraw. The magistrate denied his request and his appeal to the district court and Court of Appeals was unsuccessful. Can the court compel attorney Mallard to represent an indigent civil litigant? [*Mallard* v. *U.S. Dist. Court for Southern District of Iowa*, 109 S.Ct. 1814 (1989)]

10. What factors should an attorney consider in establishing the fee to charge a prospective client? Should the services of an attorney be provided by one's employer as a fringe benefit? Should all attorney fees be regulated by government?

FURTHER READING

1. Clark, W. *The Ox-Bow Incident*. New York: New American Library, 1960. Classic book on mob justice contrasted to the order of and the rule of law.

2. Lewis, A. *Gideon's Trumpet*. New York: Vintage, 1966. The account of the case of *Gideon* v. *Wainwright*. This case prompted the U.S. Supreme Court to extend the right of an accused to an attorney in all important criminal cases. The book provides an example of the importance of counsel in a trial and the nobility of some members of the bar.

3. Mayer, M. *The Lawyers*. New York: Harper & Row, 1967. Informed third-party account of the legal profession.

4. Mellinkoff, D. *The Conscience of a Lawyer*. St. Paul, MN: West, 1973. Fascinating look at the legal profession using a murder case and an ethical dilemma of the defendant's lawyer to provide the background.

5. Nizer, L. *My Life in Court*. New York: Doubleday, 1961. Interesting and entertaining depiction of the cases and strategies of a well-known American attorney.

6. Osborn, J. *The Paper Chase*. New York: Avon, 1971. Popular account of how much fun it is to be a Harvard law student. Much to debate and think about.

7. Turow, S. *Presumed Innocent*. New York: Farrar, Straus, Giroux, 1987. Best-selling novel about law and lawyers in a criminal prosecution.

8. Verrone, P. "The 12 Best Trial Movies, 75 *American Bar Association Journal* 96 (November 1989). All right, enough books already. How about a movie? While not agreeing on all selections, how can one ignore VCR suggestions that include *M, A Man For All Seasons,* and *To Kill a Mockingbird*?

NOTES

1. Curran, B. "Survey of the Public's Legal Needs," 61 *American Bar Association Journal* 848 (June 1978).

2. In re Keenan, 50 N.E.2d 785 (Massachusetts, 1943).

3. *Cord* v. *Gibb*, 254 S.E.2d 71 (Virginia, 1979).

4. *Sacramento Bee*, February 9, 1977.

5. See, for example, *Littell* v. *Morton*, 519 F.2d 1399 (Maryland, 1978); *Goldman* v. *Kane*, 329 N.E.2d 770 (Massachusetts, 1975); and *In re Czachorski*, 244 N.E.2d 164 (Illinois, 1969).

6. *State* v. *Alexander*, 503 P.2d 777 (Arizona, 1972).

7. *Baltes* v. Doe, 4 *Lawyers Manual of Professional Conduct* 356 (Fla. Cir. Ct. 1988).

8. Hazard, H. and W. Hodes, *The Law of Lawyering* (Englewood Cliffs, NJ: Prentice-Hall, 1989), § 90.2.

9. Carlin, J. *Lawyer's Ethics* (New York: Russell Sage Foundation, 1966).

10. A copy of the published quotation is available (contact this text's authors), although the source cannot be identified.

11. See, generally, Englade, K. "The LSC under Siege," 73 *American Bar Association Journal* 66 (December 1987).

12. *United Transportation Union* v. *State Bar of Michigan*, 401 U.S. 576, 91 S.Ct. 1076 (1971).

13. Hazard, H., and W. Hodes, op cit., p. 866.

14. Excerpt from the Model Rules of Professional Conduct, American Bar Association, adopted August 1983.

15. Citations are arranged to correlate with the examples given. *In the matter of Wallace Larson*, 589 P.2d 442 (Arizona, 1979); *In the matter of Charles Glick*, 413 N.Y.S.2d 753 (1979); *Tormo* v. *Yormark*, 398 F.Supp. 1159 (New Jersey, 1975); *State* v. *Martindale*, 527 P.2d 703 (Kansas, 1974); and *In re Hall*, 438 P.2d 874 (Washington, 1968).

16. Citations are arranged to correlate with the examples given. *In re Mitchell*, 370 N.Y.S.2d 99 (1975); *In re Kline*, 477 P.2d 881 (Montana, 1970); *In re Thompson*, 209 N.W.2d 412 (Minnesota, 1973); *Kentucky State Bar* v. *Scott*, 409 S.W.2d 293 (Kentucky, 1966); *The Florida Bar* v. *Jenkins*, 254 So.2d 785 (Florida, 1971); *In re Corey*, 515 P.2d 400 (Hawaii, 1973); *In re Safran*, 133 Cal.Rptr. 9 (1966); and *In re Michael Cohen*, 113 Cal.Rptr. 485 (1974).

17. *Maryland State Bar* v. *Agnew*, 318 A.2d 811 (Maryland, 1974).

18. *Pineda* v. *State Bar of California*, 263 Cal.Rptr. 377 (1989).

19. Ibid.

20. Schnapper, E. "The Myth of Legal Ethics," 64 *American Bar Association Journal* 202 (February 1978).

21. *In the matter of Edward McIver Leppard*, 252 S.E.2d 143 (South Carolina, 1979).

22. *Oklahoma Bar Association* v. *Haworth*, 593 P.2d 765 (Oklahoma, 1979).

23. *Bates* v. *State Bar of Arizona*, 433 U.S. 350, 97 S.Ct. 2691 (1977).

24. Although individual attorneys in all states presently are restricted from solicitation, the U.S. Supreme Court has ruled that the American Civil Liberties Union (ACLU) and similar organizations of attorneys may solicit directly [*In re Primus*, 436 U.S. 412, 98 S.Ct. 1893 (1978)]; that the National Association for the Advancement of Colored People (NAACP) may solicit parents of schoolchildren in desegregation cases [*NAACP* v. *Button*, 371 U.S. 415, 83 S.Ct. 328 (1963)]; and that a union may solicit its members to funnel their injury claims to a particular attorney [*United Mine Workers* v. *Illinois*, 389 U.S. 217, 88 S.Ct. 353 (1967)].

25. See California Business and Professions Code §§ 6147 and 6148.

26. *Baron* v. *Mare*, 120 Cal.Rptr. 675 (1975).

27. "Validity and Effect of Contract for Attorney's Compensation Made After Inception of Attorney-Client Relationship", 13 *American Law Reports* 3d 701 (Lawyer's Cooperative Publishing Co. 1967).

28. *Kansas* v. *Mayes*, 531 P.2d 102 (Kansas, 1975).

29. *Bushman* v. *State Bar*, 113 Cal.Rptr. 904 (1974); and *Florida Bar* v. *Winn*, 208 So.2d 809 (Florida, 1968).

30. *American Trial Lawyers Association* v. *New Jersey Supreme Court*, 330 A.2d 350 (New Jersey, 1974).

31. California Business & Professions Code § 6146.

32. See, for example, California Civil Code § 1717.

33. American Bar Association, CPR 5, DR 5–103(b).

34. *The Wall Street Journal*, November 22, 1989.

35. 14 American Jurisprudence 2d § 3.

36. *Harrop and Lewis* v. *Western Airlines Inc.* 550 F.2d 1143 (California, 1977).

37. *U.S. ex rel Baez* v. *Circuit Court of Cook County,* 395 F.Supp. 1285 (Illinois, 1975).

38. The American Bar Association claims that 11 percent of malpractice complaints involve a failing to calendar and also a missing of deadlines. Gates, W., "Charting the Shoals of Malpractice," 73 *American Bar Association Journal* 62 (July 1987).

39. J. Shannon, *Texaco and the $10 Billion Jury* (Englewood Cliffs, NJ: Prentice-Hall, 1988).

40. Warren Burger, Chief Justice of the U.S. Supreme Court, in a speech to the American Law Institute, May 1978, as reported in 64 *American Bar Association Journal* 847 (1978).

41. *The Wall Street Journal,* July 24, 1988.

42. Ibid.

43. *In re William R. Thompson et al,* 574 S.W.2d 365 (Missouri, 1978).

44. Rout, L., "Obsession Pays Off, Sort of, for Plaintiff Who Wouldn't Quit," *The Wall Street Journal,* October 23, 1980, p. 1.

45. Ibid.

Appendix A

The Declaration of Independence

In Congress, July 4, 1776.

A Declaration by the Representatives of the United States of America, in General Congress assembled.

When in the Course of human Events, it becomes necessary for one People to dissolve the Political Bands which have connected them with another, and to assume among the Powers of the Earth, the separate and equal Station to which the Laws of Nature and of Nature's God entitle them, a decent Respect to the Opinions of Mankind requires that they should declare the causes which impel them to the Separation.

We hold these Truths to be self-evident, that all Men are created equal, that they are endowed by their Creator with certain unalienable Rights, that among these are Life, Liberty, and the Pursuit of Happiness—That to secure these Rights, Governments are instituted among Men, deriving their just Powers from the Consent of the Governed, that whenever any Form of Government becomes destructive of these Ends, it is the Right of the People to alter or to abolish it, and to institute new Government, laying its Foundation on such Principles, and organizing its Powers in such Form, as to them shall seem most likely to effect their Safety and Happiness. Prudence, indeed, will dictate that Governments long established should not be changed for light and transient Causes; and accordingly all Experience hath shewn, that Mankind are more disposed to suffer, while Evils are sufferable, than to right themselves by abolishing the Forms to which they are accustomed. But when a long Train of Abuses and Usurpations, pursuing invariably the same Object, evinces a Design to reduce them under absolute Despotism, it is their Right, it is their Duty, to throw off such Government, and to provide new Guards for their future Security. Such has been the patient Sufferance of these Colonies; and such is now the Necessity which constrains them to alter their former Systems of Government. The History of the present King of Great-Britain is a History of repeated Injuries and Usurpations, all having in direct Object the Establishment of an absolute Tyranny over these States. To prove this, let Facts be submitted to a candid World.

He has refused his Assent to Laws, the most wholesome and necessary for the public Good.

He has forbidden his Governors to pass Laws of immediate and pressing Importance, unless suspended in their Operation till his Assent should be obtained; and when so suspended, he has utterly neglected to attend to them.

He has refused to pass other Laws for the Accommodation of large Districts of People, unless those People would relinquish the Right of Representation in the Legislature, a Right inestimable to them, and formidable to Tyrants only.

He has called together Legislative Bodies at Places unusual, uncomfortable, and distant from the Depository of their public Records, for the sole Purpose of fatiguing them into Compliance with his Measures.

He has dissolved Representative Houses repeatedly, for opposing with manly Firmness his Invasions on the Rights of the People.

He has refused for a long Time, after such Dissolutions, to cause others to be elected; whereby the Legislative Powers, incapable of Annihilation, have returned to the People at large for their exercise; the State remaining in the mean time exposed to all the Dangers of Invasion from without, and Convulsions within.

He has endeavoured to prevent the Population of these States; for that Purpose obstructing the Laws for Naturalization of Foreigners; refusing to pass others to encourage their Migration hither, and raising the Conditions of new Appropriations of Lands.

He has obstructed the Administration of Justice, by refusing his Assent to Laws for establishing Judiciary Powers.

He has made Judges dependent on his Will alone, for the Tenure of their offices, and the Amount and Payments of their Salaries.

He has erected a Multitude of new Offices, and sent hither Swarms of Officers to harrass our People, and eat out their Substance.

He has kept among us, in Times of Peace, Standing Armies, without the consent of our Legislatures.

He has affected to render the Military independent of and superior to the Civil Power.

He has combined with others to subject us to a Jurisdiction foreign to our Constitution, and unacknowledged by our Laws; giving his Assent to their Acts of pretended Legislation:

For quartering large Bodies of Armed Troops among us:

For protecting them, by a mock Trial, from Punishment for any Murders which they should commit on the Inhabitants of these States:

For cutting off our Trade with all Parts of the World:

For imposing Taxes on us without our Consent:

For depriving us, in many Cases, of the Benefits of Trial by Jury:

For transporting us beyond Seas to be tried for pretended Offences:

For abolishing the free System of English Laws in a neighbouring Province, establishing therein an arbitrary Government, and enlarging its Boundaries, so as to render it at once an Example and fit Instrument for introducing the same absolute Rule into these Colonies:

For taking away our Charters, abolishing our most valuable Laws, and altering fundamentally the Forms of our Governments:

For suspending our own Legislatures, and declaring themselves invested with Power to legislate for us in all Cases whatsoever.

He has abdicated Government here, by declaring us out of his Protection and waging War against us.

He has plundered our Seas, ravaged our Coasts, burnt our Towns, and destroyed the Lives of our People.

He is, at this Time, transporting large Armies of foreign Mercenaries to compleat the Works of Death, Desolation, and Tyranny, already begun with circumstances of Cruelty and Perfidy, scarcely paralleled in the most barbarous Ages, and totally unworthy the Head of a civilized Nation.

He has constrained our fellow Citizens taken Captive on the high Seas to bear Arms against their Country, to become the Executioners of their Friends and Brethren, or to fall themselves by their Hands.

He has excited domestic Insurrections amongst us, and had endeavoured to bring on the Inhabitants of our Frontiers, the merciless Indian Savages, whose known Rule of Warfare, is an undistinguished Destruction, of all Ages, Sexes and Conditions.

In every stage of these Oppressions we have Petitioned for Redress in the most humble Terms: Our repeated Petitions have been answered only by repeated Injury. A Prince, whose Character is thus marked by every act which may define a Tyrant, is unfit to be the Ruler of a free People.

Nor have we been wanting in Attentions to our British Brethren. We have warned them from Time to Time of Attempts by their Legislature to extend an unwarrantable Jurisdiction over us. We have reminded them of the Circumstances of our Emigration and Settlement here. We have appealed to their native Justice and Magnanimity, and we have conjured them by the Ties of our common Kindred to disavow these Usurpations, which, would inevitably interrupt our Connections and Correspondence. They too have been deaf to the Voice of Justice and of Consanguinity. We must, therefore, acquiesce in the Necessity, which denounces our Separation, and hold them, as we hold the rest of Mankind, Enemies in War, in Peace, Friends.

We, therefore, the Representatives of the UNITED STATES OF AMERICA, in GENERAL CONGRESS Assembled, appealing to the Supreme Judge of the World for the Rectitude of our Intentions, do, in the Name, and by Authority of the good People of these Colonies, solemnly Publish and Declare, That these United Colonies are, and of Right ought to be, FREE AND INDEPENDENT STATES; that they are absolved from all Allegiance to the British Crown, and that all political Connection between them and the State of Great-Britain, is and ought to be totally dissolved; and that as FREE AND INDEPENDENT STATES they have full Power to levy War, conclude Peace, contract Alliances, establish Commerce, and to do all other Acts and Things which INDEPENDENT STATES may of right do. And for the support of this Declaration, with a firm Reliance on the Protection of Divine Providence, we mutually pledge to each other our Lives, our Fortunes, and our sacred Honor.

Appendix B

Constitution of the United States of America*

We the People of the United States, in Order to form a more perfect Union, establish Justice, insure domestic Tranquility, provide for the common defence, promote the general Welfare, and secure the Blessings of Liberty to ourselves and our Posterity, do ordain and establish this Constitution for the United States of America.

Article I

Section 1. All legislative Powers herein granted shall be vested in a Congress of the United States, which shall consist of a Senate and House of Representatives.

Section 2. The House of Representatives shall be composed of Members chosen every second Year by the People of the several States, and the Electors in each State shall have the Qualifications requisite for Electors of the most numerous Branch of the State Legislature.

No Person shall be a Representative who shall not have attained to the Age of twenty five Years, and been seven Years a Citizen of the United States, and who shall not, when elected, be an Inhabitant of that State in which he shall be chosen.

Representatives and direct (Taxes)[1] shall be apportioned among the several States which may be included within this Union, according to their respective Numbers (which shall be determined by adding to the whole Number of free Persons, including those bound to Service for a Term of Years, and excluding Indians not taxed, three fifths of all other Persons).[2] The actual Enumeration shall be made within three Years after the first Meeting of the Congress of the United States, and within every subsequent Term of ten Years, in such Manner as they shall by Law direct. The Number of Representatives shall not exceed one for every thirty Thousand, but each State shall have at Least one Representative; and until such enumeration shall be made, the State of New Hampshire shall be entitled to chuse three, Massachusetts eight, Rhode Island and Providence Plantations one, Connecticut five, New York six, New Jersey four, Pennsylvania eight, Delaware one, Maryland six, Virginia ten, North Carolina five, South Carolina five, and Georgia three.

When vacancies happen in the Representation from any State, the Executive Authority thereof shall issue Writs of Election to fill such Vacancies.

The House of Representatives shall chuse their Speaker and other Officers; and shall have the sole Power of Impeachment.

Section 3. The Senate of the United States shall be composed of two Senators from each State (chosen by the Legislature thereof),[3] for six Years; and each Senator shall have one Vote.

Immediately after they shall be assembled in Consequence of the first Election, they shall be divided as equally as may be into three Classes. The Seats of the Senators of the first Class shall be vacated at the Expiration of the second Year, of the second Class at the Expiration of the fourth Year, and of the third Class at the Expiration of the sixth Year, so that one third may be chosen every second Year (and if Vacancies happen by Resignation, or otherwise, during the Recess of the Legislature of any State, the Executive thereof may make temporary Appointments until the next Meeting of the Legislature, which shall then fill such Vacancies).[4]

No Person shall be a Senator who shall not have attained to the Age of thirty Years, and been nine Years a Citizen of the United States, and who shall not, when elected, be an Inhabitant of that State for which he shall be chosen.

The Vice President of the United States shall be President of the Senate, but shall have no Vote, unless they be equally divided.

The Senate shall chuse their other Officers, and also a President pro tempore, in the Absence of the

---

* The spelling, capitalization, and punctuation of the original have been retained here. Brackets indicate passages that have been altered by amendments to the Constitution.
1. Modified by the Sixteenth Amendment.
2. Modified by the Fourteenth Amendment.

3. Repealed by the Seventeenth Amendment.
4. Modified by the Seventeenth Amendment.

Vice President, or when he shall exercise the Office of President of the United States.

The Senate shall have the sole Power to try all Impeachments. When sitting for that Purpose, they shall be on Oath or Affirmation. When the President of the United States is tried, the Chief Justice shall preside: And no Person shall be convicted without the Concurrence of two thirds of the Members present.

Judgment in Cases of Impeachment shall not extend further than to removal from Office, and disqualification to hold and enjoy any Office of honor, Trust or Profit under the United States; but the Party convicted shall nevertheless be liable and subject to Indictment, Trial, Judgment and Punishment, according to Law.

Section 4. The Times, Places and Manner of holding Elections for Senators and Representatives, shall be prescribed in each State by the Legislature thereof; but the Congress may at any time by Law make or alter such Regulations, except as to the Places of chusing Senators.

(The Congress shall assemble at least once in every Year, and such Meeting shall be on the first Monday in December, unless they shall by Law appoint a different Day.)[5]

Section 5. Each House shall be the Judge of the Elections, Returns and Qualifications of its own Members, and a Majority of each shall constitute a Quorum to do Business; but a smaller Number may adjourn from day to day, and may be authorized to compel the Attendance of absent Members, in such Manner, and under such Penalties as each House may provide.

Each House may determine the Rules of its Proceedings, punish its Members for disorderly Behaviour, and, with the Concurrence of two thirds, expel a Member.

Each House shall keep a Journal of its Proceedings, and from time to time publish the same, excepting such Parts as may in their Judgment require Secrecy; and the Yeas and Nays of the Members of either House on any question shall, at the Desire of one fifth of those Present, be entered on the Journal.

Neither House, during the Session of Congress, shall, without the Consent of the other, adjourn for more than three days, nor to any other Place than that in which the two Houses shall be sitting.

Section 6. The Senators and Representatives shall receive a Compensation for their Services, to be ascertained by Law, and paid out of the Treasury of the United States. They shall in all Cases, except Treason, Felony and Breach of the Peace, be privileged from Arrest during their Attendance at the Session of their respective Houses, and in going to and returning from the same; and for any Speech or Debate in either House, they shall not be questioned in any other Place.

No Senator or Representative shall, during the Time for which he was elected, be appointed to any civil Office under the Authority of the United States, which shall have been created, or the Emoluments whereof shall have been encreased during such time; and no Person holding any Office under the United States, shall be a Member of either House during his Continuance in Office.

Section 7. All Bills for raising Revenue shall originate in the House of Representatives; but the Senate may propose or concur with Amendments as on other Bills.

Every Bill which shall have passed the House of Representatives and the Senate, shall, before it becomes a Law, be presented to the President of the United States; If he approve he shall sign it, but if not he shall return it, with his Objections to the House in which it shall have originated, who shall enter the Objections at large on their Journal, and proceed to reconsider it. If after such Reconsideration two thirds of that House shall agree to pass the Bill, it shall be sent, together with the Objections, to the other House, by which it shall likewise be reconsidered, and if approved by two thirds of that House, it shall become a Law. But in all such Cases the Votes of both Houses shall be determined by yeas and Nays, and the Names of the Persons voting for and against the Bill shall be entered on the Journal of each House respectively. If any Bill shall not be returned by the President within ten Days (Sundays excepted) after it shall have been presented to him, the Same shall be a Law, in like Manner as if he had signed it, unless the Congress by their Adjournment prevent its Return, in which Case it shall not be a Law.

Every Order, Resolution, or Vote to Which the Concurrence of the Senate and House of Representatives may be necessary (except on a question of Adjournment) shall be presented to the President of the United States; and before the Same shall take Effect, shall be approved by him, or being disapproved by him, shall be repassed by

---

5. Changed by the Twentieth Amendment.

two thirds of the Senate and House of Representatives, according to the Rules and Limitations prescribed in the Case of a Bill.

Section 8. The Congress shall have Power To lay and collect Taxes, Duties, Imposts and Excises, to pay the Debts and provide for the common Defence and general Welfare of the United States; but all Duties, Imposts and Excises shall be uniform throughout the United States;

To borrow money on the credit of the United States;

To regulate Commerce with foreign Nations, and among the several States, and with the Indian Tribes;

To establish a uniform Rule of Naturalization, and uniform Laws on the subject of Bankruptcies throughout the United States;

To coin Money, regulate the Value thereof, and of foreign Coin, and fix the Standard of Weights and Measures;

To provide for the Punishment of counterfeiting the Securities and current Coin of the United States.

To establish Post Offices and Post Roads;

To promote the Progress of Science and useful Arts, by securing for limited Times to Authors and Inventors the exclusive Right to their respective Writings and Discoveries;

To constitute Tribunals inferior to the supreme Court;

To define and punish Piracies and Felonies committed on the high Seas, and Offences against the Law of Nations;

To declare War, grant Letters of Marque and Reprisal, and make Rules concerning Captures on Land and Water;

To raise and support Armies, but no Appropriation of Money to that Use shall be for a longer Term than two Years;

To provide and maintain a Navy;

To make Rules for Government and Regulation of the land and naval Forces;

To provide for calling forth the Militia to execute the Laws of the Union, suppress Insurrections and repel Invasions;

To provide for organizing, arming, and disciplining the Militia, and for governing such Part of them as may be employed in the Service of the United States, reserving to the States respectively, the Appointment of the Officers, and the Authority of training the Militia according to the discipline prescribed by Congress;

To exercise exclusive Legislation in all Cases whatsoever, over such District (not exceeding ten Miles square) as may, by Cession of Particular States, and the Acceptance of Congress, become the Seat of the Government of the United States, and to exercise like Authority over all Places purchased by the Consent of the Legislature of the State in which the Same shall be, for the Erection of Forts, Magazines, Arsenals, dock-Yards, and other needful Buildings;—And

To make all Laws which shall be necessary and proper for carrying into Execution the foregoing Powers, and all other Powers vested by this Constitution in the Government of the United States, or in any Department or Officer thereof.

Section 9. The Migration or Importation of Such Persons as any of the States now existing shall think proper to admit, shall not be prohibited by the Congress prior to the Year one thousand eight hundred and eight, but a Tax or duty may be imposed on such Importation, not exceeding ten dollars for each Person.

The Privilege of the Writ of Habeas Corpus shall not be suspended, unless when in Cases of Rebellion or Invasion the public Safety may require it.

No Bill of Attainder or ex post facto Law shall be passed.

(No Capitation, or other direct, Tax shall be laid, unless in Proportion to the Census or Enumeration herein before directed to be taken.)[6]

No Tax or Duty shall be laid on Articles exported from any State.

No Preference shall be given by any Regulation of Commerce or Revenue to the Ports of one State over those of another; nor shall Vessels bound to, or from, one State, be obliged to enter, clear, or pay Duties in another.

No Money shall be drawn from the Treasury, but in Consequence of Appropriations made by Law; and a regular Statement and Account of the Receipts and Expenditures of all public Money shall be published from time to time.

No Title of Nobility shall be granted by the United States; And no Person holding any Office of Profit or Trust under them, shall, without the Consent of the Congress accept of any present, Emolument, Office, or Title, of any kind whatever, from any King, Prince, or foreign State.

---

6. Modified by the Sixteenth Amendment.

Section 10. No state shall enter into any Treaty, Alliance, or Confederation; grant Letters of Marque and Reprisal; coin Money; emit Bills of Credit; make any Thing but gold and silver Coin a Tender in Payment of Debts; pass any Bill of Attainder, ex post facto Law, or Law impairing the Obligation of Contracts, or grant any Title of Nobility.

No State shall, without the Consent of the Congress, lay any Imposts or Duties on Imports or Exports, except what may be absolutely necessary for executing its inspection Laws; and the net Produce of all Duties and Imposts, laid by any State on Imports or Exports, shall be for the Use of the Treasury of the United States; and all such Laws shall be subject to the Revision and Controul of the Congress.

No State shall, without the Consent of Congress, lay any Duty of Tonnage, keep Troops, or Ships of War in time of Peace, enter into any Agreement or Compact with another State, or with a foreign Power, or engage in War, unless actually invaded, or in such imminent Danger as will not admit of delay.

Article II

Section 1. The executive Power shall be vested in a President of the United States of America. He shall hold his Office during the Term of four Years, and, together with the Vice President, chosen for the Same Term, be elected, as follows:

Each State shall appoint, in such Manner as the Legislature thereof may direct, a Number of Electors, equal to the whole Number of Senators and Representatives to which the State may be entitled in the Congress; but no Senator or Representative, or Person holding an Office of Trust or Profit under the United States, shall be appointed an Elector.

(The Electors shall meet in their respective States and vote by Ballot for two Persons of whom one at least shall not be an Inhabitant of the same State with themselves. And they shall make a List of all the Persons voted for, and of the Number of Votes for each; which List they shall sign and certify, and transmit sealed to the Seat of the Government of the United States, directed to the President of the Senate. The President of the Senate shall, in the Presence of the Senate and House of Representatives, open all the Certificates, and the Votes shall then be counted. The Person having the greatest Number of Votes shall be the President, if such Number be a Majority of the whole Number of Electors appointed; and if there be more than one

who have such Majority, and have an equal Number of Votes, then the House of Representatives shall immediately chuse by Ballot one of them for President; and if no Person have a Majority, then from the five highest on the List the said House shall in like Manner chuse the President. But in chusing the President, the Votes shall be taken by States, the Representation from each State having one Vote; A quorum for this Purpose shall consist of a Member or Members from two thirds of the States, and a Majority of all the States shall be necessary to a Choice. In every Case, after the Choice of the President, the Person having the greater Number of Votes of the Electors shall be the Vice President. But if there should remain two or more who have equal Votes, the Senate shall chuse from them by Ballot the Vice President.)[7]

The Congress may determine the Time of chusing the Electors, and the Day on which they shall give their Votes; which Day shall be the same throughout the United States.

No person except a natural born Citizen, or a Citizen of the United States, at the time of the Adoption of this Constitution, shall be eligible to the Office of President; neither shall any Person be eligible to that Office who shall not have attained to the Age of thirty five Years, and been fourteen Years a Resident within the United States.

(In Case of the Removal of the President from Office, or of his Death, Resignation, or Inability to discharge the Powers and Duties of the said Office, the Same shall devolve on the Vice President, and the Congress may by Law provide for the Case of Removal, Death, Resignation or Inability, both of the President and Vice President, declaring what Officer shall then act as President, and such Officer shall act accordingly, until the Disability be removed, or a President shall be elected.)[8]

The President shall, at stated Times, receive for his Services, a Compensation, which shall neither be increased nor diminished during the Period for which he shall have been elected, and he shall not receive within that Period any other Emolument from the United States, or any of them.

Before he enter on the Execution of his Office, he shall take the following Oath or Affirmation: "I do solemnly swear (or affirm) that I will faithfully execute the Office of President of the United States, and will to the best of my Ability, preserve, protect and defend the Constitution of the United States."

7. Changed by the Twelfth Amendment.
8. Modified by the Twentieth-fifth Amendment.

Section 2. The President shall be Commander in Chief of the Army and Navy of the United States, and of the Militia of the several States, when called into the actual Service of the United States; he may require the Opinion, in writing, of the principal Officer in each of the Executive Departments, upon any Subject relating to the Duties of their respective Offices, and he shall have Power to grant Reprieves and Pardons for Offences against the United States, except in Cases of Impeachment.

He shall have Power, by and with the Advice and Consent of the Senate, to make Treaties, provided two thirds of the Senators present concur; and he shall nominate, and by and with the Advice and Consent of the Senate, shall appoint Ambassadors, other public Ministers and Consuls, Judges of the Supreme Court, and all other Officers of the United States, whose Appointments are not herein otherwise provided for, and which shall be established by Law; but the Congress may by Law vest the Appointment of such inferior Officers, as they think proper, in the President alone, in the Courts of Law, or in the Heads of Departments.

The President shall have Power to fill up all Vacancies that may happen during the Recess of the Senate, by granting Commissions which shall expire at the End of their next Session.

Section 3. He shall from time to time give to the Congress Information of the State of the Union, and recommend to their Consideration such Measures as he shall judge necessary and expedient; he may, on extraordinary Occasions, convene both Houses, or either of them, and in Case of Disagreement between them, with Respect to the Time of Adjournment, he may adjourn them to such Time as he shall think proper; he shall receive Ambassadors and other public Ministers; he shall take Care that the Laws be faithfully executed, and shall Commission all the Officers of the United States.

Section 4. The President, Vice President and all civil Officers of the United States, shall be removed from Office on Impeachment for, and Conviction of, Treason, Bribery, or other high Crimes and Misdemeanors.

Article III

Section 1. The judicial Power of the United States, shall be vested in one supreme Court, and in such

inferior Courts as the Congress may from time to time ordain and establish. The Judges, both of the supreme and inferior Courts, shall hold their Offices during good Behaviour, and shall, at stated Times, receive for their Services, a Compensation, which shall not be diminished during their Continuance in Office.

Section 2. The judicial Power shall extend to all Cases, in Law and Equity, arising under this Constitution, the Laws of the United States, and Treaties made, or which shall be made, under their Authority;—to all Cases affecting Ambassadors, other public Ministers and Consuls;—to all Cases of admiralty and maritime Jurisdiction;—to Controversies to which the United States shall be a Party;—to Controversies between two or more States; [—between a State and Citizens of another State;—][9] between Citizens of different States,—between Citizens of the same State claiming Lands under the Grants of different States, (and between a State, or the Citizens thereof, and foreign States, Citizens or Subjects.)[10]

In all Cases affecting Ambassadors, other public Ministers and Consuls, and those in which a State shall be a Party, the supreme Court shall have original Jurisdiction. In all the other Cases before mentioned, the supreme Court shall have appellate Jurisdiction, both as to Law and Fact, with such Exceptions, and under such Regulations as the Congress shall make.

The Trial of all Crimes, except in Cases of Impeachment, shall be by Jury; and such Trial shall be held in the State where the said Crimes shall have been committed; but when not committed within any State, the Trial shall be at such Place or Places as the Congress may by Law have directed.

procedural law

Section 3. Treason against the United States, shall consist only in levying War against them, or in adhering to their Enemies, giving them Aid and Comfort. No Person shall be convicted of Treason unless on the Testimony of two Witnesses to the same overt Act, or on Confession in open Court.

The Congress shall have Power to declare the Punishment of Treason, but no Attainder of Treason shall work Corruption of Blood, or Forfeiture except during the Life of the Person attainted.

---

9. Modified by the Eleventh Amendment.
10. Modified by the Eleventh Amendment.

Article IV.

Section 1. Full Faith and Credit shall be given in each State to the public Acts, Records, and judicial Proceedings of every other State. And the Congress may by general Laws prescribe the Manner in which such Acts, Records and Proceedings shall be proved, and the Effect thereof.

Section 2. The Citizens of each State shall be entitled to all Privileges and Immunities of Citizens in the several States.

A Person charged in any State with Treason, Felony, or other Crime, who shall flee from Justice, and be found in another State, shall on Demand of the executive Authority of the State from which he fled, be delivered up, to be removed to the State having Jurisdiction of the Crime.

(No Person held to Service or Labour in one State, under the Laws thereof, escaping into another, shall, in Consequence of any Law or Regulation therein, be discharged from such Service or Labour, but shall be delivered up on Claim of the Party to whom such Service or Labour may be due.)[11]

Section 3. New States may be admitted by the Congress into this Union; but no new State shall be formed or erected within the Jurisdiction of any other State; nor any State be formed by the Junction of two or more States, or Parts of States, without the Consent of the Legislatures of the States concerned as well as of the Congress.

The Congress shall have Power to dispose of and make all needful Rules and Regulations respecting the Territory or other Property belonging to the United States; and nothing in this Constitution shall be so construed as to Prejudice any Claims of the United States, or of any particular State.

Section 4. The United States shall guarantee to every State in this Union a Republican Form of Government, and shall protect each of them against Invasion, and on Application of the Legislature, or of the Executive (when the Legislature cannot be convened) against domestic Violence.

Article V.

The Congress, whenever two thirds of both Houses shall deem it necessary, shall propose Amendments

11. Repealed by the Thirteenth Amendment.

to this Constitution, or, on the Application of the Legislatures of two thirds of the several States, shall call a Convention for proposing Amendments, which, in either Case, shall be valid to all Intents and Purposes, as Part of this Constitution, when ratified by the Legislatures of three fourths of the several States, or by Conventions in three fourths thereof, as the one or the other Mode of Ratification may be proposed by the Congress; Provided that no Amendment which may be made prior to the Year One thousand eight hundred and eight shall in any Manner affect the first and fourth Clauses in the Ninth Section of the first Article; and that no State, without its Consent, shall be deprived of its equal Suffrage in the Senate.

Article VI.

All Debts contracted and Engagements entered into, before the Adoption of this Constitution, shall be as valid against the United States under this Constitution, as under the Confederation.

This Constitution, and the Laws of the United States which shall be made in Pursuance thereof; and all Treaties made, or which shall be made, under the Authority of the United States, shall be the supreme Law of the Land; and the Judges in every State shall be bound thereby, any Thing in the Constitution or Laws of any State to the Contrary notwithstanding.

The Senators and Representatives before mentioned, and the Members of the several State Legislatures, and all executive and judicial Officers, both of the United States and of the several States, shall be bound by Oath or Affirmation, to support this Constitution: but no religious Test shall ever be required as a Qualification to any Office or public Trust under the United States.

Article VII.

The Ratification of the Conventions of nine States, shall be sufficient for the Establishment of this Constitution between the States so ratifying the Same.

Done in Convention by the Unanimous Consent of the States present the Seventeenth Day of September in the Year of our Lord one thousand seven hundred and Eighty seven and of the Independence of the United States of America the Twelfth. In witness whereof we have hereunto subscribed our Names,

Go. WASHINGTON
Presid't. and deputy from Virginia
Attest
WILLIAM JACKSON
Secretary

DELAWARE	VIRGINIA
Geo. Read	*John Blair*
Gunning Bedford jun	*James Madison Jr.*
John Dickinson	
Richard Basset	NORTH CAROLINA
Jaco. Broom	*Wm. Blount*
	Richd. Dobbs Spaight.
	Hu. Williamson
MASSACHUSETTS	
Nathaniel Gorham	
Rufus King	SOUTH CAROLINA
	J. Rutledge
	Charles Cotesworth
CONNECTICUT	*Pinckney*
Wm. Saml. Johnson	*Charles Pinckney*
Roger Sherman	*Pierce Butler.*
NEW YORK	
Alexander Hamilton	GEORGIA
	William Few
NEW JERSEY	*Abr. Baldwin*
Wh. Livingston	
David Brearley.	NEW HAMPSHIRE
Wm. Paterson.	*John Langdon*
Jona. Dayton	*Nicholas Gilman*
PENNSYLVANIA	MARYLAND
B. Franklin	*James McHenry*
Thomas Mifflin	*Dan of St. Thos Jenifer*
Robt. Morris	*Danl. Carroll.*
Geo. Clymer	
Thos. FitzSimons	
Jared Ingersoll	
James Wilson.	
Gouv. Morris	

Amendment I[12]

Congress shall make no law respecting an establishment of religion, or prohibiting the free exercise thereof; or abridging the freedom of speech, or of the press; or the right of the people peaceably to assemble, and to petition the Government for a redress of grievances.

12. The first ten amendments were passed by Congress on September 15, 1789, and were ratified on December 15, 1791. Collectively they are referred to as the *Bill of Rights*.

Amendment II

A well regulated Militia, being necessary to the security of a free State, the right of the people to keep and bear Arms, shall not be infringed.

Amendment III

No Soldier shall, in time of peace be quartered in any house, without the consent of the Owner, nor in time of war, but in a manner to be prescribed by law.

Amendment IV   *Search & Seizure*

The right of the people to be secure in their persons, houses, papers, and effects, against unreasonable searches and seizures, shall not be violated, and no Warrants shall issue, but upon probable cause, supported by Oath or affirmation, and particularly describing the place to be searched, and the persons or things to be seized.

Amendment V

No person shall be held to answer for a capital, or otherwise infamous crime, unless on a presentment or indictment of a Grand Jury, except in cases arising in the land or naval forces, or in the Militia, when in actual service in time of War or public danger; nor shall any person be subject for the same offence to be twice put in jeopardy of life or limb; nor shall be compelled in any criminal case to be a witness against himself, nor be deprived of life, liberty, or property, without due process of law; nor shall private property be taken for public use, without just compensation.   *"iminant domain"*

Amendment VI   *Procedural law*

In all criminal prosecutions, the accused shall enjoy the right to a speedy and public trial, by an impartial jury of the State and district wherein the crime shall have been committed, which district shall have been previously ascertained by law, and to be informed of the nature and cause of the accusation; to be confronted with the witnesses against him; to have compulsory process for obtaining witnesses in his favor, and to have the Assistance of Counsel for his defence.   *Subpoena*

Amendment VII

In Suits at common law, where the value in controversy shall exceed twenty dollars, the right of trial by jury shall be preserved, and no fact tried by a

jury law comes from Magna Carta (ChpT. 39?) 1215

jury, shall be otherwise reexamined in any Court of the United States, than according to the rules of the common law.

Amendment VIII

Excessive bail shall not be required, nor excessive fines imposed, nor cruel and unusual punishments inflicted.

Amendment IX

The enumeration in the Constitution, of certain rights, shall not be construed to deny or disparage others retained by the people.

Amendment X

The powers not delegated to the United States by the Constitution, nor prohibited by it to the States, are reserved to the States respectively, or to the people.

Amendment XI—(Ratified February 7, 1795)

The Judicial power of the United States shall not be construed to extend to any suit in law or equity, commenced or prosecuted against one of the United States by Citizens of another State, or by Citizens or Subjects of any Foreign State.

Amendment XII—(Ratified June 15, 1804)

The Electors shall meet in their respective states, and vote by ballot for President and Vice-President, one of whom, at least, shall not be an inhabitant of the same state with themselves; they shall name in their ballots the person voted for as President, and in distinct ballots the person voted for as Vice-President, and they shall make distinct lists of all persons voted for as President, and of all persons voted for as Vice-President, and of the number of votes for each, which lists they shall sign and certify, and transmit sealed to the seat of the government of the United States, directed to the President of the Senate;—The President of the Senate shall, in the presence of the Senate and House of Representatives, open all the certificates and the votes shall then be counted;—The person having the greatest number of votes for President, shall be the President, if such number be a majority of the whole number of Electors appointed; and if no person have such majority, then from the persons having the highest numbers not exceeding

three on the list of those voted for as President, the House of Representatives shall choose immediately, by ballot, the president. But in choosing the President, the votes shall be taken by states, the representation from each state having one vote; a quorum for this purpose shall consist of a member or members from two-thirds of the states, and a majority of all the states shall be necessary to a choice. (And if the House of Representatives shall not choose a President whenever the right of choice shall devolve upon them, before the fourth day of March next following., then the Vice-President shall act as President, as in the case of the death or other constitutional disability of the President.)[13]—The person having the greatest number of votes as Vice-President, shall be the Vice-President, if such number be a majority of the whole number of Electors appointed, and if no person have a majority, then from the two highest numbers on the list, the Senate shall choose the vice-President; a quorum for the purpose shall consist of two-thirds of the whole number of Senators, and a majority of the whole number shall be necessary to a choice. But no person constitutionally ineligible to the office of President shall be eligible to that of Vice-President of the United States.

Amendment XIII—(Ratified on December 6, 1865)

Section 1.   Neither slavery nor involuntary servitude, except as punishment for crime whereof the party shall have been duly convicted, shall exist within the United States, or any place subject to their jurisdiction.

Section 2.   Congress shall have power to enforce this article by appropriate legislation.

Amendment XIV—(Ratified on July 9, 1868) ✳

Section 1.   All persons born or naturalized in the United States, and subject to the jurisdiction thereof, are citizens of the United States and of the State wherein they reside. No State shall make or enforce any law which shall abridge the privileges or immunities of citizens of the United States; nor shall any State deprive any person of life, liberty, or property, without due process of law; nor deny to any person

---

13. Changed by the Twentieth Amendment.

✳ Gitlow vs NY used.

within its jurisdiction the equal protection of the laws.

Section 2. Representatives shall be apportioned among the several States according to their respective numbers, counting the whole number of persons in each State, excluding Indians not taxed. But when the right to vote at any election for the choice of electors for President and Vice President of the United States, Representatives in Congress, the Executive and Judicial offices of a State, or the members of the Legislature thereof, is denied to any of the male inhabitants of such State, being (twenty-one)[14] years of age, and citizens of the United States, or in any way abridged, except for participation in rebellion, or other crime, the basis of representation therein shall be reduced in the proportion which the number of such male citizens shall bear to the whole number of male citizens twenty-one years of age in such State.

Section 3. No person shall be a Senator or Representative in Congress, or elector of President and Vice President, or hold any office, civil or military, under the United States, or under any State, who having previously taken an oath, as a member of Congress, or as an officer of the United States, or as a member of any State legislature, or as an executive or judicial officer of any State, to support the Constitution of the United States, shall have engaged in insurrection or rebellion against the same, or given aid or comfort to the enemies thereof. But Congress may by a vote of two-thirds of each House, remove such disability.

Section 4. The validity of the public debt of the United States, authorized by law, including debts incurred for payment of pensions and bounties for services in suppressing insurrection or rebellion, shall not be questioned. But neither the United States nor any State shall assume or pay any debt or obligation incurred in aid of insurrection or rebellion against the United States, or any claim for the loss or emancipation of any slave, but all such debts, obligations and claims shall be held illegal and void.

Section 5. The Congress shall have power to enforce, by appropriate legislation, the provisions of this article.

14. Changed by the Twenty-sixth Amendment.

Amendment XV—(Ratified on February 3, 1870)

Section 1. The right of citizens of the United States to vote shall not be denied or abridged by the United States or by any State on account of race, color, or previous condition of servitude.

Section 2. The Congress shall have power to enforce this article by appropriate legislation.

Amendment XVI—(Ratified on February 3, 1913)

The Congress shall have power to lay and collect taxes on incomes, from whatever source derived, without apportionment among the several States, and without regard to any census or enumeration.

Amendment XVII—(Ratified on April 8, 1913)

The Senate of the United States shall be composed of two Senators from each State, elected by the people thereof, for six years; and each Senator shall have one vote. The electors in each State shall have the qualifications requisite for electors of the most numerous branch of the State legislatures.

When vacancies happen in the representation of any State in the Senate, the executive authority of such State shall issue writs of election to fill such vacancies: *Provided,* That the legislature of any State may empower the executive thereof to make temporary appointments until the people fill the vacancies by election as the legislature may direct.

This amendment shall not be so construed as to affect the election or term of any Senator chosen before it becomes valid as part of the Constitution.

Amendment XVIII—(Ratified on January 16, 1919) Repealed Dec 5 1933

Section 1. After one year from the ratification of this article the manufacture, sale, or transportation of intoxicating liquors within, the importation thereof into, or the exportation thereof from the United States and all territory subject to the jurisdiction thereof for beverage purposes is hereby prohibited.

Section 2. The Congress and the several States shall have concurrent power to enforce this article by appropriate legislation.

Section 3. This article shall be inoperative unless it shall have been ratified as an amendment to the Constitution by the legislatures of the several States, as provided in the Constitution, within seven years from the date of the submission hereof to the States by the Congress.[15]

Amendment XIX—(Ratified on August 18, 1920)

The right of citizens of the United States to vote shall not be denied or abridged by the United States or by any State on account of sex.

Congress shall have power to enforce this article by appropriate legislation.

Amendment XX—(Ratified on January 23, 1933)

Section 1.   The terms of the President and Vice President shall end at noon on the 20th day of January, and the terms of Senators and Representatives at noon on the 3d day of January, of the years in which such terms would have ended if this article had not been ratified, and the terms of their successors shall then begin.

Section 2.   The Congress shall assemble at least once in every year, and such meeting shall begin at noon on the 3d day of January, unless they shall by law appoint a different day.

Section 3.   If, at the time fixed for the beginning of the term of the President, the President elect shall have died, the Vice President elect shall become President. If the President shall not have been chosen before the time fixed for the beginning of his term, or if the President elect shall have failed to qualify, then the Vice President elect shall act as President until a President shall have qualified; and the Congress may by law provide for the case wherein neither a President elect nor a Vice President elect shall have qualified, declaring who shall then act as President, or the manner in which one who is to act shall be selected, and such person shall act accordingly until a President, or Vice President shall have qualified.

Section 4.   The Congress may by law provide for the case of the death of any of the persons from whom the House of Representatives may choose a President whenever the right of choice shall have devolved upon them, and for the case of the death of any of the persons from whom the Senate may choose a Vice President whenever the right of

choice shall have devolved upon them.

Section 5.   Sections 1 and 2 shall take effect on the 15th day of October following the ratification of this article.

Section 6.   This article shall be inoperative unless it shall have been ratified as an amendment to the Constitution by the legislatures of three-fourths of the several States within seven years from the date of its submission.

Amendment XXI—(Ratified on December 5, 1933)

Section 1.   The eighteenth article of amendment to the Constitution of the United States is hereby repealed.

Section 2.   The transportation or importation into any State, Territory, or possession of the United States for delivery or use therein of intoxicating liquors, in violation of the laws thereof, is hereby prohibited.

Section 3.   This article shall be inoperative unless it shall have been ratified as an amendment to the Constitution by conventions in the several States, as provided in the Constitution, within seven years from the date of the submission hereof to the States by the Congress.

Amendment XXII—(Ratified on February 27, 1951)

Section 1.   No person shall be elected to the office of the President more than twice, and no person who has held the office of President, or acted as President, for more than two years of a term to which some other person was elected President shall be elected to the office of President more than once. But this Article shall not apply to any person holding the office of President when this Article was proposed by the Congress, and shall not prevent any person who may be holding the office of President, or acting as President, during the term within which this Article becomes operative from holding the office of President or acting as President during the remainder of such term.

Section 2.   This article shall be inoperative unless it shall have been ratified as an amendment to the

---

15. The Eighteenth Amendment was repealed by the Twenty-first Amendment.

Constitution by the legislatures of three-fourths of the several States within seven years from the date of its submission to the States by the Congress.

Amendment XXIII—(Ratified on March 29, 1961)

Section 1. The District constituting the seat of Government of the United States shall appoint in such manner as the Congress may direct:

A number of electors of President and Vice President equal to the whole number of Senators and Representatives in Congress to which the District would be entitled if it were a State, but in no event more than the least populous State; they shall be in addition to those appointed by the states, but they shall be considered, for the purposes of the election of President and Vice President, to be electors appointed by a State; and they shall meet in the District and perform such duties as provided by the twelfth article of amendments.

Section 2. The Congress shall have power to enforce this article by appropriate legislation.

Amendment XXIV—(Ratified on January 23, 1964)

Section 1. The right of citizens of the United States to vote in any primary or other election for President or Vice President, for electors for President or Vice President, or for Senator or Representative in Congress, shall not be denied or abridged by the United States or any State by reason of failure to pay any poll tax or other tax.

Section 2. The Congress shall have power to enforce this article by appropriate legislation.

Amendment XXV—(Ratified on February 10, 1967)

Section 1. In case of the removal of the President from office or of his death or resignation, the Vice President shall become President.

Section 2. Whenever there is a vacancy in the office of the Vice President, the President shall nominate a Vice President who shall take office upon confirmation by a majority vote of both Houses of Congress.

Section 3. Whenever the President transmits to the President pro tempore of the Senate and the Speaker of the House of Representatives his written declaration that he is unable to discharge the powers and duties of his office, and until he transmits to them a written declaration to the contrary, such powers and duties shall be discharged by the Vice President as Acting President.

Section 4. Whenever the Vice President and a majority of either the principal officers of the executive departments or of such other body as Congress may by law provide, transmit to the President pro tempore of the Senate and the Speaker of the House of Representatives their written declaration that the President is unable to discharge the powers and duties of his office, the Vice President shall immediately assume the powers and duties of the office as Acting President.

Thereafter, when the President transmits to the President pro tempore of the Senate and the Speaker of the House of Representatives his written declaration that no inability exists, he shall resume the powers and duties of his office unless the Vice President and a majority of either the principal officers of the executive department or of such other body as Congress may by law provide, transmit within four days to the President pro tempore of the Senate and the Speaker of the House of Representatives their written declaration and the President is unable to discharge the powers and duties of his office. Thereupon Congress shall decide the issue, assembling within forty-eight hours for that purpose if not in session. If the Congress, within twenty-one days after receipt of the latter written declaration, or, if Congress is not in session, within twenty-one days after Congress is required to assemble, determines by two-thirds vote of both Houses that the President is unable to discharge the powers and duties of his office, the Vice President shall continue to discharge the same as Acting President; otherwise, the President shall resume the powers and duties of his office.

Amendment XXVI—(Ratified on July 1, 1971)

Section 1. The right of citizens of the United States, who are eighteen years of age or older, to vote shall not be denied or abridged by the United States or by any State on account of age.

Section 2. The Congress shall have power to enforce this article by appropriate legislation.

Glossary

abandonment When a tenant leaves rented premises with no intent to return or meet his or her legal obligations.

abortion, illegal Termination of a human pregnancy in a manner that contravenes the law of the state in which it occurs (for example, during the minority of the female without prior notification to one or more of her parents or, in the alternative, without the consent of a judge).

abortion, legal Termination of a human pregnancy in conformity with the law of the state in which it occurs (for example, by a licensed physician during the first trimester—three months from conception).

absolute liability A theory of liabiity under which the victim need not prove negligence or wrongful intent to hold the tortfeasor liable.

absolute privilege to defame Protection from liability for defamation, extended, for example, to legislators in official session and to judges and others in judicial proceedings. (See also, "conditional or qualified privilege to defame.")

abstract of title A chronological history of recorded documents affecting the title to real property.

acceptance Affirmative response to the terms of an offer, creating a contract. (See also, "offer.")

accessories after the fact Persons who harbor, conceal, or otherwise voluntarily and intentionally aid a known perpetrator of a crime to escape arrest or punishment. They are guilty of criminal conduct, but not of the perpetrator's crime.

accessories before the fact Persons who encourage or assist a perpetrator of a crime, for example, by planning, advising, or standing guard. They are guilty as principals, but in some states to a lesser degree and with lesser punishment.

accident A sudden, unexpected, unintended happening that causes injury and/or death and/or loss of property. Depending on the circumstances, legal fault may or may not exist.

accomplice A person who, in cooperation with the principal offender, is associated in a crime before, during, or after its commission. An aider and abettor. (See "aid and abet.")

accord and satisfaction A party agrees (by accord) to accept some substitute for a promised performance, which is then provided (the satisfaction).

accusation Formal commencement of a criminal case, made by a specified public official, such as a district attorney, or by a grand jury.

accusatory pleading A document specifying the crime committed and accusing the defendant of its commission.

acquitted Found not guilty of a crime by judgment of the court following jury verdict or a judge's decision.

adhesion contract A contract drafted solely by one party who has superior bargaining power and offered to another party on a take it or leave it basis.

adjudicate To hear and decide in a judicial action (court proceeding).

administrative agencies Units of federal, state, and local government that may possess legislative, executive, and judicial powers in specialized technical areas in which regulation requires action by experts.

administrator A person appointed by a court to supervise disposition of the estate of a decedent who dies without leaving a valid will, i.e., intestate.

adultery Sexual intercourse by a married person with someone other than the offender's spouse.

adversary system The system in which the parties to a legal dispute are opponents. Their attorneys advocate all conceivable theories of benefit to their clients both before and during the trial, and on any appeal. This system is widely believed to be the best method of producing the truth and a just result.

adverse possession The creation of ownership of real property through its possession for a prescribed number of years without consent of the owner.

affidavit A sworn and signed statement under oath.

affirmative action Policies and practices designed to assure employment of women and of minorities until their percentages in the work force approximate their percentages in the community.

affirmative action employment programs Programs that require efforts to hire and to promote women and minorities.

Age Discrimination in Employment Act of 1967. Federal law that added "advanced age" (40 to 70 years) to the factors listed in the Civil Rights Act of 1964 that may not be used in employment decisions.

497

agency Fiduciary relationship in which, by mutual consent, an employee (the agent) is authorized to represent and bind an employer (the principal) in business dealings with third parties.

agency shop A company or department in which all employees in the bargaining unit must pay union dues whether they are union members or not.

agent A person employed by a principal to deal with third parties and to make contracts binding the principal to the third parties.

aid and abet To help or assist another in committing a crime or tort.

alimony Maintenance payment paid by one spouse to the other spouse following a dissolution or divorce. Alimony may be rehabilitative (terminates at a specified time) or permanent (indefinite in duration). Alimony is also called maintenance.

allegations of fact Plaintiff's statement of alleged facts, contained in the complaint that serves to commence a civil action.

alternative dispute resolution (ADR) A term describing various methods of resolving disputes through means other than the judicial process.

Americans with Disabilities Act of 1990. Federal law that bars discrimination in the employment of capable handicapped persons by both private and public employers, and requires provision for reasonable accommodations for their needs.

amicus curiae [Latin: friend of the court] One who is not a party to a lawsuit, who submits a brief containing arguments in favor of the plaintiff's position or the defendant's. Usually found at the appellate level when a case has generated broad public interest.

amnesty Action by a legislature or chief executive to abolish and forget a specified offense, generally of a political nature such as treason or desertion by a large group. Contrasted to a pardon, which remits or abates punishment imposed on an individual, generally for a felony.

amortization Method of paying off a debt with a series of regular, periodic partial payments of interest and principal.

annulment A court decree cancelling a marriage because of some defect that existed when the marriage was entered. The court decrees that no valid marriage ever existed, whereas a divorce or dissolution terminates a valid marriage.

answer A document containing a defendant's denial and his or her allegations of fact. It is filed by a defendant, with the clerk of the court, after receiving a summons and complaint. A copy is supplied to the plaintiff.

antenuptial agreement A contract whereby two persons who are contemplating marriage define their future mutual rights and obligations as marriage partners. For example, a person entering marriage might desire to provide how they will divide assets if a divorce occurs. These agreements are also called premarital agreements.

anti-deficiency law A state law protecting a homeowner from payment of any deficiency if a mortgage foreclosure sale fails to produce sufficient money to satisfy the underlying debt in full.

Anti-Injunction Act of 1932 (Norris-LaGuardia Act) Federal law that restricts the issuance of injunctions in labor disputes and exempts unions from legal attack as monopolies.

appeal A request to a higher court for review of the actions of a lower court.

appellant The party who appeals to a higher court for review of questions of law decided by the judge of a trial court.

appellate courts Courts of review, as distinguished from trial courts.

appellee The party on appeal who defends the trial court judgment. Also called the respondent.

appraisal Professional estimate of the value of property.

appraised value The formal opinion of a professional appraiser of the fair market value of personal or real property.

arbitration A method of resolving disputes whereby disputing parties agree to select a neutral third party to hear and decide the dispute. Can be binding or nonbinding.

arbitrator A private person selected by disputing parties to hear and decide their dispute. Usually selected on the basis of expertise in the area of the dispute.

arraignment A criminal court proceeding prior to a trial during which the charge is read to the accused. The defendant will be advised of his or her constitutional rights at this time, and will enter a plea.

arrest To take a person into custody in order to charge him or her with commission of a crime. May be done with or without a warrant depending on the circumstances.

arson The intentional and malicious burning of a building or other property.

articles of incorporation Document that minimally states the name, address (for service of legal process), purposes, and capital structure of a proposed profit-seeking corporation. When dated and signed by the incorporator(s), it is filed in the proper state office, at which moment the corporation comes into existence.

as is A phrase which indicates that property is sold without warranty as to quality or condition.

assault, criminal The crime of unlawful attempt, coupled with present ability to commit a battery. There is no touching.

assault, civil The tort of creating apprehension in the mind of the victim of some harmful or offensive touching. There is no requirement of present ability of the actor to inflict actual harm.

assessed value The value assigned to real property by a local official, called the "assessor," for purposes of property tax assessment. Often a designated fraction (e.g., one-fourth) of the appraised or full cash value.

asset Any thing of value owned. Distinguished from liability, which is indebtedness.

assigned risk A high risk applicant seeking automobile liability insurance who is rejected by an insurance company and is then directed, by random rotating choice, to a designated insurer from a pool that includes all insurers in the state. Minimal coverage must be provided, although higher premiums may be charged.

assignment (a) The transfer of some or all rights under a contract to another person. (b) Transfer by a tenant of his or her leasehold interest for its unexpired time. (See also "sublease.")

assumption of loan An agreement by one person (usually a buyer) to assume all the obligations of an existing loan of another person (usually the seller). In periods of rising interest rates, it is desirable for a buyer to assume an existing loan on a home to be purchased rather than to obtain current financing at a higher interest rate.

assumption of risk When a plaintiff knowingly exposes herself or himself to a particular risk of injury.

attempt A crime in itself when the accused intends to commit a crime and takes a substantial step toward its commission. Evil thought and even simple preparations are not enough to constitute an attempt. If the crime is completed, the attempt "merges" into the crime.

attorney at law A person licensed to practice law. Also called a lawyer, counselor, or barrister.

attractive nuisance doctrine The doctrine under which trespassing minors may collect damages if attracted onto the defendant's premises by a man-made instrumentality that has special appeal to children and may cause injury (such as a railroad turntable or swimming pool).

auction sale Public sale in which an auctioneer solicits offers, or bids; normally the goods are sold to the highest bidder.

automobile insurance Insurance against hazards flowing directly from the ownership and operation of motor vehicles.

automobile medical payments coverage Automobile insurance that pays the medical expenses of the insured and of other occupants of the insured's vehicle who are injured in an accident.

bad faith The deliberate failure to fulfill some duty or contractual obligation owed to another. Often used to describe a purposeful failure to pay a lawful insurance claim.

bail Security posted with the court to assure that the accused, if released, will voluntarily return for further criminal proceedings.

bail bond A document signed by both the accused and a bail bondsman binding the bail bondsman to pay to the state a specified sum of money if the accused fails to appear in court as directed.

bailee One rightfully in possession of the personal property of another.

bailment A temporary right to possess the personal property of another.

bailor One who transfers possession of his or her personal property to another.

balloon payment The unpaid balance of a mortgage loan due in one payment at the end of an agreed-on period of time. For example, an interest-only loan for three years will require a balloon payment of the entire amount of principal originally borrowed.

bankruptcy Proceedings under federal law whereby all assets of a debtor (excluding certain exempt property) are distributed to his or her creditors. The debtor is then discharged or excused from the legal obligation to pay most of the debts.

  Chapter 7 bankruptcy Voluntary or involuntary proceeding whereby a debtor surrenders all property, excluding certain exempt property, to the court for liquidation. Proceeds are distributed to creditors and most debts are discharged.

  Chapter 13 adjustment of debts Bankruptcy court-approved plan whereby an individual or a small business is shielded against involuntary bankruptcy while unsecured creditors receive at least as much as they would in Chapter 7 liquidation bankruptcy. Payments are normally made over a period up to 3 years, but no longer than 5 years.

bar association A professional organization of attorneys who are members of the "bar," that is, licensed to practice law.

bargaining unit The department of a company or other employee group that is deemed appropriate for collective bargaining purposes, based on common interests or related skills and duties.

battery Any harmful or offensive touching of another human being without excuse or consent; usually involves violent infliction of injury.

beneficiary (a) The person designated by the insured to receive the proceeds of an insurance policy. (b) The person designated by a settlor or testator to receive the benefit of the property in a trust or a will. (c) A person who receives the benefit of a contract between two other persons.

beneficiary of deed of trust The lender who has advanced funds to a homebuyer to purchase a home, and whose loan is secured by deed of trust.

benefit of the bargain The respective consideration that each party in a contractual agreement is entitled to receive.

bequest A gift of personal property by will.

Better Business Bureau A voluntary private agency sponsored by the Chamber of Commerce to, among other things, help inform consumers of fraudulent sales schemes.

beyond a reasonable doubt Full satisfaction that the weight of evidence shows the guilt of the accused. There is no reasonable doubt of innocence.

bigamy The crime of being married to two or more persons at the same time.

bilateral contract Agreement in which both parties make binding promises.

bilateral mistake See "mutual mistake."

Bill of Attainder Act of the legislature punishing a named person or member of a specific group. Such a law is unconstitutional.

Bill of Rights The first ten amendments to the U.S. Constitution.

blue collar crime Crimes committed by persons of comparatively lower social status and economic wealth, often involving violence (such as robbery and assault). Contrasted to white collar crimes such as income tax evasion.

blue laws Statutes that regulate commercial activities and amusements on Sundays.

blue sky laws Statutes designed to regulate and sometimes prevent the fraudulent promotion and sale of highly speculative or worthless stock and other securities.

board of directors A group of usually three or more persons elected by the stockholders to manage a business corporation.

bodily injury and property damage insurance Automobile insurance that protects against the risk of incurring liability for injuring or killing someone else in a negligent manner, or for damaging someone's property.

bond (a) a written obligation to pay a sum of money upon the happening of specified events. (b) A written promise by a borrower to pay a lender a fixed sum of interest for a prescribed time, and to repay the principal on a stated date. (If payable within a year, it may be referred to as a note.)

booking Police practice of fingerprinting, photographing, testing of blood for alcohol of an accused person after arrest.

breach of contract Failure to fulfill one's part of a legally binding agreement.

breach of legal duty Failure to act as an ordinary prudent person is required to act by law.

briefs Written arguments addressed to the appellate court by counsel for appellant and for appellee, including points of law and authoritative case support for their respective positions.

burden of proof The duty to produce evidence as a trial progresses. In a civil case, facts are proved by a preponderance of the evidence. In a criminal case, the measure of proof is beyond a reasonable doubt and to a moral certainty.

burglary The crime of unlawfully entering into premises, structures, and vehicles with intent to commit larceny (theft) or any other felony.

business invitee A person invited onto the premises by the occupier of land for business purposes designed to produce a profit.

busing Movement of children to and from school to achieve racial integration. Less controversial purposes include safety of the children and economy in the utilization of facilities.

buy and sell agreement A contract under which business partners (or stockholders in a closely held corporation) reciprocally agree to buy and sell their interests in the firm to each other upon the death of either.

by-laws Private rules for the internal government of a business corporation. Normally adopted by the board of directors of the corporation.

cancel (contract) After breach by seller, buyer may cancel to return parties to their original status. Buyer may still sue for damages.

capital (a) Money and credit needed to start and continue a business. (b) Total assets of a business. (c) Shares of stock representing ownership in a corporation.

capital crime A crime for which the death penalty may be imposed in states where authorized.

capital gain The profit realized from the sale or exchange of a capital asset (i.e., generally a thing of value owned). The profit is the excess of the proceeds received over the cost (or other tax basis) to the owners.

capital punishment Death penalty.

case A controversy brought before a court for decision. There are two broad categories of cases:

at law The relief sought is monetary damages, and a jury may be used to decide questions of fact.

in equity The plaintiff seeks specific performance, injunction, accounting, dissolution of marriage, or other nonmonetary relief because the remedy at law is inadequate or not available. The judge decides questions of law and of fact.

case citation A reference that identifies a legal case and tells where it may be found in a reporter system that publishes opinions of appellate cases. For example: *Burnett* v. *National Enquirer,* 144 Cal.App.3d 991, 193 Cal.Rptr. 206 (1983).

case-in-chief The case presented by each party in a trial, includes calling witnesses and introducing into evidence documents, photographs, or whatever else is pertinent to the issues in a trial.

causation The act or means by which a specified effect is produced.

actual causation When injury to person or property results from some action or failure to act by the alleged tortfeasor.

proximate causation When injury results from the defendant's action in a close, natural, and continuous sequence, unbroken by an intervening force or cause, and without which the result would not have occurred.

cause of action A right that exists to seek and receive judicial relief in a civil action, assuming the factual allegations of the plaintiff are true.

caveat emptor [Latin: let the buyer beware] A buyer should investigate and rely on his or her own judgment regarding the shortcomings of goods before purchase.

caveat venditor [Latin: let the seller beware] A seller should exercise appropriate care to assure that goods sold are of fair value and suitable for human use, or be subjected to possible legal sanctions.

certificate of incorporation (See "charter.")

certificate of ownership A legal document issued by a state government showing who owns a vehicle (that is, who has title to it).

certificate of registration A legal document issued by a state government permitting operation of a motor vehicle on the highways of the state.

certiorari [Latin: to be informed of] The process by which the U.S. Supreme Court uses its discretionary power to decide which lower court cases it will hear.

challenge of a juror Any prospective trial juror may be challenged for cause when his or her bias or prejudice is established. Any prospective trial juror also may be challenged peremptorily for any reason other than racial bias. The decision to exclude a juror for cause is made by the judge; the decision to exclude a juror peremptorily is made by a party acting through his or her attorney. Peremptory challenges are limited by statute.

champerty An illegal agreement with a party to a suit for a portion of any recovery in exchange for paying the litigant's lawsuit expenses.

charter (of corporation) A permit to do business as a corporation, issued by government. Also known as a certificate of incorporation and articles of incorporation.

chattel See "Property."

checkoff Authorized withholding of union dues from wages by the employer and direct payment to the union.

citizen's arrest The taking into custody by a private citizen of a person who committed a felony in the citizen's presence, or of a person who committed a misdemeanor that constitutes a breach of the peace then in progress.

civil action A lawsuit commenced for the purpose of resolving a civil dispute. Distinguished from a criminal action.

civil law (a) The branch of law dealing with civil rights, civil duties, and their enforcement. (b) The total system of law embracing civil and criminal matters, used in the ancient Roman Empire and copied on the continent of Europe in modern times. The law was defined by experts and imposed from above by the Emperor. Contrasted to English common law.

Civil Rights Act of 1964 Federal law (specifically in Title VII) that makes it unlawful for employers of 15 or more persons and engaged in interstate commerce to discriminate with respect to employment against any individual because of such person's race, color, religion, sex, or national origin.

class action A representative suit in which one, or a limited number of parties sue on behalf of a larger group to which they belong.

clemency A formal act of kindness, mercy, and leniency by a governor or the President in commuting a criminal penalty or granting a pardon.

client One who employs an attorney to provide legal advice or assistance.

close corporation A corporation whose stock is owned by one person or very few persons. Also known as a closely held corporation.

close of escrow The time when all required monies and documents from all interested persons are distributed by the escrow agent to the appropriate persons in connection with the sale of real property.

closed shop A place of employment where workers must join the union before they can be hired.

closing costs Charges for various services that arise in connection with the purchase and sale of a home. The charges are paid upon close of escrow by the buyer and seller in accordance with the terms of their agreement and escrow instructions. Examples of closing costs are termite inspection charges, loan fees, title insurance premiums, notary public fees, and transfer taxes.

codicil A document prepared to change an existing will.

cohabitation Living together as husband and wife without complying with the legal formalities of marriage.

cohabitation agreement An agreement between cohabiting persons concerning financial or property matters.

collateral Money or property (security) made available by a debtor to a creditor through possession or right, to guarantee payment of a loan.

collaterals Relatives who are brother, sister, uncle, aunt, cousins, and so forth. (See also "lineals.")

collective bargaining Negotiation of an employment contract between representative(s) of the union and representative(s) of the employer.

collision insurance Automobile insurance that protects against the risk of negligently damaging one's own automobile.

commercial impracticability When performance as agreed is rendered impracticable by occurrence of a contingency, the nonoccurrence of which was a basic assumption of the parties to the contract.

commercial property Property used in trade or commerce, contrasted to residential or industrial property.

commingling The mixing together of community property and separate property to the extent that the properties cannot be traced back to their original status. Commingled property becomes totally community property.

commission, real estate The compensation a home seller agrees to pay the listing agent if a ready, willing and able buyer is found. The commission rate is negotiable and is a function of the sales price of the home, not the seller's equity in the home.

common carrier A carrier of passengers who agrees to transport for payment all persons applying for passage, assuming available space and no legal excuse for refusal.

common law The total system of law that originated in medieval England and was adopted by the United States at the time of the Revolution. Expressed originally in opinions and judgments of the courts, it is judge-made law that reflects the customs and usages of the people. Contrasted to Roman civil law, it is found throughout the English-speaking world. Also called unwritten law.

common law marriage The bond formed when a man and a woman live together as husband and wife for the number of years prescribed by state laws, but without observing the legal formalities of marriage. This is a legal method of creating marriage in some states.

common stock Shares representing ownership in a business corporation. They have no contractual rate or amount of dividend payment, but usually do have voting power.

community property All property acquired (in a community property state) by the husband or the wife during marriage other than by gift or inheritance, or as profits or income from separate property. (See also "separate property.")

commutation Reduction, by the chief executive, of punishment for a crime—for example, changing a death sentence to life imprisonment.

comparable worth theory Basis for payment of the same wage or salary for jobs that have equal social and economic value based on such factors as required preparation, skill, effort, responsibility, and working conditions.

comparative negligence Where the negligence of the plaintiff does not bar recovery of damages but may reduce the amount of recovery proportionally.

competent parties Parties who are legally qualified to make a binding agreement.

complaint, civil A document filed by the plaintiff with the court and served on the defendant to inform him or her of the facts constituting the cause of action.

complaint, criminal (a) A written statement filed by complainant containing facts that indicate a crime has been committed and that the accused committed it. (b) An accusation of a misdemeanor by a government official.

composition of creditors A plan whereby all or most of the creditors of a defaulting debtor mutually agree to accept less than the full amount due, and sometimes also grant an extension of time for payment.

comprehensive insurance Automobile insurance that protects against losses from having one's car stolen or damaged by other listed means such as vandalism.

compulsory arbitration See "arbitration."

conciliation and mediation of labor disputes Process by which a neutral third party attempts to negotiate a voluntary settlement of a labor dispute.

conditional or qualified privilege to defame Protection from liability for defamation extended, for example, to employers who, in good faith and without negligence, discuss employee qualifications with third parties. See "absolute privilege to defame."

condominium A building in which individuals own, and receive title to, separate units or apartments. Each owner is responsible for his or her own financing. Common areas (such as the land and elevators) are owned in common and managed collectively by all owners of the individual units.

conservatorship A legal relationship created by a court to allow a person, the conservator, to manage the assets and personal affairs of another, the conservatee, who is not competent to manage his or her own affairs.

consideration The price or inducement (for example, reciprocal promises) to enter a contract.

consortium The reciprocal right of companionship, affection, and sexual relations of each spouse from the other.

conspiracy An agreement by two or more persons to commit a crime. In most states, one or more of the conspirators must commit an overt act in furtherance of the criminal plan.

constitution A written document defining fundamental legal principles for governance of the people. It may include grants of power and limitations of power.

constitutionalism Actual restrictions and limitations on governmental power.

Consumer Credit Protection Act Also known as the Truth in Lending Act. Federal law requiring full disclosure to borrower or consumer of the cost of credit as an annual percentage rate (APR) and in dollars.

Consumer Product Safety Commission Independent federal agency charged with implementing the Consumer Product Safety Act of 1972. Authorized to set safety standards for most consumer products.

contempt of court Willful defiance of the authority or affront to the dignity of a court, or willful disobedience of its lawful orders.

contingent fee A fixed percentage of the monetary recovery obtained by a lawyer for a client which is accepted in full settlement for service rendered. If there is no recovery, no fee is due.

continuation agreement Contract between partners to permit continuation of a partnership business after dissolution, thus avoiding winding up and forestalling termination. (See also "winding up period.")

contract A legally enforceable agreement to do or not to do a specified thing.

contributing to the delinquency of a minor Any conduct by an adult that assists a person under 18 years in any unlawful activity.

contributory negligence When a plaintiff is also guilty of negligence. In many states such a plaintiff is therefore barred from claiming damages if injured.

covenant of good faith and fair dealing Agreement implied under the Uniform Commercial Code that contracting merchants shall always act with honesty and observe standards of fair dealing in the trade.

conversion Unauthorized taking of the personal property of another and wrongfully exercising rights of ownership. An intentional tort.

convicted Found guilty of a crime by a judgment of the court following jury verdict or judge's decision. (See also "acquitted.")

cooling-off period Three-day period during which a person who borrows money on the security of a second mortgage on the borrower's home may rescind.

cooperative apartment An apartment owned by a corporation formed to acquire land and erect the building. Interested persons buy shares in the corporation to obtain the right to live in one of the units.

corporation A legal entity with rights of a person, created by compliance with applicable law, for some designated purpose. May or may not seek profits. Generally characterized by unlimited life, transferable shares, limited liability for owners, and centralized management.

***corpus* (of a trust)** [Latin: body] The principal or capital sum of the trust estate, as distinguished from income.

corpus delicti [Latin: body of a crime] Two essential elements of every crime: (1) evidence that harm has occurred, (2) most probably because of a criminal act. It may be indicated by a corpse or burned building, for example.

corrective advertising Advertisements required by order of the Federal Trade Commission to inform the public of errors or misstatements in earlier advertisements by the same company.

court A place staffed by judges who hear and decide legal claims.

court-annexed arbitration A type of nonbinding arbitration required by some courts before the parties may proceed to trial.

creative financing Any financing for the purchase of a home in which the seller accepts a note secured by mortgage for all or part of the purchase price. Also called seller's financing.

credit Legal right given by one person (the creditor) to another (the debtor) to incur a debt and pay it later.

credit card A small card, usually made of plastic, identifying the holder by signature and issued by banks, stores, and other agencies. It permits the holder to obtain goods, services, or money on credit, to a prescribed limit.

Credit Card Act of 1970 Federal law that regulates issuance and enforcement of credit cards.

crime An offense against the public; violation of a criminal statute.

criminal action, case or dispute A trial held with a jury (if demanded by either party) in which the government (state or federal) prosecutes a person charged with a crime.

criminal facilitation The crime of facilitating the commission of a crime by another person.

criminal intent Intent to commit a crime; *mens rea* (Latin: guilty mind).

criminal law The branch of law dealing with crimes and their punishment.

criminal negligence Conduct that is without criminal intent and yet sufficiently careless, or in reckless disregard of other's safety, that criminal penalties are prescribed by statute.

cruel and unusual punishment Criminal punishment in which the sentence in jail is totally disproportionate to the offense, or the prisoner is subjected to cruel abuse, or the method of the punishment is unacceptable to society, or the punishment is arbitrary. Cruel and unusual punishment is prohibited by the U.S. Constitution.

damages Money awarded by a court to a plaintiff for injury or economic loss caused by the defendant. There are various types, including:

   compensatory Amount awarded sufficient to make good or replace the loss suffered.

   consequential After a breach of a sales contract by a seller, the losses resulting from the needs of the buyer that the seller knew of or should have known of when the contract was made.

   general Amount awarded to pay the plaintiff for nonmonetary losses that resulted from an injury without reference to any special circumstances of the plaintiff (e.g., pain and suffering).

   incidental After a breach of a sales contract, reasonable expenses incurred by a party (as, for example, to inspect, transport, and care for goods rightfully rejected by a buyer).

   liquidated Amount that contracting parties have previously agreed would be fair in case of breach. Unacceptable by courts if it is so large as to constitute a penalty.

   nominal or token Insignificant amount (such as $1) awarded when the defendant has violated the rights of the plaintiff but no monetary loss has been suffered or can be proved.

   punitive or exemplary Amount in addition to compensatory damages, awarded to the victim of an intentional tort to punish the tortfeasor and serve as an example to others.

   special Amount awarded to pay for monetary out-of-pocket losses resulting from the specific or special circumstances of the plaintiff (e.g., for medical expenses, loss of wages, and destruction of property).

   treble Amount of actual damages as determined by a jury or judge, multiplied by three, in order to punish the wrongdoers and serve as an example to others. Available by statute for federal antitrust law violations.

dangerous instrumentality A gun or other object that may cause harm when given to a child without instruction as to its proper use.

dangerous propensity A child's habit that may injure others, such as throwing rocks at trains.

death taxes Taxes imposed upon death on the estate of the decedent (that is, an estate tax on the privilege of giving) and on the gifts received by the donees (that is, an inheritance tax on the privilege of receiving).

decedent A deceased person.

deceit Fraudulent misrepresentation made knowingly to mislead another person who is misled and injured. Also called fraud.

declaratory judgment A judicial action where a court states the rights and duties of parties without specifically ordering that anything be done. Also called declaratory relief.

decree of dissolution A court judgment ending a marriage.

deductible clause A provision in an insurance policy whereby the insured bears the initial loss up to a prescribed sum (e.g., $50, $100, or more) in exchange for reduced premiums.

deed In general, a document that is used to transfer any ownership interest in real property. Many types of deeds are used in a variety of property transfers. For example, grant deeds and warranty deeds are commonly used in the transfer of homes; they include certain guarantees by the transferor that are implied by law. A trustee's deed transfers ownership to the purchaser or property at a foreclosure sale. (See also "deed of reconveyance," "deed of trust," and "quitclaim deed.")

deed of reconveyance A deed used by a trustee to return title to real property to the trustor (borrower) when he or she pays off a loan that was secured by a trust deed. (See also "deed.")

deed of trust A deed used by a borrower (called trustor) to transfer the legal title to real property to a disinterested stakeholder (the trustee) to hold as security or collateral for the benefit of the lender (the beneficiary). When the loan is paid in full, the legal title is reconveyed to the trustor. Also called a trust deed. (See also "deed.")

de facto [Latin: in fact, or actually.] (See also "*de Jure.*")

de jure [Latin: by law, or lawfully.] (See also "*de facto.*")

defamation False statement, either oral (called slander) or written (called libel), which tends to injure the reputation of the victim. It may be civil (a tort) as well as criminal (a crime).

default Failure of a party to do what is legally required such as to keep a contractual agreement or to file an answer to a complaint.

default judgment Judgment of a court awarded because the defendant failed to answer the summons and complaint or to appear at the trial to contest the claim of the plaintiff.

defective or voidable marriage A marriage that may be legally nullified by the innocent party through court action, thereby restoring both parties to the legal status of unmarried persons.

defendant (a) In a civil trial, the person from whom money damages or other relief is sought by the plaintiff. (b) In a criminal trial, the accused.

deficiency judgment Judgment against a debtor for the unpaid balance still due after repossession and resale of goods, or after judicial foreclosure of a real estate mortgage.

delegation Transfer of some or all duties under a contract to another person.

democracy Greek: rule by the people.

demurrer A motion filed by a defendant in response to a summons and complaint when allegations of the complaint, even if true, are insufficient to state a cause of action. In federal courts, and in many states, the same result is achieved by a motion to dismiss.

deposit receipt A misleading term commonly used to describe a contract to purchase real property.

deposition Questioning under oath by the opposing attorney before the trial, of a witness or adverse party to an action in the presence of a court reporter and the person's own counsel. A type of discovery procedure.

depreciated value The value of property after deduction of a percentage of its original value because of aging and/or use.

depreciation (a) In tax law, a tax deduction allowed by law for taxpayers who own certain kinds of assets. Such a tax deduction permits a taxpayer to pay a smaller income tax than otherwise would be due, for example, apartment house owners are entitled to large income tax deductions for depreciation. (b) In other than tax law, decline; the opposite of appreciation.

devise A gift of real property by will.

dictum **or** *dicta* [Latin: by the way] Any part of a court opinion that is unnecessary to the resolution of dispute before the court. A judicial digression that is not binding on later courts.

diminished capacity Reduced ability to exercise one's freedom of will or choose between right and wrong (perhaps because of delusion induced by drugs or the like). It may negate the presence of specific criminal intent, which is required for first degree murder.

directive to physicians A document communicating a person's wishes regarding the use of life support systems in the treatment of a terminal illness.

director (of corporation) One of a group of persons who are legally charged with the determination of major policies and overall management of a business corporation, including the declaration of dividends to distribute profits to stockholders.

directors (of corporation) Persons elected by stockholders to manage and direct the business affairs of a corporation. Collectively referred to as the board of directors.

disability insurance A form of insurance that provides replacement income for a person who is unable to work because of a disability (illness or injury).

disbarment Revocation of an attorney's license to practice law. A disbarred attorney may seek reinstatement at a future date.

discharge of contract Completion of contractual obligation(s).

disclaimer A written or oral statement that a warranty does not exist.

discovery procedures Methods used during the period between commencement of a lawsuit and the date of trial to learn facts about the dispute. (See also "deposition," "motion to produce," "request for admission of facts," and "written interrogatories.")

disputants Parties in conflict.

dissolution Termination of marriage relationship by court judgment. Called divorce in some states.

diversity of citizenship A basis of jurisdiction in federal courts. It requires that plaintiff and defendant be involved in an actual controversy, be citizens of different states, and that there be a minimum of $50,000 in damages.

divided interest Interest in property such as a parcel of land, held separately, or in severalty, by a person—for example, by the owner of a condominium.

dividend (a) Profit of a corporation distributed proportionally to stockholders by order of the board of directors. (b) Refund of overpaid premiums by an insurance company.

divorce Termination of a marriage relationship by court judgment. Called dissolution in some states.

divorce from bed and board A partial termination of marriage in which the spouses live apart while support is paid. Property is divided as in a divorce. (See also "separate maintenance.")

doctrine of supremacy The constitutional doctrine that applies whenever the United States and a state or local government enact conflicting laws on the same subject. Under the doctrine the federal law prevails.

donee The person to whom a gift is made in life or by will.

donor A person who makes a gift.

double taxation of corporate income After corporate net income has already been taxed if it is then distributed to the shareholder as dividends it is taxed again as personal income.

dower and curtesy The common law right of a married woman to a life estate in the property of her husband upon his death. Curtesy is the comparable right of a husband to property of his wife upon her death. Dower and curtesy have no application in community property jurisdictions and have been abolished or modified in most states.

dramshop statute A state law making it a crime for a tavern proprietor or employee to serve intoxicants to an obviously inebriated patron.

driving under the influence (DUI) Violating the law by driving while one's judgment and ability to react are impaired by alcohol or other mind-altering drugs.

due process of law The requirement that legal proceedings (including arrest, civil and criminal trials, and punishment) comply with the U.S. Constitution and other applicable substantive and procedural laws.

durable power of attorney A document authorizing another person to make health care and other decisions for a person who becomes incapacitated.

duress Any threat of or actual physical harm that deprives a person of the freedom of will to choose and decide.

duty, legal The obligation to recognize and respect the person, property, and other interests of other persons; enforceable in court. Reciprocal of legal right.

easement The right to use the real property of another for a limited purpose, usually access.

economic strike A strike in which workers seek a change in wages, hours, and/or conditions of employment.

emancipation Parental consent to a minor to handle his or her own financial affairs. It normally also ends parental duties of care.

embezzlement The crime of stealing property that is lawfully in the possession of the thief. For example, a cashier embezzling money from the cash register.

eminent domain The inherent power of the government to take private property for the public use, upon payment of the fair market value.

Employment Act of 1946 Federal law that committed the federal government to encourage employment for all persons able to, willing to, and seeking work.

employment at will Typical employment contract under which both the employee and the employer may end the relationship at any time without liability (other than payment for services already rendered, generally).

Employment Retirement Income Security Act (ERISA) Federal legislation that regulates private pension plans which supplement social security.

Employee Stock Ownership Plans (ESOPs) Plans encouraged by federal income tax benefits whereby employees become owners of stock in the corporation that employs them.

enact To establish a law by proper vote of members of the legislative branch of government.

endorsements, policy Clauses that supplement standard policies of insurance. May appear as printed forms.

entrapment A defense to criminal charges if the crime resulted from police encouragement, but not if police merely provided an opportunity for the accused to commit the criminal act.

entrepreneur One who initiates and owns a business.

Equal Credit Opportunity Act of 1976 Federal law that forbids discrimination in extension of credit because of sex, marital status, race, or other specified factors.

Equal Employment Opportunity Act of 1972 (EEOA) Federal law that created the Equal Employment Opportunity Commission.

Equal Employment Opportunity Commission (EEOC) Federal agency created by the Equal Employment Opportunity Act of 1972 that authorized the federal government to use its resources to enforce the Civil Rights Act of 1964 for private persons.

equal pay laws Statutes that prohibit discrimination in wages for equal work because of the sex of the employee. The federal Equal Pay Act of 1963 led the way.

equal protection clause The clause in the Fourteenth Amendment to the U.S. Constitution declaring that "no state shall . . . deny to any person within its jurisdiction the equal protection of the laws." Basis for much civil rights litigation by minorities and women.

equitable distribution The division and distribution by the court of marital property to the spouses upon divorce. Not applicable to community property states in which each spouse owns one-half of the community property.

equitable title Title possessed by the beneficial owner of goods who has possession and use, as in credit sales where the seller may retain the legal title as security.

equity The excess of the value of property over loans or other legal claims outstanding against it.

equity, action in A civil trial held without a jury when relief sought by the plaintiffs is equitable in nature, such as an injunction or a divorce or dissolution of a marriage.

escrow [From Old French, escrow: roll of writings] An arrangement in writing common in real estate transactions whereby the buyer and seller (and/or the borrower and lender) designate an agent to carry out instructions for gathering and distributing documents and funds as necessary.

estate tax A tax imposed by the federal government and some states on the privilege of giving property to another person after death of the donor.

ethics Norms of just and honest conduct.

eviction, legal A legal proceeding to terminate a leasehold and remove the tenant because of a default in the lease (usually failure to pay rent).

eviction, wrongful Any unlawful conduct designed to evict a tenant for any reason. An example is changing locks on doors.

evidence Everything that the finder-of-fact is entitled to consider in arriving at a determination of the facts.

  hearsay Evidence not based on personal observation or knowledge of the witness, but consisting of repetition of what someone else has said. Generally not admissible to prove a fact, but exceptions exist.

  immaterial Evidence that is not important or essential to the proof of facts in dispute. Counsel may successfully object to its introduction by the opponent.

  incompetent Evidence that the court will not permit counsel to present during trial because of some defect relating to the witness or the evidence.

  irrelevant Evidence that does not relate to or have a bearing upon a question of fact in dispute during a trial.

ex post facto **law** [Latin: after the fact] A statute that retroactively makes previously lawful conduct a crime. Such a statute is unconstitutional.

exempt assets or property Property that a debtor can protect from a creditor's attempt to collect, or in a personal bankruptcy.

exclusionary rule The court-made rule that precludes the use in court of any evidence improperly obtained by the prosecution.

exculpatory clause A provision in an agreement (e.g., a lease) in which a party agrees not to hold the other party responsible for his or her negligence.

executed contract A contract that has been fully performed by both parties.

executive branch The government department that is responsible for carrying laws into effect.

executive order or directive A lawful order by the President of the United States, the governor of a state, or the head of a local government, given without the concurrence of the legislative branch. An example is the 1990 executive order of President Bush calling certain units of the U.S. military reserve to active duty in the Middle East.

executive privilege The right of the president of the United States not to disclose information because of national security considerations, providing that there is no overriding reason for disclosure as determined by judicial review.

executor A person named by a testator to dispose of his or her estate after death, as directed in his or her will and in compliance with law.

executory contract A valid contract in which something remains to be done by either or both parties.

express contract An agreement stated in words, spoken or written.

express powers The powers expressly delegated to the U.S. government by the Constitution.

express warranty A warranty given by a seller to a buyer orally or in writing.

extortion The crime of obtaining money or property by threatening harm to the victim or the victim's family. The threat may be to accuse the victim of a crime or to expose some deformity or other serious matter of privacy.

fair comment A privilege that legitimatizes certain statements on matters of public concern that might otherwise be considered defamatory. (See also "privileged communication.")

Fair Credit Billing Act of 1974 Federal act that permits users of credit cards to challenge correctness of charges without penalty.

Fair Credit Reporting Act of 1970 Federal law that enables consumers to check and correct credit information about themselves in the files of credit reporting companies.

Fair Debt Collection Practices Act of 1977 Federal law that outlaws certain unreasonably harsh collection practices used by professional debt collectors.

false arrest Taking custody of another, without proper legal authority, to be held or restrained in order to answer a civil claim or criminal charge.

Because this action restrains the person's liberty, it is also false imprisonment.

false imprisonment The wrongful restraint of the personal liberty of another.

featherbedding Causing or attempting to cause an employer to pay for services by employees that are not performed or are not to be performed such as requiring unneeded extra workers.

federal Refers to the U.S. government and its activities. The United States is a federation of 50 sovereign states.

federal law Includes the U.S. Constitution, statutes enacted by Congress, international treaties, presidential orders, rules promulgated by federal agencies, and decisions of federal courts.

Federal Insurance Contribution Act (FICA) Federal tax to finance Social Security benefits (unemployment, disability, retirement, and survivors' benefits payments).

Federal Register Volumes containing federal written law enacted by independent administrative agencies.

Federal Reporter Volumes containing decisions and opinions of U.S. courts of appeals.

Federal Savings and Loan Insurance Corporation (FSLIC) A federal agency charged with assuring the collectibility of deposits and saving accounts (up to $100,000 per covered account) in savings and loans associations. The failure of hundreds of these associations led Congress to create and fund in 1990, the Resolution Trust Corporation, an agency responsible for liquidating and selling off insolvent thrifts.

Federal Trade Commission (FTC) Federal agency charged with regulating business to prevent unfair competition and to protect consumers against false advertising and other unfair trade practices.

federalism A political arrangement in which two or more levels of government direct the affairs of the same people in the same location.

fee; fee simple Complete ownership of real property. Distinguish, for example, a life estate, which is ownership limited in its duration.

felon One convicted of a felony.

felony A serious crime (such as murder) that is punishable by death or imprisonment for more than one year.

felony-murder rule Under this rule, all participants in a dangerous felony are guilty of murder in the first degree if an unlawful killing occurs during its commission.

fictitious name A name other than the true name(s) [i.e., the forename(s) and family surname(s)] used to identify a sole proprietorship or partnership. State statutes generally require filing with the county clerk the true name(s) along with the assumed name(s) to inform the public of the facts.

fidelity bond A bond insuring against losses caused by a faithless performance of duties by a personal representative (for example, an executor or guardian).

fiduciary relationship A relationship between two persons wherein one has an obligation to perform services with scrupulous good faith and honesty: e.g., attorney toward a client; partner toward partner in a partnership.

field sobriety test A simple test used to determine the reactions of a motor vehicle driver who is suspected of driving under the influence of alcohol or another drug. The test is administered at the scene.

financial responsibility law A statute requiring that, after an automobile accident, any driver not covered by insurance must post cash or bond, or lose his or her driver's license and vehicle registration until released from potential liability.

financial statement A written summary of the financial condition or operating results of a business. Most commonly the balance sheet and income statement.

firm offer A written offer signed by a merchant that remains open for a specified time, up to three months. It is binding even though the offeree does not pay for the right.

first degree murder Premeditated murder perpetrated with malice aforethought; e.g., by an explosive device or poison or while lying in wait or during commission of a specified dangerous felony such as robbery, rape, or arson.

foreclosure, judicial The involuntary sale, following a court proceeding, of an owner's real property to raise money to satisfy the unpaid balance of the loan that is in default.

foreclosure, nonjudicial The involuntary sale, without court proceedings, of an owner's real property to raise money to satisfy the unpaid balance of the loan that is in default.

foreseeability The ability of a reasonably prudent person to anticipate in advance that injury to person and/or property is likely to result from specified acts or failure to act. Essential for tort of negligence.

form prescribed by law Any written expression or particular language that may be required for a valid, fully enforceable contract.

formal contract Agreement that must use prescribed language.

formal will A typewritten will executed in compliance with law and signed or acknowledged by the creator of the document in the presence of witnesses who also sign the document.

franchise (a) The right obtained by a person or group through contract with a manufacturer or distributor to sell a branded item in a given location. (b) The right granted by government to conduct certain activities (such as gas or electric utilities) as monopolies. (c) The right to vote for candidates for public office.

franchisee A person or group who obtains a franchise from a manufacturer or distributor-franchisor.

franchisor A manufacturer or distributor who grants a franchise to a franchisee.

fraud A knowingly false representation of a material fact, made through words or conduct, with intent to deceive a victim who is induced to contract in reliance on the lie and who is, thereby, injured. Also called deceit.

fringe benefits Direct and indirect compensation of employees by an employer for services rendered, other than in money wages. Examples include insurance, vacations, and stock purchase plans.

full cash value The appraised value of real property for property tax purposes.

garnishment A legal proceeding in which a plaintiff-creditor gets a court order compelling a third party (such as the employer of the defendant-debtor) to pay monies earned by the defendant to the plaintiff.

general partner Partner who manages the firm, shares equally with other general partners in its profits and losses (unless otherwise agreed), and is liable to third parties without limit for partnership debts.

general partnership A partnership in which all members are general partners. (See also "limited partnership.")

genuine assent Consent of both parties is freely given, and not negated by fraud, duress, undue influence, and/or certain mistakes.

gift tax A tax imposed at the federal and state level on the value of gifts made by living persons.

good faith A general obligation imposed by the Uniform Commercial Code on both seller and buyer to practice honesty in conduct and contract.

good samaritan Reference to a biblical story where a person (samaritan) came to the aid of a stranger in desperate need. Use refers to statutes which protect volunteers from liability for their ordinary negligence while aiding persons in need.

goodwill, business Intangible asset of a business that is developed through customer satisfaction with sales and service, and that stimulates future sales and profits.

grand jury See "jury, grand."

grand theft The stealing of personal property of substantial value.

grandfather clause Any provision in a statute that exempts a certain class of persons from some change or new requirement in the law.

grant deed A deed of real property that impliedly warrants the grantor has not previously conveyed the property to another and the property is free from undisclosed encumbrances.

guardian A person appointed by the court (in a guardianship proceeding) to supervise and take care of another.

guardian *ad litem* [Latin: for the suit] A guardian appointed by the court to prosecute or defend any action for a minor as party.

guardianship A court-established arrangement whereby an adult guardian is appointed to take care of the person and/or the estate of a minor.

guest A person who rides for free in another person's vehicle.

guest statute Laws that pertain to guests of a driver of motor vehicle. In some states a guest cannot sue the driver if injured, unless the driver is guilty of intoxication, willful misconduct, or gross negligence that causes the accident and resulting injury or death. In other states a guest may sue the driver for ordinary negligence.

habeas corpus [Latin: you have the body] A legal writ or court order to release a prisoner from allegedly unlawful confinement, for appearance before a court for proper action. The petitioner seeks release.

habitability, implied warranty of The implied duty imposed on a landlord to keep residential rental property in a condition fit for use and enjoyment by the tenant.

hearsay See "evidence."

heirs Persons designated by law to receive the estate of a decedent who leaves no will (that is, dies intestate).

holographic will An unwitnessed will. States that allow such a will usually require it to be written in long hand by the testator, signed, and dated.

homicide Killing of a human being by another human being.

hung jury A jury that cannot reach a verdict because of inability or unwillingness of a sufficient number of jurors to agree on disputed facts.

immunity from prosecution The granting by a court of freedom from liability for crime. A person who has been granted this immunity possesses no privilege against self-incrimination and may be compelled to testify about the event in question.

implied in law contract Not a true contract, but an obligation is imposed on one party to prevent unjust enrichment of another. Also called "quasi-contract."

implied powers The authority of Congress to make laws that are "necessary and proper" for executing powers to make other laws under an express grant.

implied warranty A warranty required by law whether or not it is mentioned in a contract. (See also "warranty.")

impossibility When it is impossible to perform as promised in a contract.

in *loco parentis* [Latin: In the place of a parent]

in *propria persona* [Latin: in one's own person] Representing oneself in a legal action without the services of an attorney. Also in *pro se* [Latin: for him or herself].

incest Sexual intercourse between relatives who are lineals (grandparents, parents, children, etc.) or collaterals (brothers/sisters, aunts/uncles, etc.) of those degrees of closeness in which marriage is prohibited by state law.

indemnification Payment by one person (e.g., an employer) to another person (e.g., an employee) to make up for a loss suffered by the other.

independent contractor A person employed to do a specific job, and who retains control over how the job is done.

indeterminate sentence law A statute that provides for a range (such as one to five years) rather than a specific period of incarceration for a crime, the exact time to be determined by a designated authority after confinement begins.

indictment An accusation of felony filed by a grand jury. (See also "information.")

Individual Retirement Account (IRA) Federally authorized private pension plans supplementing Social Security whereby qualified employees contribute a certain percentage of their income, tax free, to their retirement accounts until retirement.

information An accusation of a criminal offense issued following a preliminary hearing which determines if the defendant should be made to stand trial or be released. (See also "indictment.")

informed consent Agreement of a patient before surgical procedures or administration of experimental drugs, and after full disclosure of the risk involved and alternatives available. Thus, the patient can intelligently decide on a course of action.

infraction Any minor crime that is not punishable by incarceration, but only by fine.

inheritance tax A tax imposed by most states on the privilege of receiving property from a decedent.

initiative A democratic process for making law that bypasses the legislature.

injunction An order of a court of equity forbidding an action that is considered injurious to the plaintiff, when dollar damages would be unavailable or inadequate.

insanity, legal Mental disease or defect that causes the accused to lack substantial capacity either to appreciate the criminality (wrongfulness) of his or her conduct or to conform his or her conduct to the requirements of the law. Definitions of insanity vary among the states.

installment land contract A method of selling real property in which the seller retains title for the years during which the buyer in possession makes monthly payments. Also called a contract-for-deed.

intentional infliction of mental distress Outrageous conduct that causes mental, if not immediate physical, suffering by the victim.

intentional tort Where the tortfeasor deliberately and wrongfully injures the person and/or property of another.

interest The payment, usually expressed as an annual rate (percentage), by a borrower for use of a principal sum of money obtained from a lender.

interference with an economically advantageous relationship When a tortfeasor knowingly and wrongfully interferes with the promised performance of another person's contract. As used here the term also includes violations of antitrust laws and other unfair competitive practices.

international law The branch of law governing relations between sovereign nations.

interpleader A legal proceeding to resolve conflicting claims to an escrow or other funds.

interrogatories A form of discovery using written questions directed to a party or witness who is expected to reply with written answers.

inter-spousal immunity The traditional ban on lawsuits between spouses to avoid possible resulting disruption of family harmony. Modern trend is to allow such lawsuits.

inter-vivos [Latin: among the living]

    ***inter vivos* gift** A gift from one living person to another; a way to acquire personal property.

***inter vivos* trust** A trust created during the life of the trustor.

interstate commerce Commercial trading or transportation between or among two or more states. The U.S. Constitution (Article I) delegates to the Congress power to regulate such commerce.

intestacy Dying without having made and left a valid will.

intestate law Statutory prescription for distribution, among heirs, of the estate of a decedent who has died leaving no will.

intrastate commerce Commercial trading or transportation within any one state. Under the Tenth Amendment of the U.S. Constitution the power to regulate intrastate commerce is reserved to the respective states.

invidious discrimination A governmental or private discrimination based on ethnic, religious, or national origin for which there is a legal remedy.

invitee One who enters another's land with the permission (implied or express) of the owner or occupier, for a business benefiting the owner.

involuntary manslaughter The unintentional killing of another person because of gross negligence, or as a result of dangerous and unlawful conduct (such as killing a pedestrian while speeding).

irrelevant Not pertinent to anything of consequence in the proof of facts in dispute. Valid reason for objecting to a question during a trial.

irresistible impulse The motivation whereby an accused, because of a diseased mind, could not avoid committing a criminal act even if he or she knew it was wrong. An acceptable test of legal insanity in a few states.

irrevocable trust A trust that may not be terminated or revoked by the trustor who created it.

joint tenancy A method of co-ownership of property by two or more persons. Upon the death of any co-owner, his or her percentage interest goes to the surviving joint tenant(s) regardless of the decedent's last will. This right of survivorship is the primary incident of joint tenancy ownership.

joint tortfeasors Two or more persons who together commit a tort.

judge The official who presides over a trial court. (See also "court.")

judgment The final determination or decision of the court as to the rights and duties of the parties in a lawsuit.

judgment debtor A person against whom a judgment has been entered, but payment has not yet been made or completed.

judgment creditor One who has won a judgment but has not been fully paid.

judgment non obstante veredicto or judgment n.o.v. [Latin: notwithstanding the verdict] A judgment by a judge that overrules the verdict of the jury.

judgment proof A person who lacks the assets to pay any judgment acquired against them.

judicial branch The government department that is responsible for determining the constitutionality of legislative and executive actions, and adjudicating rights and duties of persons involved in disputes. It interprets and applies the laws. (See also "executive branch" and "legislative branch.")

judicial review Powers of the U.S. Supreme Court to declare an act of Congress, presidential order, or state law unconstitutional.

jurisdiction The power of a court to decide a controversy and to award appropriate relief. Also, the scope of power to govern.

jury, grand A group of up to 23 adults selected and sworn to review, under court supervision, evidence of alleged criminal conduct, and to indict (formally accuse) persons who they believe should stand trial.

jury, trial A group, usually consisting of 12 adults, but sometimes a smaller number, who are selected and sworn to review evidence in civil and criminal trials, and to determine the facts by verdict. Also called *petit* [French: small] jury.

justices Judges in appellate courts.

juvenile court A court with jurisdiction over delinquent and neglected children.

Keogh Retirement Plan Federally authorized private pension plans whereby a self-employed person may contribute a percentage of their earnings, tax free, to a trust account until retirement.

kidnapping The crime of unlawful seizure of a victim and movement from one place to another against his or her will.

Labor-Management Relations Act of 1947 (Taft-Hartley Act) Federal law that lists unfair labor practices of unions. It outlaws the closed shop and secondary boycott.

Labor-Management Reporting and Disclosure Act of 1959 (Landrum-Griffin Act) Federal law that mandates open, democratic internal government of unions.

laches A doctrine that bars stale lawsuits in civil cases in equity. Analogous to the statute of limitations that bars stale, or old, claims for damages in civil cases at law.

land contract An agreement by an owner of real property to sell to a buyer who takes possession but does not obtain legal title until all or most payments have been made to the seller. (See also "installment land contract.")

landlord The owner of residential property who leases it to a tenant, or renter, in exchange for rent.

larceny The crime of stealing property from another who is not then present. Also called theft.

last will See "will."

laws Principles and detailed rules of human conduct that are enforceable in the courts and by administrative agencies.

lease A contract, usually written, by which the relationship of landlord and tenant is created. Also called rental agreement.

leasehold The legal interest a tenant has in residential property leased from the landlord. A leasehold is usually created by a written contract called a lease.

legal separation A court order permitting spouses to live apart with necessary related orders for child custody and support, support of the wife (or husband) and division of property (as in dissolution), but the marriage endures.

legislative branch The government department that is responsible for enacting statutory laws. (See also "executive branch" and "judicial branch.")

legitimate A person who is the issue of his or her natural, married parents. The child of an unmarried mother is illegitimate.

legitimation Irrevocable acknowledgement by a natural father that, although not married, he is the male parent of a child.

lemon Something, usually a product, that proves to be unsatisfactory or undesirable.

lemon laws State statutes designed to assist buyers of seriously defective goods to obtain a replacement or full refund.

letter of last instructions A document prepared by a person to instruct his or her personal representative (executor or administrator) as to the nature and location of assets and liabilities and to suggest appropriate action to be taken after death. Not legally binding.

liability Any legal obligation.

libel The written form of defamation.

licensee One who enters another's land with permission (implied or express) of the owner or possessor, for the visitor's convenience.

lien See "mechanic's lien."

life estate An ownership interest in property characterized by the right to its possession for the duration of the owner's life. At the death of the owner (called the life tenant) possession may (a) revert to the person (called the grantor) who created the life estate (b) go to a designated person (called the remainderman), or (c) go to a successor life tenant. For example, the conveyance may read: A (grantor) to B for life (life tenant), remainder to C (remainderman). Upon death of a life tenant, the value of the estate is extinguished and, therefore, no death taxes are payable. A life estate may be created by deed or will, and may be created so as to continue until the death of someone other than the life tenant.

limited liability of stockholders Regardless of the number of shares owned, a stockholder is normally not liable for the debts of the corporation beyond the extent of his or her investment. Considered a primary advantage of corporate ownership.

limited partner Partner whose liability for partnership debts extends only to his or her capital investment. Substantial limitations exist on the extent such partners may participate in partnership management.

limited partnership A partnership form authorized by state statute in which at least one member is a general partner who manages the firm and has unlimited liability for its debts, but the liability of the other partner(s) is limited to the amount of their capital investment(s). (See also "general partnership.")

lineals Relatives who are in a direct line of descent, as parents, children, grandchildren. (See also "collateral.")

liquidated damages A pre-arranged amount of damages in case of a contract breach.

listing agreement An employment contract between the owner of real property and a licensed agent authorizing the latter to hunt for a buyer of the property on specified terms. Pre-printed types of listing forms include:

  exclusive-agency listing The owner may find a buyer and sell the property without liability for payment of commission, but must pay the listing agent if any other agent finds a buyer to whom the owner sells.

  exclusive listing The owner must pay the listing agent the agreed upon commission regardless of who finds the buyer to whom the property is sold.

  net listing The agent retains as compensation for finding a ready, willing and able buyer all sums received by the seller that are in excess of a specified net amount.

  open listing Owner agrees to pay a commission only to the agent who produces a ready, willing, and able buyer. Thus an owner may sign several open listings, each with a different agent.

litigation Any pending lawsuit.

living trust A popular term for a revocable *inter vivos* trust whose primary purpose is to avoid probate.

living will A document usually authorized by state statute directed to a physician communicating the wishes of the drafter regarding the use of life support systems in the treatment of a terminal illness. Also called a directive to physicians.

loan shark A person who charges exorbitantly usurious interest for the loan of money, and commonly threatens or uses violence to compel payment.

lobbying Efforts by individuals and representatives of special interest groups to persuade legislators (and sometimes administrators) to enact, amend, or rescind specified laws.

lockout A shutdown of operations by an employer in response to union demands or to achieve other changes in an employment contract.

magistrates (a) State judges of the justice court or other lower courts with jurisdiction over relatively minor offenses and small claims (b) A U.S. official who performs specified judicial services in the prosecution of federal crimes.

Magnuson-Moss Warranty Act of 1975 Federal law that protects ultimate consumers of personal, family and household goods by defining effects of full and limited warranties.

maintenance Financially supporting or promoting litigation in which one has no legitimate interest. (See also "alimony.")

maker The creator of promissory note.

malice aforethought The highest degree of criminal culpability characterized by a cold and malignant heart.

malicious prosecution A sham lawsuit brought for the purpose of vexing or harassing the defendant.

malpractice Violation of a duty of due care by a professional person.

manslaughter The unlawful killing of another person without malice aforethought. Usually classified as voluntary or involuntary, depending on the degree of culpability involved. Vehicular manslaughter is a special category for negligent killings by automobile.

marital life estate trust Reciprocal trusts executed by a husband and wife with the other spouse as a life beneficiary. Also called an A and B trust.

marital property Property earned during marriage.

market value The price a home or other property would bring if offered for sale in a normal market without compulsion of buyer or seller. Also called fair market value.

material alteration Any deliberate, unilateral, important change in a written contract, without legal excuse.

mayhem The crime of unlawfully depriving the victim of some member of his or her body, or disfiguring, disabling, or rendering the member useless.

mechanic's lien A legal claim of a contractor or worker who helped construct a building (or repair a product, such as a car). It may be asserted against the property itself for any sum unpaid. A similar lien is given by law to suppliers of materials for construction projects.

mediation The use of a neutral third party to assist parties to voluntarily resolve their disputes.

medical payments insurance Coverage available in conjunction with automobile insurance—for example, to pay medical, surgical, dental, and funeral expenses suffered by the insured or by any member of the insured's household who is injured while occupying or being struck by an automobile. Coverage may be extended to other persons occupying the owned automobile.

meretricious Describes a relationship of persons living as man and wife including sexual relations without benefit of marriage. Suggests an immoral relationship.

mini-trial A nonbinding ADR process where the parties, usually sizable business organizations, agree to an informal trial-like proceeding. Each side agrees to the procedural rules, an exchange of information and a neutral advisor. The presentation is made to officials of each party possessing settlement authority.

minor A person below the age of legal competence. For most purposes in most states, minority ends at age 18; for some purposes, such as the purchase and consumption of alcoholic beverages, it may end later, up to the age of 21.

Miranda warnings Warnings directed to a suspect by police before a custodial (while in custody) interrogation may occur. The warnings include the right to remain silent, that anything said can and will be used against the person in court, and that the accused is entitled to a lawyer.

misdemeanor A crime that is punishable by fine or by incarceration in a county jail for up to a year, or by both.

misrepresentation A false statement made intentionally, knowing it is not true. A negligent misrepresentation is a false statement made carelessly. (See also "deceit" and "fraud.")

mistrial A trial that has failed to conclude properly because of some defect or because of the inability of the proper number of jurors to concur in a verdict. For example, inflammatory remarks by an attorney to a jury may result in a mistrial. A new trial usually will be scheduled to follow a mistrial.

mobile home A compact movable home, available at a relatively low price. Generally set down in a "mobile home park" and not removed thereafter.

Model Business Corporations Act A model act first drafted in 1933. Although not adopted in full by any state, it has significantly influenced the corporation codes of most states.

money Coins and paper currency authorized by the federal government as a medium of exchange and as legal tender for payment of debts.

moot question (a) A question open to argument, not settled by court decision, (b) purely hypothetical or academic question, or (c) a question no longer important.

mortgage A security agreement between a borrower (called mortgagor) and a lender (called mortgagee) that creates a lien on specified real property to guarantee repayment of the loan. If the borrower fails to repay the loan as agreed, the mortgagee may foreclose the mortgage and apply the proceeds of a foreclosure sale to repayment of the loan. In some states the same function is served by a deed of trust. The terms mortgage, real mortgage, and deed of trust are frequently used interchangeably.

> **fixed rate mortgage** A home loan (secured by a mortgage or deed or trust) that features a constant interest rate during its term.
>
> **graduated payment mortgage** A home loan (secured by a mortgage or deed or trust) that features an artificially low payment for several years as an inducement.
>
> **variable interest rate mortgage (VIRM)** A home loan (secured by a mortgage or deed or trust) that features an interest rate that may increase or decrease during its term.

Mosaic code The Ten Commandments, Decalogue, delivered to Moses on Mt. Sinai. Some ethicists consider the commandments a succinct statement of the natural law.

motion A formal request addressed to a court or other tribunal for a particular decision or act (e.g., motion for mistrial, motion for new trial, motion for directed verdict).

motion for a directed verdict Request to a judge that he or she enter a verdict instead of allowing the jury to do so because there are insufficient facts to allow any other verdict.

motion for summary judgment Request to a judge that the moving party be awarded judgment because there are no significant questions of fact in the lawsuit, and that applicable law requires the ruling.

motion to dismiss See "demurrer."

motion to produce An order made by a court at the request of counsel compelling the opposing party to provide specified evidence to the court. A type of discovery procedure.

motive A reason for doing, or not doing, an act; not synonymous with criminal intent. Intent is essential for crime; motive is not. A good motive is no excuse.

moving party The party making a request of a court.

multiple listing An organization of real estate brokers who exchange information about listings of property they have obtained. All member brokers (and their sales agents) may hunt for buyers for any of the properties multiple listed. Any agent who finds a ready, willing, and able buyer of a listed property shares in the commission earned with the agent who got the original listing agreement with the seller.

murder The unlawful killing of an human being with malice aforethought. Usually classified as first degree (or capital murder) or second degree (or noncapital murder) depending on the degree of culpability involved.

mutual assent A proper offer and acceptance by the parties forming a contract.

mutual mistake Where both parties to a contract labor under the same error about an important fact in their agreement. Also called a bilateral mistake.

National Labor Relations Act of 1935 (Wagner Act) Federal law that recognizes the right of workers to organize into unions and the duty of employers to bargain collectively with the unions over wages, hours, and conditions of employment. Lists unfair labor practices of managers.

natural law The higher law above and beyond man's power to change.

necessaries Goods and services ordinarily required by and appropriate to an incompetent person's station in life, yet not available or provided by parent or guardian.

negative injunction An order of a court of equity forbidding certain action.

negligence Failure to act as a reasonable, careful person would act under the same or similar circumstances, thereby causing injury that was foreseeable.

negligence *per se* [Latin: of itself] The proof of the act establishes the duty.

negotiation Communication for the purposes of persuasion. Bargaining.

net worth The difference between total assets and total liabilities of a person or organization. (If liabilities exceed assets, the negative difference is called a deficit. In a corporation, a deficit is the excess of liabilities and capital stock over assets.)

neutral An unbiased third party who assists parties in the resolution of disputes. Includes arbitrators, mediators and ombudsmen.

neutral expert fact finding A nonbinding ADR process in which an appointed third party expert investigates, or hears facts on, selected issues and makes advisory findings of fact.

no-fault divorce A type of divorce that may be granted by a court even though both spouses are innocent of any wrongdoing. The rapidly disappearing traditional type of divorce would be granted only to an innocent spouse on proof that the other spouse was guilty of some misconduct, such as infidelity, mental cruelty, or desertion.

no-fault insurance A type of automobile insurance that provides benefits to the insured, regardless of fault of parties to the accident.

***nolo contendere*, plea of** [Latin: I will not contest it] Equivalent to a plea of guilty, but cannot be regarded as admission of guilt in a subsequent civil trial against the defendant.

nonbinding arbitration A form of arbitration in which the arbitrator's finding is not binding on the parties.

nonsupport Failure to contribute money, in accordance with one's ability, to the maintenance of a parent or child as required by law.

notice of default Notice used to inform the public of an impending private foreclosure sale.

novation A three party agreement in which a creditor accepts a new party who agrees to assume the debt and to release the prior debtor.

nullification of marriage A court judgment terminating a defective or voidable marriage (for example, involving a person below the age of legal consent).

nuncupative will An oral will.

obscene Material or conduct is obscene if, considered as a whole, its predominant appeal is to prurient interest, i.e., a morbid interest in nudity, sex, or excretion. Community standards, as distinguished from national standards, are used by the jury in applying this definition to material or conduct alleged to be obscene.

Occupational Safety and Health Administration (OSHA) Federal agency charged with defining and enforcing minimum standards of health and safety in the work place. Assisted by state OSHA organizations in some states.

offer A promise by one person (the offeror) to do or to give something in exchange for sought-for acceptance by another person (the offeree). (See "acceptance.")

offeree In contracts, a party to whom an offer is made by the offeror.

offeror In contracts, a party who makes an offer.

officers (of a corporation) Persons selected by directors and given delegated authority to manage the day-to-day business affairs of a corporation. Typically include president, vice-president(s), secretary, and treasurer.

ombudsman A proactive neutral who investigates and determines facts and suggests resolutions to a dispute.

open shop A company or department where union membership is not required to get or keep a job. The employer does not necessarily bargain collectively with any union, although it may.

opening statements Summaries by counsel of plaintiff and of defendant indicating what they expect to prove in the ensuing trial.

option The right to purchase property at an established price at any time within a specified period. The optionee (potential buyer) pays option money to the owner in exchange for this right.

option contract An agreement the subject matter of which is the right to buy or sell something to another at a certain price at a certain time.

order of examination A judicially authorized inquiry as to the assets of a judgment debtor.

ordinance Written laws enacted by local government, such as cities and counties.

ordinary wear and tear Deterioration in a residential rental property that is attributable to the passage of time, not through any abuse by the tenant. The fading of draperies is an example.

outrageous conduct Intentional conduct that does not involve assault or battery yet inflicts extreme emotional trauma on the victim.

owner A person who has legal and equitable title to property, with related rights and duties, or benefits and burdens. Two basic subtypes of owner are:

equitable owner Has possession and use of the property although another may have the legal title.

legal owner Has legal title, for example, as security for repayment of a loan, or payment of the purchase price of real property or personal property, such as an automobile. Legal title is transferred to the equitable owner when the debt is paid.

paralegal A person qualified to perform a wide range of legal tasks under the guidance of an attorney.

pardon Release of a convicted criminal from all punishment for his or her crime through an act of the chief executive. Includes restoration of political rights.

parol evidence rule When contracting parties have put their complete agreement into writing, no prior or contemporaneous oral or written terms may be unilaterally added later to change the written contract, absent proof of fraud, mistake or illegality.

parole Release from a prison on specified conditions involving good behavior. If these conditions are violated, the prisoner is returned to complete the original sentence.

participating preferred stock Shares of preferred stock, the owners of which are entitled to receive additional dividends (beyond the regular agreed amount) when payments are made to common stockholders.

partnership An association of two or more persons to carry on, as co-owners, a business for profit. Also known as a general partnership.

paternity action A lawsuit to determine whether or not the defendant is the natural father of a child as alleged.

Pensions Benefit Guaranty Corporation (PBGC) Created under the Employee Retirement Income Security Act to assure financial soundness of all private pension plans under that act.

peremptory challenge See "challenge of juror."

performance Party to a contract does what he or she promised.

periodic tenancy A leasehold interest that continues indefinitely for successive periods (usually monthly), until properly terminated by either the lessor or lessee.

perjury Lying about material facts when testifying under oath.

personal liability insurance Protects the insured from liability arising from his or her injuring or killing a person.

personal property See "property."

petty theft The theft of personal property of value less than the value that would qualify the crime as a felony.

picketing Patrolling by strikers or sympathizers, generally at the entrances to a business plant during a labor dispute. Pickets usually carry cards urging workers to join the strikers and urging suppliers and customers to refuse to deal with the employer.

pilferage Stealing of small goods from storage, usually by employees of the owner or of the warehouse operator.

pimping The crime of enticing a female to engage in prostitution. Also called pandering and procuring.

plaintiff In trial, the person trying to recover money damages or other relief from a defendant.

plea Response of the accused to criminal charges, it may be (1) guilty, (2) not guilty, (3) *nolo contendere,* or (4) not guilty by reason of insanity.

plea bargain A binding agreement in which an accused agrees to plead guilty (or nolo contendere) if the court agrees to a specified punishment in advance. Plea bargains avoid the time, expense, and uncertainty of a trial.

pleadings The complaint of the plaintiff and answer of the defendant in a lawsuit.

points A one-time charge made by a lender when a home loan is originated. One point is one percent of the loan.

police power The inherent power of the government to subject individual rights to reasonable regulation for the health, safety, morals, or general welfare of the public.

polygraph (tests) "Lie detector" tests using a mechanical device for recording dramatic changes in body functions during interrogation.

possession The custody and control of property coupled with the right to use it.

power of appointment Authority given to a person (the donee) under a trust or will to designate or appoint the person(s) who shall receive specified assets after a specified event (such as death of the donee or death of the testator.)

power of attorney A document authorizing another to act as one's agent. A general power of attorney authorizes the agent (called the attorney-in-fact) to do all acts not prohibited by law for another (called the principal). A special power of attorney authorizes the attorney-in-fact to do a limited and specified class of acts for the principal.

preemption Assertion by the federal government of authority to regulate a field (such as labor relations). States may not enforce conflicting laws in such fields. (The same principle applies between state and local governments.) Also called supremacy.

preferred stock Shares that represent ownership in a business corporation and are entitled to dividends of a fixed amount before any payment to common stockholders.

preliminary hearing An examination in open court by a judge to determine whether sufficient evidence exists to hold the accused for trial. Not used when a grand jury issues an indictment.

preponderance of the evidence Standard of evidence that the weight of the evidence is more probable than not. Used in most civil trials.

pretermitted heir statute A statute giving rights of inheritance to children (or grandchildren) of a testator not named in the will and not provided for by settlement in life.

pretrial proceeding In the months before a civil trial is scheduled to begin, several pretrial proceedings may occur. One is a settlement conference attended by the attorneys, parties, and judge for the purpose of determining whether the case can be amicably settled without a trial. Another type of proceeding is a conference attended by the attorneys and judge for the purpose of formalizing the issues to be determined at trial and deciding whether to have a jury or not and other important matters.

prima facie [Latin: on first appearance] The proof of the initial case.

principal The person who empowers an agent to enter contracts on his or her behalf.

prior restraint Legal measures to prevent anticipated illegal conduct before it takes place, such as the banning of a parade expected to cause a riot.

privacy, invasion of right of Violation of the fundamental right of every person who has violated no law to be left alone.

private judging The use of a legally trained arbitrator who follows formal judicial procedures in hearing a case. The final award is entered as a judgment in many states with the right of judicial appeal allowed.

private law That body of law regulating the rights and duties that exist between private persons (including private corporations). Contract law is an example of private law.

privilege against self-incrimination The right of any person, including one accused of a crime, to remain silent when what might be said could indicate guilt. "No person . . . shall be compelled in any criminal case to be a witness against himself. . . ." (Fifth Amendment).

privileged communication A right and duty one has to withhold communications from disclosure in legal proceedings because of some special relationship. Examples include attorney/client, physician/patient, and husband/wife.

privity Where parties are in a direct contractual relationship, e.g., a consumer buyer dealing with the retail seller, but not with the wholesaler or with the manufacturer of the goods.

pro bono publico [Latin: for the public good] An attorney providing legal services free of charge.

probate The process of proving the validity of a will in court, coupled with the related matter of administering the decedent's estate. Involves payment of debts to creditors and distribution of remaining assets to heirs or beneficiaries.

probation Release of a convicted criminal before sentence begins, on condition of good behavior and under supervision of a probation officer. If this condition is violated, incarceration begins.

procedural law Principles and detailed rules that define the methods of administering substantive law.

process Legal documents or writs used to compel a defendant in a lawsuit to answer a complaint and appear in court.

process server A person who serves (delivers) a copy of the summons and complaint upon a defendant at the request of a plaintiff.

profits The excess of revenues or receipts of a business over costs or expenses. Also called net income.

promisee A person to whom a promise has been made. See "offeree."

promisor A person who makes a promise. See "offeror."

promissory note A written promise to pay another a sum of money in the future. The note contains all of the terms of the loan, such as the due date, repayment rate, interest rate, and so forth. Home loans evidenced by notes are secured by a mortgage or deed of trust.

property Anything that may be owned. Classified broadly as:

    real property Land and things permanently attached to it. Includes air space above, surface water, and subsurface waters, gasses, and minerals.

    personal property All property that is not real property.

property damage insurance Protects the insured from liability arising from his or her damaging the property of another.

prosecutor An attorney employed by the government to pursue legal proceedings against persons accused of crime. Represents the state or the people in criminal trials.

prospectus A formal report, published prior to the issuance of securities by a corporation, containing important facts about the company and its operations.

provocative act rule Under this rule, all participants in a dangerous felony are guilty of murder in the first degree if a lawful killing occurs in response to some threatening act of one of the felons. An example is a killing by a police officer who fires in response to gun-waving by one of the fleeing felons.

proximate cause A cause which, in natural and continuous sequence, produces the injury, and without which the effect or result would not have occurred.

proxy A written form signed by a stockholder designating another person to vote regarding his or her share(s) of stock.

public defender A lawyer provided by the community for a person who is accused of a crime and cannot afford to hire counsel.

public law That body of law directly concerned with public rights and obligations, such as constitutional, administrative, criminal, and international law.

public policy A fundamental guideline under which courts condemn or invalidate actions deemed to be contrary to the commonweal or good of society.

publication of defamatory material Communicating defamatory material about the victim to one or more third persons.

purchase money mortgage A loan the proceeds of which are used to purchase a home. The lender retains a non-possessory interest in the home as security for repayment of the loan.

quasi [Latin: as if] Used in conjunction with other words; for example, "quasi-contract" means an agreement that resembles a contract and may be enforced as one even when some essential element of a contract is missing.

questions of fact Circumstances or matter surrounding and involved in a case being tried by a court. Historical events in dispute. Decided by a jury.

questions of law Principles and rules of human conduct determined by the judge to be applicable in a case. For example, the definition of murder is a question of law within the province of the judge and not the jury.

quitclaim deed A deed to real property in which the transferor conveys whatever interest he or she may possess, which may be none. The transferor makes no warranties and therefore cannot be held liable if the title transferred proves to be faulty. Commonly used to correct errors in recorded titles. (See also "deed.")

Racketeer Influenced and Corrupt Organizations Act of 1970 (RICO) A federal law passed to control attempts by organized crime to invest money from the fruits of crime in legitimate business activities. Scope of the law is broad and creates both civil and criminal remedies for activities defined as racketeering.

racial quota Legally imposed requirement for the hiring of a specific number of minorities to rectify past discrimination against these groups. Quotas also may apply to women.

rape, forcible An unlawful act of sexual intercourse against the will of the victim. Consent obtained by trick or threat or through the use of intoxicants or narcotics is not true consent.

rape shield statute A statute that protects victims from courtroom questioning about prior sexual experiences with persons other than the defendant.

reasonable person A hypothetical person used in the law as a standard for reasonable conduct. For example, failure to act as a reasonable person under the given circumstances usually is negligence; negligent conduct may result in liability to an injured victim.

recall A democratic process for removing officials from their elective positions.

receiving stolen property The crime of knowingly receiving stolen property. Proof of knowledge may be inferred from the circumstances.

recidivist A criminal who is a repeat offender. Recidivist statutes may enhance a lesser penalty to life imprisonment.

recognizance A written promise by the accused, if released, to return voluntarily for further criminal proceedings. (See also "bail.")

referendum A democratic process submitting certain proposed laws to the electorate for approval.

registered buyer-owner The buyer of a car on time who gets possession and use while making payments. (See also "owner.")

regulations Rules created by an administrative agency consistent with the authority given to the agency by statute.

regulatory offense A violation of a rule promulgated by an administrative agency.

reinstatement of mortgage The payment of all delinquent sums and related fees within a prescribed period of time to a foreclosing creditor. Upon payment, the original loan terms are reinstated as if no default had occurred. The right of reinstatement belongs to the debtor or his assigns.

relevant Related to the fact in dispute. (See also "evidence.")

remainderman The person designated to receive complete ownership of property upon termination of a life estate; for example when a man, in his will, leaves real property to his widow for her life, and then to their children. The children are called remaindermen. (See also "life estate.")

remedies Relief provided by courts to redress wrongs and to enforce rights. Includes monetary damages, orders for specific performance, injunctions, and other appropriate relief.

rent Money paid by a renter to the landlord in exchange for the possession and use of rental property. Rent also may take the form of personal services or any asset in lieu of money.

rental agreement A contract, usually written, between a landlord and tenant. Technically it is a lease. (See also "lease.")

replevin Legal action to recover possession of goods wrongfully taken or retained by a defendant.

reprieve Postponement or stay of execution of judgment, after conviction for a crime.

republic A representative system of government in which the rulers are chosen by popular vote.

request for admission of facts Submitted to counsel by the opposing attorney before trial for the acknowledgment of facts that are not in dispute and yet are relevant and material. A type of discovery procedure.

res ipsa loquitur [Latin: the thing speaks for itself] The doctrine under which negligence is inferred. To avoid liability the defendant must prove he or she was not negligent. Available when the instrumentality causing the injury was under control of the defendant and an injury occurred that normally would not occur in the absence of negligence. Frequently relied on by victims of medical malpractice.

rescission An equitable remedy that annuls a contract and returns the parties to the relationship they had before the contract.

residual powers Any power not expressly delegated to the United States by the U.S. Constitution nor prohibited by it to the states, and hence reserved to the states, or to the people.

respondeat superior [Latin: let the master answer] A legal doctrine holding employers liable for injuries caused third persons by their employees who are negligent while acting in the course and scope of their employment.

Restatement of the Law A series of authoritative volumes on major areas of law (e.g., contracts, agency, and torts) written by scholars of the American Law Institute.

restitution Return of what has been received, as when a contract is rescinded, or when a thief repays stolen money.

retainer fee A sum of money paid an attorney for a promise to remain available for the client's consultation, if needed.

retaliatory eviction Termination of a month-to-month lease (periodic tenancy) in retaliation for some lawful act (e.g., organizing a tenant's union) by the tenant. Prohibited to some extent in most states.

reverse discrimination Label given to affirmative action programs by opponents who claim affirmative action discriminates against male and white workers.

reversionary interest (a) Something of value (such as the right to borrow against the policy) that a life insurance policyholder may retain when giving the policy to another person. (b) The future interest in real property retained by the grantor of a life estate.

revocable trust A trust that may be terminated or revoked by the trustor who created it.

rights

　　civil Rights that a person has as a human being and by virtue of U.S. citizenship. These rights are found in constitutions and state and federal civil rights laws. They include equal protection of law and due process of law.

　　fundamental Basic rights that a person has under the U.S. Constitution, such as the rights of freedom of speech, press, religion, and assembly.

　　legal Claim for recognition and protection of one's person, property, and other interests; enforceable in court. May include civil, natural, and political rights. Reciprocal of legal duty.

　　natural Rights that a person has by virtue of being human, such as the right to life, liberty, and the pursuit of happiness.

　　political Rights that citizens share in government, including the right to vote and to hold public office.

right of retraction A defense against libel favoring certain publications, such as newspapers. Even if a paper defames someone, publication of a retraction, or admission of error, may be a complete or partial defense against a claim for damages.

right-to-know-law Statute that requires informing workers of the hazards from chemicals that they are likely to be exposed to on the job.

right-to-work law Statute enacted in some 20 states that provides that a person need not join a union to get a job.

robbery The crime of stealing property from another person through the use of force or fear.

Roman civil law See "civil law."

rule against perpetuities A rule that requires remainder interests in property to vest no later than a life or lives in being, plus 21 years.

S corporation A closely held corporation that is treated as a partnership for federal tax purposes. Income is regarded as taxable personal income to the stockholders, whether distributed or retained in the business. One effect is to avoid the customary double taxation of corporation net income.

sale A contract in which title (ownership) of property passes from seller to buyer. Possession usually transfers at the time of sale.

satisfaction of judgment Proof that a debt created by a judgment of the court has been paid by the defendant.

search and seizure A phrase that describes any search of one's person or property and the process of taking evidence into custody by an officer of the law. Evidence obtained by an unreasonable search and seizure is tainted with illegality and may not be used against the accused under the so-called "exclusionary rule."

secondary boycott When striking workers picket or use other pressure against a neutral third party that supplies or buys from the struck employer.

secured loan Money borrowed with a pledge by the borrower of specific assets that may be forfeited if repayment is not made as promised.

seduction The criminal act of enticing a person to engage in sexual intercourse by means of false promise (as of marriage), but without force.

segregation Isolation or separate treatment, usually unequal, on the sole basis of race, color, creed, or national origin.

self-defense The legal right to use whatever force appears to be reasonably necessary to protect oneself (or specified others) from great and imminent bodily injury by an assailant.

self-incrimination See "privilege against self-incrimination."

separate maintenance A partial termination of marriage on which the spouses live apart while support is paid. Property normally is not divided between the spouses. (See also "divorce from bed and board." See also "legal separation.")

separate property Property, real or personal, either brought into a marriage at the outset or acquired during marriage by gift or inheritance, together with the profits therefrom. Separate property must be kept separate to retain this status. (See also "community property.")

separation agreement A contract between spouses who are contemplating a divorce. (See also "antenuptial agreement.")

separation of powers The constitutional doctrine dividing and confining certain powers of the U.S. government into the legislative, executive and judicial.

Service Core of Retired Executives (SCORE) A large group of experienced retired business executives who provide expert counselling and training to new small business entrepreneurs without charge, under the auspices of the federal Small Business Administration.

settlor A person who establishes a trust. Also called a trustor.

severalty Ownership of real property by one unmarried person, or by a married person of separate property.

sex perversion Violation of state law prohibiting sodomy, oral copulation, and lewd or lascivious acts with a child.

shareholder See "stockholder."

shares See "stock."

shoplifting Surreptitiously stealing merchandise from a retail store.

slander Spoken defamatory statement. (See also "defamation.")

simple contract All oral and written contracts not otherwise formal contracts.

Simplified Employee Pension Plans (SEP's) Private employee pension plans authorized by federal law whereby employers contribute to their employees' individual retirement accounts.

sitdown strike Illegal strike in which strikers remain in their place of employment but refuse to work.

Small Business Administration (SBA) Federal administrative agency that provides information, advice, and financial assistance to business managers and qualified small business firms.

small claims court A court with jurisdiction to decide civil controversies of a relatively minor or insignificant nature. Although a civil claim may be insignificant to society in general, it may be extremely important to the individuals involved.

social contract An agreement setting forth rights, duties, and obligations of government and the people (e.g., a constitution).

sole proprietorship A business owned and typically operated by one person who receives all profits and is liable for all losses.

solicitation The crime of assisting or encouraging another person to commit a crime.

sovereign immunity Traditional legal rule that "the king can do no wrong," hence, government is not liable for the torts of its agents and employees. Modern trend is away from recognition of such immunity.

specific performance Remedy available in a court of equity to get possession and title to goods that are unique when seller refuses to deliver under a valid sales contract. Real estate is deemed to be unique. Dollar damages are deemed an inadequate remedy for the plaintiff.

standard of care Duty required in negligence actions to act as a reasonable person would under the same or similar circumstances.

stare decisis [Latin: to stand by things settled] The common law doctrine that binds an inferior (subordinate) court to follow and apply decisions and interpretations of higher courts when similar cases arise. Also called the doctrine of precedents.

state law Includes state constitutions, statutes enacted by state legislatures, rules promulgated by state agencies, and the decisions of state courts.

statute of frauds A state statute requiring defined contracts to be evidenced by a signed writing.

statutes of limitations Statutes limiting the time during which a cause of action can be filed with a court.

statutes Written laws of federal and state legislatures.

statutory rape Sexual intercourse between a male, usually 18 or older, and an agreeing female, usually 17 or younger. State statutes vary the penalties depending on the age of the victim. Also called unlawful intercourse.

statutory will A form will authorized by state law with blanks to be completed by the testator.

stock Certificate of ownership of a share or interest in a business corporation. May be common or preferred with further subdivisions depending on rights.

stock dividend When directors of a corporation declare a dividend in the form of shares of the corporation's stock. An appropriate transfer is made from the earned surplus account to the capital account. The dividend is not taxable to the recipient unless a share received is sold.

stock split When directors of a corporation divide each share of stock into a larger number of shares. There is no transfer from the earned surplus account to the capital account. However, if the stock has par value or stated value, such values are accordingly changed.

stockholder A person who owns one or more shares of the capital stock of a profit-seeking corporation. The stockholder's liability for losses is normally limited to the amount of the capital investment made through purchase and retention of the stock.

strict liability A legal theory applicable where the tortfeasor sells a defective or hazardous product and the user-victim is thereby injured. The victim need not prove negligence, wrongful intent, breach of warranty, or privity of contract.

strike A concerted refusal by employees to perform the services for which they were hired, in order to gain recognition or improvements in wages, hours, or conditions of employment.

strike breakers Persons hired to take the place of workers who are out on strike. If it is an economic strike, the strike breakers may be retained as permanent replacements.

strike, sympathy A strike called by workers in a company or department where there is no labor dispute, in sympathy and to support workers employed elsewhere.

sublease Transfer by a tenant of his or her leasehold interest for less than its unexpired term. (See also "assignment.")

subornation of perjury Persuading another person to commit perjury.

subpoena A court order directing a person to appear at a certain time and place for the purpose of giving testimony as a witness.

subpoena *duces tecum* [Latin: under penalty bring with you] An order that one bring specified documents or physical evidence to court.

subrogation The substitution of a third party for the creditor in a claim against a debtor. For example, the insurer may pay the claim of its insured against the defendant and then sue the defendant in the name of the insured for damages resulting from an auto accident.

subsequent illegality When terms of a contract, legal at inception, cannot be performed legally.

substantial performance Party to a contract honestly performs most essentials of the contract but there is some important omission or deviation.

substantive law Principles and detailed rules that define legal rights and duties. Contrasted to procedural law.

summary jury trial A nonbinding ADR process in which parties present their cases to a private mock jury, who then advises the parties as to their advisory verdict.

summons A document issued by a clerk of the court at the request of the plaintiff when a complaint is filed. After service on the defendant judgment will be taken if the complaint is not answered within the statutory time (e.g., 15 or 30 days). Prepared by the plaintiff's attorney. (See also "complaint.")

surrogate mother A female who is artificially inseminated, carries the fetus to term, and who then relinquishes her parental rights to the biological father. Surrogacy services are performed pursuant to a contract in return for money.

sustain Where a judge agrees with an argument by one of the attorneys. For example, if an attorney objects to the introduction of evidence and the judge agrees to the objection, the judge sustains the objection.

tenancy at sufferance A tenant remaining in possession of a tenancy without permission after the expiration of a lawful term.

tenancy at will A lawful possession of a tenancy without a definite duration. Can be terminated by either the landlord or the tenant.

tenancy by the entirety A form of co-ownership of property between husband and wife. Like joint tenancy ownership, there is a right of survivorship. (See also "joint tenancy.")

tenancy in common A form of co-ownership of property by two or more persons. Upon the death of any co-owner, his or her percentage interest passes by intestate succession or by last will. Unlike joint tenancy, there is no right of survivorship.

tenancy for years A leasehold interest that expires at a specified time.

testamentary trust Trust created by a valid operative will.

testator (a) Person who makes a will. (b) Person who dies leaving a will.

theft The crime of stealing property from another who is not then present. Depending on the nature or value of the property stolen, it is either petty theft (misdemeanor) or grand theft (felony).

third party beneficiary One who is not a party to a contract, yet benefits from it. May be (a) a donee beneficiary, a third party who receives the benefit as a gift; or (b) a creditor beneficiary named because of an existing enforceable claim against one of the parties; or (c) an incidental beneficiary who may benefit from the contract but has no legally enforceable rights under it.

title Full and complete ownership of property. It may be separated into legal title (ownership) and equitable title (possession). For example, the purchaser of a home may agree to make payments for years before receiving full ownership from the seller. While waiting for legal title from the seller, the buyer is enjoying possession (equitable ownership) of the home. (See also "owner.")

title insurance A variety of insurance designed to insure against losses suffered by a homeowner or mortgage lender if title to the property is not as described by the insurer. Unlike most insurance, the premium is paid in total at the beginning of the period to be covered, it is measured in amount by the value of the property rather than by the risk of its loss, and it extends for as long as the insured continues to own the property, be it a week or 50 years.

tort A private wrong committed by one person (the tortfeasor) that injures another (the victim) in person and/or property, and for which society allows the legal remedy of monetary damages.

tortfeasor A wrongdoer who commits a private injury to another person by breaching a duty recognized by law.

trespass Wrongful interference with the real or personal property of another. Commonly refers to entry on another's land without authority.

trespass to chattel A brief, temporary, unauthorized interference with the personal property rights of another.

trial Formal procedure before a court conducted to resolve disputed questions of fact and of law.

trial courts Tribunals that conduct trials, as distinguished from courts that conduct appeals.

trust A legal relationship in which one party (trustor or settlor) transfers legal title in property to a second party (trustee) for the benefit of a third party (beneficiary).

trustee A person who holds property in a trust for the benefit of another, the beneficiary.

trustor The person who creates a trust. Also called a settlor.

Truth in Lending Act See "Consumer Credit Protection Act."

unconscionable contract A contract in which one party is treated unfairly, oppressively, and with bad faith. The court may refuse to enforce the contract, or modify it to eliminate the part that is unconscionable.

undue influence Wrongful persuasion, often by a fiduciary or other trusted individual, which deprives the victim of freedom of will in making a contract.

unenforceable contract A contract that was initially valid but can no longer be enforced, e.g., because of the statute of limitations.

unfair labor practice Certain practices of employers and unions that are prohibited by federal or state law.

unfair labor practice strike A strike in which the workers are protesting an unfair labor practice of their employer.

Uniform Commercial Code (UCC) One of several uniform laws drafted by the National Conference of Commissioners of Uniform State Laws. It covers a wide range of commercial activity and has been generally adopted by all states.

unilateral contract A contract formed by the performance of a requested act. The party who requested the act is thereby obligated to fulfill his or her promise.

unilateral mistake A situation in which one of the parties to a contract labors under some error about an important fact in their agreement.

uninsured motorist insurance Automobile insurance that protects against the risk of loss from bodily injury suffered by an insured because of the negligence of either an uninsured driver or a hit-and-run driver.

union Association of workers formed to bargain collectively with employers over wages, hours, and conditions of employment.

union shop A place of employment where newly hired workers must join the union within 30 days of being hired.

unlawful detainer A statutory remedy for a landlord to evict a renter who has defaulted in the payment of rent or who has broken the terms of the lease in some other manner. It is a summary judicial proceeding (i.e., not full-blown trial on all issues before a jury), which also may be called dispossessory warrant proceedings or forcible entry proceedings, depending on the state.

unwritten law Laws that are enforced by courts and found in their written opinions (cases) but not in statutes or ordinances. Also called common law.

usury Interest charge for the use of money in excess of maximum rates allowed by state law.

valid Legally enforceable (for example, a contract).

valid contract An agreement that complies with all requisites of the law for enforceability.

venue, change of Transfer of a case for trial to another county or judicial district.

verdict The expressed decision of the jury on questions of fact submitted to it for determination, based on evidence presented during trial.

vicarious liability The responsibility of one person for the wrongful acts of another. For example, the owner of a vehicle may be vicariously liable for the damages caused by the negligence of the driver.

vicarious murder rule A rule holding that an aider and abettor of a murder is guilty of the murder actually committed by another person.

victimless crime Any crime that allegedly hurts only the wrongdoer, if anyone (e.g., unusual sexual practices by consenting adults in private, prostitution, public drunkenness, use of marijuana, usury, and illegal gambling). Reformers contend that such acts should be decriminalized.

void Without legal force or binding effect.

void contract A misnomer, because it is a nullity. One or more essential elements is missing in the attempted contract.

voidable contract An agreement that may be legally rejected by a party because an essential element is missing.

voir dire [Old French: to speak the truth] Process of questioning prospective jurors to ascertain whether they have any bias or prejudice that would make difficult or unlikely their impartiality in determining questions of fact during a trial.

voluntary arbitration See "arbitration."

voluntary rescission When both parties voluntarily agree to return to the status quo as it existed before a contract was made. (See also "rescission.")

wage earner receivership A plan under which a court-appointed trustee collects all nonexempt wages of the debtor and distributes them pro rata to the creditors who meanwhile may not garnishee or repossess goods.

waive To give up a right, such as a trial by jury.

ward A person, usually a child, subject to a guardianship.

warrant A written authorization of a judge, or magistrate, to arrest or search a specific person.

warranty Assurance given by the seller of goods concerning the title to, or the quality or performance of, the product sold. A warranty may be express (oral or written) or implied by law even if not mentioned by the seller.

warranty against encumbrances An implied warranty that goods will be delivered free of liens and encumbrances, not otherwise noted.

warranty against infringement An implied warranty by a merchant seller that goods are free of any rightful claim, such as a patent.

warranty of fitness for particular purpose A warranty that arises when the buyer relies on the seller's selection of goods having stated the intended use of the goods.

warranty of merchantability An implied warranty in a sale by a merchant that the goods are of fair, average quality, and fit for the ordinary purpose(s) for which such goods are used.

warranty of title An implied warranty to a buyer that the seller has and is transferring good title.

warranty deed A type of deed with several warranties implied by the seller to protect the buyer.

white collar crimes Illegal acts committed by persons of comparatively higher social status and economic wealth, usually without violence, such as embezzlement, fraud, and tax evasion. Contrasted to blue collar crimes such as robbery.

wildcat strike An unlawful strike of union members without the approval of the union.

will Legal expression of a person's directions as to how property owned is to be disposed of after death; usually written. Also called the last will and testament.

winding up period After dissolution of a partnership, the time during which outstanding debts are paid, assets are sold, and partners' investments returned if possible. The partnership is then legally terminated.

Worker Adjustment and Retraining Notification Act of 1989 (WARN) Federal law that requires business managers to give employees 60 days advance notice of a plant closing or mass layoff.

workers compensation Medical treatment, rehabilitation benefits, and disability payments for workers injured on the job; paid for by employer-financed insurance.

writ of execution Order of the court directing the sheriff to confiscate property of the defendant. The property is then sold to satisfy the award of dollar damages given to the plaintiff at a trial.

written interrogatories Pretrial questioning of a witness or adverse party to an action by means of written questions submitted to counsel by the opposing attorney, to be answered in writing under oath. A type of discovery procedure.

wrongful death statute A law allowing the heirs of a deceased to sue the person(s) who caused the decedent's death.

wrongful discharge The wrongful dismissal of a permanent employee without good cause. A tort.

yellow dog contract An employment contract in which a worker agrees not to join a union. Outlawed by the Anti-Injunction Act of 1932.

Index